Issues in
Comparative Politics

Los Angeles | London | New Delhi
Singapore | Washington DC

SELECTIONS FROM **CQ RESEARCHER**

Los Angeles | London | New Delhi
Singapore | Washington DC

FOR INFORMATION:

CQ Press
An Imprint of SAGE Publications, Inc.
2455 Teller Road
Thousand Oaks, California 91320
E-mail: order@sagepub.com

SAGE Publications Ltd.
1 Oliver's Yard
55 City Road
London, EC1Y 1SP
United Kingdom

SAGE Publications India Pvt. Ltd.
B 1/I 1 Mohan Cooperative Industrial Area
Mathura Road, New Delhi 110 044
India

SAGE Publications Asia-Pacific Pte. Ltd.
33 Pekin Street #02-01
Far East Square
Singapore 048763

Printed in the United States of America

ISBN: 978-1-60871-831-3
Library of Congress Control Number: 2011936891

This book is printed on acid-free paper.

12 13 14 15 16 10 9 8 7 6 5 4 3 2 1

Acquisitions Editor: Elise Frasier
Production Editor: Mirna Araklian
Typesetter: C&M Digitals (P) Ltd.
Cover Designer: Judy Myers, Graphic Design
Marketing Manager: Chris O'Brien

Contents

ANNOTATED CONTENTS   vii

PREFACE   xiii

CONTRIBUTORS   xv

COMPARATIVE DEMOCRATIZATION AND DICTATORSHIPS

1. Turmoil in the Arab World   **1**

    Can Western-style democracy take root in Arab countries?   7

    Is the current upheaval in the best interests of the Western powers and Israel?   8

    Will the upheaval in the Middle East help Islamic extremists?   12

    Background   13

        Imperialism and Colonialism   13

        Triumph   14

        Contagion   17

        Conflict   18

        Intervention   19

    Current Situation   20

        The Second Act   20

        Islamist Threat   20

        Economic Fallout   22

    Outlook: A Collection of Irans?   23

    Notes   24

    Bibliography   26

    Voices From Abroad   29

2. Democracy in Southeast Asia   **31**

    Should political parties boycott unfair elections?   34

    Can Singapore and Malaysia become liberal democracies?   36

    Does democracy mean greater accountability and less corruption?   39

    Background   41

        Corruption and Violence   41

        Shaky Democracy   42

        Free But Corrupt   46

        Newest Democracy   47

    Current Situation   47

        Thai Violence   47

        New Philippine President   49

    Outlook: Pressuring Myanmar   51

    Notes   52

    Bibliography   54

    Voices From Abroad   57

3. Sub-Saharan Democracy   **59**

    Can Africa move beyond ethnic politics?   64

    Does natural resource wealth hamper African democracy?   66

    Is democracy the best form of government for spurring economic growth in Africa?   68

    Background   69

        Ancient Africa   69

The Slave Trade 72
'Scramble for Africa' 72
Bumpy Road to Independence 73
'Big Men' 74
'Second Liberation' 75
Current Situation 78
Democracy Retreats 78
Doing Elections 79
Outlook: Cheetahs vs. Hippos 81
Notes 82
Bibliography 84
Voices From Abroad 87

ACCOUNTABILITY, CIVIL LIBERTIES, AND CIVIL SOCIETY

4. Press Freedom 89
Can governments control media coverage? 92
Will new government cyber controls effectively censor journalists? 95
Is press freedom a prerequisite for economic development? 97
Background 98
Fall of the Wall 98
Latin America Cracks Down 99
Chinese 'Schizophrenia' 99
Current Situation 103
Press Freedom Today 103
Deadliest Country 106
Outlook: 'Critical Juncture' 108
Notes 109
Bibliography 112
Voices From Abroad 114

5. Separatist Movements 117
Should there be a right of self-determination? 124
Are globalization and regional integration fueling separatism? 126
Does separatism lead to more violent conflict? 128
Background 129
Emerging Nations 129
Decolonization 133
Ethno-centrism Surges 136
Current Situation 137
Balkan Pandora's Box 137

Frozen Conflicts 138
Asian Disputes 140
Secession in the Americas 141
Outlook: Ethnocentric Separatism 141
Update 143
Notes 145
Bibliography 148
Voices From Abroad 151

6. Gay Rights 153
Are governments and society more receptive to gay rights? 157
Does a backlash threaten advances made by gays? 160
Should the United Nations and other international bodies be promoting gay rights? 162
Background 165
Ancient Practice 165
Modern Movement 168
Current Situation 170
Same-Sex Marriage 170
The Americas 170
Western Influence? 173
Outlook: Sweeping Transformation? 173
Notes 174
Bibliography 176
Voices From Abroad 179

THE GLOBAL MARKET: DEVELOPMENT, POVERTY, AND INEQUALITY

7. Rapid Urbanization 181
Does urbanization make people better off? 185
Should governments limit migration to cities? 187
Can we make large cities greener? 188
Background 190
From Farm to Factory 190
End of Empires 193
Population Boom 193
New Solutions 196
Current Situation 197
Economic Shadow 197
Slum Solutions 199
Outlook: Going Global 201
Notes 202

Bibliography 206
Voices From Abroad 209

8. Brazil on the Rise **211**
Is Brazil's economy a model for
developing countries? 217
Is Brazil doing enough to stop
deforestation? 219
Can Brazil be a superpower? 221
Background 222
Colony to Republic 222
Economic Expansion 222
Democracy and Drugs 227
The Lula Years 227
Current Situation 229
Rousseff Era 229
Evolving Global Relations 229
Fighting Crime, Poverty 230
Outlook: In Lula's Shadow 232
Notes 233
Bibliography 237
Voices From Abroad 240

9. India Rising **243**
Can India match China's economic
growth? 249
Is India doing enough to help its poor? 250
Should India conclude the nuclear deal
with the United States? 253
Background 256
Socialist Experiment 256
Reform Era 257
Foreign Policy 258
Current Situation 260
Congress Party Returns 260
Neo-Nonalignment 261
Outlook: Full Speed Ahead? 262
Update 263
Notes 265
Bibliography 267
Voices From Abroad 269

10. Future of the Euro **271**
Will the Eurozone survive in its current
form? 276
Are some countries worse off under the
euro? 278
Will the EU approach solve the debt crisis? 279

Background 281
Bending Union Rules 281
Bloodshed Averted 282
Birth of the Euro 285
Bubbles and Bailouts 287
Current Situation 288
Cutting Deals 288
Government Killer? 290
Outlook: Nationalist Obstructionism? 291
Notes 292
Bibliography 295
Voices From Abroad 297

11. Evaluating Microfinance **299**
Does microcredit help the poor,
especially women, out of poverty? 302
Will for-profit investors continue to
benefit the very poor and women? 304
Should microfinance lenders be more
tightly regulated? 308
Background 310
Early Beginnings 310
Power of Peer Pressure 310
The 'Debt Treadmill' 312
After the Flood 314
Current Situation 315
Rising Delinquencies 315
Looming Crisis? 316
Government Crackdowns 316
Outlook: Soaring Needs 318
Notes 319
Bibliography 322
Voices From Abroad 324

SOCIAL POLICIES AND SOCIAL ISSUES

12. Religious Fundamentalism **327**
Is religious fundamentalism on
the rise? 332
Is religious fundamentalism a reaction
to Western permissiveness? 334
Should religious fundamentalists have
a greater voice in government? 337
Background 339
'Great Awakening' 339
Islamic Fundamentalism 341
Fundamentalist Jews 345
Fundamentalism in India 348

Current Situation 348
    Political Battles 348
    Rising Violence 350
Outlook: More of the Same? 352
Notes 353
Bibliography 357
Voices From Abroad 359

13. Europe's Immigration Turmoil 361
    Does Europe need its immigrants? 366
    Should European governments do more
        to integrate immigrants? 370
    Should immigrants be required to follow
        local customs? 373
Background 375
    Colonial Roots 375
    'Immigration Stop' Policies 379
    Radical Islam Emerges 379
    Examining Multiculturalism 380
Current Situation 383
    Rise of Extremists 383
    Roma Dispute 385
    Migration Slowdown 387
Outlook: 'Temporary Blip?' 387
Notes 388
Bibliography 392
Voices From Abroad 394

14. Honor Killings 397
    Are honor killings a form of domestic
        violence? 402
    Are governments doing enough to deter
        honor killings? 404
    Is the international community doing
        enough to combat honor killings? 406
Background 407
    Early Origins 407
    Medieval Prejudices 408
    Killings Spread 413
Current Situation 413
    Providing Shelter? 413
    Legal Efforts 414
Outlook: Needed: Three 'Ps' 417
Notes 417
Bibliography 421
Voices From Abroad 423

15. Social Welfare in Europe 425
    Do Europe's generous social welfare
        programs make its economies
        less productive than the
        United States? 429
    Do European welfare states have less
        social mobility than the
        United States? 433
    Can European welfare states afford
        their generous benefits? 434
Background 437
    Rise of Welfare in Britain 437
    Welfare Reform 438
    Debating Welfare Success 440
    Helping Working Mothers 441
    U.S. vs. EU Spending 441
Current Situation 442
    Cuts to Welfare States 442
    Britain's Reform Moment 442
    The European Model 445
Outlook: 'Grand Bargain' 445
Notes 446
Bibliography 447
Voices From Abroad 450

16. The Graying Planet 453
    Should official retirement ages be
        increased? 457
    Do younger generations bear most of
        the cost of aging populations? 458
    Can aging nations increase their
        birthrates? 460
Background 463
    Demographic Transitions 463
    Population Boosterism 463
    Population Control 464
    Falling Fertility 466
Current Situation 468
    Aging States 468
    Exporting Jobs 468
    'Six Elders Per Child' 470
    Aging Workforces 470
Outlook: Age Adjustment 471
Notes 472
Bibliography 474
Voices From Abroad 476

Annotated Contents

COMPARATIVE DEMOCRATIZATION AND DICTATORSHIPS

Turmoil in the Arab World

Massive, largely peaceful demonstrations in January and February 2011 forced longtime autocrats in Tunisia and Egypt from power, including Hosni Mubarak, who had dominated Egypt for more than 30 years. Subsequently, protests erupted in at least a dozen other countries across the Arab world, several of which continue. Using social media to organize, young demonstrators have called for the removal of long-entrenched corrupt regimes, greater freedom and more jobs. They have been met with violent government crackdowns in Syria, Yemen and Bahrain, while in Libya strongman Moammar Gadhafi is battling a ragtag rebel force backed by NATO. As the region reverberates with calls for change, scholars say some key questions must be answered: Will the region become more democratic or will Islamic fundamentalists take control? And will relations with the West and Israel suffer? Then, a few months later on May 1, al Qaida chief Osama bin Laden was killed in a U.S. raid in Pakistan. Once, such news might have triggered anti-U.S. protests across the region. Now, it seemed, those bin Laden had tried to radicalize were more interested in jobs and freedom than in bin Laden's dream of a vast, new Muslin caliphate.

Democracy in Southeast Asia

Indonesia is the world's third-largest democracy and one of its newest. But while Indonesia is consolidating its democratic institutions and slowly making progress against endemic corruption, democracy elsewhere in Southeast Asia is in distress. High-level corruption and politically motivated murders are obstructing democracy in the Philippines. In Thailand, 14 years of turbulent democracy ended with a military coup in 2006. Elections eventually resumed, but after anti-government protesters camped in Bangkok's commercial center for months in the spring of 2010 demanding new elections, the government finally broke up the demonstrations and began shooting and arresting protesters. True democracy is largely a fiction in Cambodia, Singapore and Malaysia, and Myanmar (Burma) is run by a brutal authoritarian regime. Against this backdrop, opposition politicians, scholars and human rights activists debate how best to encourage democracy in Southeast Asia.

Sub-Saharan Democracy

Despite a recent economic renaissance, some say much of sub-Saharan Africa is drifting toward a new age of authoritarianism. After the Cold War — when the superpowers propped up African dictators as proxy pawns in a global ideological chess match — the seeds of democracy rapidly spread across the continent. By 2000, nearly half of sub-Saharan Africa's 48 countries were considered electoral democracies. But democratic progress stalled and even regressed in the 2000s. By one measure, freedom in the region has retreated to about the same level it was in 1992–1993. Human rights are eroding in influential countries like Nigeria, South Africa, Zimbabwe and Ivory Coast. Experts blame Africa's continuing ethnic tensions and the emergence of China as a major trading partner. Western governments are skittish about pressing for democratic reforms now that they must compete for Africa's natural resources with China, which ignores such issues in its business dealings.

ACCOUNTABILITY, CIVIL LIBERTIES, AND CIVIL SOCIETY

Press Freedom

Press freedom around the globe declined for the eighth year in a row in 2009, with more than three-quarters of the world's population now living in countries without a free press. It was once thought that new technologies — such as cell phones and the Internet — would help to open up repressive societies. But as fast as reporters in those countries adopt technologies that enable them to connect to the outside world, authoritarian governments like China, Iran and Russia devise sophisticated new tools to control the flow of online information. Meanwhile, dictatorial regimes continue to use heavy-handed, old-school methods to control the world's media, including intimidation and violence. Fifty-two journalists were murdered in 2009, most of them while investigating corruption or politics. Another 136 journalists were jailed — the highest number since 2003 and a 68-percent increase over 2000. Such trends alarm media experts, who say press freedom is a prerequisite for economic development and a harbinger for the future direction of political and social freedoms.

Separatist Movements

When Kosovo declared its independence on Feb. 17, 2008, thousands of angry Serbs took to the streets to protest the breakaway region's secession from Serbia. Less than a month later, Chinese authorities battled Buddhist monks in Lhasa, the legendary capital of Tibet, where separatist resentments have been simmering since China occupied the Himalayan region more than 50 years ago. The protests were the latest flashpoints in some two dozen separatist "hot spots" — the most active of roughly 70 such movements around the globe. They are part of a post-World War II independence trend that has produced a nearly fourfold jump in the number of countries worldwide, with 27 of those new countries emerging just since 1990. Some nations, like the far-flung Kurds, are fighting fiercely to establish a homeland, while others — like Canada's Québécois — seem content with local autonomy. The Sri Lankan Tamils finally experienced defeat by government forces after a 26-year struggle for independence. A handful have become de facto states that are as-yet-unrecognized by the U.N., including Somaliland, Taiwan, South Ossetia and Nagorno-Karabakh, while South Sudan became the 193rd member of the U.N. in July 2011.

Gay Rights

By some measures, the last 10 years could be considered the "Gay Rights" decade, with countries around the world addressing concerns of the lesbian, gay, bisexual, transgender (LGBT) community. Beginning with the Netherlands in 2001, gay marriage metamorphosed almost overnight from a largely ridiculed notion to a legal reality in at least 10 countries. Sixteen other nations recognized same-sex civil unions. Nevertheless, homosexual acts remain illegal in most of Africa and the Muslim world, with severe penalties for anyone found guilty of the crime. If Uganda approves a proposal to criminalize repeated homosexual activity, it will join the five other countries (and parts of Somalia and Nigeria) where homosexual activity is punishable by death. In Russia and other Eastern European countries, gay and lesbian "pride parades" have sometimes met with violent responses, leading some observers to believe a backlash against rapid gay and lesbian advances may be developing in parts of the world.

THE GLOBAL MARKET: DEVELOPMENT, POVERTY, AND INEQUALITY

Rapid Urbanization

About 3.3 billion people — half of Earth's inhabitants — live in cities, and the number is expected to hit 5 billion within 20 years. Most urban growth today is occurring in developing countries, where about a billion people live in city slums. Delivering services to crowded cities has become increasingly difficult, especially in the world's 19 "megacities" — those with more than 10 million residents. Moreover, most of the largest cities are in coastal areas, where they are vulnerable to flooding caused by climate change. Many governments are striving to improve city life by expanding services, reducing environmental damage and providing more jobs for the poor, but some still use heavy-handed clean-up policies like slum clearance. Researchers say urbanization helps reduce global poverty because new urbanites earn more than they could in their villages. The global recession could reverse that trend, however, as many unemployed city dwellers return to rural areas. But most experts expect rapid urbanization to resume once the economic storm has passed.

Brazil on the Rise

Centuries ago, Brazil was a remote Portuguese colony. Today the biggest nation in Latin America has evolved into a stable democracy, a regional power and an important U.S. and European Union partner. Economic growth has been steady, fueled by rising food exports, and the burgeoning oil and ethanol industries have helped the country become energy independent. Twenty-eight million Brazilians have been lifted out of poverty in the past decade. Globally, Brazil participates in numerous peacekeeping missions and is becoming an aid donor rather than recipient. The picture is not all rosy, however. Brazil needs major infrastructure upgrades before it hosts the 2014 FIFA World Cup and the 2016 Summer Olympics. The Amazon rain forest continues to disappear, drug gangs control many city slums and the country increasingly relies on cheap Chinese imports. Nevertheless, as Brazil's new President Dilma Rousseff — a former guerrilla fighter — begins to make her mark, Brazil is a booming regional power.

India Rising

India's stars appear to have aligned. The World Bank projects that India is expected to overtake China as the world's fastest growing economy. India also recovered from the 2008 global meltdown faster than either the U.S. or Europe. Experts say if India stays on its current path it could be a global power by mid-century. Yet, India remains exceedingly poor. Per capita income is less than half of China's, and a quarter of the more than 1 billion Indians live below the poverty line. Government pledges to extend the benefits of growth to all are hampered by corruption and red tape. So, while the world's second-most populous country and largest democracy is headed in the right direction, it still has a long way to go.

Future of the Euro

Portugal has become the third eurozone government to seek a bailout loan from the European Union, which is struggling to prevent a debt crisis from crippling its poorest members and spreading to richer euro countries. Historically impoverished nations such as Ireland, Portugal and Greece experienced a surge of wealth in the 1990s after adopting the euro. But in the wake of the worldwide economic crash and recession, that wealth proved to be an illusion based on cheap credit from Germany and other stronger economies. The euro's defenders say the crisis has created a new determination to fix the eurozone's defects, particularly its lack of strong centralized governance. But the rise of nationalist parties in richer countries opposed to bailouts could hamper a solution. And despite years of rhetoric about European unity, critics say individual nations will never give up enough of their sovereignty — especially their right to tax and spend on liberal social programs — to become part of a United States of Europe.

Evaluating Microfinance

Since the 1980s, millions of impoverished people around the world without access to banks have been able to take out tiny loans to start businesses. Nobel Prize-winning economist Muhammad Yunus, who established the first microfinance bank in Bangladesh and launched the modern microlending movement, claims microloans have lifted millions — especially women — out of poverty and spurred economic growth. But recent studies cast doubt on microcredit's effectiveness. Borrowers have been saddled with multiple loans at exorbitant interest rates, often having to borrow from loan sharks to make their microcredit payments. Economists fear overindebtedness could make borrowers even poorer and that a possible credit bubble could burst. Others worry that in recent years, for-profit investors have swarmed to the field, attracted by high returns on investment. Some governments have capped microlenders' interest rates, but the industry hopes to forestall regulation by adopting voluntary consumer protection measures.

SOCIAL POLICIES AND SOCIAL ISSUES

Religious Fundamentalism

People around the world are embracing fundamentalism, a belief in the literal interpretation of holy texts and, among the more hard-line groups, the desire to replace secular law with religious law. At the same time, deadly attacks by religious extremists in India, Uganda, Somalia and Nigeria are on the rise — and not just among Muslims. Meanwhile, political Islamism — which seeks to install Islamic law via the ballot box — is increasing in places like Morocco and in Muslim communities in Europe. Christian evangelicalism and Pentacostalism — the denominations from which fundamentalism derives — also are flourishing in Latin America, Africa, Central Asia and the United States. Ultra-Orthodox Jewish fundamentalists are blamed for exacerbating instability in the Middle East and beyond by establishing and expanding settlements on Palestinian lands. And intolerance is growing among Hindus in India, leading to deadly attacks against Christians and others. As experts debate what is causing the spread of fundamentalism, others question whether fundamentalists should have a greater voice in government.

Europe's Immigration Turmoil

Recent gains by European right-wing political parties advocating halts in immigration from Muslim countries signal a growing resentment against foreigners as Europe faces an economy with fewer jobs to go around. Anti-immigrant parties have received unprecedented shares of the vote in famously tolerant Sweden and the Netherlands. Mainstream politicians in France, Germany and Britain have vowed to cut immigration, complaining that many immigrants — especially conservative Muslims — fail to integrate into mainstream society. Ironically, anti-immigrant fervor is rising just as the economic downturn is slowing immigration to many countries. Some economists argue that aging Europe needs young immigrants to fill its work force and support its growing pension costs. Other experts say governments need to do more to integrate Muslims, many of whom are native-born. As governments pass laws to ban burqas, headscarves and minarets, many are asking how much cultural conformity Europe can demand in an increasingly globalized world. Immigrant advocates say language requirements and citizenship tests discriminate against Muslim immigrants and, together with immigration caps, send a hostile message to the skilled workers Europe needs to attract from abroad.

Honor Killings

Each week brings horrific new headlines stating that, somewhere around the world, a woman or girl has been killed by a male relative for allegedly bringing dishonor upon her family. According to the U.N. High Commissioner for Human Rights, "In the name of preserving family 'honor,' women and girls are shot, stoned, burned, buried alive, strangled, smothered and knifed to death with horrifying regularity." Between 5,000 and 20,000 so-called honor killings are committed each year, based on long-held beliefs that any female who commits — or is suspected of committing — an "immoral" act should be killed to "restore honor" to her family. Honor killings are deeply rooted in ancient patriarchal and fundamentalist traditions, which some judicial systems legitimize by pardoning offenders or handing out light sentences. Human-rights organizations are demanding that governments and the international community act more forcefully to stop honor killings, but officials in some countries are doing little to protect women and girls within their borders.

Social Welfare in Europe

The Euro debt crisis and calls for fiscal austerity are putting a harsh new light on Europe's gold-plated welfare and pension programs. According to some economists, Europeans pay for their generous welfare programs — such as national health insurance and universal preschool — with more sluggish economies and higher unemployment than in the United States, which has among the industrialized world's least generous welfare safety nets. But in recent years, Scandinavian countries, the most generous with subsidized child care and paid parental leave, have grown at least as fast as the free-market United States. And, contrary to popular opinion, workers there have a better chance than Americans of climbing further up the economic ladder than their parents. Now Greece, Spain, France and Portugal have all proposed welfare austerity measures — mainly delaying early retirement ages and freezing pensions — not

cutting core programs like free child care or unemployment safety nets. Cutbacks in pensions have already spurred angry street protests, but most experts agree Europe has little choice as it faces a demographic time bomb of aging societies supported by a diminishing number of workers.

The Graying Planet

The world's populations are aging rapidly, triggering demographic changes that will have a profound impact on economies, government expenditures and international migration patterns. In the past century, life expectancy has doubled, while the average family size has shrunk. By 2050, the number of children under 5 is expected to drop by 49 million, while the number of adults over 60 will skyrocket — by 1.2 billion. An unprecedented number of senior citizens will be depending on diminishing numbers of younger workers to contribute to pension and health care programs for the elderly. And it's not just a problem for wealthy countries: Developing countries' elderly populations are growing faster than in the developed world. For example, in 20 years, China will have 167 million senior citizens — more than half the current U.S. population. On the positive side, some demographers believe aging societies will be more peaceful, since seniors suffer fewer crime and drug-abuse problems. And with fewer children, there could be more money per capita for their education.

Preface

Will democracy emerge from the "Arab Spring"? Is religious fundamentalism on the rise? Is Europe becoming intolerant of foreigners? These questions—and many more—are what make comparative politics so interesting and important to today's world. Students must first understand the facts and contexts of these and other issues if they are to analyze and articulate well-reasoned positions.

The first edition of *Issues in Comparative Politics* includes sixteen up-to-date reports by *CQ Researcher,* an award-winning weekly policy brief that explains difficult concepts and provides balanced coverage of competing perspectives. Each article analyzes past, present and possible political problems and is designed to promote in-depth discussion and further research to help readers formulate their own positions on crucial international issues.

This collection is organized into four subject areas—comparative democratization and dictatorships; accountability, civil liberties, and civil society; the global market: development, poverty, and inequality; and social policies and social issues—to cover a range of topics found in most comparative politics courses. Citizens, journalists and business and government leaders also can turn to the collected articles to become better informed on key issues, actors and policy positions.

CQ RESEARCHER

CQ Researcher was founded in 1923 as *Editorial Research Reports* and was sold primarily to newspapers as a research tool. The magazine was renamed and redesigned in 1991 as *CQ Researcher*. Today, students are its primary audience. While still used by hundreds of journalists and newspapers, many of which reprint portions of the reports, *Researcher*'s main subscribers are now high school, college and public libraries. In 2002, *Researcher* won the American Bar Association's coveted Silver Gavel Award for magazine excellence for a series of nine reports on civil liberties and other legal issues.

Researcher staff writers — all highly experienced journalists — sometimes compare the experience of writing a *Researcher* report to drafting a college term paper. Indeed, there are many similarities. Each report is as long as many term papers — about 11,000 words — and is written by one person without any significant outside help. One of the key differences is that the writers interview leading experts, scholars and government officials for each issue.

Like students, staff writers begin the creative process by choosing a topic. Working with *Researcher*'s editors, the writer identifies a controversial subject that has important public policy implications. After a topic is selected, the writer embarks on one to two weeks of intense research. Newspaper and magazine articles are clipped or downloaded, books are ordered and information is gathered from a wide variety of sources, including interest groups, universities and the government. Once the writers are well informed, they develop a detailed outline and begin the interview process. Each report requires a minimum of ten to fifteen interviews with academics, officials, lobbyists and people working in the field. Only after all interviews are completed does the writing begin.

CHAPTER FORMAT

Each issue of and therefore each selection in this book, is structured in the same way. A selection begins with an introductory overview, which is briefly explored in greater detail in the rest of the report.

The second section chronicles the most important and current debates in the field. It is structured around a number of key issues questions, such as "Will aging populations cause economic upheaval?" and "Do small loans for poor entrepreneurs help end poverty?" This section is the core of each selection. The questions raised are often highly controversial and usually the object of much argument among scholars and practitioners. Hence, the answers provided are never conclusive, but rather detail the range of opinion within the field.

Following those issue questions is the "Background" section, which provides a history of the issue being examined. This retrospective includes important legislative and executive actions and court decisions to inform readers on how current policy evolved.

Next, the "Current Situation" section examines important contemporary policy issues, legislation under consideration and action being taken. Each selection ends with an "Outlook" section that gives a sense of what new regulations, court rulings and possible policy initiatives might be put into place in the next five to ten years.

Each report contains features that augment the main text: sidebars that examine issues related to the topic, a pro/con debate by two outside experts, a chronology of key dates and events and an annotated bibliography that details the major sources used by the writer.

CUSTOM OPTIONS

Interested in building your ideal CQ Press Issues book, customized to your personal teaching needs and interests? Browse by course or date, or search for specific topics or issues from our online catalog of *CQ Researcher* issues at http://custom.cqpress.com.

ACKNOWLEDGMENTS

We wish to thank many people for helping to make this collection a reality. Tom Billitteri, managing editor of *CQ Researcher,* gave us his enthusiastic support and cooperation as we developed this edition. He and his talented staff of editors and writers have amassed a first-class collection of *Researcher* articles, and we are fortunate to have access to this rich cache. Some readers may be learning about *CQ Researcher* for the first time. We expect that many readers will want regular access to this excellent weekly research tool. For subscription information or a no-obligation free trial of *Researcher,* please contact CQ Press at www.cqpress.com or toll-free at 1-866-4CQ-PRESS (1-866-427-7737).

We hope that you will be pleased by the first edition of *Issues in Comparative Politics.* We welcome your feedback and suggestions for future editions. Please direct comments to Elise Frasier, Acquisitions Editor for International Relations and Comparative Politics, College Publishing Group, CQ Press, 2300 N Street, NW, Suite 800, Washington, DC 20037; or send e-mail to *efrasier@cqpress.com.*

—*The Editors of CQ Press*

Contributors

Brian Beary —a freelance journalist based in Washington, D.C.—specializes in European Union (EU) affairs and is the U.S. correspondent for the daily newspaper, *Europolitics*. Originally from Dublin, Ireland, he worked in the European Parliament for Irish MEP Pat "The Cope" Gallagher in 2000 and at the EU Commission's Eurobarometer unit on public opinion analysis. Beary also writes for the Brussels-based *Parliament Magazine* and *The Globalist* magazine. His last report for *CQ Global Researcher* was "Religious Fundamentalism." He also wrote CQ Press' recent book, *Separatist Movements, A Global Reference*.

Roland Flamini is a Washington-based correspondent who writes on foreign-affairs for *The New Republic* and other publications. Fluent in six languages, he served as *Time* bureau chief in Rome, Bonn, Beirut, Jerusalem and the European Common Market and later served as international editor at United Press International. His previous reports for *CQ Researcher* were on Afghanistan, NATO, Latin America, Nuclear Proliferation and U.S.-Russia Relations. His most recent reporting trip to China was in November-December 2009.

Sarah Glazer, a London-based freelancer, is a regular contributor to *CQ Global Researcher*. Her articles on health, education and social-policy issues also have appeared in *The New York Times* and *The Washington Post*. Her recent *CQ Global Researcher* reports include "Radical Islam in Europe" and "Social Welfare in Europe." She graduated from the University of Chicago with a B.A. in American history.

Alan Greenblatt covers foreign affairs for National Public Radio. He was previously a staff writer at *Governing* magazine and *CQ Weekly*, where he won the National Press Club's Sandy Hume Award for political journalism. He graduated from San Francisco State University in 1986 and received a master's degree in English literature from the University of Virginia in 1988. For the *CQ Researcher*, his reports include "Confronting Warming," "Future of the GOP" and "Immigration Debate." His most recent *CQ Global Researcher* reports were "Attacking Piracy" and "Rewriting History."

Reed Karaim, a freelance writer living in Tucson, Arizona, has written for *The Washington Post, U.S. News & World Report, Smithsonian, American Scholar, USA Weekend* and other publications. He is the author of the novel, *If Men Were Angels*, which was selected for the Barnes & Noble Discover Great New Writers series. He is also the winner of the Robin Goldstein Award for Outstanding Regional Reporting and other journalism awards. Karaim is a graduate of North Dakota State University in Fargo.

Robert Kiener is an award-winning writer whose work has appeared in the London Sunday Times, The Christian Science Monitor, The Washington Post, Reader's Digest, Time Life Books, Asia Inc., and other publications. For more than two decades he lived and worked as an editor and correspondent in Guam, Hong Kong and England and is now based in the United States. He frequently travels to Asia and Europe to report on international issues. He holds an M.A. in Asian Studies from Hong Kong University and an M.Phil. in International Relations from Cambridge University.

Jennifer Koons teaches journalism at Northwestern University's satellite campus in Doha, Qatar. Previously, she was a Washington, D.C.-based journalist writing about national politics and legal issues, including cases before the U.S. Supreme Court, the 2008 and 2004 presidential campaigns and congressional action on Capitol Hill. Her work has appeared in *The New York Times, The Washington Post, San Diego Union Tribune*

and *Inside Mexico*, among other publications. She earned a master's degree in journalism from Northwestern's Medill School of Journalism and a master's degree in law from Northwestern's School of Law. She was the McCormick Journalism Fellow at the Reporters Committee for Freedom of the Press in Rosslyn, Va.

Barbara Mantel is a freelance writer in New York City whose work has appeared in *The New York Times*, the *Journal of Child and Adolescent Psychopharmacology* and *Mamm Magazine*. She is a former correspondent and senior producer for National Public Radio and has won several journalism awards, including the National Press Club's Best Consumer Journalism Award and the Front Page Award from the Newswomen's Club of New York for her April 18, 2008, *CQ Researcher* report "Public Defenders." She holds a B.A. in history and economics from the University of Virginia and an M.A. in economics from Northwestern University.

Jason McLure has been an Africa correspondent since 2007, reporting for publications including Bloomberg News, *Newsweek* and *The New York Times*. Currently based in Ghana, he previously worked for *Legal Times* in Washington, D.C., and in *Newsweek*'s Boston bureau. His writing has appeared in *The Economist, Business Week*, the *British Journalism Review* and *National Law Journal*. His last *CQ Global Researcher* was "The Troubled Horn of Africa." His work has been honored by the Washington, D.C., chapter of the Society for Professional Journalists, the Maryland-Delaware-District of Columbia Press Association and the Overseas Press Club of America Foundation.

Ken Moritsugu, based for three years in New Delhi as special correspondent for McClatchy Newspapers, is now the Asia-Pacific enterprise editor for the Associated Press in Bangkok. Until August 2004, he was the national economics correspondent for McClatchy's Washington Bureau. He previously was a staff reporter at the *St. Petersburg Times, The Japan Times* in Tokyo and *Newsday*, where he was part of a reporting team that won the Pulitzer Prize in 1996 for coverage of the crash of TWA Flight 800.

Jennifer Weeks is a Massachusetts freelance writer who specializes in energy, the environment, science and technology. She has written for *The Washington Post, Audubon, Popular Mechanics* and more than 50 other magazines and websites and worked for 15 years as a public policy analyst, congressional staffer and lobbyist. She has an A.B. degree from Williams College and master's degrees from the University of North Carolina and Harvard.

1

Turmoil in the Arab World

Roland Flamini

An Egyptian citizen smiles proudly after voting in the historic constitutional referendum on March 19. Voters overwhelmingly approved the measures, including one that establishes presidential term limits, one of the major demands of tens of thousands of mostly youthful pro-democracy protesters. Their 18-day demonstration in downtown Cairo earlier in the year led to the Feb. 11 resignation of President Hosni Mubarak, who had ruled for 30 years.

From *CQ Researcher*,
May 3, 2011.

Will the current turmoil in the Arab world turn out to be the best of times or the worst of times — the Arab Spring or the Arab Winter?

Not since the collapse of the Soviet Union in 1989 and the turn to democracy of its Central and Eastern European satellite states has an entire region been plunged into such tumultuous change. From the Atlantic to the Persian Gulf, long-entrenched regimes have suddenly faced popular uprisings. Starting in Tunisia in December and spreading to Egypt and a dozen other countries, political unrest has swept across the region like a desert sandstorm, roiling each country differently but with common characteristics: youth-driven demonstrations aided by online social networks and alliances forming across religious, class and tribal lines. So far, two long-entrenched autocratic regimes have been toppled, and others appear to be on shaky ground. At least four have struck back violently to suppress the protesters.

Egyptian historian Khaled Fahmy of the American University in Cairo rates the events as momentous for the region as the collapse of Ottoman control in 1923. The incident that lit the first fuse was the Dec. 17 suicide of a street vendor in Tunisia, unleashing a torrent of pent-up public frustration over government corruption and abuse. Within weeks President Zine El Abidine Ben Ali had quit and left the country, after 23 years in power. Then, following an epic 18 days of mass protests, Egypt's President Hosni Mubarak resigned on Feb. 11, ending his 30-year autocratic rule. From there the protests spread to at least a dozen other countries.

"This was about police brutality, about human rights and personal dignity, equal opportunities and social justice," says Fahmy.

Countries With Unrest Have Youthful Populations

Young demonstrators have played key roles in the recent pro-democracy protests in 14 Middle Eastern and North African countries that so far have toppled two longtime dictators — in Tunisia and Egypt. Throughout the region, nearly half — or more — of the citizens are under age 25. Yemen has the largest "youth bulge," with 65 percent of the population under 25. Although most of the protests have been peaceful, four countries — Libya, Syria, Yemen and Bahrain — have cracked down violently on demonstrators.

Countries With Pro-Democracy Demonstrations
(and percentage of population under age 25)

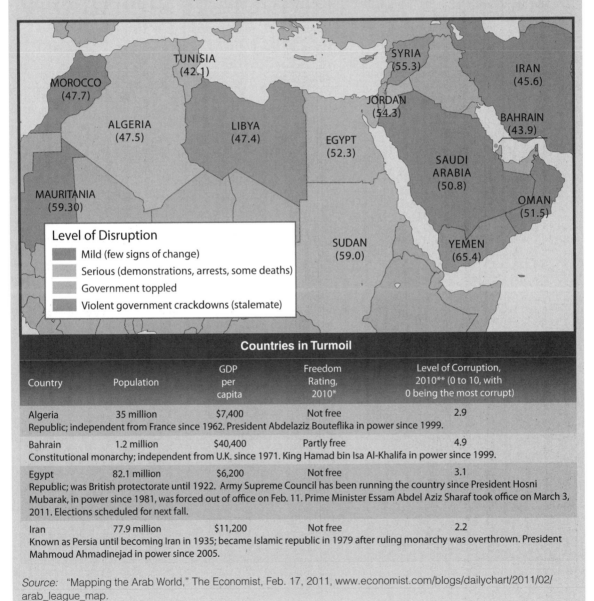

Country	Population	GDP per capita	Freedom Rating, 2010*	Level of Corruption, 2010** (0 to 10, with 0 being the most corrupt)
Algeria	35 million	$7,400	Not free	2.9
Republic; independent from France since 1962. President Abdelaziz Bouteflika in power since 1999.				
Bahrain	1.2 million	$40,400	Partly free	4.9
Constitutional monarchy; independent from U.K. since 1971. King Hamad bin Isa Al-Khalifa in power since 1999.				
Egypt	82.1 million	$6,200	Not free	3.1
Republic; was British protectorate until 1922. Army Supreme Council has been running the country since President Hosni Mubarak, in power since 1981, was forced out of office on Feb. 11. Prime Minister Essam Abdel Aziz Sharaf took office on March 3, 2011. Elections scheduled for next fall.				
Iran	77.9 million	$11,200	Not free	2.2
Known as Persia until becoming Iran in 1935; became Islamic republic in 1979 after ruling monarchy was overthrown. President Mahmoud Ahmadinejad in power since 2005.				

Source: "Mapping the Arab World," The Economist, Feb. 17, 2011, www.economist.com/blogs/dailychart/2011/02/arab_league_map.

Countries in Turmoil (Cont.)

Country	Population	GDP per capita	Freedom Rating, 2010*	Level of Corruption, 2010** (0 to 10, with 0 being the most corrupt)
Jordan	6.5 million	$5,300	Not free	4.7
Constitutional monarchy; independent from British mandate since 1946. King Abdallah II in power since 1999.				
Libya	6.6 million	$13,800	Not free	2.2
Dictatorship run by revolutionary leader Moammar Gadhafi since 1969.				
Mauritania	3.3 million	$2,100	Not free	2.3
Military junta; independent from France since 1960. President Mohamed Ould Abdel Aziz in power since 2009.				
Morocco	32 million	$4,999	Partly free	3.4
Constitutional monarchy; independent from France since 1956. King Mohammed VI in power since 1999.				
Oman	3 million	$25,800	Not free	5.3
Monarchy; independent since mid-1700s following Portuguese and Persian rule. Sultan Qaboos bin Said Al-Said in power since 1970.				
Saudi Arabia	26.1 million	$24,200	Not free	4.7
Monarchy; founded in 1932 after several attempts to unify the Arabian Peninsula. King and Prime Minister Abdallah bin Abd al-Aziz Al Saud has been in power since 2005.				
Sudan	45 million	$2,200	Not free	1.6
Independent from U.K. since 1956. Power-sharing government in place since 2005 peace agreement. President Omar al-Bashir has ruled since 1993. Southern part of country will become independent on July 9, 2011, following a referendum in January.				
Syria	22.5 million	$4,800	Not free	2.5
Authoritarian regime; was a French mandate until 1946. President Bashar Assad's family has been in power for 40 years.				
Tunisia	10.6 million	$9,500	Not free	4.3
Republic; independent from France since 1956. Interim President Fouad M'Bazaa took office in January after protests forced Zine El Abidine Ben Ali from office. Next election: October 2014.				
Yemen	24.1 million	$2,600	Not free	2.2
Republic; independent from Ottoman Empire since 1918. South Yemen unified with North Yemen in 1990. President Ali				

* According to Freedom House

** Transparency International

Source: "The World Factbook," Central Intelligence Agency, 2011, www.cia.gov/library/publications/the-world-factbook/index.html; "Map of Freedom in the World," Freedom House, 2010, www.freedomhouse.org/template.cfm?page=363&year=2010; "Corruption Perceptions Index Results 2010 Results," Transparency International, October 2010, www.transparency.org/policy_research/surveys_indices/cpi/2010/results.

"What people in [Cairo's] Tahrir Square were chanting was 'dignity, freedom, social justice.'"

But it was also about economics. "The Arab group [of countries] is not a monolithic group . . . but we face the same challenges in terms of employment, in terms of investing in our people," declared Taieb Fassi Fihri, the foreign minister of Morocco, where some minor outbreaks also occurred. "More than 50 percent of our citizens are less than 25 years old, and we have to respond to the legitimate ambitions of our youth."[1]

Although initially peaceful, the demonstrations have not been without violence. At least 872 people died and 6,400 were injured during the nearly three weeks of turmoil in Egypt, largely the result of a government crackdown on the demonstrators, according to a recent fact-finding mission.[2] In Syria and Yemen, more than 635 have been killed in government backlashes, and untold thousands have died in what has devolved into a civil war in Libya.

The unrest has shown that autocracies don't last forever. They are stable — until they are not. But the

Women Played Key Roles in Demonstrations

"We went through everything our brothers went through."

If the upheaval in the Middle East has done nothing else, it has seriously challenged the image of Arab women as second-class citizens in a male-dominated society. In Cairo, Egypt, women joined men in the pro-democracy demonstrations in Tahrir Square, and several female doctors and nurses helped to staff the four field hospitals in the square. Even more striking because of their greater seclusion, young women in Yemen started the protesters' encampment at Sanaa University, in the nation's capital.

In Cairo and Sanaa, as well as in Tunis, Tunisia, and Benghazi, Libya, television coverage showed women wearing blue jeans as well as traditional black, mixing with the men in a collective outburst of yearning for change. "We — the girls — spoke with the media, arranged protests, slept in Tahrir Square," Shehata, a young communications graduate, was quoted as saying. "Some of us got detained. So we went through everything our brothers [went] through." [1]

Says political scientist Alanoud Al-Sharekh, who works in the Chatham House think tank office in Bahrain's capital, Manama, "The traditional view is that Arab women remained in the background; a heavy nationalist movement with women in the fore means that this label can be removed: women have gained legitimacy."

And Gawdat Bahgat, an Egyptian-born professor of political science at the National Defense University in Washington, D.C., says women's role in the demonstrations "begs the question about women in the Arab world. Women demonstrators were not demanding equal rights: They were shouting the same slogans as the men. They were part of the revolution."

Even so, Nadje Al-Ali, a London-based author of studies on Egyptian and Iraqi women, warns against generalizing about the status of Arab women because the situation is different in virtually every country, and even between different social groups within the same country. "Middle-class women in Cairo probably have a better life than middle-class women in New York because they can get more domestic help and have more time to follow their own pursuits; it's the working-class women that have more problems," she says.

AFP/Getty Images/Miguel Medina

Women, who have not traditionally been active in Egyptian politics, helped organize and participated in the massive protests in Cairo's Tahrir Square against the regime of President Hosni Mubarak.

But can Arab women consolidate their gender gains? The first signs are not encouraging. On March 8, a large gathering of women in Tahrir Square to mark International Women's Day was heckled and taunted by a sea of angry men, who ultimately chased them off the square. "Go home and make mahshy [stuffed vegetables]," the men shouted, to the astonishment of the women. Some of the men even grabbed the placards held by the women — demanding a fair constitution, wide-ranging participation in government and an end to sexual harassment — and tore them to shreds. [2]

Women were particularly disappointed that no females were included in the commission appointed to reform the Egyptian constitution. "Women need to get in there right away because there are some gender-specific issues in the constitution, and women need to be involved in reviewing them," says Al-Ali. Some of the obvious legal inequalities include "getting rid of male guardians [which every Muslim woman must have], and reforming the laws of marriage, divorce and inheritance derived by interpretation of Sharia law," she adds.

Under Sharia family law, for example, a woman's testimony is not acceptable in court. However, a husband can get a unilateral divorce simply by verbally repudiating his wife, but a woman must give justifications. Child custody reverts to the father at a preset age — unless a woman has already lost custody by re-marrying. Sons inherit twice the amount as daughters.

But since 2004 Arab women's-rights activists have been able to point to Morocco, where family-law reforms overturned many discriminatory provisions. The minimum age for Moroccan women to marry was raised from 15 to 18, the same as for men; women are now allowed to marry without approval from a guardian; men can no longer unilaterally divorce their wives, and women were given the right to divorce their husbands. Men can still have multiple wives, but they must first get permission from a judge.

Although female followers of the Egyptian Muslim Brotherhood were among the demonstrators in Cairo, the prospect of the Brotherhood playing what will likely be a significant political role in post-Mubarak Egypt raises fears among some Egyptians that the radical Muslim movement might find a way to impose Sharia law.

Al-Ali concedes that while women historically have taken part in revolutionary movements, "when [the] aims are achieved, women are often pushed aside." Yet she is cautiously optimistic that this time Arab women will make some gains, but not to the same degree in every country. "Women in Saudi Arabia are starting from a different point from women in Egypt," she says.

Laura Guazzone, a Middle East specialist at the Institute of International Affairs and an associate professor of Arab history at Sapienza University in Rome, is equally cautious in her predictions. "The presence of women in the demonstrations was a step forward; I would expect it to translate into a modest amount of liberalization in the national context."

Female Literacy Rates Differ

More than 80 percent of the women in Jordan and Bahrain can read and write — the highest rates among the countries in turmoil in the Middle East and North Africa. Morocco and Yemen have the lowest female literacy rates — below 40 percent. Only about 11 percent of the members of parliament in the region are women, about half the global rate.

Female Literacy Rates in Countries With Unrest*			
Jordan	84.7%	Tunisia	65.3%
Bahrain	83.6%	Algeria	60.1%
Syria	73.6%	Egypt	59.4%
Oman	73.5%	Sudan	50.5%
Libya	72%	Mauritania	43.4%
Saudi Arabia	70.8%	Morocco	39.6%
Iran	70.4%	Yemen	30%

Percentage of Women Serving in Parliament

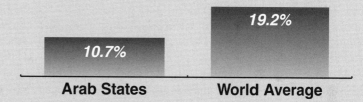

10.7% **Arab States**   19.2% **World Average**

* Based on the most recent post-2000 census available.

Sources: The World Factbook, CIA; Inter-Parliamentary Union, www.ipu.org/wmn-e/world.htm

Even so, in Cairo, prize-winning Egyptian novelist Ahdaf Soueif shrugs off nervousness about the Brotherhood's intentions. "Things can only get better," she says. "This is not a Brotherhood movement, this is an inclusive movement, and when the time comes we'll sort it out."

— Roland Flamini

[1] "Sisters aspire to equality within Egypt's Muslim Brotherhood," *Al Masry Al Youm*, March 16, 2011, www.almasryalyoum.com/en/node/354388.

[2] Hania Sholkamy, "From Tahrir square to my kitchen," *50.50 inclusive democracy*, March 14, 2011, www.opendemocracy.net/5050/hania-sholkamy/from-tahrir-square-to-my-kitchen.

euphoria generated across the region by the popular uprisings in Tunisia and Egypt quickly turned bleak, as Egyptians grappled with the challenges of rebuilding their nation from the ground up, and entrenched leaders elsewhere fought back against spiraling street demonstrations. With the death toll and arrests mounting daily, there was growing concern in the international community — and, in the case of Libya, a decision by the United Nations and NATO to intervene to protect civilians, which some see as a scenario that could well be repeated elsewhere before the dust settles in the Arab world.

In four countries, security forces and demonstrators have clashed repeatedly. More than 140 demonstrators have died in three months of unrest in Yemen, where protesters are calling for the departure of President Ali Abdullah Saleh (32 years in office).[3] One of the worst incidents occurred on March 18 in Sanaa, the capital, when government snipers firing from rooftops killed at least 45 demonstrators and injured 200.[4] In an effort to halt demonstrations in Syria, President Bashar Assad has promised some reforms, including lifting emergency law, but the unrest continued into late April. In the tiny Gulf kingdom of Bahrain, King Hamad Al Khalifa faces public pressure from a Shiite majority to reform the constitution.[5] In Amman, Jordan, a man was killed when riot police forcibly dismantled a protesters' camp. Demonstrators want King Abdullah II to hasten promised electoral reforms.

But nowhere has the government backlash been as violent as in Libya, where the cost in deaths, injuries and refugees continues to climb, as a rag-tag opposition defies longtime leader Moammar Gadhafi. The fighting has split the oil-rich desert nation, with the rebels in tenuous control of the eastern part, centered in Benghazi. On March 19, urged by the Arab League and armed with a U.N. Security Council resolution, Western nations imposed a no-fly zone over Libya. Initially, U.S. forces destroyed Gadhafi's air operations, and then six NATO countries and one Arab nation — Qatar — began attacking Gadhafi's forces in an effort to protect civilians. The government advance has been stalled, but rebels have been unable to progress. The Obama administration later agreed to send unmanned drones to support the insurrection. Meanwhile, Britain, France and Italy sent advisers to train the fighters.

The international community called on Gadhafi to step down, but the 68-year-old Libyan leader became more defiant daily. The fear, among some experts, is that the Libyan stand-off could encourage other embattled leaders to stay put at all cost, transforming the wave of pro-democracy demonstrations into a series of civil wars.

The Obama administration finds itself caught between old alliances and newly emerging opposition movements. Virtually all the region's dictators — except for Assad in Syria — were U.S. allies, including, most recently, the now demonized Gadhafi. Many of the old regimes cooperated with the United States in the ongoing war against terrorism. But the future shape of the Arab world also has global implications. The Middle East and North Africa provide a third of the 86 million barrels of oil consumed worldwide each day, with 13 million coming from Saudi Arabia and the United Arab Emirates alone.[6] And Egypt and Jordan are key participants in the perennial search for a solution to the Palestinian-Israeli conflict.[7] Although no anti-Israel slogans have been seen in the demonstrations so far, the Arab-Israeli issue has certainly not disappeared from the Arab radar screen.

The new governments in the region "are going to take a fresh look at Arab-Israeli relations," says David Aaron, a former deputy national security adviser and now a Middle East specialist at the RAND Corporation think tank offices in Washington, D.C. "They're going to see that the Israelis had 30 years to do something about implementing the Camp David agreements and — from their perspective — haven't done anything." A new Pew Research Center poll of Egyptians, conducted during the uprising, showed that 54 percent favor canceling the 1979 peace treaty with Israel.[8]

And what can the United States expect from the changes? "What struck me about the Tahrir Square protests was that for the first time the demonstrators didn't burn U.S. flags," comments Gawdat Bahgat, an Egyptian-born professor of political science at the National Defense University in Washington, D.C. "There was no anti-American sentiment." Even so, weeks later, when U.S. Secretary of State Hillary Rodham Clinton visited Tahrir Square, young demonstrators' groups refused to meet with her —"due to her initially negative stance toward the revolution during its inception and the approach of the U.S. administration towards the Middle East region," they said in a statement. On the first day of the uprisings Clinton had called the Egyptian regime "stable."[9]

Both activists and Western powers worry the upheaval will open the way for radical Islamists to gain control across the Arab world. But the demonstrations so far have been secular — so secular, in fact, that female demonstrators mixed freely with the men. Still, Bahgat believes, "Post-Mubarak Egypt will be more Islamic, and there will be less cooperation in the war on terrorism," which "is seen by many as war on Islam."

In Egypt, Islamist activism is led by the Muslim Brotherhood, the largest religious-political organization in the region. But Jean-Pierre Filiu, head of Middle East studies at the Political Science Institute in Paris (known as Sciences Po), does not see it as a threat. "There is no [Islamist] bogeyman in Egypt or Tunisia," he says. "I don't see any place where the Brotherhood will win a majority. They will end up part of coalitions."

Fear of rising Islamist influence stems in part from the fact that the regimes under siege had suppressed political opposition for so long that the democratic credentials of protest leaders are unknown and untested. But a more immediate anxiety, says historian Fahmy, is "fear of a counter-revolution, with the old regime coming back under a different guise."

So far, the revolution has raised more questions than it has answered, among them:

Can Western-style democracy take root in Arab countries?

Decades of autocratic government in the region have led to the widely held view that democracy cannot take hold in the Arab world. The familiar arguments include:

- Islam is not a democratic religion;
- There is no Arabic word for "democracy;"
- Abundant oil and gas revenue has meant citizens of some countries do not pay taxes and thus have no expectations of government accountability; and
- Western democracies had reinforced the very autocratic regimes that the protesters are trying to bring down.

Supporting those arguments, Bernard Lewis, a prominent American authority on the Middle East, recently told *The Jerusalem Post* that "the Arab masses are simply not ready for free and fair elections." He recommended that political reform follow traditional regional practices, such as consultative councils between rulers and other officials, with the circle of those consulted gradually expanding.

But Larry Diamond, a senior fellow at Stanford University's conservative Hoover Institution and an expert on democracy, says, "Support for democracy is very broad in the Arab world, and it does not vary by degree of religiosity. Look at the way Iraqis turned out to vote three times in 2005 amid widespread and dire risks to their physical safety, and it is hard to conclude that Arabs do not care about democracy."[10]

Two Middle East scholars — writing in *Survival*, the magazine of the International Institute of Strategic Studies in London — argue that the recent turmoil "has convincingly demonstrated that the Arab world yearns, too, for dignity and better governance. Arab citizens, long thought to be either hopelessly apathetic or uniquely prone to violent political rage, proved to be relentless and, in most cases, peaceful protesters."[11]

And Egyptian historian Fahmy says in recent weeks Egyptians have amply indicated that they understand the essence of democracy. They have consistently demanded "human rights and dignity, social justice, equal opportunities, and the end to police brutality," he says.

But what shape will Arab-style democracy take? "There is no one-size-fits-all, such as U.S.-style democracy," the National Defense University's Bahgat says. "What needs to happen is the start of democratization, which is not the same as democracy; it's the process of getting there — and there will be many bumps along the way."

The Economist doesn't foresee a smooth transition either. "No perfectly formed democracy is about to emerge from the detritus of Mr. Mubarak's regime," the magazine commented recently. "But Egypt, though poor, has a sophisticated elite, a well-educated middle class and a strong sense of national pride." All those factors indicate that "Egyptians can pull order out of this chaos."[12]

Former British Prime Minister Tony Blair, the troubleshooter for the international Quartet (the U.S., Russia, the U.N., and the EU) responsible for advancing the Palestinian-Israeli peace process, said it was important for the Arabs to understand what constitutes democracy. "It's not just about the freedom to vote," said Blair. "It's about freedom of expression, free markets, freedom of religion, the rule of law and a whole series of things that go to make up a genuine democracy."[13]

Most Egyptians View U.S. Unfavorably

More than three-quarters of Egyptians say they have an unfavorable view of the United States while the ratio of those who believe the U.S. response to the revolution in Egypt had a negative rather than positive impact is about 2 to 1. Egyptians are about evenly split over Islamic fundamentalists, and more than half believe Egypt should annul its peace treaty with Israel. Among potential political leaders, Mohammad Tantawi and Amr Moussa were clear favorites.

How favorable is your opinion of the United States?

Very favorable	9%
Somewhat favorable	11%
Somewhat unfavorable	30%
Very unfavorable	49%

What kind of impact has the U.S. response made in Egypt?

Positive	22%
Negative	39%
Neither	35%

Do you empathize with the Islamic fundamentalists in Egypt or with those who disagree with them?

With Islamic fundamentalists	31%
With those who disagree	30%
Both	11%
Neither	15%
Don't know/didn't answer	14%

Should Egypt maintain or annul its peace treaty with Israel?

Annul	54%
Maintain	36%
Don't know/didn't answer	10%

How favorable is your opinion of the following political leaders?

Mohammad Tantawi, chairman of the Supreme Council of the Armed Forces
Amr Moussa, secretary-general of the Arab League
Ayman Nour, chairman of the El Ghad party
Mohamed ElBaradei, former director general of the International Atomic Energy Agency
Omar Suleiman, former vice president
Hosni Mubarak, former president

- Very favorable
- Somewhat favorable
- Somewhat unfavorable
- Very unfavorable

* Figures may not total 100 due to rounding.

Source: Pew Research Center, April 2011, pewglobal.org/files/2011/04/Pew-Global-Attitudes-Egypt-Report-FINAL-April-25-2011.pdf.

Laura Guazzone, an expert on the Middle East at Rome's Sapienza University, says the best outcome would be that some countries will evolve "through a succession of compromises into quasi-democracies, politically much more liberal than the previous regimes but still largely based on the same power structures and orientations in their respective economic and foreign policies." Potential worst-case scenarios range "from a tightening of the existing repression under the same regime (Bahrain, Syria) to secession and Somalia-style fragmentation (Yemen, Libya)."

Is the current upheaval in the best interests of the Western powers and Israel?

Before the current unrest, the status quo in the Middle East and North Africa had served Western strategic interests for decades. Successive American administrations had tacitly supported, and funded, many of the regimes under assault, turning a blind eye to corruption, cronyism and torture.

"Let's face it: Mubarak was a strategic asset to the United States," says Steven A. Cook, a senior fellow at the New York-based Council on Foreign Relations think tank. "He ensured access to the Suez Canal, upheld the Egypt-Israel peace treaty and kept the Islamists down. . . . The fact that the United States supported this now-discredited government for three decades is not lost on Egyptians."

For decades, "U.S. policy has been to divide the moderate Arabs (Egypt, Jordan, Saudi Arabia) from the extremist Arabs (Syria)," says Bahgat, of the National Defense University.

Now, however, "the moderate camp is collapsing." Whoever assumes power will likely be unknown quantities to Washington and the European capitals.

If the region has become a daunting new challenge, the main issues have remained the same: terrorism, the Arab-Israeli conflict and Iran's nuclear ambitions. The crucial nature of that challenge may account for the Obama administration's initial ambivalence toward the protest movement. *Newsweek* columnist Niall Ferguson called Obama's handling of the situation in Egypt "a foreign policy debacle" by one day urging Mubarak to quit and the next day calling for an "orderly transition."[14]

But the demonstrators in Egypt weren't paying much attention to the United States, recalls Fahmy, of the American University in Cairo. Initially, they were too determined to stay on message; after Mubarak's departure, they were too euphoric. "The 'street' couldn't care less what Obama was saying," he says. "The U.S. had clearly been caught unawares and was ill-equipped to deal with the situation because of Washington's obsession with Islam and terrorism. We kept on saying: There is something else in these societies besides Islam and terrorism."

Washington Post foreign affairs columnist David Ignatius urged Obama to "go to the Middle East and embrace this moment. I understand his desire to stay out of the limelight, but it's proving to be a mistake. This is a world-historical event, as powerful as the fall of the Berlin Wall."[15]

U.S. Defense Secretary Robert Gates, who had maintained close contact with the Egyptian army throughout the uprising, has visited Cairo and reassured the interim government that U.S. aid ($1.3 billion a year in military support and hundreds of millions in other assistance) will continue.[16]

But most experts say the United States should tread warily. "Regionally, American foreign initiatives are viewed with suspicion, and too ambitious or inconsistent a policy agenda could end up backfiring in a region as volatile as the Arab world," warns Naveed Sheikh, a professor of international politics at Britain's Keele University. Obama is limited by the wars in Iraq and Afghanistan, which Sheikh calls "imperial projects that were neither economically, militarily or morally sustainable."

Though Israel was not a target of the protesters in Tahrir Square, Mubarak's commitment to the Israeli-Palestinian

To show the nondenominational nature of their pro-democracy movement, Coptic Christians and Muslims in Cairo's Tahrir Square raise a cross and the Quran on Feb. 6, the 13th day of protests calling for President Hosni Mubarak to resign. He stepped down five days later. Some "Copts" — an Egyptian Christian sect that predates Islam — fear that they could continue to be persecuted, as they were under the Mubarak regime, if the Islamist Muslim Brotherhood gains power in Egypt.

peace process clearly was: Some demonstrators waved placards in Hebrew, claiming the only language the Egyptian president understood was that of Israel's leaders. One of the first acts of Egypt's Supreme Council of the Armed Forces was to reassure Washington and Tel Aviv that it will respect Egypt's international commitments, a reference to the 1978 Camp David Accords and the 1979 Egypt-Israel peace treaty. Experts say the Egyptians probably will not want to return to war with Israel, but will they be prepared to let the peace agreements stand?

"Washington has lost an unconditional ally," wrote Alain Gresh, editor of the French foreign policy journal *Le Monde Diplomatique*. "U.S. regional strategy has relied on Egypt, along with Israel, . . . for the last 30 years. . . . Mubarak was at the forefront of the fight against the 'Iranian threat.' He maintained the illusion of the Middle East 'peace process,' putting pressure on the Palestinian Authority to continue negotiations."[17]

"Egypt under Mubarak participated in the economic blockade of Gaza and helped scuttle all attempts at reconciliation by Hamas and Fatah, even one negotiated by another 'moderate' country, Saudi Arabia [the Mecca accord of 2007]," Gresh continued. "A more representative

CHRONOLOGY

1950s-1960s *Egyptian strongman Gamal Abdel Nasser challenges West, strives to unite Arab world under his leadership.*

1952 Military coup led by Lt. Col. Nasser deposes King Farouk II, establishes Egyptian Republic.

1956 Nasser nationalizes Suez Canal in July. . . . In October, Britain, France and Israel attack Egypt in a bid to re-take control of the canal; hostilities cease after United States threatens sanctions against Britain.

1961 Sheikh Isa bin Salman Al Khalifa becomes emir of Bahrain.

1967 Mounting tension between Israel and its Arab neighbors culminates in six days of hostilities: Israel launches surprise air attack on Egypt and then seizes Gaza from Egypt and the Golan Heights from Syria and pushes Jordanian forces out of East Jerusalem and the West Bank.

1970s-1980s *Historic, U.S.-brokered Middle East peace accords halt hostilities between Israel and Egypt.*

1970 Air Force chief Hafez Assad seizes power in Syria. A year later, he is elected president for seven-year term.

1973 In effort to regain territory lost in 1967, Egypt and Syria launch major offensive against Israel on Yom Kippur, the Jewish Day of Atonement. After initial successes, the attack fails.

1975 In Bahrain, emir dissolves National Assembly and rules by decree after Prime Minister Sheikh Khalifah bin Salman Al Khalifah says it is impeding the government's work.

1978 U.S.-led negotiations lead to Camp David Accords between Israel and Egypt. "Framework for Peace" in the Middle East includes limited autonomy for Palestinians.

1981 Egyptian President Anwar al-Sadat is assassinated by jihadist Army officers for his role in signing Camp David Accords. Vice President Hosni Mubarak, wounded during the assassination, becomes president.

1982 Syria's Hafez Assad suppresses Muslim Brotherhood uprising in Hama; tens of thousands of civilians are reported killed.

1987 Tunisian Prime Minister Zine El Abidine Ben Ali takes power after having the aged President Habib Bourguiba declared mentally unfit. Two years later, Ben Ali wins the first of four presidential elections.

1990s-2000s *United States fights two wars against Iraq and opens a new front against al-Qaida after 9/11 jihadist attacks in the United States.*

1990 Iraq invades Kuwait; Syria and Egypt join U.S.-led coalition against Iraq. U.S.-Egyptian relations improve.

1990 Ali Abdullah Saleh, president of North Yemen, proclaims the Unified Republic of Yemen, with himself as president.

1991 Bahrain's port becomes base for U.S. Fifth Fleet.

1992 Aden hotel used by U.S. marines is bombed in first known al-Qaida attack in Yemen. Two Austrian tourists are killed.

2002 Shiite opposition wins 40 percent of Bahrain's parliamentary seats in first election in nearly 30 years. A Shiite is appointed deputy prime minister.

2003 U.S.-led coalition invades Iraq, claiming President Saddam Hussein has stockpiled weapons of mass destruction; none are found.

2009 Saudi and Yemeni al-Qaida branches merge into Al-Qaida in the Arabian Peninsula.

2010 Syria sentences human-rights lawyer Mohannad al-Hassani to three years in jail for "weakening national morale." . . . Former U.N. nuclear chief Mohammed ElBaradei returns to Egypt and forms alliance of activists and opposition politicians for political change; says he might run for president in 2011. . . . Bahrain arrests more than 20 Shiite opposition leaders in broad crackdown for allegedly plotting to overthrow the monarchy.

Dec. 17 A Tunisian vegetable vendor, who had been harassed by police for years, sets himself on fire after a policewoman slaps him. Public frustration over police abuses and lack of jobs erupts into protests that spread across Tunisia. Government cracks down, resulting in more than 60 deaths. Bouazizi dies on Jan. 4.

Jan. 14 Tunisian President Zine El Abidine Ben Ali flees to Saudi Arabia.

Jan. 25 Thousands of Egyptians march to Tahrir Square in Cairo, chanting "Down with Mubarak." Similar protests erupt across the country.

Jan. 27 Thousands of protesters in Sanaa, Yemen's capital, call for end of 32-year regime of autocratic President Ali Abdullah Saleh.

Jan. 31 At least 250,000 demonstrators occupy Tahrir Square, in defiance of military-imposed curfew.

Feb. 11 Demonstrators in Tahrir Square cheer announcement that Mubarak has resigned and handed over power to the army. . . . Protests continue in Yemen; by Feb. 20, seven protesters have been killed in clashes with police.

Feb. 15 Demonstrators break out in Benghazi, Libya. Police break up protest, causing many injuries.

Feb. 19 Benghazi protests degenerate into street fighting, with numerous deaths and injuries. Government officials flee the next day, leaving the city in "rebel" hands.

Feb. 20 Street protests erupt in Libyan capital of Tripoli.

Feb. 22 Libyan leader Moammar Gadhafi blames unrest on Islamists; vows to die as a martyr.

Feb. 26 Mass unrest breaks out in Bahrain, where Shiite majority presses Sunni ruling family for reforms. King Hamad al Khalifa dismisses several ministers, but opposition is not satisfied.

Feb. 26 President Barack Obama says Gadhafi should step down to avoid further bloodshed. Despite aerial bombings, anti-Gadhafi fighters make initial territorial gains, advancing toward Tripoli.

March 7 France and U.K. ask U.N. Security Council to establish a no-fly zone in Libya; Obama administration is hesitant but agrees after Arab League endorses proposal on March 12.

March 10 Well-armed pro-Gadhafi counter-offensive repels rebels.

March 15 Anti-government protests spread in Syria, the first since a state of emergency was issued 48 years ago.

March 18 In Yemen, police snipers kill at least 45 demonstrators near Sanaa University, prompting top military defections.

March 19 U.S. and British ships fire cruise missiles at more than 20 coastal targets in Libya as U.N. no-fly zone goes into effect. . . . Egyptians approve constitutional amendments; one limits presidency to two terms.

April 8 Yemen's Saleh rejects resignation plan brokered by neighboring Gulf States.

April 13 Egypt's Mubarak and his sons are detained after allegations of corruption and abuse of power.

April 17 Eleven killed in Homs, Syria, as unrest continues against regime of President Bashar Assad.

April 20 Pro-Gadhafi forces continue fighting, despite no-fly zone and NATO attacks on troops and armor. U.S., NATO and Qatar agree to fund Libyan revolutionary movement.

April 21 Yemen's Saleh considers second resignation scenario proposed by Gulf States: creation of a national unity government led by the opposition, with Saleh quitting in one month. . . . Assad ends emergency law in Syria, abolishes state security courts and allows citizens to protest peacefully.

April 22 United States decides to use armed drones in Libya.

April 25 Thousands of troops, backed by tanks, confront demonstrators in Syria.

future government in Egypt . . . will probably be more wary of U.S. attempts to form a common (if undeclared) front between Arab countries and Israel against Iran."[18]

A Cairo-brokered unity pact announced on April 27 between rival Palestinian groups seemed to confirm Gresh's predictions. The announcement that secret reconciliation talks had succeeded between the mainstream West Bank-controlling Fatah and its radical Islamist rival Hamas, which runs Gaza, surprised the international community. The two groups said they had reached an accord in part because of recent large pro-unity demonstrations staged by young Palestinians inspired by events in Egypt. Fatah leader Mahmoud Abbas and his Hamas counterpart Khaled Mashaal agreed to a joint interim government and possible combined elections in December.[19]

However, the deal could alienate Western support for Fatah, since both Israel and the United States call Hamas a terrorist organization and refuse to negotiate with it unless its leaders denounce violence. Nevertheless, analysts say the negotiating role played by Egypt's new government and its recognition of the pro-Hamas Muslim Brotherhood indicate that Egypt's evolving foreign policy could shift the political landscape in the Middle East.

U.S. relations with several other former allies likely will be pricklier as well. For example, Bahrain is immensely important to the United States strategically because it is home to the U.S. Fifth Fleet, which patrols Gulf and Central Asian waters. And Yemen plays a key role in Washington's ongoing anti-terrorism offensive by fighting the supposedly large al-Qaida presence in its rugged hinterlands. But if President Saleh is toppled — as seems likely — will the new regime be so cooperative?

The European Union might have easier relations with the new governments. As soon as Mubarak stepped down, the EU — the second-largest aid donor in the Middle East — immediately promised the interim government $670 million in aid. While the European governments also did business with autocratic Arab regimes, Arabs generally think the EU has tried harder than Washington to reach a solution in the Arab-Israeli conflict and sympathizes more with the Palestinians.

Moreover, "No one has more experience than Europeans do in difficult transitions from dictatorship to democracy," writes *Guardian* newspaper columnist

Timothy Garton Ash. "No region has more instruments at its disposal to affect developments in the Arab Middle East. The U.S. may have special relationships with the Egyptian military and Arab ruling families, but Europe has more trade, gives a lot of aid, and has a thick web of cultural and person-to-person ties across what the Romans called *Mare Nostrum*, our sea." Moreover, he continues, Europe is where most young Arabs "want to come — to visit, to study, to work. Their cousins are here already."[20]

Will the upheaval in the Middle East help Islamic extremists?

For years, most Arab dictators told Washington they were the only bulwarks against an Islamist extremist takeover in the region. Mubarak's bogeyman was the Muslim Brotherhood; Saleh's was al-Qaida, which has also been taken up by Gadhafi — when he isn't blaming youths on hallucinogens.

Three leading Egyptian political figures — Naguib Sawiris, founder and chairman of the giant Egyptian telecom company Orascom, who has just launched his own political party, and presidential candidates Amr Moussa and Mohamed ElBaradei — recently echoed their concern about the Brotherhood. They told *Washington Post* columnist Ignatius they worried that it and other Islamist groups could hijack Egypt's nascent democracy. Sawiris — a Coptic Christian — said he has "a real fear" that "we will get an Iranian type regime here."[21]

"Copts [an Egyptian Christian sect] are definitely concerned about the Brotherhood," affirms historian Fahmy. Egypt's 7 million indigenous Christians were persecuted during the Mubarak regime. Nadje Al-Ali, a gender expert at the School of Oriental and Asian Studies at the University of London, says some Egyptians worry that "the Brotherhood could push for women and Copts not to be able to run for president."

But Sciences Po's Jean-Pierre Filiu says the Brotherhood is not homogeneous, and that internal differences could weaken its influence. "I doubt very much that the Brotherhood will remain unified," he predicts.

Keele University's Sheikh says being in government will make the Brotherhood less militant. "Radical voices flourish if denied public space, legitimacy and responsibility," he explains. "There is a moderating influence in having to compete in the open market place for ideas." In Turkey and Indonesia, for instance, conservative Islamic governments have tended "to focus on 'deliverables' once given a stake in the state," he argues.

Not so, says Ray Takeyh, a senior fellow for Middle Eastern Studies at the Council on Foreign Relations. The theory that the responsibility of governance inevitably moderates Islamic political groups is "a liberal conceit" that denigrates their "commitment to their dogma," he says. Islamist parties can be expected to "menace an inexperienced democratic order" and likely will campaign against women's rights, and their militias "will threaten secular politicians . . . who do not conform to their template."

The danger is not that Islamist tactics would gain them absolute power, Takeyh continues, but that a nervous military would intervene "in the name of stability and order," taking the region's new democracies back to autocratic rule. So the United States and its allies must "strengthen the political center." A massive package of economic assistance to countries such as Tunisia and Egypt could "tether these nations to the United States" — as long as they steer clear of extremism, he suggests.

Meanwhile, the perceived threat level from al-Qaida varies depending on the country. "Al-Qaida will move, will try, will test, will intervene, taking the opportunity of any uncertainties," Moroccan Foreign Minister Fihri warns. "Al-Qaida looks for the space where there is no strong, democratic national power."

That danger could come to fruition in Yemen, where al-Qaida is said to have a firm foothold. "The four provinces where Al-Qaeda is believed to be hiding and strengthening . . . are out of the control of the central government in Sanaa," the *Egyptian Al-Ahram Weekly* reported.[22] The U.S. view is that Al-Qaida in the Arabian Peninsula (AQAP) was behind last fall's attempt to detonate bombs on a Chicago-bound plane and the attempt to blow up a passenger jet over Detroit on Christmas Day 2009. The group also shelters the American-born preacher Anwar al-Awlaki, who has been in Yemen since 2004.

Sapienza University's Guazzone agrees that al-Qaida will try to exploit any vacuum but sees "no structural, long-term way in which al-Qaida networks can reap major political benefits" as a result of the turmoil. The

uprisings have been instigated and sustained by "non-ideological, nonviolent" youth movements that are "very concrete in their demands" for freedom, dignity and employment, she points out. "They have no ties nor sympathies with jihadism and its fantasy of restoring a global caliphate through armed struggle."

BACKGROUND
Imperialism and Colonialism

The modern Arab world is, in part, a patchwork of countries carved out of the old Ottoman Empire, the precursor of modern Turkey. At its height in the 17th century, Ottoman power extended from Croatia in the Balkans to Algeria in the western Mediterranean. By 1900, the empire had shrunk dramatically. Then Turkey sided with Germany in World War I, giving the victorious powers the excuse to divide it up into European-controlled "mandates."[23]

Britain controlled the lion's share: Egypt, Transjordan (modern Jordan), Palestine (including modern Israel and the West Bank) and Iraq. France's sphere of influence included Syria and Lebanon (Algeria and Tunisia had been in French hands since the 1830s.) Italy got Cyrenaica — today's Libya. Artificial borders were delineated, compliant dictators and monarchs installed in power and modest political reforms imposed.

However, wrote historian William Cleveland in *A History of the Modern Middle East*, "The same elite that had enjoyed power and prestige before 1914 — the European-educated landed and professional classes in Egypt and the traditional notables in Syria, Lebanon and Palestine — continued to exercise their privileges during the 1920s and 1930s."[24]

The discovery of vast oil deposits in the Arab world in the early 1900s changed the equation. Oil and the machines it powered had proved critical to the world's militaries during World War I. The industrialized Western powers now had a powerful incentive to protect their interests in the region, just as the Arabs began to turn to nationalism and pan-Arabism as political organizing principles.

After World War II, countries in the Arab world, Africa and elsewhere became independent. During the 1950s-1970s, a wave of Arab nationalist leaders and

Spotting the Next Generation of Arab Leaders

By crushing opposition, autocratic leaders eliminated likely successors.

Above all else, the autocratic leaders of the Middle East were masters at suppressing opposition. As a result, few obvious leaders are waiting to fill the power vacuums left by regimes collapsing across the region. Still, some names have surfaced among the demonstrators either as influential king makers or as likely presidential candidates themselves.

The lack of a successor is probably most evident in Tunisia, where former President Zine El Abidine Ben Ali kept a tight grip on his country. An interim government is in place, but the powerful labor union UGTT has come into its own, with Ali Ben Romdhane, the union's joint leader, as a spokesman for the reformers.[1]

In March, in advance of the July 24 election for a constituent assembly to reform the constitution, the government legalized the reportedly moderate Islamic organization Ennahdha ("Renaissance"), banned by the Ben Ali regime. The group's leader, Rachid Ghannouchi, who returned from 22 years of exile in London, is considered a presidential contender.[2]

In Egypt, the most widely known politician at Tahrir Square was without question Nobel Peace Prize winner Mohamed ElBaradei, former head of the U.N. International Atomic Energy Agency. He gained world prominence in 2002 and 2003 for being one of the first to challenge the Bush administration's claim that Saddam Hussein had stockpiled weapons of mass destruction. Following his retirement, he returned to his native Cairo in 2010 and was immediately seen as a possible challenger to President Hosni Mubarak in the November 2011 presidential race. ElBaradei, 68, said he would consider running if there were reforms to guarantee a fair election.

A one-time Egyptian national squash champion, ElBaradei has support among the younger generation of demonstrators, but an online poll on the website of al-Ahram newspaper showed 74-year-old Amr Moussa, departing secretary general of the Arab League and the other declared presidential candidate, as the current front runner.

Both men had distinguished diplomatic careers. As Egyptian foreign minister Moussa occasionally rocked the boat by being quite critical of Israel (much to Washington's annoyance). Mubarak tactfully replaced him after a pop song came out titled, "I hate Israel, and I love Amr Moussa."[3]

The younger generation of Egyptian politicians is represented by Islam Lutfi, 33, and the already legendary Wael Ghonim. Lutfi, a 33-year-old lawyer, heads the youth wing of the Muslim Brotherhood and represents the once-outlawed organization on the recently formed constitutional reform panel. During the demonstrations Lutfi addressed Christian groups in Tahrir Square, saying Egyptians should be united. Under his direction the youth wing of the Brotherhood has pushed the organization's leadership to tackle issues of immediate concern to Egyptians — such as such as corruption and freedom of expression — and, more tentatively, to distance itself from more violent Islamic fundamentalists.

If any one individual launched Egypt's mass protests it was Ghonim, Google's head of marketing for the Middle East. The mild-mannered, 30-year-old father of two moved sideways into politics by designing first ElBaradei's website, which calls for democratic reforms, and then the famous web page memorializing Khaled Said, a young Egyptian who was beaten to death by two Alexandria policemen after he filmed them sharing the proceeds of a drug bust.

Ghonim's Facebook page, "We are all Khaled Said," went viral, making the young man's death a cause célèbre. Ghonim also set the date for the first Tahrir Square demonstration on Jan. 25th — ironically National Police Day. Ghonim himself was arrested in the square and held for 12 days, emerging to find himself a hero of the revolution.

dictators came to power, beginning with Gamal Abdel Nasser in Egypt in 1956, followed later by Moammar Gadhafi (1969) in Libya, Syria's Hafez Assad (1971) and Saddam Hussein in Iraq (1979).

Meanwhile, Western oil companies remained anchored in Saudi Arabia and the other oil-rich Persian Gulf monarchies and in Iran — the latter until the ayatollahs took over in 1979.[25]

Triumph

Today's Arab protesters owe a historic debt to 26-year-old Mohamed Bouazizi, a Tunisian fruit and vegetable

"This revolution started on Facebook," he said in a recent interview. "I always said, if you want to liberate a society, just give them the Internet."[4]

Ghonim's political future is uncertain. There are "Ghonim for president" websites in Egypt, but he doesn't seem to have political ambitions and wants to get back to his work at Google.

If the Egyptian political landscape is complicated, the scenario in Libya is hopelessly chaotic. A 30-member national council was established in Benghazi headed by former Justice Minister Mustapha Abdul Jalil, described by Western media as a conservative Islamist. The council also includes liberal and left-wing members.

The two international front men for Libya's revolution — who have toured foreign capitals lobbying for support and have met with U.S. Secretary of State Hillary Rodham Clinton, British Prime Minister David Cameron and France's President Nicolas Sarkozy — are Ali al-Essawi, former Libyan ambassador to India, and Mahmoud Jibril, a U.S.-educated former Benghazi university professor.[5]

Adding to the chaos, the rag-tag rebel military has rival commanders — Abdul Fattah Younis, a former interior minister and once a friend of Libyan leader Moammar Gadhafi, and Khalifa Heftar, a former general recently returned to Libya from a long exile in Virginia. Heftar proclaimed himself top army commander and is said to have a following among the fighters.

News reports describe meetings of the opposition leadership as little more than shouting matches between rivals at every level. But that, too, may be part of the revolutionary experience. Nobody ever argued with Gadhafi.

— *Roland Flamini*

AFP/Getty Images/Aris Messinis

Arab League secretary-general Amr Moussa votes in Egypt's constitutional referendum on March 19. He received favorable ratings from 89 percent of the respondents in a recent poll.

---

[1] "Tunisie: la nomination de nouveau Premier," Le Pointe.com, Feb. 28, 2011, www.lepoint.fr/monde/tunisie-la-nomination-du-nouveau-premier-ministre-critiquee-sit-in-a-tunis-28-02-2011-1300546_24.php.

[2] "Tunisia to elect constituent team," *Al Jazeera*, Feb. 28, 2011, http://english.al jazeera.net/news/africa/2011/03/20113405133628865.html.

[3] "Amr Moussa," *The New York Times*, March 10, 2011, http://topics.nytimes.com/topics/reference/timestopics/people/m/amr_moussa/index.html.

[4] Joyella, Mark, "First Tunisia, now Egypt, What's Next?" *Media ITE*, Feb. 11, 2011, www.mediaite.com/tv/first-tunisia-now-egypt-whats-next-wael-ghonim-says-ask-facebook/.

[5] "Mahmoud Jibril: the international face of Libya's rebels," CBS News, March 30, 2011, www.cbc.ca/news/world/story/2011/03/29/f-libya-jibril.html.

---

seller. Fed up after years of police bullying, Bouazizi set himself ablaze on December 17 to protest abuse from a female police woman who slapped and harassed him in public. The humiliating incident sparked popular frustrations that quickly spun out across the Arab world.[26]

Each Middle East country is different, but Mustapha K. Nabli, the newly appointed governor of the Tunisian Central Bank, says that Arab unrest is rooted in some common grievances. "The first was blatant and increasingly strong corruption that had created a deep sense of unfairness in the population," he says. "Second, the employment-education nexus: Unemployment in the Middle East and North Africa had been high for a long time and we are in a demographic [youth] bulge."

Autocratic Arab regimes also were vulnerable because of "the rapid growth of new communications technologies and social networks," he adds. Without the Internet, "the corruption of [President] Ben Ali and his cronies would not have inflamed the way [it] did, leading to the sudden eruption of outrage following the death of Mohamed Bouazizi." Lucrative government contracts went to the president's cronies, and his supporters and party members got even the lowest government jobs. The family's penchant for building palatial homes was legendary.

In Egypt, Nabli points out, the police murder of Khaled Said, a young blogger who posted a video of two police-men sharing the spoils of a drug bust, became an instant Internet cause célèbre.[27] Before the Internet, Said's death could well have gone unnoticed. "But in the new age, half a million Egyptians joined the We Are All Khaled Said Facebook page, [which] initiated the January 25 revolution," he says.

The discontent that spread across the Middle East, North Africa and the Persian Gulf also bore a common demographic characteristic. Nearly 60 percent of the 360-million-strong Arab population is under 25 — and largely better educated than in the past.[28] Meanwhile, the Arab unemployment rate of 25 percent in the 15-29 age bracket is the highest in the world.[29] In Yemen, about 75 percent of the population is under 30, and the poverty rate exceeds 45 percent; in Egypt, two-thirds of the population is under 30, while 18-22 percent of the country's 82 million citizens lives on less than $2 per day.[30]

Eleven days after President Ben Ali stunned the Arab world on January 14 by stepping down and leaving Tunisia, protests began in Cairo, spurred by online criti-cism of the Mubarak regime. The president, 82, hadn't announced whether he would run for a sixth term in the spring elections, which would have taken him past 30 years as president, and it seemed likely that he would nominate his 47-year-old son Gamal to run in his stead. Presidential elections in Egypt were widely known to be rigged anyway, so the succession was seen — resentfully — as inevitable.

In hindsight, the elements were there for a showdown. Maha Azzam, a Middle East expert at the London think tank Chatham House, wrote last November, "The

government's heavy-handed tactics, such as detention without trial and allegations of police brutality, have become commonplace. Ahead of the elections, there have been new controls." Nilesat, Egypt's leading satellite operator, had been ordered to shut down 12 television channels. "Newspaper editors have been removed from their jobs, bloggers and SMS [text] messaging have been restricted," Azzam reported. Egypt had experienced 1,600 labor protests since 2006, amid growing social and economic discontent.[31]

But early in 2011, when anti-Mubarak demonstrators defied tear gas and armed pro-Mubarak thugs assailed the demonstrators — even charging the crowd in Tahrir Square on camels and horseback — an emboldened Egyptian press joined the campaign.

"Everything that has happened in Egypt points to a dream come true for us," wrote Fahmy Howeidi, a leading Arab columnist, reflecting the general excitement. "A dream that had been stolen from us for several decades, a dream that permits us to speak with one voice as we call for moving away from pharaonic rule to democratic rule."[32]

In the end, 30 years of dictatorship disappeared in 30 seconds. That's how long it took Vice President Omar Suleiman to announce that Mubarak had resigned and that the Supreme Council was taking over as head of state. "The Young People have done it. Mubarak has stepped aside," proclaimed the Pan Arab newspaper *Al-sharq al-Awsat* [*The Middle East*], as jubilant crowds in Tahrir Square chanted "Egypt is free!"[33]

On the day Mubarak resigned, Saad Eddin Ibrahim, a leading Egyptian activist who had twice been imprisoned by the regime and was living outside of the country, flew to Cairo and went directly to Tahrir Square. "It was just like the day of judgment," he said later. "The way the day of judgment is described in our scripture, the Quran, you have all of humanity in one place, and nobody rec-ognizes anybody else, just faces, faces."[34]

The revolution — like the earlier one in Tunisia — would not have succeeded if the Egyptian army had not been willing to side with the Egyptian people. "The generals were confronted with a serious choice: They could defend Mubarak against the crowd, or defend the crowd against Mubarak," says Professor Fahmy. "The military controls between 5 and 8 percent of the Egyptian economy through weapons manufacturing . . . and other enterprises, and the stand-off was bad for business."

With Mubarak's ouster, Field Marshal Mohamad Hussein Tantawi, chairman of the ruling Supreme Council, became Egypt's fifth consecutive leader to come from the military since a 1952 army coup deposed King Farouk I.*

Almost as soon as Mubarak stepped down, cracks appeared in the protest movement over the nature and pace of reforms and the question of who speaks for the new Egypt. For example, despite the youth movement's demands, the army seemed in no hurry to live up to its promise to lift Egypt's 29-year-old emergency laws. But when the army moved quickly to organize a referendum on March 19 to amend parts of the Egyptian constitution, many of the nascent political groups protested that it was too early. They campaigned to boycott the vote on the grounds that it would only benefit the Muslim Brotherhood, the country's only organized party.

Egyptian voters overwhelmingly approved the referendum. More than 14.1 million people, or 72 percent of those voting, approved the amendments, with 4 million (22.8 percent) opposed. But, partly because of the boycott, only 41 percent of the 45 million eligible voters went to the polls, a disappointment for some commentators but a record for Egypt.[35] The 10 new amendments establish presidential term limits, give the judiciary greater electoral oversight and require a public referendum before a state of emergency can be introduced. The entire constitution is expected to be overhauled next year.

The result reflected a widespread desire for a return to normal life and showed members of the young revolutionary movement that if they wanted to have an impact on reforms they had to be better organized. "The revolutionary dream is now over, and politics must be embraced and welcomed," wrote former Egyptian ambassador Ashraf Surlam. "The battle for the soul and future is on."[36]

Shortly after the referendum, Mubarak and his two sons were detained in connection with allegations of corruption and abuse of power, including — in the former president's case — the killing of demonstrators during the 18 days of unrest.[37] A number of senior regime officials had been detained already for alleged corruption. According to reports, Mubarak was to be moved to the hospital ward of a military prison in Cairo from the

hospital in Sharm al-Sheik where he was taken in March after a heart attack. A commission of inquiry into the demonstrations has determined that 846 civilians and 26 members of Egyptian security were killed in the clashes. A commission spokesman said the security forces would have needed Mubarak's permission to use live ammunition.

Contagion

Tahrir Square and Tunisia sent a strong message to other Arabs that "they had the ability to change things if they were prepared to sacrifice themselves for their freedom and if there was unity of purpose," says Ahmed Ibrahim Rizk, who heads the Ibn Khaldun Center, a Cairo research institute. By March anti-government demonstrations had broken out in Jordan, Libya, Bahrain and Syria. Eventually, sporadic protests also were reported in Algeria, Sudan, Morocco, Mauritania, Saudi Arabia, Iran and Oman.

In Bahrain's tiny, oil-rich archipelago the unrest has had sectarian overtones. The minority Sunni-led monarchy is being challenged by the country's Shiite majority, which represents 70 percent of the 1.2 million population. But unlike the protesters in Cairo, who demanded the removal of Mubarak, Bahrain's protesters were not calling for the overthrow of the King Hamad. They wanted better economic conditions, a switch to a constitutional monarchy, curbs on royal power and the ability to replace the prime minister through elections. The king's nephew has occupied the post for 40 years.

"Bahrain remains a very nanny state with free health care, free education and free housing, but there's a perceived distinction in the level of nanny care," explains Alanoud Al Sharekh, a political scientist at the Chatham House office in Bahrain. The Shiite majority feels it doesn't get as much as it's entitled to, she says, so they want "better benefits, and other legitimate demands — not regime change."

But in early March, the mood darkened considerably after clashes between demonstrators and Bahraini security forces resulted in several deaths and injuries. The more militant protesters then began calling for the removal of the royal family and establishment of a Shiite state. "The Sunni-Shia divide is particularly problematic because of the close family connections many Shiites have to Iran," said a London *Daily Telegraph* report. In the past this has led to Iran's Revolutionary Guards establishing terrorist cells in

---

*The others were Mohammed Neguib, Nasser, Anwar Sadat and Mubarak.

Resisting Dictators

A rebel fighter near Ajdabiya, in northeastern Libya, celebrates as a rocket barrage streaks toward pro-government troops on April 14, 2011 (top). The North African nation is embroiled in civil war that grew out of demonstrations against the 42-year-long regime of dictator Moammar Gadhafi. In Yemen, a soldier who defected to the opposition joins protesters in the capital Sanaa on March 31, demanding that President Ali Abdullah Saleh resign. Saleh, who has ruled the country for 32 years, is considering a proposal negotiated by representatives of the Gulf States offering him immunity if he will resign, but the opposition is skeptical of the plan.

the kingdom, the paper said. Further complicating matters, Iran has long claimed Bahrain as part of its territory.[38]

In Saudi Arabia, an absolute monarchy without an elected parliament, King Abdullah combined stick and carrot to stifle a nascent protest movement. After some

demonstrations and cyber calls for reform, the government banned all demonstrations and public meetings. On February 26 at least 330 prominent Saudi professionals and businessmen demanded reforms, and on March 5 the Saudi e-zine *Jadaliyya* published an open letter to the king, "Demands of Saudi Youth for the Future of the Nation," seeking jobs, the release of political prisoners, the introduction of a constitutional monarchy and a top-to-bottom campaign against corruption.[39]

The Saudis, typically, responded to the challenge with cash, promising to add 75,000 government jobs, increase government employees' pay by up to 15 percent, initiate a massive infrastructure program and improve benefits for low-income citizens — essentially Saudi Arabia's restive Shiite minority.

Conflict

In neighboring Yemen — the poorest country in the Middle East — another kind of dynasty was under threat, with a potentially very different outcome. After weeks of violent anti-regime demonstrations, President Saleh, a key U.S. anti-terrorism ally, could be the next domino to topple. For years, the United States has financed and trained elite security and intelligence units that launch counterterrorism operations against al-Qaida camps in Yemen's rugged interior.

Opposition groups repeatedly demonstrated against Saleh's hard-line regime, even building their own Tahrir Square-like tent city at Sanaa University. As in Egypt and Tunisia, the groups demanded that Saleh step down immediately. Saleh was said to be grooming his son as his successor, and the notion of a hereditary presidency had further fueled opposition anger.

Saleh first tried a page out of Mubarak's playbook and said he would remain in office for the remainder of his term, but would not run again in 2013. When that was rejected, he offered to resign at the end of the year and call elections. Amid clashes with security forces, the opposition groups insisted that Saleh leave immediately, just as Mubarak had been quickly forced out.[40]

Then on March 18, at least 45 demonstrators were killed by government snipers stationed on rooftops, and the encampment in the square was bulldozed. Several ministers, diplomats and parliamentarians deserted Saleh in protest, including Brig. Gen. Ali Mohsin al-Ahmar, commander of the army's powerful 1st Armored Division and Yemen's top soldier. The general declared his support for the protesters and urged troops to do the same. His defection was seen not just as a major blow to Saleh but also provided a possible candidate to lead an interim government.

After the defection, Saleh in late April was said to be considering a proposal by the foreign ministers of the Gulf Cooperation Council. It would allow him to step down after 30 days in exchange for immunity from prosecution for him, his family and his aides. But by May 1 the deal appeared to have unraveled.[41]

Intervention

In Libya, a unique system of government through local councils had left the aging Gadhafi in effective control, with his Western-educated son Seif al-Islam seemingly destined to succeed him, and other offspring in command of elite forces. To fortify Gadhafi's control, a pervasive security apparatus suppressed all opposition, but the universities had become restless even before the protests began.

The West ended a long period of estrangement when Gadhafi in 1999 allowed the extradition of two Libyans involved in the 1988 bombing of a U.S.-bound airliner over Lockerbie, Scotland, killing 270 people. But sanctions against Libya were not eased until 2002, when Tripoli paid $1.5 billion in compensation to relatives of Lockerbie victims, and Gadhafi abandoned his nuclear weapons program and pledged to destroy a chemical weapons stockpile. Normal diplomatic relations with the United States were resumed in 2008.

Hemmed in between Egypt and Tunisia, Libya inevitably was infected by the unrest affecting its neighbors. Street demonstrations calling for Gadhafi's ouster quickly met with a tough response, and what started as a protest burgeoned into a rebellion. In Benghazi, Libya's second-largest city and long a hotbed of tribal opposition to Gadhafi, a protest by lawyers swelled into open insurrection. Anti-government demonstrators quickly occupied the eastern coastal area. In a series of bizarre radio broadcasts and television appearances, Gadhafi vowed to re-take his country, claiming the rebels were on drugs and working with al-Qaida.

As opposition casualties mounted, international concerns grew. President Nicolas Sarkozy of France and British Prime Minister David Cameron urged the imposition of

Reuters/Wael Hmeden

Tens of thousands of Syrians gather for a pro-government rally under a giant image of President Bashar Assad in downtown Damascus on March 29, 2011. The rally followed nearly two weeks of unprecedented anti-government demonstrations and demands that Assad end his family's 40-year rule of the country. At least 450 people have been killed since the protests began, according to human rights groups. On April 25, troops using tanks and artillery attacked the mostly unarmed protesters in the southern city of Daraa, reportedly killing at least 100 people.

a no-fly zone over Libya to ground Gadhafi's air force. EU Commissioner for Competition John Dalli, a former Maltese foreign minister with close Libyan ties, warned, "I know the Libyans, and as much as they believe in forgiveness, they also preach retribution."[42]

On March 3, President Obama called on Gadhafi to quit. "So let me just be very unambiguous about this," Obama declared. "Colonel Gadhafi needs to step down from power and leave."[43]

But Obama, who had already inherited two wars in Iraq and Afghanistan, hesitated to commit America to another seemingly open-ended military action. Then the momentum shifted decisively in favor of the Libyan leader, when a government counteroffensive spearheaded by special forces commanded by Gadhafi's sons pushed back the lightly armed rebellion almost to Benghazi itself, causing many casualties. The uprising seemed close to collapse.

In an unprecedented action against one of its own members, the 22-member League of Arab States asked the U.N. Security Council to authorize a no-fly zone that would effectively ground Libya's air force. On March 17, U.N. Resolution 1973 was passed, asking U.N. members to "take all necessary measures to protect civilians" and extending sanctions on the Gadhafi regime.

Obama agreed to use the U.S. Mediterranean fleet and planes to enforce the no-fly zone, but then handed over operations to a group of NATO countries (Britain, France, Canada, Demark, Italy and Spain) plus Qatar. "The president ordered the best available option," said Secretary of State Clinton. "NATO assuming the responsibility for the entire mission means the United States will move to a supporting role."[44]

"Obama considered that he had two options," Rand's Aaron says. "One was to stand aside and watch the bloodbath and take the criticism for not having done anything, and the other was to get involved, but not too deeply." Later, however, it was revealed that CIA agents had been in Benghazi almost from the start, working with the rebels, and that armed Predator drones were being used against Gadhafi's forces. As Gadhafi continued to defy the international community, the prospect of a costly, long-drawn-out confrontation loomed, and questions were raised whether the limited NATO operation could lead to a resolution.

In Syria, the unrest has larger implications because of the regime's direct involvement in the Arab-Israeli conflict. Protests against Assad's government are unprecedented, and conventional wisdom had suggested that past repression, ethnic-religious diversity and Assad's relative popularity would shield him. As in the early days of the Egyptian unrest, Assad offered concessions every few days — a lifting of the reversal of the ban on the *niqab* (face veil), citizenship for Kurds and ending emergency law.

But much like Mubarak, Assad appears to constantly lag "a step behind the protesters' demands," says Feryal Cherif, a political science assistant professor at the University of California, Riverside. Bottom line, he concludes, "A loyal military and the legacy of limited association rights significantly diminish the prospects of a successful revolution in the country."

CURRENT SITUATION

The Second Act

As a result of the protest movement, millions of Arabs now could have a chance — albeit a precarious one — at democracy.

"Toppling two of the Middle East's tyrants in little more than two months is no mean achievement," opined the *Guardian*. "Initially, that raised hopes extraordinarily high, and the regimes' fight back has injected a dose of realism. It does not mean the revolution is failing or fizzling out, but it does show that many people were expecting too much too soon."[45]

Meanwhile, as several countries face a new beginning, the unanswerable question is: the beginning of what? In Egypt, Mubarak's departure raises questions but few solid answers. And because of Egypt's importance in the region, a successful transition there will serve as a model for other countries.

"How things are going to turn out across the region will depend on how things turn out in Egypt," says Al-Ali, of the Centre for Gender Studies at the School of Oriental and African Studies in London.

When Prime Minister Ahmed Shafiq, a prime target of the Egyptian protest movement, resigned from the Supreme Council of the Armed Forces, the council appointed as his successor Essam A. Sharaf, a former transportation minister and engineering professor at Cairo University. The move was approved in advance by the protesters.

Nevertheless, some hard-core activists continue to press the Supreme Council to speed up the pace of reforms. "The younger generation of activists wants urgent action," says Rizk at the Ibn Khaldun Center. "They feel the army is being too slow in responding to some of the main requests of the revolution, such as corruption trials of former members of the regime and a full reform of the constitution before any elections."

The army recently announced that it had barred Mubarak from leaving the country and has disbanded the hated State Security Investigations Service — a top priority with the protest movement. And, responding to complaints from new groups that more time was needed to organize political parties, the army postponed elections from a tentative date in July to September.

The desire for more time to organize reflected the disarray of the rebellion. "The youth movement, whose amorphous leadership was decisive in its success on the streets, is discovering that it is a weakness when it comes to political deal-making," says Emile Hokayem, a Middle East expert at the London International Institute for Strategic Studies.

Islamist Threat

Shifting the election date also may have been designed to counter suspicions that the army has formed a tacit

Is the Arab world changing for the better?

YES
Khaled Fahmy
Chairman, Department of History, The American University in Cairo, and Chairman, Committee on Documenting the Revolution, Egyptian National Library and Archives

Written for *CQ Global Researcher*, April 2011

In my mind, the turmoil is a positive thing and long overdue — by about 50 years. What is happening is a fundamental restructuring of how the Middle East has been run for the past 100 years.

The map of the Middle East was drawn following the collapse of the Ottoman Empire. The borders that were established, the countries that were made up and, later on, the regimes that were put in place did not reflect the forces and demographics of the region in any genuine, natural way. This was all imposed by outside players, mostly by the European victors of the First World War.

Thirty years later reformers attempted to cast off the old political system: That is when Gamal Abdel Nasser in Egypt, and later Moammar Gadhafi in Libya, Hafez Assad in Syria and Saddam Hussein in Iraq all came to power promising a new dawn. But these post-independence states ended up failing. The biggest example of that failure was their defeat by Israel in the Six Day War of 1967.

But it was not only the military failure that signaled the end of the post-independence Arab state. These new states also failed to secure a decent standard of living for their citizens and, in most cases, developed police structures that violated their citizens' basic rights.

Hence, we see the recent attempts to restructure the political landscape, wherein millions of Arabs are struggling to have their voices heard in regard to how their countries are to be run. We have witnessed things in the past weeks that Egypt has not seen in a hundred years. We have brought down two governments and demanded constitutional amendments that will put in place the mechanism leading to a completely new constitution in a year.

For some people the changes are not happening fast enough, but I see this moment as the same in importance as the collapse of the Ottoman Empire.

The discovery of oil allowed these countries to buy some time, and so did the appearance of Israel. Finally, we have seen the largest of the Arab countries rise up against oppression, corruption and mismanagement.

And who knows? Maybe if our revolution succeeds, and there is no setback, it can have a very serious impact on the situation in Syria, Yemen and Saudi Arabia.

NO
David Aaron
Senior Fellow specializing in the Middle East, RAND Corporation; Former White House Deputy National security adviser

Written for *CQ Global Researcher*, April 2011

One can hope the turmoil is a good thing, but it's far too soon to be sanguine. First, the Arab Spring may prove to be as transitory as the European revolutions of 1848, which did not immediately produce functioning democracies. Second, if some measure of democracy does result, the elected governments likely will reflect the popular antipathy that the "Arab street" has for both the United States and Israel.

As a result, the United States could face some unpleasant consequences. Western and American counterterrorism efforts could be undermined. The regimes that are being swept away devoted considerable resources to battling terrorist extremists and collaborated closely with the United States in that effort. Unfortunately, these same security services often were also oppressive. They undoubtedly will be purged, and — given popular hostility to the Bush administration's War on Terror — serious anti-terrorism programs could be reconstituted. Al-Qaida could have far more room to organize, recruit, train and even develop new terrorist weapons to attack the West.

A standoffish regime in Egypt could create many problems for the United States. Denial of automatic overflight rights and priority transit through the Suez Canal could seriously compromise U.S. military flexibility and capability further east. U.S. efforts to turn back the genocide in Sudan's Darfur region have depended heavily on Egyptian cooperation, which always seemed reluctant, but now may prove unavailable.

Most important, a popular government in Cairo is likely to adversely affect relations with Israel. It would be remarkable if politicians do not exploit popular anti-Israel hostility. The Muslim Brotherhood is already a major player in post-Mubarak politics and is on record as wanting to renegotiate the Camp David Accords, which have helped to maintain peace in the region for more than 30 years.

As a harbinger of the future, Egypt is no longer cooperating in Israel's embargo of Gaza. The possibility of war is far from likely, but the Israelis are certain to seek even more material and overt diplomatic support from the United States. This will complicate U.S. efforts to build new relationships of trust with the regimes that emerge from the maelstrom of change sweeping the Arab World.

One can pray that this turmoil will lead to the advance of the values America cherishes — democracy and a better life for all in the Arab world. But celebrations are not yet in order.

Reuters/Hamad I Mohammed

A Bahraini woman holds a Quran over her head as she shouts anti-government slogans during a protest on March 25, 2011, in the predominantly Shiite village of Diraz. The Sunni-led government of King Hamad Al Khalifa called in troops from Saudi Arabia — another Sunni-dominated monarchy — to help crush the Shiite-majority-led opposition movement. Bahrain is home to the U.S. Fifth Fleet, which patrols Gulf and Central Asian waters, and a key U.S. strategic partner.

alliance with the Muslim Brotherhood, reflecting fear across the Arab world that Islamists are positioning themselves to hijack the "new order."

That is unlikely, says Rizk of the Ibn Khaldun Center. "The transformation of the Arab world today doesn't have a religious orientation. Particularly in Egypt, there are a variety of political currents involved — Islamic, Christian and secular."

Or, as the Cairo journalist Yosri Fouda texted from Tahrir Square during the protests, "This is an Allahu-Akbar-free revolution."[46]*

But will the protests remain Allahu-Akbar-free? Fahmy at the American University of Cairo says, "If this revolution has shown anything it's that the Muslim Brotherhood does not control the street as everybody believed. Within a very short space of time, using the Internet, secular forces managed to do what the Brotherhood couldn't do since 1920. Given some openness in the political system, it [would] represent about 25 percent of the electorate."

---

*The common Islamic Arab expression is often translated as "God is the greatest."

As for bin Laden and al-Qaida, Filiu of Sciences Po says with the fall of Arab autocrats the terrorists are losing their best publicists. "These are hard times for al-Qaida," he says. "Consider: peaceful movements managed to topple regimes in Tunisia and Egypt in a few weeks — regimes the jihadis could not destabilize over the past two decades; masses went bravely into the streets to demand democracy, transparency and accountability — concepts alien and even heretical for al-Qaida."

Filiu points out that during the occupation of Tahrir Square, with Egyptian flags flying everywhere, al-Qaida in Iraq warned the protesters against "the putrid idolatry of nationalism." But nobody took any notice.

In Tunisia, Filiu says, "the power is secular. I'm not talking about the army or the government: The unions are very powerful, and they are secular. The moment there is any move to Islamicize, they will react."

Economic Fallout

Economic hardship caused by the political upheavals poses a more immediate challenge. Egypt's mainstay tourist sector, which accounts for 11 percent of GDP and 10 percent of jobs, has been hardest hit. Tourism dropped by 75 percent during the uprising. "We've had group and individual cancellations up through the winter of 2011," said Laila Nabhan, head of a family-owned tour operation. "Tourists will not return until there is stability in the country."[47]

Each of the 18 days of Egypt's uprising cost the economy $1 billion in lost capital as foreign investors withdrew money from the country, according to the Egyptian stock market. Banks estimate the Egyptian economy lost more than $30 billion overall.[48]

In Tunisia, the banks continued to function, even though 105 branches were looted and burned and 280 ATMs vandalized. Growth has dropped to 2-3 percent — from more than 5 percent — but the financial market was functioning normally. Foreign reserves had fallen somewhat, but the currency has preserved its value.[49]

In Morocco, King Mohammed VI said in a televised speech in March that he was appointing a special committee to work with political parties, civil society groups and trade unions to recommend, by June, amendments to Morocco's constitution that would allow for a multiparty system and an independent judiciary. But the Moroccan Human Rights Association told Al Jazeera in April that it would not cooperate with the committee because it "lacked democratic legitimacy" and "the qualities of a representative body" necessary to draft a new constitution.[50]

In Jordan, as in Bahrain and Oman, the opposition wants more open government and a constitutional monarchy. Reacting to the demonstrators, King Abdullah II sacked the cabinet and asked Marouf Bakhit — a well-regarded ex-general untainted by corruption allegations — to form a new Jordanian cabinet. He also appointed as chief of his court an official experienced in tribal politics. The tribes are the king's biggest supporters and the backbone of the Jordanian security forces and the army.

In Bahrain, negotiations between the protesters and government have failed in part because "the protesters didn't have clear ideas what they wanted," according to Chatham House's Al Sharekh.

But in Yemen, demonstrators know what they want: Saleh's departure. Brig. Gen. al-Ahmar's defection split the army, but some units remained loyal to the beleaguered president. Rival tanks have been deployed in Sanaa, resulting in a stand-off amid rumors that the army was negotiating Saleh's departure. Whether that outcome would satisfy pro-democracy protesters remains to be seen. If the military chooses a successor without substantial reforms, their popular revolution will have been in vain.

OUTLOOK

A Collection of Irans?

Washington's nightmare — as expressed recently by Secretary of State Clinton — would be the transformation of the brave, new Arab world into a collection of Irans. But the 1979 Iranian revolution against Shah Mohammed Reza Pahlavi was mullah-driven from the start, with the formation of an Islamic theocracy under strict clerical control as its undisputed objective. While there is no question that Islamic parties will form part of the new political mix in the region, whether — and where — they will gain dominance is anybody's guess.

Keele University's Sheikh believes, "Iran may benefit from a change in the status quo, but only in the Shia-heavy countries — Bahrain in the Gulf and Lebanon in the Levant. But in general, revolutions, once successful, tend to be nationalist rather than internationalist."

In Egypt, historian Fahmy hopes his country's political course is now clear. "Once we have elected a parliament and a president, then we will have a constitutional assembly, followed by a referendum," he says.

Reforms will need generous financial support from the outside to strengthen ailing economies and create jobs. There are calls for a Western-financed reconstruction program modeled on the Marshall Plan, which enabled Europe to recover from World War II. "The price of democracy is not easy," says Hussein Hassouna, the Arab League's ambassador to the United States. "I would like to see the United States lead the effort to rally support for Egypt's economy."

The United States is being forced to re-think its approach to an entire region. For example, the Obama administration is aiding the Libyan rebels but has yet to officially recognize the temporary government in Benghazi. The same poll that found a majority of Egyptians want to annul the 1979 peace treaty with Israel showed that 79 percent of Egyptians have a somewhat or very unfavorable opinion of the United States, suggesting that the Obama administration faces a major task in repairing a once-close relationship.

Second only in importance to developments in Egypt is the civil unrest in Syria, where Assad has abandoned an earlier carrot-and-stick approach of combining some concessions with tough handling of the demonstrators. In an escalated crackdown, troops backed by tanks began attacking civilians in a week-long assault that began on April 25 in the southern city of Daraa and spread to other cities. Eyewitnesses said they could not retrieve dead bodies lying in the street because of government snipers who were shooting at random. Human-rights groups said soldiers seemed to be firing at random, even entering homes to pursue protesters. Unlike in Egypt, the Syrian military — commanded for the most part by officers from the same Alawite sect as the president — has sided with the government. But witnesses told the Associated Press on April 28 that some soldiers were refusing to shoot civilians and instead were fighting among themselves.[51]

Continued disturbances in Syria — which serves as Iran's channel of communications with Hezbollah in Beirut and Hamas in Gaza — will inevitably affect its neighbors. Historian Patrick Seale, a leading British specialist on Syrian affairs, pointed out, "If the Syrian regime were to be severely weakened . . . Iran's influence in Arab affairs would almost certainly be reduced — in both Lebanon and the Palestinian territories."[52]

The Obama administration's initial response to the bloody clashes in Syria was to consider adding "targeted sanctions" to those already in force.[53] Seale urged Obama to "forget Libya" and pay more attention to Syria. "If there's one country where unrest could truly set the Middle East alight, it's Syria," he wrote.[54]

As with Afghanistan, NATO's role in Libya has sparked internal debate on how far each member state is prepared to go to in assuming a combat role. The larger concern at NATO headquarters in Brussels is that the alliance could be bogged down in Libya for a long time. "A no-fly zone is not an indicator of an early resolution," says Keele University's Sheikh.

The bottom line: No one knows what will happen in the Middle East. Arabs themselves grow up knowing that nothing there is what it seems. Egyptian journalist Tariq Hameed captured this sense of unreality in his February 10 column in the Pan Arab newspaper *Al-Sharq al-Awsat*: "When we look at what is happening in Egypt, do we comprehend it? Egypt isn't in the process of changing; Egypt has changed. We just don't know where it's going.[55]

"There is optimism; there is pessimism," he continued. "We are all clinging to hope; however, what worries us is that our region has yet to grasp that Egypt has changed."

NOTES

1. Taeib Fassi Fihri, "Embracing Reform: A message from King Mohammed VI of Morocco," Minister of Foreign Affairs of Morocco, Brookings Institution, March 23, 2011, www.brookings.edu/events/2011/0323_morocco.aspx.

2. "Events in the Mideast and North Africa," *The New York Times*, April 20, 2011, p. A10.

3. "More protesters slain in Yemen as exit plan is weighed," Reuters, *The Washington Post*, April 26, 2011, p. A8.

4. Laura Kasinof, "In Yemen, Opposition Encourages Protesters," *The New York Times*, March 20, 2011, p. A18.

5. Ethan Bronner, "Bahrain Tears Down Monument as Protesters Seethe," *The New York Times*, March 13, 2011, www.nytimes.com/2011/03/19/world/middleeast/19bahrain.html.

6. "The 2011 Oil Shock," *The Economist*, March 3, 2011, www.economist.com/node/18281774; and "Oil Industry Reassured on Middle East Stability," CNNMoney, March 9, 2011, http://money.cnn.com/2011/03/09/news/international/oil_middle_east/index.htm.

7. For background, see Irwin Arieff, "Middle East Peace Prospects," *CQ Global Researcher*, May 1, 2009, pp. 119-148.

8. "Egyptians Embrace Revolt Leaders, Religious Parties and Military, As Well; U.S. Wins No Friends, End of Treaty With Israel Sought," Pew Research Center, April 25, 2011, http://pewresearch.org/pubs/1971/egypt-poll-democracy-elections-islam-military-muslim-brotherhood-april-6-movement-israel-obama.

9. Mohamed Abdel Salam, "Egypt youth refuse to meet U.S. Sec of State," *Bikyamasr*, March 15, 2011, http://bikyamasr.com/wordpress/?p=30571.

10. Larry Diamond, "Why are there no Arab democracies?" *Journal of Democracy*, January 2010, www.journalofdemocracy.org/articles/gratis/Diamond-21-1.pdf.

11. Elkham Fakhro and Emile Hokayem, "Waking the Arabs," *Survival 2011*, Issue 2, February 2011, www.iiss.org/publications/survival/survival-2011/year-2011-issue-2/waking-the-arabs/.

12. "Egypt rises up; The West should celebrate, not fear, the upheaval in Egypt," *The Economist*, Feb. 3, 2011, www.economist.com/node/18070190.

13. "Interview with Tony Blair," Council on Foreign Relations, CFR Multimedia, April 7, 2011, http://blogs.cfr.org/coleman/2011/04/07/csmd-launch-event-with-tony-blair/.

14. Niall Ferguson, "Wanted: A Grand Strategy for America," *Newsweek*, Feb. 14, 2011, www.newsweek.com/2011/02/13/wanted-a-grand-strategy-for-america.html.

15. David Ignatius, "Obama's fuzzy narrative in the Mideast," *The Washington Post*, March 25, 2011, www.washingtonpost.com/opinions/obamas-fuzzy-narrative-in-the-mideast/2011/03/24/AFt0DRYB_story.html.

16. "Background Note: Egypt," Department of State, Nov. 10, 2010, www.state.gov/r/pa/ei/bgn/5309.htm.

17. Alain Gresh, "Neither with the West, nor against it," *The Morung Express*, www.morungexpress.com/analysis/63756.html.

18. *Ibid.*

19. Ethan Bronner and Isabel Kershner, "Rival Factions of Palestinians Reach an Accord," *The New York Times*, April 28, 2011, p. A1.

20. Timothy Garton Ash, "If this is young Arabs' 1989, Europe must be ready with a bold response," *The Guardian*, Feb. 2, 2011, www.guardian.co.uk/commentisfree/2011/feb/02/egypt-young-arabs-1989-europe-bold.

21. David Ignatius, "Three voices of Egypt's future," *The Washington Post*, April 14, 2011, www.washingtonpost.com/todays_paper/A%20Section/2011-04-14/A/19/18.0.2395308719_epaper.html.

22. Nasser Arrabya, "Saleh stalls as Yemen unravels," *Al-Ahram Weekly* (English version), March 31, http://weekly.ahram.org.eg/2011/1041/re1.htm.

23. For background, see Kenneth Jost and Benton Ives-Halperin, "Democracy in the Arab World," *CQ Researcher*, Jan. 30, 2004, pp. 73-100.

24. William Cleveland, *A History of the Modern Middle East* (2000), p. 170.

25. D. Teter, "Iran between East and West," *Editorial Research Reports*, Jan. 26, 1979, available at *CQ Researcher Plus Archive*.

26. Yasmine Ryan, "The tragic life of a street vendor," *Al-Jazeera*, Jan. 20, 2011, http://english.al jazeera.net/indepth/features/2011/01/201111684242518839.html.

27. Cynthia P. Schneider and Nadia Oweidat, "Why Washington was blindsided by Egypt's cry for freedom,' " CNN, Feb. 10, 2011, http://articles.cnn.com/2011-02-10/opinion/schneider.egypt.us_1_pro-mubarak-egyptian-people-president-hosni-mubarak?_s=PM:OPINION.

28. "Arab Human Development Report 2009: Challenges to Human Security in the Arab Countries," U.N. Development Programme, 2009, pp. 35-36.

29. "Experts raise concern about Middle East youth unemployment," *World Learning*, January 2010, http://worldlearningnow.wordpress.com/2010/01/29/experts-raise-concern-about-mideast-youth-unemployment/.

30. See "Egypt, Arab Rep.," The World Bank, http://data.worldbank.org/country/egypt-arab-republic.

31. Azzam, Maha, "Egypt's Elections: A Challenge to the Regime?" Chatham House, Nov. 25, 2010, www.chathamhouse.org.uk/media/comment/mazzam1110/-/1181/.

32. Fahmy Howeidi, "Egypt: From Pharaonic Rule to Democracy," http://fahmyhoweidy.blogspot.com/2011/02/blog-post.html.

33. "Mubarak Resigns," "Archive for the 'Arabic Press' Category," *Islamic Middle East Blog*, Northfield Mount Herman School, Feb. 11, 2011.

34. Bari Weiss, "A Democrat's Triumphal Return to Cairo," *The Wall Street Journal*, Feb. 26, 2011, http://online.wsj.com/article/SB10001424052748703408604576164482658051692.html.

35. "Egypt Constitutional Referendum — What the Results Mean," VOA News, March 21, 2011, www.voanews.com/english/news/middle-east/Egypt-Constitutional-Referendum--What-the-Results-Mean-118376644.html.

36. Ashraf Swelam, "Egypt's Referendum: Why 'No' lost, and what to do about it," *Ahramonline*, March 26, 2011, http://english.ahram.org.eg/NewsContentPrint/4/0/8622/Opinion/0/Egypt%E2%80%99s-referendum-Why-%E2%80%9CNo%E2%80%9D-lost-and-what-to-do-ne.aspx.

37. "Mubarak to be moved to military hospital," Agence France-Press, April 24, 2011, www.focus-fen.net/index.php?id=n247970.

38. Con Coughlin, "Why the Bahrain rebellion could prove calamitous to the West," *Daily Telegraph*, March 17, 2011, www.telegraph.co.uk/comment/columnists/concoughlin/8389222/Why-the-Bahrain-rebellion-could-prove-calamitous-for-the-West.html.

39. "Demands of Saudi Youth for the Future of the Nation," *Jadaliyya*, March 5, 2011, www.jadaliyya.com/pages/index/818/demands-of-saudi-youth-for-the-future-of-the-nation.

40. "Yemen President Ready to Step Down at End of Year," VOANews.com, March 22, 2011, www

.voanews.com/english/news/Yemen-President-Ready-to-Step-Down-at-End-of-the-Year-118431164.html.

41. "More protesters slain in Yemen as exit plan is weighed," *op. cit.*

42. Kurt Sansone, "Wrong for anyone to tell the Libyans what to do: John Dalli," *TimesofMalta.com*, March 4, 2011, www.timesofmalta.com/articles/view/20110304/local/libya-events-amount-to-civil-war-john-dalli.353091.

43. Aamer Madhani, "Obama says Libya's Gadhafi must go," *National Journal*, March 3, 2011, http://nationaljournal.com/obama-says-libya-s-qaddafi-must-go-20110303.

44. " 'This Week' Transcript: Hillary Clinton, Robert Gates and Donald Rumsfeld," ABCNews.com, March 27, 2011, http://abcnews.go.com/ThisWeek/week-transcript-hillary-clinton-robert-gates-donald-rumsfeld/story?id=13232096&page=6.

45. Brian Whitaker, "The Arab spring is brighter than ever," *The Guardian*, March 14, 2011, www.guardian.co.uk/commentisfree/2011/mar/14/arab-spring-protest-crackdown-freedom.

46. Ash, *op. cit.*

47. Effat Mostafa, "Europe looks for ways to support Egypt's reforms, boost youth initiatives," Caravan, American University of Cairo, March 23, 1011, http://academic.aucegypt.edu/caravan/story/europe-looks-ways-support-egypt%E2%80%99s-reforms-boost-youth-initiatives.

48. *Ibid.*

49. Economist Intelligence Unit, "Tunisia: Civil unrest damages the economy," March 14, 2011, http://country.eiu.com/article.aspx?articleid=297893414&Country=Tunisia&topic=Economy&subtopic=Recent+developments&subsubtopic=Economic+performance%3A+Civil+unrest+damages+the+economy.

50. "Moroccan Human Rights Group Says King's Reform Panel 'Illegitimate,' " BBC Monitoring International Reports, April 10, 2011.

51. Scott Wilson, "Syria escalates lethal crackdown," *The Washington Post*, April 26, 2011, p. A1. See also Elizabeth A. Kennedy and Diaa Hadid, "Activists report clashes between Syrian army units," The Associated Press, April 28, 2011.

52. Patrick Seale, "The Syrian Time Bomb," *Foreign Policy*, March 28, 2011, www.foreignpolicy.com/articles/2011/03/28/the_syrian_timebomb.

53. David Morgan, "U.S. treads cautiously amid Syria violence," CBS World Watch, April 26, 2011, www.cbsnews.com/8301-503543_162-20057418-503543.html.

54. Seale, *op. cit.*

55. Ted Thornton, "Arab Columnist: Where is Egypt Going?" *Islamic Middle East Blog*, Feb. 10, 2010, http://islamicmiddleeast.nmhblogs.org/2011/02/09/arab-columnist-where-is-egypt-going/.

BIBLIOGRAPHY

Books

Calvert, John, *Sayyid Qutb and the Origins of Radical Islamism*, Columbia/Hurst, 2010.
A Middle East scholar from Creighton College in Omaha, Neb., argues that one of Egypt's most influential — and most misunderstood — Islamist radicals, had he lived, would not have supported Osama bin Laden.

Clark, Victoria, *Yemen: Dancing on the Heads of Snakes*, Yale University Press, 2010.
A British journalist examines Yemen's current problems and their daunting complexity.

Gubser, Peter, *Saladin: Empire and Holy War*, Gorgias Press, 2011.
The late Middle East expert and co-founder of the National Council on U.S.-Arab Relations chronicles the life of the 12th-century Islamic leader who was the architect of Islam's greatest empire.

Lawrence, T. E., *Seven Pillars of Wisdom: A Triumph: The Complete 1922 Text*, Wilder Publications, 2011.
This re-issued classic, first-person account of the World War I Arab uprising against the Ottoman Empire by the famous British Army officer describes Lawrence's role (and that of the European powers) in creating the new Middle East.

Osman, Tarek, *Egypt on the Brink*, Yale University Press, 2010.
An Egyptian writer and commentator sets the scene for the current turmoil by describing the political situation

in Egypt and the rift between the cosmopolitan elite and the mass of the younger, underemployed population.

Smith, Lee, *The Strong Horse: Power, Politics, and the Clash of Arab Civilizations, Doubleday,* **2010.**
The Middle East correspondent for the conservative *Weekly Standard* contends somewhat tendentiously that the Middle East is not ready for democracy because its populations gravitate instinctively towards autocratic leadership.

St. John, Ronald Bruce, *Libya: Continuity and Change,* *Routledge,* **2011.**
A Middle East scholar from the United States examines the socioeconomic and political development of Libya.

Articles

"Into Libya: The Birth of an Obama Doctrine," **Lexington's Notebook blog,** *The Economist,* **March 28, 2011, www.economist.com/blogs/lexington/2011/ 03/libya_4.**
A columnist finds much to commend in President Obama's speech explaining the U.S. decision to intervene in Libya.

Halimi, Serge, "No Good Choices," *Le Monde Diplomatique* **(English Edition), April 2011, http:// mondediplo.com/2011/04/01libyawar.**
The democratic Arab revolts are redrawing political, diplomatic and ideological boundaries in the Middle East.

Noun, Fady, "Unrest in Muslim Nations: Multinationals, dictators, and the social doctrine of the church," *AsiaNews,* **Feb. 8, 2011, www.asianews.it/ news-en/Unrest-in-Muslim-nations:-multinationals,- dictators-and-the-social-doctrine-of-the-Church- 20715.html.**
A prominent Lebanese economist discusses the consequences of the shake-up in the Middle East.

Reports and Studies

Azzam, Maha, *et al.,* **"Egypt and the Road Ahead: Era of Change?"** *Chatham House,* **Feb. 7, 2011.**
Current developments in Egypt and their long-term implications are discussed in a symposium held by the London think tank.

Ghallouni, Burham, "Arab Popular Uprisings, Or the Arab incoming to political modernity," *Middle East Studies Online,* **Issue 4, Vol. 2, 2011.**
A French Middle East scholar at the Sorbonne-Nouvelle University in Paris examines why Arabs have so far failed to build a modern state.

Jerome, Deborah, "Understanding Tunisia's Tremors," *Analysis Brief, Council on Foreign Relations,* **Jan. 14, 2011, www.cfr.org/democracy-and-human-rights/ understanding-tunisias-tremors/p23798.**
The deputy editor of CFR.org, the council's website, examines the Tunisian uprising that triggered the region's current turmoil.

Kumetat, Dennis, "The Arab Region as Part of a Nuclear Renaissance: Outlooks and Alternatives," *Perspectives,* **Heinrich Boll Institute, April 2011, www .boell-meo.org/downloads/01_Perspectives_ME_ 2011-Nuclear_Energy_and_the_Arab_World.pdf.**
A German Green Party think tank examines the prospects of nuclear power in the Middle East.

Lindsay, James, "Guest Post: Turmoil in the Middle East and Implications for the Israeli-Palestinian Peace Process," *Council on Foreign Relations,* **March 14, 2011, http://blogs.cfr.org/lindsay/2011/03/14/guest-post- turmoil-in-the-middle-east-and-implications-for- israeli-palestinian-peace-process/.**
A senior fellow for Middle East and Africa Studies at CFR, offers 10 observations on how the current unrest could affect the Israeli-Palestinian peace process, perhaps the region's most important issue.

For More Information

Al-Ahram Center for Political and Strategic Studies, Al-galaa St., Cairo, Egypt; 20-2-257 86037, http://acpss .ahram.org.eg/eng/index_Eng.asp. A think tank that focuses on broad international and strategic issues, particularly trends between Arab countries and the international community.

Arab-American Institute, 1600 K St., N.W., Suite 601, Washington, DC 20006; (202) 429-9210; www.aaiusa.org. Committed to the civic and political empowerment of Americans of Arab descent. Its founder, James Zogby, is a leading Arab voice in the United States.

Center for Arab Unity Studies, Beit al-Nahda Bldg., Basra St., Hamra, P.O. Box 113-6001 Beirut 2034 2407, Lebanon; 961 1 750088; http://caus.org.lb/Home/index.php?Lang=en. Conducts "independent, scientific research into all aspects of Arab society and Arab unity, free of ties to any government."

Chatham House, The Royal Institute of International Affairs, 10, St. James's Square, London SW1Y4LE, United Kingdom; 44 (207) 7957 5710; www.chathamhouse.org. Leading source of independent analysis on global and domestic issues.

Council on Foreign Relations, The Harold Pratt House, 58 East 68th St., New York, NY 10065; (212) 434-9400; www.cfr.org. An independent think tank that "promotes understanding of foreign policy and America's role in the world."

Emirates Center for Strategic Studies and Research, Abu Dhabi, P.O. Box 4567, United Arab Emirates; 97 12 404 4444, www.ecssr.ac.ae/ECSSR/appmanager/portal/ecssr?_ nfpb=true&_pageLabel=ECSSRPortal_portal_page_1076. An institute dedicated to helping to modernize UAE society.

School of Oriental and African Studies, University of London, Thornhaugh St., Russell Square, London WC1H OXG, United Kingdom; 44 207 637 2388; www.soas.ac .uk. Studies such issues as democracy, development and human rights in Asia, Africa and the Near and Middle East.

Voices From Abroad:

BAN KI-MOON

Secretary General United Nations

Lack of opportunities a root cause

"We have seen the wide[spread] demonstrations, outbursts of demonstrations and voices are now on the streets. That means they have been frustrated enough by the lack of freedom, lack of opportunities. That is the lesson, which the leaders should learn and try to change, as soon as possible, reflecting such strong voices from their own people."

Press Trust of India, February 2011

MOHAMED SAAD KITATNI

Spokesman, Muslim Brotherhood, Egypt

A collective effort

"No single political trend can claim to speak on behalf of the revolution. All segments of the Egyptian public participated in the uprising, and it was this broad-based participation that ensured its success."

Inter Press Service (South Africa) February 2011

SALEH IBRAHIM

President, Graduate Academy, Libya

The people rule in Libya

"But in Egypt, Tunisia or other traditional countries, there is no possibility for change except through the collapse of the ruling party and the coming to power of another party. In Libya, it is the people who rule and can sack people's committees anytime or hold them accountable."

Al Jazeera (Qatar), February 2011

MIKHAIL GORBACHEV

Former President Soviet Union

The people will prevail

"First in Tunisia and now in Egypt, the people have spoken and made clear that they do not want to live under authoritarian rule and are fed up with regimes that hold power for decades. In the end, the voice of the people will be decisive. The Arab elites, Egypt's neighboring countries and the world powers should understand this and take it into account in their political calculations. The events now unfolding will have far-reaching consequences for Egypt itself, for the Middle East and for the Muslim world."

International Herald Tribune February 2011

ALEKA PAPARIGA

General Secretary, Communist Party of Greece

Solutions necessary

"An uprising, in order to have a positive political outlet, first wants to have the people in the street but definitely in order for an outlet to come there have to be political forces, a political force such that they have a real alternative solution. Now the alternative solution being prepared is a succession formation that will not change politics fundamentally."

ANA-MPA news agency (Greece), January 2011

BORHANODDIN RABBANI

Chairman, High Peace Council, Afghanistan

Changes abound

"There is no doubt that these uprisings will not only bring some considerable changes in those countries, but some changes will also emerge in the Arab World, in the Middle East and even there will be considerable changes in those countries' international relations."

Noor (Afghanistan), February 2011

EYAL ZISSER

Chair, Department of Middle East and African Studies, Tel Aviv University, Israel

Storm has hit Syria

"Clearly the storm has arrived in Syria. I don't know whether it will develop to a full storm, but clearly Syria is not immune. We will have to wait a few more days or weeks to see if it goes on or things calm down."

Xinhua news agency (China) March 2011

SAIF AL-ISLAM GADHAFI

Son of Leader Moammar Gadhafi, Libya

Libya is different

"We will take up arms . . . we will fight to the last bullet. We will destroy seditious elements. If everybody is armed, it is civil war, we will kill each other. . . . Libya is not Egypt, it is not Tunisia."

Press Trust of India, February 2011

2

Democracy in Southeast Asia

Barbara Mantel

I t was a bizarre, unsettling scene and, inevitably, it turned ugly. For months, thousands of red-shirted anti-government protesters demanding new elections had camped amid the shimmering skyscrapers of downtown Bangkok, one of Southeast Asia's most modern urban centers. In recent weeks, however, the protests exploded into some of the worst political violence in Thailand's modern history. The clashes erupted on May 13, after a sniper shot a renegade Thai general as he stood talking with a *New York Times* reporter.

The next day troops blockaded the area and "fired tear gas and bullets at protesters, who responded with stones, slingshots and homemade rockets, turning parts of downtown Bangkok into a battlefield," a reporter wrote.[1] After nearly a week of violent street fighting, the military reclaimed the city and arrested several protest leaders. Nearly 100 people were killed and more than 1,000 injured during the nine weeks of demonstrations.[2]

After protest leaders surrendered on May 19, restaurant owner Wanpamas Boonpun, 39, tried to explain why some of the demonstrators felt let down by protest leaders. "We want democracy," she said. "True democracy, free democracy. Why is it so hard? Why?"[3]

Drawn mostly from the country's rural and urban poor, the red shirts support former Prime Minister Thaksin Shinawatra, a billionaire businessman elected in 2001 after promising services to the country's poor. He was ousted five years later in a military coup and eventually fled abroad to avoid arrest for a corruption conviction.

AFP/Getty Images/Ted Aljibe

A grieving woman fondly touches a banner honoring former Philippines President Corazon ("Cory") Aquino, who died last August. Aquino is revered for leading the nonviolent People Power movement in 1986 that toppled dictator Ferdinand Marcos and restored democracy. Her son Benigno ("Noynoy") was elected president on May 10, vowing to end widespread government corruption.

From *CQ Researcher*,
June 2010.

Indonesians Are Freest in Southeast Asia

Indonesia is Southeast Asia's freest country, according to the latest annual survey of global political rights and civil liberties published by Freedom House, a U.S.-based human rights organization. The 2009 survey found that Cambodia, Laos, Myanmar (formerly Burma) and Vietnam were the least free, and the Philippines, Malaysia, Thailand and Singapore were partly free.

Levels of Freedom in Southeast Asia

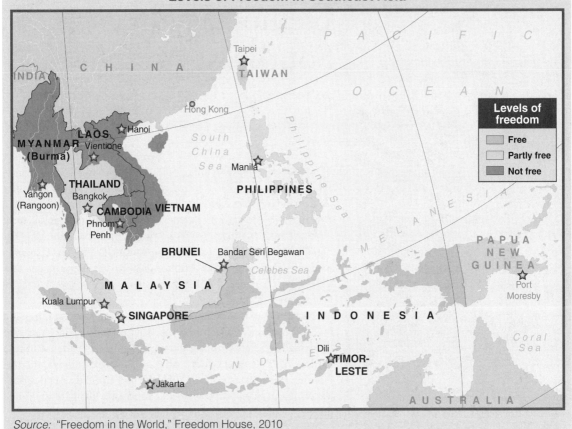

Source: "Freedom in the World," Freedom House, 2010

He has denied government accusations that he masterminded the protests.

The violence exposed a deep rift in Thai society. The protesters argue that political power in Thailand "has long been dominated by the elite in Bangkok who have . . . neglected the voice of the majority poor in the rural north and northeast regions," says Pavin Chachavalpongpun, a fellow at the Institute of Southeast Asian Studies in Singapore. On the other hand, says Thongchai Winichakul, professor of history at the University of Wisconsin-Madison, Thailand's elites — including government bureaucrats, military leaders, the intelligentsia and members of the royal family — don't trust rural voters and think democracy "is a sophisticated set of systems that needs to be taught."

Indeed, elites hold tight to the reins of power across a diverse swath of Southeast Asia, from the military junta in brutally authoritarian Myanmar (formerly Burma) to the family dynasties who compete, often violently, for power in the chaotic elections of the Philippines. Both Laos and Vietnam are legally one-party states, while Cambodia and Singapore, despite elections, are effectively so. Malaysia holds competitive elections, but the media and freedom of assembly are so restricted the opposition cannot win at the national level. "I call that competitive authoritarianism," says Larry Diamond, a senior fellow at Stanford University's Freeman Spogli Institute for International Studies.

"The next rung up the ladder is electoral democracy," says Diamond. Indonesia and East Timor are the only electoral democracies in Southeast Asia, according to Freedom House, an independent watchdog organization that advocates for democracy and human rights. The Philippines and Thailand were considered electoral democracies until campaign violence in the former and the military coup in the latter caused Freedom House to change their status a few years ago.

Freedom House defines an electoral democracy as a state with:

- a competitive multiparty political system,
- universal adult suffrage for all citizens,
- regular elections with secret and secure ballots,
- absence of massive voter fraud,
- significant access of major political parties to the electorate through the media and open political campaigning.[4]

"But this designation of electoral democracy is in essence the minimum standard for democracy," says Christopher Walker, Freedom House's Director of Studies. "It does not suggest a full, consolidated democracy with all the checks and balances one would look for."

To determine which countries meet that higher standard, Freedom House analyzes political rights, which include the electoral process, government operations and political pluralism and participation. It also analyzes civil liberties, which include freedom of expression and belief, associational and organizational rights, the rule of law and personal autonomy and individual rights. It then determines whether a country is considered "free," "partly

free," or "not free."[5] At the moment Indonesia is Southeast Asia's only "free" country.

Southeast Asian countries can rise in the rankings depending on how each faces its particular challenges. For instance, "for a repressive regime like Vietnam," says Walker, the challenge "is whether economic growth will translate into meaningful political liberalization or reform. The evidence to date suggests that it is not." Vietnam's gross domestic product (GDP) grew by an average of 7 percent a year during the past decade, until the 2009 global economic slowdown. Economic growth has occurred even faster in Cambodia, but it is not rising in the rankings; opposition parties are increasingly weak and elections far from fair.[6]

Problems with corruption and the rule of law confront the "free" and "partly free" countries, says Walker. "In Indonesia there have been efforts by senior law enforcement to hamper the work of anti-corruption bodies," says Walker, and several other countries "have had some tragedies and horrors," like the massacre in the Philippines last November when a powerful political family allegedly slaughtered 57 people, nearly half of them journalists, and the rest relatives and supporters of a political rival.[7]

Democratization depends on the public's support and desire for change. According to Diamond, pollsters have found that the public generally supports democracy in five of the region's "free" and "partly free" countries — Indonesia, the Philippines, Thailand, Singapore and Malaysia — with the highest levels of support, perhaps not surprisingly, in Indonesia.[8]

But what do respondents understand democracy to mean? The pollsters asked a series of questions to assess that, and the results vary markedly. For example, Indonesians have a high level of support for liberal values, like freedom of the press and judicial independence, according to Diamond.

However, in Thailand, "The data suggest there is a lot of support for democracy, but it is shallow," Diamond said in late April. "There is not a lot of commitment to democratic values like tolerance of opposition and freedom of the press and of association," he says, "and I think that is perfectly exhibited on the streets of the country now."

With democracy in most of Southeast Asia in distress, scholars, opposition parties, human rights activists and democracy advocates are asking these questions:

Defining Freedom

Each year, Freedom House ranks countries as Free, Partly Free and Not Free. The group assigns each country a ranking of between 1 and 7. Nations with scores of between 1 and 2.5 are designated as "free" and considered electoral and liberal democracies. Countries between 3 and 5 are "partly free;" some may actually be electoral democracies, like Timor-Leste. Those with scores between 5.5 and 7 are "not free." [1]

Here are the three categories:

A *Free* country allows open political competition, a climate of respect for civil liberties, significant independent civic life and an independent media.

A *Partly Free* country has limited respect for political rights and civil liberties and often a high rate of corruption, weak rule of law, ethnic and religious strife and a dominant political party despite the façade of pluralism.

A *Not Free* country allows no basic political rights, and basic civil liberties are widely and systematically denied.

Source: "Freedom in the World, 2010," Freedom House

1 "Freedom in the World 2009, Methodology," Freedom House, 2009

Should political parties boycott unfair elections?

In Southeast Asia, only Indonesia and East Timor are seen by international observers as holding free and fair elections.

Malaysia restricts press freedom and compresses campaigning into a two-week period that favors the ruling party; Singapore bankrupts opponents with defamation lawsuits and restricts freedom of assembly and the press. In the Philippines — where elections last month were marred by politically motivated murders — elections historically have been "corrupt and rife with rigging," says Bob Templer, director of the Asia Program at the International Crisis Group, a Brussels-based nonprofit that works to prevent and resolve deadly conflicts.

Myanmar's elections are perhaps drawing the most international scrutiny at the moment. The repressive military junta is expected to hold its first election in 20 years in October. In the last election — in 1990 — the regime lost in a landslide to the opposition National League for Democracy (NLD), but the junta refused to cede power and jailed dozens of NLD members, including party leader Daw Aung San Suu Kyi, who has spent 14 of the past 20 years under house arrest.[9]

But unlike the 1990 elections, which were considered to be free and fair, the upcoming polls are being condemned both inside and outside Myanmar as "a sham"[10] and "an insult to democracy."[11] The country's two-year-old constitution reserves 25 percent of parliamentary seats for the military, allows for the declaration of martial law and preserves draconian laws prohibiting freedom of speech, association and assembly. Three-month-old election rules bar candidates with criminal convictions, effectively eliminating Aung San Suu Kyi and any of the estimated 2,100 political prisoners from running for legislative office.[12]

The rules also require political parties to register with the state or be declared illegal, putting the opposition in the difficult position of having to decide whether to participate in elections it considers political theater or to boycott and become politically inconsequential.[13] In late March, the NLD leadership announced its controversial decision: It would boycott.

"Would political parties in the United States or other truly democratic states participate in an election that has laws that are so absurdly skewed in favor of one party?" asks Roshan Jason, executive director of the ASEAN Inter-Parliamentary Myanmar Caucus,* based in Kuala Lumpur, Malaysia. Caucus members — from parliaments across the region — press for democratic reform in Myanmar. "The NLD was left without a choice really."

"The NLD has only one [source of] leverage with the junta and that is depriving the generals of credibility and legitimacy in the eyes of the international community,"

---

*The caucus is a separate organization from ASEAN — the Association of Southeast Asian Nations — which was founded in 1967 to promote economic cooperation in the region. ASEAN now has 10 members: Indonesia, Malaysia, the Philippines, Singapore and Thailand, Brunei, Myanmar (Burma), Cambodia, Laos and Vietnam.

says Muang Zarni, a research fellow at the London School of Economics and a visiting fellow at Chulalongkorn University in Bangkok. "In that sense, the boycott is the right thing to do."

But Templer disagrees. "There was very little internal democracy within the NLD when it came to this decision. It may well doom the NLD to political irrelevance," he says. In fact, when the party did not register by the May 7 deadline, it was officially dissolved, left to transform itself into a nonpolitical social service group. A day later, a senior NLD member formed a splinter group to run in the elections, joining other small opposition parties seeking a place at the polls.[14]

Participating in the elections with a clear statement of regret at their limitations would have allowed the NLD to get into Parliament, "where they might have a more public political voice in the future," Templer says. "Parliaments can evolve into much more representative bodies."

But Zarni replies, "The army is the state. Even with an elected Parliament, you would still have the military in control of the bureaucracy. Every single top position in every single field is occupied either by a military officer or an ex-officer."

Between 1975 and 2006, about 7 percent of multiparty elections in developing nations experienced major boycotts, according to Emily Beaulieu, a professor of political science at the University of Kentucky, who has studied election boycotts around the world. They don't all produce results, she says, but where they "motivate active support from the domestic electorate, beyond simply staying home on election day, and/or lead influential international actors like the U.S. or the European Union to press the government for democratic reform, they seem to work to further democratization in the countries where they occur."

Beaulieu cites the Philippines as an example of a successful boycott. In 1981, the main opposition party boycotted elections on the grounds that it had not been given enough time to campaign and had not had equal access to the media. The Catholic Church lent its support, and "domestic pressure proved strong enough to press [President Ferdinand] Marcos to enact several electoral reforms," says Beaulieu, which eventually helped pave the way for his 1986 downfall.

If a boycott were to succeed in Myanmar, says Beaulieu, it would have to motivate such a massive domestic protest that a government crackdown would not be a viable option. "But I suspect that any partial

AFP/Getty Images

Bank worker Prita Mulyasari (right) reacts gleefully to the news that an Indonesian court threw out a criminal defamation case against her for e-mailing her friends complaining about an erroneous diagnosis at a local hospital. The court erupted with applause as the judges dismissed Omni International Hospital's complaint. Indonesians were outraged by the case, which was brought under a roundly criticized new law that imposes penalties of up to six years' imprisonment and a $106,000 fine on anyone who communicates defamatory statements over the Internet.

mobilization of the population would just invite government repression," she says.

Opposition parties also face untenable choices in Cambodia, where they threatened to boycott elections in the late 1990s but eventually participated, according to Beaulieu. Since then the opposition has continued to fragment. "If the opposition can pull itself together before the 2011 elections [for Senate], a boycott there may not be out of the question," says Beaulieu.

But a boycott might not get much popular support. Prime Minister Hun Sen dominates national politics through his Cambodian People's Party (CPP), which has ruled the country since 1979 and has quashed any challenges to its authority "with lawsuits, prosecutions, or extralegal actions," according to a Freedom House report. "Opposition figures, journalists, and democracy advocates were given criminal sentences or faced violent attacks by unknown assailants in public spaces."[15]

While many Cambodians in the capital of Phnom Penh oppose the CPP, "Many of the settled rural areas, which make up about 70 percent of the electorate, have been brought into the CPP system," says Duncan McCargo, a professor of Southeast Asian politics at the University of Leeds in the United Kingdom. It's a very

Rating Press Freedom in Southeast Asia

Timor-Leste has the freest press in Southeast Asia, according to the democracy-advocacy group Freedom House. The media in Laos, Myanmar (Burma) and Vietnam are the least free in Southeast Asia.

Press Freedom in Southeast Asia, 2010

Country	Freedom House rating*	World ranking**	Freedom status
Timor-Leste	35	78	Partly Free
Philippines	48	97	Partly free
Indonesia	52	107	Partly free
Thailand	58	124	Partly free
Cambodia	61	134	Not free
Malaysia	64	141	Not free
Singapore	68	151	Not free
Brunei	75	163	Not free
Vietnam	82	177	Not free
Laos	84	181	Not free
Burma	95	194	Not free

* The lower the rating the freer the press.

** Out of 196, with 1 being most free

Source: "Freedom the Press 2010," Freedom House, May 2010

simple patronage system, he says: "If your village elects somebody from the CPP to run the local village council, then your village gets roads built and electricity. If you support the opposition Sam Rainsy Party, then your village doesn't get those benefits." In 2008, the CPP won 90 of 123 national assembly seats.

McCargo says a boycott in 2011 would probably just play into Hun Sen's hands, leaving the opposition to pin its hopes on socioeconomic change. "I suppose the opposition's other hope is that as education levels rise and people in settled villages become more middle class, more educated and gain access to a wider range of information," he says, "they might change their political allegiance."

Can Singapore and Malaysia become liberal democracies?

Democracy-promotion experts today disagree over whether, as societies grow richer, citizens joining the educated middle class demand democratic governments — a premise once considered conventional wisdom.

Erik Kuhonta, a Southeast Asia specialist at McGill University in Montreal, Canada, is doubtful. "It is not clear to me that as economic development proceeds and you get a middle class, that the middle class will be a force for democracy," he says. While the middle class has at times challenged authoritarian regimes, as in Indonesia after the Asian financial crisis in 1997-1998, one can't assume that it always will, he says, citing Singapore as a case in point.

"If the state provides certain public goods, such as economic development, political stability, some degree of accountability and especially rule of law, this will satisfy, for the most part, the interests of the middle class, whether the state is democratic or authoritarian," says Kuhonta.

Singapore has the largest middle class as a percent of its population in Southeast Asia. Its thriving free market economy is built on exports, particularly consumer electronics, information technology products and pharmaceuticals, and on a growing financial services sector.[16]

The People's Action Party (PAP), led by Lee Kuan Yew, has ruled this city-state since 1959 and is responsible for its economic transformation. Lee served as prime minister for 30 years and is now "minister mentor" to his son Lee Hsien Loong, who became prime minister in 2004. The PAP holds 82 of the 84 seats in Parliament.

With newspapers, radio stations and television channels owned by government-linked companies, a limited nine-day campaign period and defamation lawsuits hampering opposition candidates, the 2006 polls "resembled past elections in serving more as a referendum on the prime minister's popularity than as an actual contest of power," according to Freedom House.[17]

While the opposition Singapore Democratic Party acknowledges that pocket-book issues drive elections, Chee Siok Chin, a party leader, says most Singaporeans don't protest the lack of civil liberties because they "have very little idea of what it means to have rights." The PAP tells them they have democracy, and they believe it, she says.

According to Ori Sasson, chair of the PAP Policy Forum Committee, "The essence of democracy is not the number of parties represented in Parliament, or the number of seats held by opposition parties, but rather how the actions of a country's government impacts on the daily lives of the people."[18]

Many seats in Parliament go uncontested, and Chee attributes that to a climate of fear. Chee, her brother Chee Soon Juan and other party leaders have served multiple prison terms this year on charges of unlawful assembly for peaceful protests confined to no more than half a dozen people. "Our party had a team member whose wife threatened to commit suicide should he stand as a candidate in elections," says Chee.

In addition, the government and former prime ministers have aggressively sued Chee and her brother for defamation, and what many outside experts say is a pliant judiciary has awarded massive fines that have forced the Chees into bankruptcy, seriously undermining their ability to challenge the PAP. "Bankrupts are not allowed to stand as candidates for elections," says Chee. "We are not even allowed to campaign for our party's candidates in the next elections.

"Singapore is one of the most artfully controlled societies on Earth," says Stanford's Diamond. Punishment of critics can be much subtler than taking someone to court. "You may find that you are not promoted in your government job, you may not get tenure, and benefits that flow to other citizens may not flow to you," he says.

Singapore Is Least Corrupt in Southeast Asia

Singapore ranks as the least corrupt country in Southeast Asia, and Malaysia ranks second. Myanmar (Burma) ranks 178th in the world, with only Afghanistan and Somalia being rated more corrupt.

Corruption in Southeast Asia, 2009

Country	Corruption rating*	World ranking**
Singapore	9.2	3
Brunei	5.5	39
Malaysia	4.5	56
Thailand	3.4	84
Indonesia	2.8	111
Vietnam	2.7	120
Philippines	2.4	139
Timor-Leste	2.2	146
Cambodia	2.0	158
Laos	2.0	158
Myanmar (Burma)	1.4	178

* On a 1-10 scale, with 10 being least corrupt.

** Out of 180, with 1 being the least corrupt

Source: "Corruption Perceptions Index 2009," Transparency International, 2009

While coercion is an important reason for a quiescent middle class, says Kuhonta, it's not enough. As long as middle-class needs are met, he does not expect any kind of revolt. "There is a lot of wishful thinking in terms of Singapore becoming democratic," says Kuhonta. "For that to happen, the state would have to show it could no longer manage the economy."

But Diamond and Chee are more optimistic. Lee Kuan Yew is in his mid 80s. "When Lee Sr. passes on, there will be fissures in the ruling party," says Chee. "The executive will not be as compliant, the legislature less acquiescent, the judiciary more independent. I am confident that Singapore will one day be a 'free' country," she says.

Diamond believes change will come as the next generation matures. "Young people are tired of living in a stale place, where its very rich and prosperous adult citizens are treated like children," says Diamond. "And if

Social Networking Can Help Boost Democracy

But it must be accompanied by real grassroots action, experts say.

Social media are exploding in parts of Southeast Asia — a trend being hailed by some democracy advocates as a helpful tool for promoting more open government.

"We were the first political party to make use of Twitter in 2008," says Chee Siok Chin, one of the leaders of the opposition Singapore Democratic Party. "We have also been uploading our videos on YouTube, spreading our message via Facebook."

Driven by declining prices for computers, cell phones and access fees, the use of social media such as Twitter[1] and Facebook[2] has seen spectacular growth in Indonesia and the Philippines, although it's still used by only a fraction of the population.

Social networking also is catching on in some of the more closed nations. More than a fifth of Malaysians now use Facebook,[3] and tiny Singapore accounts for nearly 1 percent of all Twitter users worldwide.[4]

While most people use social media primarily for entertainment and networking, political and social activists have begun to harness its power. Internet access has transformed coverage of events in Myanmar, which is ruled by an iron-fisted military junta. Hundreds of young people used Internet blogs to share news with the world about the Saffron Revolution, which began in late August 2007 when Buddhist monks, students and others took to the streets in peaceful protests and ended a month later with the military's brutal crackdown, according to Kyaw Yin Hlaing, a professor at City University of Hong Kong.

"Thanks to these young activists, the international media came to realize the gravity of the situation in Myanmar," wrote Hlaing.[5]

In Malaysia, the Internet strengthened the democratic opposition in 2007, according to James Chin and Wong Chin Huat of Monash University in Malaysia. "Mushrooming political web blogs . . . together with a handful of online news portals, were providing an alternative to the tightly controlled mainstream print and broadcast media," they wrote. By exposing the ruling party's "misdeeds and corruption," bloggers and online news outlets helped drive the middle class and sections of the working class "toward a major change in attitudes and voting behavior."[6] A series of unprecedented street protests took place, and in the 2008 election the ruling party lost its historic two-thirds parliamentary majority.

Malaysia makes a transition to democracy, right on Singapore's doorstep, I think psychologically this will have an impact on the Singapore model."

Malaysia is in political crisis at the moment, says Diamond. "Democratic ferment . . . is sweeping the country," he says, "and there is a very good chance of some kind of democratic change, if the regime doesn't use even more extreme authoritarian, abusive measures."

The Barisan Nasional (BN) coalition has governed Malaysia since the multiethnic country gained independence from Britain in 1957. At its core is the United Malays National Organization (UMNO), whose leader, Mahathir bin Mohamad, served as premier from 1981 until retirement in 2003. Mahathir is credited with Malaysia's impressive economic growth, but "the physician-turned-politician never hesitated to assault or undermine any democratic institution that got in his way," according to James Chin and Wong Chin Huat of Monash University in Malaysia. He eventually turned the UMNO-dominated Malaysian state into "something resembling a personal dictatorship."[19]

Elections are free, but not fair. Opposition parties compete at the polls, but they do so during a compressed campaign period, with no free press or freedom of assembly. "You need a police permit before you can get out there and protest," says William Case, director of the Southeast Asia Research Centre at City University of Hong Kong, "and there are a whole slew of draconian amendments to enforce all this." In addition, the judiciary often delivers "arbitrary or politically motivated verdicts," according to Freedom House, "with the most prominent case being the convictions of [opposition leader] Anwar Ibrahim in 1999 and 2000 for corruption and sodomy."[20]

But the Malaysian government is more corrupt and less astute at managing the economy than Singapore,

Technology also helped the anti-government demonstrators in Thailand in April and May, drawn mostly from the rural and urban poor. "In the past they were upset, but they weren't cohesive as a force and coherent in their agenda," said Thitinan Pongsudhirak, a leading political scientist in Thailand and visiting scholar at Stanford University. "New technologies have enabled them to unify their disparate voices of dissatisfaction."[7]

But social networking also has significant limits as a democratizing force. First of all, says Preetam Rai, an educator and technology researcher based in Southeast Asia, online activists' reach is limited, especially in countries where Internet penetration is low. And most people use the Internet for entertainment or socializing. "People get interested in serious issues when certain incidents happen, like the Burmese protests in 2007 or the current Thai situation," says Preetam, "but they go back to their regular online consumption pattern when the situation is normal."

Mong Palatino — a Filipino blogger, youth activist and member of parliament — participated in a student uprising that helped to topple the corrupt Estrada regime in 2001. "We sent rally updates through e-mail and e-groups," he recalls. "For the first time, texting became an important tool in organizing protest activities."

But Palatino warned in his blog earlier this year that "cyber-activism becomes a potent force only if it is fused with grassroots activism." Unfortunately, he said, too many young people are seduced into thinking that signing an online petition or adding a cause to Facebook is enough, and in that sense, cyber-activism can actually be counterproductive by keeping young people from becoming active in the real world.

"Activism in the 21st century features new action words like texting, re-tweeting, clicking, chatting and social networking," blogged Palatino. "But 20th-century action words are still more persuasive and powerful — like talking, organizing, marching, pushing and rallying."[8]

— *Barbara Mantel*

[1] "Twitter Enjoys Major Growth and Excellent Stickiness," *Sysomos*, March 29, 2010, http://blog.sysomos.com/2010/03/29/twitter-enjoys-major-growth-and-excellent-stickiness/.

[2] "Facebook Sees Solid Growth Around the World in 2010," *Inside Facebook*, April 6, 2010, www.insidefacebook.com/2010/04/06/facebook-sees-solid-growth-around-the-world-in-march-2010.

[3] *Ibid.*

[4] "Twitter Enjoys Major Growth and Excellent Stickiness," *op. cit.*

[5] Donald K. Emmerson, ed., *Hard Choices: Security, Democracy, and Regionalism in Southeast Asia* (2008), p. 172.

[6] James Chin and Wong Chin Huat, "Malaysia's Electoral Upheaval," *Journal of Democracy*, July 2009, pp. 79-84.

[7] Thomas Fuller, "Widening Disparity Strains Traditional Bonds of Thai Society," *The New York Times*, April 1, 2010, p. A4.

[8] Mong Palatino, "Online and Offline Activism," *Mong Palatino blog*, Jan. 12, 2010, http://mongpalatino.com/2010/01/online-and-offline-activism/.

and the public has become increasingly frustrated with its political leaders. Disillusionment with the Anwar verdict and with a dishonest police force, rampant corruption, UMNO slurs against Malaysians of Chinese and Indian descent and rising crime and inflation led to a shocking result in the 2008 elections. For the first time since 1969, the BN lost its two-thirds majority in the lower house of Parliament.[21] One major reason for the shift was "the ethnic Indians who had always been staunch supporters of the BN had swung in a big way to the opposition," says Terence Gomez, a professor at the University of Malaya in Kuala Lumpur.

"For about six months after the 2008 election we thought there was a chance that Malaysia would become a two-party democracy," says Case, but he now calls the prognosis for democracy "not good." After the election, opposition parties formed a coalition called the People's Alliance, and Anwar vowed it would capture a parliamentary majority by accepting defectors from the BN and form a new government by September 2008. However, he failed, undermining his credibility. He is now in court fighting new government accusations of sodomy that Diamond says are "completely false."

"People talk about a loss of hope since 2008," says Gomez. "The opposition has to get its act together and show that it has the capacity to govern."

Does democracy mean greater accountability and less corruption?

Democracy advocates once thought that democracy automatically led to greater government accountability and less corruption. Today, many are much more pessimistic. And few are surprised by the level of corruption in authoritarian regimes such as those in Cambodia and Myanmar.

"You basically have a predatory government in Cambodia," says Philip Robertson, deputy director of

Human Rights Watch's Asia Division. "If I'm a minister who wants to obtain a piece of land to build a shopping mall with some friends who are developers, I would just say, 'hey, here's a little bit of money, and if you don't move, we'll move you,'" says Robertson.

Citizens must routinely pay bribes for basic services, and senior state and military personnel demand kickbacks from foreign companies in the petroleum, gas and logging industries.[22] In fact, Cambodia is ranked near the bottom of Transparency International's Corruption Perceptions Index: 158 out 180 countries.[23]

Myanmar is even worse, considered one of the world's most corrupt regimes, ranking 178th. "Every single sector is corrupt," says Maureen Aung-Thwin, director of the Burma Project at the Open Society Institute, a New York-based nonprofit that works to build democracies. Top military officers siphon off natural gas revenues, and poorly paid government workers demand petty bribes.

"You have to bribe your teacher to get a good grade; you have to pay a bribe to get a passport for travel; soldiers will stop people to check their registration and ask for a bribe," Aung-Thwin says. "The only way to purge the corruption is regime change."

But regime change elsewhere in Southeast Asia has not necessarily brought more accountability and less corruption. Indonesia and the Philippines, which were once authoritarian like Myanmar and Cambodia, are considered more corrupt than some of their less democratic neighbors.

"If you look at Transparency International's Corruption Perceptions Index, Singapore is high up and not democratic at all, and the Southeast Asia country that performs second best is Malaysia," says Case of the City University of Hong Kong. "They are well ahead of the Philippines, which is sometimes understood to be democratic, and well ahead of Indonesia, which is the only democracy in the region."

There is no correlation between democracy and reduced corruption, says Danang Widoyoko, deputy coordinator of Indonesia Corruption Watch, a nongovernmental organization in Jakarta. "We inherited the corruption problem that was practiced widely and systematically by President Suharto's New Order regime," says Danang. Gen. Suharto controlled Indonesian politics for 32 years in one of Southeast Asia's most repressive

dictatorships before it collapsed in 1998 following the Asian financial crisis.[24] "Corruption in Indonesia is a way of life," says Danang.

Since Suharto's rule ended, "the country has been trying to break with its past experience of centralized power vulnerable to oligarchic abuse," reports Transparency International. Political power has been decentralized, and Indonesia now consists of 33 provinces, each with its own legislature and governor. "The responsibility for most public services such as health, education, culture, public works, land management, manufacturing and trading has been transferred to districts, cities and villages."[25]

While decentralization has helped Indonesia become a relatively liberal democracy with fair elections and extensive freedom of the press and association, it has had the perverse effect of increasing corruption opportunities. "With decentralization, . . . there are more people you have to pay off," says Bridget Welsh, a professor of political science at Singapore Management University.

Last year, Indonesia's Corruption Eradication Commission (KPK), formed in 2002, caught on wiretap Gen. Susni Duadji, then chief of detectives in the national police force, asking for a $1 million bribe. Susni was then reported to have tried to frame two of the anti-corruption commissioners.[26] "If you check the KPK's cases, there have been scandals in the election commission, corruption in the Indonesian Central Bank, bribery of prosecutors, and more," says Danang.

Likewise, the Philippines has had its own corruption scandals, starting with former strongman Marcos. During his 14-year rule from 1972 to 1986, Marcos and his family "are alleged to have stolen between $5-10 billion worth of state assets," reports Transparency International.[27] Even after mass nonviolent street demonstrations known as the People Power revolution restored democracy, corruption remained. In 2001, President Joseph Estrada resigned amid accusations of graft; he was later charged with stealing more than $80 million in state funds. Convicted in 2007, he was pardoned by his successor, Gloria Macapagal-Arroyo, an economist who was elected in hopes of battling corruption, but who has suffered her own scandals during two terms that ended in May.[28]

The Center for People Empowerment in Governance (CenPEG), a watchdog group based in Quezon City, has called the Arroyo government a kleptocracy that specialized "in awarding contracts and civil service posts to allies and friends."[29]

Transparency International reports that "all levels of corruption, from petty bribery to grand corruption, patronage and state capture, exist in the Philippines at a considerable scale and scope."[30]

The problem is not a lack of laws. "The country has many laws and about 17 agencies that fight corruption, and yet it remains near the top of the list of most corrupt countries in the region if not the whole world," says Bobby Tuazon, CenPEG's director of policy studies.

What's needed is a new mass "people power" movement, says Tuazon, to press for a complete overhaul of the bureaucracy and the creation of "a powerful, independent anti-corruption watchdog that has powers to arrest, jail and prosecute suspects, including the powerful." However, he points out, "the use of threats and legal coercion by those in power are a deterrent to this democratic undertaking by the people. In the Philippines, . . . the 'whistle-blowers' . . . get arrested and threatened."

Danang is more hopeful about Indonesia. "I'm quite optimistic that corruption can be curbed in the future," he says, pinning his hopes on the pressure of continued public outrage expressed through a free media. Both Danang and Welsh see the need for campaign-finance reform to reduce reliance on the private donations of businessmen, and civil service reform to raise salaries and increase professionalism. "It just takes time," says Welsh, "and it is not easy."

In fact, a study examining the role of democracy as a check on corruption comes to basically the same conclusion. Its authors argue that democracy helps to minimize corruption eventually, but that it takes time, sometimes several generations. New democracies must establish the necessary campaign-finance reform, accountable executive branches, independent judiciaries and auditors and the free flow of information.[31]

The challenge is to maintain democracy long enough to do the job. "Corruption deprives people of services and facilities, and when these are not delivered, democracy is eroded because people have less access to economic and social rights," says Edna Estifania A. Co, a professor at the National College of Public Administration and Governance at the University of the Philippines Diliman.

BACKGROUND
Corruption and Violence

"Democracies . . . become consolidated only when both significant elites and an overwhelming proportion of ordinary citizens see democracy . . . as 'the only game in town,'" write the authors of *How East Asians View Democracy*.[32] But in Southeast Asia, that prerequisite for legitimacy is extremely fragile.

In Thailand and the Philippines, for instance, "a significant number of citizens harbor professed reservations about democracy and lingering attachments to authoritarianism," according to surveys. Although Freedom House once ranked both countries liberal democracies, it has not done so since 2005, and by 2007 it no longer considered them electoral democracies either, a less stringent category. In all of Southeast Asia, only Indonesia is now viewed as a liberal democracy, and East Timor an electoral democracy.

Yet the Philippines has the longest experience with democracy of any Southeast Asian nation. When the Philippines gained independence from the United States in 1946, it retained an American-style democratic system that had been put in place under colonial rule.

But by the late 1960s "it became apparent that procedural democracy had not generated social justice and equity," according to Philippine political pollster Linda Luz Guerrero and Rollin Tusalem, an assistant political science professor at Arkansas State University. Powerful families held most of the economic and political power, and half the population lived in poverty. A civil war was brewing on the southern island of Mindanao, and communist insurgents on the northern island of Luzon were demanding land reform.

In 1970, demonstrators tried to storm the presidential palace in Manila, and an attempt was made on the life of visiting Pope Paul VI; the following year grenades were thrown at a political rally. In September 1972, President Ferdinand Marcos declared martial law.[33] Throughout the decade, poverty and government corruption increased, and Marcos' "friends and associates monopolized major industries," write Guerrero and Tusalem.

The 1980s marked a turning point for the Philippines. The military's assassination of opposition leader and democratic reformer Benigno "Ninoy" Aquino in August 1983 as he returned to Manila from self-exile in the United States triggered a funeral procession attended by

atlas.colorado.edu

Hundreds of thousands of Filipinos pack Manila streets in 1986, demanding that dictator Ferdinand Marcos step down from power. After Marcos fled the country four days later — following 20 years of autocratic rule — the so-called People Power movement became the inspiration for other nonviolent demonstrations around the world, including those that ended several communist dictatorships in Eastern Europe.

hundreds of thousands of people. Months of massive demonstrations followed, in which protesters demanded Marcos' resignation and the restoration of democracy. The protests continued intermittently over the next three years, until Aquino's widow, the late Corazon Aquino, led the nonviolent "People Power" uprising that finally toppled Marcos in 1986.

The People Power movement inspired similar movements around the world, including people's rallies in South Korea, the pro-democracy demonstration in China's Tiananmen Square in 1989, the Solidarity movement in Poland and the Velvet Revolution in the former Czechoslovakia.

But reform-minded Aquino was unable to turn back the crony capitalism of the Marcos era. Since the return of democracy, the Philippines has struggled with the same "violence, bossism, and corruption" that plagued the country during martial law, writes Stanford's Diamond. A few dozen clans continue to dominate politics and the economy, and many control private armies responsible for election-year violence; corruption pervades all levels of government; organized crime often operates with official collusion; social injustice feeds a communist insurgency in the north; and in the south, Muslim insurgents agitate for autonomy.[34]

Almost every president since Aquino has been accused of corruption. In January 2001 the Supreme Court ended the presidency of former movie actor Joseph Marcelo

Estrada, elected in 1998, after he was found to have taken payoffs from illegal gambling operations. His successor, economist Gloria Macapagal-Arroyo, suffered through her own series of accusations — that she rigged her reelection in 2004; that her husband was involved in illegal gambling, logging and smuggling and that she fabricated her claim of a coup attempt in February 2006 so she could declare a state of emergency to stop anti-government demonstrations.[35]

This May, Corazon Aquino's son Benigno "Noynoy" Aquino was elected to succeed Arroyo on a campaign pledge — made by almost every other Philippine president — to fight corruption and strengthen democracy.

Shaky Democracy

Thailand is the only nation in Southeast Asian never to have been colonized. An absolute monarchy until a palace coup in 1932, Thailand, like the Philippines, has had an uneven experience with democracy.

What followed the coup was not a genuine participatory democracy, write Thailand scholars Robert Albritton and Thawilwadee Bureekul. "Political power was monopolized by an exclusive elite in a one-party state, . . . which promised full electoral democracy only when at least half the population had completed primary education or 10 years had passed."

Albritton and Thawilwadee write that only six of the years leading up to 1985 could be considered truly democratic. Otherwise, a series of military-supported authoritarian regimes governed Thailand, until public disaffection with the "excesses of the authoritarian right again revived the demand for democracy among the Thai public," culminating in "fully democratic elections" in 1988 and the formation of a coalition government.

But three years later a military coup, supported by Thailand's middle class, dismissed the elected government after the media relentlessly criticized it for corruption. Eventually, popular pressure forced the military junta to promise new elections, and Freedom House once again categorized Thailand as an electoral democracy in 1993. Lawmakers passed a new constitution in 1997 that "radically revised the electoral system" and created a Constitutional Court, an Election Commission and the National Anti-Corruption Commission.

Freedom House raised Thailand's status in 1998 from "partly free" to "free," and in 2001 the polarizing billionaire

CHRONOLOGY

1940s-1950s *Independence arrives in Southeast Asia after World War II.*

1960s-1970s *Authoritarian regimes dominate Southeast Asia.*

1962 Gen. Ne Win leads coup in Burma; military takes control; country is renamed Myanmar.

1964 America's military support of South Vietnam escalates when U.S. bombs North Vietnam; U.S. pulls out in 1973; North Vietnam prevails in 1975 to form the Socialist Republic of Vietnam.

1968 Gen. Suharto becomes president of Indonesia, assumes authoritarian control.

1972 Philippine President Ferdinand Marcos declares martial law.

1975 Khmer Rouge seizes power in Cambodia; up to 2 million people are killed or die from disease, overwork, starvation; Vietnam eventually overthrows the regime and installs new communist government in 1979.

1980s-1990s *Democracy returns to some countries in Southeast Asia.*

1983 Philippine democracy advocate and former Sen. Benigno Aquino is assassinated; mass pro-democracy demonstrations ensue.

1986 "People Power" revolution in Philippines topples Marcos; Aquino's widow Corazon is elected president.

1988 Thailand holds democratic elections after decades of authoritarian rule.

1990 National League for Democracy (NLD) wins parliamentary elections in Myanmar but junta rejects results; and places NLD leader Daw Aung San Suu Kyi under house arrest.

1991 Military coup overthrows elected government in Thailand.

1997 Thailand adopts reformist constitution.

1998 Riots erupt in Indonesia after Asian financial crisis; Suharto is forced to resign.

2000-Present *Corruption scandals and election violence hit Philippines; coup roils Thailand.*

2001 Philippine Supreme Court ends corrupt presidency of Joseph Marcelo Estrada; Gloria Macapagal-Arroyo takes power. . . . Billionaire businessman Thaksin Shinawatra becomes Thailand's prime minister.

2002 East Timor gains independence from Indonesia.

2006 Military coup overthrows Thaksin in Thailand amid accusations of corruption.

2008 Courts remove Thaksin allies from power; opposition politician Abhisit Vejjajiva becomes prime minister. . . . Malaysia's Barisan Nasional party loses its majority in parliamentary election.

November 2009 Fifty-seven people — including journalists and relatives and supporters of a political candidate — are massacred in Philippines, reportedly by supporters of a rival candidate.

2010 Myanmar's military junta imposes restrictive rules for upcoming elections; opposition NLD announces election boycott (March 8). . . . Anti-government protesters begin demonstrations in Bangkok, demanding that Thai Prime Minister Abhisit step down and call new elections (March 12); 25 people die and more than 800 are injured when soldiers and police try to disperse the protesters (April 10). . . . NLD disbands in Myanmar after failing to register for upcoming elections (May 7). . . . Sen. Benigno Aquino, son of former president Corazon Aquino, is elected president in country's first computerized election (May 10) . . . . Central Bangkok becomes a battleground as soldiers disperse crowds and protesters burn buildings. . . . Thai government imposes curfews, closes opposition media outlets and issues arrest warrant on terrorism charges for self-exiled former prime minister Thaksin Shinawatra (May 14-May 27). In all, 88 people are killed and more than 1,000 injured during the nine weeks of protests.

Indonesia's Defamation Laws Stifle Democracy

"Truth is not a defense if an official finds the content of your statement 'insulting.'"

Human Rights Watch (HRW) examines Indonesia's harsh defamation laws in a report issued in April, "Turning Critics Into Criminals: The Human Rights Consequences of Criminal Defamation Law in Indonesia." CQ Global Researcher *writer Barbara Mantel discussed the report with Elaine Pearson, deputy director of HRW's Asia Division.*

CQGR: Indonesia has eliminated many of the most pernicious laws that officials once used to silence critics, but criminal defamation and insult laws remain.

EP: Six criminal defamation and "insult" provisions are commonly invoked by powerful people in Indonesia. These include provisions in the Criminal Code on slander or libel, with higher penalties invoked if the person is a public official. There are also specific provisions against insulting a public authority and a particularly harsh provision that punishes the communication of defamatory statements over the Internet, with up to six years' imprisonment and a fine of up to 1 billion rupiah (approximately $106,000).

CQGR: What if the statements are true?

EP: Under Indonesia's "insult" laws, truth is not a defense if an official finds the content of your statement "insulting." Under the other defamation laws, if defendants want to use truth as a defense they have to both prove their claim is true and also that they acted in the "general interest" or out of necessity. And this is risky; if the judge hears a truth defense but is not convinced, the defendant can be found guilty of "calumny," which carries a more severe penalty of up to four years imprisonment.

CQGR: Why is the penalty higher for defamation over the Internet?

EP: One justification is that Internet defamation has the potential to be far more harmful than regular defamation because the Internet can be used to communicate content to an infinite number of people. Human Rights Watch believes that it is precisely because the Internet can dramatically expand the channels for communication and sharing of information that laws on Internet use should not seek to repress the peaceful airing of grievances.

CQGR: How have officials and powerful private citizens used these laws to silence criticism and opposition?

EP: Because the laws contain extremely vague language, powerful people can use criminal defamation laws to retaliate against people who had made allegations of corruption, fraud or misconduct against powerful interests or government officials. These laws are also open to manipulation by individuals with political or financial power who can influence the behavior of investigators. For instance, in some cases the police aggressively pursued the criminal defamation complaint without properly investigating the validity of the underlying complaint of corruption or fraud.

CQGR: Can you give an example of a government official using the laws to silence opposition?

EP: Three activists from the Coalition of Students and People of Tasikmalaya were put on trial in 2009 for criminal defamation on a complaint filed by a local education official after they held an anti-corruption demonstration related to corruption charges they had made against him. Tukijo, a farmer, was convicted of defamation earlier this year. The charges were brought by a local official whom he asked for the results of a land assessment. He had previously argued with the local official.

CQGR: Can you give an example of these laws' use against the media?

EP: Bersihar Lubis, a veteran reporter, was convicted of defaming the attorney general when he criticized his

Thaksin Shinawatra, who had made his fortune in telecommunications, was elected prime minister. He had appealed to the majority electorate in rural northern and northeastern Thailand with promises of development programs and health care reform. But while Thaksin improved the conditions of the rural poor, critics accused him and his associates of undercutting the reformist 1997 constitution, abusing power for personal gain, conducting a brutal "war on drugs" that resulted in at least 2,500 deaths in 2003 and responding with a heavy hand to a Muslim insurgency in Thailand's four southernmost provinces.[36]

When the Thaksin family sold its share of Shin Corp. — one of Southeast Asia's most important information

decision to ban a high school history textbook in an opinion column. Journalist Risang Bima Wijaya was convicted of defamation and served six months in prison after he published unflattering articles about a local media figure in Yogyakarta who had been accused of a crime.

CQGR: What impact do these criminal defamation laws have on democracy in Indonesia?

EP: All those accused of defamation engaged [in conduct] that included holding peaceful demonstrations against officials accused of corruption, publicizing consumer complaints and disputes with businesses, requesting information from the authorities and lodging complaints with them and reporting in the media on subjects of public importance. Democracy requires a vibrant civil society that can monitor the performance of public officials and a free press that shares information about prominent people and events, even when the news is negative. And democracy requires an atmosphere in which people are free to speak their minds and participate in public discourse. But under Indonesia's defamation laws, people who do these things can be found guilty of a crime if they offend the wrong person.

These laws have a chilling effect on free speech in Indonesia. This is harmful to every individual who has something to say but is afraid to do so because they fear imprisonment. Journalists told us how they are afraid to get an exclusive story on sensitive topics because they fear going to jail.

CQGR: What other countries in Southeast Asia have criminal defamation laws?

EP: Many countries — such as Singapore, Malaysia, Cambodia and Thailand — have criminal defamation laws or other "insult" or national security laws that have a similar chilling effect. However from what we have seen in Indonesia, the use of criminal defamation laws is more widespread. Also Indonesia has more criminal defamation offenses than any other country in the region.

CQGR: Human Rights Watch wants to see criminal defamation laws eliminated. Why is there no place for criminal penalties?

Elaine Pearson, deputy director of Human Rights Watch's Asia Division, denounces Indonesia's new defamation laws, saying that they repress peaceful airing of grievances.

EP: Criminal penalties are always disproportionate punishments for reputational harm and should be abolished. International human rights law allows for restrictions on freedom of expression to protect the reputations of others, but such restrictions must be necessary and narrowly drawn. As repeal of criminal defamation laws in an increasing number of countries shows, such laws are not necessary. Civil defamation and criminal incitement laws are sufficient for the purpose of protecting people's reputations and maintaining public order and can be written and implemented in ways that provide appropriate protections for freedom of expression.

— Barbara Mantel

technology firms — to the investment arm of the Singapore government in January 2006, a wave of anti-Thaksin protests in the capital — led by the People's Alliance for Democracy (PAD) — resulted. After snap elections, boycotts and street protests, a military coup forced Thaksin from office, and judicial and parliamentary maneuvering eventually led Abhisit Vejjajiva, leader of

the opposition Democratic Party, to take over as prime minister.[37]

Ever since, Thaksin's supporters have been demanding that Abhisit step down and call new parliamentary elections, and demonstrations have been a periodic feature of Bangkok life. They turned violent in April and May as soldiers and protestors battled in the capital's

Protesting Repression

Demonstrators in Manila display a photograph of Burmese pro-democracy leader Daw Aung San Suu Kyi (top) as they denounce Myanmar's new election law on March 19. Under the new law, Nobel Peace Prize winner Suu Kyi, who has been held under house arrest for 14 years, cannot run in elections expected to be held in October or November. Supporters of slain UNTV journalist Daniel Tiamzon — one of 57 people killed in an election-related massacre in the southern Philippines in November — demonstrate during his funeral (bottom). They are demanding that the killers, allegedly associated with a politically powerful family, be brought to justice.

streets. The government dispersed the crowds on May 19, arresting protest leaders, imposing curfews and shutting down opposition media outlets. It also issued an arrest warrant on terrorism charges for Thaksin,

accusing him of masterminding the March-through-May street protests. Thaksin, who is in self-exile abroad to avoid arrest on a post-coup corruption conviction, denies the charges.

Free But Corrupt

In marked contrast to the Philippines and Thailand, Indonesia, which became an electoral democracy only in 1999, has become "a surprising political success story," according to Diamond.

"Today, Indonesia is not only a reasonably stable democracy . . . but it is even in some respects a relatively liberal democracy, with reasonably fair elections and extensive freedoms of press and association," Diamond writes.[38] In 2005, Freedom House raised its status to "free."

Indonesia won independence from the Dutch in 1949, and the republic's first president, known only as Sukarno, assumed authoritarian powers in 1957. After Gen. Suharto crushed a coup attempt by the Communist Party of Indonesia (PKI) in 1965, "mass acts of violence followed, ostensibly against suspected PKI members, resulting in an estimated 500,000 deaths," according to Freedom House.[39] Suharto became president in 1968.

Under Suharto, Indonesia was an "authoritarian success story," with average annual economic growth of 7 percent. But "three decades of development and sure-handed economic management imploded in just a matter of months under the strain of the 1997 East Asian financial crisis," writes Diamond. Stories began to circulate of "colossal corruption and monopolistic practices" of the president's children and associates, and riots erupted when the government announced cuts in fuel and electricity subsidies.[40] In 1998, Suharto was forced to resign, and the country soon held its first free legislative elections since 1955.

Graft remains endemic, especially in the government bureaucracy, yet new legislation signed into law last September dilutes the authority and independence of the Corruption Eradication Commission and the Anticorruption Court. The rule of law is seriously undermined "by rampant corruption in the judiciary, and politically well-connected elites rarely face consequences of abuses of power," according to Freedom House. According to its most recent report, the security forces and the military abuse human rights with impunity. "In short, corruption, collusion and nepotism continue to constitute the modus operandi of Indonesian politics," Freedom House's Indonesia analyst writes.[41]

Newest Democracy

While predominantly Muslim Indonesia was building its own democracy, its military was brutally suppressing an independence movement in East Timor, a Catholic enclave that occupies half an island on the eastern edge of the Indonesian archipelago. In 1999, the people of East Timor voted for independence from Indonesia, which had invaded and annexed the country in 1975 as the Portuguese were relinquishing control. But after the referendum, "the territory descended into chaos as pro-Indonesian militias and the army engaged in a campaign of terror and brutality, killing supporters of independence, looting and burning buildings and causing thousands to flee their homes."[42]

Indonesia eventually allowed a United Nations peacekeeping force to enter East Timor, and the country slowly transitioned to an electoral democracy, finally becoming independent on May 20, 2002.

East Timor's struggle to build a democracy and a functioning state has been punctuated by violence. The country has made significant progress and is considered an electoral democracy, but — as in other Southeast Asian countries — it has experienced "threatening episodes of armed rebellion, attempted assassination of the president and prime minister, and violent communal conflict," not to mention high-level corruption, according to Freedom House.[43]

CURRENT SITUATION

Thai Violence

Bangkok streets damaged by bloody battles have been scrubbed, the fires from buildings torched by retreating protesters put out, the demonstrators dispersed and their leaders arrested. But the divisions within Thai society that are at the root of this spring's anti-government protests — which left at least 88 people dead and more than 1,000 wounded — remain.

"I am mourning my fellow protesters who were killed by the government like vegetables and fish," said a middle-aged resident of Thailand's rural northeast region, a stronghold of anti-government sentiment. "Watch out," she said. "People are going to go underground and fight with arms. This is the beginning of a very long war."[44]

The protesters, known as red shirts, took over an area of commercial Bangkok in late March, disrupting hotel service, shopping, tourism and, ultimately, the economy. They numbered tens of thousands at their peak, and for the first weeks they were carefully nonviolent; the military was cautious as well. In fact, many Bangkok residents became increasingly critical of the government for not trying to take back control of that crucial part of the capital.

But on April 10, when soldiers finally did try to disperse the crowds, the protesters counterattacked, repulsing the troops. At the end of the day, at least 25 civilians and

Economies Grew Rapidly Across Region

Per capita gross national income (GNI) in Southeast Asia grew dramatically between 2005 and 2008, with Timor-Leste posting more than a 200 percent increase. GNI throughout the region grew at least 26 percent during the period, with eight countries growing at 40 percent or more. Experts disagree on whether economic growth in a country leads to democracy in the government.

Per Capita Gross National Income in Southeast Asia, 2005-2008*

Country	2005	2008	% increase
Brunei	$22,770	n/a	n/a
Cambodia	$450	$640	42%
Indonesia	$1,170	$1,880	61%
Laos	$450	$760	69%
Malaysia	$5,210	$7,250	39%
Philippines	$1,260	$1,890	50%
Singapore	$27,670	$34,760	26%
Thailand	$2,580	$3,670	42%
Timor-Leste	$740	$2,460	232%
Vietnam	$620	$890	44%

* Figures not available for Myanmar (Burma)

Source: The World Bank

Philippine Election Violence Declined

The recent election season in the Philippines was one of the country's least violent, despite a shocking, election-related massacre last Nov. 23, when 57 people — 30 of them journalists — were killed in Maguindanao Province. During the past decade, the bloodiest year for Philippine elections was 2004, when nearly 200 people were killed.

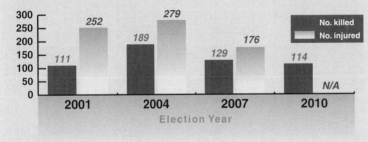

Source: Philippine Institute for Peace, Violence and Terrorism Research

soldiers were killed and more than 800 wounded in what was, at that point, the worst violence the country had seen in 20 years. Sporadic fighting continued, with grenade attacks in parts of the city, until on May 14th the protests turned bloody as the military once again moved in. Within a week, dozens more were killed and hundreds wounded, and on May 19, many protest leaders surrendered.

The demonstrators were mostly farmers and small business people from rural Thailand, who account for the majority of the electorate, joined by some of Bangkok's poorer residents, students and professionals. Thailand is a constitutional monarchy, and the red shirts want the current prime minister and his government, which they view as illegitimate, to step down and call new elections. "I used to think we were born poor and that was that," Thanida Paveen, who grew up in rural Thailand and now lives in the capital's outskirts, told a reporter. "I have opened my mind to a new way of thinking: We need to change from the rule of the aristocracy to a real democracy."[45]

The roots of their protest can be traced to 2006, when a military coup ousted then Prime Minister Thaksin Shinawatra, who had introduced universal health care and brought investment to rural areas. But Bangkok's elite, composed of middle class professionals, military leaders, bureaucrats and members of the royal family, long accustomed to controlling politics and the country, accused Thaksin of vote buying, corruption and undermining the rule of law in a deadly anti-drug campaign. Many took to the streets under the banner of the People's Alliance for Democracy (PAD), also known as the "yellow-shirts," setting the stage for the coup that eventually sent Thaksin into self-exile to avoid arrest on a corruption conviction.[46]

New elections were held a year later. But after Thaksin allies won, the PAD returned to the streets, this time incapacitating the government and shutting down Bangkok's airports for a week. Through a series of court rulings and parliamentary moves, Thaksin's allies were forced from power and their party disbanded. Abhisit became prime minister.

Even though the violence in Bankok has ended, Thai society will remain deeply polarized, say analysts. During its street protests in 2008, the PAD called for "a revamping of the democratic system to prevent the rural sector from dictating the outcome of the elections."[47] It advocated an indirect voting system based on occupation.

"The elites have a very low opinion of people who are not highly educated," says Robert Albritton, an expert on Thailand at the University of Mississippi. "They were asking, 'Are we going to let these uneducated people in the rice fields run the government?' " The elites prefer "guided democracy," he says, with a strong government bureaucracy loyal to the monarchy and a weak, rubber-stamp Parliament.

The Thai bureaucracy often is unaccountable to the prime minister and his appointees, says Thawilwadee Bureekul, director of research and development at King Prajadhipok's Institute in Nonthaburi, which promotes democracy and good governance. For instance, a politically appointed minister of agriculture would have at his side a permanent secretary, who ascended to his position after years of civil service. "Sometimes the minister will have a difficult time enforcing his policies," says Thawilwadee, "because these government officials won't always support him. We need to reform the bureaucracy."

Thaksin tried to reform the bureaucracy by reshuffling ministries, says Thawilwadee. That's one reason "the bureaucracy had grown to hate him," says Albritton. But Thaksin also had a "dark side" and did not tolerate criticism, opposition or the constraints of the rule of law, according to Diamond of Stanford. He intimidated journalists and critical nongovernmental organizations and infuriated a nationalist public when he sold his business holdings to a Singaporean firm for nearly $2 billion while paying no tax.[48]

Now the government is accusing Thaksin of terrorism for masterminding the street protests and encouraging violence, charges he has denied. It has issued an arrest warrant and hopes that one of the countries where Thaksin travels in self-exile will extradite him.[49]

Meanwhile Thai authorities have shut down publications linked to the red shirt movement and blocked scores of websites and community radio stations under a state of emergency currently in place in Bangkok and 23 provinces.[50] Yet schools and other buildings continue to be attacked across the country. "The land will go up in flames," said Sa-at, a farmer who participated in the Bangkok protests.[51]

New Philippine President

Opposition Sen. Benigno "Noynoy" Aquino was decisively elected the next president of the Philippines on May 10, delivering a sharp rebuke to outgoing President Gloria Macapagal-Arroyo, who had been embroiled in corruption scandals since taking office in 2001.

Aquino is the son of the late Corazon Aquino, who led the "People Power" uprising that finally toppled Marcos in 1986. Known for her honesty and integrity, Mrs. Aquino promised to clean up the "crony capitalism" that had riddled the Marcos dictatorship, but she largely failed. Her son campaigned on the slogan "No corruption means no poverty," but his lackluster record in Congress led some analysts to doubt his ability to rid the Philippines of endemic graft. "It simply will take overhauling the entire state bureaucracy, and I don't see him ready to undertake this monumental fight," says Tuazon of CenPEG.

It took only two days for voters to learn that Aquino had likely won, an unprecedented brief time compared to past elections, when it took weeks to tally the votes. Voters used computerized optical scanning machines this time, installed not just to shorten the reporting time but also to prevent the rampant election fraud associated with the pencil and paper ballots of the past. In the 2004

Christians in Timor-Leste — Southeast Asia's newest democracy — carry crucifixes during a procession in Dili to mark Palm Sunday on March 16, 2008. The predominantly Roman Catholic country has made significant progress toward democracy since it gained independence from Muslim-dominated Indonesia. Although it is considered an electoral democracy, Timor-Leste — like other Southeast Asian countries — has experienced "threatening episodes of armed rebellion, attempted assassination of the president and prime minister, and violent communal conflict," according to Freedom House.

AFP/Getty Images/Mario Jonny Dos Santos

elections, Arroyo was accused of massive vote rigging, later supported by an audiotape that surfaced of a conversation between the president and the head of the Commission on Elections (Comelec).

Many of those who were originally skeptical of the largely untested computerized system and of the tainted Comelec's oversight hailed this year's election as a success. Newspaper columnist Conrado de Quiros wrote, "I was wrong about the automation, I was wrong about the Comelec commissioners . . . and, boy, am I absolutely ecstatic to be so."[52]

But several losing presidential candidates are calling for an audit of the results, claiming that 8 million Filipinos failed to cast their ballots due to technical glitches and long lines on election day.[53] And CenPEG said it had received numerous reports from its field researchers and poll watchers of significant problems, including machine malfunctions and shutdowns, power outages and failed electronic transmission of results, leaving an estimated 15 percent of registered voters unable to vote.

The computerized system could not prevent other ills typically associated with Philippine elections. "Vote

Should the United States, European Union and Australia maintain sanctions on Myanmar?

YES
Wylie Bradford
Editor, Burma Economic Watch Senior Lecturer, Department of Economics, Macquarie University, Sydney, Australia

Written for *CQ Global Researcher*, May 31, 2010

The most obvious and compelling, yet typically neglected, reason to maintain sanctions against the Burmese regime is simple: morality. The military rulers of Burma are criminals of the most violent and rapacious kind, with decades of murder, torture, rape, oppression and pillage on their records. Common human decency ought to be enough to compel legitimate states to make it as hard as possible for the junta and its cronies to continue to profit from evil.

Sadly, the all-too-common mélange of special pleading, anti-Western propaganda and outright hypocrisy has driven a campaign against sanctions on the grounds that sanctions don't work, impose excessive burdens on the Burmese people and ought to be dropped in favour of greater "engagement" with the regime. The intellectual bankruptcy of these positions is another powerful argument for retaining and extending sanctions.

Nobody argues that limiting trade and financial interaction with Burma will lead in itself to democratisation. Hence any claim that sanctions don't work made on those grounds is no more than a straw man. Sanctions — especially targeted financial sanctions — certainly do work by denying the regime access to our financial systems for the purposes of storing and laundering their blood money.

The claim that sanctions hurt the Burmese population is uninformed at best and dishonest at worst. Five decades of military rule have rendered Burma's economy barely functional, a process of destruction set in motion long before any sanctions were imposed. The extent of regime control over economic activity means there are no sectors immune either to their rapacity or their policy incompetence. The junta is the Burmese people's greatest enemy in every sense.

The pro-engagement case is an exercise in sophistry and distortion. The mechanism through which greater "engagement" will produce change is never spelt out. The fact that flourishing trade with nonsanctioning states has yielded precisely no political gains is elided when arguing for greater Western engagement. The demonstrable ineffectiveness of aid is ignored in favour of unfounded assertions to the contrary, and scholarly access to Burma yields papers that few read and none cite and the indulgence of the *National Geographic* fantasies of tourists seeking cheap holidays masquerade as blows for freedom.

Any and all forms of pressure must be maintained until change occurs. The idea that if we enable the generals' malfeasance long enough they will stop of their own accord can only charitably be regarded as stunningly naïve.

NO
Sreeradha Datta
Fellow, Institute of Defence Studies and Analyses, New Delhi, India

Written for *CQ Global Researcher*, May 31, 2010

Once considered Asia's rice bowl, Myanmar today barely manages economic growth of 3 percent. The ruling junta spends 40 percent of its budget on defense, with marginal spending on sectors that could have stimulated the economy. The lack of economic opportunities has been cited by the junta to argue for removal of the sanctions imposed on Myanmar. Indeed, the lack of development can be attributed to the chronic political instability brought on by the ruling generals and their mismanagement of resources and inept economic decision-making.

The generals, meanwhile, enjoy an envious lifestyle, amassing wealth in several bank accounts — clearly sanitized from the surrounding impoverishment. Arguably, the sanctions have affected the junta's commercial projects, but the biggest hit has been taken by the common masses. The generals, the real targets of the sanctions, are the least affected and continue to hold complete sway, economically and politically. They not only run the country with utter disdain toward any democratic or human rights norms but also continue to isolate political opponents with impunity.

Although the international community exudes a sense of disapproval towards the junta, the sanction regime has found limited appeal. In contrast to the Western nations who have persisted with sanctions for over the last two decades, the regional powers and Myanmar's immediate neighbors have chosen to engage with the generals. Although international sanctions are supported by the opposition groups, sanctions have undermined the reformists' position and reinforced the hardliners within the ruling establishment.

The elections announced for the end of the year likely will be farcical. Not only has the junta engineered the absence of the strongest opposition leaders, but it also has simultaneously planted its own men in several of the political parties contesting the elections. Despite this, the eventual rise of new power centers — even a multiparty system — holds some prospects.

Undoubtedly, Myanmar is in dire need of better governance and pluralism. In the face of splintered opposition the junta's overthrow is not an immediate option. Rather, it needs persuasion towards undertaking some reforms. Concerted peer pressure involving regional players and stakeholders holds greater promise of eliciting a response from the generals. Thus, dialogue is a good beginning, not as a supplement to sanctions but rather as a genuine attempt to engage the ruling elite. The stick failed. How about guided inducement?

buying remains rife," according to a May report from the International Crisis Group. For instance, a candidate in Maguindanao province described "a system of 'assists,' whereby the heads of families or town mayors would be paid to deliver a certain number of votes."[54]

Violence also marred the campaign season, although there were fewer deaths than in the recent past, surprising some observers. "Our institute forecasted more violence in the May 2010 elections because of the continuing presence of illegally armed groups all over the country," says Rommel Banlaoi, director of the Philippine Institute for Peace, Violence and Terrorism Research. "But we were proven wrong because the police and military seriously prepared themselves in deterring these armed groups." Banlaoi says law enforcement initiated peace covenants between competing politicians and made their presence felt in election hotspots.

But Co of the University of the Philippines disagrees that election violence was reduced. "One should look at the 'quality' of violence, and I thought it was more grim and horrid compared to the past," she says.

The worst case of political violence in the country's recent history occurred last November, when 100 armed men ambushed the wife of a local politician while she traveled with family members, supporters and journalists to file her husband's candidacy for the Maguindanao provincial governorship. A total of 57 people were massacred, their bodies found in graves that appeared to have been dug in advance. "Evidence soon emerged to implicate the Ampatuan clan, which dominated the province's politics and was closely allied with the Arroyo administration," according to Freedom House.[55] More than 60 people were arrested, including the provincial governor, Andal Ampatuan Sr.

"Local polls are essentially an intense competition for political power among the country's political dynasties," says Tuazon, like the Marcoses, the Ampatuan clan and the Cojuangco-Aquinos, the family of the next president, which owns Southeast Asia's biggest sugar plantation.

Many of these families, particularly in the southern Philippines, have their own armies, says Tuazon. "These private armies were mobilized by the government for the counterinsurgency campaigns against the Marxist New People's Army and rebels from the Moro National Liberation Front and Moro Islamic Liberation Front." But families like the Ampatuans have also used their armies to intimidate rival politicians and deliver votes, says Tuazon, who adds that laws meant to disband the armies are "toothless."

"The practice of electoral democracy in the Philippines is still messy, and that implies that our democratic foundation remains fragile," says Banlaoi. "The Philippines is still a young democracy, and we need more time to mature," he says.

OUTLOOK
Pressuring Myanmar

Pressure is mounting for the Association of Southeast Asian Nations (ASEAN) to aggressively push for meaningful change in Myanmar. Last year, U.S. Secretary of State Hillary Rodham Clinton called for the organization to consider expelling Myanmar if it did not release pro-democracy leader Aung San Suu Kyi from house arrest.[56]

In April, 106 lawmakers from across Southeast Asia signed a petition criticizing the Burmese elections expected for October as designed "to do nothing more than firmly entrench the military's role in the future governance of Myanmar." The petitioners demanded that ASEAN suspend Myanmar and impose sanctions against its military government.[57]

The goal is to "force the military to the negotiating table with democracy proponents . . . to ensure fairer and more inclusive elections," says Jason, whose ASEAN Inter-Parliamentary Myanmar Caucus sponsored the petition.

ASEAN was founded in 1967 during the height of the Cold War to reduce the region's "risk of falling victim to global rivalry among the great powers."[58] But economic cooperation, cultural exchange and security between its members were the main objectives; interfering in each other's internal politics was not, and in fact is prohibited in the organization's charter.

Another obstacle to ASEAN sanctioning Myanmar: It would require more than a simple majority. "The problem with any serious sanctions or expulsion is that it requires a full consensus," says Evan Laksmana, a researcher at the Centre for Strategic and International Studies, a think tank in Jakarta. "And that is nearly impossible."

"Unlikely, but not impossible," says Jason. "It will take political will by big ASEAN states such as Thailand, Indonesia, Malaysia, Singapore and Philippines to make this happen."

Ever since ASEAN admitted Myanmar in 1997, the group's leaders have engaged in behind-the-scenes diplomacy with the military junta, and, more recently, have publicly expressed concerns over Myanmar's exclusionary election rules unveiled in March. But the policy of "constructive engagement" and mild public rebuke "has been a failure," says McGill's Kuhonta. "ASEAN leaders had argued that if junta leaders were incorporated into ASEAN, back-room diplomacy would make them less coercive," he says. "But not only did it not have any effect, human rights abuses actually increased."

Both Laksmana and Kuhonta are unsure whether sanctions and expulsion, even if possible, would be wise. "It would not change what's happening in Myanmar," says Laksmana, "because Myanmar can survive without ASEAN" as long as China and India continue to provide economic and military aid and invest in the country. Kuhonta calls expulsion too extreme. "ASEAN would lose all leverage with Myanmar," he says. He thinks perhaps stronger public criticism might be the right path for ASEAN now.

Jason disagrees, arguing that sanctions and expulsion from ASEAN would change things quite a bit. "Can China and India continue to defend Myanmar when its closest allies begin to pull away?" he asks. Jason says Myanmar's political and economic support needs to be broken down "brick by brick."

The election could force ASEAN's hand. "What sort of effort will there be to protest? If the death toll runs into the hundreds and the troops lose their cool, then what will ASEAN do?" asks Donald Emmerson, director of the Southeast Asia Forum at Stanford University.

Emmerson notes that Indonesia, Southeast Asia's only "free" democracy, takes over the leadership of ASEAN next January. "Indonesia may say we cannot tolerate a situation where we look like a club of dictators, and we have to do something about that," he says, adding that he cannot predict what shape that response would take.

NOTES

1. Seth Mydans, "With Guns, Slingshots and Rocks, Thai Troops and Protesters Clash, to Lethal Effect," *The New York Times*, May 15, 2010, p. A4.

2. Eric Talmadge, "Thais up Red Shirt watch: no warrant on ex-PM yet," Associated Press, May 28, 2010, www.google.com/hostednews/ap/article/ALeqM5g3j-vAVG1fg3kEfnogTiH8_4EXvwD9FVOQJ02.

3. Thomas Fuller, Seth Mydans and Kirk Semple, "Violence Spreads in Thailand After Crackdown," *The New York Times*, May 19, 2010, www.nytimes.com/2010/05/20/world/asia/20thai.html?pagewanted=1.

4. Arch Puddington, "Freedom in the World 2010: Erosion of Freedom Intensifies," Freedom House, Jan. 12, 2010, p. 4, www.freedomhouse.org/uploads/fiw10/FIW_2010_Overview_Essay.pdf.

5. "Freedom in the World 2009, Methodology," Freedom House, 2009, www.freedomhouse.org/template.cfm?page=351&ana_page=354&year=2009.

6. "The World Factbook," Central Intelligence Agency, www.cia.gov/library/publications/the-world-factbook/.

7. Mark Tran, "Clan allied to Philippine president suspected of being behind massacre," *The Guardian*, Nov. 25, 2009, www.guardian.co.uk/world/2009/nov/25/death-toll-philippines-massacre-57.

8. Since 2001, pollsters across Southeast Asia have been surveying popular opinion in a project called the Asian Barometer Survey (ABS), based at National Taiwan University, www.asianbarometer.org.

9. "Freedom in the World: Burma," Freedom House, 2010, www.freedomhouse.org.

10. "SPDC Election Laws Set the Stage for Sham Elections," ALTSEAN-Burma, April, 2010, www.altsean.org/Docs/PDF%20Format/Thematic%20Briefers/SPDC%20election%20laws%20set%20the%20stage%20for%20sham%20elections.pdf.

11. "Burmese Election Laws an Insult to Democracy and Rule of Law," International Federation for Human Rights, March 12, 2010, www.fidh.org/Burmese-Election-Laws-an-Insult-to-Democracy-and.

12. "SPDC Election Laws Set the Stage for Sham Elections," *op. cit.*

13. *Ibid.*

14. "Myanmar Opposition to Form New Party," *The Wall Street Journal*, May 8, 2010, http://online.wsj

.com/article/SB100014240527487033380045752
29613786634410.html.

15. "Freedom in the World: Cambodia, 2010," Freedom House, www.freedomhouse.org/template.cfm?page=363&year=2010&country=7794.

16. "The World Factbook," Central Intelligence Agency, www.cia.gov/library/publications/the-world-factbook/geos/sn.html.

17. "Freedom in the World: Singapore," Freedom House, 2009, www.freedomhouse.org.

18. "The best system for Singapore is . . .," Ori Sasson, People's Action Party, Sept. 6, 2009, www.pap.org.sg/articleview.php?id=4950&cid=85.

19. "Malaysia's Electoral Upheaval," *Journal of Democracy*, July 2009, Vol. 20, No. 3, pp. 71-85.

20. "Freedom in the World: Malaysia," Freedom House, 2010, www.freedomhouse.org/template.cfm?page=363&year=2009&country=7654.

21. "Malaysia's Electoral Upheaval," *op. cit.*

22. "Countries at the Crossroads: Cambodia," Freedom House, 2010, p. 15, www.freedomhouse.org/uploads/ccr/country-7794-9.pdf.

23. "Corruption Perceptions Index 2009," Transparency International, www.transparency.org/policy_research/surveys_indices/cpi/2009/cpi_2009_table.

24. "Countries at the Crossroads: Indonesia," Freedom House, 2010, www.freedomhouse.org/uploads/ccr/country-7841-9.pdf.

25. "Corruption Challenges at Sub-National Level in Indonesia," U4 Expert Answer, Transparency International, July 21, 2009, www.u4.no/helpdesk/helpdesk/query.cfm?id=210.

26. Norimitsu Onishi, "Exposing Graft, but His Motives Are Murky," *The New York Times*, May 8, 2010, www.nytimes.com/2010/05/08/world/asia/08general.html.

27. "Overview of Corruption and Anti-Corruption in the Philippines," U4 Expert Answer, Transparency International, August 2008, p. 3, www.u4.no/helpdesk/helpdesk/query.cfm?id=212.

28. "Global Integrity Report: Philippines," *Global Integrity*, 2008, http://report.globalintegrity.org/philippines/2008/timeline.

29. "Using corruption for political power and private gain," CenPEG, June 29, 2008.

30. "Overview of Corruption and Anti-Corruption in the Philippines," *op. cit.*, p. 1.

31. Charles H. Blake and Christopher G. Martin, "The Dynamics of Political Corruption: Re-examining the Influence of Democracy," *Democratization*, Feb. 2006, Vol. 13, No. 1, p. 4.

32. Unless otherwise stated, the following material is drawn from Yun-Han Chu, *et al.*, *How East Asians View Democracy* (2010).

33. "Philippines," *The New York Times*, http://topics.nytimes.com/top/news/international/countriesandterritories/philippines/index.html.

34. Larry Diamond, *The Spirit of Democracy: The Struggle to Build Free Societies Throughout the World* (2008), p. 221. For background, see Brian Beary, "Separatist Movements," *CQ Global Researcher*, April 2008, pp. 85-114.

35. *Ibid.*, p. 223.

36. "Freedom in the World: Thailand," Freedom House, 2009, www.freedomhouse.org.

37. *Ibid.*

38. Larry Diamond, "Indonesia's Place in Global Democracy," in Edward Aspinall and Marcus Mietzner, eds., *Problems of Democratization in Indonesia: Elections, Institutions and Society*, ISEAS, 2010, pp. 21-49.

39. "Freedom in the World: Indonesia," Freedom House, 2010, www.freedomhouse.org.

40. Diamond, *The Spirit of Democracy, op. cit.*, p. 92.

41. "Countries at the Crossroads: Indonesia," *op. cit.*

42. "Indonesia," *The New York Times*, http://topics.nytimes.com/top/news/international/countriesandterritories/indonesia/index.html.

43. "Countries at the Crossroads: East Timor," Freedom House, 2010, www.freedomhouse.org.

44. Hannah Beech and Khon Kaen, "Raising a Red Flag in Thailand," *Time* in partnership with CNN, June 7, 2010, www.time.com/time/magazine/article/0,9171,1992244,00.html.

45. Thomas Fuller, "Widening Disparity Strains Traditional Bonds of Thai Society," *The New York Times*, April 1, 2010, p. A4.

46. Erik Kuhonta, "Is the Middle Class a Harbinger of Democracy? Evidence from Southeast Asia," presented at the Annual Meeting of the Association for Asian Studies, March 25-28, 2010, p. 15.

47. *Ibid.*

48. Diamond, *The Spirit of Democracy, op. cit.*, pp. 80-81.

49. Eric Talmadge, "Thais up Red Shirt watch; no warrant on ex-PM yet," The Associated Press, May 28, 2010, www.google.com/hostednews/ap/article/ALeqM5g3j-vAVG1fg3kEfnogTiH8_4EXvwD9FVOQJ02.

50. Martin Petty, "Thailand extends censorship against anti-govt protesters," Reuters, May 27, 2010, http://uk.reuters.com/article/idUKTRE64Q1VU2010 0527.

51. Beech and Kaen, *op. cit.*

52. TJ Burgonio, *et al.*, " 'Eating Humble Pie': Poll automation naysayers 'thrilled to be wrong,' " *Inquirer.net*, May 13, 2010, http://newsinfo.inquirer.net/inquirerheadlines/nation/view/20100513-269687/Poll-automation-naysayers-thrilled-to-be-wrong.

53. "Philippine lawmakers to probe poll fraud allegations," Reuters India, May 18, 2010, http://in.reuters.com/article/worldNews/idINIndia-48581920100518.

54. "Philippines: Pre-Election Tensions in Central Mindanao," International Crisis Group, May 4, 2010, p. 5, www.crisisgroup.org/en/regions/asia/south-east-asia/philippines.aspx.

55. "Freedom in the World: Philippines," Freedom House, 2010, www.freedomhouse.org.

56. Boonradom Chitradon, "ASEAN rejects Clinton's call to expel Myanmar: Thai PM," Agence France-Presse, July 23, 2009, www.saigon-gpdaily.com.vn/International/2009/7/72733/.

57. "Petition to ASEAN Leaders attending 16th ASEAN Summit," April 7, 2010, www.aseanmp.org/wp-content/uploads/2008/07/Petition-to-ASEAN-on-Myanmar-2010-election.pdf.

58. Donald K. Emmerson, ed., *Hard Choices: Security, Democracy, and Regionalism in Southeast Asia* (2008), p. 59.

BIBLIOGRAPHY

Books

Chu, Yun-han, *et al.*, ed., *How East Asians View Democracy, Columbia University Press*, 2008.
Contributors dissect polling data from the Asian Barometer Survey, a comparative examination of democratization and values across the region.

Diamond, Larry, *The Spirit of Democracy: The Struggle to Build Free Societies Throughout the World, Henry Holt*, 2008.
With democracy in many parts of the world under pressure, a Stanford University professor examines why and how it is achieved and what conditions sustain it.

Emmerson, Donald K., ed., *Hard Choices: Security, Democracy, and Regionalism in Southeast Asia, The Walter H. Shorenstein Asia-Pacific Research Center*, 2008.
Contributors debate the role of the Association of Southeast Asian Nations (ASEAN) in ensuring security and encouraging democracy in the region.

Articles

"Myanmar Opposition To Form New Party," *The Wall Street Journal*, May 8, 2010, p. A9.
Myanmar's main opposition movement decides to boycott upcoming elections, and former members launch a splinter group to contest the polls.

"Worsening violence closes Bangkok bank and businesses," *The Guardian*, April 23, 2010, www.guardian.co.uk/world/2010/apr/23/violence-closes-bangkok-banks.
In Thailand's worst violence in 20 years, protesters and soldiers clash, leaving scores dead or wounded.

Boonradom, Chitradon, "ASEAN rejects Clinton's call to expel Myanmar: Thai PM," *Agence France-Presse*, July 23, 2009.
U.S. Secretary of State Hillary Rodham Clinton calls for the Association of Southeast Asian Nations to consider expelling Myanmar if its military junta does not release Nobel laureate and opposition leader Daw Aung San Suu Kyi from house arrest.

Onishi, Norimitsu, "Exposing Graft, but His Motives are Murky," *The New York Times*, May 8, 2010, www.nytimes.com/2010/05/08/world/asia/08general.html.
A former chief of detectives in Indonesia's national police force, accused of soliciting a bribe, threatens to release details of high-level police and government corruption.

Sasson, Ori, "The Best System for Singapore Is . . . ," *People's Action Party*, www.pap.org.sg, Sept. 6, 2009, www.pap.org.sg/articleview.php?id=4950&cid=85.
A member of Singapore's ruling party argues that democracy exists when the dominant party provides for citizens' needs and that a two-party system is not necessary in a democracy.

Reports and Studies

"Freedom in the World: Cambodia," *Freedom House*, 2010, www.freedomhouse.org/template.cfm?page=363&year=2010&country=7794.
Land grabs, official corruption and government harassment of critics worsen in Cambodia as a new law makes defamation a criminal offense.

"Freedom in the World: Singapore," *Freedom House*, 2009, www.freedomhouse.org.
An opposition politician must pay defamation damages to the prime minister and his father, while another opposition politician draws jail time for insulting two judges on his blog.

"SPDC Election Laws Set the Stage for Sham Elections," *ALTSEAN-Burma*, April 2010, www.altsean.org/Reports/2010Electionster.php.
This briefing paper contends that Burma's repressive election laws, along with restraints placed on the media, ensure unfair elections in the fall.

Blake, Charles H., and Christopher G. Martin, "The Dynamics of Political Corruption: Re-examining the Influence of Democracy," *Democratization*, February 2006.
The authors argue that the consolidation of a vital democracy over time exercises a more powerful influence over corruption than past research had indicated.

Buehler, Michael, "Countries at the Crossroads — Indonesia," *Freedom House*, 2010, www.freedomhouse.org.
The author reviews how Indonesia has established a liberal democracy since the fall of Gen. Suharto in 1998 but describes how the quality of that democracy remains low.

Chin, James, and Wong Chin Huat, "Malaysia's Electoral Upheaval," *Journal of Democracy*, July 2009, www.journalofdemocracy.org/articles/gratis/Chin-20-3.pdf.
The authors assess what the ruling party's surprising loss of its two-thirds parliamentary majority in the 2008 election means for the future of quasi-democratic Malaysia.

Nawaz, Farzana, "Overview of Corruption and Anti-Corruption in the Philippines," *U4 Expert Answer, Transparency International*, Aug. 17, 2009, www.u4.no/helpdesk/helpdesk/query.cfm?id=212.
The author describes the endemic corruption that is a significant obstacle to good governance in the Philippines.

For More Information

Asia Society, 725 Park Ave., New York, NY 10021; (212) 288-6400; www.asiasociety.org. A leading global and pan-Asian organization working to strengthen relationships and promote understanding among the people, leaders and institutions of the United States and Asia.

Asian Barometer Survey, Department of Political Science, National Taiwan University, 21 Hsu-Chow Rd., Taipei, Taiwan 100; (886) 2 2357 0427; www.asianbarometer.org. An applied research program on public opinion about political values, democracy and governance in Asia.

Association of Southeast Asian Nations (ASEAN), 70A Jl. Sisingamangaraja, Jakarta 12110, Indonesia; (6221) 7262991; www.aseansec.org. Established in 1967 to accelerate economic growth, social progress and cultural development in the region and to promote regional peace and stability.

Center for People Empowerment in Governance (Cen-PEG), 3/F CSWCD Bldg., Magsaysay St., University of the Philippines Diliman, 1101 Quezon City, Philippines; (632) 929-9526; www.eu-cenpeg.com. A public policy center that monitors elections in the Philippines and advocates for the democratic representation of the poor.

Centre for Strategic and International Studies, The Jakarta Post Bldg., 3rd Floor, Jl. Palmera Barat 142-243, Jakarta 10270, Indonesia; (62-21) 5365 4601; www.csis.or.id. An independent nonprofit organization in Indonesia focusing on policy-oriented studies and dialogue on domestic and international issues.

Freedom House, 1301 Connecticut Ave., N.W., Floor 6, Washington, D.C. 20036; (202) 296-5101; www.freedomhouse.org. An independent watchdog organization that supports democratic change, monitors freedom, and advocates for democracy and human rights.

Global Voices, Atrium, Strawinskylaan 3105, Amsterdam ZX 1077, The Netherlands; http://globalvoicesonline.org. A community of more than 300 bloggers and translators who publicize citizen media from around the world, with emphasis on voices not ordinarily heard in international mainstream media.

Human Rights Watch, 50 Fifth Ave., 34th Floor, New York, NY 10118; (212) 290-4700; www.hrw.org. A leading independent organization dedicated to defending and protecting human rights.

Institute of Southeast Asian Studies, 30 Heng Mui Keng Terrace, Pasir Panjang, Singapore, 119614; (65) 6778 0955; www.iseas.edu.sg. A regional research center dedicated to the study of sociopolitical, security and economic trends and developments in Southeast Asia.

International Crisis Group, 149 Avenue Louise, Level 24, B-1050 Brussels, Belgium; (32) 2 502 90 38; www.crisisgroup.org. An independent, nonprofit, nongovernmental organization committed to preventing and resolving deadly conflict.

Transparency International, Alt-Moabit 96, 10559 Berlin, Germany; (49) 30 3438 20 0; www.transparency.org. A global coalition of more than 90 national offices around the world that fight corruption.

Voices From Abroad:

STEPHEN LILLIE

British Ambassador to the Philippines

A maturing system

"Through their high turnout at the elections, the Filipino people have demonstrated their commitment to the democratic process and their determination to shape their own destiny. This is a good day for politics in the Philippines. . . . This is a welcome sign of the increasing maturity of the Philippine political system."

Philippines News Agency May 2010

IAN STOREY

Senior Fellow, Institute of Southeast Asian Studies, Singapore

A new democratic leader

"It would have been incredible to conceive a few years ago, but this election is showing just how far Indonesia has come. Any hopes about Thailand or Malaysia emerging as democratic voices have fallen away and now Indonesia is the standout."

South China Morning Post July 2009

CHRIS PURANASAMRIDDHI

Construction company manager, Thailand

Embarrassed for my country

"Thailand is the land of smiles, easygoing, and I want it back. The red shirts, they are quite aggressive, and we are not an aggressive country, as everyone knows. For the first time, I am embarrassed for Thailand in front of the world."

The New York Times, April 2010

SOMYOT PRUKSAKASEMSUK

Red Shirt Leader, Thailand

A crisis of faith

"Initially, independent movements of the masses in Bangkok and the regions will begin, then riots will ensue. For

The National Herald, India/Paresh Nath

Thailand in the long term, there will be major changes due to the crisis of faith."

The Boston Globe, May 2010

WALDEN BELLO

Senior Analyst, Focus for the Global South Philippines

China's leverage

"ASEAN has not yet managed to consolidate itself as an economic bloc. Yet, here we are launching a free trade area with China that will mean eventually bringing our tariffs down to zero. ASEAN is already noncompetitive with China across a whole range of manufactured goods and agricultural products."

Philippine Daily Inquirer January 2010

RIZAL SUKMA

Executive Director, Centre for Strategic and International Studies, Indonesia

Institutionalize democratic culture

"While the people have once again demonstrated the ability to practice democracy, there is still the challenge of institutionalizing democratic culture, norms and values among the political elite. In the long run, the merit of Indonesia as a full-fledged democracy will also depend on the ability of the elected government to deliver economic prosperity and social justice."

Jakarta (Indonesia) Post July 2009

SHITA LAKSMI

**Program Officer, Hivos
Foundation, Netherlands**

"Long dear friends"

"It seems that Indonesian people and criminal defamation are long dear friends. It would be difficult to separate them as long as freedom of expression is a dream and the exercise of criticizing or being open to criticism is not a part of our tradition."

Jakarta (Indonesia) Post, January 2010

IRENE KHAN

**Secretary General, Amnesty
International, England**

A symbol of hope for all

"In those long and often dark years, Daw Aung San Suu Kyi has remained a symbol of hope, courage and the undying defense of human rights, not only to the people of Myanmar but to people around the world."

The New York Times, July 2009

CHARLES CHONG

**Member, ASEAN Inter-Parliamentary Myanmar
Caucus, Indonesia**

Impatient with Burma

"More and more parliamentarians within ASEAN are beginning to lose their patience with Burma. And, we are calling upon our governments to do more than just expressions of dismay, regret, grave concern and so on, and seriously look at suspending Burma's membership of ASEAN."

Thai Press Reports, May 2009

3

Sub-Saharan Democracy

Jason McLure

Zimbabwe's authoritarian President Robert Mugabe (center), refused to accept defeat during his country's disputed 2008 presidential election, setting a bad precedent, according to democracy advocates, for other African leaders seeking to retain power. After international condemnation, Mugabe agreed to appoint his opponent, Morgan Tsvangirai as prime minister. Like many of Africa's other post-independence dictators — so-called "Big Men" — Mugabe has ruled Zimbabwe for 28 years as a one-party authoritarian.

From *CQ Researcher*, February 15, 2011.

Elections are supposed to choose one winner. But the presidential run-off in Ivory Coast last Nov. 28 left a bizarre predicament: Two candidates claimed victory. Each held an inauguration and appointed separate cabinets, leaving the lush West African country in limbo.

The farce continued after the country's electoral commission declared opposition leader and former Prime Minister Alassane Ouattara the winner on Dec. 2. Incumbent President Laurent Gbagbo, who had postponed elections for five years, promptly challenged the results in a constitutional court, which declared him the winner, with 51 percent of the vote. Street protests and a violent crackdown by security forces ensued. Most foreign leaders congratulated Ouattara, a U.S.-educated economist and technocrat, but the Ivorian army remained with Gbagbo.

Meanwhile, Gbagbo remained in the presidential palace in the nation's commercial and administrative capital, Abidjan, surrounded by security forces, while Ouattara holed up in the nearby Golf Hotel, surrounded by barbed wire and guarded by U.N. peacekeepers.

But the standoff was not new for the world's largest cocoa producer, known officially as Côte d'Ivoire. During the 2000 presidential election, Gbagbo and Gen. Robert Guei both claimed victory and held competing swearing-in ceremonies — though street protests eventually persuaded Guei to step aside.

"It's a shame that as Africa tries hard to tear itself away from despotism, leaders are reluctant to uphold democracy," Kenya's second-largest newspaper, *The Standard*, editorialized. "It is another statistic on the continent's soaring catalogue of shame."[1]

Few Sub-Saharan Nations Are 'Free'

Only nine of the 48 countries in Sub-Saharan Africa are rated as "free" by the human rights organization Freedom House. The free countries — three in West Africa, three in southern Africa and three island nations — represent 12 percent of the vast region's population. More than 750 million people — more than three-quarters of sub-Saharan inhabitants — live in countries deemed "not free" or "partly free."

Levels of Freedom in Sub-Saharan Africa, 2010

Source: "Freedom in the World 2011," Freedom House, Jan. 13, 2011

Ivory Coast gained independence from France in 1960. The nation of 22 million people was for decades among Africa's wealthiest and most stable countries, often called the "Ivorian miracle." Its history exemplifies the political difficulties experienced in much of sub-Saharan Africa. Félix Houphouët-Boigny, the country's first president, ruled as a moderate, anti-communist dictator for 33 years, well into his eighties.

But as is often the case in the region, the eventual transition of leadership was chaotic. Houphouët-Boigny did not groom a successor nor prepare for a transition to democracy, and after his death in 1993, the introduction of elections and multiparty politics contributed to instability. The country fractured along ethnic and religious lines, largely between the predominantly Christian south and Muslim north. Gbagbo, a Christian from the Bete ethnic group, comes from the south. Supporters of Ouattara, a Muslim and a Dioula, live mostly in the north, held by rebels who initiated a civil war less than two years after Gbagbo became president.[2]

Autocratic "Big Men" like Houphouët-Boigny ruled much of Africa during the decades after independence in the 1960s and '70s. When the Berlin Wall fell in 1989, signaling the beginning of the Soviet Union's disintegration, not a single African president had permitted his people to vote him out of power.[3]

"The old saying was that at independence Africa pursued the one-person, one-vote, one-time approach to free elections," says Tibor Nagy, a former U.S. ambassador to Ethiopia and Guinea. "That lasted until the collapse of the Soviet Union [in 1991], when African states could no

Press Freedom Is Rare in Sub-Saharan Africa

Only two mainland sub-Saharan countries — Mali and Ghana — enjoy press freedom, a major prerequisite for democracy, according to the international human rights organization Freedom House. Three other countries in the 48-nation region have a free press: the island nations of Cape Verde, São Tomé/Príncipe and Mauritius. Eritrea, Equatorial Guinea and Zimbabwe have the least media freedom in the region.

Sub-Saharan Countries With the Freest, Least Free Media, 2010
(The lower the rating the freer the press)

Country	Freedom House rating	Press Freedom status
TOP 10 (Most Press Freedom)		
Mali	25	Free
Ghana	26	Free
Mauritius	27	Free
Cape Verde	28	Free
São Tomé and Príncipe	28	Free
South Africa	32	Partly Free
Benin	33	Party Free
Namibia	34	Partly Free
Botswana	39	Partly Free
Burkina Faso	41	Partly Free
BOTTOM 10 (Least Press Freedom)		
Swaziland	76	Not Free
Chad	77	Not Free
Ethiopia	78	Not Free
Democratic Republic of the Congo	81	Not Free
The Gambia	81	Not Free
Rwanda	83	Not Free
Somalia	84	Not Free
Zimbabwe	84	Not Free
Equatorial Guinea	90	Not Free
Eritrea	94	Not Free

Source: "Freedom of the Press 2010," Freedom House, May 2010

longer play off the East vs. the West, and the dictators realized things had to change or their days were numbered."

As the Cold War ended and the superpowers no longer felt compelled to support dictators who supported them, democracy began to surge in Africa.

Before and After

Kenya's disputed 2007 presidential election triggered ethnic violence that left at least 1,000 people dead and 600,000 homeless, sparking international outrage over alleged ethnic cleansing (top). Stability returned after an awkward power-sharing arrangement left incumbent Mwai Kibaki as president and opposition leader Raile Odinga as prime minister. The 2008 peace agreement that ended the violence also called for a new constitution, along with other wide-ranging electoral, judicial and land reform measures to improve governance in East Africa's largest economy. A supporter of the new constitution (bottom) participates in a rally in Nairobi on Aug. 1, 2010. Three days later the voters overwhelmingly approved the constitution in a peaceful referendum.

Between 1990 and 1994, more than half of Africa's sub-Saharan nations underwent regime change, sparking an expansion of civil liberties through the decade, according to Freedom House, a Washington-based advocacy group

that tracks human rights and democratic reforms around the world. [4]

"One clear measure of the spread of democratic politics is the acceptance of the ballot box as the only means of acquiring political legitimacy," says Emmanuel Gyimah-Boadi, director of the Ghana Center for Democratic Development, which oversees the Afrobarometer opinion poll monitoring African attitudes toward democracy. "It's also clear from the Afrobarometer data that popular rejection of alternative forms of rule has also been resoundingly strong. Military rule, one-person rule, one-party rule — all these other forms of government have been quite thoroughly repudiated."

The march to freedom stalled, however, in recent years and has begun to reverse. "The trajectory has been basically positive until about 2005, and in the last three or four years there has been a decline," says Arch Puddington, research director at Freedom House.

To be sure, political systems have been successfully transformed in some African countries, notably Mali, South Africa, Ghana and Benin. All four have had at least two consecutive democratically elected governments.

But there have been more backsliders than success stories. For instance, Kenya's disputed 2007 election triggered ethnic violence that left 1,000 people dead. Zimbabwe's 2008 presidential election ended in a months-long standoff after President Robert Mugabe lost a first-round of voting and then terrorized the opposition into withdrawing before a run-off. More recently, Ethiopia's ruling party and its allies won more than 99 percent of parliamentary seats in rigged national elections in 2010, only five years after holding the freest polls in the country's history. [5]

According to Freedom House, only nine of sub-Saharan Africa's 48 countries were "free" in 2010, down from 11 in 2005. Sixteen African countries had declining scores in civil rights and political liberties, such as freedom of expression and quality of elections, while only four nations showed improvement, according to Freedom House's 2010 report. The decline occurred even as the continent experienced 5.8 percent annual economic growth between 2004 and 2009, considerably higher than the 3.7 percent average global growth rate. [6]

"It's been a case of two steps forward in the early 1990s and one step back in the past decade," says Kathryn Sturman, a researcher at the South African Institute of International Affairs in Braamfontein. "You have people holding elections, so the issue in 2010 is not whether there will be an election, it's whether it will be free and fair."

Africa's intense ethnic loyalties present a major obstacle to democratic development. Many Africans identify first with their tribe, not with their nationality. When Europeans colonized Africa at the end of the 19th century, they arbitrarily lumped rival ethnic groups together into single political entities and divided some groups between multiple countries. Colonial administrations then operated as autocratic fiefdoms focused on the maximum production of raw materials.

"Not only do you throw together people who are historical enemies, but you create all infrastructure and lines of communications to focus on extracting the countries' natural resources," says Nagy. "You send colonial officials who are the dregs of the service and can't make it anywhere else, and you empower them with dictatorial powers and security laws that the Africans inherit after independence."

Today foreign powers continue to play a significant role in African governance. The United States, China and former colonial powers France and the United Kingdom have major economic and political interests on the continent, and the U.N. operates six peacekeeping missions in sub-Saharan Africa (one each in Western Sahara, Ivory Coast, Liberia and Democratic Republic of Congo and two in Sudan).

And some experts say booming world prices and increased demand for African

Demand for Democracy Outstrips Supply

An average of 70 percent of the residents in 20 select sub-Saharan African countries prefer democracy over other forms of government (top), but only 59 percent say they live in a full or almost full democracy (bottom). The highest support for democracy was in southern African countries such as Botswana and Zambia.

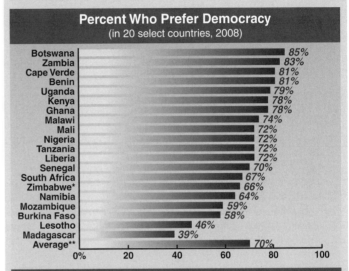

Percent Who Prefer Democracy
(in 20 select countries, 2008)

Country	Percent
Botswana	85%
Zambia	83%
Cape Verde	81%
Benin	81%
Uganda	79%
Kenya	78%
Ghana	78%
Malawi	74%
Mali	72%
Nigeria	72%
Tanzania	72%
Liberia	72%
Senegal	70%
South Africa	67%
Zimbabwe*	66%
Namibia	64%
Mozambique	59%
Burkina Faso	58%
Lesotho	46%
Madagascar	39%
Average**	70%

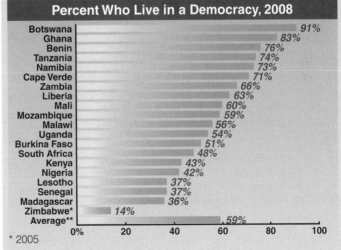

Percent Who Live in a Democracy, 2008

Country	Percent
Botswana	91%
Ghana	83%
Benin	76%
Tanzania	74%
Namibia	73%
Cape Verde	71%
Zambia	66%
Liberia	63%
Mali	60%
Mozambique	59%
Malawi	56%
Uganda	54%
Burkina Faso	51%
South Africa	48%
Kenya	43%
Nigeria	42%
Lesotho	37%
Senegal	37%
Madagascar	36%
Zimbabwe*	14%
Average**	59%

* 2005

** Does not include Zimbabwe

Source: "Neither Consolidating Nor Fully Democratic: The Evolution of African Political Regimes, 1999-2008," Afrobarometer, May 2009

Democratic Models Are All in West Africa

Ghana, Mali and Benin have peacefully turned over party power.

It was the closest presidential election in African history, and the campaign preceding it was marked by harsh rhetoric. But Ghana's 2008 election bore little resemblance to Kenya's 2007 election, with its deadly aftermath of ethnic violence.[1]

The race between Nana Akufo-Addo of the ruling New Patriotic Party and John Atta Mills of the opposition National Democratic Congress was nail-bitingly close after Akufo-Addo narrowly won a first round of voting. But in the run-off election three weeks later, Mills squeaked by him, winning by 50.2 percent to 49.8 percent.

But despite the razor-thin margin of victory, Akufo-Addo conceded. So too did outgoing President John Kufuor, who was from the same party as Akufo-Addo. There were no outbreaks of ethnic violence, no barrage of lawsuits demanding recounts and no interference by security forces. The media was free to report, and the electoral commission operated independently and transparently.

"Very often when we look at Africa we lose hope," Jean Ping, chairman of the African Union Commission, told a press conference following badly flawed 2010 elections in Sudan. "We don't need to lose hope."

Indeed, nine sub-Saharan African countries are consolidating democratic gains, according to the Washington-based democracy advocacy group Freedom House.[2] South Africa, Namibia, Botswana, Mauritius, Cape Verde and São Tomé/Príncipe are often rightfully praised for their political freedoms and smooth transitions from one leader to the next. However, politics in all three of the southern African countries are dominated by a single party, while Mauritius, Cape Verde and São Tomé/Príncipe are tiny island states.

That makes the achievements of West Africa's Ghana, Mali and Benin all the more impressive. All three have successfully transferred presidential power from one party to another via the ballot box. In Ghana, it's happened twice, in Benin three times.

They also provide counter-examples to the widely held view that nations must first attain a level of economic security before democracy can take root. Mali is among the world's poorest nations, while Ghana only attained the status of "middle-income" country (as defined by the World Bank) in 2010 — a full decade after its first democratic transition.

Even as many other countries on the continent have seen democratic freedoms retreat, multiparty systems in

commodities have hurt African democracy, even though they have boosted economic growth. Western buyers are less inclined to push the region's authoritarian leaders to democratize when facing stiff competition from other buyers like China, which remains neutral on democratic reforms.

As sub-Saharan Africa has begun to regress politically, here are some of the questions being debated:

Can Africa move beyond ethnic politics?

Africa has unparalleled human diversity — an estimated 2,000 languages are spoken on the continent, with more than 200 spoken in Democratic Republic of Congo (DRC) alone. But ethnic differences have long been a source of political friction.

Ethnic tension in Rwanda between Hutus and Tutsis led to the 1994 genocide that killed some 800,000 Tutsi and moderate Hutus.[7] In Sudan, an estimated 2 million people died in a 20-year-long civil war between the predominately Arab and Muslim north and the black and mainly Christian and animist south. Another 300,000 reportedly have died over the past decade due to war between the Sudanese government and rebels from several ethnic minority groups in the western region of Darfur.[8] Somalia has been in a state of constant civil war since 1991, driven largely by clan rivalries.[9]

Even in countries such as Kenya and Ivory Coast, which experienced decades of stability after independence, ethnic tensions have led to political crises in recent years. "Ethnicity is holding its own as a potent political force in Africa," says David Shinn, a former U.S. ambassador to Burkina Faso and Ethiopia. "Few African countries have managed to overcome this scourge."

In fact, many Africans — even in the continent's most stable and democratic countries — consider their ethnic identity as equally or more important than their

Mali, Benin and Ghana seem to be strengthening with each passing election. The success of those nations' democracies provides a powerful example to strongmen elsewhere on the continent, who cling to power by arguing that only authoritarianism can bring Africa stability and that Africans are not ready for democracy.

Having military men who are willing to exit politics gracefully seems to help. Benin's Lt. Gen. Mathieu Kérékou was Africa's first post-independence leader to allow himself to be voted from office. In Ghana, former president Jerry Rawlings came to power via a coup d'etat, ruled as a military leader for 11 years before twice winning disputed elections in the 1990s. But he stepped down in 2000, after then opposition leader Kufuor beat Mills, Rawlings' vice president.

Mali also had military leaders who were willing to step aside for civilians. After leading a coup that ousted former dictator Moussa Traore in 1991, Gen. Amadou Toumani Touré held multiparty polls the following year and handed power over to former opposition leader Alpha Konaré. A grateful population elected Touré to succeed Konaré in 2002.

"It's something of an achievement for Africa that you can count a handful of countries that have gone through power alternations," says Emmanuel Gyimah-Boadi, director of the Ghana Center for Democratic Development, who oversees the Afrobarometer opinion poll monitoring

AFP/Getty Images/Andreas Solaro

Election officers count votes at a polling station in Accra, Ghana, on Dec. 7, 2008. The West African country has twice transferred presidential power peacefully from one party to another via the ballot box, providing a counter-example to recent African elections marred by intimidation and violence.

African attitudes toward democracy. "It's no longer unthinkable."

— Jason McLure

[1] Jeffrey Gettleman, "Disputed Vote Plunges Kenya Into Bloodshed," *The New York Times*, Dec. 31, 2007, www.nytimes.com/2007/12/31/world/africa/31kenya.html?_r=1.

[2] "Freedom in the World 2011 Survey Release," Freedom House, Jan. 13, 2011, www.freedomhouse.org/template.cfm?page=594.

national identity: Slightly more than half of Africans polled by Afrobarometer in 2005 and 2006 said they had a stronger or equally strong attachment to their ethnic group as their national identity.[10] Strong ethnic attachments can hamper the development of democracy if elections become mere ethnic headcounts, with winners dividing the spoils.

Further hampering the development of democracy, experts say, are the arbitrary boundaries of African states — imposed when colonial powers divvied up the continent in the late 1800s. The selection of boundaries that were not based on existing ethnic or cultural geography prevented the emergence of strong national identities in African countries. Moreover, where ethnic groups were left straddling national boundaries, civil wars often have spilled over into neighboring states, as occurred in 2006, when Chad was drawn into the conflict in neighboring Sudan's Darfur region.[11]

"Africa as it exists today is a pure fiction," says Barak Hoffman, executive director of the Center for Democracy and Civil Society at Georgetown University. "The lines are ones that Europeans drew. Prior to the 20th century, states lived and died on their own internal organization. Post-World War II African states don't die, because we've used an enormous amount of foreign aid and U.N. troops to prop up the governments."

Africans have rarely determined their own national borders. In fact, it has only happened twice since the colonial era. In 1993, Eritreans voted overwhelmingly for independence from Ethiopia (which itself had never been colonized by Europeans, although it was occupied by Italy from 1936-1941). And in January of this year, South Sudan voted to secede from the north, an election mandated by an internationally brokered peace agreement following Sudan's 20-year civil war.

In many cases, colonial administrators used rivalries between African ethnic groups, playing one group against another in order to consolidate colonial rule. Belgium used traditional Tutsi rulers to control its Rwandan colony, exacerbating tensions with the country's Hutu majority.

In other cases, European colonizers lumped hostile groups together into a single nation, setting the stage for eventual civil war. In Nigeria, for example, seven years after independence the country's third-largest ethnic group, the Igbo, tried to secede and form their own country of Biafra. At least 500,000 people died of starvation and related causes after the Nigerian government blockaded the breakaway region. The rebels surrendered in 1970 after two and a half years of war.

But some sub-Saharan countries have overcome their ethnic conflicts. In South Africa, where colonial rule lasted the longest, national liberation parties such as the African National Congress were able to effectively unite previously competing black ethnic groups against European colonial governments and white rule.

Yet the strength and cohesiveness that helped such parties overcome ethnic divisions sometimes has harmed post-independence democracy, says Sturman, of the South African Institute of International Affairs. In Zimbabwe, for instance, liberation leader Mugabe became president after wresting power from the white-ruled Rhodesian government. After independence, however, he created a one-party state under the Zimbabwe African National Union-Patriotic Front (ZANU-PF).

"Following independence, people vote for the national liberation movement year after year until it's entrenched," Sturman says. "The problem is very visible in Zimbabwe, where for 20 years people voted for [Mugabe's] ZANU-PF, and then by 2000 it was too late for real democracy because ZANU was too strong, and they could gerrymander constituencies."

Strategies to mitigate the effects of ethnicity in politics vary from country to country. Two states with poor democratic records, Ethiopia and Nigeria, have nonetheless won praise from some for their efforts to defuse ethnic tensions. Under a system known as ethnic federalism, Ethiopia has been divided into regions based on ethnicity. Control of land, local policing, elementary education and marriage devolves to local authorities. However, the

system has been criticized for not protecting the rights of minority groups in the regions and for overemphasizing ethnicity in decisions, such as who should receive university scholarships and government jobs.

"This is highly controversial, but given the abject failure of centralized African states, it's well-worth pursuing," says former U.S. ambassador to Ethiopia Nagy.

Similarly in Nigeria, he says, the ruling People's Democratic Party's unwritten requirement to rotate the presidency between the Muslim north and Christian/animist south every two terms has helped the once-coup-plagued country maintain civilian rule for 11 years. Until the policy was adopted, no civilian government had left power peacefully in Nigeria's first four decades of independence from Britain.

But Nigeria's system will be tested this year: Southerner Goodluck Jonathan, the incumbent, has upset the rotational principle by seeking reelection to a term informally reserved for a northern candidate.

Does natural resource wealth hamper African democracy?

Despite sub-Saharan Africa's reputation as an economic basket-case, the region averaged 5.8 percent growth per year from 2004 to 2009, significantly higher than the rate in U.S. and major European economies.[12] Oil-exporting countries grew the fastest — averaging 7.9 percent per year — thanks to rising crude prices and new production in Angola, Chad and Equatorial Guinea.

But, as in other regions, the discovery of oil has not coincided with an expansion of democratic rights. Seven of the eight-largest oil producers in Africa — Chad, Sudan, Equatorial Guinea, Angola, Cameroon, Gabon and DRC — are classified as "not free" by Freedom House. The exception — Nigeria — draws a "partly free" designation.

"There is a myth out there, I call it the 'Beverly Hillbillies' myth, that the discovery of oil is going to lead to democracy and prosperity," says Stephen Kretzmann, executive director of OilChange International, a Washington-based group that monitors the oil industry. "Unfortunately you can't just drill your way to democracy and prosperity."

Indeed, Kretzmann's research parallels other studies showing oil-exporting countries less likely to be democratic and more prone to conflict.[13] In many countries oil benefits only a politically connected few in the capitals and ports that support the oil industry. The establishment of a large middle class is often viewed as a key element in democracy building. Yet oil production creates few jobs for local people. It requires expensive equipment such as offshore drilling platforms but only a small work force, often mainly foreign workers and engineers with specialized training.[14] Instead of investing oil wealth in improving education, health and infrastructure, most leaders use it to strengthen security forces so they can overpower political opponents.

Oil also has fueled ethnic conflict in Africa, notably in Nigeria's oil-rich Niger Delta and the Angolan enclave of Cabinda. In both regions people living closest to the oil production have been angered by the persistence of local poverty and pollution, despite their proximity to billions of dollars in petroleum wealth.

Further, the demand for oil from China's rapidly expanding economy has heightened competition with oil-importing Western nations, such as the United States, Britain and France. Indeed, resource-hungry China has become a major trading partner in Africa in recent years, buying timber, so-called rare earth minerals and oil, including the majority of Sudan's petroleum exports. And because communist China doesn't complicate its business dealings with political demands, Africa's other major trading partners — the United States and European Union — have quieted their demands for democratic reforms in exporting countries like Angola.[15]

"There has been a lessening of international pressure for democracy," says the South African Institute of International Affairs' Sturman. "The U.S. and EU countries that previously would have imposed more conditions before investing in a country are now investing anywhere" they can.

The decline of democracy is especially evident in oil-rich Equatorial Guinea, where opponents of dictator Teodoro Obiang Nguema face "abduction, detention, torture and execution," according to Amnesty International. Obiang and his cronies deposited tens of millions of dollars of the country's oil wealth into overseas bank accounts, according to a 2004 probe by the U.S. Senate Government Affairs Permanent Subcommittee on Investigations, while nearly two-thirds of the population live in extreme poverty, and infant and

AFP/Getty Images/Pius Utomi Ekpei

Rebels in Nigeria's oil-rich Niger Delta have declared a full-scale "oil war" until the government addresses poverty and pollution in the region. The discovery of oil in Africa has brought neither democracy nor peace and prosperity. Seven of the eight-largest African oil producers are classified as "not free" by the human rights advocacy group Freedom House. Nigeria is considered "partly free" but has fought the rebels in the delta region for years.

child mortality equals that of the war-ravaged Democratic Republic of Congo.[16] Meanwhile, according to *Foreign Policy* magazine, Obiang's son spent more on real estate and cars between 2004 and 2006 than the government spent on education.[17]

Nonetheless, doing business with American oil producers such as Exxon Mobil and Hess has kept U.S. relations with Obiang's government warm. The Obama administration's ambassador to Equatorial Guinea recently called the country an "ally," even as he urged Obiang to develop a "more robust civil society."[18]

Last June, in what some are calling an attempt at image doctoring, Obiang promised to carry out political reforms in the coming decade, spend more on the poor and allow the International Red Cross to investigate alleged human rights violations.[19]

Equatorial Guinea's African neighbors have been no more critical than the United States. On January 30 they elected Obiang to a one-year term as president of the African Union.

But some analysts hope Africa's most democratic countries, at least, can beat the so-called resource-curse. South Africa (gold), Zambia (copper) and Botswana (diamonds) have all scored high on democracy indicators, despite their rich natural resources.

"Botswana would seem to be a good model," says John Harbeson, a former U.S. Agency for International Development (USAID) official who oversaw democracy programs in Africa. "While Botswana is maintaining its democratic credentials, its corruption ranking remains strong."

A key test of the resource curse will be Ghana, a democratic country with a much larger and more diverse population than Botswana. Ghana began pumping offshore oil from its Jubilee field in December. Flanking Ivory Coast on the east, Ghana has functioned as a democracy for nearly two decades and peacefully transferred power between rival parties in 2000 and 2008. Though corruption is a problem, the country is considered less corrupt than more developed countries like Italy, Thailand and Brazil, according to Transparency International.[20] "Ghana is an important test case if it can be the first in Africa to maintain relatively democratic government and avoid the oil curse," says former ambassador Shinn.

In addition to its experience with democracy, Ghana is also fortunate, ironically, that its oil find, which will generate about 120,000 barrels of crude per day and about $1 billion in revenue, is relatively modest compared with Nigeria or Angola, which each receive more than 15 times as much oil money.[21] Many hope Ghana's smaller find won't overwhelm the country's political class and small-farmer-led cocoa sector, while allowing strong oversight over how the new revenue is spent.

Is democracy the best form of government for spurring economic growth in Africa?

Africa is the poorest continent in the world, with about half its population living in poverty, according to the World Bank. Moreover, poverty levels have remained stable since 1981, despite recent economic growth.[22]

China's Rising Inflence Could Slow Democracy

China's share of Sub-Saharan Africa's trade quadrupled between 2000 and 2009, even though the European Union remained Africa's largest trading partner. Some experts say the growth of China's economic influence in the region relieves pressure on authoritarian African governments to democratize, because — unlike the U.S. and other Western trading partners — China does not link progress toward democratization to its business dealings with other countries.

China's Share of Trade in Sub-Saharan Africa, 2000-2009

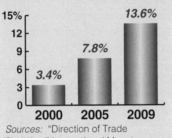

Sources: "Direction of Trade Statistics," International Monetary Fund

The persistence of hunger, disease and low living standards in Africa underscores the question of how tightly democracy and poverty are linked. Since the 1950s the debate has been shaped by "modernization theory," which argues that rising wealth leads to an educated middle class that demands political freedom and control over its governance, eventually ousting repressive governments.

But the rapid economic development of nondemocratic societies, such as China — and to a lesser degree Russia — in the past two decades has challenged that idea. The Chinese Communist Party lifted more than 600 million people out of poverty between 1981 and 2005, even as the party retained its authoritarian grip over the political system.[23] That success hasn't gone unnoticed in Africa.

"They're providing a model by their own success as an authoritarian, state-driven capitalist system that does provide an alternative," says Freedom House's Puddington.

Indeed, recent research has shown that the link between economic growth and political freedom is actually quite weak — and may be getting weaker.[24] Some of the African countries that have made the greatest strides in reducing poverty in recent years — such as Rwanda, Ethiopia and Uganda — have been the most notable backsliders on democratic freedoms.[25]

Ethiopia, which appears to be modeling its political and economic system on China, says it has averaged more than 10 percent growth per year for the past five years — in what is one of the world's poorest countries. Even allowing for some exaggeration, such growth is remarkable. By contrast, economic growth in Senegal, Benin and Ghana — three of the continent's freest states — has averaged about half that over the same period.

Ethiopia's Prime Minister Meles Zenawi criticizes what he calls the failure of "neo-liberal" reforms advocated by the World Bank and other Western-dominated institutions, which promote free markets and, to a lesser degree, free politics.[26] Meles has instead shifted the continent's second-most populous country toward that of a "developmental state," which mixes foreign investment with the championing of government- and ruling-party-owned companies in key sectors. He's similarly shifted Ethiopia away from the path of liberal democracy towards "revolutionary democracy," virtually eliminating the organized opposition.[27]

Angola, one of China's biggest oil suppliers, has also moved toward greater authoritarianism as its trade ties with China have grown.[28]

"A number of African leaders who would like to maintain pseudo-democracies are looking at the Chinese model," says former Ambassador Nagy. "They know that economic advancement is a much higher goal for their people than genuine democracy, so the China factor can at least delay Africa's political transformation."

China's influence in Africa has grown along with its trade presence. Trade with Africa (including North Africa) topped $115 billion in 2010, up from $18.5 billion in 2003.[29] "It is apparent to me that the Chinese are indifferent to democratization," former USAID official Harbeson says. "At best they may be helping African leaders to thumb their noses at the whole architecture of Western human rights and democracy norms."

The Chinese economy's resilience during the global economic crisis that began in 2008 and the backlash against the U.S. invasion of Iraq in 2003 have also changed perceptions. "The financial and economic crisis has increased the attractiveness of the Chinese model of authoritarian capitalism," the Economist Intelligence Unit's 2010 report on global democracy said.[30] "Democracy promotion by the Western world was already discredited by the experience in the Middle East in recent years. The economic crisis has undermined further the credibility of efforts by developed nations to promote their values abroad."

Yet, democracy advocates warn, what's succeeded in China, with its ethnic homogeneity and centuries of history as a nation-state, may not prove as durable in multiethnic Africa.

For the Chinese Communist Party, economic growth is key to its survival. "The party knows that it needs to create jobs," says Hoffman, of Georgetown University. "If governments in Africa faced that same exigency, they'd find the same way to create those jobs. Governments in Africa don't face that same pressure, in part because Western aid gives them alternative" sources of government funds.

In addition, China's model shows that while some authoritarian governments can drive economic growth and rapidly reduce poverty, its model doesn't allow governments that don't produce growth to be replaced. Zimbabwe's gross domestic product dropped by half between 2000 and 2009, as President Mugabe's government stole elections, seized farmland from whites and printed money so rapidly that inflation reached 231 million percent in 2008.[31]

"Authoritarianism begets more authoritarianism," says Shinn. "At some point, there is a breaking point unless there is movement, even slow movement, toward increasing participation of the people in government."

BACKGROUND

Ancient Africa

The rise of complex political entities in Africa came at different times in different regions. The first great kingdom south of the Sahara emerged at Axum, in what is now northern Ethiopia, as early as the 2nd century A.D. By the 4th century the Axumites had converted to Christianity and would eventually expand their empire across the Red Sea to include parts of the Arabian Peninsula.[32]

In West Africa the first empire to emerge was the kingdom of Ghana, established around 800 A.D in what is now western Mali and southeastern Mauritania.[33] Ghana's kings drew their wealth from the region's vast gold deposits and control of the trans-Saharan salt trade. The empire was destroyed in 1240 A.D. by a Mandingo chieftain named Sundiata Keita, who then established the Kingdom of Mali, the region's first great Muslim state, reflecting the spread of Islam to the lands just south of the Sahara Desert.[34]

CHRONOLOGY

1400s-1700s *Europeans begin trading with Africa, eventually shifting focus from trading in gold and ivory to slaves, taking an estimated 11.5 million people from Africa, undermining local governance.*

1800s *Europeans begin colonizing Africa.*

1807 Slavery is banned in British Empire.

Nov. 1884-January 1885 European powers meet in Berlin to establish rules for colonizing Africa; "scramble for Africa" begins.

1950s-1960s *Era of independence begins. U.S. and Soviet pressure forces Europeans to give up their African colonies.*

1957 Britain grants independence to Ghana. Most British colonies become independent by 1965.

1958 Guinea becomes independent. Most French African colonies gain independence by 1960.

1960 Belgian Congo gains independence but plunges into civil war.

1970s-1980s *One-party governments or dictatorships take control in most of Africa, usually supported by the Cold War superpowers.*

1975 Portugal's last African colonies — Angola and Mozambique — become independent.

1980 Zimbabwe is established with black-majority rule after guerrilla war.

1990s *End of the Cold War eliminates U.S.-Soviet rivalries. African democracy grows.*

1990 Namibia becomes independent after civil war against South Africa's apartheid government. Benin's long-time president Mathieu Kérékou becomes first incumbent president in Africa to be peacefully voted out of power.

1991 Rebels depose Ethiopia's military dictator Mengistu Haile Mariam. . . . Zambian President Kenneth Kaunda is defeated in multiparty elections.

1994 South Africa holds first multiracial parliamentary elections; Nelson Mandela becomes president. Malawi's "Life President" H. Kamuzu Banda loses office in multiparty elections.

1999 Military rule in Nigeria ends after multiparty elections.

2000s *Democratic gains slow, begin to reverse.*

2002 Kenya's Daniel arap Moi retires after 24 years as president; his chosen successor Uhuru Kenyatta loses multiparty elections to Mwai Kibaki. Mali has second democratic transition since 1991.

2005 Following disputed elections, Ethiopian security forces shoot unarmed protesters, helping to extend 14-year rule of Prime Minister Meles Zenawi. Allies of Uganda's Yoweri Museveni, already in power for 19 years, eliminate presidential term limits. Togo's Gnassingbé Eyadéma, leader for 38 years, dies and is succeeded by his son.

2007 Nigerian presidential elections are marred by large-scale fraud, installing political unknown Umaru Yar'Adua — anointed by his predecessor Olusegun Obasanjo. Disputed Kenya elections trigger ethnic violence that kills 1,000 and displaces up to 600,000.

2008 Massive crackdown on supporters of opposition leader Morgan Tsvangirai, winner of a first-round poll, leads him to withdraw from presidential run-off. He and President Robert Mugabe eventually establish a power-sharing government.

2010 Deeply flawed elections enable incumbents to win more than 90 percent of the vote in Rwanda, Burundi and Ethiopia. Opposition parties boycott Sudan's first election in 24 years. Ivory Coast President Laurent Gbagbo refuses to cede power after losing election.

2011 Presidential elections are scheduled to take place in 15 African countries.

Africa's Gulag State Shuns Democracy

Tiny Eritrea hasn't held an election in 17 years.

A former ambassador died when he didn't receive medicine for his chronic asthma. The former vice president died after not receiving medicine for a swelling on his neck. A journalist hung himself in a doorway with his tee-shirt. One of the highest-ranking women in the liberation movement and a former transportation minister both died of heat exhaustion.

Such was the fate of just a few of the 35 prisoners at Eritrea's secret Era-Ero prison camp, operated by one of the world's most repressive regimes, according to Eyob Bahda, a former prison guard. Little more than a collection of metal shipping containers and cement-block structures on a broiling desert plain near the Red Sea, the camp houses the country's most sensitive political prisoners.

"They are left for death," Bahda said in a meeting with reporters in Ethiopia in May 2010. "The government knows everything."

The camp was built to house senior government officials and journalists arrested over the past decade for demanding reforms from President Isaias Afewerki, who for 17 years has ruled the tiny, tulip-shaped, former Italian colony with an iron fist.[1] Of the 35 prisoners who have been taken into custody by the military intelligence group that runs the camp, only 20 are still alive, according to Bahda.

Eritrea's ministry of information did not respond to e-mails requesting comment on Bahda's report. But his story is consistent with reports by human rights organizations, even as it provides a greater degree of detail.

The weakest prisoners at Era-Ero are kept in the shipping containers, he says. All are kept in their three-square-yard cells 23-hours a day. Though prisoners are not tortured, they also do not receive medical treatment, and temperatures often reach 115 degrees Fahrenheit. Food rations are meager.

While nearly every African government now holds regular elections — regardless of how flawed — Eritrea's insular regime has not held a single national poll since the country gained independence from Ethiopia after a 1993 referendum. The vote followed a 30-year war of independence — Africa's longest civil war — in the country located on the northwestern tip of Africa's Horn.

However, the absence of polls is just one in a variety of alleged human rights abuses by Afewerki's government, which has turned the country into a "giant prison," according to Ben Rawlence, an Africa researcher for New York-based Human Rights Watch.[2]

According to the human rights advocacy group, independent media offices were shuttered in 2001, when the first group of political detainees were arrested. Foreign journalists are regularly kicked out of the country or denied access, and a veil of secrecy blankets the regime. Freedom of religion is restricted — with the president appointing Christian and Muslim religious leaders — and citizens need permits to travel inside the country or go overseas. Those fleeing the country face a shoot-to-kill policy by the security forces, according to Human Rights Watch. Nearly all men age 18 and over are conscripted into the army or the government's national service.[3]

Bahda escaped from his guard unit under the pretext of attending a wedding. He then snuck across the border into Ethiopia, well-aware that his family would be fined for his desertion. Even the prison guards, he says, aren't free in Eritrea.

"We were also prisoners there," he says. "I was afraid I'd die with those people."

— *Jason McLure*

---

[1] For background, see Jason McLure, "The Troubled Horn of Africa, *CQ Global Researcher*, June 2009, pp. 149-176.

[2] Ben Rawlence, "Slender Land, Giant Prison," Human Rights Watch, www.hrw.org/en/news/2009/05/06/eritrea-slender-land-giant-prison.

[3] "Service for Life," Human Rights Watch, April 16, 2009, www.hrw.org/en/reports/2009/04/16/service-life-0.

Meanwhile, in Central Africa's Great Lakes region, near present-day Rwanda and Uganda, the Bantu people established their first kingdoms around 1300. In southern Africa, the first major empire was that of Great Zimbabwe, which reached its height in the mid-15th century along the Zambezi River.[35]

These precolonial-era African kingdoms and other entities practiced various forms of governance. Many

Africans lived in stateless societies, clusters of villages or towns where people did not recognize a supreme leader beyond that of the village chief. And in some of the African kingdoms, such as the Solima Yalunka in Sierra Leone, a monarch ruled but consulted on important decisions with a council of elders. In the area near modern Guinea, Liberia and Sierra Leone, secret societies known as *poro* made important decisions such as war declarations.[36]

States usually did not have standing armies that allowed monarchs to impose their will. At the local level, a village headman, aided by heads of families and community leaders, handled governance.

In most precolonial African societies, women had little voice in governance, although there were exceptions. Among the Yoruba of modern Nigeria the *iyalode*, or female representative, had jurisdiction over women's issues and a place on the ruling council. In some cases women also fought in armies — with the Dahomey Amazons of modern Benin being the best known example.

The first Europeans to make contact with Africa were the Portuguese, who began exploring coastal African communities in the 15th century. In 1469, Portugal granted a Lisbon merchant, Fernã Gomes, a five-year monopoly on trade south of the island of Arguin, off Mauritania. In return Gomes promised to pay the crown 500 crusados and explore 100 leagues (about 300 miles) of coastline per year — a seemingly stiff price, given that almost nothing was known of the area. But the potential for profits from an unexplored region fueled discoveries: Within 20 years the explorer Bartholomew Diaz had rounded the Cape of Good Hope, and by 1498 Vasco de Gama had reached India by sailing around southern Africa.[37]

The Slave Trade

Contact with Europeans would have a profound impact on the political life of Africans. The English, French and Dutch soon followed the Portuguese in pursuit of African gold and ivory. But by the 17th century the Europeans had shifted to trade in a more lucrative cargo: human beings.[38]

Up to 11.5 million Africans were exported from Africa between 1600 and 1870 to work as slaves in plantations in the Americas.[39] The impact of the slave trade on Africa's Atlantic coast varied. The area near modern Senegal and Gambia provided many of the slaves in the early years of the trade.[40] In the 1700s, civil war among the Yoruba in

what is now Nigeria provided a large number of slaves for export via ports in today's Benin, as did British slave forts in Ghana. Portugal's abolition of the slave trade north of the equator in 1815 fueled commerce in human beings from areas further south in modern-day Angola, Gabon and Democratic Republic of Congo.

The slave trade fomented warfare and ethnic tension within Africa and upended political stability in many affected areas, as increasingly wealthy traders prospered at the expense of less powerful groups. The trade even felled the mighty kingdoms of the Ngoyo and Kakongo in what today are Angola and the DRC. But for others — such as the Ashanti kingdom in what is now Ghana, the Dahomey kingdom of modern Benin and the Oyo kingdom of modern Nigeria — the slave trade with Europeans helped local monarchs consolidate control and expand their influence.[41]

Southern and eastern Africa were largely unaffected by the trans-Atlantic slave trade. In South Africa, however, contact with Europeans brought Dutch (in 1657) and later British (beginning in 1820) settlers who would clash both with each other and with Bantu-speaking groups who had migrated south from central Africa.[42] In East Africa, Ethiopia would remain largely insulated from European contact until the mid-19th century, while the Swahili-speaking coast of what is now Kenya and Tanzania had greater links with the Arabian Peninsula until the age of European imperial control in the late 1800s.

'Scramble for Africa'

From the 1500s onward, Africans and Europeans were increasingly bound in a series of unequal relationships. However, beyond a few coastal areas and swathes of white-settled South Africa, Europeans did not exert direct political control over sub-Saharan Africa until the late 1800s.

By that time European rivalries and hunger for natural resources had led to a "scramble for Africa," with its abundant gold, ivory, timber and empty tracts of fertile land for farming. In November 1884 the main European powers in Africa: Great Britain, France, Germany, Portugal and Belgium's King Leopold II[43] attempted to formalize their conflicting commercial, missionary and diplomatic interests at a conference in Berlin.[44] Underpinning the colonial mission were pseudo-scientific ideas of European racial superiority, a desire to "civilize" African societies that were technologically primitive and the hope that

Europe might gain economically from exploiting Africa's raw materials while selling manufactured goods to its inhabitants.

By 1912, Europeans ruled virtually all of sub-Saharan Africa except independent Ethiopia.[45] An estimated 10,000 independent African political/ethnic groups had been consolidated into 40 European colonies, often with disregard to the location of common ethnic and language groups. France alone claimed 3.75 million square miles of African territory, primarily in the West.[46]

The Europeans faced armed resistance in virtually every colony and maintained power only through the use of superior arms and strategic alliances with traditional rulers. The British favored a system of indirect rule, whereby British district administrators used local African leaders to collect taxes and keep order in their domains. Incredibly, the system allowed Britain to rule its 43 million African colonial subjects in the 1930s with only 1,200 British officials.[47]

Financial self-sufficiency was the primary goal of European colonial administrations; public services such as health and education largely were left to small groups of missionaries. European-owned companies controlled most commerce and emphasized the production of cash crops such as coffee, cocoa and rubber or raw materials such as timber and minerals — an economic system whose legacy is still visible today in much of Africa.

Bumpy Road to Independence

World War I altered the colonial map by stripping Germany of its colonial possessions in what are now Namibia, Cameroon, Togo, Tanzania, Rwanda and Burundi. Italian dictator Benito Mussolini briefly occupied Ethiopia in the late 1930s.

But World War II — a catalyst for African independence — was to have a profound, long-term impact on Africa. Nearly 400,000 Africans joined the British army, and African units helped defeat the Italians in Ethiopia and restore the rule of Emperor Haile Selassie. They also noted that independence movements in other poor countries, like India and Burma, had won pledges of self-governance from the Crown.[48]

The war also crippled the British and French economies and spurred the rise of the United States and Soviet Union — emerging superpowers that opposed colonialism. Under the 1941 Atlantic Charter between President Franklin D. Roosevelt and British Prime Minister Winston Churchill, Britain and the United States would "respect the right of all peoples to choose the form of government under which they will live."[49] Anti-colonialism, meanwhile, was a tenet of Soviet communism and inspired the establishment of pro-communist African nationalist movements.

Belated reform efforts by colonial administrations — ending slave labor, investing in infrastructure and social services and offering a larger governance role to Africans — proved to be too little too late. Independence in sub-Saharan Africa came first in Ghana, formerly Britain's Gold Coast colony. There Kwame Nkrumah, a charismatic U.S.-educated lawyer, emerged from a British prison in 1951 to become prime minister of the country's colonial government and lead it to independence in 1957.

Ghana's relative wealth, its sizable number of educated leaders and its ethnic homogeneity helped smooth its transition as Africa's first independent state. Ghana's experience became a model for others as Nkrumah used his new position to help spur a wave of independence for European colonies elsewhere in Africa.

By 1960 France had granted independence to most of its colonies in West and Central Africa, and by the mid-1960s Belgium had exited from its territories. British rule had ended in East and West Africa. In 1963, the Organization of African Unity was established in Ethiopia by 32 now-independent African states (including those of North Africa) with a mandate to support the freedom of Africa's remaining colonies and to foster continental unity.

In many cases the transition of political authority was remarkably peaceful. Nonetheless, the newly independent states faced enormous challenges, including the need for infrastructure, health care and education for their largely illiterate populations. They also faced the question of how they might integrate politically. In French-speaking West Africa, Ivorian Houphouët-Boigny — leader of the region's wealthiest territory at the time — defeated an attempt to form a union among France's eight West African states.[50] While the move guaranteed that Ivory Coast wouldn't have to share its lucrative cocoa and coffee revenues with its poorer neighbors, it ensured that the region would be divided into several small, weak states vulnerable to foreign domination.

Ethnic tensions, competition for influence between the United States and the Soviet Union and the lingering influence of European colonial governments created a toxic and more violent environment elsewhere in Africa. While Ghana and Ivory Coast managed their transitions to nation-states relatively smoothly, the DRC, Angola and South Africa had rough going.

The sprawling DRC, one of Africa's wealthiest nations in natural resources, gained its independence in June 1960. But it was among the continent's least-governable, with dozens of ethnic groups living in an area more than three times the size of France, a tiny group of educated citizens and virtually no roads or phones. Riots against the colonial authorities and a mutiny by security services followed, and the copper-rich Katanga region, backed by European business interests, tried to secede from the new state.[51]

Prime Minister Patrice Lumumba, who led the country's sole national democracy movement, was arrested in December of 1960 and murdered in early 1961, reportedly with the complicity of U.S. and Belgian officials. In 1965, Col. Joseph-Désiré Mobutu took power in a coup, renamed the country Zaire and ruled as a pro-U.S. dictator (under the name Mobutu Sese Seko) until the 1990s.

According to former congressional staffer and Africa policy specialist Stephen R. Weissman, "The murder of Patrice Lumumba . . . crystallized an eventual 35-year U.S. commitment to the perpetuation of that regime [which] would tear civil society apart, destroy the state and help pave the way for a regional war that would kill millions of people." Noting the role played by the U.S., Belgian and Congolese governments in the assassination, Weissman said Lumumba "continues to be honored around the world because he incarnated — if only for a moment — the nationalist and democratic struggle of the entire African continent against a recalcitrant West."[52]

In Angola, Portuguese rule slowly disintegrated during the 1960s and '70s as Europe's weakest colonial power battled three rival nationalist groups. During that period the conflict morphed from a war of liberation against colonial forces into a civil war between competing Angolan groups. Although Portugal officially granted Angola independence in 1975, the conflict between Angolan factions hardly paused.

The United States, white-ruled South Africa and Zaire's Mobutu supported two Angolan factions — Uniao Nacional para a Independencia Total de Angola (UNITA)

and Frente Nacionale de Licertacao de Angola (FNLA) — while the Soviet Union and Fidel Castro's Cuba provided cash and troops to the Movimento Popular de Libertacao de Angola (MPLA).[53] By the time the conflict ended in 2002 — 27 years after independence — up to 1.5 million people had died and 4 million had been displaced.[54]

South Africa's history was vastly different from that of much of the continent, because of large-scale white settlement in the 1800s. By 1911, there were more than a million whites — about a fifth of the population — and the country had become a self-governing part of the British Commonwealth in 1910. But only whites were allowed to vote.[55]

In 1948, a vicious policy of racial categorization and segregation known as apartheid was instituted. It required blacks to carry passes when traveling and live in racially zoned areas. Blacks, mixed-race people and those of Indian or Asian background were barred from jobs, schools and public facilities reserved for whites. Backed by an extensive police state, apartheid would endure for nearly five decades, until black resistance and the collapse of U.S. support for the government at the end of the Cold War led to the end of apartheid and the selection of Nelson Mandela as president in the country's first multiracial elections in 1994.

'Big Men'

Cold War rivalry between the United States and the Soviet Union seriously hampered the development of democracy across the African continent. Angola's civil war was not the only African conflict fomented by Cold War tensions. South Africa and Zaire (today's DRC) were not the only authoritarian regimes propped up by the superpowers.

Foreign aid and arms from the U.S. and Soviet blocs ensured that authoritarian rulers had the means to violently repress their opponents — and, hence, little need to win popular support. In the process, Western democracies found themselves providing military and financial support to some of the continent's most dictatorial — albeit staunchly anti-communist — governments.[56]

As a result, the first-generation of post-independence African leaders often came to power talking of democracy and then promptly turned away from it after assuming control. Successive leaders in many countries came to power either through military coups or civil war, sometimes with superpower funding.

From the early 1960s until the collapse of the Soviet Union, Africa was ruled by the so-called Big Men who dealt ruthlessly with political opponents, feisty media and disloyal military officers. They stacked electoral commissions, cowed the judiciary and universities, enriched their families and top deputies, squandered money on arms and secret police and used state-owned television stations as outlets for one-sided demagoguery. The United States and its European allies nominally pushed for democratic reforms, fearing a leadership change would weaken anti-Soviet governments or even usher in communist governments.

Among the client regimes supported by the United States and its Cold War allies, France and the United Kingdom, were Zaire's Mobutu (1965-1997), Ethiopia's Haile Selassie (1930-1974), Gabon's Omar Bongo (1967-2009), Ivory Coast's Houphouët-Boigny (1960-1993), Central African Republic's Jean-Bedel Bokassa (1966-1979), Cameroon's Ahmadou Ahidjo (1960-1982) and Malawi's Hastings Kamuzu Banda (1966-1994).

Soviet-backed dictators included Mozambique's Samora Machel, Ethiopia's Mengistu Haile Mariam (1974-1991) and Guinea's Ahmed Sékou-Touré (1958-1984).

Still others — such as Tanzania's Julius Nyerere (1961-1985), Zambia's Kenneth Kaunda (1964-1991) and Ghana's Kwame Nkrumah (1957-1966) — tried to chart a middle-path and joined the Non-Aligned Movement, though they created single-party states to remain in power.[57]

'Second Liberation'

The collapse of the Soviet Union in the late 1980s and early '90s led to sweeping political changes across Africa. The United States and Russia both scaled back military and diplomatic support for presidents with dubious human rights records, and international pressure grew for real democratic reforms and multiparty elections around the world. Televised images of former dictators fleeing from office across Eastern Europe put Africa's autocrats on notice.

The change set the stage for what some hoped would be Africa's "second liberation." Benin, a small former French colony in West Africa, was the first to break the

AFP/Getty Images

Mobutu Sese Soku — who took power in the Belgian Congo in a coup d'etat in 1965 — is sworn in for his third seven-year term on Dec. 5, 1984. The dictator renamed the country Zaire (renamed Democratic Republic of Congo after he was deposed) and ruled for 32 years — one of many strongmen who led Africa during the post-independence era. The United States and its allies supported Mobutu and others during the Cold War because of their anti-communist stance.

mold. Lt. Gen. Mathieu Kérékou had ruled autocratically since taking power in a 1972 coup. Yet in March of 1991, after being beaten in an election 2 to 1 by former World Bank economist Nicephore Soglo, Kérékou stepped down. It was the first peaceful removal of an incumbent president in Africa since independence from colonial rule.[58]

By the fall of 1994, a dozen African nations had established multiparty democracies. In Zambia, Kaunda, the country's president since independence, stepped down after being defeated in October 1991 by union leader Frederick Chiluba. In April 1994, South Africa held its first multiracial elections following the end of apartheid, and the following month in Malawi, self-styled "Life President" Banda was defeated by businessman Bakili Muzuli.

Africa's Newest Nation Faces a Tough Road Ahead

Peaceful vote leads to South Sudan's secession from the Arab north.

South Sudan's road to independence was one of the longest and bloodiest in the history of Africa's liberation movements. About 2 million people died — one in five of the inhabitants — during the 22-year war between the Arab, Muslim-dominated north and the black, Christian and animist south, which ended when a peace accord was signed in 2005.

The horrific death toll made south Sudan's January independence referendum all the more emotional for the 3.9 million people who supported independence. "We lost a lot of people," Lt. Col. William Ngang Ayuen, a soldier, told The Associated Press, as he struggled to maintain his composure outside a polling place. "Today is good for them."[1]

Final results of the referendum, announced on Feb. 7, showed that 98.8 percent of the voters chose to separate from the north, clearing the way for Africa's newest nation to become independent on July 9.[2]

But, while jubilation over independence was testimony to the restorative power of the ballot box, the new nation faces massive challenges. Decades of warfare have left the landlocked region one of the poorest and least-developed corners of the world.

A 15-year-old girl in southern Sudan has a higher chance of dying in childbirth than of completing school, according to the United Nations.[3] Only 8 percent of women are literate, and one in seven children die before age 5. The Texas-size new country has less than 50 miles of paved roads and an estimated 5 billion barrels of petroleum reserves. But the pipelines that transport the crude to ports on the Red Sea run through territory controlled by its old enemies in Khartoum.[4]

The prospects for democracy are as bleak as the country's development indicators. The government of southern Sudan depends on oil revenue for 98 percent of its budget.[5] Corruption in the south is rampant, and the government is dominated by former rebels from the Sudanese People's Liberation Army. Tension remains rife in a region with dozens of ethnic groups, some of whom were armed by Khartoum to attack their neighbors during the country's civil war.[6]

"To have an oil economy in a newly independent state without institutions is not a recipe for stability," says one European diplomat, who declined to be identified. Pessimists predict

Kyodo via AP Images/Tomoaki Nakano

Residents in Juba, South Sudan, celebrate the news that 98.8 percent of voters peacefully chose in a January referendum to secede from the north. The oil-rich south — scene of a brutal 20-year civil war with the north — will become Africa's newest country in July.

South Sudan could descend into chaos and become a failed state like nearby Somalia.

For the moment, the people of southern Sudan appear optimistic about the future. "We have suffered for 55 years at the hands of our Arab brothers," Augustine Ngor, a 70-year-old man in Bahr el Ghazal state, told *The Guardian* newspaper. "And now at last we will have our freedom."[7]

— Jason McLure

---

[1] Jason Straziuso and Maggie Fick, "For Jubilant Voters in S. Sudan, New Country Nears," The Associated Press, Jan. 10, 2011, www.msnbc.msn.com/id/40990533/ns/world_news-africa/.

[2] " 'A New Country Is Being Born,' " *The Washington Post*, Feb. 8, 2011.

[3] "Scary Statistics — Southern Sudan," United Nations, September 2010, www.unsudanig.org/library/index.php?fid=documents.

[4] Alan Boswell, "South Sudan Buys Russian Helicopters Ahead of a Planned Vote on Secession," Bloomberg News, Sept. 3, 2010, www.bloomberg.com/news/2010-09-03/southern-sudan-buys-russian-helicopters-ahead-of-planned-secession-vote.html.

[5] Maram Mazen and Jared Ferrie, "South Sudan Votes in Referendum to Declare Oil-Rich Region's Independence," Bloomberg News, Jan. 9, 2011, www.bloomberg.com/news/2011-01-08/sudan-s-referendum-begins-as-oil-rich-southern-region-eyes-independence.html.

[6] "Sudan: Mounting Ethnic Tensions in the South," IRIN, June 24, 2009, www.irinnews.org/PrintReport.aspx?ReportID=84971.

[7] Xan Rice, "Sudan Vote: Celebrations Across South as Millions Flock to Polling Stations," *The Guardian*, Jan. 9, 2011, www.guardian.co.uk/world/2011/jan/09/sudan-vote-celebrations-south.

AT ISSUE

Does Western aid improve African democracy and good governance?

YES
Gregory Adams
Director of Aid Effectiveness Oxfam America
Hussein Khalid Executive Director Muslims
for Human Rights Kenya

Written for *CQ Global Researcher*, February 2011

Aid to Africa does not create democracy and good governance. Africans create democracy and good governance by holding their leaders accountable, respecting the rule of law, defending basic rights and meeting citizens' needs. But Africans often have used Western aid to better govern their countries.

- In Mozambique the Administrative Tribunal has received aid from Sweden, Germany, Norway, Finland and others to better scrutinize government actions and reduce corruption. By 2008, it was conducting 350 audits, covering about 35 percent of the budget. The tribunal's latest annual report found increasing accountability across the political spectrum.
- In Liberia, the U.S. Treasury Department's Office of Technical Assistance helped create an electronic link between the Ministry of Finance and the Central Bank in 2005. The change eliminated reliance on easily-forged paper receipts, and provided for electronic cross-checks between accounts. This reduced the potential for fraud and offered taxpayers a one-stop tax preparation and payment option.
- In Kenya, Muslims for Human Rights (MUHURI) received Western aid to conduct social audits of funds intended to promote grassroots development. By involving local communities in evaluating their elected representatives, MUHURI is empowering Kenyans to hold their leaders accountable. During the 2007 elections, a majority of those audited lost their seats as a direct result of findings that exposed corruption among leaders.
- In Malawi, donors have supported community scorecards, enabling citizens to provide feedback on government services. In one stakeholder meeting, the scorecard revealed that teachers were sending students nearly two miles away from the school to fetch water for the teachers' houses before classes. Since the scorecards were implemented, the community has appealed for a water borehole near the school and the practice of having students fetch water for teachers has mostly stopped.

In each example, success was contingent upon Africans themselves — both inside and outside government — seizing the initiative for change. If donors invest the time and energy to find capable and willing partners from both government and civil society, these partnerships can yield significant lasting change to help Africans take charge of their own futures.

NO
Babatunde Olugboji
Long-time African human rights
activist; Recently joined Human Rights Watch

Written for *CQ Global Researcher*, February 2011

Sub-Saharan Africa receives the highest share of foreign aid globally — about one-third of net foreign aid in 2000-2007 — and receives the most aid per capita. But I am not convinced that aid furthers the growth of African democracy.

African aid has multiple, contradictory effects. It affects state formation and disintegration, state-society relations and regional geopolitics. Aid also helps in emergencies, prevents (and fuels) conflict and provides services, infrastructure and capital.

But, according to some critics, aid can also be a tool of foreign policy or represent economic and cultural domination. Countries like Uganda and Ethiopia, which receive a substantial portion of their budgets from foreign aid, are hailed by Western donors as economic models. But both are virtually one-party states.

Africa's problems cannot be solved from Washington, London or Paris. Internally-generated solutions are far more sustainable. Moreover, foreign aid often favors the giver rather than the receiver. About 75 percent of the $27.7 billion spent by the United States on foreign assistance in the 1980s "was spent in the United States to purchase food and equipment sent abroad or the salaries of aid workers," according to a Clinton Administration report.

In addition, the number of major official donors' implementing agencies has expanded exponentially over the last three decades, to more than 100. Each recipient country deals with an average of 26 different official donors. More than 35,000 separate official aid transactions occurred in 2004, said one study, which quotes astonishing figures showing how African ministries are overloaded by aid proliferation. For example, Tanzania had more than 2,000 ongoing donor projects in the early 1990s, while Mozambique's ministry of health was managing more than 400 projects at one point.

The resources Africa desperately needs for self-sustaining growth can be found in Africa itself. While African leaders are — rightly — being blamed for corruption, little attention has been paid to Western nations and institutions that indirectly aid corruption in Africa. Many Western nations happily accommodate corrupt African companies and officials when they are allies, especially in the so-called war on terror. Western banks gladly open their vaults to illicit deposits from African dictators, safe in the knowledge that age-old banking secrecy laws will block prying eyes. Bank executives know that in all probability such monies will never be repatriated.

The real question should be: Does the West really care if Africa is democratizing?

Progress, however, was uneven. In Niger and Mali, newly elected governments still struggled with ethnic conflict. In Cameroon, Gabon and Ghana, incumbents clung to power amid charges of election irregularities. In the DRC, ethnic divisions stifled under the Mobutu regime led to clashes and eventually a horrific civil war that continues two decades later.

Nevertheless, by 2005 the number of African countries categorized as "free" had grown to 11, up from 2 in 1988.

CURRENT SITUATION

Democracy Retreats

The declining trend toward democracy that began earlier in the decade appears to be continuing, calling into question the durability of the progress made in the 1990s and the legitimacy of the 15 African elections that will be held this year.

"The year 2010 featured a continued pattern of volatility and decline for sub-Saharan Africa," said Freedom House in its "Freedom in the World 2011" report. "The region as a whole registered declines in both political rights and civil liberties indicators."

While more than half of African countries introduced presidential term limits between 1990 and 1994, 12 governments reversed themselves and abolished term limits in the 10 years ending in 2009, according to the South African Institute of International Affairs.[59] The backsliders include Cameroon's President Paul Biya, who had the distinction of instituting term limits on his rule in 1996 and then abolishing them in 2008 as his scheduled retirement loomed.

"The stars that people were looking to a decade ago — Ethiopia, Kenya, Uganda — they're not going in the right direction," says Georgetown University's Hoffman. "These were going to be the generation of reformers. But power corrupts."

Experts say a variety of factors in the early 2000s tripped up Africa on its way to democracy, starting with the U.S. government's long and bloody military effort to install democracy in Iraq. Many began to question the moral authority of the West's efforts to promote democracy. "Our misadventure in Iraq, democracy at the barrel of a gun, did much to de-legitimize democracy promotion

in the U.S. and the welcoming of democracy support by recipient countries," says former USAID official Harbeson.

Meanwhile, after the Soviet Union collapsed, African leaders watched in alarm as so-called "color revolutions" erupted in one former communist regime after another. Between 2003 and 2005, popular uprisings ousted authoritarian leaders in Ukraine ("Orange Revolution"), Georgia ("Rose Resolution") and Kyrgyzstan ("Tulip Revolution"). The Africans could not help but note that after the uprisings, long-simmering ethnic tensions — held in check by years of one-party rule — frequently burst to the surface.

"There is not going to be a 'Rose Revolution' or a 'Green Revolution' or any colour revolution in Ethiopia after the election," Ethiopian Prime Minister Meles Zenawi said in May 2005 as the opposition took to the streets to protest his reelection, which extended his 14-year rule.[60] The election had widely been seen as the freest ever in Africa's second-most-populous country. Security forces responded to the protests by killing nearly 200 people and arresting much of the opposition leadership.

Western donors did not withdraw aid to the regime, and within days Uganda's leading opposition leader Kizza Besigye was arrested on treason charges, less than four months before the first multiparty elections since President Yoweri Museveni took power in 1986. Museveni won an easy victory in February 2006 after his allies amended the constitution to allow him to stand for a third term. The charges against Besigye were later dropped.

In 2007 two key countries held flawed elections, despite having held internationally lauded polls earlier in the decade. In Nigeria, Africa's most-populous country, efforts by the incumbent Olusegun Obasanjo to change the constitution so he could remain in office for a third-term were defeated. His handpicked successor, Umaru Yar'Adua, an obscure state governor, won the election with 70 percent of the vote, despite concerns over his health. A European Union (EU) electoral observation mission concluded the results were not credible, due to a "lack of essential transparency, widespread procedural irregularities, substantial evidence of fraud, widespread voter disenfranchisement, lack of equal conditions for political parties and candidates and numerous incidents of violence" that killed at least 200 people. The report said political parties should "end the practice of hiring thugs to perpetrate electoral violence."[61]

Even more disturbing was the widespread violence that broke out in December 2007 after a disputed election in Kenya, long one of Africa's most stable and prosperous nations. President Mwai Kibaki, elected five years earlier in a widely lauded poll, appeared to have been beaten by opposition leader Raile Odinga, who was backed by the long-marginalized Luo ethnic group in the country's west and Muslims along its Indian Ocean coast.

Yet, according to EU election observers, the country's electoral commission swung tens of thousands of votes to Kibaki by altering results, giving him a 2-percentage-point victory.[62] He was hastily sworn-in for a second term in a secret ceremony televised by the state broadcaster.[63] A wave of ethnic violence ensued, leaving more than 1,000 people dead across the country and displacing up to 600,000. A modicum of stability returned two months after the election when Kibaki and Odinga agreed to an awkward power-sharing arrangement, under which Kibaki remained president and Odinga was named prime minister. Though it ended the bloodshed, the deal set an unfortunate precedent for Africa: An incumbent president need not stand down just because he lost an election.

African democracy also began to falter when the broad coalitions that helped force the Big Men from power had little to unify them once an autocrat stepped down. In Kenya Odinga and Kibaki — who had been allies against the 24-year rule of former President Daniel arap Moi — later became political enemies. "You have coalitions who throw out autocrats, but then they have to decide how to rule themselves," says Hoffman. The new leaders then rule less through repression and more by "throwing around a lot of patronage and corruption."

Kenya's power-sharing agreement helped set the stage for a similar problematic electoral outcome in Zimbabwe in 2008. Mugabe, who had led the liberation movement to topple the white-minority run Rhodesian government in 1980, was expected to face his toughest electoral challenge, given the country's economic collapse during the previous decade. In a first round of voting, opposition leader Morgan Tsvangirai topped Mugabe by a significant 48 percent to 43 percent margin.

But Tsvangirai halted his bid to end Mugabe's 28-year rule after Mugabe's security forces and supporters unleashed a wave of violence, beating thousands of opposition supporters and leaving at least 86 dead. Tsvangirai withdrew

"No to a dictatorship. Long life to democracy," says a placard during post-election protests outside the U.N. offices in Bouake, Ivory Coast, on Dec. 2, 2010. During the 33-year rule of longtime President Felix Houphouët-Boigny, the Ivory Coast was a bastion of peace and relative prosperity, the so-called "Ivoirian miracle." After Houphouët-Boigny's death in 1993, the country eventually descended into a civil war that has divided the nation along ethnic and religious lines. U.N. peacekeepers are monitoring the uneasy peace.

AFP/Getty Images/Sia Kambou

from the run-off, taking refuge briefly in the Dutch embassy in Harare.[64] Mugabe claimed victory, despite international condemnation.

Under pressure from African and Western governments and with food supplies in the country running low, Mugabe signed a Kenya-style power-sharing deal with Tsvangirai, under which Mugabe remained president but Tsvangirai was given the less powerful post of prime minister.[65]

Botswana President Ian Khama was one of the few African leaders to directly criticize Mugabe's actions. "If a ruling party thinks it's likely to lose, and then uses its position as a ruling party to manipulate the outcome of the election . . . , [it is] not the way to go," he told the *Financial Times* in 2009.[66] "This power-sharing thing is a bad precedent for the continent."

Doing Elections

Since 2008, the number of authoritarian regimes in sub-Saharan Africa has grown from 22 to 25, according to

> *Africa's post-colonial rulers include an "assortment of military fufu-heads, Swiss Bank-socialists, crocodile liberators [and] vampire elite."*
>
> — **George Ayittey, Ghanaian economist**

the Economist Intelligence Unit's 2010 Democracy Index. And just five out of 44 countries measured by the London-based consulting group had free and fair elections: Botswana, South Africa, Ghana and the island nations of Mauritius and Cape Verde.

"Many elections are rigged, and defeated incumbents often still refuse to accept defeat," the report said. [67]

"The democratization process on the continent is not faring very well," says Jean Ping, the Gabonese chairman of the African Union Commission, which helped to craft the power-sharing agreements in Kenya and Zimbabwe and pushes African governments to adhere to pan-African treaties on democracy and human rights. "The measures that we take here are taken in a bid to make sure that we move forward. The crises, they are repeating themselves."

The problems in Kenya, Nigeria, Ivory Coast and Ethiopia are particularly distressing because those countries are among the continent's most influential. "A disturbing development is the failure of the largest and most strategically significant African countries to develop stronger and more mature democratic institutions," says Puddington, the Freedom House researcher. "They do have elections, but they are inevitably flawed, with high levels of political violence."

Ivory Coast's wasn't the only election in 2010 to highlight current difficulties. In Rwanda, Burundi and Ethiopia, incumbent leaders Paul Kagame, Pierre Nkurunziza and Zenawi used a mix of coercion and threat to systematically exclude opposition parties from taking part in the vote while stacking the courts and electoral commissions to ensure they would ratify the results. All three leaders won more than 90 percent of the vote. [68]

"The really powerful governments learned how to do elections," Richard Dowden, director of the London-based Royal African Society, said after Ethiopia's most recent poll. [69]

Meanwhile in Togo President Faure Gnassingbé, who took power in 2005 when his father, Gnassingbé Eyadéma, died after ruling the country for 38 years, handily won reelection in an election in which the fairness was disputed by the opposition. [70] A similar "hereditary presidency" exists in Gabon, where Ali Ben Bongo won a disputed presidential election in 2009 after the death of his father, Omar Bongo, who had ruled for 42 years. Likewise in Senegal, President Abdoulaye Wade, 84, once viewed as a staunch democrat, now appears to be grooming his son Karim to succeed him. [71]

"African socialism and single-party democracy didn't really change underlying colonial patterns of authoritarian executive rule so much as adapt them to new purposes and fly them under new ideological covers," says Harbeson. "We now know beyond a shadow of a doubt that multiparty elections per se don't undo these colonial structures either."

Polls elsewhere in 2010 had more positive outcomes. In Guinea — where a politically inspired massacre and mass rapes occurred in 2009 — the country teetered on the brink of open ethnic warfare after the announcement of its election results in November. [72] Yet tensions eased after Cellou Dalein Diallo, the loser of the run-off, conceded.

War-torn Sudan's first election in 24 years in April 2010 was largely peaceful, albeit tainted by a boycott by major opposition parties. Although President Omar al-Bashir — under indictment by the International Criminal Court for war crimes in Darfur — was returned to power, the election set the stage for southern Sudan's peaceful independence vote in January. [73]

In Tanzania, President Jakaya Kikwete — whose Chama Cha Mapinduzi (CCM) party has ruled the country in varying forms since 1964 — was reelected with 61 percent of the vote. Yet opposition parties ran unexpectedly strong in urban areas and among educated voters — heralding more competitive elections in the future. [74]

As 2011 begins, all eyes will be focused on the 15 presidential elections scheduled to take place in sub-Saharan Africa this year. Polls are expected to be held in Benin, Cameroon, Cape Verde, Central African Republic, Chad, DRC, Djibouti, Gambia, Liberia, Madagascar, Niger, Nigeria, Uganda, Zambia and Zimbabwe.

OUTLOOK

Cheetahs vs. Hippos

How governance in Africa evolves in the coming decades will depend on the outcome of the conflict between what Ghanaian economist George Ayittey calls the continent's "cheetahs" and "hippos."

Cheetahs, as Ayittey defines them, are a new generation of meritocratic African elites. "They brook no nonsense about corruption, inefficiency, ineptitude, incompetence or buffoonery," he writes. "The Cheetahs do not look for excuses for government failure by wailing over the legacies of the slave trade, Western colonialism, imperialism, the World Bank, or an unjust international economic system."[75]

Hippos, Ayittey continues, represent the post-colonial African ruling class that enriched themselves through corruption, manipulation of state-power and donor funds. They are, as he colorfully described them in a 2007 speech, "an assortment of military fufu-heads, Swiss Bank-socialists, crocodile liberators [and] vampire elite."[76]

"Hippos are near-sighted — and sit tight in their air-conditioned government offices, comfortable in their belief that the state can solve all of Africa's problems," he wrote earlier this year.[77] "All the state needs is more power and more foreign aid. And they would ferociously defend their territory, since that is what provides them with their wealth. . . . They care less if the whole country collapses around them, but are content as long as their pond is secure."

Analysts disagree as to what extent hippos will continue to shape the future of African governance. "There was a certain sense that we're going to see democracy grow and grow," says Gyimah-Boadi, of Afrobarometer. "But I think, in the end, autocratic rulers have found ways to forestall progress, especially by . . . keeping political power largely concentrated at the center."

Gyimah-Boadi foresees a continuation of "super-tense elections, all kinds of attempts to abridge constitutions so as to enable rulers and governments to exercise power, and very dramatic . . . attempts to evade constitutional limits on tenure."

Bruce Gilley, an African politics researcher at Portland State University, argues that Mugabe's ability to cling to power despite diplomatic isolation and sanctions has set a bad precedent for leaders like Kagame, Museveni, Gbagbo and Zenawi.

"It is easy to dismiss him as a relic of the past, but Mugabe is actually an augur of the future," writes Gilley.[78] "At independence Mugabe was a great conciliator who spoke of good governance and an end to conflict. Over time, this cheetah became a hippo. Others are now following."

The growing influence in Africa of rising global economic powers is bringing greater demand for African oil, minerals and coffee, but less international pressure for democratic reforms. "China's involvement — and perhaps that of countries like Brazil, India and the Arab world as well — may be problematic for democracy," says, former USAID democracy expert Harbeson.

But others foresee a brighter future, as the continents' governments are eventually turned over to a less-insular, better prepared group of leaders. "Africa has had several generations of truly abysmal political leadership," says Puddington of Freedom House. "As you move further from the post-colonial generation and get young people who are educated and see how other countries work, I think you'll see more leaders who are committed to democracy."

"Enlightened African leaders will spur democratic reforms," says Shinn, the longtime U.S. African diplomat. "Without enlightened leadership that really believes in democratic principles, I doubt there will be much improvement. Too many leaders are interested in remaining in power at any cost."

The challenge for Africa's democrats now is not to oust independence-leaders-turned-Big-Men but to provide a check on presidential powers by strengthening democratic institutions such as parliaments, the judiciary, electoral commissions and citizens' groups, some experts say.

Others see the recent retreat in political freedoms as just a temporary recession in a trend towards greater democratic governance, citing countries like Ghana and Mali, whose free press and domestic human rights groups will provide a model for their neighbors.

"Most of Africa will be greatly improved. Overall trends will be more positive than the last decade," says Nagy, the former U.S. diplomat in Africa. "The scales have finally tipped. The Ghana models will become much more the norm than the Ivory Coast or Kenya models."

NOTES

1. "Ivory Coast: Africa's Latest Case of Bungled Elections," *The Standard* (Nairobi, Kenya), Dec. 4, 2010, www.standardmedia.co.ke/editorial/InsidePage .php?id=2000023976&cid=16&story=Ivory%20 Coast:%20Africa.

2. George E. Curry, "Exclusive Interview: Embattled Ivory Coast President Explains His Victory," *New Journal and Guide*, 2011, www.njournalg.com/index .php?option=com_content&view=article&id=4503: exclusive-interview-embattled-ivory-coast-president-explains-his-victory&catid=41:national-news& Itemid=29.

3. Martin Meredith, *The Fate of Africa* (2005), pp. 378-379.

4. Michael Bratton and Nicolas van de Walle, *Democratic Experiments in Africa* (1997), p. 4.

5. Jason McLure, "Ethiopia: Supreme Court To Hear Election Challenge," *The New York Times*, June 16, 2010, p. A6.

6. "Freedom in the World 2011 Survey Release," Freedom House, Jan. 13, 2011, www.freedomhouse .org/template.cfm?page=594.

7. For background, see Sarah Glazer, "Stopping Genocide," *CQ Researcher*, Aug. 27, 2004, pp. 685-708.

8. For background, see Karen Foerstel, "Crisis in Darfur," *CQ Global Researcher*, Sept. 1, 2009, pp. 243-270.

9. For background, see Jason McLure, "The Troubled Horn of Africa," *CQ Global Researcher*, June 1, 2009, pp. 149-176.

10. Amanda Lea Robinson, "National Versus Ethnic Identity in Africa," *Afrobarometer Working Papers*, September 2009, www.isn.ethz.ch/isn/Digital-Library/ Publications/Detail/?ots591=0C54E3B3-1E9C-BE1E-2C24-A6A8C7060233&lng=en&id=106155.

11. Alan Boswell, "Chad, Sudan Signal End to Proxy Wars," VOANews.com, Voice of America, www .voanews.com/english/news/africa/east/Chad-Sudan-Signal-End-to-Proxy-Wars-84017867.html.

12. "Regional Economic Outlook: Sub-Saharan Africa," International Monetary Fund, October 2010, www .imf.org/external/pubs/ft/reo/2010/AFR/eng/sreo

1010.htm. Note: IMF regional data does not include Sudan.

13. Stephen Kretzmann, "Drilling into Debt," OilChange International, July 2005, available at: http://priceofoil .org/educate/resources/drilling-into-debt/.

14. John Ghazvinian, *Untapped: The Scramble for Africa's Oil* (2007).

15. For background, see Karen Foerstel, "China in Africa," *CQ Global Researcher*, Jan. 1, 2008, pp. 1-26.

16. Terence O'Hara and Kathleen Day, "Ex-Riggs Manager Won't Testify About Accounts," *The Washington Post*, July 16, 2004, p. A1, www.washingtonpost .com/wp-dyn/articles/A53345-2004Jul15.html. Also see "Money Laundering and Foreign Corruption: Enforcement and Effectiveness of the Patriot Act, Case study involving Riggs Bank," Permanent Subcommittee on Investigations, Senate Government Affairs Committee, July 14, 2004, http://levin.senate.gov/newsroom/supporting/2004/ 071504psireport.pdf.

17. Tutu Alicante and Lisa Misol, "Resource Cursed," *Foreign Policy*, Aug. 26, 2009.

18. Alberto M. Fernandez, "Remarks by Ambassador Alberto M. Fernandez at the 4th of July Reception," U.S. State Department, http://malabo.usembassy.gov/ ambassador/statements.html.

19. Celia W. Dugger, "African Leader Hires Adviser and Seeks an Image Change," *The New York Times*, June 28, 2010.

20. "Transparency International's 2010 Corruption Perceptions Index," www.transparency.org/policy_ research/surveys_indices/cpi/2010/results.

21. Jason McLure, "Ghana's New Oil Wealth May Trigger Borrowing Spree," Bloomberg.com, Dec. 15, 2010, www.bloomberg.com/news/2010-12-15/ ghana-oil-wealth-may-trigger-borrowing-spree-not-fund-future-generations.html.

22. Shaohua Chen and Martin Ravallion, "The Developing World Is Poorer Than We Thought, But No Less Successful in the Fight Against Poverty," World Bank, August 2008, http://siteresources.worldbank .org/JAPANINJAPANESEEXT/Resources/ 515497-1201490097949/080827_The_Developing_ World_is_Poorer_than_we_Thought.pdf.

23. *Ibid.*

24. Bruce Bueno de Mesquita and George Downs, "Development and Democracy," *Foreign Policy*, September/October 2005.

25. "Efficiency Versus Freedom," *The Economist*, Aug. 5, 2010, www.economist.com/node/16743333.

26. Akwe Amosu, "China in Africa: It's (Still) the Governance, Stupid," *Foreign Policy in Focus*, March 9, 2007, www.fpif.org/reports/china_in_africa_its_still_the_governance_stupid.

27. Helen Epstein, "Cruel Ethiopia," *New York Review of Books*, May 13, 2010.

28. "Angola: Authoritarian Alliances," *Africa Confidential*, March 2, 2007.

29. "China-Africa Trade Hits Record High," *People's Daily Online*, Dec. 24, 2010, http://english.people-daily.com.cn/90001/90776/90883/7241341.html.

30. "The Democracy Index 2010: Democracy in Retreat," *The Economist Intelligence Unit*, 2011.

31. Sebastien Berger, "Zimbabwe Inflation Hits 231 Million Percent," *The Telegraph*, Oct. 9, 2008.

32. Colin McEvedy, *The Penguin Atlas of African History* (1995), p. 40.

33. John Addison, *Ancient Africa* (1970), p. 37.

34. Basil Davidson, *The African Past* (1964), p. 73.

35. Addison, *op. cit.*, pp. 99-103, 115-116.

36. Unless otherwise noted, this section is drawn from C. Magbaily Fyle, *Introduction to the History of African Civilization: Precolonial Africa*, University Press of America (1999), pp. 86-97.

37. McEvedy, *op. cit.*, pp. 70-73.

38. Davidson, *op. cit.*, pp. 176-177.

39. For further detail see: Philip Curtin, *The Atlantic Slave Trade: A Census* (1969).

40. Roland Oliver and Michael Crowder (eds.), *The Cambridge Encyclopedia of Africa* (1981), pp. 146-148.

41. *Ibid.*, p. 149.

42. Gideon Were, *A History of South Africa* (1974), pp. 22, 53.

43. The Congo Free State, which lasted from 1885 to 1909, was a private colonial project of King Leopold II,
though the Belgian government provided financing. For further reading on Leopold's brutal rule, see Adam Hochschild, *King Leopold's Ghost* (1998).

44. Thomas Pakenham, *The Scramble for Africa: White Man's Conquest of the Dark Continent from 1876 to 1912* (1991), pp. 239-255.

45. Parts of South Africa were under independent white rule. Liberia, established as a homeland for freed American slaves in the 1840s, was nominally independent at this time though in practice it functioned as a U.S. protectorate.

46. Meredith, *op. cit.*, p. 2.

47. *Ibid.*, pp. 5-6.

48. *Ibid.*, p. 8.

49. The Atlantic Charter, Aug. 14, 1941, U.S. National Archives, www.archives.gov/education/lessons/fdr-churchill/images/atlantic-charter.gif.

50. Meredith, *op. cit.*, p. 64.

51. Oliver and Crowder, *op. cit.*, p. 260.

52. Stephen R. Weissman, "New Evidence Shows U.S. Role in Congo's Decision to Send Patrice Lumumba to His Death," *allAfrica.com*, Aug. 1, 2010, http://allafrica.com/stories/201008010004.html.

53. Meredith, *op. cit.*, pp. 312-318.

54. "Angola," *The World Factbook*, CIA, www.cia.gov/library/publications/the-world-factbook/geos/ao.html.

55. Leonard Thompson, *A History of South Africa* (2001), p. 298.

56. See Michael Clough, *Free at Last? U.S. Policy Toward Africa and the End of the Cold War* (1992).

57. Meredith, *op. cit.*

58. For background on post-Cold War democratization in Africa, see Kenneth Jost, "Democracy in Africa," *CQ Researcher*, March 24, 1995, pp. 241-272.

59. Kathryn Sturman, "Term Limits — Who Needs Them?" South African Institute of International Affairs, Aug. 25, 2009, www.saiia.org.za/diplomatic-pouch/term-limits-who-needs-them.html.

60. "Protests Banned in Ethiopia," Agence France-Presse, May 15, 2005, www.news24.com/Africa/News/Protests-banned-in-Ethiopia-20050515.

61. John Attard-Montalto and Vittorio Agnoletto, "Presidential and National Assembly Elections in Nigeria," (and accompanying press release) European Parliament, May 8, 2007, www.europarl.europa.eu/intcoop/election_observation/missions/2004-2009/20070421_nigeria_en.pdf.

62. "Kenya: Final Report on the General Elections 27 December, 2007," European Union Election Observation Mission, April 3, 2008, www.eueomkenya.org/Main/English/PDF/Final_Report_Kenya_2007.pdf.

63. "Kenya's Elections: Twilight Robbery, Daylight Murder," *The Economist*, Jan. 3, 2008, www.economist.com/node/10438473.

64. Alan Cowell and Barry Bearak, "A Grim Image of Politics in Zimbabwe," *The New York Times*, June 27, 2008, www.nytimes.com/2008/06/27/world/africa/27zimbabwe.html.

65. Karin Brulliard, "Power-Sharing Deal is Signed in Zimbabwe," *The Washington Post*, Sept. 16, 2008, www.washingtonpost.com/wp-dyn/content/article/2008/09/15/AR2008091500504.html.

66. Tom Burgis, "Harare Power-Sharing Comes Under Fire," *Financial Times*, March 8, 2009, www.ft.com/cms/s/0/c4eb75d8-0c01-11de-b87d-0000779fd2ac.html#axzz1D0JpjuYO.

67. Economist Intelligence Unit, *op. cit.*,

68. "U.S. Expresses Concern About Rwanda Election," Reuters, Aug. 14, 2010, www.reuters.com/article/2010/08/14/us-rwanda-election-usa-idUSTRE67D0DX20100814?type=politicsNews&feedType=RSS&sp=true; also see Jina Moore, "Burundi Election Lacks Critical Ingredient: Presidential Candidates," *The Christian Science Monitor*, June 23, 2010, www.csmonitor.com/World/Africa/2010/0623/Burundi-election-lacks-critical-ingredient-presidential-candidates; "Premier's Party Sweeps Ethiopian Vote," *The New York Times*, May 26, 2010, www.nytimes.com/2010/05/26/world/africa/26ethopia.html.

69. Jason McLure, "Why Democracy Isn't Working," *Newsweek*, June 18, 2010, www.newsweek.com/2010/06/18/why-democracy-isn-t-working.html.

70. John Zodzi, "Togo Leader Gnassingbe Re-elected in Disputed Poll," Reuters, March 6, 2010, www.reuters.com/article/2010/03/06/us-togo-idUSTRE62520G20100306?pageNumber=2.

71. "President's Son Says He'll Join Senegal's Government," Agence France-Presse, May 1, 2009, www.france24.com/en/20090501-presidents-son-says-he-will-join-new-government-.

72. Ougna Camara and Jason McLure, "Guinea President Konate Declares State of Emergency," Bloomberg News, Nov. 17, 2010, www.bloomberg.com/news/2010-11-17/guinea-s-president-konate-declares-emergency-amid-post-election-violence.html. For background, see Jina Moore, "Confronting Rape as a War Crime," *CQ Global Researcher*, May 1, 2010, pp. 105-130.

73. Opheera McDoom, "Sudan Poll Does Not Meet World Standards: Observers," Reuters, April 17, 2010, www.reuters.com/article/2010/04/17/us-sudan-elections-idUSTRE63F1FC20100417?feedType=RSS&feedName=topNews.

74. "Tanzania's Kikwete Wins Second Presidential Term," VOA News, Nov. 5, 2010, www.voanews.com/english/news/africa/Tanzanias-Kikwete-Extends-Lead-in-Presidential-Election-106760463.html.

75. George Ayittey, "Why Africa Needs 'Cheetahs,' Not 'Hippos,'" CNN.com, Sept. 6, 2010, http://edition.cnn.com/2010/OPINION/08/25/ayittey.cheetahs.hippos/index.html.

76. "George Ayittey on Cheetahs vs. Hippos," Speech to TEDGlobal 2007 Conference in Arusha, Tanzania. Video available at www.ted.com/talks/george_ayittey_on_cheetahs_vs_hippos.html.

77. *Ibid.*, Ayittey, CNN.com.

78. Bruce Gilley, "The End of the African Renaissance," *Washington Quarterly*, October 2010, www.twq.com/10october/docs/10oct_Gilley.pdf.

BIBLIOGRAPHY

Books

Ayittey, George, *Africa Unchained: The Blueprint for Africa's Future*, Palgrave MacMillan, 2006.
Ghanaian economist George Ayittey is unsparing in his criticism of the failures of modern African governance, 50 years after the end of colonialism. Freeing African

economies from their governments' shackles would raise living standards for the continent's poorest, he argues.

Collier, Paul, *Wars, Guns, and Votes, HarperPerennial*, 2009.

Oxford Professor Paul Collier argues that sham democracies in the world's poorest countries, many of them in Africa, are prone to higher levels of political violence. Rigged elections lead to disillusionment, resentment and eventually bad governance.

Maathai, Wangari, *The Challenge for Africa, Pantheon*, 2009.

Nobel prize-winning environmentalist and human rights campaigner sees hope for the continent in reforming local governance and promoting grassroots development. She criticizes colonialism and Western hypocrisy towards Africa but also finds fault with modern African cultures tolerate corruption and environmental degradation.

Meredith, Martin, *The Fate of Africa, PublicAffairs*, 2005.

This sweeping history takes the reader on a continent-wide journey, beginning at independence and ending with civil wars in Darfur, Liberia and Sierra Leone. Key leaders, including Ghana's Kwame Nkrumah, Zimbabwe's Robert Mugabe and Ivory Coast's Felix Houphouët-Boigny are given unflinching treatment.

Pakenham, Thomas, *The Scramble for Africa: White Man's Conquest of the Dark Continent from 1876 to 1912, RandomHouse*, 1991.

This classic history of African colonialism — from King Leopold's grab for the Congo to British domination of South Africa — details how the continent was divided arbitrarily by the European powers, with long-lasting effects on African governance.

Wrong, Michela, *It's Our Turn to Eat: The Story of a Kenyan Whistleblower, HarperCollins*, 2009.

This biography of Kenyan journalist and iconoclastic anti-corruption activist John Githongo illuminates the failed dream of democracy in Kenya — once considered East Africa's most stable government — and highlights the corruption and ethnic division that plague Kenyan politics.

Articles

Epstein, Helen, "Cruel Ethiopia," *The New York Review of Books*, May 13, 2010.

The writer documents in detail how the World Bank and other Western aid agencies were complicit in Ethiopia's development into an authoritarian one-party state after the country's abortive multiparty elections in 2005.

McLure, Jason, "Why Democracy Isn't Working," *Newsweek*, June 18, 2010.

The United States and its allies are accepting democracy's retreat in Africa. Confirmed autocrats remain close U.S. allies in part because of the need for natural resources, help in fighting terrorists like al-Qaeda and an entrenched aid bureaucracy.

Sanders, Edmund, "Democracy is Losing Ground Across Africa," *Los Angeles Times*, July 13, 2008.

China's growing influence, along with African leaders' reluctance to criticize each other, helps explain why many democratic gains on the continent have been reversed.

Reports and Studies

"Freedom in the World 2011: The Authoritarian Challenge to Democracy," *Freedom House*, 2011, www.freedomhouse.org/template.cfm?page=594.

The democracy promoting advocacy group's annual report shows that only nine of 48 sub-Saharan countries were considered "free" in 2010. Last year was the fifth consecutive year liberties declined globally, the longest regression in the report's nearly four-decade history.

Bratton, Michael, and Robert Mattes, "Neither Consolidating Nor Fully Democratic: The Evolution of African Political Regimes, 1999-2008," *Afrobarometer*, May 2009, www.afrobarometer.org/index .php?option=com_docman&Itemid=37.

A polling project founded by a network of African research organizations provides a wealth of survey data on how citizens in 19 (mostly free or partly free) countries view their own governance.

Rawlence, Ben, and Chris Albin-Lackey, "Nigeria's 2007 General Elections: Democracy in Retreat," *African Affairs 106* (424), 2007, pp. 497-506.

Two Human Rights Watch officials painstakingly detail the myriad ways the ruling party in Africa's most populous state cheated in its last election.

For More Information

African Union, P.O. Box 3243, Addis Ababa, Ethiopia; +251 11 551 77 00; www.africa-union.org. Pan-African body that promotes political and economic cooperation between the 53 member nations; mediates election disputes.

Freedom House, 1301 Connecticut Ave., N.W., Sixth Floor, Washington, DC 20036; (202) 296-5101; www.freedomhouse.org. Founded in 1941, tracks liberties across the globe based on a checklist of political and civil rights; publishes an annual survey, "Freedom in the World."

Human Rights Watch, 350 Fifth Ave., 34th Floor, New York, NY 10118-3299; (212) 290-4700; www.hrw.org. Uses its own on-the-ground research to provide periodic reports on human rights developments in Africa and around the world.

Institute for Security Studies, P.O. Box 1787, Brooklyn Square, Tshwane (Pretoria) 0075, South Africa; +27 012 346 9500; www.iss.co.za. One of Africa's leading foreign policy think tanks; provides a range of views on democracy and other African issues.

Mo Ibrahim Foundation, 3rd Floor North, 35 Portman Square, London W1H 6LR, United Kingdom; +44 20 7535 5088; www.moibrahimfoundation.org. Sudanese-born telecom tycoon Ibrahim has donated part of his fortune to improving African governance. Foundation offers the world's richest prize — $5 million over 10 years and $200,000 for life thereafter — to democratically-elected African heads of state who serve their countries well and then leave office. The organization also publishes an index ranking African countries on their governance.

National Endowment for Democracy, 1025 F St., N.W., Suite 800, Washington DC 20004; (202) 378-9700; www.ned.org. A private, nonprofit foundation funded mainly by the U.S. Congress; finances democracy projects in more than 90 countries and publishes the *Journal of Democracy*.

South African Institute of International Affairs, P.O. Box 31596, Braamfontein 2017, South Africa; +27 11 339 2154; www.saiia.org. An Africa-focused think tank that studies African governance, parliamentary performance and natural resource management.

Voices From Abroad:

GUILLAUME SORO

Prime Minister Ivory Coast

At a crossroads

"This is what's at stake: Either we assist in the installation of democracy in Ivory Coast or we stand by indifferent and allow democracy to be assassinated."

Virginian-Pilot, January 2011

DONKRIS MEVUTA

Executive Director Friends of the Land (environmental NGO), Ghana

Blessing or curse?

"Politicians have left people expecting very high returns. The very limited space the people have for participation [in managing the impact of the oil industry] is a recipe for disappointment and conflict. Oil is a blessing, but the way we manage the environmental and social impacts will show whether it is a curse."

The Christian Science Monitor December 2010

HAJO ANDRIANAINARIVELO

Minister of Land Management, Madagascar

No advice wanted

"One has the right to strike if one feels his liberty is not respected, so we had the right to take the future in our hands. As for SADC [the Southern African Development Community], we don't need democracy lessons from the likes of Zimbabwe or Swaziland."

The Christian Science Monitor November 2010

CHINUA ACHEBE

Novelist, Nigeria

Patience needed

"This is not a time to bemoan all the challenges ahead. It is a time to work at developing, nurturing and

Florida Today/Parker

sustaining democracy. But we also must realize that we need patience and cannot expect instant miracles. Building a nation is not something a people do in one regime, in a few years, even. . . . Sustaining democracy in Nigeria will require more than just free elections. It will also mean ending a system in which corruption is not just tolerated, but widely encouraged and hugely profitable."

The New York Times January 2011

KAMALI

Resident, Nairobi, Kenya

Coups still necessary

"Coups are there because of lack of democracy. To avoid coups, [the African Union] should emphasize building true democratic institutions. Currently, coups are still needed in Africa."

New York Amsterdam News February 2010

PACOME BIZIMUNGU

Physiotherapy student
Kigali Health Institution Rwanda

Steps toward democracy

"We make our decision according to the strength of the candidates — there is no issue of ethnicity. We are in a process. We have not reached real democracy yet, but I think this is the first step to democracy."

The Christian Science Monitor August 2010

DAVID DADGE

Director, International Press Institute, Austria

Democracy leads to development

"From the statistics, it is now clear that there's a correlation between poor leadership of a country and press freedom. It is high time these leaders cultivated some sense of democracy as this will ultimately lead to the development of their nations."

The Nation (Kenya), March 2010

ELIJAH OMAGOR

Partner Ezel Associates (think tank) Uganda

Oil curse makes leaders unresponsive

"Oil revenues therefore turn out to be a curse when leaders enjoy free reign over national resources. This lack of accountability is a recipe for the oil curse because personalisation of national resources always results in politicians becoming unresponsive and unaccountable to their electorate. This is especially so because political relationships in our part of the world tend to be vertical such that those in power allocate resources downwards in exchange for political support. This means that even basic functions of government are fulfilled in exchange for political support and those who are politically well-connected reap big."

The Monitor (Uganda) March 2010

4

Press Freedom

Jennifer Koons

Freed U.S. journalist Euna Lee is reunited with her husband and daughter upon her arrival in the United States on Aug. 5, 2009. She and fellow journalist Laura Ling were arrested in North Korea in March and sentenced to 12 years of hard labor for allegedly entering the country illegally. Released after former U.S. President Bill Clinton pleaded their case in North Korea, the two were among the 136 journalists jailed worldwide in 2009.

From *CQ Researcher*, November, 2010.

A s the editor of Ciudad Juárez's leading daily newspaper, Pedro Torres had seen enough. After a second journalist at the paper was murdered recently, Torres published a startling open letter to the drug cartels ravaging the Mexican city just across the border from El Paso, Texas. "Tell us what we should try to publish or not publish, so we know what to expect," he pleaded in a front-page editorial.[1]

In September, suspected cartel gunmen had killed 21-year-old photographer Luis Carlos Santiago in the parking lot of a shopping mall where he planned to attend a photography workshop.[2] In November 2008, hitmen shot the paper's crime reporter, José Armando Rodríguez, outside his home.[3]

Mexico overall has experienced the greatest decline in press freedom in Latin America during the last five years, according to the press freedom watchdog groups Freedom House and the Committee to Protect Journalists (CPJ). More than 30 reporters investigating crime, drug trafficking and official corruption have been murdered or gone missing since Mexican President Felipe Calderón took office in 2006 and cracked down on the cartels. Many other journalists have been kidnapped or threatened, making Mexico one of the world's most dangerous places for journalists, according to CPJ.[4]

Moreover, rampant corruption within law enforcement and the judiciary has left most of the murderers unpunished.[5] The growing danger has led to increased self-censorship, and many Mexican newspapers no longer publish bylines on stories involving organized

Western Countries Have the Most Press Freedom

Media freedom worldwide has declined for the eighth year in a row, according to the pro-democracy watchdog group Freedom House. The United States, Canada, Australia, Japan and the European Union had the most media freedom in 2009, while the Middle East, Russia and much of Asia had the least.

Global Press Freedom Rankings, 2009

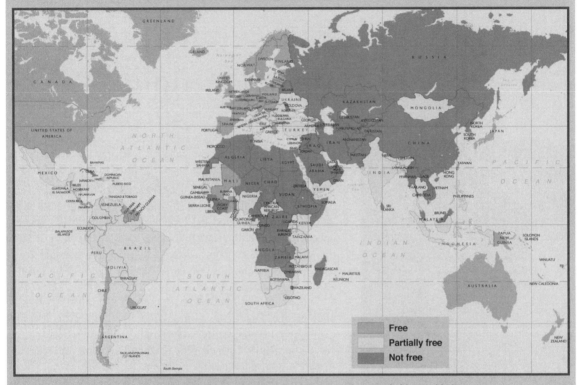

Free
Partially free
Not free

Source: "Freedom of the Press 2010," Freedom House, www.freedomhouse.org/template.cfm?page=363&year=2010

crime. "You love journalism, you love the pursuit of truth, you love to perform a civic service and inform your community. But you love your life more," an editor in Reynosa, a city just across the Rio Grande from McAllen, Texas, told the *Los Angeles Times* recently. "We don't like the silence. But it's survival."[6]

The lack of accountability for the murders encourages further bloodshed, according to a CPJ report released in September.[7] "It is not a lack of valor on the part of the journalists. It is a lack of backing," TV reporter Jaime Aguirre told the *Times*. "If they kill me, nothing happens."[8]

The dire conditions for Mexican journalists are reflected worldwide. According to Freedom House, 72 journalists died last year in the line of duty — 52 of them murdered. Of those, 33 were killed in the Philippines in the run-up to the presidential election, 32 of them gunned down in a premeditated massacre by more than 60 heavily armed gunmen on Mindanao Island in the southern Philippines. Besides the Philippines, the other deadliest places for journalists in 2009 were countries in conflict, such as Somalia — where nine reporters died while doing their jobs — and Iraq and Pakistan, where four died in each country.[9] This year also promises to be bloody: As of October 29, 37 journalists have been killed in the line of duty in 2010.[10]

In addition to violence, journalists also face imprisonment for reporting on unpopular subjects. A total of 136 reporters, editors and photojournalists were imprisoned worldwide in 2009, including 24 in China and 23 in Iran, many jailed during Iran's crackdown on dissent following the disputed 2009 election.[11] Governments in Belarus, Myanmar, China, Cuba, Eritrea, North Korea, Tunisia, Uzbekistan and Venezuela also imprisoned journalists for publishing stories critical of governments.

"The numbers of journalists killed and jailed are both up, which is very alarming," says CPJ Executive Director Joel Simon. "You will typically see the killings of journalists along with the killings [of dissidents], and the common factor is impunity or systemic violence without consequence."

In Russia, journalists know exactly what topics will put them in danger — organized crime, government corruption and the conflict in Chechnya — the subjects covered by nearly all of the 52 journalists killed in Russia since 1992.[12] Two of the journalists killed in 2009 had worked for Moscow's independent *Novaya Gazeta* (New Newspaper), including Natalya Estemirova, 50, an award-winning human rights activist who was kidnapped and shot execution-style.[13]

But violent retribution and imprisonment aren't the only threats limiting media freedom. The globalization of censorship and restrictions on the Internet also constrain press freedom, especially for journalists working in countries engulfed in political conflict.

Criminal defamation laws, for instance, frighten journalists into self-censorship. Such laws make it illegal — punishable by imprisonment and fines — to defame or libel private citizens, public officials or even countries. In

Turkey, for instance, it is illegal to "insult Turkishness." In industrialized countries, defamation and libel cases are litigated in civil courts, punishable only by fines.

Criminal libel or defamation laws, popular among the 57-member Organisation of the Islamic Conference, are punishable by both imprisonment and fines. "If you look at the more than 20 countries from Morocco to Turkey and Iran . . . every single one of [them] has criminal defamation laws on the books," says Mohamed Abdel Dayem, CPJ program coordinator for the Middle East and North Africa. "When journalists are charged

---

Philippines Was Deadliest Country for Journalists

Fifty-two journalists were murdered in 2009 — 32 of them in the Philippines during a bloody massacre allegedly ordered by provincial officials during the presidential campaign. Killers of journalists were convicted in only 6 percent of the murder cases in 2009. Politics was the most dangerous beat for reporters: That was the subject covered by 67 percent of the 72 journalists killed in the line of duty worldwide in 2009.

No. of Journalists Killed in Eight Deadliest Countries, 2009		Beats Covered by Journalists Killed in 2009*	
Philippines	33	Corruption	11%
Somalia	9	Crime	8%
Iraq	4	Culture	8%
Pakistan	4	Human rights	10%
Mexico	3	Politics	67%
Russia	3	Sports	1%
Afghanistan	2	War	25%
Sri Lanka	2		

Impunity in Journalist Murder Cases

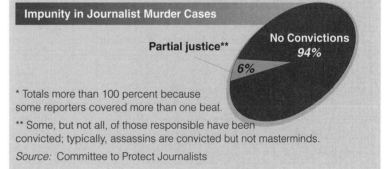

Partial justice** 6%

No Convictions 94%

* Totals more than 100 percent because some reporters covered more than one beat.

** Some, but not all, of those responsible have been convicted; typically, assassins are convicted but not masterminds.

Source: Committee to Protect Journalists

AFP/Getty Images/Ronaldo Schemidt

Journalists enact a mock murder during a protest in Mexico City on Aug. 7, 2010, against violence toward journalists in Mexico. More than 30 reporters have been murdered or gone missing since Mexican President Felipe Calderón took office in 2006 and began cracking down on the nation's powerful drug cartels. Many others have been kidnapped or threatened — mostly by drug traffickers — making Mexico one of the world's most dangerous places for journalists.

with libel, they go before a criminal court. If they are found guilty, they are fined and/or imprisoned — with an emphasis on the imprisonment. This should really be a matter for civil courts, but it's not."

Also, in some Muslim countries any expression that can be interpreted as an insult to Islam — and therefore blasphemous — is widely criminalized and punishable by death, powerful motivations for self-censorship.

When Yemen established a special press and publications court in 2009 to examine media-related disputes, more than 150 cases — some from as far back as 2006 — were brought before the judicial body.[14] In one of its first rulings, the court banned a U.S.-based reporter from ever practicing journalism in Yemen. Munir Mawari, a contributor to the independent weekly *Al-Masdar*, had described President Ali Abdullah Saleh's leadership style as a "weapon of mass destruction."[15]

Also in 2009, the Yemeni government shuttered eight newspapers it said were inciting separatism in the southern part of the country, charging the editors with instigating violence and upsetting national unity.[16] "All kinds of semantic cat-and-mouse business takes place in this part of the world, which doesn't change the fact that journalists have to operate under a climate of fear," CPJ's Dayem says.

The advent of the Internet and the growing popularity of social networking sites have created a countervailing trend that is helping to offset government censorship. With reporters and editors blogging and posting to Facebook and Twitter and online media outlets posting stories around the clock, governments are having a harder and harder time suppressing negative stories. "The current 24/7 news cycle is way too fast for most governments anyway, and their voices get drowned in the general noise," said Wilfried Ruetten, director of the European Journalism Centre in Maastricht, the Netherlands. "If Paris Hilton's dog dies and, on the same day, Obama speaks on U.S. relations with, say, Syria, you know what Google News will look like."

As journalists around the world face violent attacks and government censorship, here are some of the questions being asked:

Can governments control media coverage?

Journalists and press-freedom advocates spent the summer battling the creation of a proposed media tribunal in South Africa, which currently enjoys one of Africa's freest press climates. Warning the tribunal would restrict press coverage, Raymond Louw, chairman of South Africa's Press Council, said the country is headed toward becoming "the kind of state where we want to criminalize information and . . . put editors behind bars."[17]

Louw and fellow South African journalists have launched a campaign against what they say amounts to reinstating apartheid-era press laws. During the apartheid era, the now-ruling African National Congress (ANC) strongly defended media freedom. But after 16 years in power, it has lobbied for creation of the tribunal.[18]

"We need stronger measures where . . . people have been defamed, where . . . malicious intents have driven reporting by media houses or reporters," ANC spokesman Jackson Mthembu told reporters in August.[19]

South Africa's proposed tribunal and Yemen's new special press and publications court both represent overt government attempts to influence media coverage. And the persistent threat of prosecution in one of those media courts triggers self-censorship.

"Governments are becoming increasingly more sophisticated at dictating the terms and the content of media coverage," says Byron Scott, a professor emeritus at the University of Missouri School of Journalism. And governments are aided in those efforts by such journalistic practices as "professional laziness, the blurring of the line between significant news and entertaining and, in many nations under stress, the most important of all, self-censorship."

Self-censorship often reaches its peak during wartime. Prominent American media outlets self-censored their reporting during the first year and a half of the Iraq War, largely due to concerns about public reaction to graphic images and content, according to a 2005 survey of more than 200 journalists by American University's School of Communications.[20]

"Mixed with patriotism, self-censorship becomes the easiest, cheapest and most pernicious of all," Scott says. "It tends to take root during times of national stress and distort news values for some time afterward."

The growing popularity of social media websites has changed how journalists work in the countries with repressive regimes, such as Malaysia, which falls near the bottom of most international rankings on press freedom. While the government-controlled mainstream media previously screened out criticism in newspapers and on TV and radio programs, opposing views increasingly are appearing on blogs and mobile phone messages.

"All our reporters have BlackBerrys and use them to follow these tweets. The social media [have] changed the way journalists work in fundamental ways," said Premesh Chandran, founder of the online news source Malaysiakini.[21] The prevalence of real-time updates from critics and opposition sources inhibited officials from controlling the flow of information, he said.

In fact, legislators today "are forced to engage and debate their counterparts across the aisle in social media like Twitter and Facebook, allowing us to report on the opposition and avoid much censorship," said a veteran reporter at one of Malaysia's leading newspapers, who spoke on condition of anonymity. "Although the restrictions and controls are still in place, it's become much

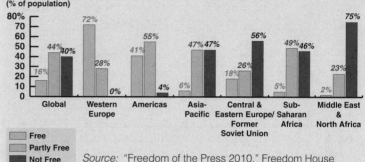

Press Freedom Is Limited in Most of the World

Only 16 percent of the world's population — mainly in Western Europe or the Americas — enjoys a free press. More than three-quarters of the people on Earth live in countries where the press is not free or only partly free. The Middle East and North Africa have the least freedom of the press.

Press Freedom by Percentage of Population, 2009

Source: "Freedom of the Press 2010," Freedom House

harder to censor what the opposition or rights groups say in the media."[22]

In 2009, Reporters Without Borders (Reporters Sans Frontières, or RSF) — a Paris-based group that promotes press freedom around the world — ranked Malaysia 131st out of 175 countries on press freedoms.[23] The low ranking reflected Malaysia's implementation in 2009 of a publishing-permit system that made it easier to censor publications, according to RSF.[24]

Still, the situation is better than it used to be. To promote its information-technology sector, Malaysian officials pledged in 1996 to limit online censorship, which has significantly opened up the country's reporting landscape.

RSF regional correspondent Patrice Victor said Malaysia's experience could be recreated in other nations where authoritarian regimes allow reasonable Internet access.[25]

"We are seeing social media free the way journalists report in this region, and the trend in Malaysia can also be seen happening in Singapore, Thailand and Burma," she said. "Governments here are slowly realizing that it is very hard to censor and restrict information once people have access to the Net, and this trend of using social

Freelance Journalists Have Few Protections

A handful of press-freedom organizations offer help.

After police in Kasensero, Uganda, arrested Sengooba Eddie in September in connection with the murder and robbery of a motorcycle taxi driver, a group of angry fellow drivers gathered at Eddie's home. In an act of vigilantism recorded by freelance radio reporter Paul Kiggundu, the bikers burned Eddie's house to the ground.

Assuming Kiggundu was a spy for the police, the mob turned on him, kicking and beating him until he was unconscious, ignoring his screams that he was only a journalist, according to witnesses. He later died of internal bleeding at nearby Kalisizo hospital.[1]

Shocked by the incident, the chairman of Uganda's Human Rights Network for Journalists, Robert Ssempala, said: "Injustice cannot be used to obtain justice."[2] The Committee to Protect Journalists (CPJ) called on the Ugandan police to bring the perpetrators to justice. "No journalist should be killed simply for carrying out their profession," said CPJ East Africa Consultant Tom Rhodes.[3]

Kiggundu's death reflects the dangers faced by freelancers and journalists who work for small, independent media outlets around the world. They report on critical issues but often lack the support provided to staff reporters employed by larger news organizations. Furthermore, in an era of shrinking foreign and domestic news bureaus, struggling media organizations increasingly are relying on freelance journalists. Nine freelancers were among the 72 journalists killed in 2009.[4]

The CPJ said impunity is the greatest threat to local journalists because it leads potential murderers to believe they will never be held accountable. "The perpetrators assumed, based on precedent, that they would never be punished," said CPJ. "Whether the killings are in Iraq or the Philippines, in Russia or Mexico, changing this assumption is the key to reducing the death toll."[5]

Several international press-freedom organizations help journalists and freelancers cope with threats, injuries and other obstacles. For instance, when Mikhail Beketov, editor of a suburban Moscow newspaper, was viciously attacked for his coverage of local government policies, he suffered a skull fracture, concussion and leg and finger injuries that required partial amputations. CPJ's Journalist Assistance Program provided ongoing financial support to Beketov during his long rehabilitation. Similarly, during the Iranian government's post-election crackdown on journalists in 2009, photojournalist Ehsan Maleki was forced to flee his home in the face of likely imprisonment. CPJ helped him resettle in another country.[6]

Other journalist assistance programs include:

- **International Federation of Journalists** — Based in Brussels, Belgium; promotes international action to defend press freedom and social justice through independent journalist trade unions. (www.ifj.org/en/splash)
- **International Freedom of Expression Exchange** — A clearinghouse based in Toronto, Canada, providing accurate, timely information on freedom of expression issues and abuses worldwide. (www.ifex.org)
- **Media Legal Defence Initiative** — A nongovernmental organization based in London that provides legal support to journalists and media outlets around the world. (www.mediadefence.org/index.html)
- **The Rory Peck Trust** — Supports freelancers around the world from its base in London; promotes good practices on behalf of freelancers, supports their right to work safely and provides them with assistance when needed. (www.rorypecktrust.org)
- **World Press Freedom Committee** — An international umbrella organization of press-freedom groups; fights against press restrictions such as the licensing of journalists and imposition of mandatory codes of conduct. (www.wpfc.org)

— Jennifer Koons

---

[1] Nangayi Guyson, "Uganda: Journalist Beaten to Death," AfricaNews.com, Sept. 14, 2010, www.africanews.com/site/list_message/30344?data[source]=rss.

[2] "Radio reporter beaten to death," IFEX, Sept. 13, 2010, www.ifex.org/uganda/2010/09/13/kiggundu_killed/.

[3] "Freelance journalist beaten to death in Uganda," Committee to Protect Journalists, Sept. 13, 2010, http://cpj.org/2010/09/freelance-journalist-beaten-to-death-in-uganda.php.

[4] "72 Journalists Killed in 2009/Motive Confirmed," Committee to Protect Journalists, http://cpj.org/killed/2009/.

[5] *Ibid.*

[6] "Making an Impact; CPJ aids dozens of journalists worldwide in 2009," Journalist Assistance Program, Committee to Protect Journalists, www.cpj.org/campaigns/assistance.

media to break down censorship looks like it is here to stay."[26]

Will new government cyber controls effectively censor journalists?

Free-press advocates say the most troubling press censorship trend centers around government efforts to restrict communication online, according to Simon of the Committee to Protect Journalists.

"Nowadays, more and more newsgathering and dissemination is being done on the Web," he says. "It doesn't matter if it's print or broadcast or nonprofit or for-profit. . . . It's all online. And governments recognize that."

During a crackdown on months-long demonstrations last spring, Thai officials expanded Internet controls to further restrict a wide range of online speech, including commentary and newsgathering. To protect national security, said Prime Minister Abhisit Vejjajiva, the government ordered security forces to block access to at least 36 websites and broadcasts of the People's Channel satellite news station, which had been supporting antigovernment protests.[27]

Political protests moved online as more Thai citizens have gained access to the Internet. By 2009, nearly a quarter of the population (or 16.1 million people) had Internet access.[28] Even exiled former Prime Minister Thaksin Shinawatra and Prime Minister Abhisit's spokesman post competing messages to Twitter.[29]

The Thai government is not the only government instituting cyber controls. Iran, China, Russia and Venezuela — among others — have developed highly advanced techniques to monitor citizens' online activities and block critical websites.

"At first, the perception was that the Internet could not be controlled and was highly resistant to regulation," Simon says. "No one believes that anymore. Governments have taken effective measures to curtail free speech online." Some countries are more heavy-handed than others, he says. "Cuba and Burma do it in a very unsophisticated way — they simply block people from going online."

Simon is encouraged that the Internet is dominated by a handful of fairly large companies, some of which "have demonstrated a commitment to — at least in principle — privacy and freedom of expression," he

says. The companies generally "understand that they are in the business of providing information and guaranteeing that this information will be protected," he added, despite some glaring shortcomings. Yahoo! Inc., for example, on four occasions was accused of helping the Chinese government track down dissidents that were using its search engine, triggering outcries from Internet users around the world concerned about growing U.S. corporate acceptance of repressive Chinese media laws. The last incident, in 2005, enabled the government to identify online journalist Shi Tao, who was subsequently arrested and jailed. Since then, Google and Microsoft also have been criticized for censoring their content within China.[30]

But the European Journalism Centre's Ruetten says that even the most restrictive government controls can be skirted. "China in particular shows how to turn the Web into a controlled intranet," he said. "But there is always a way around censorship if you are somewhat tech-savvy."

David Bandurski, a researcher at the University of Hong Kong's China Media Project, says "Internet controls are not, in fact, the core issue facing journalists in terms of what they can and cannot report." Rather, government censorship of print and broadcast news sources, which is much easier, directly impacts what's available on the Internet, he says. "In China, Internet sites are still prevented from doing their own news reporting, which means they rely on the reporting done by traditional media." Thus, he explains, restricting traditional investigative reporting or examinations of the deeper causes behind news stories will "directly impact the Web."

In Syria, where the state controls most print publications, the government began restricting digital speech when Syrians began using the Internet in large numbers. By 2008, with more than 2 million Syrians online, the Web had emerged as a platform for dissent, so authorities began to beef up online monitoring and censorship.

Although no Syrian laws specifically regulate online content, reporters and bloggers face prosecution under the nation's emergency laws, penal code and press law, which lists topics or lines of inquiry journalists are forbidden to discuss and the punishments for violating those restrictions.[31] "The Internet represents the final frontier in the Middle East, and a lot of governments are really uncomfortable," says CPJ's Dayem. "Satellite TV

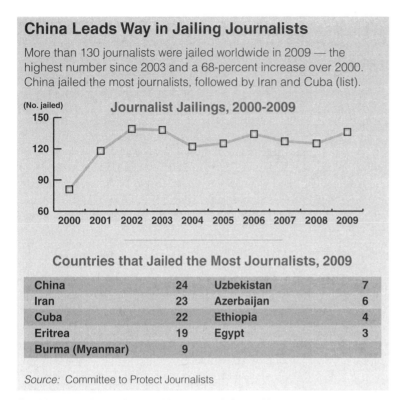

China Leads Way in Jailing Journalists

More than 130 journalists were jailed worldwide in 2009 — the highest number since 2003 and a 68-percent increase over 2000. China jailed the most journalists, followed by Iran and Cuba (list).

Journalist Jailings, 2000-2009

(No. jailed)

Countries that Jailed the Most Journalists, 2009

China	24	Uzbekistan	7
Iran	23	Azerbaijan	6
Cuba	22	Ethiopia	4
Eritrea	19	Egypt	3
Burma (Myanmar)	9		

Source: Committee to Protect Journalists

felt like something they couldn't control, but a blog is even worse."

In 2008 the Syrian Ministry of Communications ordered Internet cafe owners to keep records of their customers' personal information along with the exact time they accessed the Web.[32] In March 2009, authorities sentenced online journalist Habib Saleh to three years in prison for writing articles that "weakened national feeling" and "incited civil and religious warfare."[33] In May 2009, Syrian officials set out to expand the existing press law to cover Internet users.

Many governments, especially in the Gulf states, monitor and limit Internet access by retaining monopoly ownership of local Internet service providers (ISPs). But Abdul Rahman al-Rashed, general manager of the Dubai-based satellite TV channel Al-Arabiya, said governments are wrong to think they can control the spread of information online.

"A lot of information is getting through to the average person, in Cairo, in Jeddah and Dubai. Censorship will not stop the free flow of information, in my opinion," he said.[34]

Al-Rashed cited the rising influence of the telecommunications sector, including the critical role played by the Internet in growing economies and businesses and the increasing demand for new technology tools from the middle class. Remote areas of the world that still lack basic access to the Web could be the last refuge for strict government control, he said.[35]

Iran is the Middle East's poster child for repression of online activity, combining old-school detention and harassment with newer techniques such as blocking and monitoring Internet behavior. The theocratic government has also moved aggressively to extend the longstanding legal restrictions on print and broadcast journalism to online media.

As in Iran, officials in Egypt, Saudi Arabia, Syria and elsewhere are experimenting with old press statutes and new strategies like blocking and monitoring bloggers from disseminating information, according to a 2009 CPJ survey.[36]

"As Internet connectivity mushrooms in the region, the popularity of blogs has rivaled that of traditional news media," Dayem says. "This is especially true with sensitive topics such as sexual harassment, torture and HIV/AIDS. On topics such as these, bloggers have pushed boundaries and provided cover for traditional journalists."

Governments are pushing back, hard. They're expanding existing legal restrictions, writing new Web-specific laws and requiring service providers to police customers, according to CPJ. In addition, officials are using technology to monitor and block online content and employing old-school tactics such as harassment and detention against bloggers, most of whom are isolated and vulnerable.

"The tactics of authorities may vary, but the goal is often the same: Convince a blogger that the cost of doing battle with the state far outweighs any benefit," Dayem says.

In Cuba, however, bloggers are finding ways to share news and views online, despite widespread legal and technical restrictions. "A lively blogging culture has emerged over the last three years, despite Havana's attempts to control the Internet," says CPJ's Simon. "Some bloggers are examining controversial subjects considered off-limits by the mainstream media, like official corruption and human rights abuses — a risky enterprise considering that the majority of imprisoned Cuban journalists were targeted for work distributed online."[37]

The bloggers, mainly young professionals, have opened a new space for free expression in Cuba. "I am heartened by the rise of a new generation of blogger/journalists," says Scott, of Missouri's journalism school. They are getting an audience."

In November 2009, President Barack Obama took the unusual step of answering questions submitted by Cuban blogger Yoani Sánchez, who has gained international acclaim for criticizing Cuba online, despite government harassment.[38]

"Your blog provides the world a unique window into the realities of daily life in Cuba," Obama wrote. "It is telling that the Internet has provided you and other courageous Cuban bloggers with an outlet to express yourself so freely. The government and people of the United States join all of you in looking forward to the day all Cubans can freely express themselves in public without fear and without reprisals."[39]

Is press freedom a prerequisite for economic development?

Indian Nobel laureate Amartya Sen and other economists say a free press is a central condition for the development and maintenance of transparent and honest government and lasting economic growth.[40] It is no coincidence, they say, that repression of information and opinion is most severe in the poorest, least-developed countries, where journalists are persecuted, murdered, beaten, arrested and imprisoned, often for reporting on corruption.

Yet many autocratic and repressive governments — notably China — say a free press hampers economic and social development. The free flow of information and expression should be postponed, they argue, until a satisfactory level of economic development has been achieved.

Media experts from 100 countries gathered in Jordan in October 2005 for the Global Forum for Media Development, which explored the link between media development and economic, political and overall development.[41] The World Bank Institute presented empirical evidence to show that independent, financially stable media are essential to good governance and that they succeed when the business environment in which they operate is strengthened.[42]

"Unstable economies invariably breed irresponsible journalism. Studies by Freedom House, Transparency International and others clearly show that the more stable a nation is economically, the better the public perception of the press," says Missouri's Scott. "A press that cannot afford to live cannot thrive."

But oil-rich Gulf nations such as Oman and Qatar would appear to buck that trend: They continued to prosper while keeping a firm hold on the media. Qatar's government-owned Al Jazeera, which has become one of the most popular Arabic satellite television channels in the Middle East, generally does not cover Qatari politics, focusing instead on regional issues, such as the situation in Iraq and the Arab-Israeli conflict.

"There are countries in the region that are entirely closed, politically and economically speaking, or underdeveloped economically and have a media landscape that is nearly the most repressive in the region," says Dayem, CPJ's Middle East program coordinator. "Others are open [but] have virtually a nonexistent media landscape. Look at Saudi Arabia and Kuwait or Saudi Arabia and the United Arab Emirates," he continues. "Economically, neither is lagging behind the other. Saudi Arabia is a much bigger country, but the media landscape is completely different" in the three countries.

Al Jazeera Director General Wadah Khanfar summed up the situation in the Middle East: "As long as our governments are not convinced that free media could help in developing society, and as long as they see us [as] potential recruits for their propaganda, and as long as there are journalists around who will seek grants from governments to act on their behalf and to deceive and to disinform, I think we are going to have a problem."[43]

China also provides a counterargument to those who contend a free press precedes economic prosperity, according to Ruetten, of the European Journalism Centre.

"The theory was, once you get middle classes, they will want more freedoms and that, again, can lead to more economic development," Ruetten says. "But looking at China seems to prove the opposite. Substantial economic development happens even though there is no free press. The same goes for Singapore and the Gulf states. And how free is 'the press' anyway in countries like yours [in the United States] when its [media] institutions have to generate quarterly profits for shareholders?"

BACKGROUND

Fall of the Wall

After World War II, most of Eastern Europe disappeared behind an "Iron Curtain" of Soviet communist authoritarian rule, which barred press freedom. Berlin was sliced in half by an 11-foot wall, erected in 1961 to keep East Berliners away from the influences — and freedoms — enjoyed by West Berliners. By the early 1980s, military dictators ruled throughout Latin America, and Cold War-fueled conflicts raged across Africa and Asia. Press freedom was largely unknown outside the United States, Western Europe and Japan.

In the late 1980s and early '90s, press freedom began to expand greatly, after a wave of democratization swept the globe — first in Latin America where military juntas were replaced by democratic governments and then in the former Soviet Union and its satellite states. Later, some parts of Africa and Asia saw some relaxation of media restraints.

Beginning in 1989, popular discontent toppled communist governments in rapid succession. "Ironically, I was playing poker with a bunch of journalists and journalism professors the night the Berlin Wall fell," remembers Missouri's Scott. "Sadly, none of us paused to exclaim what a seminal event it would prove to be; probably because none of us anticipated those consequences. The subsequent rapid collapse of the Soviet Union rewrote the rules for all of us, not just those behind the Iron Curtain. Suddenly, we all had access, each to the other. We could talk, question and report on an equal basis. At least, that was the naïve theory.

"The reality was that there were virtually no journalists in the former Communist bloc trained . . . in the principles of press freedom, at least as we in the West considered it," Scott says. "The subsequent couple of decades have been about mutual adjustment."

The fall of the wall mainly benefited younger journalists, since so many older journalists in Eastern Europe had pledged allegiance to the communist regimes or suffered in silence.

"Those reporters and editors lost their jobs, since they were all totally discredited," the European Journalism Centre's Ruetten says. "This is especially true for public broadcasting operations. That is why you find only very few journalists in Eastern Europe who are above age 50 or so. So it did benefit all the younger guys. As for [Western] publishers, they all went east with their papers and magazines, trying to establish new ventures in the new countries," he says. "Some worked, some failed: The jury is still out on whether this has been a success or not."

With Eastern Europe opening up, Western governments and agencies, such as the U.S. Agency for International Development, sent visiting journalists to train local news organizations in how to operate in a free society.

But unforeseen problems quickly emerged. "Neither journalists nor their governments had much prior experience with press freedom, so they changed their constitutions but not their practices," Scott says. "Laws were adopted but never followed. In many nations, press freedom was a Potemkin Village erected for foreign visitors and their funding agencies.

"As computer technology spread, benefits and abuses have walked side-by-side," he said. "Hacking, copyright abuse and Internet fraud emanate from many computer cafes and newsrooms" in the former Eastern bloc countries. "No longer supported by the state, journalists have taken second and third jobs, some with the very news sources on which they report."

As Eastern Europeans fell into old patterns, press freedom suffered. "If you look at the annual rankings of Freedom House, Reporters Without Borders and IREX [a Washington-based nonprofit specializing in media development], for example, not much has changed in recent years. However, we know from looking at post-Salazar Portugal and post-Franco Spain that true change comes more slowly, with the passing of generations," he added, citing the repressive regimes of former Portuguese

Prime Minister António de Oliveira Salazar and Spanish dictator Francisco Franco.

"We have begun to see this in the nations of Central Europe that got a head start under *perestroika* and *glasnost*," he continued, referring to the economic reform and government transparency, respectively, instituted by Soviet leader Mikhail Gorbachev in the mid-1980s. "That process also is progressing in the Balkans with the influence of the European Union and Europeanization" — the process whereby former Soviet bloc countries must liberalize their press-freedom laws to qualify for EU membership. But such media reforms have "hardly begun in Central Asia and the Caucasus region, although there are some heartening examples of success."

Latin America Cracks Down

As communist governments were collapsing in Eastern Europe, authoritarian regimes in Latin America were disappearing as well. Over the past 30 years, all of Latin America's military juntas, except in Cuba, have been replaced by democratically elected governments that adopted more liberal press policies.

Then, as the 20th century drew to a close, "a veritable left-wing tsunami" appeared ready to hit the region, observed former Mexican Foreign Minister Jorge Castañeda. And, indeed, beginning with Hugo Chávez's victory in Venezuela in 1998, "a wave of leaders, parties and movements generically labeled 'leftist' swept into power in one Latin American country after another."[44]

But the news media have not always benefited from the new leftist governments. Despite widespread protests by Bolivian journalists, President Evo Morales recently signed into law a controversial measure allowing news outlets to be shut down and journalists jailed for publishing or writing about statements or acts deemed racist. Several Bolivian papers published blank front pages protesting, "There is no democracy without freedom of expression."[45]

Since taking office, Chávez has frequently vilified the press, while using politicized administrative procedures to force critical broadcasters off the air. Last year, authorities arrested Guillermo Zoloaga, president of the 24-hour opposition television news network Globovisión, and his son. Media watchdog organizations called the move part of a systematic campaign of harassment of the private media that also resulted in the closure of Radio Caracas

Palestinian photojournalist Nasser Shiyuki's camera goes flying as Israeli soldiers try to stop him from photographing a protest against Jewish settlements in the West Bank village of Beit Omar, near Hebron, on Sept. 25, 2010.

Televisión Internacional (RCTV), Venezuela's main critical cable television network, and dozens of private radio stations.[46] Chávez has also worked to closely align his country with Iran and Cuba, two nations with similarly restrictive press laws and policies.

With 22 reporters and editors in prison, Cuba is the third-biggest jailer of journalists in the world, after Iran and China.[47] Most of the Cuban journalists were imprisoned in March 2003, when 75 dissidents — including 29 journalists — were arrested in the so-called Black Spring roundup. After summary trials held within weeks, the journalists were sentenced to up to 28 years in prison on vague antistate charges connected to their reporting.[48]

Over the past seven years, Cuba has freed a small number of journalists in exchange for international political concessions, according to the Committee to Protect Journalists.[49] But in a country where the government has complete control of the media, independent journalists working for foreign-based news websites are routinely threatened and harassed by security police. Laws and regulations restricting Internet access continue to be among the most repressive in the world.[50]

Chinese 'Schizophrenia'

As China continues to make its mark on the global economy, leaders in Beijing are struggling to balance the

CHRONOLOGY

1980s *Press freedom reaches great heights and even greater lows as the Cold War comes to an end.*

1986 Colombian journalist Guillermo Cano Isaza is assassinated in front of his newspaper's offices in Bogotá on Dec. 17, after his writings offend Colombia's powerful drug barons. Since then the U.N. has marked World Press Freedom Day each year by conferring the UNESCO/Guillermo Cano World Press Freedom Prize.

1987 U.N. General Assembly adopts Article 19 of the Universal Declaration of Human Rights, declaring: "Everyone has the right to freedom of opinion and expression; . . . to hold opinions without interference and to seek, receive and impart information and ideas through any media and regardless of frontiers."

1989 Press freedom expands in former Soviet bloc after Berlin Wall falls.

Early 2000s *After the Sept. 11 terrorist attacks in the United States, journalists covering the wars in Afghanistan and Iraq encounter increased violence.*

2002 *Wall Street Journal* reporter Daniel Pearl is kidnapped and murdered in Pakistan by Muslim extremists. . . . More than 200 people die in riots in the Nigerian capital of Abuja after fashion writer Isioma Daniel, in an article about the Abuja Miss World beauty contest, writes that the Prophet Mohammed probably would have married one of the contestants.

2003 U.S. invasion of Iraq begins in March; more than 220 journalists and media assistants die during the six-and-a-half-year war.

Late 2000s *Olympic Games in Beijing and the Iranian presidential election draw the world's attention back to press censorship.*

2006 U.N. Security Council unanimously adopts Resolution 1738, which calls for war correspondents and associated personnel to be protected as civilians under the Geneva Conventions. . . . Russian Journalist Anna Politkovskaya is shot dead at her Moscow apartment, provoking international outrage. Politkovskaya had written frequently about human rights abuses in Chechnya for the *Novaya Gazeta* newspaper. In February 2009, three men were acquitted in her murder, but the Russian Supreme Court later ordered a new trial.

2008 Olympic Games in China shine international spotlight on limited press freedom in the communist country. Some official concessions are made toward foreign correspondents covering the Games, but Chinese journalists still face wide-ranging restrictions.

2009 On March 24 American TV journalists Euna Lee and Laura Ling are taken into custody by North Korean officials after "illegal intruding" from across the border with China. Both are pardoned on August 4 after former U.S. President Bill Clinton intercedes. . . . Disputed reelection of Iranian President Mahmoud Ahmadinejad on June 12 triggers a wave of antigovernment protests and the arrests of more than 170 journalists and bloggers. . . . In November, 32 journalists are murdered in a massacre during the run-up to the presidential election by gunmen linked to municipal leaders in a southern Philippine province. . . . Fourth World Electronic Media Forum in Mexico calls "for sustained and concrete international action to address the murder of journalists and media support staff . . . in peacetime and war."

2010 President Barack Obama in May directs U.S. State Department to cover press freedom in its annual global human rights reports. . . . About 60-70 of the journalists arrested after the 2009 Iranian election are still awaiting trial. The others are either in prison or were fined; many are forbidden from ever practicing journalism in Iran again. . . . Trial begins in the Philippines of accused murderers of 32 journalists. . . . In October, World Association of Newspapers and News Publishers awards its annual press freedom prize to Iranian journalist/political analyst Ahmad Zeid-Abadi, sentenced to six years in prison and banned from journalism on charges that he plotted to overthrow the government during his coverage of the 2009 election protests in Iran. . . . Twenty-three Chinese Communist Party elders release an open letter calling for an end to restrictions on free speech and the media in China.

Journalism Proves Lethal in the Philippines

Will the alleged murderers of 32 journalists be convicted?

Luis Teodoro, director of the Manila-based Center for Media Freedom and Responsibility, discusses the ongoing challenges facing journalists in the Philippines following the massacre on Nov. 23, 2009, of 57 unarmed civilians — including 32 journalists. They were shot to death in broad daylight by a group of gunmen allegedly hired by the politically powerful Ampatuan family of Maguindanao Province. Teodoro, who answered reporter Jennifer Koons' questions via e-mail, teaches journalism at the University of the Philippines' College of Mass Communication, where he was dean from 1994 until 2000. He is also editor of the Philippine Journalism Review.

Has journalism in the Philippines changed since the massacre?

Journalism hasn't changed since Nov. 23, 2009. Many journalists assume that what happened to others won't happen to them, which I suppose is a cultural trait. Filipinos are basically optimistic despite their historical and current experience. So they persist in writing their usual stories.

Do you believe those responsible for the Maguindanao massacre will be found guilty?

Because there are 197 accused of planning and participating in the massacre, and more than 200 prosecution witnesses, the trial will take at least five years, during which anything can happen, including the witnesses' being killed or bought off. I am not optimistic that anyone will be punished, but some people say the Ampatuans are prepared to sacrifice Andal Ampatuan Jr., since the evidence against him at this point is overwhelming.

What are the biggest obstacles faced by journalists in your country?

One of the reasons the killing of journalists persists — 117 have been murdered since 1986 — is the failure to

Bodies mark the grisly scene of a politically motivated massacre on Mindanao Island in the southern Philippines on Nov. 23, 2009. Of the 57 victims, 32 were journalists. Members of a powerful local clan were charged with masterminding the murders and are being held in Manila, where their trial is expected to last several years.

Reuters/Erik de Castro

punish the killers. Only nine of these murders have led to the trial and imprisonment of the guilty, and no mastermind has ever been arrested and tried.

How much do Filipino journalists rely on the Internet and social networking sites like Twitter for stories?

Few of the several thousand journalists in the country, especially those in the provinces, rely on the Internet and social networking sites, but that's slowly starting to change as we get better access to these technologies.

---

need for more information while controlling content and maintaining power. The balancing act makes the government appear to be in a state of "schizophrenia" about media policy, said Council on Foreign Relations Senior Fellow Elizabeth C. Economy. It "goes back and forth, testing the line, knowing they need press freedom — and

the information it provides — but worried about opening the door to the type of freedoms that could lead to the regime's downfall."[51]

As a result, the past few years have been rocky for press freedom in China, where the government operates what is widely regarded as the world's most extensive

More Countries Now Have a Free Press

The percentage of countries with a free press has risen from 25 percent in 1980 to 35 percent in 2010, while the percentage without a free press has dwindled from 53 percent to 32 percent. The biggest improvement occurred in Russia and the former Soviet bloc countries, which went from having no press freedom in 1980 to 66 percent enjoying a free or partly free press in 2010. The Middle East and North Africa saw the least improvement: Only 5 percent of the countries had a free press in 1980 — a figure that has not changed in three decades.

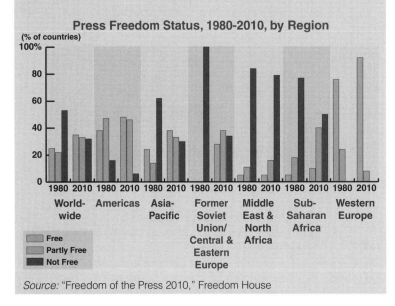

Press Freedom Status, 1980-2010, by Region

Source: "Freedom of the Press 2010," Freedom House

of this scale would mean only tighter controls."

The temporary loosening of controls on both local and foreign media leading up to the Olympics — and then the welcome announcement that the less restrictive regulations for foreign media would remain in force past October 2008 — generated hope for positive change on the press-freedom front. But the optimism quickly faded early in 2009, as authorities sought to reexert control, focusing in particular on the rising power of the Internet as a means for social expression and organizing.[52]

According to Bandurski, "2009 was a year of intensified control of the Internet and new media in China. These controls had a devastating effect on many small and medium-sized websites in China and sent a general chill through China's Internet sector."

Then, last January, Google executives suddenly announced that the company would end its four-year practice of blocking search results that the Chinese government considered subversive or pornographic. Google reached the decision, it said, after Chinese computer hackers tried to steal

system of Web monitoring and filtering, blocking both pornographic sites and those seen as subversive to communist rule. The controls were relaxed temporarily before and during the 2008 Olympic Games in Beijing, but as soon as the international spotlight faded, authorities clamped down again.

"The issue of press freedom and the Beijing Olympics was decided when China was awarded host status years earlier," the University of Hong Kong's Bandurski says. "In fact, China never promised press freedom for the Beijing Olympics." China only committed to allowing foreign journalists to have access to the Olympics. "The core issue for press freedom in China is the environment that faces China's own journalists, and Chinese journalists understood from the beginning that an international event

the company's technology and e-mail information from Chinese human rights activists.[53] Eventually, Google won permission to continue operating in the country after agreeing to eliminate an automatic detour around China's online censorship requirements.

Starting in March, Google began automatically rerouting search requests from the Google.cn site on the mainland to its Hong Kong service, which isn't subject to Beijing's censorship rules.*

---

* Chinese censorship rules don't apply to Hong Kong, which is recognized by international treaty as being vested with independent judicial power.

After Chinese officials threatened not to renew the company's operating license, Google compromised. Search requests from within mainland China now require an extra click to get to the Hong Kong site.[54] Since Google must renew its license with China on an annual basis, the issue could arise again if the authorities become displeased with the current arrangement.

Some observers have pointed out that because all companies must comply with China's censorship demands as a condition of doing business in China, "Google knew, or should have known, what kind of environment it was dealing with when it entered the country," Bandurski notes. "But 2009 demonstrated just how capricious China's Internet sector is as a result of political controls, and that undoubtedly forms some of the background for Google's confrontation."

President Hu Jintao at first seemed flexible. Shortly after assuming office in 2003, Hu told Chinese lawmakers, "The removal of restrictions on the press, and the opening up of public opinion positions, is a mainstream view and demand held by society; it is natural, and should be resolved through the legislative process. If the Communist Party does not reform itself, if it does not transform, it will lose its vitality and move toward natural and inevitable extinction."[55] In the past seven years, however, Hu has taken a tougher stance than some expected in regulating content and prosecuting journalists.

Nevertheless, some of China's staterun media have been allowed to pursue some level of commercialization — to profit from selling ads while remaining tied to the state structure. According to a government report, there are more than 2,000 privately owned newspapers, 8,000 magazines and 374 TV stations.[56]

"Journalists in China face a host of struggles — social, economic, political and personal. But the most important restrictions are still political, and these are many-faceted," Bandurski says. "Media receive daily directives from propaganda authorities about what they can and cannot report, or what they must.

"However, controls are much less ideologically driven today than in the past," he explains. "They are no longer about violations of Marxist ideology or the party line but more often about protecting the vested interests of entrenched party leaders." As a result, many of today's press restrictions are carried out "to protect commercial and political interests, which are often one and the same. So the protection of journalists and their professional work must be dealt with ultimately through political reforms."

CURRENT SITUATION

Press Freedom Today

After two decades of progress, mostly in former Soviet bloc countries, press freedom recently has begun declining in almost every part of the world, according to Freedom House's most recent annual report.

"Only 16 percent of the world's citizens live in countries that enjoy a free press," the report said. "In the rest of the world, governments as well as non-state actors control the viewpoints that reach citizens and brutally repress independent voices who aim to promote accountability, good governance, and economic development."[57]

As fast as reporters in repressive societies adopt new technologies — like cell phones, the Internet, Facebook and Twitter — to connect to the outside world, governments like China, Iran and Venezuela devise sophisticated new tools to control the flow of online information. Or regimes take the easier route: Using heavy-handed, old-school methods such as intimidation and violence to control the media.

The 10 nations that made Freedom House's "worst of the worst" list were Belarus, Burma (or Myanmar), Cuba, Equatorial Guinea, Eritrea, Iran, Libya, North Korea, Turkmenistan and Uzbekistan. In these countries — scattered across the globe —"independent media are either nonexistent or barely able to operate, the press acts as a mouthpiece for the regime, citizens' access to unbiased information is severely limited and dissent is crushed through imprisonment, torture and other forms of repression," according to the report. Despite hope that the advent of the Internet and other new media would lead to improvements in these countries, most of their scores have remained stagnant.

In one notable development, however, Iran replaced Zimbabwe in the worst-performing group. Zimbabwe's score improved slightly after the new "government of national unity" led to "small openings in media coverage and editorial bias, as well as less stringent application of

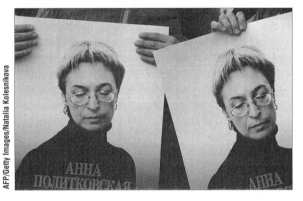

Murdered Journalists

Prominent Iraqi TV anchorman Riad al-Saray (top) is shown anchoring an Al-Iraqiya news broadcast before he was shot while driving his car on Sept. 7 in Baghdad, bringing to 15 the number of Al-Iraqiya reporters murdered since the Iraq War began. Not considered a controversial journalist, al-Saray sought to reconcile Shiites and Sunnis in his broadcasts. Of the 735 journalists killed worldwide in the past decade because of their jobs, 170 died in Iraq — many during war coverage — making it the most dangerous country in the world for journalists over the 10-year period. Russian human rights activists (bottom) rally in Moscow on Oct. 7 to mark the fourth anniversary of the assassination of celebrated Russian investigative journalist Anna Politkovskaya, known for her critical coverage of the war in Chechnya.

Here is the situation elsewhere around the globe, according to Freedom House:

Sub-Saharan Africa —The steepest overall drop in press freedom occurred in this vast region. South Africa's ongoing battle over a proposed media tribunal pushed the country's press freedom ranking from "free" to "partly free," leaving southern Africa with no "free" countries for the first time in 20 years. Last year, incidents of violence, prosecutions, imprisonment and censorship occurred in Angola, Burundi, Cameroon, Democratic Republic of Congo, Ethiopia, Eritrea, Ghana, Nigeria, Somalia, Sudan and Uganda.[58] Press freedom in Kenya increased slightly after the post-election violence in 2008. In August 2010, Kenyans approved a new constitution, which ensures the right to freedom of expression and information.[59] Meanwhile, Nigerian officials sponsored a three-day national conference on promoting press freedom across the country.[60]

The Americas — In Latin America, where a deep-rooted culture of impunity prevails and authoritarian and populist regimes tolerate minimal scrutiny or criticism, reporting on organized crime, drug cartels and high-level corruption is fraught with danger. With chilling regularity, Mexican journalists are murdered, threatened, assaulted and harassed. Five journalists were killed in Honduras last year,[61] and Venezuelan radio journalist Orel Sambrano was shot in the back of the head on his way home from work in January 2010.[62] The United States continues to have a free press, but it faces several challenges, including the lack of a federal shield law to protect confidential sources, an economic threat from the nation's poor economic conditions and the increased polarization of news content.

Central and Eastern Europe/Former Soviet Union — Russia remains one of the world's more repressive and dangerous media environments. In April, an antiterrorism measure was proposed that would broaden the definition of "extremism" to include criticism of officials, punishable by fines and jail terms.[63] In Bulgaria, journalists are threatened by pervasive organized crime, assaults and death threats.[64] And six newspapers in Estonia published blank pages in March to protest a proposed law reducing protections for journalists' confidential sources.[65] On the other hand, the National Assembly of Armenia decriminalized defamation, including libel. If the legislation is signed into law, journalists could no longer be imprisoned for defamation.[66]

harsh media laws," while press freedom in Iran "suffered a dramatic deterioration, as both official and unofficial avenues for news and information sharing were severely curtailed" after the disputed presidential election. Journalists were arrested, imprisoned and tortured.

Is the climate for Chinese journalists worsening?

YES
Madeline Earp
Senior Asia Program Researcher, Committee to Protect Journalists

Written for *CQ Global Researcher*, October 2010

The climate for journalists in China is worsening in some ways, even as many Chinese journalists have more freedom than in the past. Foreign journalists operate more easily since regulations were relaxed during the 2008 Beijing Olympics, although local authorities still try to obstruct them, and their local news assistants and sources are often questioned or monitored.

Many Chinese journalists say the press-freedom climate has improved immeasurably over the last 30 years, partly because of the Internet and partly because more commercial news outlets exist. Yet, as distribution methods become more sophisticated, so do the state's information authorities. Censorship regulations have increased around sensitive events, including the Olympics, in the past three years, handed down to newsrooms (and increasingly to Internet portals) answerable to state sponsors. So while the Committee to Protect Journalists (CPJ) is finding professional journalists less likely to be imprisoned than a decade ago, that's partly because the system to stifle aggressive reporting in-house is strengthening.

When editors and journalists cross the line, they may be reprimanded, demoted or fired — punitive actions that are less visible to the outside world. Banned news stories circulate online, but censors work to erase them. When the story is too big — like imprisoned Chinese dissident Liu Xiaobo winning the Nobel Peace Prize — propaganda to undermine it ("Nobel win criticized") appears in the mainstream media. So the version that remains on record is the one selected to favor the Communist Party.

Journalists who work independently online are especially vulnerable. The CPJ counted 24 journalists in Chinese prisons in 2009, many of them activists or minorities who published online. Gheyret Niyaz, a Uighur website editor, was sentenced last summer to 15 years for endangering state security after he wrote about 2009 ethnic unrest in the Xinjiang Uighur Autonomous Region.

In an October report, the CPJ found a debate raging in the Chinese media on "press rights." The government has pledged to protect journalists — and many media outlets are publicizing cases in which reporters are harassed by local police or security guards. This is a positive development. CPJ also found that while the state continues to repress the media, it remains a superficial development.

Journalists in China are energetically overcoming many restrictions. But that will not amount to an improved climate until the state allows a genuinely independent media.

NO
David Bandurski
Researcher, China Media Project, University of Hong Kong

Written for *CQ Global Researcher*, October 2010

China's media environment is a very complicated terrain. It doesn't lend itself to simplistic characterizations of tightening vs. opening. To really understand the situation facing journalists in China, one must balance a very complex equation involving many factors, not just state controls.

For example, media commercialization – allowing commercial spin-offs of state-run newspapers that survive by selling advertising, but are still formally tied into the state structure — is changing the relationship between media and society in China. The Chinese media consumer now has greater power than ever before: Journalistic professionalism is increasing, and technology is advancing, enabling the growth of the Internet and new tools such as Twitter-like microblogs. And while the Chinese Communist Party (CCP) has remained determined to control the media to maintain party rule, which leaders call "public opinion guidance," broader social and economic change in China has complicated this goal and opened up interesting new spaces for journalism.

Nevertheless, Chinese journalists face new hurdles. The Chinese government has imposed new curbs on investigative reporting, which enjoyed rather strong growth from the late 1990s to 2004. In 2004, the CCP officially curbed the practice of what it calls "extra-territorial reporting" (*yidi jiandu*), which refers to journalists from one city or province reporting hard news or exposés in another region. In a country where media are still controlled directly by party officials in their jurisdiction, "extra-territorial reporting" has been an important tool of professional journalists, allowing them to report harder-hitting stories without fear of reprisals from their immediate party superiors.

But provincial party leaders complained that the practice was hindering their work. The government has not banned extra-territorial reporting, but it has given officials extra leverage in fighting back against tough news stories. Secondly, Chinese media and journalists are facing much greater resistance from both local governments and corporations.

The resistance reflects the development and entrenchment of special-power interests during the country's economic boom in the absence of substantial political reforms — what some have characterized as "market-Leninism." Vested party, government and commercial entities now work aggressively to contain news and information that contravenes their interests. As a result, officials now restrict reporting on corporations, and some companies now intimidate or even attack journalists. Thus, say some Chinese journalists, while the space for reporting on certain issues such as corporate corruption has formally expanded in China, in other instances reporting has become more hazardous.

AFP/Getty Images/Sabah Arar

Iraqi journalists protest attempts to muzzle journalists on Aug. 14, 2009, after an influential Shiite political leader reportedly threatened violence against a local journalist for reporting that the cleric was linked to a deadly July 28, 2009, bank robbery. The cartoon reads "Don't kill the truth."

Middle East and North Africa — In the aftermath of the crackdown on protests following its disputed 2009 election, Iran remains one of the world's most inhospitable countries for journalists. Hundreds of local journalists have been arrested, and Iranian newspapers have been explicitly warned to stay away from touchy subjects. The rapidity with which the press-freedom situation deteriorated in Iran has been shocking, says CPJ's Simon. "Imprisoned journalists are held incommunicado, abused, tortured, some die in custody, . . . it's a very, very alarming situation," he says. "While Iran was never an open society, there was a certain level of tolerance for critical journalism and some thriving independent media outlets. Those are gone, many leading journalists are in jail, and the future for freedom of expression in Iran looks very bleak indeed."

Neighboring Iraq is also a dangerous place to practice journalism; two local TV anchors were murdered in September.[67] Harassment, defamation suits and other measures are commonly used in Bahrain, Yemen, the Palestinian Territories, Egypt and Tunisia to control the press and limit freedom of information.

Asia-Pacific — As China continues to closely monitor journalists, 23 Communist Party elders, in a surprising development, released an open letter in October calling for an end to restrictions on free speech and the media. "If the Communist Party does not reform itself, does not

transform, it will lose its vitality and die a natural death," warned the letter, which was posted on the Internet. The signers included a former secretary to Mao Zedong and a former publisher of the *People's Daily*, the official Communist Party newspaper.[68]

Meanwhile, other governments across Asia continue to impose various press restrictions, including state interference in day-to-day newsgathering and impunity for violent retribution against journalists. Kidnapping and the deliberate targeting of journalists make Pakistan — where six journalists have been killed so far this year — one of the more dangerous countries for media professionals in 2010.[69] North Korea continued its tight control over the media and even arrested two U.S. journalists, Euna Lee and Laura Ling, caught near the North Korean-Chinese border region where they were reporting on the trafficking of North Korean women into China's sex trade industry. They were found guilty and sentenced to 12 years of hard labor for allegedly entering the country illegally. But after 140 days in custody, the reporters were freed on humanitarian grounds after former President Bill Clinton flew to Pyongyang and met with North Korean leader Kim Jong Il on their behalf.[70]

Deadliest Country

But the most dangerous place on Earth for journalists in 2009 was the Philippines, where in September the first trial began in Manila against some of the nearly 200 suspects charged in connection with the 2009 slaughter of 57 people, including 32 journalists.[71]

The gruesome, premeditated massacre was "a shocking display of barbarism apparently motivated by political clan rivalries," said the Committee to Protect Journalists. It was the bloodiest attack on journalists since CPJ began documenting violence against the press 18 years ago.[72] The journalists were apparently caught up in a long-running feud between powerful rival political clans in a lawless region of Muslim-dominated Mindanao, one of the poorest islands in the Southeast Asian archipeligo.

On Nov. 23, 2009, the reporters were traveling in an eight-car convoy with family members and relatives of mayoral candidate Esmael Mangudadatu to watch him file papers to run for governor of Maguindanao Province. The convoy was stopped at a checkpoint, said a farmer who lives nearby, when nearly a dozen vehicles — including police cars and a Hummer outfitted with a .50-caliber sniper rifle — with more than 60 heavily armed, camouflage-wearing men arrived and ordered the reporters and others out of their cars. According to the witness, the local mayor, Andal Ampatuan, Jr., his uncle and the police chief were among those who slapped, kicked and punched the 57 victims before forcing them at gunpoint to an isolated field where pits had been dug by backhoes.[73] The victims — 15 of whom were women, including the candidate's wife — were then shot dead, he told the court, and most were buried in the mass graves.[74]

Another witness — former Ampatuan employee Lakmudin Salio — told the court that six days before the massacre he overheard the Ampatuans planning the murders at dinner. Later, he said, family patriarch Andal Sr. — the mayor's father and former Maguindanao governor — tried to bribe national and local officials in an effort to keep his family from being prosecuted. However, both Andal Jr. and Sr. have been charged in connection with the murders, as was the uncle, 16 policemen and more than 170 others. At least 100 people who have been indicted are still at large. Five potential witnesses have been murdered.[75]

But those weren't the only journalists killed in the Philippines recently. In June, seven months after the Maguindanao massacre, two outspoken radio broadcasters who had criticized corruption among local officials were killed in separate attacks at opposite ends of the country during a 24-hour period.[76] Police found no suspects, but Filipino media groups pointed out that the attacks appeared to follow a typical pattern in which journalists are targeted for exposing corruption, and their murderers are rarely prosecuted.

The Filipino journalists killed this past year are just the latest of 145 to die in the line of duty in the 25 years since the late dictator Ferdinand Marcos left office and press freedom was restored to the country, according to Journalists of the Philippines (NUJP) Vice Chairman Nonoy Espina.[77] There is scant accountability in a nation where journalists — like human rights attorneys and advocates — often face violence and intimidation, says Luis Teodoro, director of the Philippines-based Center for Media Freedom and Responsibility.

"The conditions which make these killings possible must be removed," Teodoro told Agence France-Presse in June 2010. "That means you are going to have to punish the guilty and show that the justice system works. You

Targeted in Pakistan

Eight years after American journalist Daniel Pearl — being remembered in a musical tribute in Islamabad in October (top) — was kidnapped and beheaded by Muslim extremists in Pakistan, the country is still a dangerous place for journalists. A Pakistani journalist calls for help (bottom) after a suicide bomb attack at the gate of the Peshawar Press Club last Dec. 22 killed three people and wounded 17.

must show that one cannot just kill anybody and get away with it."[78]

To fight the deep-seated climate of impunity in the Philippines, CPJ has worked for three years with local Filipino partners in its Global Campaign Against Impunity. The program presses government officials for greater

AFP/Getty Images/Reinnier Kaze

Cameroonian journalists continue their demonstration on May 3, 2010, in another part of the capital city of Yaoundé after police forcefully prevented several hundred of them from staging a sit-in at the prime minister's office. The journalists are marking World Press Freedom Day and protesting the death in prison earlier in the year of popular newspaper editor Bibi Ngota.

resolve, provides legal support and assistance to victims' families and pursues legal tactics that improve the odds for arrests and convictions.[79]

OUTLOOK

'Critical Juncture'

As the beleaguered news business struggles to survive in the Internet age, media organizations are expected to rely increasingly on local journalists, particularly freelancers and bloggers — the very people who are least protected by big media institutions.

"We're at a very critical juncture right now," says Simon of the Committee to Protect Journalists. "You're seeing several trends simultaneously. First, media institutions in most developed countries around the world are facing the deepest threat to their business model in a generation [so] they are cutting resources. And one of the resources they are cutting is international coverage. Those who step into the breach are freelancers and local journalists."

While international journalists are often well-protected — with flak jackets, armored cars and armed guards, not to mention lawyers — local journalists usually do not have the means to protect themselves sufficiently,

either from gunshots or from government action. Thus, they have traditionally been the easiest targets for censorship, harassment — and even murder. In 2009, more than 90 percent of the unsolved murders of journalists were local reporters killed in their home countries, according to CPJ.[80]

That is especially true in conflict zones. "In Afghanistan, Iraq and now Pakistan . . . those being killed are almost exclusively local journalists," says Sherry Ricchiardi, a senior writer specializing in international affairs for the *American Journalism Review* and a professor of journalism at Indiana University. "They are targeted by all sides." While several foreign correspondents were killed at the beginning of the Iraq War in 2003 and 2004, Iraqi journalists are now the primary targets, especially photographers and TV journalists who are easier to spot. And in Pakistan and Afghanistan local journalists who have consistently provided much of the frontline coverage have been exposed to greater risk.

Moreover, according to Simon, nine out of 10 journalist murders show signs of premeditation — such as careful planning, groups of assailants and gang-style executions. Journalists can be targeted by rebel groups, militias, drug traffickers, extremists or corrupt politicians — both in conflict zones and in countries where press freedom is not sufficiently valued.

Government officials realize that local reporters, who speak the language and are known in their communities, can uncover damaging information, so "they're taking steps to limit this kind of information," he adds. But in repressive societies, he adds, "institutions that would normally protect journalists are not there. So when governments take steps against bloggers and freelancers in their own countries, they are vulnerable. There will be an increase in the number of journalists in jail in places like Iran."

As a result, he predicts, "Five years from now we could have a Balkanized world confined to certain spheres where information does not reach the vast majority of society."

Jennifer Windsor, executive director of Freedom House, describes the declining press freedom around the world as inherently troubling but also emblematic of more serious problems.[81]

"Freedom of expression is fundamental to all other freedoms. Rule of law, fair elections, minority rights, freedom of association and accountable government all depend on an independent press, which can fulfill its watchdog function," she says. "When the Iranian Revolutionary Guards torture a journalist, or communist authorities in China imprison a blogger or criminal elements in Russia assassinate yet another investigative reporter, it sends a clear message that every person fighting for basic rights is vulnerable to a similar fate."[82]

NOTES

1. Katherine Corcoran, "Juarez editorial ignites a beleaguered Mexico," The Associated Press, Sept. 25, 2010, www.google.com/hostednews/ap/article/ALeqM5jm93hjH5nQsBSdR19AJyiQSmfV8gD9IDQVC82; and "¿Qué quieren de nosotros?" *El Diario de Juarez*, Sept. 18, 2010, www.diario.com.mx/notas.php?f=2010/09/18&id=6b124801376ce134c7d6ce2c7fb8fe2f.

2. "Luis Carlos Santiago," Committee to Protect Journalists, Sept. 16, 2010, http://cpj.org/killed/2010/luis-carlos-santiago.php.

3. "Journalist Murdered by Drug Gang in Cuidad Juarez," Reporters Without Borders, Nov. 14, 2008, http://en.rsf.org/mexico-journalist-murdered-by-drug-gang-14-11-2008,29293.

4. "Silence or Death in Mexico's Press," Committee to Protect Journalists, Sept. 8, 2010, http://cpj.org/reports/2010/09/silence-or-death-in-mexicos-press.php.

5. *Ibid.*

6. Tracy Wilkinson, "Under Threat From Mexican Drug Cartels, Reporters Go Silent," *Los Angeles Times*, Aug. 16, 2010, http://articles.latimes.com/2010/aug/16/world/la-fg-mexico-narco-censorship-20100816.

7. "Silence or Death in Mexico's Press," *op. cit.*

8. Wilkinson, *op. cit.*

9. "Freedom of the Press 2010," Freedom House, www.freedomhouse.org/template.cfm?page=251&year=2010.

10. "37 Journalists Killed in 2010/Motive Confirmed," Committee to Protect Journalists, 2010, www.cpj.org/killed/2010/.

11. "CPJ's 2009 Prison Census: Freelance Journalists Under Fire," Committee to Protect Journalists, Dec. 8, 2009, www.cpj.org/reports/2009/12/freelance-journalists-in-prison-cpj-2009-census.php.

12. "52 Journalists Killed in Russia Since 1992," Committee to Protect Journalists, www.cpj.org/killed/europe/russia/.

13. "Getting Away With Murder," Committee to Protect Journalists, http://cpj.org/killed/europe/russia/murder.php.

14. For background, see "Attacks on the Press 2009: Yemen," Committee to Protect Journalists, www.cpj.org/2010/02/attacks-on-the-press-2009-yemen.php.

15. *Ibid.*

16. *Ibid.*

17. Andrew Geoghegan, "Journalists Fear Return to Apartheid-Era Laws," ABC News Online, Aug. 18, 2010, www.abc.net.au/news/stries/2010/08/18/2986773.htm.

18. *Ibid.*

19. *Ibid.*

20. M. J. Bear and Jane Hall, "Media coverage of the War in Iraq," American University School of Communication, March 17, 2005, http://ics.leeds.ac.uk/papers/vp01.cfm?outfit=pmt&folder=193&paper=2246.

21. "Malaysians Use Social Media to Bypass Censorship," Agence France-Presse, Aug. 18, 2010, www.asiaone.com/News/Latest%2BNews/DigitalOne/Story/A1Story20100818-232717.html.

22. *Ibid.*

23. "Press Freedom Index 2009," Reporters Without Borders, http://en.rsf.org/press-freedom-index-2009,1001.html.

24. "Authoritarianism Prevents Press Freedom Progress in Much of Asia," Reporters Without Borders, Oct. 20, 2009, http://en.rsf.org/asia-authoritarianism-prevents-press-20-10-2009,34788.html.

25. *Ibid.*

26. *Ibid.*

27. "Government Uses State of Emergency to Escalate Censorship," Reporters Without Borders, April 8, 2010, http://en.rsf.org/thailand-government-uses-state-of-emergency-08-04-2010,36968. For background, see Barbara Mantel, "Democracy in Southeast Asia," *CQ Global Researcher*, June 1, 2010, pp. 131-156.

28. Danny O'Brien, "In Censoring Web, Thailand Could Worsen Crisis," Committee to Protect Journalists, April 12, 2010, http://cpj.org/blog/2010/04/in-censoring-Web-thailand-could-worsen-crisis.php.

29. *Ibid.*

30. Robert Marquand, "Yahoo, Chinese police, and a jailed journalist," *The Christian Science Monitor*, Sept. 9, 2005, www.csmonitor.com/2005/0909/p01s03-woap.html. Also see Ilya Garger, "Yahoo China is under fire again," Marketwatch, Wall Street Journal Digital Network, April 28, 2006, www.marketwatch.com/story/yahoo-helps-china-jail-dissidents-says-rights-group.

31. Anthony Mills, "World Press Freedom Review: Syria," International Press Institute, Feb. 9, 2010, www.freemedia.at/publications/world-press-freedom-review/singleview/4749/.

32. *Ibid.*

33. "Cyber Dissident Sentenced Habib Saleh To Three Years Jail," Reporters Without Borders, March 16, 2009, http://en.rsf.org/syria-cyber-dissident-habib-saleh-16-03-2009,30591.html.

34. Joe Sterling, "Report: Mideast, North African Countries Censor, Control Media," CNN.com, Feb. 12, 2010, http://insidethemiddleeast.blogs.cnn.com/2010/02/12/report-mideast-north-african-countries-censor-control-media/.

35. *Ibid.*

36. Mohamed Abdel Dayem, "Middle East Bloggers: The Street Leads Online," Committee to Protect Journalists, Oct. 14, 2009, www.cpj.org/reports/2009/10/middle-east-bloggers-the-street-leads-online.php.

37. For background, see "Press Freedom in the Americas," Committee to Protect Journalists' Executive Director Joel Simon's Testimony before the House Subcommittee on the Western Hemisphere, June 16, 2010, http://foreignaffairs.house.gov/111/sim061610.pdf.

38. Sara Miller Llana, "Obama Grants Interview to Cuban Blogger Yoani Sanchez," *The Christian Science Monitor*, Nov. 20, 2009, www.csmonitor.com/World/Global-News/2009/1120/obama-grants-interview-to-cuba-blogger-yoani-sanchez.

39. "Obama Responses Stun Cuban Blogger Yoani Sanchez," Carlos Lauria, Committee to Protect Journalists, Nov. 19, 2009, http://cpj.org/blog/2009/11/obama-responses-stun-cuban-blogger-yoani-sanchez.php.

40. For background, see Amartya Sen, *Development as Freedom* (1999).

41. For background, see the Global Forum for Media Development, October 2005, http://70.87.64.34/~intint/gfmd_info/index.php?option=com_content&task=view&id=40&Itemid=93.

42. See *Right to Tell: The Role of Mass Media In Economic Development* (2002).

43. Claire Ferris-Lay, "No Progress on Press Freedom, Al Jazeera Chief," *ArabianBusiness.com*, July 4, 2010, www.arabianbusiness.com/591970-no-progress-on-mideast-press-freedom---al-jazeera-chief.

44. Jorge G. Casteñada, "Latin America's Left Turn," *Foreign Affairs*, May/June 2006, www.foreignaffairs.com/articles/61702/jorge-g-castaneda/latin-americas-left-turn. For background, see Roland Flamini, "The New Latin America," *CQ Global Researcher*, March 1, 2008, pp. 57-84.

45. Carlos A. Quiroga, "Bolivia's Morales signs racism law as media fret," Reuters, Oct. 8, 2010, www.reuters.com/article/idUSN0822976220101008.

46. "Press Freedom in the Americas," *op. cit.*

47. *Ibid.*

48. Sara Miller Llana, "Cuba Prisoner Release: Seven 'Black Spring' Dissidents are Freed in Spain," *The Christian Science Monitor*, July 13, 2010, www.csmonitor.com/World/Americas/2010/0713/Cuba-prisoner-release-Seven-Black-Spring-dissidents-are-freed-in-Spain.

49. "Newly Freed, Six Cuban Journalists Arrive in Spain," Committee to Protect Journalists, July 13, 2010, http://cpj.org/2010/07/newly-freed-six-cuban-journalists-arrive-in-spain.php.

50. *Ibid.*

51. Carin Zissis, Corinne Baldwin and Preeti Bhattacharji, "Media Censorship in China," Council on Foreign Relations, May 27, 2010, www.cfr.org/publication/11515/media_censorship_in_china.html.

52. "China: New Restrictions Target Media," Human Rights Watch, March 18, 2009, www.hrw.org/en/news/2009/03/18/china-new-restrictions-target-media.

53. Ellen Nakashima, Steven Mufson and John Pomfret, "Google Threatens to Leave China After Attacks on Activists' E-Mail," *The Washington Post*, Jan. 13, 2010, www.washingtonpost.com/wp-dyn/content/article/2010/01/12/AR2010011203024.html.

54. Michael Liedtke, "Google Wins Permission to Keep Website in China," The Associated Press, July 9, http://abcnews.go.com/Technology/wireStory?id=11123889.

55. Li Rui, *et al.*, "China Must Abandon Censorship," *Guardian*, Oct. 13, 2010, www.guardian.co.uk/commentisfree/2010/oct/13/china-censorship-freedom-speech.

56. *Ibid.*

57. "Freedom of the Press, 2010," *op. cit.*

58. *Ibid.*

59. Dennis Itumbi, "Kenya's new constitution good news for media," *Journalism.co.za*, August 2010, www.journalism.co.za/index.php?option=com_content&Itemid=51&catid=168&id=3367&view=article.

60. "National Conference Could Herald Start of New Era for Niger's Media," Reporters Without Borders, April 1, 2010, http://en.rsf.org/niger-national-conference-could-herald-01-04-2010,36931.html.

61. Roy Greenslade, "Two More Journalists Killed in Honduras," *Guardian*, March 29, 2010, www.guardian.co.uk/media/greenslade/2010/mar/29/honduras-press-freedom.

62. "Ole Sambrano," Committee to Protect Journalists, Jan. 16, 2009, http://cpj.org/killed/2009/orel-sambrano.php.

63. "Freedom House Calls on Medvedev to Veto FSB Legislation," Freedom House, July 16, 2020, www.freedomhouse.org/template.cfm?page=70&release=1210.

64. Clive Leviev-Sawyer, "Bulgaria Has Lowest Press Rankings in EU," *Sofia Echo*, Oct. 20, 2009, http://sofiaecho.com/2009/10/20/802401_bulgaria-has-lowest-press-freedom-ranking-in-eu-reporters-without-borders.

65. "Estonian Press Protests Against the Source Protection Act," Estonian Free Press, March 2010, www.estonianfreepress.com/2010/03/estonian-press-protests-against-the-source-protection-act/.

66. "CPJ Welcomes Armenian Vote to Decriminalize Defamation," Committee to Protect Journalists, May 19, 2010, http://cpj.org/2010/05/cpj-welcomes-armenian-vote-to-decriminalize-defama.php.

67. "Second TV Anchor Gunned Down in Two Days in Iraq," Committee to Protect Journalists, Sept. 8, 2010, http://cpj.org/2010/09/second-tv-anchor-gunned-down-in-two-days-in-iraq.php.

68. "Open Letter from Party Elders Calls for Free Speech," China Media Project, Oct. 13, 2010, http://cmp.hku.hk/2010/10/13/8035/.

69. "Abducted British Journalist Freed in Pakistan," Committee to Protect Journalists, Sept. 9, 2010, http://cpj.org/2010/09/abducted-british-journalist-freed-in-pakistan.php.

70. Laura Ling and Euna Lee, "Hostages of the Hermit Kingdom," *Los Angeles Times*, Sept. 1, 2009, www.latimes.com/news/opinion/la-oe-lingleeweb2-2009sep02,0,7489638.story.

71. Oliver Teves, "Nearly 200 People Indicted in Philippine Massacre," The Associated Press, Feb. 9, 2010, http://news.yahoo.com/s/afp/20100908/wl_asia_afp/philippinespoliticsmassacretrial.

72. "Attacks on the Press 2009: Philippines," Committee to Protect Journalists, www.cpj.org/2010/02/attacks-on-the-press-2009-philippines.php.

73. "Philippine massacre victims 'begged for mercy,' "Agence France-Presse, Sept. 7, 2010, http://news.yahoo.com/s/afp/20100908/wl_asia_afp/philippinespoliticsmassacretrial.

74. Simon Montlake, "Philippines massacre trial: a test for justice and accountability," *The Christian Science Monitor*, Sept. 29, 2010; www.csmonitor.com/World/Asia-Pacific/2010/0929/Philippines-massacre-trial-a-test-for-justice-and-accountability. See also "2nd prosecution witness in Maguindanao massacre trial resumes testimony," Philippines News Agency, Oct. 6, 2010.

75. Montlake, *op. cit.*

76. Roy Greenslade, "Filipino Radio Journalists Murdered," *Guardian*, June 18, 2010, www.guardian.co.uk/media/greenslade/2010/jun/18/press-freedom-philippines.

77. Cecil Morella, "Outrage as Two More Journalists Killed in Philippines," Agence France-Presse, June 15, 2010, www.google.com/hostednews/afp/article/ALeqM5hiJCKV53HtMJgAwi8pylquJFi8uA.

78. *Ibid.*

79. "Attacks on the Press 2009: Philippines," *op. cit.*

80. "Getting Away With Murder," Committee to Protect Journalists, April 20, 2010, www.cpj.org/reports/2010/04/cpj-2010-impunity-index-getting-away-with-murder.php.

81. "Restrictions on Press Freedom Intensifying," Freedom House, April 29, 2010, www.freedomhouse.org/template.cfm?page=70&release=1177.

82. *Ibid.*

BIBLIOGRAPHY

Books

Bollinger, Lee C., *Uninhibited, Robust, and Wide-Open: A Free Press for a New Century*, Oxford University Press, 2010.
The president of Columbia University argues for spreading freedom of the press around the world.

Heinemann, Arnim, Olfa Lamloum and Anne Francoise Weber, eds., *The Middle East in the Media: Conflicts, Censorship and Public Opinion*, Saqi Books, 2010.
The rise of satellite television and the Internet have forced Middle Eastern governments to adapt their censorship methods. The editors are a researcher at the Orient-Institut (Heinemann), a researcher at the Institut Français du Proche-Orient (Lamloum) and a program manager at the Friedrich Ebert Foundation — all in Beirut.

Shirk, Susan L., ed., *Changing Media, Changing China*, Oxford University Press, Dec. 7, 2010.
A leading authority on contemporary China edited this collection of essays.

Articles

" 'Blogfather,' columnist get heavy prison terms in Iran," Committee to Protect Journalists, Sept. 28, 2010, http://cpj.org/2010/09/iranian-journalist-and-blogfather-receive-heavy-pr.php.
Two prominent journalists were jailed for comments about leading Iranian clerics.

"Philippine massacre victims 'begged for mercy,' " Agence France-Presse, Sept. 7, 2010, http://news.yahoo.com/s/afp/20100908/wl_asia_afp/philippinespoliticsmassacretrial.
During the first trial in the killings of more than 30 journalists in the Philippines, a witness said the victims begged for mercy before being shot.

Aumente, Jerome, "Lessons in Teaching Foreign Journalists," Nieman Reports, summer 2005, www.nieman.harvard.edu/reportsitem.aspx?id=101136.
A professor emeritus at the School of Communication, Information and Library Studies at Rutgers University reflects on his experience teaching foreign journalists how to avoid the party line and deal with threats of reprisals and kidnappings.

Baldauf, Scott, "Global News Agencies Uneasy over South Africa's Press Freedom," *The Christian Science Monitor*, Sept. 7, 2010, www.csmonitor.com/World/Africa/Africa-Monitor/2010/0907/Global-news-agencies-uneasy-over-South-Africa-s-press-freedom.
In a letter to South African President Jacob Zuma, four syndicated news services express concern over South Africa's plan to create a media tribunal to punish inaccurate reporting and limit scrutiny on much of the government's activities.

Bhattacharji, Preeti, *et al.*, "Media Censorship in China," Council on Foreign Relations, May 27, 2010, www.cfr.org/publication/11515/media_censorship_in_china.html.
A study of China's media climate finds growing demand for information is testing the regime's media controls.

Dehghan, Saeed Kamali, "Iran's Fight for Press Freedom," *Guardian*, Feb. 26, 2010, www.guardian.co.uk/commentisfree/2010/feb/26/iran-press-freedom-fight.

An Iranian reporter examines the crackdown on journalists in Iran, where more than 100 journalists and bloggers have been imprisoned since last year's disputed election.

Londoño, Ernesto, "Iraqi Journalist Sees Threats to Press Freedom," *The Washington Post*, Feb. 26, 2010, www.washingtonpost.com/wp-dyn/content/article/2010/02/25/AR2010022505730.html?sid=ST2010022506210.

Iraqi journalists continue to struggle with government restrictions and targeted violence.

Reports and Studies

"Freedom of the Press 2010," Freedom House, April 29, 2010, www.freedomhouse.org/templatecfm?page=533.

In its 2010 annual report, the pro-democracy watchdog organization found that global media freedom has declined for the eighth year in a row.

"World Press Freedom Index 2010," Reporters Without Borders, Oct. 20, 2010, http://en.rsf.org/press-freedom-index-2010,1034.html.

The press freedom watchdog organization's ninth annual report listed the 10 worst countries for journalists: Rwanda, Yemen, China, Sudan, Syria, Burma, Iran, Turkmenistan, North Korea and Eritrea. These countries were selected because of their "persecution of the media and a complete lack of news and information."

Lauría, Carlos, and Mike O'Connor, "Silence or Death in Mexico's Press," Committee to Protect Journalists, Sept. 8, 2010, http://cpj.org/reports/2010/09/silence-or-death-in-mexicos-press.php.

A special report on the impact of crime, violence and corruption on Mexican journalism concludes that systemic failures, if left unaddressed, will further erode freedom of expression and the rule of law.

For More Information

Arab Media Watch, P.O. Box 36134, London SW7 1WY, United Kingdom; (44) 7956 455 528; www.arabmediawatch.com. A media watchdog organization seeking objective British media coverage of the Arab world.

Committee to Protect Journalists, 330 Seventh Ave., 11th Floor, New York, NY 10001; (212) 465-1004, ext. 128; www.cpj.org. A nonprofit organization dedicated to the defense of press freedom around the world.

Division for Freedom of Expression, Democracy & Peace, UNESCO, Street 1, Rue Miollis, 75732 Paris, France; (33) 1 45 68 42 03; http://portal.unesco.org. The division of UNESCO dedicated to promoting freedom of expression.

Freedom House, 1301 Connecticut Ave., N.W., Floor 6, Washington, DC 20036; (202) 296-5101; www.freedomhouse.org. International organization that researches and advocates democracy, political freedom and freedom of expression worldwide.

Index on Censorship, Free Word Centre, 60 Farringdon Road, London EC1R 3GA, United Kingdom; (44) 20 7324 2522; www.indexoncensorship.org. A nongovernmental organization that covers news and issues related to freedom of expression across the globe.

International Press Institute, Spiegelgasse 2, A-1010 Vienna, Austria; (43) 1 512 90 11; www.freemedia.at. A global network of editors, journalists and media executives dedicated to protecting press freedom.

National Union of Journalists of the Philippines, 4/L Penthouse, FSS Building #89, Sct. Castor, Barangay Laging Handa, Quezon City 1103, Philippines; www.nujp.org. An organization dedicated to looking out for the interests of Filipino journalists.

Reporters without Borders, 47 rue Vivienne, 75002 Paris, France; (33) 1 44.83.84.84; http://en.rsf.org. An organization dedicated to promoting global press freedom

Voices From Abroad:

ROBERT KABUSHENGA

CEO, New Vision newspaper, Uganda

Finances for defense

"Press freedom issues go far beyond the quarrels between the state and the media. . . . It also revolves around the financial might of a media house. Those with a huge financial base cannot easily be intimidated. They can withstand oppression."

The Nation (Kenya) March 2010

NAY MYO WA

General Secretary, Peace and Diversity Party, Myanmar (formerly Burma)

Freedom equals truth

"There is a sense in the mind of the people that they all know there will be less inequality and injustice if they can enjoy greater press freedom. If there is press freedom, we can know the truth, and we can consider what is right and what is wrong."

Mizzima News Agency (India), September 2010

VIRGINIE JOUAN

Executive Director, World Association of Newspapers and News Publishers Darmstadt, Germany

How to silence journalists

"Journalists who find themselves facing harassment, death threats, attacks and imprisonment rightly fear for their lives and often are forced into exile. This frequently deprives them of the means to continue working as journalists, and effectively silences them. That's why we have dedicated our World Press Freedom Day initiative to exiled journalists, and are asking colleagues around the world to show support by focusing attention on their plight."

New Zealand Press Association April 2010

ARES.
caglecartoons.com/espanol

Caglecartoons.com/Ares

MOHAMMAD TAL

Editor-in-Chief, Ad Dustour Jordan

Freedom must seek truth

"The media of all types have a remarkable margin of freedom, and this must be utilized in the service of the profession through high-quality and professional performances that seek the truth."

Jordan Times, May 2010

GARY OLIVAR

Presidential Economic Spokesperson, Philippines

Our country remains free

"I hope it is clear that the Philippine press is one of the freest in the world and has nothing to fear from the national government, nor from a President who only last year — and all by herself — opposed the right to reply bill."

Philippine Star, January 2010

JIANG YU

Spokeswoman, Chinese Foreign Ministry

Stop the accusations

"The number of press staff has increased continuously. We urge the U.S. to respect the facts, view China's press freedom correctly and stop groundless accusations against China."

Xinhua News Agency, May 2010

AIDAN WHITE

General Secretary, International Federation of Journalists Brussels, Belgium

Intimidation tactics are unacceptable

"Intimidation and threats against the media led to a closure. It is unacceptable to happen in any country, and certainly not to happen in Ethiopia, which is the center of the coming together of African states in the new landscape they are trying to create in terms of world diplomacy."

Voice of America, January 2010

BOBBY GODSELL

Chairman, Business Leadership South Africa

More questions raised

"We just dispelled so many stupid ideas about our country. Now we've got people raising questions about whether our government believes in press freedom."

Miami Times, August 2010

YAVUZ BAYDAR

Ombudsman, Sabah (newspaper), Turkey

Freedom requires good relations

"There are several layers of problems in Turkey that cause curbs on press freedom. But the most important factor is the polluted relations between the media owners and Ankara that make editorial independence impossible."

The Washington Post, July 2010

5

Separatist Movements

Brian Beary

The American Embassy in Belgrade is set ablaze on Feb. 21 by Serbian nationalists angered by U.S. support for Kosovo's recent secession from Serbia. About 70 separatist movements are under way around the globe, but most are nonviolent. Kosovo is one of seven countries to emerge from the former Yugoslavia and part of a nearly fourfold jump in the number of countries to declare independence since 1945.

From *CQ Global Researcher*,
April 2008. (Updated 7/21/2011)

Angry protesters hurling rocks at security forces; hotels, shops and restaurants torched; a city choked by teargas. The violent images that began flashing around the world on March 14 could have been from any number of tense places from Africa to the Balkans. But the scene took place high in the Himalayas, in the ancient Tibetan capital of Lhasa. Known for its red-robed Buddhist monks, the legendary city was the latest flashpoint in Tibetan separatists' ongoing frustration over China's continuing occupation of their homeland. [1]

Weeks earlier, thousands of miles away in Belgrade, Serbia, hundreds of thousands of Serbs took to the streets to vent fury over Kosovo's secession on Feb. 17, 2008. Black smoke billowed from the burning U.S. Embassy, set ablaze by Serbs angered by Washington's acceptance of Kosovo's action. [2]

"As long as we live, Kosovo is Serbia," thundered Serbian Prime Minister Vojislav Kostunica at a rally earlier in the day. [3] Kosovo had been in political limbo since a NATO-led military force wrested the region from Serb hands in 1999 and turned it into an international protectorate after Serbia brutally clamped down on ethnic Albanian separatists. Before the split, about 75 percent of Serbia's population was Serbs, who are mostly Orthodox Christian, and 20 percent were ethnic Albanians, who are Muslim. [4]

Meanwhile, war-torn Iraq witnessed its own separatist-related violence on Feb. 22. Turkish forces launched a major military incursion into northern Iraq — the first big ground offensive in nearly a decade — to root out Kurdish separatist rebels known as the PKK,

Separatist Movements Span the Globe

Nearly two dozen separatist movements are active worldwide, concentrated in Europe and Asia. At least seven are violent and reflect ethnic or religious differences with the mother country.

Selected Separatist Hot Spots

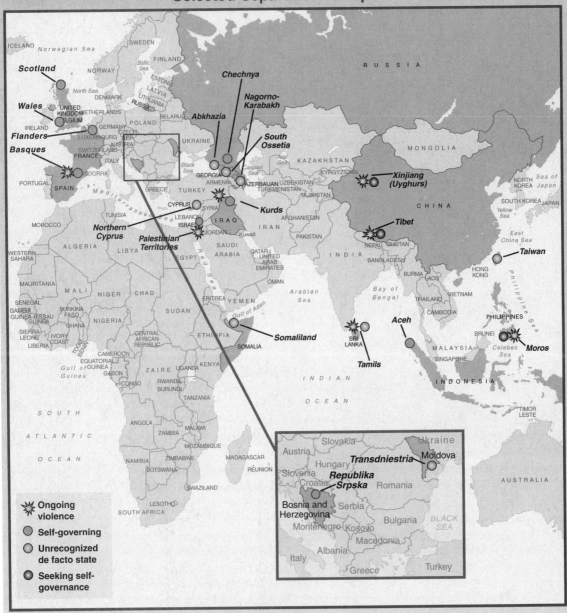

Legend:
- ☀ Ongoing violence
- ◯ Self-governing
- ◯ Unrecognized de facto state
- ◯ Seeking self-governance

Sources: Unrepresented Nations and People's Organization, www.unpo.org; *Political Handbook of the World 2007,* CQ Press

Ongoing Separatist Movements

Africa

Somaliland — Militants in this northern Somalia territory established an unrecognized de facto state in the 1990s after the government of Somalia collapsed. The area was ruled by the United Kingdom from 1884 to 1960 and then became unified with the former Italian-ruled Somalia from 1960 to 1989.

Asia/Eurasia

Abkhazia — Independent Soviet republic briefly in 1921. Subsequently united with Georgia. Declared independence in 1992; war with Georgia ensued, which the Abkhaz won with Russian support. Since then, a stalemate has persisted. Up to 300,000 Georgians have fled since the 1990s, leaving an estimated 100,000 Abkhaz as the dominant force.

Aceh — One of the first places where Islam was established in Southeast Asia. Indonesia annexed the territory in 1949 upon becoming independent. Aceh was granted autonomy in 1959 and declared independence in 1976, with thousands dying in violence since then. A further 100,000 were killed in the 2004 Indian Ocean tsunami. A peace agreement was signed in 2005 granting autonomy.

Chechnya — A Muslim region in southern Russia, Chechnya was briefly independent in 1922. It declared independence after the collapse of the Soviet Union, but Russia opposed the secession and went to war with Chechnya from 1994-1996 and again in 1999. It became an autonomous Russian republic after a 2003 referendum.

Kurds — The world's largest ethnic group without its own country resides in Iraq, Iran, Turkey and Syria. The Iraqi Kurds have had autonomy since 1991. In Iran and Turkey they have no autonomy but are relatively free to speak Kurdish. The language is banned in Syria.

Moros — Muslims in the southern Philippines who live primarily on the island of Mindanao. Migration by Christian Filipinos from the north has diluted the Moro population. A militant Islamic fundamentalist group, Abu Sayyaf, is fighting the government to create a Moro Muslim state. Malaysia has committed the most international peacekeeping forces to stem the violence.

Nagorno-Karabakh — Declared independence from Azerbaijan in 1991, followed by a three-year war, during which most of the Azeris fled. A ceasefire has existed since 1994. It is now a de facto independent republic — unrecognized by the international community — populated mostly by ethnic Armenians.

Palestinian Territories — Since the largely Jewish state of Israel came into being in 1948, Arabs from the former Palestine have had no country of their own. The Palestinians live mainly in two non-contiguous areas, the Gaza Strip and West Bank, which Israel occupied in 1967 after a war with Egypt, Jordan and Syria. While the Palestinians have their own civilian administration and neither Israel nor neighboring Arab countries claim sovereignty over them, there is no independent Palestinian state yet because the terms cannot be agreed upon. A violent conflict between Israelis and Palestinians has persisted for decades.

South Ossetia — This region, which became part of Georgia in 1922, tried to become autonomous in 1989, but Georgia refused. After a war from 1990 to 1992 it became a de facto independent republic. Referenda in 1992 and 2006 confirming independence have not been recognized by any other country. Ossetian towns are governed by the separatist government; Georgian towns are overseen by Georgia.

Taiwan — The island off China's southeastern coast was established as a rival Chinese government in 1949 following the defeat of Chiang Kai-shek's Nationalists by Mao Tse-tung's communists. Between 1949 and 1971, it was recognized by most countries as the official government of China, but in 1971 mainland China replaced it as China's representative in the United Nations. In the 1990s, the Taiwanese government started a campaign to become a U.N. member again. Politics is polarized between those favoring unification with China — who won two recent elections — and those seeking official independence.

Tamils — Militant separatists known as the Liberation Tigers of Tamil Eelam (LTTE) have run a de facto state in northern Sri Lanka for many years. The LTTE assassinated Indian Prime Minister Rajiv Gandhi in 1991 for helping Sri Lanka crack down on the Tamils and Sri Lankan Prime Minister Ranasinghe Premadasa in 1993. A ceasefire was declared in 2002, but violence resumed in 2005. The Tamils are predominantly Hindu whereas the majority-Sinhalese community is Buddhist.

(Continued)

(Continued)

Asia/Eurasia (*Cont.*)

Tibet — China took over the Buddhist region in western China by force in the 1950s. Tibet's spiritual leader, the Dalai Lama, fled in 1959 and set up a government-in-exile in India. Recent separatist violence has been fueled by resentment over Chinese immigration into the autonomous region and the government's continued refusal to grant independence. The violence has prompted the Dalai Lama to consider resigning as the head of the exiled government.

Xinjiang — Known as East Turkestan or Chinese Turkistan, this vast region on China's northwest border with Central Asia — which comprises one-sixth of China's land mass — was annexed by China in the 18th century. Its 18 million inhabitants include 47 ethnic groups, including the Turkic-speaking Muslim Uyghurs — who once comprised 90 percent of the population. Today the Uyghurs make up only 40 percent of the inhabitants due to government policies that encourage Han Chinese to migrate there. Although the region has been officially autonomous since 1955, ethnic tensions have escalated in recent years. The U.S. State Department complains of serious human rights abuses against the Uyghurs due to Beijing's efforts to forcibly assimilate them and undermine their culture. China says Uyghur separatists are Islamic terrorists.

Europe

Basque Country — Basques in northeast Spain and southwest France have been pushing for greater autonomy or independence for more than a century. The militant separatist group ETA has killed about 1,000 people since 1968. Spain has granted its Basques extensive political and cultural autonomy but France has not.

Flanders — Flemish nationalism has grown in recent decades in Flanders, the northern part of Belgium where 60 percent of the population lives, most of them Dutch-speaking. Flanders, which has grown wealthier than French-speaking Wallonia to the south, already has extensive autonomy, but most Flemings would like more; many favor full independence.

Northern Cyprus — When Cyprus gained independence from British rule in 1960, relations between the Turks and Greeks on the island quickly deteriorated. Turkey's invasion in 1973 led to the Turkish Cypriots creating their own de facto state in the north that is only recognized by Turkey.

Republika Srpska — This self-governing territory within Bosnia, created in 1992, is populated mainly by ethnic Serbs who opposed Bosnia's secession from Yugoslavia. Moves to integrate it with the rest of Bosnia have failed so far.

Scotland and Wales — Demands by Celtic peoples in the northern and western corners of the United Kingdom for greater control over their affairs resulted in a devolution of power in 1999: A parliament was installed in Scotland and an assembly in Wales.

Transdniestria — First became a part of Moldova in 1812 when Russia captured both territories. From 1917 to 1939 it was part of the Soviet Union, while the rest of Moldova was ruled by Romania. From 1945 to 1991 both parts fell under Soviet rule. In 1992, when Moldova became an independent country Transdniestria seceded amid fear that Moldova would unify with Romania. The Moldovan army was repelled with the support of the Russian army. Its secession has not been recognized internationally. The area is dominated by Russian-speakers, with the Russian military also present.

The Americas (not shown on map)

Bolivia — After Evo Morales, Bolivia's first indigenous president, proposed changing the constitution last year to share more of the country's natural resources with the nation's indigenous highlanders, the mainly European-descended lowlanders have been threatening to secede.

Lakota Nation — This Indian nation of eight tribes living in South Dakota and neighboring states signed a treaty with the United States in 1851 granting them land rights. In 1989 they were awarded $40 million for losses incurred based on an 1868 land-rights treaty. In December 2007 a group of dissident Lakota delivered a declaration of independence to the State Department, which did not respond.

Québec — This majority French-speaking province has been threatening to secede from Canada since the 1960s. In two referenda on independence — in 1980 and 1995 — the Québécois voted to remain part of Canada. Today, they have a large degree of regional autonomy.

Sources: Unrepresented Nations and People's Organization, *www.unpo.org;* Political Handbook of the World 2007, CQ Press

who have waged a bloody independence campaign against Ankara since 1984.[5]

The three hotspots reflect the same worldwide phenomenon — the almost inevitable conflict caused when a group of people want to separate themselves from a state that refuses to let them go. Despite today's oft-heard mantra that mankind is living in a global community where borders no longer matter, having a homeland of one's own clearly remains a dream for millions.

Out of more than 70 separatist movements around the globe, about two dozen are active, most in Europe and Asia, and seven of them are violent. And since 1990, more than two dozen new countries have emerged from separatist movements, mostly the result of the disintegration of the Soviet Union and the breaking apart of the former Yugoslavia.[6] Almost half of the 25 successful separatist movements were accompanied by some amount of violence, most of it ethnically based.

In fact, the number of independent countries around the globe has waxed and waned over the past 150 years. During the 19th century, the number declined as the European colonial powers gobbled up territories in Asia and Africa. Then after World War II the number mushroomed as those empires disintegrated. The United Nations has grown from 51 members when it was founded in 1945 to 192 members today (not counting Kosovo).[7]

Among the groups fighting for independence today, the Kurds are the largest, with approximately 25 million dispersed in Turkey, Iraq, Iran and Syria.[8] Other separatist movements are microscopic by comparison: The South Ossetians — who have seceded from Georgia and formed a de facto but as-yet-unrecognized government — number just 70,000, for example. Some movements, like the Québécois in Canada and the Scottish in the United Kingdom, have been peaceful, while others, like the Tamils in Sri Lanka and Palestinians in Israel, have been violent. Indonesia has had two separatist movements with very different destinies: East Timor (Timor Leste) on Indonesia's eastern tip became independent in 1999 — although it is still struggling to fend for itself, relying on international aid to make up for its severe food shortages — while Aceh in the west has opted for autonomy within Indonesia.[9]

Separatism often triggers serious rifts between the world's major powers. In the case of Kosovo, the United States and its NATO allies — including the United

AFP/Getty Images/Vano Shlamov

Protesters at a March rally in Tbilisi, Georgia, want Russia to stop supporting South Ossetia and Abkhazia, two Georgian regions that seceded and formed de facto states. Their placards — which say "Russia! Stop Dealing With the Fates of Small Nations!" — indicate how a separatist movement can become a pawn in a geopolitical tug-of-war. Russia supports the two breakaway states, while most of the international community does not recognize them.

Kingdom, France, Germany, Italy and Turkey — backed the secession. U.S. Assistant Secretary of State Daniel Fried has dubbed it "the last chapter in the dissolution of Yugoslavia," while acknowledging "many things can go wrong and probably will."[10] In stark contrast, Russia steadfastly opposes independence for Kosovo and is standing shoulder-to-shoulder with its historical ally, Serbia.

Outgoing Russian President Vladimir Putin has said, "If someone believes that Kosovo should be granted full independence as a state, then why should we deny it to the Abkhaz and the South Ossetians?" According to Matthew J. Bryza, U.S. deputy assistant secretary of State for European and Eurasian Affairs, Russia is covertly providing material support to South Ossetia and Abkhazia — two de facto states that have emerged from within Russia's political foe, the ex-Soviet Republic of Georgia.[11] The United States and the rest of the international community don't recognize the secession of either state.

Meanwhile, the Chinese government opposes the pro-independence movement among the ethnically

World's Newest Country Remains Divided

Kosovo is struggling to be recognized.

Delaware-size Kosovo grabbed the world's attention on Feb. 17 when its ethnic Albanian-dominated government declared its independence from Serbia, triggering street protests among some Serb citizens.

Because of fierce opposition from Serbs both inside Kosovo and in Serbia, a large international presence with armies from six "framework" nations keeps an uneasy peace: The United States controls the east, Ireland the center, Turkey and Germany the south, Italy the west and France the north.[1]

"Do not trust the apparent calm, it's the main difficulty of this mission," says Captain Noê-Noël Ucheida from the Franco-German brigade of the 16,000-strong NATO force in Kosovo. "It can be calm. But it becomes tense in the morning and ignites in the afternoon."[2]

The spotlight fell on Kosovo in 1999 — several years after the break-up of Yugoslavia — when Serbian leader Slobodan Milosevic's brutal campaign to forcibly remove Kosovar Albanians led to NATO having to step in and take the province out of Serb hands. Now Kosovo's 2 million Albanians seem determined to open a new chapter in their history by implementing a U.N. plan granting them internationally supervised independence. Not for the first time, the world's leading powers are divided over a conflict in the Balkans. The United States, Germany, United Kingdom, France and Italy back independence while Serbia, Russia and China oppose it.

Further complicating the issue are the 100,000 Serbs living in Kosovo, including 40,000 concentrated in a zone north of the Ibar River; the remainder are dispersed throughout the south. Just as Kosovo's Albanians fought tooth and nail to free themselves from Serb rule, so the Serbs in north Kosovo are equally resolved to be free of Albanian rule. "They already run their own de facto state," says Nicolas Gros-Verheyde, a French journalist who toured Kosovo just before the declaration of independence. "They are heavily subsidized by the Serbian government in Belgrade, which tops up the salaries of local police officers and supplies the electricity and mobile phone network."

The Ibar River is fast becoming yet another border in the Balkans. "Cars in the north have different registration plates. When Kosovar Serbs drive south, they remove them to avoid being attacked. Our translator, who was Serbian, would not even get out of the car," says Gros-Verheyde. He notes there was much greater contact between the Serb and Albanian communities during his previous visit to Kosovo in 1990, when the Serbian military patrolled the province. "But 15 years of ethnic conflict has bred mistrust and hatred," says Gros-Verheyde.

Daniel Serwer, vice president of the Center for Post-Conflict Peace and Stability Operations at the United States Institute of Peace (USIP), feels Serbia only has itself to blame for losing Kosovo. It drove the Kosovar Albanians to secede by excluding them from the Serbian government, he argues. "If Kosovars had been included — for example by being offered the presidency of Serbia — it might not have seceded. The Serbs want sovereignty over the territory of Kosovo, but they could not care less about the people," he says.

The economy of Kosovo has suffered terribly from two decades of strife throughout the region. With unemployment

Turkic Uyghur people, who live in the western Chinese autonomous region of Xinjiang. China has tried to stifle separatism in its western provinces by promoting mass migration of ethnic Chinese to both Tibet and Xinjiang to dilute the indigenous population. Critics say China used the Sept. 11, 2001, terrorist attacks in the United States as a pretext for clamping down on the Uyghurs, who are Muslim, by claiming they were linked to Islamic terrorist movements like al Qaeda.[12]

China's separatist woes are an embarrassment just four months before the start of the Summer Olympic Games in Beijing — China's chance to shine on the world stage. The Chinese call the Tibetan protests a "grave violent crime involving beating, smashing, looting and burning" orchestrated by the Dalai Lama, the Tibetan leader-in-exile.[13] But Western leaders are not buying Beijing's line. Nancy Pelosi, Speaker of the U.S. House of Representatives, traveled to India to meet with the Dalai Lama on March 21 and declared the Tibet situation "a challenge to the conscience of the world."[14]

Despite the international condemnation of China's treatment of the Tibetans, however, the international community and the United Nations (U.N.) — which in 1945 enshrined the right to self-determination in its

at 50 percent, thousands have migrated to Western Europe and the United States, sending money back to their families. Much of the country's income is derived from trafficking in drugs, weapons and women, claims Gros-Verheyde. Roads are dilapidated, and electricity is cut off several times a week.

Meanwhile, the international community is ever-present: The mobile phone network for Kosovar Albanians is provided by the principality of Monaco, the euro is the local currency and NATO soldiers' frequent the hotels and restaurants.

"The Albanian part is livelier than the Serbian," says Gros-Verheyde. "The birth rate among the Albanians is very high. They want to increase their population to ensure they are not wiped out."

Kosovo's future remains uncertain. Most of the world's nations have not yet recognized it as an independent country, and many are unlikely to do so, including Spain, Slovakia and Romania, which fear potential secessionist movements of their own.[3] Internally, tensions between the Albanian and Serb communities are unlikely to simply melt away. In fact, relations could further deteriorate over how to divide up the country's mineral resources, most of which lie in the Serb-controlled northern part.

Meanwhile, the world will keep a watchful eye and presence. The European Union (EU) is in the process of deploying a 1,900-strong police and rule-of-law mission to replace a U.N. police force.[4] Indeed, many observers think the EU may hold out the best hope of salvation: Under a plan proposed by the European Commission — and supported virtually across the board in Europe — all Balkan nations would be integrated into the EU, ultimately diminishing the significance of borders and smoothing out ethnic tensions.

Ethnic Albanians celebrate Kosovo's declaration of independence from Serbia on Feb. 17, 2008. The new state is backed by the United States and key European allies but bitterly contested by Serbia and Russia.

In the meantime, NATO holds the fort with a "high-visibility, low-profile" doctrine. "The soldiers have bullet-proof vests but keep them in the vehicles," says Gros-Verheyde. "They carry machine guns on their back but do not walk through villages with a weapon at their hip. A soldier told me the only exception to this was the American soldiers who have been traumatized by Iraq."

---

[1] Nicolas Gros-Verheyde, "One eye on Belgrade, the other on Pristina," *Europolitics*, (EU affairs subscription-based news service), Jan. 22, 2008, www.europolitics.info/xg/europolitique/politiquessectorielles/defense/217304?highlight=true&searchlink=true.

[2] Quoted in *ibid.*

[3] Joanna Boguslawska, *Europolitics*, Dec. 14, 2007, www.europolitics.info/xg/europolitique/politiquesexternes/relationsexterieures/215424?highlight=true&searchlink=true.

[4] For details, see Web sites of NATO and U.N. forces, respectively, at www.nato.int/KFOR and www.unmikonline.org.

founding charter — have provided little support to recent separatist movements. Many countries are wary of incurring the wrath of economic giants like China, and international law on separatism is ambiguous, leading to an inconsistent and non-uniform global reaction to separatist movements.

Though several international conventions reaffirm the right to self-determination, they also pledge to uphold the "principle of territorial integrity" — the right of existing states to prevent regions from seceding. "International law grows by practice," says Thomas Grant, a senior fellow and legal scholar at the United

States Institute of Peace (USIP), an independent institution established and funded by the U.S. Congress that tries to resolve international conflicts. "The legal situation adapts itself to the factual situation."

Consequently, the international community's response to de facto separatist states varies widely. For example, most of the world refuses to deal with the Turkish Republic of Northern Cyprus, which has been punished with an economic embargo since 1973, when Turkish troops invaded Cyprus and permanently occupied the north, creating a Turkish-dominated de facto state there. Somaliland — which established a de facto state in northwestern Somalia in 1991 after the government in Mogadishu collapsed — has been largely ignored by the world community despite being a relative beacon of stability in the otherwise unstable horn of Africa.[15] The Tamils' campaign to gain independence from Sri Lanka attracts relatively little international diplomatic attention these days, in part, some say, because the area is not considered critical by the major powers.

Meanwhile, the island nation of Taiwan, off the coast of mainland China, is accepted as a global trading partner — the United States alone has 140 trade agreements with the Taiwanese — but not as an independent country. Few countries are willing to challenge Beijing's "one-China" policy, which denies any province the right to secede and sees Taiwan as its 23rd province.[16]

In addition, the world has done nothing — apart from occasionally condemning human rights violations — to prevent Russia from brutally repressing Chechnya's attempt to secede. While separatists there largely succeeded in creating their own state in the 1990s, Moscow has since regained control of it, although an insurgency continues.

The U.N. has no specific unit looking at separatism as a phenomenon. Instead, it usually waits for a conflict to break out and then considers sending a peacekeeping mission to restore law and order.

"U.N. member states are likely to be wary of separatism because of the knock-on effects it can have on themselves," says Jared Kotler, communications officer at the U.N.'s Department of Political Affairs. "Member states are very aware how one movement can encourage another — possibly in their own country."

"Thus far, territorial integrity has always won the debate," says Hurst Hannum, a professor of international law at Tufts University in Medford, Mass., and a specialist in self-determination theory. "This is why Kosovo will be an important precedent despite statements by all concerned that it should not be seen as such."

In Latin America, where most countries won wars of independence in the early 1800s, separatist movements are rare today, although one recently sprang up in Bolivia. Bolivians living in the lowlands, who are mostly of European ancestry, are threatening to secede to prevent the government from redistributing the profits from the nation's oil and gas reserves to the mainly indigenous highlanders. In North America, the United States has not experienced a serious separatist threat since 1861 when 11 Southern states seceded, provoking the Civil War. And while few predict an imminent resurgence of such movements in the United States, diverse secessionist groups are beginning to coordinate their efforts.[17]

Some separatist movements have been highly successful. For example, since declaring independence from the Soviet Union in 1990, Lithuania has liberalized and grown its economy, consolidated democracy and joined the European Union (EU) and NATO.

Seth D. Kaplan, a foreign policy analyst and author of the forthcoming book *Fixing Fragile States*, has some advice for countries struggling to put out secessionist fires. "Countries that can foster sufficient social cohesion and a common identity while minimizing horizontal inequities are the most likely to stay whole," he says. "Those that don't and have obvious identity cleavages are likely to ignite secessionist movements."

While the world confronts growing separatism, here are some key questions being asked:

Should there be a right of self-determination?

"In principle, yes," says Daniel Serwer, vice president of the Center for Post-Conflict Peace and Stability Operations at the United States Institute of Peace. "But the real question is: What form should self-determination take?"

Self-determination is often interpreted to mean the right to secede and declare independence. But it can take other forms, too, such as local autonomy, similar to what Canada has granted to Québec, or a federal system with a strong central government that protects minority rights.

"In Kosovo, after nine years under U.N. control, young people expected independence," says Serwer. But other minorities have chosen a different path, he adds. For instance, "the Kurds in Iraq were thrown out of their homes" by Saddam Hussein. "They were even gassed. But so far they have not chosen the route of independence."

Gene Martin, executive director of the Philippine Facilitation Project at USIP, notes, "Local autonomy may not be enough for some people, who feel they just do not belong to a country." Plus, he adds, the government's ability or willingness to relinquish its authority also affects whether a minority will push for local autonomy or for full independence. Martin has been involved in brokering peace between the Philippine government and the Moro Islamic Liberation Front, which has for decades fought for an independent state for the Moros, a Muslim people living in southern Philippines.

Marino Busdachin — general secretary of the Hague-based Unrepresented Nations and Peoples Organization (UNPO), which represents 70 nonviolent movements pushing for self-determination — rails against the U.N. for not upholding that right. "Self-determination exists on paper only. It is a trap," he says. "We cannot apply to anyone for it. The U.N. member states block us."

Moreover, he says, seeking self-determination should not be confused with demanding the right to secede. "Ninety percent of our members are not looking for independence," he says.

That's a significant distinction, according to Diane Orentlicher, a professor of international law at American University in Washington, D.C. Although the U.N. has enshrined the right to self-determination, it has never endorsed a right of secession, and no state recognizes such a right. Such a step would be dangerous, she writes, because it would allow minorities to subvert the will of the majority. "Minorities could distort the outcome of political processes by threatening to secede if their views do not prevail," she writes. [18]

Dmitry Rogozin, Russia's ambassador to NATO, shares that view. "If the majority wants to live in a shared state, why does the minority have the right to break away?" he has asked. [19] "Look at Berlin. You could say it's the third-largest Turkish city [because of the large number of people of Turkish origin living there]. If tomorrow the Turks living in Berlin want to create a national state in the city, who can be against it?"

"The challenge for the West in Kosovo," says self-determination legal expert Hannum at Tufts, is to recognize its independence without implicitly recognizing its right to secede — just as "the West pretended that the former Yugoslavia 'dissolved' as opposed to recognizing the secession of its various parts."

The State Department's Bryza, who deals with conflicts in Abkhazia, South Ossetia and Nagorno-Karabakh, a separatist enclave in Azerbaijan, agrees. "It is unreasonable to have self-determination as the only guiding principle," he says. "If we did, the world would live in utter barbarity."

Fixing Fragile States author Kaplan believes separatism makes sense in a few cases, such as Kosovo and

AP Photo/Al Jacinto

The Moro Islamic Liberation Front — which for decades has fought for an independent state for the Moros, a Muslim group living in the south of the predominantly Catholic Philippines — are negotiating with the government to peacefully settle the dispute.

Somaliland. "But, generally, the international community is right to initially oppose separatism," he says.

So when should a group have the right to secede? "When you are deprived of the right to participate in government, and there are serious violations of human rights, such as genocide," says the USIP's Grant. "The bar is placed very high because you want to preserve the state, as that is the mechanism you use to claim your right of secession."

This is why, argues Serwer, ethnic Albanians in Macedonia, which borders Kosovo, do not have the right to secede. "If they called for independence — and I don't think they want this — I would say 'nonsense,' because they have their rights respected. It is only when other forms of self-determination — like local autonomy — are blocked that secession becomes inevitable."

Meto Koloski — the president of United Macedonian Diaspora, which campaigns for the rights of Macedonian minorities in Greece, Bulgaria, Albania, Serbia and

More Than Two Dozen New Nations Since 1990

Since 1990, 26 new countries have declared independence — 15 of them the result of the dissolution of the Soviet Union. Yugoslavia has separated into seven new states, the last one, Kosovo, declaring its independence in February.

Successful Separatist Movements Since 1990

Emerged from Ethiopia (1993)
Eritrea

Emerged from Indonesia (2002)
Timor Leste

**Emerged from the
Soviet Union (1991)**

Armenia	Kazakhstan	Russia
Azerbaijan	Kyrgyzstan	Tajikistan
Belarus	Latvia	Turkmenistan
Estonia	Lithuania	Ukraine
Georgia	Moldova	Uzbekistan

**Emerged from Czechoslovakia
in 1993**
Czech Republic
Slovakia

Emerged from Yugoslavia
Bosnia and Herzegovina (1992)
Croatia (1991)
Kosovo (2008, from Serbia)
Macedonia (1991)
Montenegro (2006)*
Serbia (2006)*
Slovenia (1991)

* For three years, Serbia and Montenegro existed as a confederation called Serbia & Montenegro, and then split into separate countries.

Sources: Unrepresented Nations and Peoples' Organization, www.unpo.org; *Political Handbook of the World 2007,* CQ Press, 2007; Tibet Government-in-exile, www.tibet.com.

country was first founded. "The whole self-determination theology is very slippery," says a U.S. government official with extensive knowledge of the separatist conflict in Aceh, Indonesia. "We support the territorial integrity of Indonesia. We never concluded that the human rights situation in Aceh was intolerable."

Jerry Hyman, governance advisor at the Center for Strategic and International Studies in Washington, highlights an often-overlooked point: "We have to ask how economically and politically viable are states like Transdniestria? If you apply this [right to secede] to Africa, it could explode. At best, Africa is a stained-glass window." Economic viability tends to be ignored when assessing separatist claims, he says, because the "we're special" argument usually prevails.

"If they are not viable, they will end up like East Timor, relying on the international community financially," he says.

Kosovo — says, "Everyone should have a right to self-determination, their own identity, language and culture but not to their own state."

Secession also is problematic — even if backed by a clear majority of those in the seceding region — because the minority opposed to secession could end up being oppressed. "Secession does not create the homogeneous successor states its proponents often assume," writes Donald Horowitz, a professor of law and political science at Duke University in Durham, N.C. "Guarantees of minority protection in secessionist regions are likely to be illusory; indeed, many secessionist movements have as one of their aims the expulsion or subordination of minorities in the secessionist regions.[20]

"There is an inevitable trade-off between encouraging participation in the undivided state and legitimating exit from it," he continued. "The former will inevitably produce imperfect results, but the latter is downright dangerous."[21]

Some would argue that certain separatist movements have no legal basis because the people concerned already exercised their right of self-determination when their

Are globalization and regional integration fueling separatism?

Several organizations and treaties have emerged in recent years to encourage more regional integration and cross-border trade. The EU is the oldest and largest, but newer arrivals include the Association of Southeast Asian Nations (ASEAN), the African Union (AU), the Latin American trading blocs ANDEAN and MERCOSUR and the North American Free Trade Agreement (NAFTA). In addition, the World Trade Organization (WTO) is working to abolish trade barriers globally. Experts differ over whether these organizations promote or discourage separatism.

The Peace Institute's Grant believes they can encourage it. "What are the political impediments to independence?" he asks. The new states are not sustainable as a small unit, he says, adding, "If you reduce the significance of national borders and improve the free movement of people, goods and capital, you remove that impediment."

For instance, the possibility of being part of the EU's single market makes an independent Kosovo a more viable option and has seemingly suppressed Albania's desire to merge with the Albanians in Kosovo to create a Greater Albania. Asked if Albania had a plan to establish a Greater Albania, Foreign Minister Lulzim Basha said, "Yes, we do. It has a blue flag and gold stars on it," describing the EU flag. "Today's only goal is integration into NATO and the EU as soon as possible."[22]

Günter Dauwen, a Flemish nationalist who is director of the European Free Alliance political party in the European Parliament, says the EU fuels separatism by not adequately ensuring respect for regions. Dauwen is campaigning for more autonomy and possibly independence for Flanders, the mostly Dutch-speaking northern half of Belgium that already has a large degree of self-government. "The national capitals control the EU. They decide where funds for regional development go. This creates terrible tension."

Over-centralization of decision-making is particularly acute in Spain, he says, where it has triggered separatism in the region of Catalonia in the northeast and Galicia in the northwest. In addition, France suppresses regionalist parties in Brittany, Savoy and the French Basque country, he says. "When we complain to the EU, its stock answer is that only nation states can devolve power to the regions."

Dauwen points out that the European Court of Human Rights (ECHR) has condemned countries for not respecting the rights of ethnic minorities, but the EU doesn't force its members to comply with those rulings. For instance, he says, the ECHR condemned the Bulgarians for not allowing ethnic Macedonians to form their own political party. But the EU did nothing to force Bulgaria to abide by the ruling, further fueling the desire for separatism.

The State Department's Bryza disagrees. "The opposite works in my experience," he says. "As Hungary and Slovakia have deepened their integration into the EU, the desire of ethnic Hungarians who live in countries neighboring Hungary to become independent is receding. And the possibility for Turkish Cypriots in northern Cyprus [whose de facto state is only recognized by Turkey] to be part of the EU gives them an incentive to rejoin the Greek Cypriot government in the south, which is already in the EU."

AP Photo/Gemunu Amarasinghe

Female Tamil Tiger fighters undergo training at a hideout deep in Tiger-controlled territory northeast of Colombo, Sri Lanka, in 2007. The Tamils, who comprise 18 percent of Sri Lanka's population, began fighting for independence in 1983 — a struggle that has resulted in the deaths of some 70,000 people. Tamils now control large swathes of the country.

Likewise, Ekaterina Pischalnikova — special assistant to the special representative of the secretary-general at the U.N. observer mission in Georgia, which is trying to resolve the Georgia-Abkhaz conflict — says EU regional integration has helped to "mitigate rather than fuel separatist movements."

Busdachin of the Unrepresented Nations and Peoples Organization says the EU "is helping to resolve separatist conflicts in many cases because it has the most advanced regime for protecting minorities." For example, the EU has consistently pressured Turkey, which wants to join the union, to grant the Kurds the right to express their language and culture more freely. Such a move could quell some Kurds' desire for full independence, he says, adding that he would like to see ASEAN, MERCOSUR and other regional organizations follow the EU model.

Author Kaplan — who has lived in Turkey, Nigeria, China and Japan — says regional integration "is only promoting separatism in the EU. Europe is peaceful and prosperous so there is no real need for states. But when you get into the wild jungle, the state is more important." For instance, he explains, "states in Africa and Central America do not want to give up their power, even though they would benefit the most from regionalism."

In Asia, ASEAN has no clearly defined policy on separatism, leaving it up to national governments to decide how to deal with separatist movements. The Shanghai Co-operation Organization (SCO) — set up in 2001 by Russia, China, Kazakhstan, Kyrgyzstan, Uzbekistan and Tajikistan to combat separatism, terrorism and extremism — strongly opposes separatist movements like that of China's Uyghurs.[23]

Ironically, separatism also can fuel regional integration. Many of the countries that have recently joined the EU or intend to do so — Lithuania, Slovakia, Slovenia, Montenegro and Macedonia — were formed from separatist movements. Too small to be economically self-sufficient, they see integration into the EU market as the only way to ensure continued prosperity and stability.

Does separatism lead to more violent conflict?

The recent developments in the Balkans provide strong evidence that separatism can provoke violent conflict — especially when countries divide along ethnic lines, as the former Yugoslavia has done.

Serbia's festering rage over Kosovo's declaration of independence is a prime example. "If this act of secession for ethnic reasons is not a mistake, then nothing is a mistake," said Serbia's Foreign Minister Vuk Jeremic, adding, "Serbia will not go quietly. We will fight, and we will not tolerate this secession."[24]

Serwer at the United States Institute for Peace says, "If you partition a state along ethnic lines, this almost inevitably leads to long-term conflict," especially if the central government resists the separatist movement.

"Secession converts a domestic ethnic dispute into a more dangerous one," according to Duke's Horowitz. "The recurrent temptation to create a multitude of homogeneous mini-states, even if it could be realized, might well increase the sum total of warfare rather than reduce it."[25]

The State Department's Bryza says separatism doesn't have to lead to violence "if leaders of national groups exert wise leadership and temper the ambitions of nationalist groups."

The campaign by Taiwanese separatists to obtain a seat for Taiwan at the U.N. — a March 22 referendum calling for this failed — shows how even nonviolent separatism can trigger conflict. "Bizarre as it may seem, a peaceful referendum in Taiwan may portend war," according to John J. Tkacik, a policy expert at the Heritage Foundation in Washington. He predicted China would invoke a 2005 anti-secession law to justify using "non-peaceful" means to counter Taiwanese separatism.[26] Fear of provoking a war with China is probably the main reason there is so little international support for the Taiwan independence movement.

As former U.S. Deputy Secretary of State Robert B. Zoellick said in 2006, "We want to be supportive of Taiwan, while we are not encouraging those that try to move toward independence. Because I am being very clear: Independence means war. And that means American soldiers."[27]

But independence does not always mean war. With a broadly homogeneous population, its own currency, flag, army, government and airline, Somaliland is an example of how a people can effectively secede without causing chaos and violence. Somaliland's isolation from the international community has not hindered its development — indeed it has helped, argues author Kaplan.

"The dearth of external involvement has kept foreign interference to a minimum while spurring self-reliance and self-belief," he says.

Martin at the Peace Institute points out that since the end of the Cold War, "most wars have been intra-state. Sometimes borders can be shifted to solve the problem and actually prevent war."

But separatist movements also are frequently manipulated by external powers as part of a geopolitical chess game that can become violent. "People want independence because of ethnic hatred and because it is in their economic interests to separate. But outside powers help separatists, too," says Koloski, of the United Macedonian Diaspora. For example, the United States, Britain and France support Kosovo's independence because they believe this will help stabilize the region, while Russia and China support Serbia's opposition because they fear it will encourage separatist movements elsewhere, including in their territories.

In some cases — notably Québec, Flanders, Wales and Scotland — separatist movements have not boiled over into violent conflict. In each, the central government granted some self-rule to the separatist region, preventing the situation from turning violent.[28] In addition, the movements were able to argue their case through elected political representatives in a functioning democratic system, which also reduces the likelihood of violence.

"When a country is too centralized and non-democratic, this produces separatist movements that can become violent," says Busdachin at the Unrepresented Nations and Peoples Organization. "The responsibility is 50-50."

But democracy does not always prevent separatism from escalating into conflict. From the 1960s to the '90s, extreme Irish Catholic nationalists in Northern Ireland waged a violent campaign to secure independence from the U.K., all the while maintaining a political party with elected representatives.

How the global community responds to one separatist movement can affect whether a movement elsewhere triggers a war. "Violence is not inevitable," says Flemish nationalist Dauwen. "But ethnic minorities do get frustrated when they get nowhere through peaceful means, and they see those who use violence — for example the Basque separatist movement ETA in Spain — attracting all the headlines."

As a Tamil activist notes, "Whatever we have achieved so far, we have got by force."

BACKGROUND

Emerging Nations

Throughout history separatism has manifested itself in various forms as groups grew dissatisfied with their

Number of Countries Reaches All-time High

The number of countries in the world has increased sixfold since the 1800s, when European colonization was at its peak. The greatest jump occurred after World War II, when Europe gave up its colonies amid a worldwide movement for independence. The United Nations, which includes nearly all of the world's countries, now has 192 members. The U.N. has not yet recognized Kosovo, which declared its independence in February.

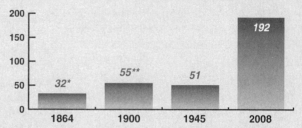

Number of Countries Recognized Worldwide, 1864-2008

* Includes several states in Australia and New Zealand that were part of the British Empire; Finland and Poland were considered part of Russia; Africa is omitted entirely, since its interior was largely unmapped at that time. Since the U.S. Civil War was in progress, the Confederate States were counted as a separate country.

** The British Empire is counted as a single country, as are the French, German and Dutch empires; Austria-Hungary is considered one country and includes both Liechtenstein and Bosnia-Herzegovina; Finland and several Asian dependencies are counted as part of Russia; Turkey includes five states.

Sources: The Statesman's Year Book, 1864 and 1900; United Nations

governments. Even the Roman Empire — which was synonymous with order, peace and civilization in most of its conquered territories — had its Celtic resisters, the Britons and Gauls.[29]

In medieval Europe, the discontented sought to extricate themselves from kingdoms, feudal domains and churches. In the 18th and 19th centuries European colonies in the Americas, Australia and New Zealand began splitting off from the "mother" countries. By the 19th century, with the Hapsburg, Romanov and Ottoman empires on the decline, groups united by ethnicity, language or culture began to cast off their imperial shackles. Then in the late 1800s and early 20th century the major European powers — and the United States — began acquiring and consolidating colonies or territories.

Just three decades after its own war for independence from Great Britain, the United States had to weather its own secessionist storms. In 1814 a handful of New

CHRONOLOGY

1776-1944 *Nation states gradually eclipse multi-ethnic empires as the dominant form of government.*

1776 Britain's American colonies declare independence, triggering war.

Early 1800s Spanish and Portuguese colonies in Latin America become independent.

1861 Eleven Southern U.S. states secede, sparking Civil War. After four years of bitter fighting, the South loses and is reintegrated into the union.

1918 At the end of World War I new European states are created from the ashes of the Hapsburg and Ottoman empires.

1919 U.S. President Woodrow Wilson champions the "right of self-determination" but fails to get it adopted by the League of Nations.

1939 World War II breaks out. Borders shift as Germany, Japan and Italy occupy neighboring countries before being defeated by the Allies.

1945-1989 *More new states emerge as colonies gain independence, but borders are left largely intact.*

1945 U.N. charter includes the right of self-determination.

1949 China invades and occupies Tibet.

1960 U.N. General Assembly proclaims a Declaration on the Granting of Independence to Colonial Countries and Peoples, heralding the end of the colonial era.

1967 Biafra secedes from Nigeria; is reintegrated after a three-year war.

1975 World's leading powers sign the Helsinki Final Act, guaranteeing peoples the right of self-determination.

1984 A new, violent Kurdish separatist revolt breaks out in Turkey.

1990-2008 *Twenty-six new countries are created after the Soviet Union and Yugoslavia break apart.*

1990 Soviet republics begin resisting Moscow's central control. Lithuania on March 11 becomes the first republic to declare its independence, setting off a chain reaction that leads to the dissolution of the U.S.S.R.

1991 Slovenia and Croatia split from Yugoslavia, accompanied by violence, especially in Croatia. . . . New states emerge from the Soviet Union, as do unrecognized breakaway republics in Nagorno-Karabakh, Chechnya, South Ossetia, Abkhazia and Transdniestria. . . . In Africa, Somaliland separates itself from rapidly disintegrating Somalia.

1992 Bosnia splits from Yugoslavia, provoking a three-year war.

1993 Czechoslovakia splits peacefully into the Czech Republic and Slovakia. . . . Eritrea secedes from Ethiopia after a U.N.-monitored referendum.

1995 A referendum in Québec advocating secession from Canada is rejected by 50.6 percent of Québécois.

1999 North Atlantic Treaty Organization seizes Kosovo from Serbia in response to Serbia's persecution of Kosovar Albanians. . . . East Timor declares independence from Indonesia after 25 years of violence.

2004 The separatist region of Aceh is granted autonomy from Indonesia after a devastating Dec. 26 Indian Ocean tsunami creates a feeling of solidarity between Aceh's separatists and the Indonesian authorities.

2005 Chinese authorize use of force to prevent Taiwan from seceding.

2007 Belgium edges closer to disintegration. . . . In Bolivia, people of European descent threaten to secede in response to fears of losing control over the country's gas reserves.

2008 Taiwanese separatists are defeated in parliamentary elections on Jan. 12. . . . Kosovo declares independence from Serbia on Feb. 17, triggering violent protests among Serbs in Belgrade. Separatist protests in Tibet turn violent on March 14; Chinese send in troops to put down the rebellion.

2008

August — Georgia fights brief war with Russia over who should govern Georgia's secessionist enclave of South Ossetia. The conflict leads Russia to recognize South Ossetia and Abkhazia, another Georgian enclave that seceded in the early 1990s.

Nov. 25 — Referendum passes in Danish-owned Greenland giving its 56,000 inhabitants full control over their natural resources.

2009

April 16 — In Bolivia, two alleged militant secessionists representing lowlanders are assassinated in a government sting, a sign of rising tensions between Bolivia's highlandbased indigenous majority and lowlanders of mostly European ancestry.

May — Sri Lankan forces defeat the Tamil Tigers, a militant separatist group that had been fighting since 1983 to create an independent Tamil homeland.

July 5 — Violent protests by China's Uyghur minority in the northwestern province of Xinjiang, triggered by

Uyghur anger over China's alleged cultural genocide policies toward the Uyghurs, lead to 197 deaths.

2010

June 13 — Secessionist parties from Flanders emerge as the largest political block in Belgian national elections, leading to protracted discussions between the Flemish and Francophone parties on granting further regional autonomy.

2011

January — In an internationally approved referendum, the South Sudanese vote overwhelmingly to form their own country

May — Parliamentary elections show mixed fortunes of constitutional separatists: In Canada, Bloc Quebecois suffer a near meltdown, but in the United Kingdom the Scottish National Party wins an overall majority in regional elections.

July 9 — South Sudan declares independence, the first separatist movement to do so since Kosovo declared its independence in February 2008.

July 14 — United Nations General Assembly recognizes South Sudan.

England states opposed to the federal government's anti-foreign-trade policies and the War of 1812 organized a convention in Hartford, Conn., and produced a report spelling out the conditions under which they would remain part of the United States. The U.S. victory against the British in 1815 took the wind out of the initiative's sails, however, and secession negotiations never actually took place.

Then in 1861, largely in response to U.S. government efforts to outlaw slavery, 11 Southern states tried to secede from the union to form their own country. After a bloody, four-year civil war, the South was forcibly reintegrated into the United States in 1865.[30] The U.S. Supreme Court cemented the union with a ruling in 1869 (*Texas v. White*) that effectively barred states from unilaterally seceding.[31]

In 1914 nationalist opposition to imperialist expansionism in Europe sparked World War I. Aggrieved at the

Austro-Hungarian Empire's annexation of Bosnia, home to many Serbs, 19-year-old Serbian Gavrilo Princip assassinated Archduke Franz Ferdinand, heir to the imperial throne. Many of the new countries created in the post-war territorial division, such as Lithuania and Poland, were constructed along broadly ethnic lines. At the same time the concept of "self-determination" — the right of a nation to determine how it should be governed — emerged, championed by President Woodrow Wilson.[32]

Wilson's effort to enshrine self-determination in the founding statute of the newly created League of Nations was defeated. The idea of holding a referendum to determine who should govern a disputed territory gained support in this period, too. And when the league set up a commission to determine the status of the Åland Islands (it determined Finnish sovereignty), the concept was developed that a people might have the right to secede

Bye-Bye Belgium?

More prosperous Flanders wants autonomy.

Belgium experienced a surreal moment in December 2006 when a spoof news program on a French-speaking TV channel announced that Flanders, the country's Dutch-speaking region, had seceded. Footage of the king and queen of Belgium hastily boarding an airplane interspersed with shocked reactions from politicians convinced many viewers that their country was no more. Some even took to the streets to spontaneously rally for the Belgian cause.

But Dutch-speaking Flemings (as those who live in Flanders are called) were offended at how quickly their francophone compatriots (called the Walloons) believed Flanders had seceded. The incident triggered months of national soul-searching about the future of the country.

Fast-forward to the June 2007 general election, when the separatist-leaning Flemish Christian Democrats won the most seats in parliament and demanded that the constitution be amended to devolve more power to the regions, escalating an ongoing dispute between French and Dutch-speaking parties. The controversy became so fierce it took six months to form a government, and even then, it was only provisional, aimed at keeping the country united until the French- and Dutch-speaking communities could agree on a more long-term program. While a coalition pact was finally approved on March 18, bringing an end to the country's nine-month political limbo, the pact says nothing about devolution of powers, so the real battle has still to be fought.[1]

"If the French do not give us more autonomy, it's bye-bye Belgium," says Flemish nationalist Gunter Dauwen, director of the European Free Alliance, a political group that represents 35 nationalist parties in Europe.

Dauwen's party, Spirit, is demanding that unemployment benefits be paid for by the regional governments rather than the federal government. The jobless rate is higher in French-speaking Wallonia. Under Dauwen's plan, the Flemish would not have to subsidize the unemployed Walloons as they do now.

But such a lack of solidarity irks the Francophones. "We are a small country. We should all get the same benefits," says Raphael Hora, an unemployed Walloon. "You can't have a guy in Charleroi (Wallonia) getting less than a guy in Antwerp (Flanders)."

There is also a growing cultural chasm between Flemings and Walloons, he says. "I speak English, Italian, Spanish, Norwegian, German and Polish — but not Dutch. My father never wanted me to learn it."

Roughly 60 percent of Belgians speak Dutch, 39 percent speak French and the remaining 1 percent speak German. The Belgian constitutional system is Byzantine in its complexity, with powers dispersed between governments organized along municipal, linguistic, provincial, regional and national lines.

Hora, who recently moved to Berlin, sees Belgium's breakup as inevitable: "When it happens, I'll come back to Belgium and campaign for Wallonia to rejoin France. We'll be stronger then."

Dauwen insists independence for Flanders is not the goal for now. "My party is not campaigning for independence yet but for a confederation." Contrary to the widespread perception of Flemings as rampant separatists, Dauwen says, "We are all peaceful and not extreme." Flanders' largest pro-independence party, Vlaams Belang, actually lost support in last June's elections, although it remains a major force, garnering about 20 percent of Flemish voters.

According to Jérémie Rossignon, a landscape gardener from Wallonia living in Brussels, "Belgians are not very proud of being Belgian. They do not boast about their achievements and culture." He feels this is a pity, because Belgium has much to be proud of — from its world-renowned beers, chocolates and restaurants to its sports stars like tennis champ

---

when the state they belonged to did not respect their fundamental rights.[33]

One group, the Kurds, fared badly in the post-war territorial settlements. Emerging without a state of their own, Kurds repeatedly staged uprisings in Iraq, Iran and Turkey but were suppressed each time. The most recent and bloody of these has occurred in Turkey, where 40,000 people have been killed in an ongoing conflict that began in 1984. The Kurds in northern Iraq also suffered widespread massacres and expulsions in the late 1980s under Iraqi President Saddam Hussein, but when the United States and its allies defeated Saddam in the 1991 Gulf War, Iraqi Kurds effectively gained self-rule after the U.N. forced Saddam to withdraw from the region.[34]

Justine Henin and the funky fashion designers of Antwerp to the eclectic euro-village that is Brussels.

"There is not much communication between the Francophones and Flemings any more," he continues. "Young Flemings speak English, not French, whereas their parents can speak French."

Meanwhile, he admits, the Francophones "are useless at foreign languages." Foreign-language movies and TV programs are dubbed into French, whereas in Flanders they are subtitled, he notes. The mostly French-speaking monarchy, which is supposed to unify the country, has become another cause of division. Belgium's Italian-born Queen Paola cannot speak Dutch, the language of 60 percent of her subjects, while Crown Prince Philippe has publicly slammed Flemish separatism.

Belgium's predominantly French-speaking capital, Brussels, is located in Flanders, and is seen alternately as a glue holding the country together or an obstacle preventing it from splitting apart. "The Walloons are trying to annex Brussels" by moving to the small strip of land in Flanders that separates Brussels from Wallonia, according to Dauwen. Elected representatives and residents in these municipalities squabble over which language should be used on official documents and street signs. And once a year the Flemings organize a bike ride — known as *Het Gordeel* (the belt) — around Brussels to send a symbolic message that Brussels must not extend itself further into Flanders.

The Francophones feel equally passionately. "The Romans conquered Brussels before the Germans did so we should stay French," says Marie-Paul Clarisse, a lifelong Bruxelloise, who works for an EU-affairs newspaper.

One compromise being floated would turn Brussels into Europe's Washington, D.C., and have it run by the EU, which is based in the city. An even wilder solution calls for tiny Luxembourg to annex Brussels and Wallonia.[2] And

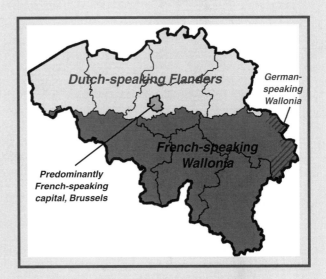

Belgians Speak Three Languages

The Dutch-speaking portion of Belgium is called Flanders. The southern portion, Wallonia, includes both Francophones and German-speaking citizens. French is the predominant language of Brussels, the capital.

as if things were not complicated enough, Belgium also has an autonomous German-speaking community living in Wallonia. No one is quite sure what they want.

Even Rossignon, an ardent defender of Belgium, doubts its future: "The separatists will win out," he predicts, and the new government "will regionalize our country even more than it already is."

---

[1] "New Belgian Coalition Government Reaches Agreement," Agence France-Presse, March 18, 2008, http://afp.google.com/article/ALeqM5jhowUtJkHEsJRfNHhaSlnCb8-Zig.

[2] Laurent Lintermans, "Un Etat federal avec le Luxembourg?" *La Libre Belgique*, Aug. 18, 2007, www.lalibre.be/index.php?view=article&art_id=364931.

The Palestinians were also dealt a poor hand in 1948 after their homeland became part of the new state of Israel, populated mainly by Jews fleeing post-war Europe. After winning the Six-Day War in 1967, Israel occupied Palestinian lands on the western bank of the Jordan River and in a narrow strip of land called Gaza. Ever since then, the Palestinians have been fighting to have a country of their own.[35]

Decolonization

The 20th century saw the number of independent countries around the globe more than triple — from the approximately 55 that existed in 1900 to the 192 that make up the United Nations today.[36] Most of the new nations were created in the post-World War II era, as the European powers shed their colonies in Africa and

Laws Are Ambiguous on Self-Determination

The right to self-determination — which allows people to secede from a mother state if they so choose — appears in various international conventions, including the founding document of the United Nations. But the international documents are ambiguous, because they also espouse the importance of "territorial integrity"— the right of countries not to have their territory dismembered.

International Texts Dealing with Self-determination and Territorial Integrity

U.N. Founding Charter (Article 1) — 1945

- One purpose of the United Nations is "to develop friendly relations among nations based on respect for the principle of equal rights and self-determination of peoples, and to take other appropriate measures to strengthen universal peace."

U.N. Resolution 2625 — 1970

- "Every State has the duty to refrain from any forcible action which deprives peoples referred to in the elaboration of the principle of equal rights and self-determination of their right to self-determination and freedom and independence."

- "Nothing in the foregoing paragraphs shall be construed as authorizing or encouraging any action which would dismember, or impair, totally or in part, the territorial integrity or political unity of sovereign and independent states conducting themselves in compliance with the principle of equal rights and self-determination of peoples and thus possessed of a government representing the whole people belonging to the territory without distinction to race, creed or color."

African Charter on Human and Peoples' Rights (Article 20) — 1981

- "All peoples shall have . . . the unquestionable and inalienable right to self-determination. They shall freely determine their political status and shall pursue their economic development according to the policy they have freely chosen."

Conference on Security and Co-operation in Europe's Charter of Paris for a New Europe — 1990

- "We affirm that the ethnic, cultural, linguistic and religious identity of national minorities will be protected."

- "We reaffirm the equal rights of peoples and their right to self-determination in conformity with the Charter of the United Nations and with the relevant norms of international law, including those related to territorial integrity of states."

Vienna Declaration and Program of Action adopted by World Conference of Human Rights — 1993

- The conference recognizes "the right of peoples to take any legitimate action, in accordance with the Charter of the U.N., to realize their inalienable right of self-determination."

Sources: Organization for Security and Co-operation in Europe, United Nations, University of Hong Kong, University of New Mexico, Unrepresented Nations and Peoples Organization

---

Asia. To ensure that the decolonization process was peaceful and orderly, the United Nations adopted the Declaration on the Granting of Independence to Colonial Countries and Peoples in 1960.[37]

But in practice the emergence of new states was often far from peaceful. Hundreds of thousands of people died in outbreaks of violence during the August 1947 partition of India and Pakistan, which within months went to war with each other over the disputed territory of Kashmir. In 1967 the Igbo people of Biafra tried to secede from Nigeria, triggering a devastating war and famine. Three years later the region was forcefully rejoined to Nigeria.

Despite accusations that Nigeria was committing genocide on the Biafrans, the international community did not back Biafra's independence.

The former British colony of Somaliland in the horn of Africa became momentarily independent in 1960 but immediately chose to unite with its fellow Somalis in the newly constituted state of Somalia to the south created from Italy's former colony. When Somalia collapsed into violent anarchy in 1991, Somaliland seceded, and separatist militants installed a civil administration. In northern Ethiopia, Eritrea's 31-year secession struggle finally ended in independence in 1993 after passage of a U.N.-monitored referendum.

In Sri Lanka, which is dominated by Sinhalese people, the minority Tamils — who make up about 18 percent of the population — have been pushing for independence since the 1970s.[38] The Tamils had wielded considerable influence when the island belonged to the British Empire but felt increasingly discriminated against after Sri Lankan independence in 1948. In the late 1970s and early '80s, when Indira Ghandi was India's prime minister, India — which is home to 70 million Tamils — supported the separatist "Tamil Tigers." But in the late 1980s her son and successor, Rajiv Ghandi, dispatched Indian troops to clamp down on the Tigers. He was later assassinated by a female Tamil suicide bomber, Thenmuli Rajaratnam.

Hopes of reconciliation were raised when Sinhalese and Tamil authorities agreed to rebuild areas devastated by the December 2004 Indian Ocean tsunami, which killed some 35,000 Sri Lankans. But the Sri Lankan Supreme Court struck down the agreement.

Dispersed across a vast plateau in the Himalayan mountains, Tibetans are a mostly Buddhist people with a 2,000-year written history and their own language, Tibetan, which is related to Burmese. China claims ownership of the region based on historical links with Tibetan leaders, which were especially strong in the 18th century. The Tibetans refute this claim and insist the region was never an integral part of China and that from 1913 until 1949 Tibet existed as an independent state.

China invaded Tibet in 1949 and 1950, annexed it in 1951 and in 1965 created the Tibet Autonomous Region — a territory less than half the size of the region Tibetans consider their homeland.

Over the past 60 years, according to the Tibetan government-in-exile, China has brutally repressed the Tibetans, killing 87,000 during the 1959 uprising against Chinese rule and destroying or closing down nearly all of the region's 6,259 monasteries by 1962. China unleashed

Yugoslavia Yields Seven New Nations

The former Yugoslavia has broken into seven new countries since 1991, and at least one additional province — the self-governing Republika Srpska in Bosnia and Herzegovina — is threatening to secede. Kosovo, on Serbia's southern border, declared its independence in February. The northern Serbian province of Vojvodina, populated by many Hungarians — is autonomous.

more death and destruction against the Tibetans in 1966 during the Cultural Revolution, the Tibetans claim.[39]

In other regions, movements to allow ethnic minorities to express their cultures and govern their own affairs have flourished since the 1960s. Such efforts have succeeded among the Welsh in Scotland and the Basques in Spain. In Belgium divisions between Dutch-speakers in Flanders, who make up roughly 60 percent of the population, and the French-speakers of Wallonia widened as more power devolved from the central government to the regions. In Canada separatist aspirations among French-speakers, who make up about 80 percent of the population in the province of Québec, culminated in a 1980 referendum on independence that was rejected by 60 percent of the voters. A subsequent referendum in October 1995 failed by a smaller margin, with 50.6 percent voting No and 49.4 percent Yes.[40]

In northern Iraq's Qandil Mountains, recruits for a splinter group of the militant Kurdish PKK separatists are training to fight government troops across the border in Iran. Some 16-28 million Kurds are dispersed in Turkey, Iraq, Iran and Syria, making them the world's largest nation without its own country. The PKK wants a single Kurdish state; other Kurds seek either greater autonomy or independence from the countries where they live.

During the Cold War, the United States, the Soviet Union and others signed the Helsinki Final Act of 1975, which established, among other things, the principle of "equal rights and self-determination of peoples." Latvia, Lithuania and Estonia would later use this to justify seceding from the Soviet Union, according to a U.S. government official involved in overseeing implementation of the act. The 1977 Soviet constitution gave the constituent republics the right to leave the U.S.S.R., but the right was not exercised for fear of reprisals from Moscow.[41]

Mikhail Gorbachev — the Soviet leader from 1985 to 1991 whose "glasnost" policy of greater openness to the West proved to be a catalyst for the break-up the U.S.S.R. — had his doubts about self-determination. In his memoirs, he wrote that "the application by a community of its right to self-determination leads regularly to a corresponding attack on the other community. . . . It is obvious that the recognition of the rights of peoples to self-determination should not be absolute."[42]

Ethno-centrism Surges

The fall of communism in Eastern Europe in the late 1980s and early '90s unleashed a wave of nationalist sentiment that destroyed the two largest multi-ethnic states in the region — Yugoslavia and the Soviet Union. Lithuania got the ball rolling, declaring independence from the Soviets in March 1990. Within two years, 15 new states had emerged from the former Soviet Union and another four in the former Yugoslavia.[43]

Soon several of the new states were experiencing their own secession movements. Russia fought fiercely and successfully to suppress the independence aspirations of the Chechens, a Muslim people with a long history of resisting subjugation by Moscow. Largely Romanian-speaking Moldova saw its Russian-dominated Transdniestria region morph into a de facto yet unrecognized state with the help of the Russian military. Ethnic Armenians in Azerbaijan's Nagorno-Karabakh region set up their own state in 1991, provoking a three-year war during which thousands of Azeris fled. Two regions — South Ossetia and Abkhazia — seceded from Georgia but have yet to be recognized by the international community.

Yugoslavia was torn asunder — eventually into seven new countries — due to the aggressive policies of nationalist leaders like Serbia's president, Slobodan Milosevic (1989-1997) and Croatia's president, Franjo Tudjman (1990-1999). The republics of Slovenia and Croatia in the northwest seceded in 1991, followed by Macedonia in the south and the triangular-shaped Bosnia and Herzegovina in 1992. The tiny republic of Montenegro seceded from Serbia in 2006. The province of Vojvodina in northern Serbia, populated by a substantial number of Hungarians, is autonomous but still part of Serbia.

Montenegro and Macedonia's splits were bloodless and Slovenia's relatively peaceful, but in Croatia and Bosnia hundreds of thousands were either killed, fled persecution or were expelled, leading to the term "ethnic cleansing." NATO helped to take Kosovo, a province in Serbia whose autonomy was withdrawn in 1989, away from the Serbs in 1999 after Milosevic brutally cracked down on Kosovo Albanian separatists. Kosovo remained an international protectorate for the next nine years.

The Yugoslav experience highlighted the danger of using referenda to determine the status of territories. The Serbs living in Bosnia, who made up about a third of the population, did not want to secede from Yugoslavia so they boycotted the 1992 plebiscite. When it passed with the overwhelming support of the Bosnian Muslims and Croats, the Bosnian Serbs violently resisted integration into Bosnia, and a three-year war ensued. The EU had helped to trigger the referendum by imposing a deadline on the Yugoslav republics to request recognition as independent countries. [44]

In 1993, Czechoslovakia split into the Czech and Slovak republics even though no referendum was held, and opinion polls indicated most citizens wanted to keep the country together. [45] The split came about because the leading politicians decided in 1992 that a peaceful divorce was easier than negotiating a new constitution with the Czechs favoring a more centralized state and the Slovaks wanting more autonomy.

In August 1999 East Timor seceded from Indonesia after a U.N.-supervised referendum. East Timor's annexation by Indonesia in 1975 had never been recognized by the U.N., and the East Timorese were Catholic, unlike the predominantly Muslim Indonesians, since the area had been colonized by Portugal.

The path to independence was a bloody one. The Indonesian military supported anti-independence militias who killed some 1,400 Timorese, causing 300,000 to flee, and destroyed much of the country's infrastructure. Australian-led international peacekeepers helped restore order in September 1999, and Timor Leste became a U.N. member on Sept. 27, 2002. [46]

By contrast, the separatist movement in Aceh has never succeeded in gaining independence, despite a decades-long struggle. Instead, the Free Aceh Movement and the Indonesian government signed a peace treaty in 2005, granting Aceh autonomy. The rapprochement was facilitated by a feeling of solidarity that grew out of the December 2004 Indian Ocean tsunami, which killed more than 130,000 people in Aceh.

CURRENT SITUATION

Balkan Pandora's Box

The shock waves emanating from Kosovo's Feb. 17 declaration of independence show that separatism remains an explosive issue. For Prime Minister Hashim

---

What Is a Nation?

The words nation, state and country are often used — incorrectly — as if they are interchangeable. But international law and usage today make clear distinctions in the concepts, as set out by U.S. lawyer and diplomat Henry Wheaton in his 1836 text Elements of International Law.

A "nation," he wrote, implies "a community of race, which is generally shown by community of language, manners and customs."

A country — or "state" — refers to "the union of a number of individuals in a fixed territory, and under one central authority," Wheaton explained. Thus a state "may be composed of different races of men" while a nation or people "may be subject to several states."

Wheaton noted that in ancient Rome, the philosopher and orator Cicero defined a state as "a body politic, or society of men, united together for the purpose of promoting their mutual safety and advantage by their combined strength."

Source: Henry Wheaton, Elements of International Law, 1836.

Thaçi, a former separatist guerrilla, "independence is everything for our country and our people. We sacrificed, we deserve independence, and independence of Kosovo is our life, it's our future." [47]

The Kosovars waited until Serbia's presidential elections were over before seceding in order to deny the more nationalistic Serb candidate, Tomislav Nikolic, the chance to make political hay out of the declaration. On Feb. 3, Nikolic narrowly lost to his more moderate opponent, Boris Tadiç. Kosovo also deliberately made its declaration before Russia assumed the presidency of the U.N. Security Council on March 1, knowing that Moscow opposes its independence.

At this stage, few expect Serbia to launch a military offensive to take back Kosovo, given the strong NATO presence in the region. The Serbs instead are vowing to diplomatically freeze out any countries that recognize Kosovo. Russia's ambassador to the EU, Vladimir Chizhov, warned in February that such recognition would be "a thorn in our political dialogue." [48] This has not prevented more than 30 countries so far from endorsing Kosovo's independence, including the United States, Canada, Australia and much of Europe.

Some fear that recognizing Kosovo will open a Pandora's box of ethnically motivated separatism. For example, the ethnic Serbs in Bosnia and Herzegovina, who have already largely separated themselves from the rest of Bosnia by creating Republika Srpska, on Feb. 21 pledged to hold

Wearing symbolic chains, a Uyghur protester in Geneva demands self-rule for the predominantly Muslim, ethnically Turkic Uyghurs in China's autonomous western region of Xinjiang. He also opposes China's one-child policy, which human rights advocates say forces some pregnant mothers to get abortions. China says recent separatist unrest in Tibet has triggered protests in Xinjiang, where some 500 Uyghurs held a demonstration in Khotan on March 23.

Frozen Conflicts

Russia's heavy clampdown on separatists in Chechnya serves as a stark warning to other ethnic groups in the region with separatist leanings not to push for independence. The predominantly Muslim Chechens had managed to gain de facto independence from Moscow in their 1994-1996 war, but Russia recaptured the territory in 1999. Tens of thousands have been killed in these conflicts and hundreds of thousands displaced.

Ethnic violence has also spread to other neighboring republics in the North Caucasus like Dagestan, North Ossetia and Ingushetiya, where disparate rebel groups are fighting for more autonomy or independence. To prevent the Balkanization of Russia, the Putin government cracked down hard on the violence.

Meanwhile, the Central Asian republics of Kazakhstan, Tajikistan, Uzbekistan, Turkmenistan and Kyrgyzstan no longer are as economically integrated as they were during the Soviet era, fueling corruption. Reportedly officials routinely demand bribes from traders and workers seeking to move goods or personnel across the new borders.[50] Some of the new states, like Kyrgyzstan, are weak and at risk of fragmenting or being subsumed by their neighbors.[51]

Transdniestria, Nagorno-Karabakh, South Ossetia and Abkhazia remain unrecognized de facto states, since Moldova, Azerbaijan and Georgia all lack the military or economic strength to recapture the four breakaway territories. The long, narrow valley of Transdniestria — which has a population of Russians, Moldovans and Ukrainians — is "like a Brezhnev museum," according to a U.S. government official involved in reconciliation efforts there, referring to the Soviet leader from 1964 to 1982 whose regime was characterized by stagnation and repression. "It is a nasty place: the rulers repress the Moldovan language, and the economy is largely black market." And Georgia's two secessionist regions — South Ossetia and Abkhazia — are egged on by Russia, according to the State Department's Bryza.

These so-called frozen conflicts have produced "an impasse of volatile stability [where] nobody is happy but nobody is terribly unhappy either, and life goes on, as neither central state nor de facto states have collapsed," writes Dov Lynch, author of a book on the conflicts and director of the U.S. Institute for Peace project. Up to a million people have been displaced, standards of living have dropped as economies barely function, organized

a referendum on secession. But the republic's chances of gaining acceptance as an independent country are slimmer than Kosovo's, because both the EU and the United States firmly oppose it.

Romania and Slovakia worry that their large Hungarian minorities could feel emboldened to demand more autonomy or even unification with Hungary. Hungarians in the Romanian region of Transylvania are already demanding that Romanian law recognize their ethnically based autonomy.[49]

Could separatism spread to the United States?

YES
Kyle Ellis
*Founder, Californians
for Independence*

Written for *CQ Global Researcher*, March 2008

Asking whether separatism will spread to the United States is a bit of an odd question to pose in a nation founded through an act of secession from the British Empire.

Secession is at the very foundation of what it means to be American, and over the years since the country was founded many secessionist organizations and movements have kept this American tradition alive.

If you think the Civil War ended the question of secession in the United States, any Internet search you run will show just how wrong you are. Dozens of groups in various states are organizing and agitating for secession.

These groups are getting larger, and more serious ones are being founded all the time. As the leader and founder of one of these new organizations, I would like to offer a little insight as to why I believe the idea of secession will become a lot more popular in the years to come.

Here in California, there is much resentment toward the federal government. People don't like how politicians who live thousands of miles away are able to involve themselves in the creation of California's laws and the allocation of local resources, not to mention the billions of tax dollars sent away each year that are never to be seen again.

Other states have other reasons for wanting independence: Vermonters see the federal government as fundamentally out of touch with their way of life; the Southern states believe their unique culture is being systematically destroyed by the actions of the federal government; and Alaska and Hawaii view the circumstances surrounding their admittance into the Union as being suspect, if not downright undemocratic.

All of these groups view the federal government as broken in such a way that it cannot be fixed from within the system — a valid view considering it is run by two political parties that are fundamentally statist in nature. The two-party system is not even democratic (as we know from the 2000 elections), because it effectively disenfranchises millions of third-party voters due to the winner-take-all nature of political contests.

The federal government also continues to encroach upon individual rights and liberties.

It is natural that marginalized and disenfranchised people will seek to break away from a system they are not a part of, just as the founders of the United States sought to break away from Britain.

NO
Seth D. Kaplan
*Foreign Policy Analyst and Business Consultant
Author,* Fixing Fragile States: A New
Paradigm for Development

Written for *CQ Global Researcher*, March 2008

Separatism requires a cohesive minority group that dominates a well-defined geographical area and possesses a strong sense of grievance against the central government. All three of these ingredients were present when the United States had its own encounter with separatism: the Confederacy's bid for independence in the 1860s. Southern whites possessed a unique identity, dominated a contiguous territory and were so aggrieved at the federal government that they were prepared to take up arms.

In recent decades, another disaffected and socioculturally distinct group in North America has waged a potent — but in this case nonviolent — campaign for independence: Canada's Québécois. Within the United States, however, no such groups exist today, and none seems likely to emerge in the foreseeable future. Puerto Rico does have a separatist movement, but Puerto Rico is already semi-autonomous and, more to the point, is only an unincorporated organized territory of the United States — not a full-fledged state. Some argue that California is close to reaching a level of economic self-sufficiency that would enable it to survive as an independent state. However, even if California could afford to be independent, neither its sense of difference nor of grievance seems likely to become strong enough to form the basis for a separatist movement.

Some Native American tribes, discontented with their circumscribed sovereignty, might wish to separate but — even if Washington raised no objections — their small populations, weak economies and unfavorable locations (inland, distant from other markets) would not make them viable as independent states.

The cohesiveness of the United States stands in marked contrast to most of the world's large, populous states. China, India, Indonesia and Pakistan all contend with separatist movements today.

Why has the United States escaped this danger? The answer lies in the impartiality of its institutions, the mobility of its people and the brevity of its history. Its robust and impartial institutions do not provide ethnic or religious groups with a strong enough sense of discrimination to ignite separatist passions. Its citizens migrate within the country at an unprecedented rate, ensuring a constant remixing of its population and tempering any geographically focused sense of difference. And its history as a relatively young, immigrant country — where people focus on the future far more than the past — means that few are fiercely loyal to any particular area.

crime flourishes and a "profound sense of psychological isolation" prevails.[52]

In one of those ongoing conflicts, the militant Kurdish separatist organization, the PKK, has stepped up its violent campaign against Turkey, which has responded with a military strike into the PKK's base in northern Iraq.[53] The Kurds in northern Iraq already govern themselves. Some pragmatic Kurdish leaders feel their best solution would be to replicate this model in Iran, Syria and Turkey — where they do not have autonomy — instead of pushing for a single Kurdish state.

Meanwhile, the Israeli-Palestinian conflict seems to be edging towards a "two-state solution" under which the Palestinians would be given a state of their own in the West Bank and Gaza in exchange for acknowledgment of Israel's right to exist. However, the region's ongoing violence makes reaching a final agreement problematic.

In Africa, Somaliland looks to be creeping towards acceptance as a state, too. An African Union mission in 2005 concluded that Somaliland's case for statehood was "unique and self-justified" and not likely to "open a Pandora's box." Nevertheless, its neighbors continue to oppose recognizing it formally.[54]

Asian Disputes

The separatist movement in Sri Lanka remains strong. The Tamil Tigers run a de facto state in the northeast and are fiercely fighting the Sri Lankan government, which wants to regain control of the whole country. On Feb. 4 — the 60th anniversary of the country's independence — Sri Lankan President Mahinda Rajapaksa affirmed his commitment to "go forward as a single, unitary state."[55]

According to a Tamil activist who asked not to be identified, Sri Lanka is squeezing the Tamil-controlled area with an economic embargo and preventing international aid organizations from providing humanitarian supplies. Though Pakistan, India and China are helping the Sri Lankan government, the Tamils are holding onto their territory, he says, with the help of Tamils who have fled the country and are dispersed throughout the world. This "diaspora" community is providing funds for weapons that the guerrillas buy covertly from Asian governments, he says.

In Aceh, the 2005 self-rule pact with Indonesia "is working to some extent," according to a U.S. official in Indonesia. With rising crime, high unemployment, little trade with the outside world and little experience in spending public money, "the challenge for the ex-rebels is to become good governors. They need help from the international community," the official says.

Separatism in Taiwan received a blow in the January 2008 parliamentary and March 2008 presidential elections when the Kuomintang Party, which supports reunification with mainland China, trounced the separatist Democratic Progressive Party (DPP), which seeks U.N. membership for Taiwan.[56]

For its part, the United States continues to sit on the fence, reflecting the international community's ambivalence toward Taiwan. According to Susan Bremner, the State Department's deputy Taiwan coordinating adviser, the United States has "not formally recognized Chinese sovereignty over Taiwan and [has] not made any determination as to Taiwan's political status."[57] In the past, however, the United States has said that if China were to bomb or invade Taiwan, it would help defend the island.[58]

In western China, the Uyghurs continue to see their proportion of the population decline as more ethnic Chinese migrate there. Chinese tourists are flooding in, too, as visiting EU official Fearghas O'Beara recently discovered in Kashgar. "The city was as foreign to the Chinese as it was to me," he said. "At times I felt a bit uneasy as well-to-do Chinese people took copious photos of the 'natives' with their quaint habits and clothing."[59]

Eclipsing all these movements are the newest round of protests by Tibetans that began in March, the 49th anniversary of a failed uprising against Chinese rule in Tibet. Protesters in Lhasa on March 14 burned, vandalized and looted businesses of ethnic Chinese immigrants, venting their seething resentment over the wave of immigration that has turned Tibetans into a minority in their capital city.[60] The Tibetans say 99 people were killed, but the Chinese put the figure at 22.[61] Though the Chinese riot police were initially slow to respond, Beijing is now cracking down hard on the protesters. It also is keeping monks elsewhere confined to their monasteries and forcing them to denounce the Dalai Lama. China accuses the exiled leader of orchestrating the violence — calling him "a vicious devil" and a "beast in human form" — even though he has condemned the violence and advocates autonomy rather than outright independence for Tibet.[62]

Before the outbreak of violence, a Chinese Foreign Ministry spokesman had urged the Dalai Lama to drop his "splittist" efforts to attain "Tibetan independence" and do more for average Tibetans. "The Dalai clique repeatedly talks about Tibetan culture and the environment being ruined. But in fact, the Tibetan society, economy and culture have prospered," said spokesman Qin Gang. "The only thing destroyed was the cruel and dark serfdom rule, which the Dalai clique wanted to restore."[63]

The 72-year-old Dalai Lama, Tibet's leader for 68 years, commands enormous respect around the world, as evidenced by U.S. President George W. Bush's decision to telephone China's President Hu Jintao on March 26 to urge the Chinese government "to engage in substantive dialogue" with the Dalai Lama.[64]

Tension over China's suppression of the Tibetans is mounting as some countries consider calling for a boycott of the Beijing Olympics in August to show solidarity with the Tibetans. European foreign ministers, meeting in Brdo, Slovenia, on March 28-29, came out against an outright boycott of the games, although the leaders of France and the Czech Republic are threatening to boycott the opening ceremony. And on April 1, U.S. House Speaker Nancy Pelosi, D-Calif., urged President Bush to reconsider his plans to attend the opening ceremony if China continues to refuse talks with the Dalai Lama.

But Bush at the time was becoming entangled in yet another separatist controversy. Stopping in Ukraine on his way to a NATO summit in Romania, Bush said he supports Georgia's entry into NATO, which Russia opposes. If Georgia were to join the alliance, the NATO allies could be forced to support any future Georgian military efforts to re-take South Ossetia and Abkhazia — also strongly opposed by Russia. That would put Georgia in the middle of the same geopolitical chess game that Kosovo found itself in.[65]

Secession in the Americas

Across the Americas, separatist movements are scarcer and weaker than in Europe, Africa and Asia. Perhaps the most significant is the recent flare-up in Bolivia, where the mainly European-descended lowlanders are pushing for greater regional autonomy and are even threatening secession.[66] They are wealthier than the mostly indigenous highlanders and fear that the centralization efforts of indigenous President Evo Morales will loosen the lowlanders' grip on Bolivia's natural resources. Already, Morales has proposed amending the constitution so that oil and gas revenues would be shared evenly across the country.[67]

There are also plans to redistribute a huge portion of Bolivia's land — beginning with its forests — to indigenous communities. Vice Minister of Lands Alejandro Almaraz, who is implementing the project, said recently the tension with the lowlanders was "very painful" and warned that "the east of Bolivia is ready to secede and cause a civil war" to thwart the government's redistribution plans.[68]

In the United States, separatism remains a marginal force, though the movement has never been more visible. "There are 36 secessionist organizations now at work," including in New Hampshire, Vermont, California, Washington state, Oregon and South Carolina, says Kirkpatrick Sale, director of the Middlebury Institute, a think tank on secessionism that he established in 2004.

In Texas, Larry Kilgore — a Christian-orientated secessionist who wants to enact biblical law — won 225,783 votes or 18.5 percent in the March 4 primary for Republican candidate to the U.S. Senate.[69] "If the United States is for Kosovo's independence, there is no reason why we should not be for Vermont's independence," says Sale. "The American Empire is collapsing. It is too big, corrupt and unequal to survive."

Some Native American tribes with limited self-government continue to push for more autonomy. For example, a group of dissident Lakota Indians traveled to Washington in December 2007 to deliver a declaration of independence to the State Department, which did not respond.[70]

OUTLOOK

Ethnocentric Separatism

The growing tendency to construct states along ethnic lines does not necessarily bode well for the future. French philosopher Ernest Renan's warning, delivered in the era of empires and grand alliances, has as much resonance today as it did in 1882: "Be on your guard, for this ethnographic politics is in no way a stable thing and, if today you use it against others, tomorrow you may see it turned against yourselves."[71]

"The Kosovo case is not unique despite the many claims to that effect by European and American diplomats," says Serwer at the United States Institute for Peace. "If people worry about it being a precedent, they should have ensured its future was decided by the U.N. Security

Council. That would have created a good precedent for deciding such things."[72]

Though some might support the creation of a U.N. body for assessing separatist claims, U.N. member states would most likely fear it would only serve to give more publicity to separatist causes, writes American University self-determination expert Orentlicher.[73]

The two Western European regions most likely to become independent within the next 10 years are Scotland and Flanders, says Flemish nationalist Dauwen. As for Transdniestria, "the more time that passes, the more likely it will become independent, because the military will resist rejoining Moldova," says a U.S. official working to promote peace in Eastern Europe. The passage of time usually increases the survival odds of unrecognized states, because entrenched elites who profit from their existence fight to preserve them regardless of how politically or economically viable the states are.[74]

The probability of separatist movements morphing into new states also depends on who opposes them. Nagorno-Karabakh, for instance, is more likely to gain independence from Azerbaijan than Chechnya is from Russia because the Azeris are weaker than the Russians.

Political leadership is another factor. When hardliners and extremists rise to power it triggers separatist movements, while the emergence of moderates willing to share power can entice separatist regions to be peacefully and consensually reintegrated into the mother country.

Ethnocentric separatism may also fuel irredentism — annexation of a territory on the basis of common ethnicity. For instance, the Albanians in Macedonia, Kosovo and Albania may push to form a single, unitary state. Ethnic Hungarians living in Romania, Serbia and Slovakia may seek to forge closer links with Hungary; Somalis scattered across Somaliland, Kenya, Ethiopia and Djibouti might decide to form a "Greater Somalia."

"The goal of attaining recognition is the glue holding it together," a State Department official said about Somaliland. "If recognized, I fear that outside powers will interfere more, and it could split."

Likewise, Kurds in Iraq, Turkey, Iran and Syria could rise up and push for a "Greater Kurdistan" encompassing all Kurds. While some countries might support the creation of a Kurdish state in theory, they would be reticent, too, knowing how much it could destabilize the Middle East.

In Southeast Asia, Myanmar (formerly Burma), Thailand and the Philippines are potential separatist hotbeds as tensions persist between the many different ethnic groups, with religious differences further aggravating the situation.[75] "If something moves in the region, it could have a tsunami effect, as happened in Eastern Europe in 1989," says Busdachin at the Unrepresented Nations and Peoples Organization. He adds that most of these groups are seeking autonomy, not independence.

Yet a U.S. official in Indonesia says of Aceh: "I would be very surprised if we would have a new country in 15 years. I don't see that dynamic. Things are moving in the other direction."

And in Taiwan, any push for U.N. membership would worry trading partners like the European Union and the United States, which are keen to maintain good relations with the island but reluctant to anger China.

As for the United States, the strong federal government that emerged during the Great Depression seems to be on the wane as state and local governments increasingly assert their powers. Yet the nation remains well-integrated, and outright secession of a state or group of states seems unlikely. Smaller changes are possible, however, such as the splitting of California into northern and southern states or the evolution of the U.S.-governed Puerto Rico into a new U.S. state or independent country.

In the long term, separatism will fade, author Kaplan believes. "Separatism always appears on the rise when new states are born because such entities do not have the deep loyalties of their people typical of older, successful countries," he says. But as states mature, he notes, the number of separatist movements usually declines.

A starkly different prediction is made by Jerry Z. Muller, history professor at The Catholic University of America in Washington. "Increased urbanization, literacy and political mobilization; differences in the fertility rates and economic performance of various ethnic groups and immigration will challenge the internal structure of states as well as their borders," he wrote. "Whether politically correct or not, ethnonationalism will continue to shape the world in the 21st century." Globalization will lead to greater wealth disparities and deeper social cleavages, he continues, and "wealthier and higher-achieving regions might try to separate themselves from poorer and lower-achieving ones." Rather than fight the separatist trend, Muller argues, "partition may be the most humane lasting solution."[76]

UPDATE

The world's newest country was born July 9, 2011, when Africa's largest nation, Sudan, split in two, with the south seceding from the north.

"We give praise to the Almighty God for making it possible for us to witness this day [for] which we have waited for more than 56 years," South Sudan President Salva Kiir Mayardit said during a proclamation ceremony in the new capital, Juba.

Diplomats from around the world attended — including northern Sudan's President, Omar Al Bashir — effectively giving the secession a universal seal of approval. [77] Five days later, the United Nations admitted South Sudan as its 193rd member.

The birth of South Sudan came six months after southerners voted for independence in an internationally sanctioned referendum and almost six decades after they mounted their first war of independence from the North in 1955. The second civil war, which lasted 20 years and ended in 2005, cost 2 million lives. However, violence between northern and southern forces continues to flare, and the north-south border is still in dispute.

But the success of the South Sudanese independence movement is not a sign that separatism is on the rise globally. Indeed, since the creation in February 2008 of the world's previous "newest" country, Kosovo, separatist movements have faced more setbacks than successes. Of the roughly 60 significant secessionist or autonomy movements, only about 10 — including the South Sudanese, Greenlanders and South Ossetians — have made significant progress toward securing greater autonomy or independence. About twice that number — including the Tamils, Quebecers and Uyghurs — have lost ground. [78]

Militant separatists have experienced major setbacks. The most drastic was the devastating defeat inflicted by Sri Lankan forces against the Tamil Tigers in May 2009, abruptly ending the Tigers' violent 26-year struggle to create an independent Tamil homeland. Some 100,000 people were killed and 1 million displaced during that conflict. [79]

Other militant separatists also are encountering difficulties, as governments confront them militarily rather than negotiate political settlements. In Africa, for example, the Ethiopian government continues to oppose the Oromo Liberation Front and the Ogaden National

Uyghur women grapple with a riot policeman during ethnic violence in Urumqi, the capital of China's remote northwest Xinjiang province, on July 7, 2009. The unrest had begun two days earlier, when the Muslim Uyghurs rose up in protest against what they deem China's cultural genocide policies toward their group, but police brutally repressed the demonstrations, and nearly 200 people were killed.

Liberation Front, which represent, respectively, Ethiopia's Oromo and Somali minorities.

In East Asia, the Christian-dominated Philippine government is clamping down on Muslim Moro separatist militancy on the island of Mindanao. In Myanmar, the military junta is showing no mercy in its campaign to crush the Karen National Union, a group that has fought to create a homeland for the Karen minority since 1947. Both the Karen and Moro movements have been undermined by splits within their ranks, as various splinter groups fight one another.

In China, home to numerous autonomy movements, two ethnic minorities — the Buddhist Tibetans and the Muslim Uyghurs — rose up in protest against the government, respectively, in March 2008 and July 2009. The Chinese government brutally repressed the protests, killing hundreds. Today, Beijing refuses to negotiate with the leaders of the Tibetan and Uyghur autonomy movements and restricts visits by foreigners, making it hard to get a clear picture of the situation.

The International Campaign for Tibet, an activist group, said, "The series of travel bans suggests a high degree of government nervousness about potential trouble and foreign witnesses and undermines efforts to portray Tibet as harmonious and open for business." [80]

In Spain, the militant group Euskadi Ta Askatasuna (ETA), which has fought for an independent Basque homeland since 1968, is seeing many of its leaders arrested and its organization dismantled by government authorities. And in Russia, the government has stepped up counter-insurgency efforts against militant separatists from the North Caucasus after a spate of terrorist attacks, including on Moscow's subway and airport. [81]

The scorecard for separatists who pursue their goals peacefully by forming political parties and competing in elections is mixed, as evidenced by the performances of separatist parties from Quebec and Scotland in recent elections. On May 2, 2011, the secessionist Bloc Quebecois suffered a near meltdown in Canada's parliamentary elections, losing all but 4 of its 47 seats. "Although many Quebecers have shown they are dissatisfied with the Bloc," *The Gazette*, a Montreal-based newspaper, said in an editorial, "it doesn't mean they want to shelve the national question." [82]

Just three days later and across the Atlantic, the Scottish National Party (SNP), which wants Scotland to split from the United Kingdom, won its first overall majority in the Scottish parliament. The SNP is pledging to hold a referendum on independence within five years.

In continental Europe, where many regional autonomy movements exist, the Dutch-speaking people of Flanders, the Flemings, have brought Belgium to the brink of break-up. Separatist Flemish parties emerged as the largest political bloc in the June 2010 Belgian elections and are demanding more autonomy. Belgium's Francophone minority is resisting, and the resulting political stalemate has prevented the formation of a new government for more than a year.

In Catalonia and the Basque region (Spain), Corsica (France) and Northern Italy, separatist parties, while not as strong as in Flanders, are significant political forces. Unlike militant separatists from past generations, such as the Basques' ETA, "the new generation . . . puts politics first," noted Doug Saunders, the European bureau chief of *The Globe and Mail*, a Canadian newspaper. "The ever-telescoped threat of separation is a means to gain more politically," he wrote, suggesting that separatist parties use secessionist threats to gain more autonomy. [83]

The success of a separatist movement can depend on the political circumstances of the country where it is based, as is the case with the 25 million-strong Kurds, the world's largest nation without its own state. In Iraq, the Kurds are using the political autonomy they won after the U.S.-led 1991 and 2003 Gulf Wars to develop their oil-rich economy and have transformed Kurdistan into Iraq's most prosperous region. In Turkey, the Kurdish nationalist party, the BDP, performed well in the June 2011 elections, picking up 35 seats, boosting its chances of gaining some kind of autonomy in a planned overhaul of Turkey's constitution. By contrast, the repressive regimes in Iran and Syria have made it more difficult for the Kurds to make progress — even on basic human rights issues, including the right to speak their own language.

Eight separatist movements have now achieved de facto independence but have not yet been accepted as a United Nations member state — the effective international badge of statehood. [84] Kosovo is probably best poised to be admitted. Seventy-six U.N. member states already recognize Kosovo's independence, including the United States and most of Europe; Russia, China and India do not.

The status of Abkhazia and South Ossetia, Georgian enclaves that seceded in the early 1990s, changed after the August 2008 Georgia-Russia war, when Moscow recognized the independence of both.

In Taiwan, which has governed itself independently from China since 1949, signals are mixed. On one hand, the pro-unity Kuomintang party has, since being re-elected in March 2008, strengthened trade ties with mainland China. However, polls show that support among Taiwanese for independence has increased, from 30.5 percent to 35.5 percent. [85] Thus, it appears that while the Taiwanese may desire better relations with mainland China, a majority still don't necessarily want reunification.

Some other movements have a chance of becoming independent in the coming decade. A frontrunner is Greenland, the huge Danish-owned Arctic island with a tiny, mostly indigenous Inuit population of 56,000. Greenlanders gained more autonomy in a November 2008 referendum and now have full control over their natural resources, which include abundant oil and gas reserves that they are beginning to exploit. Economic self-sufficiency will greatly strengthen their ability to go it alone, which the Danish government says it will not block. [86]

Meanwhile, the Palestinian territories are preparing to declare independence at the September 2011 U.N. General Assembly. That step promises to leave the world's key powers with a dilemma: While they support an independent Palestine in theory, they want it to result from a Palestinian-Israeli peace treaty and not a unilateral move by the Palestinians. For that reason, Juba's celebratory scenes in July ushering in South Sudan's independence are unlikely to be repeated in the Palestinian territories in September.

NOTES

1. For detailed accounts of the protests, see *The Economist*, "Trashing the Beijing Road," March 19, 2008, www.economist.com/opinion/displaystory.cfm?story_id=10875823 and Tini Tran, "Tibetan Protests Escalate into Violence," The Associated Press, March 14, 2008, http://news.yahoo.com/s/ap/20080314/ap_on_re_as/china_tibet.

2. Ellie Tzortzi, "US outrage as Serb protesters burn embassy," Reuters, Feb. 21, 2008, www.reuters.com/article/worldNews/idUSL2087155420080221?pageNumber=1&virtualBrandChannel=0.

3. See "In quotes: Kosovo reaction," BBC News, Feb. 17, 2008, http://news.bbc.co.uk/1/hi/world/europe/7249586.stm.

4. See European Commission's Web site for political and economic profiles of Serbia and Kosovo, http://ec.europa.eu/enlargement/potential-candidate-countries/index_en.htm.

5. Selcan Hacaoglu and Christopher Torchi, "Turkey launches ground incursion into Iraq," The Associated Press, Feb. 22, 2008, www.washingtontimes.com/apps/pbcs.dll/article?AID=/20080222/FOREIGN/297026899/1001.

6. For list of current U.N. member states, see the U.N.'s Web site, www.un.org/members/list.shtml.

7. To see growth in U.N. membership, go to www.un.org/members/growth.shtml.

8. See "Kurdistan — Kurdish Conflict," globalsecurity.org, www.globalsecurity.org/military/world/war/kurdistan.htm.

9. Lisa Schlein, "East Timor Facing Food Crisis," June 24, 2007, www.voanews.com/english/archive/2007-06/2007-06-24-voa8.cfm?CFID=213682651&CFTOKEN=33049644.

10. Fried was testifying at a hearing on the Balkans at the U.S. House of Representatives Committee on Foreign Affairs, March 12, 2008. For full testimony go to: http://foreignaffairs.house.gov/testimony.asp?subnav=close.

11. Gary J. Bass, "Independence Daze," *The New York Times*, Jan. 6, 2008, www.nytimes.com/2008/01/06/magazine/06wwln-idealab-t.html?ref=magazine.

12. Several Uyghurs were detained in the U.S. terrorist prison in Guantánamo Bay, Cuba. According to James Millward, history professor at Georgetown University, Washington, D.C., the Uyghurs' detention in Guantánamo became an embarrassment for the United States when it emerged they were pro-U.S. and anti-China. The U.S. administration decided it could not send them back to China because they would probably be mistreated. Although the United States asked more than 100 other countries to take them, all refused except Albania, where some of the detainees were ultimately expatriated in 2006.

13. Chinese Foreign Ministry spokesperson Qin Gang at press conference, March 18, 2008, www.china-embassy.org/eng/fyrth/t416255.htm.

14. Jay Shankar, "Pelosi Urges Probe of Chinese Claim Dalai Lama Behind Unrest," Bloomberg News, March 21, 2008, www.bloomberg.com/apps/news?pid=20601101&sid=aDLLITUsmrIg&refer=japan.

15. Seth D. Kaplan, "Democratization in Post-Colonial States: The Triumph of a Societal-Based Approach in Somaliland," in *Fixing Fragile States: A new paradigm for development* (scheduled for publication July 2008).

16. Harvey Feldman, fellow in China policy for the Heritage Foundation, speaking at a discussion on Taiwanese elections in Washington, D.C., Jan. 15, 2008.

17. In November 2004, a group of about 50 secessionists, gathered for a conference in Middlebury, Vt., signed a declaration pledging to develop cooperation between the various secessionist groups in the

United States, including setting up a think tank, The Middlebury Institute, devoted to studying separatism, secessionism and self-determination. See www.middleburyinstitute.org.

18. Diane Orentlicher, "International Responses to Separatist Claims: Are Democratic Principles Relevant," Chapter 1 of Stephen Macedo and Allen Buchanan, eds., *Secession and Self-Determination* (2003), p. 29.

19. Interview with Nicolas Gros-Verheyde, "Europe should develop its defence policy with Russia," *Europolitics* (EU affairs subscription-based news service), March 4, 2008, www.europolitics.info.

20. Donald L. Horowitz, "A Right to Secede," Chapter 2 of Macedo and Buchanan, *op. cit.*, p. 50.

21. *Ibid.*, p. 73.

22. Basha was speaking at the Center for Strategic and International Studies in Washington, D.C., on May 5, 2007.

23. Lecture on Shanghai Cooperation Organization by Professor Akihiro Iwashita, visiting fellow at the Brookings Institution, delivered at the Woodrow Wilson International Center for Scholars, Feb. 2, 2008.

24. Jeremic was addressing the European Parliament's Foreign Affairs Committee in Strasbourg, Feb. 20, 2008. See the press release at www.europarl.europa.eu/sides/getDoc.do?pubRef=-//EP//TEXT+IM-PRESS+20080219IPR21605+0+DOC+XML+V0//EN&language=EN.

25. Horowitz, *op. cit.*, p. 56.

26. John J. Tkacik, "Dealing with Taiwan's Referendum on the United Nations," Heritage Foundation, Sept. 10, 2007, www.heritage.org/about/staff/JohnTkacikpapers.cfm#2007Research.

27. Zoellick's remark, made at a U.S. congressional hearing on China on May 10, 2006, was quoted in John J. Tkacik, "America's Stake in Taiwan," Heritage Foundation, Jan. 11, 2007, www.heritage.org/Research/AsiaandthePacific/bg1996.cfm.

28. For background, see "Nationalist Movements in Western Europe," *Editorial Research Reports*, April

16, 1969, available at *CQ Researcher Plus Archive*, www.library.cqpress.com.

29. Adapted quote from Ernest Renan, French philosopher and theoretician on statehood and nationalism, in his discourse "What is a nation?" widely viewed as the definitive text on civic nationalism (1882).

30. For more details, see Mark E. Brandon, Chapter 10, "Secession, Constitutionalism and American Experience," Macedo and Buchanan, *op. cit.*, pp. 272-305.

31. The case is 74 U.S. 700 (1868), available at http://caselaw.lp.findlaw.com/scripts/getcase.pl?court=US&vol=74&invol=700.

32. See Patricia Carley, "Self-Determination: Sovereignty, Territorial Integrity, and the Right to Secession," *Peaceworks 7*, March 1996, p. 3, www.usip.org/pubs/peaceworks/pwks7.html.

33. Orentlicher, *op. cit.*, p. 21.

34. For more details, see Washington Kurdish Institute, "The Territorial Status of Kirkuk," position paper, November 2007, http://71.18.173.106/pages/WO-PositionPapers.htm#.

35. For background, see Peter Katel, "Middle East Tensions," *CQ Researcher*, Oct. 27, 2006, pp. 898-903.

36. Figures taken from *The Statesman's Yearbook*, an annual reference book on the states of the world that first appeared in 1864, and from the U.N. Web site, www.un.org/members/list.shtml.

37. For full text of the 1960 U.N. Declaration on the Granting of Independence to Colonial Countries and Peoples, go to www.un.org/Depts/dpi/decolonization/declaration.htm.

38. For background, see "Sri Lanka," *Political Handbook of the World*, CQ Press (2007).

39. According to the Central Tibetan Administration Web site, www.tibet.net/en/diir/chrono.html.

40. For background, see Mary H. Cooper, "Québec Sovereignty," *CQ Researcher*, Oct. 6, 1995, pp. 873-896.

41. Under Article 72 of the 1977 U.S.S.R. Constitution, "Each Union Republic retains the right freely to

secede from the U.S.S.R," www.departments .bucknell.edu/russian/const/1977toc.html.

42. Mikhail Gorbachev and Odile Jacob, ed., *Avant Memoires* (1993), p. 30.

43. The 15 ex-Soviet states could have been 16. Karelia, a region now part of western Russia bordering Finland, used to be a separate Soviet republic until 1956 when its status was downgraded to an autonomous republic within Russia.

44. Orentlicher, *op. cit.*, p. 36.

45. *Ibid.*, p. 33.

46. See CIA, *The World Factbook*, https://www.cia.gov/ library/publications/the-world-factbook/geos/tt.html.

47. Reported on CNN.com, Jan. 9, 2008, http:// edition.cnn.com/2008/WORLD/europe/01/09/ kosovo.independence/index.html.

48. Joanna Sopinska, "Russia in last-ditch bid to block Kosovo mission," *Europolitics* (EU affairs subscription-based news service), Feb. 7, 2008, www .europolitics.info.

49. See Medlir Mema, "Kosovo through Central European eyes," Jan. 2, 2008, Center for European Policy Analysis (CEPA), www.cepa.org/digest/ kosovo-through-central-european-eyes.php.

50. From lecture by researchers Kathleen Kuehnast and Nora Dudwick at the Woodrow Wilson International Center for Scholars, Nov. 27, 2006.

51. From discussion with Professors Anthony Bowyer, Central Asia and Caucasus Program Manager at IFES, the International Foundation for Election Systems, Eric McGlinchey, associate professor at George Mason University, and Scott Radnitz, assistant professor at the University of Washington, at the School for Advanced International Studies, Dec. 12, 2007.

52. Dov Lynch, *Engaging Eurasia's Separatist States* (2004), pp. 91-93.

53. Al Jazeera, "Toll rises in Turkey-PKK conflict," http://english.aljazeera.net/NR/exeres/3E14DD15-F2D1-4C65-8148-5200DFB3E975.htm.

54. Kaplan, *op. cit.*

55. The president's speech can be viewed in English at www.priu.gov.lk/news_update/Current_Affairs/

ca200802/20080204defeat_of_terrorism_is_ victory_for_all.htm.

56. See "Opposition's Ma wins Taiwan poll," BBC News, March 22, 2008, http://news.bbc.co.uk/2/ hi/asia-pacific/7309113.stm.

57. Letter from Susan Bremner, deputy Taiwan coordinating adviser at the U.S. State Department, June 26, 2007, quoted in article by Tkacik, "Dealing with Taiwan's Referendum on the United Nation," *op. cit.*

58. See Peter Brookes, "US-Taiwan Defense Relations in the Bush administration," Nov. 14, 2003, www .heritage.org/Research/AsiaandthePacific/hl808.cfm.

59. Travel diary of Fearghas O'Beara, media adviser to the president of the European Parliament, who toured the region in August 2007.

60. Jim Yardley, "As Tibet Erupted, China Security Forces Wavered," *The New York Times*, March 24, 2008, www.nytimes.com/2008/03/24/world/ asia/24tibet.html?ex=1364097600&en=58a6edae8a e26676&ei=5088&partner=rssnyt&emc=rss.

61. *Ibid.*

62. See "Chinese Crackdown on Tibetan Protests," "The Diane Rehm Show," National Public Radio, March 20, 2008, http://wamu.org/programs/dr/08/03/20 .php#19471; also see Pico Iyer, "A Monk's Struggle," *Time*, March 21, 2007, www.time.com/time/world/ article/0,8599,1723922,00.html; also see Louisa Lim, "China's Provinces Feel Crush of Tibet Crackdown," National Public Radio, March 28, 2008, www.npr .org/templates/story/story.php?storyId=89160575 &ft=1&f=1004.

63. "China urges Dalai Lama to drop splittist attempts," Xinhua News Agency, March 11, 2008.

64. See White House press release at www.whitehouse .gov/news/releases/2008/03/20080326-2.html.

65. Joanna Sopinska, "Ministers condemn Tibet crackdown, reject Olympic boycott," *Europolitics*, March 31, 2008, www.europolitics.info. See Peter Baker, "Bush Pushes NATO Membership for Ukraine, Georgia," *The Washington Post*, April 1, 2008.

66. See Kaplan, *op. cit.*, Chapter 9, "Bolivia: Building Representative Institutions in a Divided Country."

Also see Roland Flamini, "The New Latin America," *CQ Global Researcher*, March 2008, pp. 57-84.

67. Flamini, *ibid.*, p. 79.

68. Almaraz was giving a presentation on his land reform proposals at the George Washington University in Washington on March 11, 2008.

69. Primary results posted on *The Austin Chronicle's* Web site, www.austinchronicle.com/gyrobase/Issue/story?oid=oid%3A599906.

70. Bill Harlan, "Lakota group secedes from U.S." *Rapid City Journal*, Dec. 21, 2007, www.rapidcityjournal.com/articles/2007/12/21/news/local/doc476a99630633e335271152.txt.

71. Renan, *op. cit.*

72. See Daniel Serwer, "Coming Soon to a Country Near You: Kosovo Sovereignty," *Transatlantic Thinkers*, December 2007, www.usip.org/pubs/usipeace_briefings/2007/1214_kosovo.html.

73. Orentlicher, *op. cit.*, p. 37.

74. Lynch, *op. cit.*, p. 119.

75. See Joseph Chinyong Liow, "Muslim Resistance in Southern Thailand and Southern Philippines: Religion, Ideology and Politics," East-West Center, Washington, 2006, www.eastwestcenter.org/fileadmin/stored/pdfs/PS024.pdf.

76. Jerry Z. Muller, "Us and Them: The Enduring Power of Ethnic Nationalism," *Foreign Affairs*, March/April 2008, www.foreignaffairs.org/20080301faessay87203/jerry-z-muller/us-and-them.html.

77. Murithi Mutiga, "History is Made As Nation Becomes Independent State," *The Nation* (Nairobi), July 9, 2011, http://allafrica.com/ stories/201107100002.html.

78. See Brian Beary, *Separatist Movements — A Global Reference*, CQ Press (2011).

79. See Ben Doherty, "Peace a battle; Sri Lanka — 'The fighting is gone but we don't have our lives back' " *The Age* (Melbourne, Australia), May 14, 2011, www.theage.com.au/ world/peace-a-battle-20110513-1em6g.html.

80. Calum MacLeod, "Tibet prepares to reopen to foreign tourists; Annual travel ban gets lifted in August for non-Chinese visitors," *USA Today*, June 28, 2011, www.usatoday.com/ NEWS/usaedition/2011-06-28-Tibet_ST_U.htm.

81. Michael Schwirtz and Ellen Barry, "Medvedev Warns Islamic Separatists," *The New York Times*, March 30, 2011, www.nytimes.com/2011/ 03/30/world/europe/30russia.html.

82. Charles Blattberg, *et al.*, (opinion editorial), "Election 2011: Viewpoints," *The Gazette* (Montreal), May 3, 2011, www.montrealgazette.com/ news/Election+2011+Viewpoints/4715078/story.html.

83. Doug Saunders, "A new generation of separatists," *The Globe and Mail* (Canada) June 4, 2011, http://m.theglobeandmail.com/news/ opinions/opinion/a-new-generation-of-scottish-separatists/article2046767/?service=mobile.

84. They are Abkhazia (Russia), Kosovo (Serbia), Nagorno Karabakh (Azerbaijan), South Ossetia (Russia), Somaliland (Somalia), Taiwan (China), Transnistria (Moldova) and Turkish Republic of Northern Cyprus (Cyprus).

85. "Taiwan's commonsense consensus," *The Economist*, Feb. 26, 2011, www.economist. com/node/18229208.

86. Keith Nuthall, "Greenland, Denmark woo Arctic metal mining investors," *Metal Bulletin*, June 21, 2011, www.metalbulletin.com/Article/ 2851813/Greenland-Denmark-woo-Arctic-metal-mining-investors.html.

BIBLIOGRAPHY

Books

Kaplan, Seth D., *Fixing Fragile States: A New Paradigm for Development, Praeger Security International,* **2008.**
A business consultant who has founded successful corporations in Asia, Africa and the Middle East uses various case studies from around the world to analyze what makes states function and why they become dysfunctional.

Lynch, Dov, *Engaging Eurasia's Separatist States — Unresolved Conflicts and De Facto States, United States Institute of Peace Press,* **2004.**
The director of a U.S. Institute of Peace project describes the "frozen conflicts" in the breakaway republics of Transdniestra, Nagorno Karabakh, South Ossetia and Abkhazia.

Macedo, Stephen, and Allen Buchanan, *Secession and Self-Determination: Nomos XLV*, New York University Press, 2003.

In a series of essays, different authors debate whether there should be a right to secede and analyze specific secessionist cases, notably Québec and the pre-Civil War Southern U.S. states.

Articles

"The Territorial Status of Kirkuk," *Washington Kurdish Institute*, November 2007, http://71.18.173.106/pages/WO-PositionPapers.htm#.

The institute argues that Kirkuk should be unified with the Kurdish region of northern Iraq.

Mema, Medlir, "Kosovo Through Central European Eyes," *Center for European Policy Analysis*, Jan. 2, 2008, www.cepa.org/digest/kosovo-through-central-european-eyes.php.

A Balkans scholar explains how many of the countries near Kosovo that have sizeable ethnic minorities are wary of the precedent set by an independent Kosovo.

Muller, Jerry Z., "Us and Them: The Enduring Power of Ethnic Nationalism," *Foreign Affairs*, March/April 2008, pp. 18-35.

A professor of history at Catholic University argues in the magazine's cover story that ethnic nationalism will drive global politics for generations.

Ponnambalam, G. G., "Negotiation with Armed Groups: Sri Lanka and Beyond," *Tufts University symposium*, April 6, 2006, http://fletcher.tufts.edu/news/2006/04/ponnambalam.shtml.

An academic paper by a member of the Sri Lankan parliament charts the unsuccessful efforts by the Sri Lankan authorities and Tamil separatists to end their conflict.

Renan, Ernst, "What is a Nation?" March 11, 1882, www.tamilnation.org/selfdetermination/nation/renan.htm.

This classic lecture by a French philosopher and theoretician on statehood and nationalism at the Sorbonne University in Paris is viewed as the definitive text on civic nationalism.

Serwer, Daniel, "Coming Soon to a Country Near You: Kosova Sovereignty," *Bertelsmann Stiftung*

Transatlantic Thinkers series, December 2007, www.usip.org/pubs/usipeace_briefings/2007/1214_kosovo.html.

A conflict resolution expert argues for Kosovo's independence.

Tkacik, John J., "Dealing with Taiwan's Referendum on the United Nations," *Heritage Foundation*, Sept. 10, 2007, www.heritage.org/about/staff/John Tkacikpapers.cfm#2007Research.

A China policy scholar assesses how the international community should respond to the ongoing campaign by Taiwanese separatists to obtain a U.N. seat for Taiwan.

Reports and Studies

Carley, Patricia, "Self-Determination: Sovereignty, Territorial Integrity, and the Right to Secession," *United States Institute of Peace, Peaceworks 7*, March 1996, www.usip.org/pubs/peaceworks/pwks7.html.

A conflict resolution expert outlines the main issues in the self-determination debate, including the uncertainty over what the right entails and who is entitled to claim it.

Gutierrez, Eric, and Saturnino Borras, Jr., "The Moro Conflict: Landlessness and Misdirected State Policies," *East-West Center Washington*, 2004, www.eastwestcenter.org/fileadmin/stored/pdfs/PS008.pdf.

The authors explain how resentment over not having control of their land has fueled separatism among the Muslim Moros in the southern Philippines.

Millward, James, "Violent Separatism in Xinjiang: A critical assessment," *East-West Center Washington*, 2004, www.eastwestcenter.org/fileadmin/stored/pdfs/PS006.pdf.

A history professor at Georgetown University in Washington highlights the plight of the Uyghurs, a Turkic people living in western China, where separatist tensions are simmering.

Schulze, Kirsten E., "The Free Aceh Movement: Anatomy of a Separatist Organization," *East-West Center Washington*, 2004, www.eastwestcenter.org/fileadmin/stored/pdfs/PS002.pdf.

A senior history lecturer at the London School of Economics discusses the history of the separatist movement in the Indonesian province of Aceh since 1976. The paper was published just prior to the brokering of a peace agreement in 2005.

For More Information

Center for Strategic and International Studies, 1800 K St., N.W., Washington, DC 20006; (202) 887-0200; www.csis.org. Think tank focused on regional stability, defense and security.

Centre for the Study of Civil War, P.O. Box 9229, Gronland NO-0134, Oslo, Norway; +47 22 54 77 00; www.prio.no/cscw. An autonomous center within the International Peace Research Institute, Oslo, that studies why civil wars break out, how they are sustained and what it takes to end them.

Commission on Security and Co-operation in Europe (Helsinki Commission), 234 Ford House Office Building, Washington, DC 20515; (202) 225-1901; www.csce.gov. An independent agency of the U.S. government created to promote democracy, human rights and economic development.

European Free Alliance, Woeringenstraat 19, 1000 Brussels, Belgium; +32 (0)2 513-3476; www.e-f-a.org/home.php. A political alliance consisting of regionalist and nationalist parties in Europe seeking greater autonomy for regions and ethnic minorities through peaceful means.

Middlebury Institute, 127 East Mountain Road, Cold Spring, NY 10516; (845) 265-3158; http://middlebury institute.org. Studies separatism, self-determination and devolution, with a strong focus on the United States.

United Nations Observer Mission in Georgia, 38 Krtsanisi St., 380060 Tbilisi, Georgia; (+995) 32 926-700; www.un.org/en/peacekeeping/missions/past/unomig/. Established by the U.N. in 1993 to verify that the Georgian and Abkhaz authorities are complying with their ceasefire agreement.

United States Institute of Peace, 1200 17th St., N.W., Washington, DC 20036; (202) 457-1700; www.usip.org. An independent agency funded by Congress to prevent and resolve violent international conflicts and to promote post-conflict stability and development.

Unrepresented Nations and Peoples Organization, P.O. Box 85878, 2508CN The Hague, the Netherlands; +31 (0)70 364-6504; www.unpo.org. An umbrella organization that promotes self-determination for various indigenous peoples, occupied nations, ethnic minorities and unrecognized states.

Washington Kurdish Institute, 611 4th St., S.W., Washington, DC 20024; (202) 484-0140; www.kurd.org. Promotes the rights of Kurdish people and awareness of Kurdish issues.

Voices From Abroad:

ANATOLY SAFONOV

Deputy foreign minister, Russia

Recognition of Kosovo a potential security threat

"We should not forget that jihadists of terror, who lived a semi-legal life, have settled in Kosovo and in other places since the active phase of the Balkans campaign. However, at the same time, they have kept in touch with al-Qa'idah and other terrorist structures. If Kosovo is recognized, these forces will receive a signal to emerge from the underground. We shall see if our partners adhere to their principles regarding this underground."

Interfax News Agency, February 2008

VLADIMIR PUTIN

President, Russia

Putin challenges double standard for Kosovo

"I don't want to say anything that would offend anyone, but for 40 years northern Cyprus has practically had independence. Why aren't you recognizing that? Aren't you ashamed, Europeans, for having these double standards?"

The Guardian (England), February 2008

Florida Today/Parker

ZHANG QINGLI

Communist Party leader, Tibet

Tibetan communists challenge separatist Dalai Lama

"We are currently in an intensely bloody and fiery struggle with the Dalai Lama clique, a life or death struggle with the enemy. . . . As long as we . . . remain of one heart, turn the masses into a walled city and work together to attack the enemy, then we can safeguard

social stability and achieve a full victory in this intense battle against separatism."

Canberra Times (Australia), March 2008

DALHA TSERING

Campaign coordinator, Tibetan Community in Britain

Dalai Lama holds back Tibetan violence

"China is one of the most powerful countries in the world, yet it is afraid of one person, and that's the

Dalai Lama. He is the only person holding Tibetans from turning violent and confrontational. When his holiness goes, nobody can predict where the situation will go."

Los Angeles Times, March 2008

GEORGE FITZHERBERT

Tibet scholar Oxford University

China exacerbates Tibet's frustrations
"Tibetans are rapidly and reluctantly becoming a minority in their own ancestral homelands, in much the same way as Mongolians have already become an almost negligible minority in the equally "autonomous" Chinese province of Inner Mongolia. . . . [By] demonising the Dalai Lama and refusing to compromise an inch on Tibetan aspirations, the Chinese will inevitably exacerbate the already fractious ethnic relations in this vast area of western China."

www.opendemocracy.net/article/ china/democracy_power/tibet_ history_china_power, March 2008

KARMA CHOPHEL

Speaker, Tibet Parliament-in-Exile

Beware of propaganda
"They [China] use propaganda hoping to fool the world, so we must consider our actions with caution. . . . China is ready to label Tibetans as terrorists in order to win international blessing for their actions. . . . Those who know the true fact of the matter know that this is a genuine outcry and outburst over Chinese misrule."

Agence France-Presse, March 2008

DAVID MILIBAND

Foreign Secretary, Great Britain

The last piece of the puzzle
"There is a very strong head of steam building among a wide range of countries that do see [Kosovo] as the last piece of the Yugoslav jigsaw and don't see stability in the western Balkans being established without the aspirations of the Kosovar people being respected."

The Associated Press, February 2008

6

Gay Rights

Reed Karaim

Moses, a gay Ugandan seeking asylum in the United States, hides his identity out of fear for his safety as he tells a press conference in Washington, D.C., on Feb. 2, 2010, about being terrorized in his home country for being homosexual. The conference was held to kick off the American Prayer Hour, a multi-city event organized to "affirm inclusive values and call on all nations, including Uganda, to decriminalize the lives of gay, lesbian, bisexual and transgender people."

AFP/Getty Images/Jewel Samad

From *CQ Researcher*,
March 1, 2011

The movie poster shows two shirtless young men in a passionate embrace. But the film is not "Brokeback Mountain," the acclaimed Hollywood story featuring Jake Gyllenhaal and Heath Ledger as closeted, gay cowhands.

This film was produced, surprisingly, in Mumbai, India, home of the Bollywood extravaganza. Until last year, Bollywood films were long on exuberant singing and dancing, and virtually devoid of sex scenes. Even heterosexual kissing was primly avoided.

But after Delhi's high court in 2009 overturned a 148-year-old colonial law criminalizing homosexual acts between consenting adults, Bollywood moved quickly to keep up with the times. Soon afterwards, "Dunno y — Na Jaane Kyun" changed all that with the first gay kiss in an Indian movie. Indeed, the film by director Sanjay Sharma was billed as India's "Brokeback Mountain." And as Indian bloggers made clear, it had its share of both defenders and critics.

"Dunno y" reflects what could, by one measure, be considered the culmination of the "Gay Rights" decade. In a relatively short time, countries around the world have addressed concerns of homosexual or bisexual individuals.

Beginning with the Netherlands in 2001, gay marriage morphed almost overnight from a largely ridiculed notion to a legal reality in at least 10 countries. Sixteen other nations recognized same-sex civil unions. And anti-sodomy laws were struck down in nations as disparate as the United States and India. On every continent, lesbian, gay, bisexual and transgender (LGBT) people stepped out in "pride marches." The trend continued, or even accelerated, in 2010. Argentina became the first Latin American country to legalize same-sex marriage. The United States is in the process of ending its "don't

Muslim and African Nations Have Toughest Anti-Gay Laws

Africa and the Middle East have the strictest laws governing homosexual behavior. At least five countries in those regions allow the death penalty for homosexual acts, and gays can be jailed in at least 75 countries, some for life. Australia, Canada, Europe and South Africa have the most liberal laws.

Status of Lesbian and Gay Rights Around the World

Prosecution for same-sex acts

- ■ Death Penalty
- □ Imprisonment — 1 month to 10 years
- □ Imprisonment, no set term
- ■ Imprisonment — 11 years to life
- □ Unclear

Recognition of same-sex unions

- ▨ Allows marriage
- ▨ Treats about same as marriage
- ▨ Treats as inferior to marriage
- □ No specific legislation
- ▨ Prohibits discrimination

* Legislation is pending to legalize gay marriage in Nepal, following the Nov. 17, 2008, Supreme Court ruling that prohibiting same-sex marriage is unconstitutional.

Source: International Lesbian, Gay, Bisexual, Trans and Intersex Association, May 2010

ask, don't tell" policy requiring gay military personnel to hide their sexual orientation, joining at least 36 countries that allow gays and lesbians to serve openly in the armed services.[1]

Polls show growing U.S. support for same-sex marriage, and in a major policy shift on Feb. 23, the Obama administration decided it could no longer defend the Defense of Marriage Act, the 1996 law that bars federal recognition of same-sex marriages. President Barack Obama says the law is unconstitutional.[2]

But a happy Bollywood movie tells only part of the global story of gay rights. While it seems the best of times for the LGBT community in an increasing number of countries, large parts of the world continue to view same-sex relationships as unnatural, a sin and a threat to the traditional family.

Homosexual acts remain illegal and severely punished in most of Africa and the Muslim world. Uganda made international headlines last year when *Rolling Stone*, a local newspaper not connected to the U.S. publication, publicly identified 100 gays and called on the public to "hang them."[3] A member of the Ugandan parliament introduced a bill that would impose the death penalty on anyone engaging in repeated homosexual activity.[4] If approved, Uganda would join the five other countries and parts of Somalia and Nigeria where homosexual activity is punishable by death.

In the formerly communist states of Eastern Europe, gay-pride marches were met with outrage and violence, sometimes organized by far-right political groups.[5] China, where homosexuality is not illegal, still stifles public gatherings or rallies for gays.[6] And in the United States, a spate of gay teen suicides in 2010 at year's end provided evidence that, even in countries with "hate crime" laws and other legal protections for LGBT people, "coming out" remains an agonizing experience for many, often greeted with disapproval or cruelty.[7]

Within the scientific community the question of whether sexual orientation is inherent or learned — a debate often referred to as "nature vs. nurture" — is largely over. "The consistency of the genetic, prenatal and brain findings has swung the pendulum toward a biological explanation," writes David Myers, a psychology professor at Michigan's Hope College, in his textbook *Exploring Psychology*. "Nature more than nurture, most psychiatrists now believe, predisposes sexual orientation."[8]

The evidence, however, has failed to convince the most fervent opponents of treating homosexual

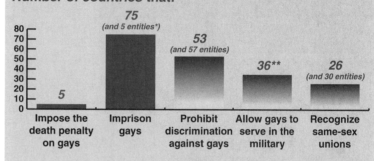

Gays Face Harsh Penalties in 75 Nations

Individuals engaging in homosexual behavior can face the death penalty in five countries and can be imprisoned in 75 others. However, more than 50 countries and 57 states, districts or other governmental entities have enacted anti-discrimination laws protecting gays. Three dozen countries allow gays to serve openly in the military, and 26 nations recognize same-sex unions.

Number of countries that:

Impose the death penalty on gays	Imprison gays	Prohibit discrimination against gays	Allow gays to serve in the military	Recognize same-sex unions
5	75 (and 5 entities*)	53 (and 57 entities)	36**	26 (and 30 entities)

* Includes part of a federation state, a district or any other administrative or territorial unit.

** Includes Israel but does not include the United States, which is repealing its ban on gays in the military.

Sources: International Lesbian, Gay, Bisexual, Trans and Intersex Association, May 2010; "Report of the Comprehensive Review of the Issues Associated with a Repeal of Don't Ask Don't Tell," Pentagon Working Group Study, Nov. 30, 2010

relationships as equal to heterosexual ones. In fact, the rhetoric seemed to grow even more heated on the most strident anti-gay edge of the debate as public animosity faded and legal rights were extended to gay couples. Gay-rights supporters speak of their battle as part of the broader movement to assure equal rights for all.

"I don't like the phrase 'LGBT rights' because what we're really talking about are fundamental human rights, like the right to privacy. When you talk about LGBT rights or gay rights, people immediately think you want something special. We don't want anything special. We want to be treated like everyone else," says Boris Dittrich, a former member of parliament in the Netherlands who initiated that country's same-sex marriage and adoption bills. He now serves as advocacy director for the LGBT program at Human Rights Watch, an international organization dedicated to defending and protecting human rights.

AFP/Getty Images/Ilmars Znotins

Waving banners and bibles, anti-gay activists hold a counter-protest during a 2009 Baltic Gay Pride rally in Riga, Latvia. The backlash against gay and lesbian rights in several former Soviet satellite states has been led by far-right parties that also have campaigned against other minorities. Government officials often cite the threat of violence from such groups to justify outlawing gay-pride parades and other events.

This perspective has gained strength in the American debate about same-sex marriage, even among conservatives. Theodore B. Olson, who served as solicitor general under President George W. Bush, argued in *Newsweek* last year that legalizing same-sex marriage would "be a recognition of basic American principles." Marriage is an "expression of our desire to create a social partnership, to live and share life's joys and burdens with the person we love," and honoring these desires in all people strengthens society's bonds, he concluded.[9]

Opponents of gay rights, not surprisingly, do not speak in unison. Some support civil unions and legal safeguards against discrimination for gays and lesbians but oppose same-sex marriage, believing it should be reserved for heterosexual couples to promote the traditional family. Others do not accept the idea of natural differences in sexual orientation or gender identity.

Religious communities around the world take a range of positions on homosexuality, from acceptance to prohibition. Many Christians and Muslims believe gay sexual relations are proscribed by God but emphasize charity and forgiveness. The Catholic Church says homosexual acts are a sin but recognizes that homosexual orientation is strongly felt and may be innate in some people.

But the Catholic Church, with 1.2 billion faithful worldwide, adamantly opposes extending certain legal rights to same-sex couples, particularly the right to marry. Pope Benedict XVI has called same-sex marriage one of the "most insidious and dangerous challenges that today confront the common good."[10]

Some American evangelical Christians take a harsher view of both homosexuality and the idea of gay rights. In a still widely disseminated 2002 essay against granting "rights" to gays, Scott Lively, president of the Springfield, Mass.-based group Abiding Truth Ministries, says the idea that homosexuals can be the subject of "discrimination" and that those who support their cause are "tolerant" distorts both words. He discounts the possibility that homosexual preference could be innate and says that, even if it is, acting on that impulse is a choice equivalent to "pedophilia, sado-masochism, bestiality and many other forms of deviant behavior."[11]

The Southern Poverty Law Center, the Montgomery, Ala.,-based anti-bigotry advocacy group, calls Lively's organization a hate group.[12] But the message of Lively and others who consider homosexuality deviant and dangerous continues to find a receptive audience overseas, particularly in Africa, where he met with Ugandan political leaders shortly before they introduced their punitive legislation.[13]

But support for allowing gay marriage or equal partnerships can be found among Christian leaders and scholars, including in the Catholic Church. More than 140 German, Austrian and Swiss Catholic theologians signed a petition earlier this year calling for reforms in the church, including acceptance of homosexual partners.[14]

Daniel Maguire, a professor of moral theology at Catholic Marquette University in Milwaukee, has argued that the love of some people for members of the same sex is a fact of God's creation and should be accepted. "Homosexuality is not a sin. Heterosexism (prejudice against people who are homosexual) is a sin," Maguire writes. "It is a serious sin because it violates justice, truth and love."[15]

Tolerance is also gaining support in some developing nations. Nepal's highest court has said gays should have the right to marry, and the Philippine Supreme Court recently ruled that an LGBT political party could field candidates for office. And there was the overturning by India's high court of a British-era anti-sodomy law, declaring it a vestige of colonialism that did not square with the country's constitution.

"People feel much freer in their minds. Their hands are untied," says Arvind Narrain, one of the lawyers who brought the case. "I never thought I'd see this in my lifetime, but we've seen how quickly things can change."

But in parts of socially conservative Eastern Europe, changes have gone in the other direction. Romania and other countries in the region have legally defined marriage as a union between a man and woman. Romania also prohibits recognition of same-sex marriages or civil unions that were entered into legally abroad.

"In the last couple of years, Romanians realized what was happening in Holland, Sweden and Spain [countries where gay marriage is legal], and they became very concerned" about the trend spreading to Romania, says Peter Costea, a lawyer and president of the Alliance of Romania's Families, which worked for adoption of the new definition. "They decided that right now, they did not wish such an institution to be legalized in Romania."

Costea believes a backlash is growing against what many conservative Europeans see as a gay-rights "agenda" that discounts the importance of the traditional family. But while resistance to same-sex marriage or civil unions remains strong in many parts of the world, far fewer countries are now willing to accept discrimination based on sexual orientation. For instance, Costea notes, it is illegal under Romanian law to discriminate against gays seeking housing or jobs.

As gay rights evolve across the globe, here are some of the questions being debated:

Are governments and society more receptive to gay rights?

LGBT activists seem generally optimistic that they are succeeding, albeit only incrementally in some places. "We are on a very positive trajectory," says Mark Bromley, chairman of the Washington, D.C.-based Council for Global Equality, founded to encourage a stronger American voice on LGBT human rights concerns. "There will be some plateaus and some inevitable backlash, and there is a gap between parts of the globe, but I think we've seen tremendous progress over all."

But opponents of gay-friendly initiatives see exactly the opposite. "We work with groups in more than 70 countries. We've been holding our world congresses since 1997, and in that time we've seen participants realize they represent a much larger voice in the world," says Larry Jacobs, managing director of the Illinois-based World Congress of Families, which insists heterosexual marriage is fundamental to society and is threatened by same-sex marriage and other social changes.

Government policies in most of the world's industrialized democracies have become far more supportive of equal treatment of gays and lesbians than would have been imaginable only a generation ago. More than 50 countries and 57 states, districts or other governmental entities have enacted anti-discrimination laws protecting gays, and 26 countries and 30 government entities recognize same-sex unions. Meanwhile, 36 countries now allow homosexuals to openly serve in the military, and the United States is in the process of repealing its ban on gays in the services.[16] Same-sex consensual sexual acts also have been decriminalized throughout these countries.

In some Western European nations the question of equal treatment under the law for same-sex couples seems largely settled. In the Netherlands, for instance, Jan Willem Duyvendak, a sociologist at the University of Amsterdam who studies the gay-rights movement, says, "The opening up of marriage to gay people will never be reversed. Even the political parties that were originally against it now support it."

Indeed, in countries where homosexuality still faces disapproval, governments have decriminalized sex between same-sex partners. In Russia, for example, authorities have refused to allow gay-pride marches and other gatherings, and public antipathy toward homosexuals remains strong, but homosexual acts have been legal since 1993.

Still, in many countries — especially in Eastern Europe — majority sentiment appears to be against taking further steps, particularly when it comes to legalizing same-sex marriage. In addition to Romania, three other countries — Bulgaria, Estonia and Lithuania — have taken legal steps to reserve marriage for heterosexuals.[17]

Reflecting much of the opinion across Eastern Europe, Costea of the Alliance of Romania's Families says, "Romania is a deeply religious country, mainly an

Five U.S. States Allow Same-Sex Marriage

Five states and the District of Columbia issue marriage licenses to same-sex couples. Twelve other states give some spousal rights to same-sex couples or recognize marriages initiated in other jurisdictions.

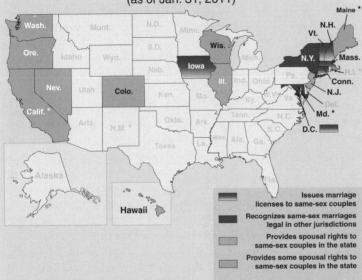

States That Recognize Same-sex Marriage
(as of Jan. 31, 2011)

Issues marriage licenses to same-sex couples

Recognizes same-sex marriages legal in other jurisdictions

Provides spousal rights to same-sex couples in the state

Provides some spousal rights to same-sex couples in the state

* California: *Marriages that took place between June 16 and Nov. 4, 2008, continue to be defined as marriages. An Oct. 12, 2009, law recognizes out-of-jurisdiction same-sex marriages that occurred in the June-November 2008 time frame as marriages in California, and all other out-of-jurisdiction same-sex marriages as domestic partnerships.*

* Maine: *Marriage equality legislation enacted May 6, 2009; repealed by a ballot measure in November 2009.*

* Maryland: *Provides certain benefits to statutorily defined domestic partners. In 2010, attorney general said the state can recognize out-of-jurisdiction marriages.*

* New Mexico: *In January 2011, attorney general issued an advisory opinion saying the state can recognize out-of-jurisdiction same-sex marriages.*

* Rhode Island: *Provides certain benefits to statutorily defined domestic partners. In February 2007 attorney general issued an opinion saying the state can recognize out-of-jurisdiction marriages. However, in December 2007 state Supreme Court refused to grant a divorce to a same-sex couple legally married in Massachusetts.*

Source: "Marriage Equality & Other Relationship Recognition Laws," Human Rights Campaign, Jan. 31, 2011

orthodox one with a fairly substantial evangelical minority. The church has retained a fairly firm position with respect to marriage, and it's a position shared by the overwhelming majority of the Romanian people."

At least one LGBT rights activist, however, believes anti-gay opinion is tempering in parts of Eastern Europe. Greg Czarnecki — a board member for the Brussels-based International Lesbian, Gay, Bisexual, Trans and Intersex Association (ILGA) in Europe — lives in socially conservative, predominantly Catholic Poland. In recent years, Polish governments have drafted a bill to punish teachers who "promoted" homosexuality. European officials criticized the measures as homophobic, and recently Czarnecki sees the tone changing.[18] "The Democratic-left alliance now supports a form of civil partnership for gays," he says, "and the conservatives have tempered some of their rhetoric, too."

But social attitudes rarely change as fast as government policy. "Most people aren't actively, violently against gay people. They just kind of say, 'Okay, if you're gay, just don't talk about it,'" he says. "That's a very Polish way to look at an issue. If there's an uncomfortable situation, we try to find a way around it. With the younger people, I see a real hunger to join the West, and I think there's definitely a more cosmopolitan, tolerant attitude."

Focusing on Europe, however, can create a false impression. In other parts of the world — especially in Africa and the Middle East — signs that policies or attitudes are becoming more supportive of the LGBT community are difficult to find. The

Sexual Orientation: Is It Due to Nature or Nurture?

Sexual Orientation: Is It Due to Nature or Nurture?

Is human sexual orientation predetermined at birth or something that is learned? That question is not only part of the scientific inquiry into the nature of human sexual relationships but, to many, central to the political debate over gay rights.

If it's an innate characteristic like left-handedness or red hair, then arguments that homosexuality is "unnatural" or against God's plan become much harder to justify, as does treating sexual relationships — and the idea of love — between adults of the same gender differently than heterosexual relationships.

Since the "nature vs. nurture" question concerning sexual orientation is so fraught, some people will never accept the answer unless it coincides with their political or religious beliefs. But within the scientific community, a consensus has emerged.

"Most of today's psychologists view sexual orientation as neither willfully chosen nor willfully changed," writes David Myers, a psychology professor at Hope College in Michigan in his textbook *Psychology.* "Sexual orientation is in some ways like handedness. Most people are one way, some the other. A very few are truly ambidextrous. Regardless, the way one is endures."[1]

A wide range of research has found biological connections to sexual orientation. Identical twins are more likely to share a homosexual orientation than fraternal twins. Another study found that a certain cell cluster in the hypothalamus of the brain is reliably larger in heterosexual men than in women or homosexual men. Hormonal activity in the womb also seems to have an effect on sexual orientation.[2]

Several organizations, mostly religion-based, claim "corrective therapy" can reorient gays and lesbians toward heterosexuality. But studies by researchers have found that same-sex attractions typically persist, as do those of heterosexuals, who are no more capable of changing their sexual orientation.[3]

Since the days of the ancient Greeks, whenever philosophers have argued against homosexual love, some have argued that it is against the natural order, in part because it was found nowhere else in the animal kingdom.

Scientists now know this is incorrect. Some birds, sheep, monkeys and more than 450 other species of animals have at least occasional same-gender sex.[4] In some cases, animals form long-lasting same-sex relationships, even raising young together. Studies have found that roughly 8 percent of male sheep are sexually attracted only to other males — an example of an animal subpopulation that seems exclusively homosexual.[5]

In his book *The Science of Sexual Attraction*, noted neurobiologist Simon LeVay examines same-sex animal behavior. "The bonobo monkeys are interesting, because they're fairly close to us (genetically)," he says, "and they're polymorphously perverse — they use sex for many interactions that aren't tied to procreation. As far as we know, you don't really have gay or straight . . . bonobos."

LeVay discovered the difference in the hypothalamus between gay and straight men and published his results in *Science* in 1991. He initially found the results — some of the earliest evidence indicating biological differences between gay and straight men — startling.

The research briefly made him a scientific celebrity. "I was really shocked when I came in the day after it was published," he says, "and saw satellite trucks waiting outside the office."

Twenty years later, in the middle of a tour promoting *The Science of Sexual Attraction* — LeVay says the reaction has been far more muted. "There was no sense of shock with my book coming out as there was when my research came out," he says. "I think a lot of people have come to accept that biology is relevant to sexual orientation."

— ***Reed Karaim***

---

[1] David Myers, *Psychology* (2010), p. 472.

[2] *Ibid.*

[3] *Ibid.*

[4] Jon Mooallem, "Can animals be gay?" *The New York Times Magazine*, March 31, 2010, www.nytimes.com/2010/04/04/magazine/04animals-t.html.

[5] John Cloud, "Yep, they're gay," *Time*, Jan. 26, 2007, www.time.com/time/magazine/article/0,9171,1582336,00.html.

proposed death-penalty legislation in Uganda has gotten the most attention, but several other African nations are considering or have adopted similar measures. LGBT activists also worry about violent public sentiment worked up by politicians and the media elsewhere in Africa.

"Genocide is brewing in Uganda, and the influence of this bill is spilling over to other countries like Zambia, Democratic Republic of Congo, and Malawi, where similar bills are being proposed," says Valentine Kalende, a Ugandan LGBT activist who was identified in the *Rolling Stone* article. "It seems like the whole world is focusing on Uganda, and ignoring what's happening to LGBT people in other African countries."

On the other side, Theresa Okafor, the CEO of Life League, a Nigerian organization that believes homosexuality is unnatural, does not think gays and lesbians should be executed; she believes counseling or therapy is in order. But she rejects the notion they are victims of prejudice in Africa. "I have heard accusations that they are being discriminated against," she says, "but this is completely false because if you think deeply about it, it is not the person that is being despised, it is the conduct."

But why does Africa seem to be growing more intolerant toward gays? That topic is hotly debated. Some blame it on the recent rise in Christian and Muslim fundamentalism in the region, while some say it is a reaction against Western influence and an expression of traditional attitudes, although others say that misrepresents the diversity of views in the African past. Some political observers say authoritarian regimes are scapegoating gays in order to redirect public ire.

"By and large, these are countries with very difficult economic and political problems, with political leaders who are not popular who can score easy victories by targeting the gays," says the Council for Global Equality's Bromley.

Meanwhile, in the Middle East there are few signs of a thaw in government policies. Homosexual acts remain illegal in most of the region and are often punished severely. Iran presents a particularly harsh case study. Human Rights Watch has documented a series of allegations of rape, torture and executions of sexual minorities by Iran's police and paramilitary forces.[19]

"Executions take place in Iran," says Human Rights Watch's Dittrich. "It's one of very few places where that happens." Four other countries and two regions — all Muslim countries — allow executions for consensual same-sex acts, according to the organization: Saudi Arabia, Yemen, Sudan, Mauritania and the ultra-conservative parts of Somalia and Nigeria.

But elsewhere in the developing world, change is happening with surprising swiftness. Marcelo Ferreyra, Buenos Aires-based program coordinator for Latin America and the Caribbean with the International Gay and Lesbian Human Rights Commission (IGLHRC), which works for LGBT rights worldwide, notes that Argentina's legalization of same-sex marriage is part of a broader trend in the region.

"Two or three years ago, Uruguay was the first country in Latin America to recognize civil unions. Mexico City allows same-sex marriages. Colombia is going through a recognition process for same-sex couples. There's a lot happening in Brazil," says Ferreyra. "This is not just coming from Argentina."

In Asia, the picture is as complex as it is in Europe. Gay-rights advocates have won important victories in Nepal, India and, to a lesser degree, the predominantly Catholic Philippines. In China, however, which has one-fifth of the world's population, the situation seems largely static. Laws criminalizing homosexuality were taken off the books in the 1997, but no law bars discrimination on the basis of sexual preference, and the government continues to block gay public gatherings and websites.[20]

In Indonesia, observers see an example of another phenomenon: a backlash against the increasing visibility of the LGBT community.

Does a backlash threaten advances made by gays?

During a regional gay-rights conference in Surabaya, Indonesia, last year, Grace Poore, IGLHRC coordinator for Asia and the Pacific Islands, got a first-hand look at how some political and religious groups are responding to the gay-rights movement.

As the conference was about to begin, protesters from hardline Islamic groups arrived at the hotel, demanding that the conference be shut down and the attendees leave the country. Conference members were told to stay in their rooms as the protesters moved through the halls. Eventually, after hearing that a larger group of protesters was on the way and that the police could not guarantee members' safety, organizers decided to cancel the conference.

"We were basically under siege in the hotel," Poore says. "We were forced to leave. We were threatened with violence. I think it's the only time I have been afraid. It was such a situation of anarchy, and the police were saying they would not protect us."

Indonesia has the world's largest Muslim population, but it is a secular state, and homosexual acts are not illegal. But conservative Muslim groups have been increasingly strident in their opposition to equal treatment of LGBT relationships. To Poore it's an example of a counteroffensive being mounted in many countries.

"We're seeing religious backlash," particularly by hardliners, whether it's Islamic hardliners or Christian fundamentalists," she says. "Even in India, where Hindu has been considered very open, the Hindu right wing has suddenly claimed that homosexuality is anathema to Indian culture and Hindu beliefs. It's all part of this trend where religious conservatives and extremists, on their own or with the support of governments, are really pushing back in severe ways."[21]

The backlash has made it harder for LGBT people to publicly make their case and complicates the political landscape. For instance, in some Eastern European countries the reaction against gay and lesbian rights has been led by the rise of far-right parties that also have campaigned against other minorities, including Roma (Gypsies) and Jews. The threat of violence from such groups has been cited by government officials to justify outlawing gay-pride parades and other events.

In some countries the backlash has resulted in hate crimes — even in countries without a hostile government and where the dominant religion, such as Catholicism, opposes homosexuality but does not condone violence against the LGBT community.

"We're facing some backlash in different ways," Ferreyra, of the International Gay and Lesbian Human Rights Commission, says about Latin America. "We are experiencing a high rate of hate crimes — in Honduras, where five LGBT activists were just murdered but also in Mexico and other places. You see it happen especially where LGBT people have become more visible."[22]

Up to 20,000 people took to the streets in Burundi's capital city of Bujumbura on March 6, 2009, to protest the failure of the Senate to outlaw homosexuality. Anti-gay sentiment is on the rise in many African countries, where Christian and Muslim fundamentalism is growing, and homosexuality is seen as foreign to many African cultures.

But even in the most dangerous countries the backlash is not suppressing the LGBT movement, say some observers. "In virtually every country, there are brave individuals who are standing up and saying I'm gay or I'm lesbian, and I have rights, too. We're seeing this activism in virtually every corner of the world," says Bromley, of the Council for Global Equality.

Activist Kalende says this is true even in Uganda. "The LGBT movement in Uganda is more organized than before," she says. Kalende believes the movement's work with other concerned groups in Uganda and abroad has helped to prevent passage of the bill so far.

Despite violent incidents, the backlash against gay rights is not just about intimidation, hatred or prejudice. "We're not anti-homosexual; they're not the 'evil people' that need to be destroyed," says Jacobs, of the World Congress of Families. "What we're saying is that what's best for society is the natural family."

In some cases the backlash is coming from people who feel their own rights are being trampled by the movement to recognize gay rights. In Great Britain, Andrea Minichiello Williams is a lawyer and the founder of Christian Concern, which represents people who feel they've been treated unjustly because of their Christian beliefs. Her organization represents British citizens

AFP/Getty Images/Esdras Ndikumana

who've been reprimanded or fired because they refused to take certain actions regarding the treatment of gays and lesbians, such as presiding over a civil union ceremony or teaching about homosexuality, required under Britain's Equality Act of 2010.

Williams says many rank-and-file Britons who feel their beliefs aren't being respected could become more extreme if they're not listened to. "My sense is that the British people are longing to get their country back, their country founded on great Christian principles," she says.

In the United States, a backlash against court rulings in favor of same-sex marriage has been evident in several states. Voters in California overturned — through referendum — a state Supreme Court ruling in favor of same-sex marriage.[23] In Iowa, voters removed three state Supreme Court judges who voted to allow same-sex marriage.[24] "We've won every time it's been put before the people of any state, including liberal states like California and Maine," says Maggie Gallagher, chairman of the board of the U.S. National Organization for Marriage, which opposes same-sex marriages.

Todd Shepard, a historian at The Johns Hopkins University in Baltimore who studies the history of sexuality, believes it's a mistake to assume the increasing freedom many LGBT people are experiencing represents an unstoppable historical current. "One of the things we want to do in America is make every story a progress story, where things are getting better and better," he says. "But there have been plenty of other times where there were all sorts of freedoms, and then — there weren't."

However, sociologist Duyvendak of the Netherlands believes history has turned a corner. "There will be local fights and backlash in some areas, but I think the trends will continue. Even in the United States we still see progress, step-by-step. Now the army is open, and marriage will be the next thing. Things may go slow, but I'm really quite optimistic. I don't think the gains that have been made will be reversed."

Should the United Nations and other international bodies be promoting gay rights?

The United Nations does not mention same-sex relations in its main human rights treaties, although the documents do include declarations of the right of all

people to be treated with dignity and respect regardless of circumstances. U.N. agencies also disseminate information on a variety of topics, including basic human rights and educational materials on sexual behavior, which includes information about homosexuality.

The European Union (EU), however, does prohibit discrimination based on sexual orientation, and the EU's Fundamental Rights Agency monitors and recommends policies to end discrimination within member countries.

Not surprisingly, gay-rights supporters and opponents view the activities of these international organizations very differently.

Human Rights Watch's Dittrich helped develop the Yogyakarta Principles, which were drawn up in 2006 by a group of international experts to apply human rights to sexual orientation and gender identity.[25] The principles are not a legally binding treaty but represent a template for treatment of the LGBT community. While acknowledging legitimate differences in cultures, Dittrich believes the responsibility of the U.N. and EU in this regard is clear.

"In many countries, they say the words 'gay' or 'homosexual' are from the West. They have this vision of the gay parades in New York or Amsterdam, and they say, 'We don't want that,' and that stops the discussion," Dittrich says. "But we're not talking about people dancing in the streets, we're talking about people being evicted or thrown into prison and being raped in prison without having access to lawyers. We are talking about fundamental human rights."

But few critics of the U.N. and EU activity on behalf of LGBT rights advocate throwing people into prison on the basis of sexual orientation or denying them lawyers. However, they do object to what they say are the bureaucracies of these international bodies adopting "agendas" that promote homosexual relationships as equivalent to heterosexual relationships, a position that enforces an ideology deeply at odds with the religious and cultural convictions of many people.

For instance, says Brussels lawyer Jakob Cornides, the European Union's Fundamental Rights Agency has pushed a "radical" gay-rights agenda that includes the false proposition that European nations must enact same-sex marriage laws to correspond to international law. "They're not reacting to the number of cases or complaints," he says. "They have their own agenda, and part of it is promotion of LGBT rights."

But the Council for Global Equality's Bromley says the agency's work has been within the legal and human rights mainstream and does not require nations to adopt same-sex marriage. "They have an agenda that is far broader than LGBT concerns. It includes programs to respond to religious discrimination, racism and other forms of discrimination that are of equal concern across the EU region," he says. "While they do not have a radical LGBT agenda, they do have an important tolerance agenda that focuses on equality for all."

Austin Ruse, president of the Catholic Family and Human Rights Institute, based in New York and founded to affect debate at the U.N., says his organization is fairly satisfied with the U.N. position "because all these agendas have been stopped. Sexual orientation and gender identity are not part of the human rights treaties, and they're not going to be anytime soon."

In December, 2008, Ruse's group joined the Vatican in opposing a nonbinding U.N. "declaration" — sponsored by France with broad support in Europe and Latin America — recommending that countries decriminalize homosexuality. It was the first time a measure specifically dealing with gay rights was discussed by the U.N. General Assembly. Proponents, who included representatives of 66 countries, said laws making it a crime to be gay conflicted with the Universal Declaration of Human Rights. But representatives from the Vatican and 60 nations opposed the declaration, saying it could lead to legalizing same-sex marriage.[26]

Some critics say the U.N. still promotes policies at odds with the Universal Declaration of Human Rights, passed by the General Assembly in 1948. It proclaims that "Men and women of full age, without any limitation due to race, nationality or religion, have the right to marry and found a family," and, "The family is the natural and fundamental group unit of society and is entitled to protection by society and the State."[27]

To some social conservatives, the two provisions were intended to establish the primacy of the heterosexual marriage and traditional family. "Many of the foundational human rights documents being used today to undermine the family actually provide a remarkable

19 Nations Allow Both Same-Sex Unions and Gays in Military

In 36 countries the military either allows gays to serve openly or does not ban homosexual conduct, and at least 26 countries recognize same-sex unions. Nineteen nations do both.

Gay Rights in Selected Countries

Country	Allows gays to serve in the military*	Recognizes same-sex unions	Country	Allows gays to serve in the military*	Recognizes same-sex unions
Albania	X		Iceland	X	X
Andorra		X	Ireland	X	
Argentina		X	Israel **	X	
Australia	X		Italy	X	
Austria	X	X	Latvia	X	
Azerbaijan	X		Lithuania	X	
Belgium	X	X	Luxembourg	X	X
Bosnia and Herzegovina	X		Netherlands	X	X
Canada	X	X	New Zealand	X	X
Colombia		X	Norway	X	X
Croatia	X		Portugal	X	X
Czech Republic	X	X	Romania	X	
Denmark	X	X	Slovakia	X	
Ecuador		X	Slovenia	X	X
Estonia	X		South Africa		X
Finland	X	X	South Korea	X	
France	X	X	Spain	X	X
Georgia	X		Sweden	X	X
Germany	X	X	Switzerland		X
Greece	X		Ukraine	X	
Hungary	X	X	United Kingdom	X	X
			Uruguay		X

* Among NATO and ISAF (International Security Assistance Force in Afghanistan) partner nations, and in Israel, which is not a member of either organization. Does not include the United States, which is in the process of repealing its ban on gays serving openly in the military.

** Israel allows a limited common-law marriage for same-sex couples.

Sources: "Report of the Comprehensive Review of the Issues Associated with a Repeal of Don't Ask Don't Tell," Pentagon Working Group Study, Nov. 30, 2010; International Lesbian, Gay, Bisexual, Trans and Intersex Association

CHRONOLOGY

1st-15th *Centuries Judeo-Christian tradition against homosexuality takes hold.*

50-58 Apostle Paul denounces homosexuality, forming foundation for subsequent religious and legal rulings.

313-380 Roman Empire converts to Christianity; adopts its views on homosexuality.

1480s Homosexuals are persecuted during Spanish Inquisition.

19th Century *Homosexuality is defined, defended and viewed as scandalous.*

1867 German intellectual Karl Heinrich Ulrichs becomes first modern openly gay activist.

1900s-1950s *Homosexuality remains largely hidden, but research illuminates its prevalence.*

1924 First U.S. gay-rights organization, Society for Human Rights, is founded in Chicago, but soon disbands.

1930s-40s Nazis imprison, murder gays.

1948-52 Pioneering sex researcher Alfred Kinsey reveals unexpectedly high prevalence of male homosexuality.

1960s-1970s *Gay-rights movement emerges.*

1967 England and Wales decriminalize sex between male adults, except in armed forces and merchant marines.

1969 Police raid Stonewall Inn, a gay bar in New York City, triggering riots and launching modern gay-rights movement.

1974 Netherlands allows gays to serve openly in the military.

1980s-1990s *Rising gay activism results in policy changes but prompts conservative backlash.*

1983 U.S. Rep. Gerry Studds, D-Mass., becomes the first openly gay member of Congress. . . . The Rev. Jerry Falwell describes AIDS, a new disease that has appeared among homosexual men, as a "gay plague."

1989 Denmark is first to grant same-sex couples rights similar to marriage.

1993 "Don't ask, don't tell" law allows gays and lesbians to serve in the U.S. military, but only if they hide their sexual orientation.

1996 U.S. adopts Defense of Marriage Act (DOMA), which allows states and the federal government not to recognize same-sex marriages legal in another state.

1997 World Congress of Families holds its first international gathering devoted to defending the heterosexual, or as the Congress terms it, "natural" family.

2000s *Worldwide gay-rights movement builds despite growing resistance.*

2001 Denmark becomes first to allow same-sex marriage.

2008 Nepal legalizes same-sex marriage. For the first time, U.N. General Assembly discusses gay rights, debating a nonbinding resolution to recommend that countries decriminalize homosexuality.

2009 India's high court overturns British-era anti-sodomy law.

2010 U.S. Congress votes to allow gays to serve openly in the military, but it does not take effect immediately. . . . Romania, Estonia and Bulgaria take legal steps to define marriage as between a man and a woman. . . . Uganda and other African nations consider stronger sanctions — including the death penalty — for homosexual acts.

2011 Ugandan gay activist David Kato is murdered in January, after he is identified by a newspaper that urged Ugandans to kill gays. . . . British government lifts ban on same-sex civil union ceremonies in churches. . . . Obama administration stops defending DOMA in court.

defense of the natural family, marriage between a man and a woman," William Saunders Jr., senior vice president for legal affairs of Americans United for Life, wrote in *The Family in America, A Journal of Public Policy.*[28]

U.N. officials have ignored the vision of human rights expressed in these documents because "they've been taken over by activists who focus 24/7 on issues that really only affect a small minority," says Jacobs, of the World Congress of Families. "They've taken over the human rights committees in the U.N. — the Committee on the Rights of the Child, the Commission on the Status of Women — all these things have been taken over by NGOs [nongovernmental organizations] that don't really represent the values of the people of the world."

Proponents of LGBT rights say their concerns warrant inclusion based on a basic concept of human rights. They note that the Universal Declaration of Human Rights says that "everyone is entitled to all the rights in this declaration without distinction of any kind," including "race, colour, sex, language, religion . . . birth or other status." The declaration also proclaims "no one shall be subjected to arbitrary interference with his privacy, family, (or) home."[29]

Gay-rights supporters say the U.N. and other international organizations must ensure that the rights expressed in these documents are applied to the LGBT community, which has suffered from discrimination and violent oppression throughout history. Current events provide regular evidence that the battle against both is far from over, they say.

For example, IGLHRC director of programs Jessica Stern points to what happened when a General Assembly committee recently was renewing a declaration condemning "extrajudicial, summary or arbitrary executions." Benin, on behalf of several African nations, tried to strike "sexual orientation" from the list of discriminatory grounds on which these killings often take place — a list that has been in the declaration for the past 10 years.

But the amendment to eliminate the reference passed, with 79 votes in favor, 70 against, 17 nations abstaining and 26 not present.[30] Only after lobbying by the United States and other nations did sexual orientation go back into the resolution.

"We were forced to mobilize the vote, and in the end we picked up three African votes." Stern says. "But the fact is, it's still the only explicit LGBT resolution passed at the U.N., and what is it about? It's about killing, and we had to fight for it. It really underscores the fragility of the whole human rights framework."

BACKGROUND

Ancient Practice

Those who oppose granting same-sex relationships equal legal and social footing with heterosexual relationships often refer to being gay or lesbian as a "lifestyle choice." If so, it's a lifestyle that has survived since the beginnings of recorded civilization, often in the face of sanctions that included torture and death.

"If you just take a look at homoerotic love, it crosses all cultures, it goes through all time. You can always find people who are having sex with members of their own sex and falling in love with them," says John G. Younger, a gay-studies scholar and professor of the classics at the University of Kansas. "What society does with it is the question."

Some cultures viewed same-sex behavior benignly, as just another aspect of human sexuality. Some have accepted it under certain conditions, for example, as part of rites of passage or initiation rituals. Others have viewed it as contrary to God's natural order but have largely tried to ignore it. Some have punished it severely.

Most of the attitudes that existed in the past can still be found today.

From ancient Greece to the early dynasties in China, historical documents make clear that homosexual behavior has been around since humanity began recording its own existence. Some of the most esteemed literature from the pre-Christian era in Greece celebrates same-sex love. Sappho's poems to young women on the island of Lesbos spawned the words "lesbian" and "Sapphic."

Some Greek philosophers considered sex between adolescent boys and older men, who also served as their intellectual and societal mentors, as the highest form of love. But other Greeks believed it represented a distortion of the natural business of sex, which was procreation.

In China, court historians recorded the homosexual affairs and infatuations of many Han Dynasty emperors, who ruled for roughly 400 years from the 2nd century B.C.[31] In the 18th century several Manchu emperors

Gays in the Military Create Few Problems Abroad

Transition has been much less wrenching than the debate.

At least 36 nations already allowed gays and lesbians to serve openly in their armed forces before the U.S. Congress in December voted to have the United States join them. Those nations included most of America's NATO allies, plus Israel and South Korea, countries where hostile neighbors make maintaining military capability a priority.[1]

During America's heated debate over whether to end "don't ask, don't tell" — the controversial U.S. policy that required gays to keep their sexual orientation hidden — opponents claimed that allowing gays to serve openly would undermine American military readiness and lead to dissent in the ranks. Congress was being "asked to impose a risky military social experiment that has not been duplicated anywhere else in the world," said Elaine Donnelly, president of the Center for Military Readiness, which opposed ending the policy.[2]

The record, however, indicates little risk. Several key U.S. allies now have more than a decade of experience with openly homosexual sailors and soldiers in uniform. Despite dire predictions by some foreign officers that would be echoed years later in the United States, the transition seems to be much less wrenching than the debate.

"It was a nonevent," retired Maj. Gen Simon Willis, the former head of personnel for the Australian Defense Force, told the Brookings Institution, "and it continues to be a nonevent."[3]

In Great Britain, a review after the policy was instituted found that only three service members, out of more than 250,000, had resigned because of the change. In addition, discussions with foreign military personnel in several nations conducted by a special Pentagon Working Group and the Rand Corporation think tank found no evidence that the shift had undermined training or morale.[4]

The study said none of the nations directly assessed the effects of the policy on combat effectiveness. "However, most of these nations have been engaged in combat operations in the years since changing their policy. Uniformly, these nations reported that they were aware of no units that had a degradation of cohesion or combat effectiveness, and that the presence of gay men and lesbians in combat units had not been raised as an issue by any of their units deployed in Iraq or Afghanistan."[5]

In Canada, the United Kingdom and Australia, the military expected "noticeable numbers" of gays and lesbians to come out following the change, "but in fact very few did so." Officials in Canada and the U.K. also said recruitment did not suffer, nor did retention of personnel.[6]

Most nations instituted the policy relatively quickly, usually after amending their training methods in order to emphasize respect for people of different sexual orientation.

A survey of American military personnel conducted by the Pentagon Working Group as part of its study found that

openly engaged in sex with both men and women.[32] Although these choices were often considered unwise, they weren't considered unnatural. The Arab world in the first millennium also took a more benign view of homosexual relations than many later cultures.

Men and women engaging in homosexual behavior in ancient times did not necessarily think of themselves as gay or lesbian in the modern sense, say scholars. Most historians of human sexuality believe the idea of sexual preference as a defining part of one's identity did not become a popular concept until much later. This was true, they say, even after Christian disapproval of homosexuality took hold in Western culture.

"People thought of sex acts primarily as sinful acts available to everyone, rather than identity," says Shepard, the Johns Hopkins University historian.

The triumph of Judeo-Christian beliefs, particularly the adoption of Christianity by the Roman Empire in the 4th century, ushered in a long period in which homosexuality was considered a sin, generally outlawed and sometimes punished by torture or death. The roots of the Judeo-Christian attitude toward gays can be found in Chapters 18 and 20 of the Old Testament book of "Leviticus," which prohibit same-sex relations. Chapter 18, verse 22, is the most succinct: "You shall not lie with a male as with a woman. It is an abomination." Chapter

70-78 percent expected the change to either improve or make little difference in the ability of their unit to work together or get along socially.[7]

Aubrey Sarvis, executive director of the Service-member's Legal Defense Network, which is dedicated to allowing gays to serve in the military, says he suspects most Americans believe that gays could serve openly as soon as President Barack Obama signed the law repealing "don't ask, don't tell." But the law requires the president, the Defense secretary and the joint chiefs of staff to certify that the military is ready for the change and then includes a 60-day transition period before open service becomes the rule.

The administration has not yet issued the certification, and groups that fought for the repeal are watching the process closely. "I don't see any foot-dragging at the Pentagon, but I think it's clear they want to have a sizeable number of the force receiving training around open service before certification can take place," says Sarvis.

Still, Sarvis expects the process to proceed quickly from here. "Moving to open service really isn't that complicated, for two reasons," he says. "One, gays and lesbians are already serving side by side with their straight counterparts, and many of them know who the gays and lesbians are, even if they haven't come out. We're talking about a lot of young people, and they have pretty good radars. Second, the education and training around open service isn't that complicated either. How many different ways do you have to say: 'Treat your fellow soldier with the respect and dignity you expect to receive?'"

— Reed Karaim

Members of the British Royal Navy march during the Euro Pride parade in London, England, on July 1, 2006. The U.K. is one of 36 nations — including most of America's NATO allies — that allow gays and lesbians to serve openly in their armed forces.

[1] "Report of the Comprehensive Review of the Issues Associated with the Repeal of 'Don't Ask, Don't Tell,'" Pentagon Working Group Study, Nov. 30, 2010, p. 89, www.defense.gov/home/features/2010/0610_gatesdadt/DADTReport_FINAL_20101130(secure-hires).pdf.

[2] Elaine Donnelly, "At Issue: Should the U.S. follow the example of nations that allow gays to serve openly in the military?" *CQ Researcher*, Sept. 18, 2009, p. 781.

[3] Charles McLean and Peter Singer, "What Our Allies Can Tell Us About the End of Don't Ask, Don't Tell," The Brookings Institution, June 7, 2010, www.brookings.edu/opinions/2010/0607_dont_ask_dont_tell_singer.aspx.

[4] "Report of the Comprehensive Review of the Issues Associated with the Repeal of 'Don't Ask, Don't Tell,'" *op. cit.*

[5] *Ibid.*, p. 92.

[6] *Ibid.*, p. 91.

[7] *Ibid.*, p. 64.

20, verse 13, adds that the two men "shall surely be put to death."[33]

But Leviticus spends more time condemning incest, adultery and consorting with evil spirits than it does on male homosexuality (female homosexuality isn't mentioned). It also establishes dietary and hygiene rules to which Christianity does not generally adhere. Nonetheless, it's hard to overstate the impact Leviticus has had on the Christian world's view of homosexuality. "The authors of Leviticus wrote two dozen words which sealed the fate of men who loved men for more than 14 centuries," wrote pioneering gay studies scholar Louis Crompton in his sweeping *Homosexuality and Civilization.*[34]

The Apostle Paul harshly condemned homosexuality in his epistles to the Romans and Corinthians. It was also defined as unnatural and morally wrong by Saint Thomas Aquinas, a 13th-century Italian priest and philosopher whose writings still form the underpinnings of Catholic philosophy.[35] In the Middle Ages and through the Renaissance, the Catholic Church and civil governments generally proscribed homosexual acts, whether by gays or heterosexuals.

The penalties were often severe, including branding, castration and death, but punishments varied from one city or country to another and from one generation to the next. The situation was far more complex than a simple reading of the laws would indicate, say historians.

"Michelangelo had male lovers; Leonardo da Vinci had lovers. Nobody cared, mostly because the people they were having sex with were young men from the lower classes," says Younger, who edited the encyclopedia *Sex in the Ancient World.* "If they had been doing it with the sons of nobles, it would have been different. The act might be illegal, but the law is applied in different ways."

For instance, during a 100-year period in Florence, a principal Renaissance city, the uncertainty surrounding how seriously to punish homosexuals is recorded in Crompton's history. The laws were changed, on the average, "more than once a decade and contain such elaborately gradated punishments that they resemble a kind of commercial tariff," Crompton wrote.[36] Records indicate 4,062 accusations of sodomy were lodged in just 24 years, at a time when the city had less than 50,000 occupants.[37]

On the other hand, officers of the Spanish Inquisition — which executed about 100 men for sexual relations with other males — were far less troubled by ambiguity, according to Crompton. Harsh punishments, primarily torture, were also common.[38]

In the ensuing centuries punishments for homosexual behavior became less severe across most of Europe, and some authorities showed far less zeal in pursuing men suspected of same-sex relations. Female homosexual behavior was of even less concern.

In Asia, Africa and elsewhere the view of same-sex behavior and of minorities that crossed traditional gender identities — such as the Hijras, men who have dressed like women for centuries in India — varied widely during this period. Heterosexual relationships, whether polygamous or monogamous, remained the dominant form of sexual pairing everywhere, however.

In the West, the most significant change in ideas about same-sex behavior since Christianity began occurred in 19th-century Germany, where the modern notion of a "homosexual" was born.

Modern Movement

Karl Heinrich Ulrichs, a 19th-century German intellectual, is considered by many historians and LGBT activists as the father of the modern homosexual-rights movement. But his journey was an intensely personal one that began as an examination of his own sexual

attraction to men. Eventually he concluded that "sexual orientation was a stable, inherent human characteristic and homosexuality a valid and natural form of sexual expression," wrote Francis Mark Mondimore, author of *A Natural History of Homosexuality.* Mondimore is an associate professor at The Johns Hopkins University medical school in Baltimore, Md.[39]

Ulrichs was considered a pioneer because he publicly acknowledged his sexual orientation and began crusading for his ideas, even arguing against anti-sodomy laws before a congress of German jurists. Although he had barely begun to speak before he was shouted down, today the International Lesbian and Gay Law Association presents an annual award in his memory.[40]

The word "homosexual" first appeared in an 1869 political pamphlet by Karl Maria Kertbeny, a German journalist and crusader who also opposed having anti-sodomy statutes included in the unified German state's proposed constitution. The word "heterosexuality" came to be used in its modern sense slightly later. Taken together, these words would eventually help to create an idea of human sexuality built around two opposite poles of attraction, with humans' sexual compass needle more or less pointing one way or the other. They would also help to tie sexuality more closely to a person's sense of identity.

The notion of sexuality as identity would flower in the 20th century. "There's this idea that there's something in you that's really you, and that sexuality is one of the key aspects of who you are as an individual," says Shepard of The Johns Hopkins University. "Sexuality, or sex, goes from being something you do to this key measure by which people can know something about you. It becomes revelatory."

The idea that sexual orientation is largely innate is widely accepted within the scientific community now but continues to be debated by the public. It was viewed even more skeptically through most of the 20th century. The American Psychiatric Association classified homosexuality as a mental disorder until 1973, and pop culture often referred to it as a disease, or an aberrant, repulsive act.

A sense of shared identity began to strengthen in homosexual subcultures, which flourished at various times and places in several countries. For instance, in Berlin in the 1920s and in Paris in the '20s and '30s attitudes toward homosexuality were relaxed, and gays and lesbians lived fairly openly.

"We're always trying to build this story where things are headed in one direction, but even if you just look at the 20th century and the West, we've really gone back and forth," Shepard says. "The fact is, there were lots of moments and places in time when people had good things happening to them and were living their lives without too much trouble."

But those periods also can end abruptly, Shepard adds, such as during the Nazi persecution of homosexuals in the 1930s. And in the United States and many European nations "the 1950s and '60s were a pretty dramatic period of repression," Shepard says. France, for example, passed its first anti-homosexual laws during that period.

Still, homosexual organizations were slowly raising their profile, both in the United States and in Europe. In 1965, a group picketed in front of the White House against U.S. policies concerning homosexuality.

But in 1969 the modern gay-rights movement was suddenly and violently born. On June 28, police raided the Stonewall Inn, a gay bar in the Greenwich Village section of Manhattan. Police raids on gay bars were hardly rare at the time and had generally been greeted with submission. But this time the patrons, who were not charged, did not disperse. A crowd quickly gathered outside the bar, and a riot eventually broke out. It raged, off and on, for several days, gathering world attention. By the time it ended, gays and lesbians were demanding fair treatment and establishing a defiantly public gay culture that included annual parades and other events.

"Stonewall was enormously influential, basically all across Europe, from Argentina to Japan," says Shepard. "You had all these people making connections. The world is much more mobile, and you're getting this massive transfer of information."

The gay-liberation movement would intersect with other social currents, such as the international youth movement seeking to overturn existing social norms and a burgeoning feminist movement. It would include an ethos of sexual freedom and experimentation that in the 1980s ran smack up against the AIDS epidemic and a growing emphasis on safe sexual practices.

AIDS (Acquired Immune Deficiency Syndrome) was originally viewed as a disease afflicting only gay men until researchers began finding cases among heterosexual women and realized it could be transmitted through blood, semen, vaginal fluid and breast milk. Gay activists played

AFP/Getty Images/Janek Skarzynski

Thousands of gays, lesbians, bisexuals and supporters of equal rights for sexual minorities march in a gay-pride parade in Warsaw, Poland, on July 17, 2010, urging the government to legalize same-sex partnerships. The socially conservative, predominantly Catholic country has not legalized gay marriage and recently tried to punish teachers who "promote" homosexuality. But the measure was condemned as homophobic by European Union officials.

a leading role in pressuring governments for more money for research and treatment.[41]

Political organizing eventually won greater legal and cultural recognition for LGBT relationships. The cause also expanded to embrace bisexuals and transgender people. Although the LGBT movement has had little or limited impact on policies or social attitudes in some countries, it has encouraged LGBT people around the globe to speak up, often at personal risk. In the West, it has led to dramatic changes in laws and attitudes. Homosexuality has been generally decriminalized in most places except Africa and the Middle East, more and more nations accept civil unions or gay marriage, and gays have won elective office and serve openly in the military in three dozen countries.[42] More significant, perhaps, are polls showing that the young are particularly unconcerned about sexual orientation.

All this has happened in about four decades. "In today's world we get so caught up in what's happening right now," says Younger at the University of Kansas, "it's easy to forget how much has changed in recent years."

CURRENT SITUATION

Same-Sex Marriage

Amid the remnants of a worldwide recession, unprecedented immigration levels and a continuing conflict between Islamic fundamentalism and secular Western democracies, the debate over sexual rights often gets caught in the political and social crosswinds. And frequently, same-sex marriage seems to be at the center of the storm.

In Europe, for instance, Hungary has shown how shifts in larger political sentiments can affect the gay-rights debate. Since the 1990s, gay-rights activists have considered Hungary one of Eastern Europe's more progressive countries. In 2010, it passed a law recognizing "registered partnerships," which give gay couples most of the benefits of marriage.

But Hungary also was hit hard by the economic downturn, fueling frustration with failed economic policies seen as imported or imposed by the West as Hungary was integrated into the EU. That anger helped the far-right Jobbik Party, known for anti-gay rhetoric, win 16.7 percent of the vote in the last general election.[43]

"I think it's sort of a Euro-fatigue," says Czarnecki, the LGBT activist in Poland. "I think overall people are a little disenchanted with the [economic and cultural] integration process."

Particularly in rejecting the idea of same-sex marriage, Eastern Europeans seem to be staking out their national identity. "To Romanians, the only thing that saved them as a nation [during communism] was the family, marriage and their faith in God," says Costea, whose Alliance of Romania's Families worked to get the law to define marriage as between a man and a woman.

On the other side of Europe's political spectrum, support for gay and lesbian rights has become a litmus test

for cultural assimilation in some countries where LGBT rights have progressed the farthest, such as the Netherlands and Scandinavia. Norway, for example, now requires asylum seekers to watch a movie on gays and lesbians. "We want to show that homosexuality is normal and accepted," said the movie's director, Mari Finnestad. "If you want to live in Norway and be part of the Norwegian society, you have to accept that."[44]

Some observers believe that in such situations LGBT rights are being used as a way to define Muslim immigrants as outsiders — not really part of the nations they have joined. Randi Gressgård, a researcher at the Centre for Women's and Gender Research at the University of Bergen, Norway, recently coauthored a paper examining the phenomenon: "Intolerable Citizens: Tolerance, Islam and Homosexuality."[45] Ironically, she says, the concept of tolerance is being used to exclude people — "as a political strategy to create a division between what are considered proper citizens, liberal and tolerant citizens, and improper or intolerant citizens."

Gressgård points out that as anti-Muslim sentiment has grown in Europe, the cause of "homo-tolerance" has been embraced even by conservative parties that originally opposed same-sex marriage and a previously indifferent general public.[46] "People don't care about gender and sexuality issues," she says, "but when it comes to Muslims it's suddenly really important. It's not enough that they follow the laws, they have to embrace the social norm."

Yet, a recent survey in the Netherlands found that most of the country's minorities, including Muslims, feel that "gay people should be free to live their lives as they wished."[47]

Still, the perceived cultural split has led even some gays to join far-right political parties and anti-Muslim groups, says Gressgård, who believes the actions reflect a shift in strategies by far-right parties across much of Europe. France's National Front Party, for example, has gained public support by changing its tune and supporting gay rights while focusing on Muslim immigration as a threat to national identity.[48]

The Americas

Gay rights have been at the center of America's culture war for at least two decades. Legislative proposals limiting gay rights, often used to whip up turnout among

Should same-sex couples be allowed to marry?

YES

Rosa M. Posa Guinea
Coordinator, Latin American Human Rights Advocacy Institute, International Gay and Lesbian Human Rights Commission, Paraguay

Written for *CQ Global Researcher*, March 2011

"we do not want to marry! And we want that that be our own choice! We do not want the State to regulate our relations in any way, even forbidding marriage!" That statement — which is how the Colombian women's community organization Mujeres al Borde qualifies its endorsement of same-sex marriage — summarizes my thoughts on equal marriage. We celebrate the progress toward equal rights that same-sex marriage indicates. But, we recognize that equal marriage is not the pinnacle of the fight for the rights of lesbian, gay and bisexual people, nor does it end discrimination on the basis of sexual orientation and gender identity.

In January a lesbian and bisexual organization in Argentina — where same-sex marriage was legalized in July 2010 — faced an unusual discrimination case. Members of the group were forbidden from entering a swimming pool because the women were wearing "non-feminine" swimwear (shorts and shirts). They were told they must "respect the family environment" and that the recent victory for the rights of same-sex couples to marry was merely "a left-wing issue!" Clearly, the legalization of same-sex marriage in Argentina had not really changed people's prejudices.

Limiting marriage to heterosexual couples encourages homophobia, discrimination and exclusion. The specter of same-sex marriage is used by opponents of lesbian, gay, bisexual and transgender (LGBT) rights to further persecute us. It is invoked in countries that criminalize homosexuality to arrest people exercising their freedom of association rights or by legislatures seeking to blame systemic problems on vulnerable minorities. In countries where same-sex marriage is a viable goal or already a reality, leaders who still oppose allowing same-sex couples to marry play on this prejudice, painting same-sex couples as less important to society.

Consider South Africa, a country that legalized same-sex marriage in 2006. There lesbian activists fight to end "corrective rape" (when a man rapes a lesbian in order to "turn" her heterosexual) and have it recognized as a hate crime. Dozens of lesbians are raped and murdered there every week, even though the South African Constitution prohibits discrimination on the basis of sexual orientation.

The right to marry a person of the same sex is not the only right LGBT people still seek. In all countries, even those where marriage equality exists, we still have a long way to go to reach real equality as citizens.

NO

Margaret Somerville
Professor, Centre for Medicine, Ethics and Law, McGill University, Montreal, Quebec, Canada

Written for *CQ Global Researcher*, March 2011

I oppose same-sex marriage but approve of "civil unions." Civil unions can provide the protections and benefits same-sex couples seek and send the message that discrimination on the basis of sexual orientation is wrong, while leaving children's rights unaffected.

Same-sex marriage presents a conflict between the claims of children and homosexual adults. Children's claims relate to their biological origins, family structure and societal norms. Homosexual adults' claims are to not be discriminated against in public recognition of their committed, intimate relationships and the benefits of such recognition. In that conflict I give children priority, since they are the most vulnerable.

In law, marriage confers two rights: to marry and create a family. Giving same-sex couples the latter right changes our societal norms regarding children's human rights. It divests all children of the right to be reared in a natural family structure, with a mother and a father, who optimally should be the child's biological parents. It also gives married, gay adults the right to use reproductive technologies to create families. Thus, a same-sex couple could potentially create a shared genetic child, contravening the child's right to have natural, biological origins — unmanipulated by science.

Rather than being defined primarily by biological ties, all parenthood would be defined primarily by legal ties, as Canada's same-sex marriage law shows. Civil unions do not establish the right to create a family, so they do not affect children's rights. Thus, they are the ethical way to deal with this conflict.

Same-sex marriage was always possible, but it's been an anomaly. Over millennia, the core of marriage across all kinds of societies, cultures and religions has been its biological, procreative reality. Same-sex marriage negates this core. Marriage is built around procreation because it is primarily intended to benefit children and only secondarily, adults. Today, marriage as a cultural construct built around a biological reality is more important than ever, due to the advent of assisted human reproductive technologies and how those can affect the rights of children resulting from their use.

Proponents of same-sex marriage correctly point out that children's rights often are not respected in opposite-sex marriages and not all opposite-sex couples procreate. But those cases do not erase existing societal norms, basic values or symbolism regarding children's rights with respect to their biological origins and family structure. Same-sex marriage does exactly that, which is why we should not introduce it.

AFP/Getty Images/Gianluigi Guercia

AFP/Getty Images/Brian Sokol

Tying the Same-Sex Knot

South Africa and Nepal are among the countries where gay marriage is legal. Sonia Souls (left) and Charmaine Weber (center) embrace after their wedding in Capetown, South Africa, on Feb. 14, 2010 (top), and Diya Mahaju and Anil Mahaju prepare to wed in Kathmandu on Aug. 26, 2006, in Nepal's first public gay marriage (bottom). Sixteen other countries recognize same-sex civil unions.

culturally conservative voters, have been a political staple during election years. They've also been convenient political sledgehammers to batter an opponent — such as the initial uproar over allowing gays to serve openly in the military that forced President Bill Clinton to accept the controversial "don't ask, don't tell" approach.[49]

Thus, the most surprising thing about the December votes by the U.S. Congress to repeal the "don't ask, don't tell" measure may be how little heat it generated. Although Sen. John McCain, R-Ariz., brandished a petition from

1,000 retired officers opposing the idea, polls showed strong public support for repeal, and a Pentagon study concluded it would cause little disruption in the ranks. In a year of bitter partisan division, eight Republicans joined with the Democratic majority to pass the Senate measure.[50]

The vote left same-sex marriage as the last flashpoint in what had once been a fiery battle over LGBT rights in the United States. Younger, director of the Women, Gender and Sexuality Studies Program at the University of Kansas, believes that's because marriage is considered more than a civil contract. "Most people think of marriage as a religious ceremony," he says. "We all know that what makes it legal is when you go in the back room and sign the papers, but it's a religious sacrament, and I think that's one reason you see people drawing the line."

Some opponents, however, stress the benefit they believe comes with having children raised by parents of both sexes, and what they consider the right of children to know their biological parents. "A child's got a right to a mother and a father, and preferably its own biological parents," says Margaret Somerville, a law and ethics professor at Canada's McGill University in Montreal, Quebec, who supports civil unions, but not same-sex marriage.

In the United States, five states and the District of Columbia currently allow same-sex marriage, and six others allow some legal spousal rights to gay couples.[51] Although some polls showed Americans inching toward a roughly even split on the issue, the fight over same-sex marriage seemed likely to continue in courts and state-houses across the nation in 2011.

LGBT activists believe they have a good chance to see gay marriage legalized in several other states, including Maryland, New York and Delaware within the next year. But opponents, pointing to their success with voter referendums, believe they will be able to prevail at the ballot box.

Surprisingly, same-sex marriage may have a better chance in some predominantly Catholic Latin American countries. The movement exists, says Ferreyra, IGLHRC's representative in Argentina, because past authoritarian regimes have left the public sensitive to the need to pro-tect human rights. "It's also related to the overall political climate," he says. "There are many left-wing governments that have taken power, in countries such as Argentina,

Brazil, Venezuela, Ecuador, and they are supporting LGBT rights."[52]

Western Influence?

David Kato — a gay activist in Uganda who had been publicly identified by the local newspaper *Rolling Stone*, which urged Ugandans to kill local gays — was murdered in January.

Claims and counterclaims about his death were still being made in mid-February, the motive uncertain. But to many gay activists, Kato's death represents the dangerous situation that exists in the homophobic climate of Uganda and several other African nations, including Cameroon, Senegal and Nigeria.[53]

Many gay activists blame a 2009 visit by American evangelist Lively, of Abiding Truth Ministries, and two other U.S. anti-gay crusaders for inflaming existing homophobic sentiment in Uganda and spurring a local lawmaker to introduce the bill imposing the death penalty for repeated homosexual offenses.

"Lively is said to have spent four hours with Ugandan parliamentarians talking to them about homosexuality," says Kalende, the Ugandan gay activist. "In April 2009, the first version of the bill was written, and the language of this first version reiterated Lively's comments." Ugandan lawmaker David Bahati, however, said on MSNBC's "Rachel Maddow Show" that he alone authored the legislation. In the same interview, Bahati claimed foreigners are coming into Uganda and spending millions of dollars to recruit children into homosexuality, but, despite repeated requests, he has provided no evidence to support the assertion.

The Rev. Kapya Kaoma, a Zambian Episcopal priest, says the foreigners spending money to spread their views about homosexuality are on the other side of the issue. "It's a political agenda being driven by so-called evangelism in the U.S. and being pushed on to Africa," Kaoma concluded after spending 16 months interviewing people in Uganda, Kenya and Nigeria. His report, "Globalising the Culture Wars; U.S. Conservatives, African Churches and Homophobia," warned that preaching intolerance could lead to mob violence against African gays.[54]

Likewise, some leaders in the Middle East see tolerance for homosexuality — and even homosexuality itself — as something imposed on them by the West. Iranian President Mahmoud Ahmadinejad notably expressed that idea at Columbia University in New York City in 2007, when responding to a question about the recent execution in Iran of two gay men. "In Iran we don't have homosexuals like in your country," he said. "In Iran we do not have this phenomenon. I do not know who has told you we have it."[55] African leaders have made similar claims.

As some Ugandans have begun speaking out in opposition to the bill, and international criticism has grown, the Ugandan anti-gay bill appears to have stalled.[56] But with homosexuality already illegal in almost all the countries of the region, and more punitive legislation pending in several, the situation for LGBT people in Africa seems unlikely to improve in the immediate future.

Meanwhile, a continent away in the world's second-largest nation, the 2009 decision of the Indian Supreme Court to strike down a colonial-era law and decriminalize homosexuality may have had as much of an effect on the lives of LGBT people as any other action in the world. The case attracted support from a broad array of public organizations, but it also was opposed by some religious groups that have continued legal efforts to restore bans on homosexual behavior.

"There's a continuing legal battle, but as far as the public is concerned, the fight is over," says Indian lawyer Narrain. "To change the law you need a public movement, and that's what we have had in India."

OUTLOOK

Sweeping Transformation?

Both proponents and opponents of gay rights seem to share the sense that things have been moving quickly. Those who feel that the changes threaten the traditional heterosexual family have developed a fierce determination to halt the process. Among those who believe they stand at the cusp of an era when gays and lesbians will see their relationships treated just like everyone else's, there is an equal determination to complete the transformation.

American psychiatrist and author Mondimore believes the arguments for discrimination are "just falling away" and that attitudes about same-sex relationships could get to the point "where it's like it is with interracial marriage. Once people got all worked up about it, and now that reaction just seems strange."

But Ruse, head of the Catholic Family and Human Rights Institute, believes the "status quo" will prevail and that gay-rights activists overestimate how much opinion is shifting. "We are told incessantly that homosexual marriage is just on the cusp of widespread acceptance," he says, "but I don't see that happening."

The University of Amsterdam's Duyvendak, however, believes a fundamental shift in attitudes has taken place in much of Europe, at least, that will help to make same-sex couples unexceptional in the near future. "Sexuality and procreation have been totally decoupled," he says. "This very idea that love and sexuality is only reserved for straight people, I cannot imagine that coming back."

In Latin America, Ferreyra of the International Gay and Lesbian Human Rights Commission sees the next 10 to 15 years of gay-rights advocacy as part of a larger regional effort to build institutions that support stable democracies and "increase the internal bonds within the countries, support civil society and human rights." And the current LGBT movement in Latin American is limited largely to urban elites, he says. The next step is to reach out to "the whole population."

The World Congress of Families' Jacobs believes LGBT activists who are optimistic about the future overlook a key factor: global demographic trends. Declining birth rates and aging populations among the largely secular Western nations contrast with higher birth rates in regions that are hostile to gay rights. Even within the developed world, he says, portions of the population that oppose equal treatment for homosexual couples are growing. "The arrow points to the natural family," he says, "because it's only the religious who are having children."

But reflecting the general sense of optimism within the LGBT community, activist Kalende looks past today's troubles in her native Uganda and sees a brighter future there, too. "Things will get better," she says, "because whenever there is a noble cause for justice, freedom finds a way."

NOTES

1. "Report of the Comprehensive Review of the Issues Associated with a Repeal of Don't Ask Don't Tell," Pentagon Working Group Study, Nov. 30, 2010, p. 89, www.defense.gov/home/features/2010/0610_gatesdadt/DADTReport_FINAL_20101130 (secure-hires).pdf.

2. "Americans split evenly on gay marriage," CNN Politics, Aug. 11, 2010, http://political ticker.blogs .cnn.com/2010/08/11/americans-split-evenly-on-gay-marriage/. Also see Charlie Savage and Sheryl Gay Stolberg, "U.S., in Shift, Sees Marriage Act as Violation of Gay Rights," *The New York Times*, Feb. 23, 2011, www.nytimes.com/2011/02/24/us/24 marriage.html.

3. Sudarsan Raghavan, "Gays in Africa face growing persecution, activists say," *The Washington Post*, Dec.12, 2010, www.washingtonpost.com/wp-dyn/content/ article/2010/12/11/ AR2010121103045.html.

4. *Ibid.*

5. Mark Lowen, "Scores arrested in Belgrade after anti-gay riot," BBC News, Oct. 10, 2010, www.bbc.co .uk/news/world-europe-11507253.

6. "Sexual Orientation/Gender Identity References, Human Rights Report for 2009," U.S. Department of State, March 10, 2010, http:// paei.state.gov/g/ drl/rls/hrrpt/2009/.

7. Jeremy Hubbard, "Fifth Gay Teen Suicide Sparks Debate," ABC News, Oct. 3, 2010, http://abcnews .go.com/US/gay-teen-suicide-sparks-debate/ story?id=11788128.

8. David Myers, *Exploring Psychology* (2007), p. 368.

9. Theodore Olson, "The Conservative Case for Gay Marriage," *Newsweek*, July 10, 2010, www.newsweek .com/2010/01/08/the-conservative-case-for-gay-marriage.html.

10. Nick Squires, "Pope says gay marriage is 'insidious and dangerous,'" *The Telegraph*, May 13, 2010, www.telegraph.co.uk/news/news topics/religion/ 7719789/Pope-says-gay-marriage-is-insidious-and-dangerous.html.

11. Scott Lively, "Deciphering 'Gay' word-speak and language of confusion," *newswithviews. com*, May 25, 2002, www.newswithviews.com/conspiracy/ conspiracy6.htm.

12. Evelyn Schlatter, "18 Anti-Gay Groups and their Propaganda," Southern Poverty Law Center, winter 2010, www.splcenter.org/get-informed/ intelligence-report/browse-all-issues/ 2010/winter/ the-hard-liners.

13. Zoe Alsop, "Uganda's Anti-Gay Bill: Inspired by the U.S.," *Time*, Dec. 10, 2009, www. time.com/time/world/article/0,8599,1946645, 00.html.

14. Thomas Fox, "140 theologians call for women's ordination, end of mandatory celibacy," *The National Catholic Reporter*, Feb. 4, 2011, www.ncronline.org/blogs/ncr-today/143-theologians-call-womens-ordination-end-mandatory-celibacy.

15. Daniel Maguire, "A Catholic Defense of Same-Sex Marriage," *The Religious Consultation*, April 20, 2006, www.religiousconsultation.org/ Catholic_defense_of_same_sex_marriage.htm.

16. "Lesbian and Gay Rights in the World," International Lesbian, Gay, Bisexual, Trans and Intersex Association, May 2010, http://ilga.org/ ilga/en/article/1161.

17. "Homophobia, Transphobia and Discrimination on Grounds of Sexual Orientation and Gender, 2010 Update," European Union Agency for Fundamental Rights, 2010, p. 7.

18. "Poland urged to halt 'homophobia,'" BBC News, April 27, 2007, http://news.bbc.co.uk/2/hi/europe/6596829.stm.

19. "We Are a Buried Generation: Discrimination and Violence Against Sexual Minorities in Iran," Human Rights Watch, Dec. 15, 2010, www.hrw.org/en/reports/2010/12/15/we-are-buried-generation.

20. Kathy Chu and Calum MacLeod, "Gay life in China is legal but remains hidden," *USA Today*, Feb. 22, 2010, www.usatoday.com/news/ world/2010-02-21-gays-China-closeted_N.htm.

21. For background, see Brian Beary, "Religious Fundamentalism," *CQ Global Researcher*, Feb. 1, 2009, pp. 27-58.

22. Rafael Romo, "Hate crimes, killings rising, say Honduras activists," CNN, Feb. 1, 2011, www.cnn.com/2011/WORLD/americas/01/31/ honduras.hate.crimes/index.html.

23. Tamara Audi, Justin Scheck and Christopher Lawton, "California Votes for Prop 8," *The Wall Street Journal*, Nov. 5, 2008, http://online.wsj. com/article/SB122586056759900673.html.

24. A. G. Sulzberger, "Ouster of Iowa Judges Sends Signal to Bench," *The New York Times*, Nov. 3, 2010, www.nytimes.com/2010/11/04/us/politics/04judges.html.

25. "The Yogyakarta Principles," www.yogyakartaprinciples.org/.

26. Neil MacFarquhar, "In a First, Gay Rights Are Pressed at the U.N.," *The New York Times*, Dec. 19, 2008, p. 22.

27. Article 16, "The Universal Declaration of Human Rights," United Nations, www.un.org/en/documents/udhr/index.shtml.

28. William J. Saunders, "Committees Gone Wild: How U.N. Bureaucrats Are Turning 'Human Rights' Against the Family," *The Family in America, A Journal of Public Policy*, winter 2010, www.familyinamerica.org/index.php?doc_id=15&cat_id=6.

29. Articles 2 and 12, "The Universal Declaration of Human Rights," *op. cit.*

30. "Governments Remove Sexual Orientation from UN Resolution Condemning Extrajudicial, Summary or Arbitrary Executions," IGLHRC press release, Nov. 17, 2010, www.iglhrc.org/ cgi-bin/iowa/article/pressroom/pressrelease/ 1257.html.

31. Louis Crompton, *Homosexuality and Civilization* (2003), location 4751 in the Kindle edition.

32. *Ibid.*, location 5161 in the Kindle edition.

33. The Holy Bible, New King James version.

34. Crompton, *op. cit.*, location 888 in the Kindle edition.

35. A concise summary of Aquinas's philosophical argument and objections to it can be found at Stephen Law's blog, under "Aquinas on Homosexuality," March 14, 2007, http://stephenlaw.blogspot.com/2007/03/aquinas-on-homosexuality.html.

36. Crompton, *op. cit.*, location 5397 in the Kindle edition.

37. *Ibid.*

38. *Ibid.*, location 6208.

39. Francis Mark Mondimore, *A Natural History of Homosexuality* (1996), p. 28.

40. "The Karl Heinrich Ulrichs Award," International Lesbian and Gay Law Association, www.ilglaw.org/cnfaward.htm.

41. For background, see Nellie Bristol, "Battling HIV/AIDS," *CQ Researcher*, Oct. 26, 2007, pp. 889-912.

42. Gay and Lesbian Leadership Institute, www.glli.org/home.

43. Dan Bilefsky, "World Briefing/Europe; Hungary: New Leader Assails Far-Right Party's Rise," *The New York Times*, April 13, 2010, www.nytimes.com/2010/04/13/world/europe/13briefs-Hungary.html.

44. "Asylum seekers have to watch gay movie," DR Forside (Danish Public Broadcasting), Feb. 10, 2010, www.dr.dk/Nyheder/Andre_ sprog/English/2011/02/10/151816.htm.

45. Randi Gressgård and Christine Jacobsen, "Intolerable citizens: Tolerance, Islam and Homosexuality," presented at the conference on Sexual Nationalisms: Gender, Sexuality and the Politics of Belonging in the New Europe, in Amsterdam, Jan. 27-28, 2011.

46. For background, see Sarah Glazer, "Europe's Immigration Turmoil," *CQ Global Researcher*, Dec. 1, 2010, pp. 289-320.

47. "Just Different, That's All, Acceptance of Homosexuality in the Netherlands," The Netherlands Institute for Social Research, August 2010, p. 17, www.scp.nl/english/Publications/Publica tions_by_year/Publications_2010/Just_different_ that_s_all.

48. Sarah Wildman, "Neo-Nazis No Longer? Marine le Pen Tones Down France's Far Right," *Politics Daily*, August 2010, www.politicsdaily.com/2010/05/31/neo-nazis-no-longer-marine-le-pen-tones-down-frances-far-right/.

49. For background, see Kenneth Jost, "Gays in the Military: Update," *CQ Researcher*, Oct. 15, 2010.

50. Ed O'Keefe, " 'Don't ask, don't tell,' is repealed by Senate; bill awaits Obama's signing," *The Washington Post*, Dec. 19, 2010, www.washingtonpost.com/wp-dyn/content/article/2010/12/18/AR2010121801729.html.

51. "Marriage and Relationships Recognition" webpage, Human Rights Campaign, www.hrc.org/issues/marriage.asp.

52. For background, see Roland Flamini, "The New Latin America," *CQ Global Researcher*, March 1, 2008, pp. 57-84.

53. Jeffrey Gettleman, "Ugandan who spoke up for gays is beaten to death," *The New York Times*, Jan. 27, 2011, www.nytimes.com/2011/01/28/world/africa/28uganda.html.

54. Jacqui Goddard and Jonathan Clayton, "Anti-gay laws in Africa are product of American religious exports, say activists," *The Times*, May 22, 2010.

55. " 'We don't have any gays in Iran,' Iranian president tells Ivy League audience," *The Daily Mail*, Sept. 25, 2007, www.dailymail.co.uk/news/article-483746/We-dont-gays-Iran-Iranian-president-tells-Ivy-League-audience.html.

56. "Uganda gay bill critics deliver online petition," BBC News, March 1, 2010, http://news.bbc.co.uk/2/hi/8542341.stm.

BIBLIOGRAPHY

Books

Carlson, Allan, and Paul Mero, *The Natural Family: A Manifesto, Spence Publishing Co.*, 2007.
Two leaders of a movement to protect the heterosexual, or what they call the "natural," family outline their view of its societal role and threats it faces from same-sex marriage.

Crompton, Louis, *Homosexuality and Civilization, Belknap Press*, 2003.
A comprehensive history of homosexuality and how different societies have responded to it, written by a professor who founded one of the first interdisciplinary gay studies programs, at the University of Nebraska, in 1970.

LeVay, Simon, *Gay, Straight and the Reason Why: The Science of Sexual Orientation, Oxford University Press*, 2010.
A neuroscientist looks at the research on the development of sexual orientation.

Mondimore, Francis Mark, *A Natural History of Homosexuality, The Johns Hopkins University Press*, 1996.
A psychologist at The Johns Hopkins University provides an accessible survey of homosexual history, along with research into sexual biology and sexual identity.

Articles

"Gay Rights in Eastern Europe: The long march," *The Economist*, Oct. 26, 2010, www.economist.com/blogs/east ernapproaches/2010/10/gay_rights_eastern_europe.
A blogger reviews the tension between European Union calls for equitable treatment of gays and antipathy toward gay rights felt in many Eastern European countries.

Kaphle, Anup, and Habiba Nosheem, "After string of gay-friendly measures, Nepal aims to tap valuable tourist market," *The Washington Post*, Jan. 9, 2011, www.washing tonpost.com/wp-dyn/content/article/2011/01/07/AR2011 010702762.html.
Reporters examine how Nepal became the first South Asian country to decriminalize homosexuality and allow same-sex marriage.

Kurczy, Stephen, "Don't ask, don't tell: How do other countries treat gay soldiers?" *The Christian Science Monitor*, May 26, 2010, www.csmonitor.com/World/Glob al-News/2010/0526/Don-t-ask-don-t-tell-How-do-other-countries-treat-gay-soldiers.
The reporter examines which countries allow gays and lesbians to serve openly in the military and how the transformation has gone.

Mooallem, Jon, "Can animals be gay?" *The New York Times Magazine*, March 31, 2010, www.nytimes.com/2010/04/ 04/magazine/04animals-t.html.
Research shows that same-gender relationships are common among many animals.

O'Flaherty, Michael, and John Fisher, "Sexual Orientation, Gender, Identity and International Rights Law: Contextualizing the Yogyakarta Principles," *Human Rights Law Review*, 2008.
Two scholars look at the significance and impact of the Yogyakarta Principles, a set of human rights standards relating to sexual orientation and gender identity.

Raghaven, Sudarson, "Gays in Africa Face Growing Persecution, activists say," *The Washington Post*, Dec. 12, 2010, www.washingtonpost.com/wp-dyn/content/article/2010/12/ 11/AR2010121103045.html.
Persecution of gays is intensifying across Africa, the author says, spurred by evangelical preachers, local politicians and a virulently anti-gay local media.

Studies and Reports

"2009 Country Reports on Human Rights Practices," *U.S. Department of State*, March 2010, www.state.gov/g/drl/ rls/hrrpt/2009/index.htm.
The annual report examines human rights issues around the world, including discrimination against LBGT people.

"Homophobia, Transphobia and Discrimination on grounds of Sexual Orientation and Gender Identity, 2010 Update," *European Union Agency for Fundamental Rights*, www.fra. europa.eu/fraWebsite/attachments/FRA-LGBT-report-up date2010.pdf.
The agency that monitors human rights across Europe reviews how the LGBT population is being treated.

"Religious Groups' Official Positions on Same-Sex Marriage," *Pew Forum on Religion and Public Life*, July 2010, http://pewforum.org/Gay-Marriage-and-Homosexuality/ Religious-Groups-Official-Positions-on-Same-Sex-Marriage. aspx.
The nonprofit Pew center looks at every major religion's position on same-sex marriage.

Tozzi, Piero, "Six Problems with the 'Yogyakarta Principles,' " *Catholic Family and Human Rights Institute*, April 2007, www.c-fam.org/publications/id.439/pub_ detail.asp.
A conservative reviews the Yogyakarta Principles, intended to provide a human rights framework for the LGBT community.

For More Information

Catholic Family and Human Rights Institute, 211 East 43rd St., Suite 1306, New York, NY 10017; (212) 754-5948; www.c-fam.org. A research and lobbying group that works "to defend life and family at international institutions" and otherwise support the values of the Catholic Church.

Council for Global Equality, 1220 L St., N.W., Suite 100-450, Washington, DC 20005; (202) 719-0511; www.globalequality.org. Brings together experts and organizations to encourage a U.S. foreign policy supportive of LGBT people around the world.

European Union Fundamental Rights Agency, Schwarzenbergplatz 11, 1040 Vienna, Austria; (+43 (1) 580 30 - 60; www.fra.europa.eu. An advisory body of the European Union that monitors human rights.

International Gay and Lesbian Human Rights Commission, 80 Maiden Lane, Suite 1505, New York, NY 10038; (212) 430-6054; www.iglhrc.org. Opposes discrimination or abuse based on a person's actual or perceived sexual orientation, gender identity or expression.

International Lesbian, Gay, Bisexual, Trans and Intersex Association (ILGA), http://ilga.org. A network of groups that have been working for LGBT rights since 1978, with regional offices throughout the world.

World Congress of Families, Howard Center for Family, Religion and Society, 934 N. Main St., Rockford, IL 61103; (815) 964-5819; www.worldcongress.org. Seeks to unite groups from around the world who believe the "natural" family is threatened by societal changes.

The Yogyakarta Principles, www.yogyakartaprinciples.org. An effort by an international group of experts to outline a broad range of human rights standards relating to sexual orientation and gender identity.

Voices From Abroad:

MORGAN TSVANGIRAI

Prime Minister, Zimbabwe

Ruling party practices homosexuality

"Nowhere in our (Movement for Democratic Change political party) principles document is there any reference to gays and lesbians. For the record, it is well-known that homosexuality is practised in Zanu PF (political party) where senior officials from that party have been jailed while others are under police probe on allegations of sodomy. It is in Zanu PF where homosexuality is a religion."

Guardian Unlimited (England) March 2010

PETER TATCHELL

Coordinator, Equal Love Campaign, England

Double standards

"If the government banned black people from getting married and offered them civil partnerships instead, it would provoke public outrage. It is equally outrageous for the government to deny gay couples the right to marry."

Yorkshire (England) Evening Post, November 2010

DAVID WATKINS

Teacher, Schools Out (LGBT organization) England

Other types of people exist

"When you have a math problem, why does it have to involve a straight family or a boyfriend and girlfriend? Why not two boys or two girls? It's not about teaching about gay sex, it is about exposing children to the idea that there are other types of people out there."

Sunday Telegraph (England) January 2011

PAUL SEMUGOMA

Physician, Uganda

A deadly policy

"In Uganda, our once-lauded AIDS programmes are failing. They refuse to serve major vulnerable populations like gay men. Puritanism may make attractive politics, but it's a deadly policy."

The Independent (Sierra Leone) February 2010

MAHMOUD AHMADINEJAD

President, Iran

No gays in Iran

"In Iran we don't have homosexuals like in your country (United States). In Iran we do not have this phenomenon. I don't know who has told you that we have it."

Agence France-Presse
September 2007

JUNG YEON-JU

Law professor Sungshin Women's University, South Korea

Consider the majority

"Yes, there are some countries making efforts to accept gay [service] members, but at the same time, many others oppose them. Especially given that Korea maintains a mandatory [military] draft system, we should think about the majority in the big picture."

Korea Times (South Korea) June 2010

NICHOLAS OKOH

Archbishop, Uganda

A threat to the church

"Homosexuality is not a new phenomenon in the society but the only trouble is that the issues dividing us (church) now are very difficult to handle. They are threatening the unity of the church because they disobey the authority of the scriptures."

The Monitor (Uganda) August 2010

ZHANG BEICHUAN

Gay-rights advocate, China

An added benefit

"To legalize same-sex marriage could help stabilize and sustain gay relationships, thereby lowering the risk of contracting HIV/AIDS."

Chinadaily.com.cn November 2010

VITIT MUNTARBHORN

Law professor Chulalongkorn University Thailand

Thailand welcomes gays

"Thailand is in a good position to promote LGBT rights internationally. We have an environment conducive to LGBT rights. Our constitution also contains a non-discrimination clause for their protection."

The Nation (Thailand) December 2010

KELVIN HOLDSWORTH

Provost, St. Mary's Episcopal Cathedral, Scotland

'The time has come'

"I am aware of couples in Glasgow who are prevented by law from celebrating their relationship in the form of marriage. The time has come for a marriage law that does not discriminate, and I look forward to the day when I can marry gay members of my congregation in church."

The Herald (Scotland) November 2010

7

Rapid Urbanization

Jennifer Weeks

Children scavenge for recyclables amid rubbish in the Dharavi slum in Mumbai, India. About a billion people worldwide live in slums — where sewer, water and garbage-collection services are often nonexistent. If impoverished rural residents continue streaming into cities at current rates, the world's slum population is expected to double to 2 billion within the next two decades, according to the United Nations.

From *CQ Researcher*, April 2009.

India's most infamous slum lives up to its reputation. Located in the middle of vast Mumbai, Dharavi is home to as many as 1 million people densely packed into thousands of tiny shacks fashioned from scrap metal, plastic sheeting and other scrounged materials. Narrow, muddy alleys crisscross the 600-acre site, open sewers carry human waste and vacant lots serve as garbage dumps. There is electricity, but running water is available for only an hour or so a day. Amid the squalor, barefoot children sing for money, beg from drivers in nearby traffic or work in garment and leather shops, recycling operations and other lightly regulated businesses.

Moviegoers around the globe got a glimpse of life inside Dharavi in last year's phenomenally popular Oscar-winning film, "Slumdog Millionaire," about plucky Jamal Malik, a fictional Dharavi teenager who improbably wins a TV quiz-show jackpot. The no-holds-barred portrayal of slum life may have been shocking to affluent Westerners, but Dharavi is only one of Asia's innumerable slums. In fact, about a billion people worldwide live in urban slums — the ugly underbelly of the rapid and haphazard urbanization that has occurred in many parts of the world in recent decades. And if soaring urban growth rates continue unabated, the world's slum population is expected to double to 2 billion by 2030, according to the U.N.[1]

But all city dwellers don't live in slums. Indeed, other fast-growing cities presented cheerier faces to the world last year, from Dubai's glittering luxury skyscrapers to Beijing's breathtaking, high-tech pre-Olympic cultural spectacle.

World Will Have 26 Megacities by 2025

The number of megacities — urban areas with at least 10 million residents — will increase from 19 to 26 worldwide by the year 2025, according to the United Nations. The seven new megacities will be in Asia and sub-Saharan Africa. Most megacities are in coastal areas, making them highly vulnerable to massive loss of life and property damage caused by rising sea levels that experts predict will result from climate change in the 21st century.

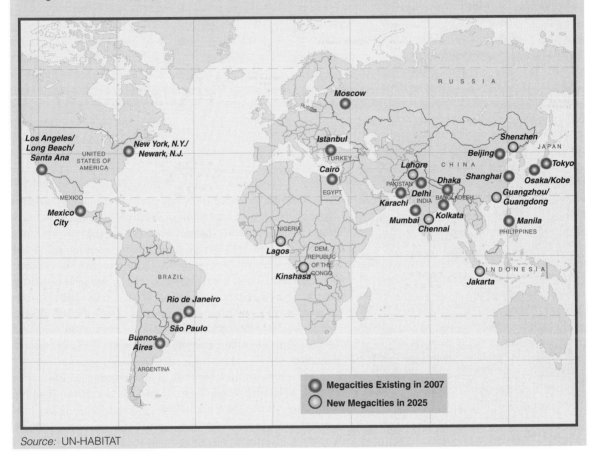

Source: UN-HABITAT

Today, 3.3 billion people live in cities — half the world's population — and urbanites are projected to total nearly 5 billion (out of 8.1 billion) worldwide by 2030.[2] About 95 percent of that growth is occurring in the developing world, especially in Africa and Asia.[3]

These regions are going through the same threefold evolution that transformed Europe and North America over a 200-year period between 1750 and 1950: the industrialization of agriculture, followed by rural migration to cities and declining population growth as life expectancy improves. But today's developing countries are modernizing much faster — typically in less than 100 years — and their cities are expanding at dizzying rates: On average, 5 million people in developing countries move to cities every month. As urban areas struggle to absorb this growth, the new residents often end up crowded into already teeming slums. For instance, 62 percent of city dwellers in sub-Saharan Africa live in slums, 43 percent in southern Asia, 37 percent in East Asia and 27 percent in Latin America and the Caribbean, according to UN-HABITAT, the United Nations agency for human settlements.[4]

UN-HABITAT defines a slum as an urban area without at least one of the following features:

- Durable housing,
- Adequate living space (no more than three people per room),
- Access to clean drinking water,
- Access to improved sanitation (toilets or latrines that separate human waste from contact with water sources), or
- Secure property rights.[5]

But all slums are not the same. Some lack only one basic necessity, while others lack several. And conditions can be harsh in non-slum neighborhoods as well. Thus, experts say, policies should focus on specific local problems in order to make a difference in the lives of poor city dwellers.[6]

Cities "are potent instruments for national economic and social development. They attract investment and create wealth," said HABITAT Executive Director Anna Tibaijuka last April. But, she warned, cities also concentrate poverty and deprivation, especially in developing countries. "Rapid and chaotic urbanization is being accompanied by increasing inequalities, which pose enormous challenges to human security and safety."[7]

Today, improving urban life is an important international development priority.[8] One of the eight U.N. Millennium Development Goals (MDGs) — broad objectives intended to end poverty worldwide by 2015 — endorsed by world leaders in 2000 was environmental sustainability. Among other things, it aims to cut in half the portion of the world's people

Tokyo Is by Far the World's Biggest City

With more than 35 million residents, Tokyo is nearly twice as big as the next-biggest metropolises. Tokyo is projected to remain the world's largest city in 2025, when there will be seven new megacities — urban areas with at least 10 million residents. Two Indian cities, Mumbai and Delhi, will overtake Mexico City and New York as the world's second- and third-largest cities. The two largest newcomers in 2025 will be in Africa: Kinshasa and Lagos.

Population of Megacities, 2007 and 2025
(in millions)

2007		2025 (projected)	
Tokyo, Japan	35.68	Tokyo, Japan	36.40
New York, NY/Newark, NJ	19.04	Mumbai, India	26.39
Mexico City, Mexico	19.03	Delhi, India	22.50
Mumbai, India	18.98	Dhaka, Bangladesh	22.02
São Paulo, Brazil	18.85	São Paulo, Brazil	21.43
Delhi, India	15.93	Mexico City, Mexico	21.01
Shanghai, China	14.99	New York, NY/Newark, NJ	20.63
Kolkata, India	14.79	Kolkata, India	20.56
Dhaka, Bangladesh	13.49	Shanghai, China	19.41
Buenos Aires, Argentina	12.80	Karachi, Pakistan	19.10
Los Angeles/Long Beach/ Santa Ana (CA)	12.50	Kinshasa, Dem. Rep. Congo	16.76
Karachi, Pakistan	12.13	Lagos, Nigeria	15.80
Cairo, Egypt	11.89	Cairo, Egypt	15.56
Rio de Janeiro, Brazil	11.75	Manila, Philippines	14.81
Osaka/Kobe, Japan	11.29	Beijing, China	14.55
Beijing, China	11.11	Buenos Aires, Argentina	13.77
Manila, Philippines	11.10	Los Angeles/Long Beach/ Santa Ana (CA)	13.67
Moscow, Russia	10.45	Rio de Janeiro, Brazil	13.41
Istanbul, Turkey	10.06	Jakarta, Indonesia	12.36
		Istanbul, Turkey	12.10
		Guangzhou/Guangdong, China	11.84
		Osaka/Kobe, Japan	11.37
		Moscow, Russia	10.53
		Lahore, Pakistan	10.51
		Shenzhen, China	10.20
		Chennai, India	10.13

New megacities in 2025

Source: UN-HABITAT

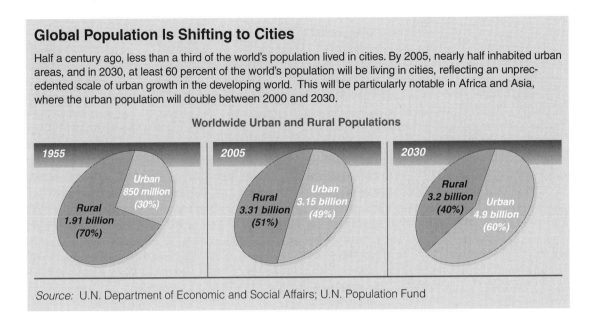

Global Population Is Shifting to Cities

Half a century ago, less than a third of the world's population lived in cities. By 2005, nearly half inhabited urban areas, and in 2030, at least 60 percent of the world's population will be living in cities, reflecting an unprecedented scale of urban growth in the developing world. This will be particularly notable in Africa and Asia, where the urban population will double between 2000 and 2030.

Worldwide Urban and Rural Populations

1955
Urban 850 million (30%)
Rural 1.91 billion (70%)

2005
Rural 3.31 billion (51%)
Urban 3.15 billion (49%)

2030
Rural 3.2 billion (40%)
Urban 4.9 billion (60%)

Source: U.N. Department of Economic and Social Affairs; U.N. Population Fund

without access to safe drinking water and achieve "significant improvement" in the lives of at least 100 million slum dwellers.[9]

Delivering even the most basic city services is an enormous challenge in many of the world's 19 megacities — metropolises with more than 10 million residents. And smaller cities with fewer than 1 million inhabitants are growing even faster in both size and number than larger ones.[10]

Many fast-growing cities struggle with choking air pollution, congested traffic, polluted water supplies and inadequate sanitation services. The lack of services can contribute to larger social and economic problems. For example, slum dwellers without permanent housing or access to mass transit have trouble finding and holding jobs. And when poverty becomes entrenched it reinforces the gulf between rich and poor, which can promote crime and social unrest.

"A city is a system of systems. It has biological, social and technical parts, and they all interact," says George Bugliarello, president emeritus of Polytechnic University in New York and foreign secretary of the National Academy of Engineering. "It's what engineers call a complex system because it has features that are more than the sum of its parts. You have to understand how all of the components interact to guide them."

Improving life for the urban poor begins with providing shelter, sanitation and basic social services like health care and education. But more is needed to make cities truly inclusive, such as guaranteeing slum dwellers' property rights so they cannot be ejected from their homes.[11]

Access to information and communications technology (ICT) is also crucial. In some developing countries, ICT has been adopted widely, particularly cell phones, but high-speed Internet access and computer use still lag behind levels in rich nations. Technology advocates say this "digital divide" slows economic growth in developing nations and increases income inequality both within and between countries. Others say the problem has been exaggerated and that there is no critical link between ICTs and poverty reduction.

Managing urban growth and preventing the creation of new slums are keys to both improving the quality of life and better protecting cities from natural disasters. Many large cities are in areas at risk from earthquakes, wildfires or floods. Squatter neighborhoods are often built on flood plains, steep slopes or other vulnerable areas, and poor people usually have fewer resources to escape or relocate.

For example, heavy rains in northern Venezuela in 1999 caused mudslides and debris flows that demolished many hillside shantytowns around the capital city of Caracas, killing some 30,000 people. In 2005 Hurricane

Katrina killed more people in New Orleans' lower-income neighborhoods, which were located in a flood plain, than in wealthier neighborhoods of the Louisiana port city that were built on higher ground. As global warming raises sea levels, many of the world's largest cities are expected to be increasingly at risk from flooding.

Paradoxically, economic growth also can pose a risk for some cities. Large cities can be attractive targets for terrorist attacks, especially if they are symbols of national prosperity and modernity, such as New York City, site of the Sept. 11, 2001, attack on the World Trade Center. Last November's coordinated Islamic terrorist attacks in Mumbai followed a similar strategy: Landmark properties frequented by foreigners were targeted in order to draw worldwide media coverage, damage India's economy and send a message that nowhere in India was safe.[12]

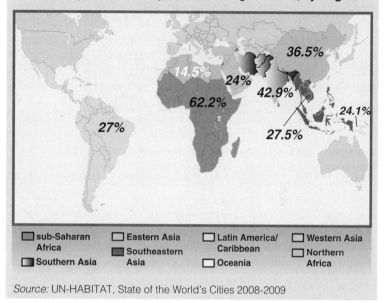

Most African City Dwellers Live in Slums

Most of the world's slum dwellers are in developing countries, with nearly two-thirds of sub-Saharan Africa's city dwellers living in slums.

Percentage of Urban Populations Living in Slums, by Region

36.5%
14.5%
24%
42.9%
62.2%
24.1%
27%
27.5%

☐ sub-Saharan Africa
☐ Eastern Asia
☐ Latin America/ Caribbean
☐ Western Asia
☐ Southern Asia
☐ Southeastern Asia
☐ Oceania
☐ Northern Africa

Source: UN-HABITAT, State of the World's Cities 2008-2009

Today the global economic recession is creating a new problem for city dwellers: Entry-level jobs are disappearing as trade contracts evaporate and factories shut down. Unable to find other jobs, many recent migrants to cities are returning to rural areas that are ill-prepared to receive them, and laborers who remain in cities have less money to send to families back home.[13]

As national leaders, development experts and city officials debate how to manage urban growth, here are some issues they are considering:

Does urbanization make people better off?

With a billion city dwellers worldwide trapped in slums, why do people keep moving to cities? Demographic experts say that newcomers hope to earn higher incomes and find more opportunities than rural areas can offer.

"Often people are fleeing desperate economic conditions," says David Bloom, a professor of economics and demography at Harvard University's School of Public Health. "And the social attractions of a city — opportunities to meet more people, escape from isolation or in

some cases to be anonymous — trump fears about difficult urban conditions. If they have relatives or friends living in cities already, that reduces some of the risk."

When nations attract foreign investment, it creates new jobs. In the 1990s both China and India instituted broad economic reforms designed to encourage foreign investment, paving the way for rapid economic growth. That growth accelerated as information technology advances like the Internet, fiber-optic networks and e-mail made it faster and cheaper to communicate worldwide in real time.[14] As a result, thousands of manufacturing and white-collar jobs were "outsourced" from the United States to India, China and other low-wage countries over the past decade.[15]

These jobs spurred major growth in some cities, especially in areas with educated, English-speaking work forces. The large southern Indian city of Bangalore became a center for information technology — dubbed "India's Silicon Valley." Other cities in India, Singapore and the Philippines now host English-language call centers that manage everything from computer technical support to lost-baggage complaints for airlines. In a

AFP/Getty Images/Shafiq Alam

Packed buses in Dhaka take residents in the Bangladeshi capital to their homes in outlying villages on the eve of the Muslim holiday Eid al-Adha — the "Festival of Sacrifice." Rapidly growing cities have trouble keeping up with the transportation needs of residents.

twist on this model, the Chinese city of Dalian — which was controlled by Japan from 1895 through World War II and still has many Japanese speakers — has become a major outsourcing center for Japanese companies.[16]

Some observers say an increasingly networked world allows people to compete for global "knowledge work" from anywhere in the world instead of having to emigrate to developed countries. In his best-seller *The World Is Flat*, author and *New York Times* columnist Thomas Friedman cites Asian call centers as an example of this shift, since educated Indians can work at the centers and prosper at home rather than seeking opportunity abroad. While he acknowledges that millions of people in developing countries are poor, sick and disempowered, Friedman argues that things improve when people move from rural to urban areas.

"[E]xcess labor gets trained and educated, it begins working in services and industry; that leads to innovation and better education and universities, freer markets, economic growth and development, better infrastructure, fewer diseases and slower population growth," Friedman writes. "It is that dynamic that is going on in parts of urban India and urban China today, enabling people to compete on a level playing field and attracting investment dollars by the billions."[17]

But others say it's not always so simple. Educated newcomers may be able to find good jobs, but migrants without skills or training often end up working in the "informal economy" — activities that are not taxed, regulated or monitored by the government, such as selling goods on the street or collecting garbage for recycling. These jobs are easy to get but come without minimum wages or labor standards, and few workers can get credit to grow their businesses. Members of ethnic minorities and other underprivileged groups, such as lower castes in India, often are stuck with the dirtiest and most dangerous and difficult tasks.[18]

And some countries have experienced urban growth without job growth. Through the late 1980s, many Latin American countries tried to grow their economies by producing manufactured goods at home instead of importing them from abroad.

"Years of government protection insulated these industries from outside competition, so they did not feel pressure to become more productive. Then they went under when economies opened up to trade," says Steven Poelhekke, a researcher with DNB, the national bank of the Netherlands. "In Africa, industrialization has never really taken off. And without job creation governments cannot deliver benefits for new urbanites."[19]

Meanwhile, when cities grow too quickly, competition for land, space, light and services increases faster than government can respond. Real estate prices rise, driving poor residents into squatter neighborhoods, where crowding and pollution spread disease. "When cities get too big, the downsides to city life are bigger than the benefits for vulnerable inhabitants," says Poelhekke.

Broadly, however, urbanization has reduced the total number of people in poverty in recent years. According to a 2007 World Bank study, about three-quarters of the world's poor still live in rural areas. Poor people are urbanizing faster than the population as a whole, so some poverty is shifting to cities. Yet, clearly, many of those new urbanites are finding higher incomes — even if they end up living in city slums — because overall poverty rates (urban plus rural) fall as countries urbanize. While the persistence of urban poverty is a serious concern, the authors concluded, if people moved to the cities faster, overall poverty rates would decline sooner.[20]

Many development advocates say policy makers must accept urbanization as inevitable and strive to make it more beneficial. "We need to stop seeing migration to cities as a problem," says Priya Deshingkar, a researcher at the Overseas Development Institute in Hyderabad, India. "These people were already vulnerable because they can't make a living in rural areas. Countries need to rethink their development strategies. The world is urbanizing, and we have to make more provisions for people moving to urban areas. They can't depend on agriculture alone."

Should governments limit migration to cities?

Many governments have tried to limit urban problems by discouraging migration to cities or regulating the pace of urban growth. Some countries use household registration policies, while others direct aid and economic development funds to rural areas. Political leaders say limiting migration reduces strains on city systems, slows the growth of slums and keeps villages from languishing as their most enterprising residents leave.

China's *hukou* system, for example, requires households to register with the government and classifies individuals as rural or urban residents. Children inherit their *hukou* status from their parents. Established in the 1950s, the system was tightly controlled to limit migration from agricultural areas to cities and to monitor criminals, government critics and other suspect citizens and groups.[21]

In the late 1970s China began privatizing farming and opened its economy to international trade, creating a rural labor surplus and greater demand for city workers. The government offered rural workers temporary residence permits in cities and allowed wealthy, educated citizens to buy urban *hukou* designations. Many rural Chinese also moved to cities without changing their registration. According to recent government estimates, at least 120 million migrant workers have moved to Chinese cities since the early 1980s.[22] Today *hukou* rules are enforced inconsistently in different Chinese cities, where many rural migrants cannot get access to health care, education, affordable housing or other urban services because they are there illegally.

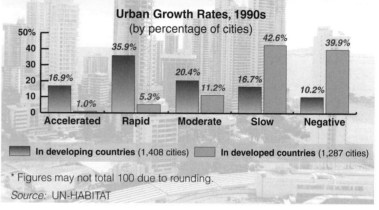

Cities in Developing World Growing Rapidly

More than half the developing world's cities experienced fast annual growth in the 1990s, compared to just 6.3 percent of those in wealthier countries. Conversely, more than 80 percent of cities in the wealthier countries had slow or negative growth, compared to about a quarter of those in developing countries.

Urban Growth Rates, 1990s
(by percentage of cities)

	Accelerated	Rapid	Moderate	Slow	Negative
In developing countries (1,408 cities)	16.9%	35.9%	20.4%	16.7%	10.2%
In developed countries (1,287 cities)	1.0%	5.3%	11.2%	42.6%	39.9%

* Figures may not total 100 due to rounding.

Source: UN-HABITAT

Chinese officials say they must manage growth so all areas of the country will benefit. In a 2007 report to the 17th Communist Party Congress, President Hu Jintao promised to promote "a path of urbanization with Chinese characteristics" that emphasized "balanced development of large, medium-sized and small cities and towns."[23]

But critics say the *hukou* system has created an urban underclass and should be scrapped. When the municipality of Chongqing (which omits an estimated 4.5 million migrant workers from its official population figures) established November 4 as Migrant Workers' Day in 2007, the *Asia Times* commented, "By not changing the [*hukou*] system and instead giving the migrant workers a special holiday, it's a bit like showing starving people menus instead of feeding them."[24]

India and Vietnam also control migration to urban areas by requiring people to register or show local identity cards to access social services. "They're both trying to promote rural development and keep from overburdening urban areas," says Deshingkar at the Overseas Development Institute. "But it doesn't work. People move despite these regulations. It just makes it harder for them, and if they can access services it's at a price."

Many experts say governments should not try to halt rural-to-city migration because when migrant workers send large shares of their wages home to their families in the country it helps reduce rural poverty and inequality. In Dhaka, Bangladesh, for example, remittances from city workers provide up to 80 percent of rural households' budgets, according to the Coalition for the Urban Poor.[25]

Urban growth also helps rural economies by creating larger markets for agricultural products — including high-value products like meat, chicken and fish that people tend to add to their diets as their incomes rise. Cities can promote economic growth in surrounding areas by creating a demand for local farmers' products. For instance, South Africa's Johannesburg Fresh Produce Market offers vendors stalls, overnight storage space, business-skills training and financing; it also requires market agents to buy at least 10 percent of their produce from small, low-income farms.[26]

However, the rootless lifestyle adopted by so-called circular migrants — those who move back and forth between the city and the country — makes people vulnerable, Deshingkar points out. "There are roughly 100 million circular migrants in India now, and they're completely missed by official statistics because the government only counts permanent migrants," she says. "They can't get any insurance or social services, so they carry all the risk themselves."

Beyond the fact that anti-migration policies usually fail, experts say the biggest factor driving population increase in many fast-growing cities is not new residents moving in but "natural increase" — the rate at which people already living there have children. Natural increase accounts for about 60 percent of urban growth worldwide, while 20 percent comes from domestic and international migration and 20 percent results from reclassification of rural areas as urban.[27]

Family-planning programs helped reduce poverty rates in several developing Asian countries — including South Korea, Taiwan, Thailand, Singapore, Indonesia and Malaysia — where having smaller families increased household savings and reduced national education costs.[28] In contrast, artificial birth control is difficult to obtain in the Philippines, where the population is 80 percent Catholic and the government supports only "natural" family planning. Several professors at the University of the Philippines have calculated that if Filipinos had

followed Thailand's example on family planning in the 1970s, the Philippines would have at least 4 million fewer people in poverty and would be exporting rice rather than importing it. Instead, the Philippine government's opposition to family planning "contributed to the country's degeneration into Southeast Asia's basket case," said economist Arsenio Balisacan.[29]

Can we make large cities greener?

Many fast-growing cities are unhealthy places to live because of dirty air, polluted water supplies and sprawling waste dumps. City governments worldwide are increasingly interested in making their cities greener and more sustainable.

Greening cities has many up-front costs but can provide big payoffs. For example, energy-efficient buildings cost less to operate and give cities cachet as centers for advanced technology and design.

Green policies also may help cities achieve broader social goals. When Enrique Peñalosa was elected mayor of Bogotá, Colombia, in 1998, the city was overrun with traffic and crime. Wealthy residents lived in walled-off neighborhoods, while workers were squeezed into shanties on the city's outskirts. Under Peñalosa's rule, the city built hundreds of new parks and a rapid-transit bus system, limited automobile use, banned sidewalk parking and constructed a 14-mile-long street for bicyclists and pedestrians that runs through some of the city's poorest neighborhoods. The underlying goal of the programs: Make Bogotá more people-friendly for poor residents as well as the rich.

"[A]nything that you do in order to increase pedestrian space constructs equality," said Peñalosa, who now consults with city officials in other developing countries. "It's a powerful symbol showing that citizens who walk are equally important to those who have a car."[30] His administration also invested funds that might otherwise have been spent building highways in social services like schools and libraries. Air pollution decreased as more residents shifted to mass transit. Crime rates also fell, partly because more people were out on the streets.[31]

"Mobility and land use may be the most important issues that a mayor can address, because to unlock the economic potential of cities people have to be able to move from one area to another," says Polytechnic University's Bugliarello. "You also have to take care of water supplies and sanitation, because cities concentrate people and pathologies. Appropriate technologies aren't always the most expensive options, especially if cities get together and form markets for them."

For example, bus rapid transit (BRT) systems, which create networks of dedicated lanes for high-speed buses, are much cheaper than subways but faster than conventional buses that move in city traffic. By 2007 some 40 cities worldwide had developed BRT systems, including Bogotá; Jakarta, Indonesia; and Guayaquil, Ecuador. Many others are planned or under construction.[32]

Some developing countries are planning entire green cities with walkable neighborhoods, efficient mass transit and renewable-energy systems. Abu Dhabi, part of the United Arab Emirates on the Persian Gulf, is designing a $20 billion project called Masdar City, which it bills as the world's first carbon-neutral, zero-waste city. Located on the coast next to Abu Dhabi's airport, Masdar City will be a mixed-use community with about 40,000 residents and 50,000 commuters traveling in to work at high-tech companies. Plans call for the city to be car-free and powered mainly by solar energy.[33]

Abu Dhabi wants to become a global hub for clean technologies, according to Khaled Awad, property development director for the Masdar initiative. "It lets us leverage our energy knowledge [from oil and gas production] and our research and development skills and adapt them to new energy markets," he said.

"If we can do it there, we can do it anywhere," said Matthias Schuler, an engineer with the German climate-engineering firm Transsolar and a member of the international Masdar City design and planning team.[34] He points out that average daytime summer temperatures in Abu Dhabi are well over 100 degrees Fahrenheit, and coastal zones are very humid. "You can't find a harsher climate."

In China, meanwhile, green urban design is gaining support as a way to attract foreign investment and demonstrate environmental awareness. But some showpiece projects are falling short of expectations.

Huangbaiyu was supposed to be a sustainable "green village" that would provide new homes for a farming town of more than 1,400 in rural northeast China. But the master plan, produced by a high-profile U.S. green architecture firm, called for 400 densely clustered bungalows without enough yard space for livestock. This meant that villagers would lose their existing income

from backyard gardens, sheep flocks and trout ponds. The plan also proposed to use corncobs and stalks to fuel a biogas plant for heat, but villagers needed these crop wastes as winter feed for their goats.

By December 2008 the Chinese builder had constructed 42 houses, but only a few were occupied. The designer blamed the builder for putting up low-quality houses, but others said the plan did not reflect what villagers wanted or needed.[35] Planners "inadvertently designed an ecologically sound plan — from the perspectives of both birds and the green movement — that would devastate the local economy and bankrupt the households whose lives were to be improved," wrote Shannon May, an American graduate student who lived in the old village of Huangbaiyu for two years and wrote her dissertation on the project.[36]

Dongtan, a larger Chinese city designed as a green project with zero-carbon-emission buildings and transit systems, has also been sidetracked. Groundbreaking on the model city of 500,000 on a Manhattan-sized island near Shanghai is more than a year behind schedule. High-rise towers are sprouting up around the site, leading some observers to call the project expensive "greenwashing" — attempting to make lavish development acceptable by tacking on environmentally friendly features.

"'Zero-emission' city is pure commercial hype," said Dai Xingyi, a professor at Fudan University in Shanghai. "You can't expect some technology to both offer you a luxurious and comfortable life and save energy at the same time. That's just a dream."[37]

Construction is also under way on a new green city southeast of Beijing for 350,000 residents, co-developed by China and Singapore. Tianjin's features include renewable-energy sources, efficient water use and green building standards. Premier Wen Jiabao attended the 2008 groundbreaking.[38]

Although China's green development projects have a mixed record so far, "The government is starting to recognize that it has responsibility for environmental impacts beyond its borders, mainly by promoting renewable energy," says Alastair MacGregor, associate vice president of AECOM, an international design firm with large building projects in China. "Chinese culture is playing catch-up on sustainability."

More than 130 buildings designed to LEED (Leadership in Energy and Environmental Design)

China Aggressively Tackles Air Pollution

"No country in developing Asia takes those challenges more seriously."

China's large cities have some of the world's worst air pollution, thanks to rapid industrial growth, heavy use of coal and growing demand for cars.

The capital, Beijing, lost its 1993 bid to host the 2000 Summer Olympic Games partly because the city was so polluted. A chronic grey haze not only sullied Beijing's international image but also threatened to cause health problems for athletes and impair their performances.

When Beijing was chosen in 2001 to host the 2008 Summer Games, it pledged to put on a "green Olympics," which was widely understood to include clearing the air.

Between 2001 and 2007, however, China's economy grew beyond all predictions, with its gross domestic product expanding by up to 13 percent a year.[1] Beijing's air pollution worsened as new factories, power plants and cars crowded into the city. Winds carried in more pollutants from other burgeoning cities, including nitrogen oxides and sulfur dioxide — which contribute to acid rain and smog — and fine particulates, which can cause or worsen heart and lung problems.

With the Olympic deadline looming, many observers predicted Beijing would not meet its targets even if it relied heavily on authoritarian measures like shutting down factories and limiting auto use.[2] International Olympic Committee President Jacques Rogge said some outdoor endurance sports might have to be postponed if they occurred on high-pollution days — an embarrassing prospect for Chinese leaders.[3]

But China met its promised target, keeping Beijing's daily air pollution index — based on combined measurements of sulfur dioxide, nitrogen dioxide and fine particulates — below 100 during the month the Olympics took place. A 100 index score means air quality will not affect daily activities, compared to a maximum score of 500, when officials warn residents to stay indoors. In fact, during the Olympics in August 2008 Beijing's daily air pollution reached the lowest August measurements since 2000, sometimes even dropping into the 20s.[4]

"No country in Asia has bigger air quality challenges than China, but no country in developing Asia takes those challenges more seriously," says Cornie Huizenga, executive director of the Clean Air Initiative for Asian Cities (CAI-Asia), an international network based in the Philippines and founded by the Asian Development Bank, the World Bank and the U.S. Agency for International Development. "China has taken a whole series of long-term structural measures to address air pollution. The Olympics put a

standards — which measure energy efficiency and healthy indoor working conditions — are planned or under construction in Beijing, Shanghai, Chongqing, Wuhan and other Chinese cities.[39] Chinese investors see LEED buildings as premium products, not as an everyday model, said MacGregor.

Some Chinese cities are developing their own green standards. About half of worldwide new construction between 2008 through 2015 is projected to occur in China, so even greening a modest share of that development would be significant.

"China could end up being a sustainability leader just by virtue of its size," MacGregor predicted.[40]

BACKGROUND

From Farm to Factory

At the beginning of the 19th century only 3 percent of the world's population lived in cities, and only Beijing had more than a million inhabitants.[41] Then new technologies like the steam engine and railroads began to transform society. As the Industrial Revolution unfolded, people streamed from rural areas to manufacturing centers in Europe and the United States seeking a better income and life. This first great wave of urbanization established cities like London, Paris and New York as centers of global commerce.

magnifying glass on Beijing and made them focus there, but its programs are much bigger."

For instance, China continuously monitors air quality in more than 100 cities, requires high-polluting provinces and companies to close small, inefficient emission sources and install pollution-control equipment and has new-car emissions standards roughly equivalent to U.S. and Western European laws.

"For the Olympics China took temporary measures on top of those policies, like closing down large facilities and keeping cars off the roads. All of this plus good weather let Beijing deliver what it promised for the Games," says Huizenga.

Now China is further expanding air pollution regulations. During the Olympics, the Ministry of Environment announced that in 2009 it would start monitoring ultrafine particle and ozone pollution — persistent problems in many developed countries. And Beijing officials plan to increase spending on public transportation.

Local pollution sources, weather patterns and geography influence air pollution, so China's policies for cleaning up Beijing's air might not work in other large cities. Mexico City, for instance, also has tried to reduce its severe air pollution but is hampered by the city's high altitude (7,200 feet). Car engines burn fuel inefficiently at high altitudes, so they pollute more than at sea level. And while automobiles are the biggest emission sources, scientists also found that leaking liquefied petroleum gas (LPG) — which most Mexican households burn for

cooking and heating — also contributes to Mexico City's air pollution.[5]

"We need better-harmonized air quality monitoring in developing countries before we can compare them," says Huizenga. "But other cities should be able to make progress on a large scale like Beijing. There's a lot of low-hanging fruit, such as switching to cleaner transportation fuels, getting rid of vehicles with [high-polluting] two-stroke engines, managing dust at construction sites and cutting pollution from coal-fired power plants. But to make them work, you also need effective agencies with enough people and money to carry [out] policies."

[1] Michael Yang, "China's GDP (2003-2007)," forum.china.org.cn, Nov. 10, 2008; "China Revises 2007 GDP Growth Rate to 13%," Jan. 15, 2009, http://english.dbw.cn.

[2] Edward Russell, "Beijing's 'Green Olympics' Test Run Fizzles," *Asia Times*, Aug. 10, 2007; Jim Yardley, "Beijing's Olympic Quest: Turn Smoggy Sky Blue," *The New York Times*, Dec. 29, 2007; David G. Streets, *et al.*, "Air Quality during the 2008 Beijing Olympic Games," *Atmospheric Environment*, vol. 41 (2007).

[3] "IOC President: Beijing Air Pollution Could Cause Events to Be Delayed During 2008 Olympics," The Associated Press, Aug. 7, 2007.

[4] "Summary: AQ in Beijing During the 2008 Summer Olympics," Clean Air Initiative for Asian Cities, www.cleanairnet.org/caiasia/1412/article-72991.html. Weather conditions are important factors in air pollution levels — for example, summer heat and humidity promote the formation of ground-level ozone, a major ingredient of smog — so to put conditions during the Olympics in context, scientists compared them to readings taken in August of previous years.

[5] Tim Weiner, "Terrific News in Mexico City: Air Is Sometimes Breathable," *The New York Times*, Jan. 5, 2001.

It also spawned horrific slums in factory towns and large cities. Tenement houses became a feature of working-class neighborhoods, with little access to fresh air or clean drinking water. Often whole neighborhoods shared a single water pump or toilet, and trash was usually thrown into the streets.[42]

German social scientist and a co-founder of communist theory Friedrich Engels graphically described urban workers' living conditions in cities like London and Manchester in 1844: "[T]hey are penned in dozens into single rooms. . . . They are given damp dwellings, cellar dens that are not waterproof from below or garrets that leak from above. . . . They are supplied bad, tattered or

rotten clothing, adulterated or indigestible food. . . . Thus are the workers cast out and ignored by the class in power, morally as well as physically and mentally."[43]

Engels and his collaborator Karl Marx later predicted in *The Communist Manifesto* that oppression of the working class would lead to revolution in industrialized countries. Instead, public health movements began to develop in Europe and the United States in mid-century. Seeking to curb repeated cholera and typhoid epidemics, cities began collecting garbage and improving water-supply systems. A new medical specialty, epidemiology (the study of how infections are spread) developed as scientists worked to track and contain illnesses. Cities built

CHRONOLOGY

1700s-1800s *Industrial Revolution spurs rapid urban growth in Europe and the U.S. Expanding slums trigger reforms and public health laws.*

1804 World population reaches 1 billion.

1854 British doctor John Snow discovers the connection between contaminated drinking water and a cholera outbreak in London.

1897 Brazil's first *favela* (shanty town), is established outside Rio de Janeiro.

1900-1960s *Europe and the United States are the most urbanized. Africa and Asia begin gaining independence and struggle to develop healthy economies.*

1906 An earthquake and subsequent fire destroy much of San Francisco, killing more than 3,000 people.

1927 World population reaches 2 billion.

1949 Chinese communists defeat nationalists, establishing the People's Republic of China, which aggressively promotes industrial development.

1960 World population hits 3 billion.

1964 Tokyo becomes first Asian city to host the Olympic Games and soon after that displaces New York as the world's largest city.

1970s-1990s *Urbanization accelerates in Asia and Africa. Many U.S. and European cities shrink as residents move to suburbs.*

1971 East Pakistan secedes from West Pakistan and becomes the independent nation of Bangladesh; populations in Dhaka and other cities grow rapidly.

1974 World population reaches 4 billion.

1979 China initiates broad economic reforms, opens diplomatic and trade relations with the United States and starts to ease limits on migration to cities.

1985 An earthquake in Mexico City kills some 10,000 people and damages water-supply and transit systems.

1987 World population reaches 5 billion.

1991 India institutes sweeping market reforms to attract foreign investors and spur rapid economic growth.

1999 World population reaches 6 billion.

2000s *Most industrialized countries stabilize at 70-80 percent urban. Cities continue to grow in Asia and Africa.*

2000 International community endorses the U.N. Millennium Development Goals designed to end poverty by 2015, including improving the lives of slum dwellers.

2001 Many international companies shift production to China after it joins the World Trade Organization; migration from rural areas accelerates. . . . Terrorists destroy World Trade Center towers in New York City, killing thousands. . . . Taiwan completes Taipei 101, the world's tallest skyscraper (1,671 feet), superseding the Petronas Towers in Kuala Lumpur, Malaysia (1,483 feet).

2005 United Nations condemns Zimbabwe for slum-clearance operations that leave 700,000 people homeless.

2007 The nonprofit group One Laptop Per Child unveils a prototype $100 laptop computer designed for children in developing countries to help close the "digital divide" between cities and rural areas.

2008 More than half of the world's population lives in cities. . . . Beijing hosts Summer Olympic Games. . . . Coordinated terrorist attacks in Mumbai kill nearly 170 people and injure more than 300.

2009 A global recession leaves millions of urban workers jobless, forcing many to return to their home villages.

2030 World's urban population is expected to reach 5 billion, and its slum population could top 2 billion.

2070 About 150 million city dwellers — primarily in India, Bangladesh, China, Vietnam, Thailand, Myanmar and Florida — could be in danger due to climate change, according to a 2008 study.

green spaces like New York's Central Park to provide fresh air and access to nature. To help residents navigate around town, electric streetcars and subway trains were built in underground tunnels or on elevated tracks above the streets.

Many problems persisted, however. Homes and factories burned coal for heat and power, blanketing many large cities in smoky haze. Horse-drawn vehicles remained in wide use until the early-20th century, so urban streets were choked with animal waste. Wealthy city dwellers, seeking havens from the noise, dirt and crowding of inner cities, moved out to cleaner suburban neighborhoods.

Despite harsh conditions, people continued to pour into cities. Economic growth in industrialized countries had ripple effects in developing countries. As wealthier countries imported more and more raw materials, commercial "gateway cities" in developing countries grew as well, including Buenos Aires, Rio de Janeiro and Calcutta (now Kolkata). By 1900, nearly 14 percent of the world's population lived in cities.[44]

End of Empires

Worldwide migration from country to city accelerated in the early-20th century as automation spread and fewer people were needed to grow food. But growth was not uniform. Wars devastated some of Europe's major cities while industrial production swelled others. And when colonial empires dissolved after World War II, many people were displaced in newly independent nations.

Much of the fighting during World War I occurred in fields and trenches, so few of Europe's great cities were seriously damaged. By the late 1930s, however, long-range bombers could attack cities hundreds of miles away. Madrid and Barcelona were bombed during the Spanish Civil War, a prelude to intensive air attacks on London, Vienna, Berlin, Tokyo and elsewhere during World War II. In 1945 the United States dropped atomic bombs on the Japanese cities of Hiroshima and Nagasaki, destroying each. For centuries cities had walled themselves off against outside threats, but now they were vulnerable to air attacks from thousands of miles away.

After 1945, even victorious nations like Britain and France were greatly weakened and unable to manage overseas colonies, where independence movements were underway. As European countries withdrew from their holdings in the Middle East, Asia and Africa over the next 25 years, a wave of countries gained independence,

including Indonesia, India, Pakistan, the Philippines, Syria, Vietnam and most of colonial Africa. Wealthy countries began providing aid to the new developing countries, especially in Asia and Latin America. But some nations, especially in Africa, received little focused support.

By mid-century most industrialized countries were heavily urbanized, and their populations were no longer growing rapidly. By 1950 three of the world's largest cities — Shanghai, Buenos Aires and Calcutta — were in developing countries. Populations in developing countries continued to rise through the late 1960s even as those nations struggled to industrialize. Many rural residents moved to cities, seeking work and educational opportunities.

In the 1950s and '60s U.S. urban planners heatedly debated competing approaches to city planning. The top-down, centralized philosophy was espoused by Robert Moses, the hard-charging parks commissioner and head of New York City's highway agency from 1934 to 1968. Moses pushed through numerous bridge, highway, park and slum-clearance projects that remade New York but earned him an image as arrogant and uncaring.[45] His most famous critic, writer and activist Jane Jacobs, advocated preserving dense, mixed-use neighborhoods, like New York's Greenwich Village, and consulting with residents to build support for development plans.[46] Similar controversies would arise later in developing countries.

By the 1960s car-centered growth characterized many of the world's large cities. "Circle over London, Buenos Aires, Chicago, Sydney, in an airplane," wrote American historian Lewis Mumford in 1961. "The original container has completely disappeared: the sharp division between city and country no longer exists." City officials, Mumford argued, only measured improvements in quantities, such as wider streets and bigger parking lots.

"[T]hey would multiply bridges, highways [and] tunnels, making it ever easier to get in and out of the city but constricting the amount of space available within the city for any other purpose than transportation itself," Mumford charged.[47]

Population Boom

In the 1970s and '80s, as populations in developing countries continued to grow and improved agricultural methods made farmers more productive, people moved to the cities in ever-increasing numbers. Some

Cities Need to Plan for Disasters and Attacks

Concentrated populations and wealth magnify impact.

Flash floods in 1999 caused landslides in the hills around Caracas, Venezuela, that washed away hundreds of hillside shanties and killed an estimated 30,000 people — more than 10 times the number of victims of the Sept. 11, 2001, terrorist attacks in the United States.

Because cities concentrate populations and wealth, natural disasters in urban areas can kill or displace thousands of people and cause massive damage to property and infrastructure. Many cities are located on earthquake faults, flood plains, fire-prone areas and other locations that make them vulnerable. The impacts are magnified when high-density slums and squatter neighborhoods are built in marginal areas. Political instability or terrorism can also cause widespread destruction.

Protecting cities requires both "hard" investments, such as flood-control systems or earthquake-resistant buildings, and "soft" approaches, such as emergency warning systems and special training for police and emergency-response forces. Cities also can improve their forecasting capacity and train officials to assess different types of risk.[1] Although preventive strategies are expensive, time-consuming and often politically controversial, failing to prepare for outside threats can be far more costly and dangerous.

Global climate change is exacerbating flooding and heat waves, which are special concerns for cities because they absorb more heat than surrounding rural areas and have higher average temperatures — a phenomenon known as the urban heat island effect. According to a study by the Organization for Economic Cooperation and Development (OECD), about 40 million people living in coastal areas around the world in 2005 were exposed to so-called 100-year floods — or major floods likely to occur only once every 100 years. By the 2070s, the OECD said, the population at risk from such flooding could rise to 150 million as more people move to cities, and climate change causes more frequent and ferocious storms and rising sea levels.

Cities with the greatest population exposure in the 2070 forecast include Kolkata and Mumbai in India, Dhaka (Bangladesh), Guangzhou and Shanghai in China, Ho Chi Minh City and Hai Phong in Vietnam, Bangkok (Thailand), Rangoon (Myanmar) and Miami, Florida. Cities in developed countries tend to be better protected, but there are exceptions. For example, London has about the same amount of flooding protection as Shanghai, according to the OECD.[2]

"All cities need to look at their critical infrastructure systems and try to understand where they're exposed to natural hazards," says Jim Hall, leader of urban research at England's Tyndall Centre for Climate Change Research. For example, he says, London's Underground subway system is vulnerable to flooding and overheating. Fast-growing cities planning for climate change, he adds, might want to control growth in flood-prone areas, improve water systems to ensure supply during droughts or build new parks to help cool urban neighborhoods. "Risks now and in the future depend on what we do to protect cities," says Hall.

In some cities, residents can literally see the ocean rising. Coastal erosion has destroyed 47 homes and more than 400 fields in recent years in Cotonou, the capital city of the West African nation of Benin, according to a local non-profit called Front United Against Coastal Erosion. "The sea was far from us two years ago. But now, here it is. We are scared," said Kofi Ayao, a local fisherman. "If we do not find a solution soon, we may simply drown in our sleep one day."[3]

national economies boomed, notably the so-called Asian tigers — Hong Kong, Singapore, Taiwan and South Korea — by focusing on manufacturing exports for industrialized markets and improving their education systems to create productive work forces. Indonesia, Malaysia, the Philippines and Thailand — the "tiger cubs" — went through a similar growth phase in the late 1980s and early '90s.

After China and India opened up their economies in the 1980s and '90s, both countries became magnets for foreign investment and created free-trade areas and special economic zones to attract business activity. Cities in those areas expanded, particularly along China's southeast coast where such zones were clustered.

As incomes rose, many Asian cities aspired to global roles: Seoul hosted the 1988 Summer Olympics, and

Social violence can arise from within a city or come as an attack from outside. For example, in 2007 up to 600 people were killed when urban riots erupted in Kenya after a disputed national election.[4]

Urban leaders often justify slum-clearance programs by claiming that poor neighborhoods are breeding grounds for unrest. Others say slums are fertile recruiting grounds for terrorist groups. Slums certainly contain many who feel ill-treated, and extreme conditions may spur them into action. Overall, however, experts say most slum dwellers are too busy trying to eke out a living to riot or join terrorist campaigns.

A Bangladeshi boy helps slum residents cross floodwaters in Dhaka. Rising waters caused by global warming pose a significant potential threat to Dhaka and other low-lying cities worldwide.

"Poverty alone isn't a sufficient cause [for unrest]," says John Parachini, director of the Intelligence Policy Center at the RAND Corp., a U.S. think tank. "You need a combination of things — people with a profound sense of grievance, impoverishment and leaders who offer the prospect of change. Often the presence of an enemy nearby, such as an occupying foreign power or a rival tribal group or religious sect, helps galvanize people."

Last November's terrorist attacks in Mumbai, in which 10 gunmen took dozens of Indian and foreign hostages and killed at least 164 people, showed an ironic downside of globalization: Wealth, clout and international ties can make cities terrorist targets.

"Mumbai is India's commercial and entertainment center — India's Wall Street, its Hollywood, its Milan. It is a prosperous symbol of modern India," a RAND analysis noted. Mumbai also was accessible from the sea, offered prominent landmark targets (historic hotels frequented by foreigners and local elites) and had a heavy media presence that guaranteed international coverage.[5]

But serendipity can also make one city a target over another, says Parachini. "Attackers may know one city better or have family links or contacts there. Those local ties matter for small groups planning a one-time attack," he says.

Developing strong core services, such as police forces and public health systems, can be the first step in strengthening most cities against terrorism, he says, rather than creating specialized units to handle terrorist strikes.

"Basic governance functions like policing maintain order, build confidence in government and can pick up a lot of information about what's going on in neighborhoods," he says. "They make it harder to do bad things."

[1] George Bugliarello, "The Engineering Challenges of Urban Sustainability," *Journal of Urban Technology*, vol. 15, no. 1 (2008), pp. 64-65.

[2] R. J. Nicholls, *et al.*, "Ranking Port Cities with High Exposure and Vulnerability to Climate Extremes: Exposure Estimates," *Environment Working Papers No. 1*, Organization for Economic Cooperation and Development, Nov. 19, 2008, pp. 7-8, www.olis.oecd.org/olis/2007doc .nsf/LinkTo/NT000058 8E/$FILE/JT03255617.PDF.

[3] "Rising Tides Threaten to Engulf Parts of Cotonou," U.N. Integrated Regional Information Network, Sept. 2, 2008.

[4] "Chronology: Kenya in Crisis After Elections," Reuters, Dec. 31, 2007; "The Ten Deadliest World Catastrophes 2007," Insurance Information Institute, www.iii.org.

[5] Angel Rabasa, *et al.*, "The Lessons of Mumbai," *RAND Occasional Paper*, January 2009.

Malaysia built the world's tallest skyscrapers — the Petronas Twin Towers, completed in 1998, only to be superseded by the Taipei 101 building in Taiwan a few years later.

Some Asian countries — including Malaysia, Sri Lanka and Indonesia — implemented programs to improve living standards for the urban poor and helped reduce poverty. However, poverty remained high in Thailand and the Philippines and increased in China and Vietnam.[48]

Cities in South America and Africa also expanded rapidly between 1970 and 2000, although South America was farther ahead. By 1965 Latin America was already 50 percent urbanized and had three cities with populations over 5 million (Buenos Aires, São Paulo and Rio de Janeiro) — a marker sub-Saharan Africa would not achieve for several decades.[49] Urban growth on both continents followed the "primacy" pattern, in which one city

Security officers forcibly remove a woman from her home during land confiscations in Changchun, a city of 7.5 million residents in northeast China, so buildings can be demolished to make way for new construction. Some rapidly urbanizing governments use heavy-handed methods — such as land confiscation, eviction or slum clearance — so redevelopment projects can proceed.

is far more populous and economically and politically powerful than all the others in the nation. The presence of so-called primate cities like Lima (Peru), Caracas (Venezuela) or Lagos (Nigeria) can distort development if the dominant city consumes most public investments and grows to a size that is difficult to govern.

Latin America's growth gradually leveled out in the 1980s: Population increases slowed in major urban centers, and more people moved to small and medium-sized cities.[50] On average the region's economy grew more slowly and unevenly than Asia's, often in boom-and-bust cycles.[51] Benefits accrued mostly to small ruling classes who were hostile to new migrants, and income inequality became deeply entrenched in many Latin American cities.

Africa urbanized quickly after independence in the 1950s and '60s. But from the mid-1970s forward most countries' incomes stagnated or contracted. Such "urbanization without growth" in sub-Saharan Africa created the world's highest rates of urban poverty and income inequality. Corruption and poor management reinforced wealth gaps that dated back to colonial times. Natural disasters, wars and the spread of HIV/AIDS further undercut poverty-reduction efforts in both rural and urban areas.[52]

New Solutions

As the 21st century began, calls for new antipoverty efforts led to an international conference at which 189 nations endorsed the Millennium Development Goals,

designed to end poverty by 2015. Experts also focused on bottom-up strategies that gave poor people resources to help themselves.

An influential proponent of the bottom-up approach, Peruvian economist Hernando de Soto, stirred debate in 2000 with his book *The Mystery of Capital: Why Capitalism Triumphs in the West and Fails Everywhere Else.* Capitalist economies did not fail in developing nations because those countries lacked skills or enterprising spirit, de Soto argued. Rather, the poor in those countries had plenty of assets but no legal rights, so they could not prove ownership or use their assets as capital.

"They have houses but not titles; crops but not deeds; businesses but not statutes of incorporation," de Soto wrote. "It is the unavailability of these essential representations that explains why people who have adapted every other Western invention, from the paper clip to the nuclear reactor, have not been able to produce sufficient capital to make their domestic capitalism work." But, he asserted, urbanization in the developing world had spawned "a huge industrial-commercial revolution" which clearly showed that poor people could contribute to economic development if their countries developed fair and inclusive legal systems.[53]

Not all experts agreed with de Soto, but his argument coincided with growing interest in approaches like microfinance (small-scale loans and credit programs for traditionally neglected customers) that helped poor people build businesses and transition from the "extra-legal" economy into the formal economy. Early microcredit programs in the 1980s and '90s had targeted mainly the rural poor, but donors began expanding into cities around 2000.[54]

The "digital divide" — the gap between rich and poor people's access to information and communications technologies (ICTs) — also began to attract the attention of development experts. During his second term (1997-2001), U.S. President Bill Clinton highlighted the issue as an obstacle to reducing poverty both domestically and at the global level. "To maximize potential, we must turn the digital divide among and within our nations into digital opportunities," Clinton said at the Asia Pacific Economic Cooperation Forum in 2000, urging Asian nations to expand Internet access and train citizens to use computers.[55] The Millennium Development Goals called for making ICTs more widely available in poor countries.

Some ICTs, such as mobile phones, were rapidly adopted in developing countries, which had small or unreliable landline networks. By 2008, industry observers predicted, more than half of the world's population would own a mobile phone, with Africa and the Middle East leading the way.[56]

Internet penetration moved much more slowly. In 2006 some 58 percent of the population in industrial countries used the Internet, compared to 11 percent in developing countries and only 1 percent in the least developed countries. Access to high-speed Internet service was unavailable in many developing regions or was too expensive for most users.[57] Some antipoverty advocates questioned whether ICTs should be a high priority for poor countries, but others said the issue was not whether but when and how to get more of the world's poor wired.

"The more the better, especially broadband," says Polytechnic University's Bugliarello.

While development experts worked to empower the urban poor, building lives in fast-growing cities remained difficult and dangerous in many places. Some governments still pushed approaches like slum clearance, especially when it served other purposes.

Notoriously, in 2005 President Robert Mugabe of Zimbabwe launched a slum-clearance initiative called Operation Murambatsvina, a Shona phrase translated by some as "restore order" and others as "drive out the trash." Thousands of shacks in Zimbabwe's capital, Harare, and other cities across the nation were destroyed, allegedly to crack down on illegal settlements and businesses.

"The current chaotic state of affairs, where small-to-medium enterprises operated outside of the regulatory framework and in undesignated and crime-ridden areas, could not be countenanced much longer," said Mugabe.[58]

But critics said Mugabe was using slum clearance as an excuse to intimidate and displace neighborhoods that supported his opponents. In the end, some 700,000 people were left homeless or jobless by the action, which the United Nations later said violated international law.[59] Over the next several years Mugabe's government failed to carry out its pledges to build new houses for the displaced families.[60]

CURRENT SITUATION

Economic Shadow

The current global economic recession is casting a dark cloud over worldwide economic development prospects. Capital flows to developing countries have declined

Slum Redevelopment Plan Stirs Controversy

Conditions for the 60,000 families living in Mumbai's Dharavi neighborhood (top) — one of Asia's largest slums — are typical for a billion slum dwellers around the globe. Slums often lack paved roads, water-distribution systems, sanitation and garbage collection — spawning cholera, diarrhea and other illnesses. Electric power and telephone service are usually poached from available lines. Mumbai's plans to redevelop Dharavi, located on 600 prime acres in the heart of the city, triggered strong protests from residents, who demanded that their needs be considered before the redevelopment proceeds (bottom). The project has stalled recently due to the global economic crisis.

sharply, and falling export demand is triggering layoffs and factory shutdowns in countries that produce for Western markets. But experts say even though the overall picture is sobering, many factors will determine how severely the recession affects cities.

In March the World Bank projected that developing countries would face budget shortfalls of $270 billion to $700 billion in 2009 and the world economy would

Reflecting China's stunningly rapid urbanization, Shanghai's dramatic skyline rises beside the Huangpu River. Shanghai is the world's seventh-largest city today but will drop to ninth-place by 2025, as two south Asian megacities, Dhaka and Kolkata, surpass Shanghai in population.

shrink for the first time since World War II. According to the bank, 94 out of 116 developing countries were already experiencing an economic slowdown, and about half of them already had high poverty levels. Urban-based exporters and manufacturers were among the sectors hit hardest by the recession.[61]

These trends, along with an international shortage of investment capital, will make many developing countries increasingly dependent on foreign aid at a time when donor countries are experiencing their own budget crises. As workers shift out of export-oriented sectors in the cities and return to rural areas, poverty may increase, the bank projected.

The recession could mean failure to meet the Millennium Development Goals, especially if donor countries pull back on development aid. The bank urged nations to increase their foreign aid commitments and recommended that national governments:

- Increase government spending where possible to stimulate economies;
- Protect core programs to create social safety nets for the poor;
- Invest in infrastructure such as roads, sewage systems and slum upgrades; and
- Help small- and medium-size businesses get financing to create opportunities for growth and employment.[62]

President Barack Obama's economic stimulus package, signed into law on Feb. 17, takes some of these steps and contains at least $51 billion for programs to help U.S. cities. (Other funds are allocated by states and may provide more aid to cities depending on each state's priority list.) Stimulus programs that benefit cities include $2.8 billion for energy conservation and energy efficiency, $8.4 billion for public transportation investments, $8 billion for high-speed rail and intercity passenger rail service, $1.5 billion for emergency shelter grants, $4 billion for job training and $8.8 billion for modernizing schools.[63]

Governments in developing countries with enough capital may follow suit. At the World Economic Forum in Davos, Switzerland, in January, Chinese Premier Wen Jibao announced a 4 trillion yuan stimulus package (equivalent to about 16 percent of China's GDP over two years), including money for housing, railways and infrastructure and environmental protection. " 'The harsh winter will be gone, and spring is around the corner,' " he said, predicting that China's economy would rebound this year.[64]

But according to government figures released just a few days later, more than 20 million rural migrant workers had already lost their jobs in coastal manufacturing areas and moved back to their home towns.[65] In March the World Bank cut its forecast for China's 2009 economic growth from 7.5 percent to 6.5 percent, although it said China was still doing well compared to many other countries.[66]

In India "circular migration" is becoming more prevalent, according to the Overseas Development Institute's Deshingkar. "Employment is becoming more temporary — employers like to hire temporary workers whom they can hire and fire at will, so the proportion of temporary workers and circular migrants is going up," she says. "In some Indian villages 95 percent of migrants are circular. Permanent migration is too expensive and risky — rents are high, [people are] harassed by the police, slums are razed and they're evicted. Keeping one foot in the village is their social insurance."

Meanwhile, international development aid is likely to decline as donor countries cut spending and focus on their own domestic needs. "By rights the financial crisis shouldn't undercut development funding, because the total amounts given now are tiny compared to the national economic bailouts that are under way or being debated in developed countries," says Harvard economist

Bloom. "Politically, however, it may be hard to maintain aid budgets."

At the World Economic Forum billionaire philanthropist Bill Gates urged world leaders and organizations to keep up their commitments to foreign aid despite the global financial crisis. "If we lose sight of our long-term priority to expand opportunity for the world's poor and abandon our commitments and partnerships to reduce inequality, we run the risk of emerging from the current economic downturn in a world with even greater disparities in health and education and fewer opportunities for people to improve their lives," said Gates, whose Bill and Melinda Gates Foundation supports efforts to address both rural and urban poverty in developing nations.[67]

In fact, at a summit meeting in London in early April, leaders of the world's 20 largest economies pledged $1.1 trillion in new aid to help developing countries weather the global recession. Most of the money will be channeled through the International Monetary Fund.

"This is the day the world came together to fight against the global recession," said British Prime Minister Gordon Brown.[68]

Slum Solutions

As slums expand in many cities, debate continues over the best way to alleviate poverty. Large-scale slum-clearance operations have long been controversial in both developed and developing countries: Officials typically call the slums eyesores and public health hazards, but often new homes turn out to be unaffordable for the displaced residents. Today development institutions like the World Bank speak of "urban upgrading" — improving services in slums instead of bulldozing them.[69]

This approach focuses on improving basic infrastructure systems like water distribution, sanitation and electric power; cleaning up environmental hazards and building schools and clinics. The strategy is cheaper than massive demolition and construction projects and provides incentives for residents to invest in improving their own homes, advocates say.[70]

To do so, however, slum dwellers need money. Many do not have the basic prerequisites even to open bank accounts, such as fixed addresses and minimum balances, let alone access to credit. Over the past 10 to 15 years, however, banks have come to recognize slum dwellers as potential customers and have begun creating microcredit

Two-thirds of sub-Saharan Africa's city dwellers live in slums, like this one in Lagos, Nigeria, which has open sewers and no clean water, electric power or garbage collection. About 95 percent of today's rapid urbanization is occurring in the developing world, primarily in sub-Saharan Africa and Asia.

Reuters/George Esiri

programs to help them obtain small loans and credit cards that often start with very low limits. A related concept, micro-insurance, offers low-cost protection in case of illness, accidents and property damage.

Now advocates for the urban poor are working to give slum dwellers more financial power. The advocacy group, Shack/Slum Dwellers International (SDI), for example, has created Urban Poor Funds that help attract direct investments from banks, government agencies and international donor groups.[71] In 2007 SDI received a $10 million grant from the Gates foundation to create a Global Finance Facility for Federations of the Urban Poor.

The funds will give SDI leverage in negotiating with governments for land, housing and infrastructure, according to Joel Bolnick, an SDI director in Cape Town, South Africa. If a government agency resists, said Bolnick, SDI can reply, " 'If you can't help us here, we'll take the money and put it on the table for a deal in Zambia instead.' "[72]

And UN-HABITAT is working with lenders to promote more mortgage lending to low-income borrowers in developing countries. "Slum dwellers have access to resources and are resources in themselves. To maximize the value of slums for those who live in them and for a city, slums must be upgraded and improved," UN-HABITAT Executive Director Tibaijuka said in mid-2008.[73]

Will redevelopment of the Dharavi slum improve residents' lives?

YES Mukesh Mehta
Chairman, MM Project Consultants

Written for *CQ Researcher*, April 2009

Slum rehabilitation is a challenge that has moved beyond the realm of charity or meager governmental budgets. It requires a pragmatic and robust financial model and a holistic approach to achieve sustainability.

Dharavi — the largest slum pocket in Mumbai, India, and one of the largest in the world — houses 57,000 families, businesses and industries on 600 acres. Alarmingly, this accounts for only 4 percent of Mumbai's slums, which house about 7.5 million people, or 55 percent of the city's population.

Mumbai's Slum Rehabilitation Authority (SRA) has undertaken the rehabilitation of all the eligible residents and commercial and industrial enterprises in a sustainable manner through the Dharavi Redevelopment Project (DRP), following an extensive consultative process that included Dharavi's slum dwellers. The quality of life for those residents is expected to dramatically improve, and they could integrate into mainstream Mumbai over a period of time. Each family would receive a 300-square-foot home plus adequate workspace, along with excellent infrastructure, such as water supply and roads. A public-private partnership between the real estate developers and the SRA also would provide amenities for improving health, income, knowledge, the environment and socio-cultural activities. The land encroached by the slum dwellers would be used as equity in the partnership.

The primary focus — besides housing and infrastructure — would be on income generation. Dharavi has a vibrant economy of $600 million per annum, despite an appalling working environment. But the redevelopment project would boost the local gross domestic product to more than $3 billion, with the average family income estimated to increase to at least $3,000 per year from the current average of $1,200. To achieve this, a hierarchy of workspaces will be provided, including community spaces equivalent to 6 percent of the built-up area, plus individual workspaces in specialized commercial and industrial complexes for leather goods, earthenware, food products, recycling and other enterprises.

The greatest failure in slum redevelopment has been to treat it purely as a housing problem. Improving the infrastructure to enable the local economy to grow is absolutely essential for sustainable development. We believe this project will treat Dharavi residents as vital human resources and allow them to act as engines for economic growth. Thus, the DRP will act as a torchbearer for the slums of Mumbai as well as the rest of the developing world.

NO Kalpana Sharma
Author, Rediscovering Dharavi: Stories from Asia's Largest Slum

Written for *CQ Researcher*, April 2009

The controversy over the redevelopment of Dharavi, a slum in India's largest city of Mumbai, centers on the future of the estimated 60,000 families who live and work there.

Dharavi is a slum because its residents do not own the land on which they live. But it is much more than that. The settlement — more than 100 years old — grew up around one of the six fishing villages that coalesced over time to become Bombay, as Mumbai originally was called. People from all parts of India live and work here making terra-cotta pots, leather goods, garments, food items and jewelry and recycling everything from plastic to metal. The annual turnover from this vast spread of informal enterprises, much of it conducted inside people's tiny houses, is an estimated $700 million a year.

The Dharavi Redevelopment Plan — conceived by consultant Mukesh Mehta and being implemented by the Government of Maharashtra state — envisages leveling this energetic and productive part of Mumbai and converting it into a collection of high-rise buildings, where some of the current residents will be given free apartments. The remaining land will be used for high-end commercial and residential buildings.

On paper, the plan looks beautiful. But people in Dharavi are not convinced. They believe the plan has not understood the nature and real value of Dharavi and its residents. It has only considered the value of the land and decided it is too valuable to be wasted on poor people.

Dharavi residents have been left with no choice but to adapt to an unfamiliar lifestyle. If this meant a small adjustment, one could justify it. But the new form of living in a 20-story high-rise will force them to pay more each month, since the maintenance costs of high-rises exceed what residents currently spend on housing. These costs become unbearable when people earn just enough to survive in a big city.

Even worse, this new, imposed lifestyle will kill all the enterprises that flourish today in Dharavi. Currently, people live and work in the same space. In the new housing, this will not be possible.

The alternatives envisaged are spaces appropriate for formal, organized industry. But enterprises in Dharavi are informal and small, working on tiny margins. Such enterprises cannot survive formalization.

The real alternative is to give residents security of tenure and let them redevelop Dharavi. They have ideas. It can happen only if people are valued more than real estate.

Nevertheless, some governments still push slum clearance. Beijing demolished hundreds of blocks of old city neighborhoods and culturally significant buildings in its preparations to host the 2008 Olympic Games. Some of these "urban corners" (a negative term for high-density neighborhoods with narrow streets) had also been designated for protection as historic areas.[74] Developers posted messages urging residents to take government resettlement fees and move, saying, "Living in the Front Gate's courtyards is ancient history; moving to an apartment makes you a good neighbor," and "Cherish the chance; grab the good fortune; say farewell to dangerous housing."[75]

Beijing's actions were not unique. Other cities hosting international "mega-events" have demolished slums. Like Beijing, Seoul, South Korea, and Santo Domingo in the Dominican Republic were already urbanizing and had slum-clearance programs under way, but as their moments in the spotlight grew nearer, eviction operations accelerated, according to a Yale study. Ultimately, the study concluded, the benefits from hosting big events did not trickle down to poor residents and squatter communities who were "systematically removed or concealed from high-profile areas in order to construct the appearance of development."[76]

Now the debate over slum clearance has arrived in Dharavi. Developers are circling the site, which sits on a square mile of prime real estate near Mumbai's downtown and airport. The local government has accepted a $3 billion redevelopment proposal from Mukesh Mehta, a wealthy architect who made his fortune in Long Island, N.Y., to raze Dharavi's shanties and replace them with high-rise condominiums, shops, parks and offices. Slum dwellers who can prove they have lived in Dharavi since 1995 would receive free 300-square-foot apartments, equivalent to two small rooms, in the new buildings. Other units would be sold at market rates that could reach several thousand dollars per square foot.[77]

Mehta contends his plan will benefit slum residents because they will receive new homes on the same site. "Give me a better solution. Until then you might want to accept this one," he said last summer.[78] But many Dharavi residents say they will not be able to keep small businesses like tanneries, potteries and tailoring shops if they move into modern high-rises, and would rather stay put.

"I've never been inside a tall building. I prefer a place like this where I can work and live," said Usman Ghani, a potter born and raised in Dharavi who has demonstrated against the redevelopment proposals. He is not optimistic about the future. "The poor and the working class won't be able to stay in Mumbai," he said. "Many years ago, corrupt leaders sold this country to the East India Company. Now they're selling it to multinationals."[79]

OUTLOOK
Going Global

In an urbanizing world, cities will become increasingly important as centers of government, commerce and culture, but some will be more influential than others. Although it doesn't have a precise definition, the term "global city" is used by city-watchers to describe metropolises like New York and London that have a disproportionate impact on world affairs. Many urban leaders around the world aspire to take their cities to that level.

The 2008 *Global Cities Index* — compiled by *Foreign Policy* magazine, the Chicago Council on Global Affairs and the A. T. Kearney management consulting firm — ranks 60 cities on five broad criteria that measure their international influence, including:

- Business activity,
- Human capital (attracting diverse groups of people and talent),
- Information exchange,
- Cultural attractions and experiences, and
- Political engagement (influence on world policy making and dialogue).[80]

The scorecard is topped by Western cities like New York, London and Paris but also includes developing-country cities such as Beijing, Shanghai, Bangkok, Mexico City and São Paulo. Many of these cities, the authors noted, are taking a different route to global stature than their predecessors followed — a shorter, often state-led path with less public input than citizens of Western democracies expect to have.

"Rulers in closed or formerly closed societies have the power to decide that their capitol is going to be a

In addition to Dubai's glittering, new downtown area filled with towering skyscrapers, the city's manmade, palm-tree-shaped islands of Jumeirah sport hundreds of multi-million-dollar second homes for international jetsetters. Development has skidded to a temporary halt in the Arab city-state, much as it has in some other rapidly urbanizing cities around the globe, due to the global economic downturn.

world-class city, put up private funds and spell out what the city should look like," says Simon O'Rourke, executive director of the Global Chicago Center at the Chicago Council on Global Affairs. "That's not necessarily a bad path, but it's a different path than the routes that New York or London have taken. New global cities can get things done quickly — if the money is there."

Abu Dhabi's Masdar Initiative, for example, remains on track despite the global recession, directors said this spring. The project is part of a strategic plan to make Abu Dhabi a world leader in clean-energy technology. "There is no question of any rollback or slowing down of any of our projects in the renewable-energy sector," said Sultan Ahmed Al Jaber, chief executive officer of the initiative, on March 16.[81] Last year the crown prince of Abu Dhabi created a $15 billion fund for clean-energy investments, which included funds for Masdar City.

Money is the front-burner issue during today's global recession. "Unless a country's overall economic progress is solid, it is very unlikely that a high proportion of city dwellers will see big improvements in their standard of living," says Harvard's Bloom. In the next several years, cities that ride out the global economic slowdown successfully will be best positioned to prosper when world markets recover.

In the longer term, however, creating wealth is not enough, as evidenced by conditions in Abu Dhabi's neighboring emirate, Dubai. Until recently Dubai was a booming city-state with an economy built on real estate, tourism and trade — part of the government's plan to make the city a world-class business and tourism hub. It quickly became a showcase for wealth and rapid urbanization: Dozens of high-rise, luxury apartment buildings and office towers sprouted up seemingly overnight, and man-made islands shaped like palm trees rose from the sea, crowded with multi-million-dollar second homes for jetsetters.

But the global recession has brought development to a halt. The real estate collapse was so sudden that jobless expatriate employees have been fleeing the country, literally abandoning their cars in the Dubai airport parking lot.[82]

Truly global cities are excellent in a variety of ways, says O'Rourke. "To be great, cities have to be places where people want to live and work." They need intellectual and cultural attractions as well as conventional features like parks and efficient mass transit, he says, and, ultimately, they must give residents at least some role in decisionmaking.

"It will be very interesting to see over the next 20 years which cities can increase their global power without opening up locally to more participation," says O'Rourke. "If people don't have a say in how systems are built, they won't use them."

Finally, great cities need creative leaders who can adapt to changing circumstances. Mumbai's recovery after last November's terrorist attacks showed such resilience. Within a week stores and restaurants were open again in neighborhoods that had been raked by gunfire, and international travelers were returning to the city.[83]

The Taj Mahal Palace & Tower was one of the main attack targets. Afterwards, Ratan Tata, grand-nephew of the Indian industrialist who built the five-star hotel, said, "We can be hurt, but we can't be knocked down."[84]

NOTES

1. Ben Sutherland, "Slum Dwellers 'to top 2 billion,'" BBC News, June 20, 2006, http://news.bbc.co.uk/2/hi/in_depth/5099038.stm.

2. United Nations Population Fund, *State of World Population 2007: Unleashing the Potential of Urban Growth* (2007), p. 6.

3. UN-HABITAT, *State of the World's Cities 2008/2009* (2008), p. xi.

4. UN-HABITAT, *op cit.*, p. 90.

5. *Ibid.*, p. 92.

6. *Ibid.*, pp. 90-105.

7. Anna Tibaijuka, "The Challenge of Urbanisation and the Role of UN-HABITAT," lecture at the Warsaw School of Economics, April 18, 2008, p. 2, www.unhabitat.org/downloads/docs/5683_16536_ ed_warsaw_version12_1804.pdf.

8. For background see Peter Katel, "Ending Poverty," *CQ Researcher*, Sept. 9, 2005, p. 733-760.

9. For details, see www.endpoverty2015.org. For background, see Peter Behr, "Looming Water Crisis," *CQ Global Researcher*, February 2008, pp. 27-56.

10. Tobias Just, "Megacities: Boundless Growth?" Deutsche Bank Research, March 12, 2008, pp. 4-5.

11. Commission on Legal Empowerment of the Poor, *Making the Law Work for Everyone* (2008), pp. 5-9, www.undp.org/legalempowerment/report/Making_ the_Law_Work_for_Everyone.pdf.

12. Angel Rabasa, *et al.*, "The Lessons of Mumbai," *RAND Occasional Paper*, 2009, pp. 1-2, www.rand .org/pubs/occasional_papers/2009/RAND_OP249.pdf.

13. Wieland Wagner, "As Orders Dry Up, Factory Workers Head Home," *Der Spiegel*, Jan. 8, 2009, www.spiegel .de/international/world/0,1518,600188,00.html; Malcolm Beith, "Reverse Migration Rocks Mexico," *Foreign Policy.com*, February 2009, www.foreignpolicy .com/story/cms.php?story_id=4731; Anthony Faiola, "A Global Retreat As Economies Dry Up," *The Washington Post*, March 5, 2009, www.washing tonpost.com/wp-dyn/content/story/2009/03/04/ ST2009030404264.html.

14. For background, see David Masci, "Emerging India, *CQ Researcher*, April 19, 2002, pp. 329-360; and Peter Katel, "Emerging China," *CQ Researcher*, Nov. 11, 2005, pp. 957-980.

15. For background, see Mary H. Cooper, "Exporting Jobs," *CQ Researcher*, Feb. 20, 2004, pp. 149-172.

16. Ji Yongqing, "Dalian Becomes the New Outsourcing Destination," *China Business Feature*, Sept. 17, 2008, www.cbfeature.com/industry_spotlight/news/ dalian_becomes_the_new_outsourcing_destination.

17. Thomas L. Friedman, *The World Is Flat: A Brief History of the Twenty-First Century*, updated edition (2006), pp. 24-28, 463-464.

18. Priya Deshingkar and Claudia Natali, "Internal Migration," in *World Migration 2008* (2008), p. 183.

19. Views expressed here are the speaker's own and do not represent those of his employer.

20. Martin Ravallion, Shaohua Chen and Prem Sangraula, "New Evidence on the Urbanization of Global Poverty," World Bank Policy Research Working Paper 4199, April 2007, http://siteresources.worldbank .org/INTWDR2008/Resources/2795087-1191427 986785/RavallionMEtAl_UrbanizationOfGlobal Poverty.pdf.

21. For background on the *hukou* system, see Congressional-Executive Commission on China, "China's Household Registration System: Sustained Reform Needed to Protect China's Rural Migrants," Oct. 7, 2005, www .cecc.gov/pages/news/hukou.pdf; and Hayden Windrow and Anik Guha, "The Hukou System, Migrant Workers, and State Power in the People's Republic of China," *Northwestern University Journal of International Human Rights*, spring 2005, pp. 1-18.

22. Wu Zhong, "How the Hukou System Distorts Reality," *Asia Times*, April 11, 2007, www.atimes .com/atimes/China/ID11Ad01.html; Rong Jiaojiao, "Hukou 'An Obstacle to Market Economy,' " *China Daily*, May 21, 2007, www.chinadaily.com.cn/ china/2007-05/21/content_876699.htm.

23. "Scientific Outlook on Development," "Full text of Hu Jintao's report at 17th Party Congress," section V.5, Oct. 24, 2007, http://news.xinhuanet.com/ english/2007-10/24/content_6938749.htm.

24. Wu Zhong, "Working-Class Heroes Get Their Day," *Asia Times*, Oct. 24, 2007, www.atimes.com/atimes/ China_Business/IJ24Cb01.html.

25. "Internal Migration, Poverty and Development in Asia," *Briefing Paper no. 11*, Overseas Development Council, October 2006, p. 3.

26. Clare T. Romanik, "An Urban-Rural Focus on Food Markets in Africa," The Urban Institute, Nov. 15, 2007, p. 30, www.urban.org/publications/411604 .html.

27. UN-HABITAT, *op. cit.*, pp. 24-26.

28. "How Shifts to Smaller Family Sizes Contributed to the Asian Miracle," *Population Action International*, July 2006, www.popact.org/Publications/Fact_Sheets/FS4/Asian_Miracle.pdf.

29. Edson C. Tandoc, Jr., "Says UP Economist: Lack of Family Planning Worsens Poverty," *Philippine Daily Inquirer*, Nov. 11, 2008, http://newsinfo.inquirer.net/breakingnews/nation/view/20081111-171604/Lack-of-family-planning-worsens-poverty; Blaine Harden, "Birthrates Help Keep Filipinos in Poverty," *The Washington Post*, April 21, 2008, www.washingtonpost.com/wp-dyn/content/story/2008/04/21/ST2008042100778.html.

30. Kenneth Fletcher, "Colombia Dispatch 11: Former Bogotá Mayor Enrique Peñalosa," Smithsonian.com, Oct. 29, 2008, www.smithsonianmag.com/travel/Colombia-Dispatch-11-Former-Bogota-mayor-Enrique-Penalosa.html.

31. Charles Montgomery, "Bogota's Urban Happiness Movement," *Globe and Mail*, June 25, 2007, www.theglobeandmail.com/servlet/story/RTGAM.20070622.whappyurbanmain0623/BNStory/lifeMain/home.

32. Bus Rapid Transit Planning Guide, 3rd edition, Institute for Transportation & Development Policy, June 2007, p. 1, www.itdp.org/documents/Bus%20Rapid%20Transit%20Guide%20%20complete%20guide.pdf.

33. Project details at www.masdaruae.com/en/home/index.aspx.

34. Awad and Schuler remarks at Greenbuild 2008 conference, Boston, Mass., Nov. 20, 2008.

35. "Green Dreams," Frontline/World, www.pbs.org/frontlineworld/fellows/green_dreams/; Danielle Sacks, "Green Guru Gone Wrong: William McDonough," *Fast Company*, Oct. 13, 2008, www.fastcompany.com/magazine/130/the-mortal-messiah.html; Timothy Lesle, "Cradle and All," *California Magazine*, September/October 2008, www.alumni.berkeley.edu/California/200809/lesle.asp.

36. Shannon May, "Ecological Crisis and Eco-Villages in China," *Counterpunch*, Nov. 21-23, 2008, www.counterpunch.org/may11212008.html.

37. Rujun Shen, "Eco-city seen as Expensive 'Green-Wash,'" *The Standard* (Hong Kong), June 24, 2008, www.thestandard.com.hk/news_detail.asp?we_cat=9&art_id=67641&sid=19488136&con_type=1&d_str=20080624&fc=8; see also Douglas McGray, "Pop-Up Cities: China Builds a Bright Green Metropolis," *Wired*, April 24, 2007, www.wired.com/wired/archive/15.05/feat_popup.html; Malcolm Moore, "China's Pioneering Eco-City of Dongtan Stalls," *Telegraph*, Oct. 19, 2008, www.telegraph.co.uk/news/worldnews/asia/china/3223969/Chinas-pioneering-eco-city-of-Dongtan-stalls. html; "City of Dreams," *Economist*, March 19, 2009, www.economist.com/world/asia/displaystory.cfm?story_id=13330904.

38. Details at www.tianjinecocity.gov.sg/.

39. "LEED Projects and Case Studies Directory," U.S. Green Building Council, www.usgbc.org/LEED/Project/RegisteredProjectList.aspx.

40. Remarks at Greenbuild 2008 conference, Boston, Mass., Nov. 20, 2008.

41. Population Reference Bureau, "Urbanization," www.prb.org; Tertius Chandler, *Four Thousand Years of Urban Growth: An Historical Census* (1987).

42. Lewis Mumford, *The City In History: Its Origins, Its Transformations, and Its Prospects* (1961), pp. 417-418.

43. Frederick Engels, *The Condition of the Working Class in England* (1854), Chapter 7 ("Results"), online at Marx/Engels Internet Archive, www.marxists.org/archive/marx/works/1845/condition-working-class/ch07.htm.

44. Population Reference Bureau, *op. cit.*

45. Robert A. Caro, *The Power Broker: Robert Moses and the Fall of New York* (1975).

46. Jane Jacobs, *The Death and Life of Great American Cities* (1961).

47. Mumford, *op. cit.*, pp. 454-455.

48. Joshua Kurlantzick, "The Big Mango Bounces Back," *World Policy Journal*, spring 2000, www.worldpolicy.org/journal/articles/kurlant.html; UN-HABITAT, *op. cit.*, pp. 74-76.

49. BBC News, "Interactive Map: Urban Growth," http://news.bbc.co.uk/2/shared/spl/hi/world/06/urbanisation/html/urbanisation.stm.

50. Licia Valladares and Magda Prates Coelho, "Urban Research in Latin America: Towards a Research Agenda," MOST Discussion Paper Series No. 4 (undated), www.unesco.org/most/valleng.htm#trends.

51. Jose de Gregorie, "Sustained Growth in Latin America," Economic Policy Papers, Central Bank of Chile, May 2005, www.bcentral.cl/eng/studies/economic-policy-papers/pdf/dpe13eng.pdf.

52. UN-HABITAT, *op cit.*, pp. 70-74.

53. Hernando de Soto, *The Mystery of Capital: Why Capitalism Triumphs in the West and Fails Everywhere Else* (2000), excerpted at http://ild.org.pe/en/mystery/english?page=0%2C0.

54. Deepak Kindo, "Microfinance Services to the Urban Poor," *Microfinance Insights*, March 2007; World Bank, "10 Years of World Bank Support for Microcredit in Bangladesh," Nov. 5, 2007; "Micro Finance Gaining in Popularity," *The Hindu*, Aug. 25, 2008, www.hindu.com/biz/2008/08/25/stories/2008082550121600.htm.

55. Michael Richardson, "Clinton Warns APEC of 'Digital Divide,'" *International Herald Tribune*, Nov. 16, 2000, www.iht.com/articles/2000/11/16/apec.2.t_2.php.

56. Abigail Keene-Babcock, "Study Shows Half the World's Population With Mobile Phones by 2008," Dec. 4, 2007, www.nextbillion.net/news/study-shows-half-the-worlds-population-with-mobile-phones-by-200.

57. "Millennium Development Goals Report 2008," United Nations, p. 48, www.un.org/millenniumgoals/pdf/The%20Millennium%20Development%20Goals%20Report%202008.pdf.

58. Robyn Dixon, "Zimbabwe Slum Dwellers Are Left With Only Dust," *Los Angeles Times*, June 21, 2005, http://articles.latimes.com/2005/jun/21/world/fg-nohomes21.

59. Ewen MacAskill, "UN Report Damns Mugabe Slum Clearance as Catastrophic," *Guardian*, July 23, 2005, www.guardian.co.uk/world/2005/jul/23/zimbabwe.ewenmacaskill.

60. Freedom House, "Freedom in the World 2008: Zimbabwe," www.freedomhouse.org/uploads/press_release/Zimbabwe_FIW_08.pdf.

61. "Crisis Reveals Growing Finance Gaps for Developing Countries," World Bank, March 8, 2009, http://web.worldbank.org/WBSITE/EXTERNAL/NEWS/0,,contentMDK:22093316~menuPK:34463~pagePK:34370~piPK:34424~theSitePK:4607,00.html.

62. "Swimming Against the Tide: How Developing Countries Are Coping with the Global Crisis," World Bank, background paper prepared for the G20 finance Ministers meeting, March 13-14, 2009, http://siteresources.worldbank.org/NEWS/Resources/swimmingagainstthetide-march2009.pdf.

63. "Major Victories for City Priorities in American Recovery and Reinvestment Act," U.S. Conference of Mayors, Feb. 23, 2009, www.usmayors.org/usmayornewspaper/documents/02_23_09/pg1_major_victories.asp.

64. Carter Dougherty, "Chinese Premier Injects Note of Optimism at Davos," *The New York Times*, Jan. 29, 2009, www.nytimes.com/2009/01/29/business/29econ.html?partner=rss.

65. Jamil Anderlini and Geoff Dyer, "Downturn Causes 20m Job Losses in China," *Financial Times*, Feb. 2, 2009, www.ft.com/cms/s/0/19c25aea-f0f5-11dd-8790-0000779fd2ac.html.

66. Joe McDonald, "World Bank Cuts China's 2009 Growth Forecast," The Associated Press, March 18, 2009.

67. "Bill and Melinda Gates Urge Global Leaders to Maintain Foreign Aid," Bill and Melinda Gates Foundation, Jan. 30, 2009, www.gatesfoundation.org/press-releases/Pages/2009-world-economic-forum-090130.aspx.

68. Mark Landler and David E. Sanger, "World Leaders Pledge $1.1 Trillion to Tackle Crisis," *The New York Times*, April 4, 2009, www.nytimes.com/2009/04/03/world/europe/03summit.html?_r=1&hp.

69. "Is Demolition the Way to Go?" World Bank, www.worldbank.org/urban/upgrading/demolition.html.

70. "What Is Urban Upgrading?" World Bank, www.worldbank.org/urban/upgrading/what.html.

71. For more information, see "Urban Poor Fund," *Shack/Slum Dwellers International*, www.sdinet.co.za/ritual/urban_poor_fund/.

72. Neal R. Peirce, "Gates Millions, Slum-Dwellers: Thanksgiving Miracle?" *Houston Chronicle*, Nov. 22,

2007, www.sdinet.co.za/static/pdf/sdi_gates_iupf_neal_peirce.pdf.

73. "Statement at the African Ministerial Conference on Housing and Urban Development," UN-HABITAT, Abuja, Nigeria, July 28, 2008, www.unhabitat.org/content.asp?cid=5830&catid=14&typeid=8&subMenuId=0.

74. Michael Meyer, *The Last Days of Old Beijing* (2008), pp. 54-55; Richard Spencer, "History is Erased as Beijing Makes Way for Olympics," *Telegraph* (London), June 19, 2006, www.telegraph.co.uk/news/worldnews/asia/china/1521709/History-is-erased-as-Beijing-makes-way-for-Olympics.html; Michael Sheridan, "Old Beijing Falls to Olympics Bulldozer," *Sunday Times* (London), April 29, 2007, www.timesonline.co.uk/tol/news/world/asia/china/article1719945.ece.

75. Meyer, *op. cit.*, pp. 45, 52.

76. Solomon J. Greene, "Staged Cities: Mega-Events, Slum Clearance, and Global Capital," *Yale Human Rights & Development Law Journal*, vol. 6, 2003, http://islandia.law.yale.edu/yhrdlj/PDF/Vol%206/greene.pdf.

77. Slum Rehabilitation Authority, "Dharavi Development Project," www.sra.gov.in/htmlpages/Dharavi.htm; Porus P. Cooper, "In India, Slum May Get Housing," *Philadelphia Inquirer*, Sept. 22, 2008.

78. Mukul Devichand, "Mumbai's Slum Solution?" BBC News, Aug. 14, 2008, http://news.bbc.co.uk/2/hi/south_asia/7558102.stm.

79. Henry Chu, "Dharavi, India's Largest Slum, Eyed By Mumbai Developers," *Los Angeles Times*, Sept. 8, 2008, www.latimes.com/news/nationworld/world/la-fg-dharavi8-2008sep08,0,1830588.story; see also Dominic Whiting, "Dharavi Dwellers Face Ruin in Development Blitz," Reuters, June 6, 2008, http://in.reuters.com/article/topNews/idINIndia-33958520080608; and Mark Tutton, "Real Life 'Slumdog' Slum To Be Demolished," CNN.com, Feb. 23, 2009, www.cnn.com/2009/TRAVEL/02/23/dharavi.mumbai.slums/.

80. Unless otherwise cited, this section is based on "The 2008 Global Cities Index," *Foreign Policy*, November/December 2008, www.foreignpolicy.com/story/cms.php?story_id=4509.

81. T. Ramavarman, "Masdar To Proceed with $15 Billion Investment Plan," *Khaleej Times Online*, March 16, 2009, www.khaleejtimes.com/biz/inside.asp?xfile=/data/business/2009/March/business_March638.xml&section=business&col=; Stefan Nicola, "Green Oasis Rises From Desert Sands," *Washington Times*, Feb. 2, 2009, www.washingtontimes.com/themes/places/abu-dhabi/; Elisabeth Rosenthal, "Gulf Oil States Seeking a Lead in Clean Energy," *The New York Times*, Jan. 13, 2009, www.nytimes.com/2009/01/13/world/middleeast/13greengulf.html.

82. David Teather and Richard Wachman, "The Emirate That Used to Spend It Like Beckham," *The Guardian*, Jan. 31, 2009, www.guardian.co.uk/world/2009/jan/31/dubai-global-recession; Robert F. Worth, "Laid-Off Foreigners Flee as Dubai Spirals Down," *The New York Times*, Feb. 12, 2009, www.nytimes.com/2009/02/12/world/middleeast/12dubai.html; Elizabeth Farrelly, "Dubai's Darkening Sky: The Crane Gods are Still," *Brisbane Times*, Feb. 26, 2009, www.brisbanetimes.com.au/news/opinion/dubais-darkening-sky-the-crane-gods-are-still/2009/02/25/1235237781806.html.

83. Raja Murthy, "Taj Mahal Leads India's Recovery," *Asia Times*, Dec. 3, 2008, www.atimes.com/atimes/South_Asia/JL03Df01.html.

84. Joe Nocera, "Mumbai Finds Its Resiliency," *The New York Times*, Jan. 4, 2009, http://travel.nytimes.com/2009/01/04/travel/04journeys.html.

BIBLIOGRAPHY

Books

Meyer, Michael, *The Last Days of Old Beijing: Life in the Vanishing Backstreets of a City Transformed*, Walker & Co., 2008.
An English teacher and travel writer traces Beijing's history and describes life in one of its oldest neighborhoods as the city prepared to host the 2008 Olympic Games.

Silver, Christopher, *Planning the Megacity: Jakarta in the Twentieth Century*, Routledge, 2007.
An urban scholar describes how Indonesia's largest city grew from a colonial capital of 150,000 in 1900 into a megacity of 12-13 million in 2000, and concludes that overall the process was well-planned.

2007. State of the World: Our Urban Future, Worldwatch Institute, Norton, 2007.

Published by an environmental think tank, a collection of articles on issues such as sanitation, urban farming and strengthening local economies examines how cities can be healthier and greener.

Articles

"The 2008 Global Cities Index," *Foreign Policy,* November/December 2008, www.foreignpolicy.com/story/cms.php?story_id=4509.

Foreign Policy magazine, the Chicago Council on World Affairs and the A.T. Kearney management consulting firm rank the world's most "global" cities in both industrialized and developing countries, based on economic activity, human capital, information exchange, cultural experience and political engagement.

"Mexico City Bikers Preach Pedal Power in Megacity," The Associated Press, Dec. 28, 2008.

Bicycle activists are campaigning for respect in a city with more than 6 million cars, taxis and buses.

Albright, Madeleine, and Hernando De Soto, "Out From the Underground," *Time,* July 16, 2007.

A former U.S. Secretary of State and a prominent Peruvian economist contend that giving poor people basic legal rights can help them move from squatter communities and the shadow economy to more secure lives.

Bloom, David E., and Tarun Khanna, "The Urban Revolution," *Finance & Development,* September 2007, pp. 9-14.

Rapid urbanization is inevitable and could be beneficial if leaders plan for it and develop innovative ways to make cities livable.

Chamberlain, Gethin, "The Beating Heart of Mumbai," *The Observer,* Dec. 21, 2008, www.guardian.co.uk/world/2008/dec/21/dharavi-india-slums-slumdog-millionaire-poverty.

Eight boys growing up in Dharavi, Asia's largest slum, talk about life in their neighborhood.

Osnos, Evan, "Letter From China: The Promised Land," *The New Yorker,* Feb. 9, 2009, www.newyorker.com/reporting/2009/02/09/090209fa_fact_osnos.

Traders from at least 19 countries have set up shop in the Chinese coastal city of Guangzhou to make money in the export-import business.

Packer, George, "The Megacity," *The New Yorker,* Nov. 13, 2006, www.newyorker.com/archive/2006/11/13/061113fa_fact_packer.

Lagos, Nigeria, offers a grim picture of urban life.

Schwartz, Michael, "For Russia's Migrants, Economic Despair Douses Flickers of Hope," *The New York Times,* Feb. 9, 2009, www.nytimes.com/2009/02/10/world/europe/10migrants.html?n=Top/Reference/Times%20Topics/People/P/Putin,%20Vladimir%20V.

Russia has an estimated 10 million migrant workers, mainly from former Soviet republics in Central Asia — some living in shanty towns.

Reports and Studies

"Ranking of the World's Cities Most Exposed to Coastal Flooding Today and in the Future," Organization for Economic Cooperation and Development, 2007, www.rms.com/Publications/OECD_Cities_Coastal_Flooding.pdf.

As a result of urbanization and global climate change, up to 150 million people in major cities around the world could be threatened by flooding by 2070.

"State of World Population 2007," U.N. Population Fund, 2007, www.unfpa.org/upload/lib_pub_file/695_filename_sowp2007_eng.pdf.

A U.N. agency outlines the challenges and opportunities presented by urbanization and calls on policy makers to help cities improve residents' lives.

"State of the World's Cities 2008/2009: Harmonious Cities," UN-HABITAT, 2008.

The biennial report from the U.N. Human Settlements Programme surveys urban growth patterns and social, economic and environmental conditions in cities worldwide.

For More Information

Chicago Council on Global Affairs, 332 South Michigan Ave., Suite 1100, Chicago, IL 60604; (312) 726-3860; www.thechicagocouncil.org. A nonprofit research and public education group; runs the Global Chicago Center, an initiative to strengthen Chicago's international connections, and co-authors the Global Cities Index.

Clean Air Initiative for Asian Cities, CAI-Asia Center, 3510 Robinsons Equitable Tower, ADB Avenue, Ortigas Center, Pasig City, Philippines 1605; (632) 395-2843; www.cleanairnet.org/caiasia. A nonprofit network that promotes and demonstrates innovative ways to improve air quality in Asian cities.

Institute for Liberty and Democracy, Las Begonias 441, Oficina 901, San Isidro, Lima 27, Peru; (51-1) 616-6100; http://ild.org.pe. Think tank headed by economist Hernando de Soto that promotes legal tools to help the world's poor move from the extralegal economy into an inclusive market economy.

Overseas Development Institute, 111 Westminster Bridge Road, London SE1 7JD, United Kingdom; (44) (0)20 7922 0300; www.odi.org.uk. An independent British think tank focusing on international development and humanitarian issues.

Shack/Slum Dwellers International; (27) 21 689 9408; www.sdinet.co.za. The Web site for the South Africa-based secretariat of an international network of organizations of the urban poor in 23 developing countries.

UN-HABITAT, P.O. Box 30030 GPO, Nairobi, 00100, Kenya; (254-20) 7621234; www.unhabitat.org. The United Nations Human Settlements Programme; works to promote socially and environmentally sustainable cities and towns.

World Bank, 1818 H Street, N.W., Washington, DC 20433, USA; (202) 473-1000; http://web.worldbank.org. Two development institutions with 185 member countries, which provide loans, credits and grants to middle-income developing countries (International Bank for Reconstruction and Development) and the poorest developing countries (International Development Association)

Voices From Abroad:

DAVID DODMAN

Researcher, International Institute for Environment and Development, England

Cities aren't to blame for climate change.
"Blaming cities for climate change is far too simplistic. There are a lot of economies of scale associated with energy use in cities. If you're an urban dweller, particularly in an affluent country like Canada or the U.K., you're likely to be more efficient in your use of heating fuel and in your use of energy for transportation."

Toronto Star, March 2009

BABATUNDE FASHOLA

State Governor Lagos, Nigeria

Megacities create many challenges.
"Because of human activities there will be conflict and there will be the issue of security, everybody fighting for control, and these are some of the challenges that come with the status of a megacity. It is really a status that creates certain challenges that the government must respond to."

This Day (Nigeria), November 2007

JONATHAN WOETZEL

Director, McKinsey & Company, Shanghai

Migration to China could cause problems.
"The fact that 40 to 50 per cent of [Chinese] cities [by 2025] could be made up of migrant workers is a real wake-up call. Smaller cities in particular are going to face a growing challenge if they are to provide equal access to social services."

Irish Times, March 2008

THE WORLD BANK

Singapore does it right.
"Improving institutions and infrastructure and intervening at the same time is a tall order for any government, but Singapore shows how it can be done. . . . Multi-year plans were produced, implemented and updated. For a city-state

Cagle Cartoons, La Prensa, Panama/Arcadio Esquivel

in a poor region, it is also not an exaggeration to assert that effective urbanization was responsible for delivering growth rates that averaged 8 per cent a year throughout 1970s and 1980s."

World Development Report 2009

THORAYA AHMED OBAID

Executive Director, U.N. Population Fund

Informal work has value.
"Many of tomorrow's city dwellers will be poor, swelling the ranks of the billion who already live in slums, but

however bad their predicament, experience shows that newcomers do not leave the city once they have moved. . . . They are also remarkably productive. Economists agree that informal work makes a vital contribution to the urban economy and is a key growth factor in developing countries."

The Guardian (England), July 2007

ZHU TONG

Environmental Scientist, Peking University

Different air standards cause confusion.
"Different countries vary in their air quality standards, and the WHO does not have a binding set of standards. China's national standards are not as high as those in developed countries, which has led to disagreements, confusion or even misunderstandings."

South China Morning Post, July 2008

SUDIRMAN NASIR

Lecturer, University of Hasanuddin, Indonesia

Opportunities lead to migration.
"The lack of job and economic opportunities in rural areas justifies migration to the cities as a survival strategy. It is a rational choice made by villagers because cities generally have more jobs to offer. It's impossible to reduce urbanization through the repressive approach."

Jakarta Post (Indonesia), October 2008

8

Brazil on the Rise

Brian Beary

Brazilian security forces search for drug dealers in a Rio de Janeiro slum on Nov. 29, 2010. They confiscated large quantities of drugs, ammunition and arms after a weeklong initiative. Brazil's ongoing crackdown on crime — which includes moving young officers into the slums to live — has helped lower the murder rate: Rio had 4,768 murders in 2010, down from 6,323 in 2006.

From *CQ Researcher*,
June 7, 2011.

Visits between leaders of Brazil and the United States are nothing new. Since the emperor of Brazil spent three months in the United States in 1876, there have been three dozen such meetings.[1]

But until *Air Force 1* touched down on March 19 in Brasília, Brazil's capital city, the pattern has always been the same: Each new Brazilian leader would travel to Washington to present credentials and establish ties.

But this time, in a sign of how far Brazil's global prestige has risen, President Barack Obama — the world's most powerful leader — was traveling to Brazil to meet its new female leader.

And 63-year-old Dilma Rousseff was about as far from an emperor as one can imagine: The daughter of a Bulgarian immigrant, she is a former guerrilla fighter who was tortured by a previous military regime.

Since independence in 1822, Brazil — with its large population and territory, vast natural resources, sweeping savanna and dense Amazon rain forest — often has been called "a country with great potential." But crippling inflation, widespread poverty, large income inequalities and political instability blocked progress.

Today, however, few still see Brazil the old way, given its enormous strides over the last generation.

"Brazil is no longer an emerging country — it has emerged," U.S. Ambassador to Brazil Thomas Shannon has said.[2]

Brazil's economy has grown robustly for more than a decade, thanks to a surge in exports of sugar, coffee, soybeans, poultry, beef, orange juice and iron ore. Trade with China, Brazil's largest export market, has grown exponentially: from just $2 billion in 2000 to

Brazil Dominates South America

Slightly smaller than China, Brazil is the world's fifth-largest country — both in area and in population. Covering a huge swath of South America, Portugese-speaking Brazil touches the borders of every other nation on the continent except Chile and Ecuador. The 4,200-mile-long Amazon River — the world's second-longest — stretches across the northern part of the country. Brazil has the world's seventh-largest economy and produces 60 percent of South America's gross domestic product.

Brazil's Major Cities and Rivers

Brazil at a Glance

Area: 3.28 million square miles, slightly smaller than China (5th-largest country in the world)

Population: 203.4 million (July 2011 est.)

Labor force: 103.6 million (2010 est.)

Unemployment rate: 7%

GDP: $2 trillion (2010); 7.5% growth (2010); 4.5% (2011, projected)

Value of top commodities (2008): beef — $18.7 billion; sugar cane — $13.3 billion; soybeans — $12.3 billion

Religions: Catholic (74%); Protestant (15%); Other (4%); None (7%)

Government: Federal republic; president elected to four-year terms.

Sources: White House Fact Sheet on Brazil-U.S. Relations; International Monetary Fund; Food and Agriculture Organization; U.N. Population Division; The World Factbook, Central Intelligence Agency; map by Lewis Agrell

$56.2 billion by 2010.[3] Iron ore makes up about 40 percent of Brazil's exports to China. Europe and the Middle East also are big buyers of Brazil's goods.

Agriculture has been at the heart of Brazil's export boom. Brazilian agricultural exports quadrupled between 2000 and 2008, from $15 billion to $61 billion.[4] By 2009, Brazil was the world's fifth-largest exporter of agricultural products, behind the United States, the Netherlands, Germany and France but ahead of Canada, China and Argentina.

But agricultural exports tend to come from large, industrial-scale agribusinesses with smaller work forces. Thus, as agriculture's share of the economy has risen, Brazilians have not been returning to the countryside. In fact, with 87 percent of its citizens now living in urban centers, Brazil boasts some of the world's fastest-growing megacities, which create both employment opportunities as well as immense housing and infrastructure challenges.[5]

The *favelas*, or slums, of Rio de Janeiro and São Paulo are infamous both for their abject poverty and for being in the iron grip of organized drug gangs. Brazil is the world's second-largest consumer of cocaine after the United States.[6] But police recently have made some inroads in arresting drug traffickers and criminals who prey on slum residents.[7]

On the plus side, Brazil is largely energy independent, having invested heavily in renewable energy sources such as ethanol refined from the nation's mammoth sugarcane crop. Since late 2008, Brazilians have been consuming more ethanol than gasoline, and more of Brazil's sugarcane is now processed into ethanol than is sold as sugar.[8] About three-quarters of Brazil's ethanol is consumed domestically, partly because the export market has been stifled by high import tariffs in Europe and the United States.[9] About 50 percent of Brazil's energy consumption now comes from renewable sources, either sugar ethanol or hydropower. By comparison, renewable energy accounts for only 14 percent of the U.S. energy mix, notes Ladislau Martin-Neto, an official with Embrapa, the Brazilian Agricultural Research Corp.[10]

In addition, Brazil soon could become a world oil power. A new offshore oil rig has been constructed nearly 200 miles off the coast of Rio de Janeiro, home to the "world's largest-known offshore deposit," according to the *Financial Times*. If Brazil is able to fully exploit the

AFP/Getty Images/Adriano Machado

Brazilian President Dilma Rousseff — shown at her Jan. 1 inauguration with outgoing President Luiz Inácio Lula da Silva — is Brazil's first female head of state. The daughter of a Bulgarian immigrant, she also is a former guerrilla fighter who reportedly was tortured by Brazil's former military regime. Considered a pragmatic, trade-friendly leader, Rousseff has said her "essential commitment is building a middle-class income society [and] assuring vocational and professional opportunities for the workers and for our immense youth population."

deposits, which lie beneath a mile-thick layer of salt, it will rise from 15th to fifth place in the rankings of the world's largest oil reserves.[11]

Brazil's growing economic wealth has enabled it to move from being a recipient of development aid to a provider. The $4 billion it doled out last year to places as diverse as Haiti, Gaza, Mozambique and Mali is considerably less than China's aid budget but more than some advanced economies, including Sweden and Canada. Moreover, Brazil's aid budget is increasing rapidly.[12]

"Brazil can speak to those countries in a way that the United States cannot," says Marcella Szymanski, foreign affairs officer for agriculture, biotechnology and textile trade at the U.S. Department of State.[13] The United

Indigenous Amazon Peoples Face Uncertain Future

Despite safeguards, traditional way of life is threatened.

Deforestation is dramatically shrinking Brazil's legendary Amazon rain forest — threatening dozens of indigenous tribes. But deforestation is only the latest threat from outsiders encroaching on native peoples' homeland.

Ever since Portuguese explorer Pedro Álvares Cabral arrived in Brazil in 1500, new diseases, slavery, warfare, loss of land and marriage to outsiders have caused native peoples' numbers to decline steadily, notes University of Maryland anthropologist Janet Chernela, an expert on indigenous Amazonian groups. Today, the Amazon's native population totals about 600,000, compared to the 2 million to 4 million who lived in Brazil when Cabral arrived.

Most recently, the biggest threat has been the loss of their culture and way of life due to depletion of their rain forest habitat.[1] As a result, native peoples are adopting multitasking lifestyles, says Jason Bremner, director of population, health and environment at the Population Reference Bureau, a Washington D.C., think tank.

"They may hunt and farm while also working as security guards for oil companies. There is a lot of diversity among them, and they all use the land differently," he says. Some support communal land rights, while others claim ownership of designated plots. "We need to understand these divergences when devising a conservation strategy."[2]

Indigenous Brazilians have traditionally lived in small settlements and made decisions by consensus. "Governance and leadership among indigenous peoples is not always understood by outsiders, who often assume the existence of a tribal chief," says Chernela. Several indigenous associations have emerged since the late 1980s, she notes, but no national-level organization represents all the groups.

Native peoples' subsistence lifestyles rely heavily on the forests for hunting, fishing and farming — activities that have a "light ecological impact," Chernela says. They usually harvest a portion of land for up to 10 years, then leave it fallow until the forest regenerates. "They are stewards of the forests," she says, in contrast to how non-native people use the land, which "is generally unsustainable."

Steve Schwartzman, director of tropical forest policy at the Environmental Defense Fund (EDF) in Washington, is an Amazon expert who lived with the Panara group for more than a year in the early 1980s. Since the 1960s, he says, when the government began building roads into the Amazon, the Panara's isolation from the rest of Brazil has been breached, with catastrophic results.

"Within five years, about 60 percent of the indigenous Panara died from common illnesses like colds, flu and measles," he says. The population nearly collapsed in the 1970s but has rebounded in recent years, largely due to higher birth rates, he says.

Adoption of the 1988 Brazilian constitution, which guaranteed collective ownership of lands originally occupied by indigenous Brazilians, was a landmark event for native groups, which now enjoy limited autonomy in several protected areas.[3] However, the process of designating indigenous lands has stalled, Chernela says, and many Amazonians have lost their land to expanding industrial agriculture. A new organization, the 1.5-million-member *Movimento dos Trabalhadores Rurais Sem Terra* (Landless Workers' Movement), supports landless populations' efforts to occupy unused lands.

But not all indigenous peoples live in the native territories. For example, three-quarters of the 40,000 people living in São Gabriel da Cachoeira, a city in northwestern Brazil, are indigenous, and the municipality has recognized three native tongues as official languages since 2002.

The constitution also removed a ban on native populations being educated in their own languages, which has triggered a rise in indigenous teachers and bilingual schooling. The Brazilian government also has adopted key global treaties that boost native peoples' rights, including the 1989

International Labor Organization's Convention 169 and the 2007 U.N. Declaration on the Rights of Indigenous Peoples.[4]

Given the global interest in maintaining the fragile Amazon ecosystem, indigenous peoples have been seeking clarification of their right to manage their own food supply, particularly with regard to subsistence farming, hunting and fishing in protected forests. Erick Fernandes, World Bank adviser on Latin America and the Caribbean on agriculture and rural development, notes that the "indigenous people asked what their legal rights were to take charge of this issue and were told they do have a right."[5]

Looking to the future, habitat changes will continue to impinge heavily on Amazonian peoples. For example, the water supply of indigenous groups appears threatened after the Brazilian government's decision in May to give next-to-final approval for Pará state's proposed Belo Monte hydro-electric dam on the Xingu River. The structure is expected to be the world's third-largest dam and to power 23 million Brazilian homes.[6] It also is expected to bring 100,000 new settlers to the area.

Indigenous groups struggle to prevent such developments, primarily because they lack strong political representation in state and national parliaments, which don't properly defend native rights, says Chernela.

However, the picture is not entirely bleak. The EDF's Schwartzman believes the Brazilian government has, over the past decade, gotten more serious about preserving the Amazon, and indigenous people have become more assertive.

"Their land rights are much stronger since 1988," he says. "Their story across the region is one of relocation, followed by ethnic reaffirmation."

— *Brian Beary*

Indigenous Brazilians protest dam projects in the Amazon that will flood their lands, including the Belo Monte hydroelectric dam on the Xingu River, expected to be the world's third-largest and to attract 100,000 new settlers to the area. The demonstration was held outside Brazil's Permanent Mission to the U.N. in New York City on April 28, 2010.

[1] Fiona Harvey, "The long road to rainforest conservation," *Financial Times,* June 28 2010, www.ft.com/cms/s/0/9195323a-7d13-11df-8845-00144feabdc0,dwp_uuid=1ab2a3bc-7d38-11df-8845-00144feabdc0.html#axzz1HWckVicv.

[2] Comments made during roundtable discussion: "Deforestation, Population and Development in a Warming World," Woodrow Wilson International Center of Scholars, Feb. 15, 2011.

[3] Brazil's constitution is at www.v-brazil.com/government/laws/title-VIII.html.

[4] See "C169 Indigenous and Tribal Peoples Convention, 1989," International Labour Organization, www.ilo.org/ilolex/cgi-lex/convde.pl?C169; and "United Nations Declaration on the Rights of Indigenous Peoples," United Nations, www.un.org/esa/socdev/unpfii/en/drip.html.

[5] Comments made at a conference organized by the Brazil Institute at the Woodrow Wilson International Center for Scholars: "Brazil and Africa: Cooperation for Innovation in Agriculture and What the U.S. Can Do," U.S. House of Representatives, May 16, 2011.

[6] Gary Duffy, "Brazil grants environmental licence for Belo Monte dam," BBC News, Feb. 2, 2010, http://news.bbc.co.uk/2/hi/americas/8492577.stm.

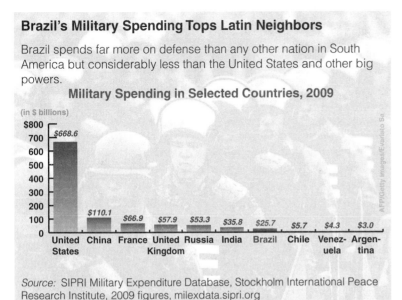

Brazil's Military Spending Tops Latin Neighbors

Brazil spends far more on defense than any other nation in South America but considerably less than the United States and other big powers.

Military Spending in Selected Countries, 2009

(in $ billions)

Country	Spending
United States	$668.6
China	$110.1
France	$66.9
United Kingdom	$57.9
Russia	$53.3
India	$35.8
Brazil	$25.7
Chile	$5.7
Venezuela	$4.3
Argentina	$3.0

Source: SIPRI Military Expenditure Database, Stockholm International Peace Research Institute, 2009 figures, milexdata.sipri.org

States and Brazil in March 2010 signed a development aid partnership agreement for Africa, she notes.

Meanwhile, the government has made significant strides in reducing poverty at home. According to Brasília-based Bruno de Saraiva, an economist at the Inter-American Development Bank (IADB), some 28 million Brazilians were raised above the poverty line between 2003 and 2010. "In terms of income inequality, Brazil now ranks in the middle compared to other Latin American countries, whereas it used to top the inequality index," he adds. Brazil now ranks 73rd out of 169 countries in the U.N. Development Program's "human development" index — higher than either China or India. The index combines life expectancy, education and income.[14]

Today, only 7 percent of Brazilians live in extreme poverty, compared to 13 percent in 2002.[15] Life expectancy has shot up by 10 years in a generation: from 63.4 years in 1980 to 73.5 years today.[16]

On Jan. 1, 2011, Dilma Rousseff became Brazil's first female leader, the nation's third in a succession of pragmatic, trade-friendly leaders. Her predecessors Fernando Henrique Cardoso (1995-2002) and Luiz Inácio Lula de Silva (2003-2010) both had great charisma that helped put Brazil on the global map.

Rousseff, on the other hand, is an intense, but low-key technocrat "who has never occupied elective office,"

notes Paulo Sotero, director of the Brazil Institute at the Woodrow Wilson Center for International Scholars in Washington. Rousseff rose through the civil service ranks before Lula tapped her as energy minister and later his chief of staff. Sotero noted that Rousseff favors "a strong state role in the economy," having helped to revamp the oil sector so that the state oil company, Petrobras, now holds a virtual monopoly over Brazil's huge new offshore oil findings. He described her as "a strong personality with a famously short temper."[17]

Since military rule ended in the mid-1980s, Brazil has strengthened its democracy. Today's politics are dominated by moderates, and elections are free, fair and noncontroversial. Even so, the administration has its problems: The state bureaucracy is widely considered to be bloated and corrupt. Brazil ranks 69th out of 178 countries in levels of corruption, (with 178th being the most corrupt), according to Transparency International.[18]

However, Brazil's infrastructure still resembles that of a developing country. A subway line in São Paulo, for example, first conceived in 1969, has yet to be completed. And just this past December, authorities shelved plans to build a train line connecting downtown São Paulo to its airport. The governor of the Rio de Janeiro state government has blamed Brazil's poor performance on infrastructure development to "absurd centralization."[19]

Internationally, Brazil is becoming more assertive in trade negotiations, climate talks and even on global security — which Brazil has historically been reluctant to discuss. The government now wants Brazil to become a permanent member of the U.N. Security Council, a move many say would make the United Nations more inclusive.

Brazil has "a lot of potential in the area of conflict resolution," says Luigi Einaudi, a fellow at the National Defense University (NDU) in Washington. Its history "has essentially been one of peaceful progress." In the 1800s, he notes, Brazil transitioned nonviolently from empire to independence and later consolidated its borders with its neighbors through treaties, rather than violence.

In many ways, Brazil is the most attractive of the four so-called BRIC emerging economies — Brazil, Russia, India and China. Unlike Russia and China, it is a stable democracy with a positive scorecard on human rights, and unlike nuclear-armed India it has no internal or external conflicts to contend with, possessing no nuclear weapons and having pacifist tendencies.

Environmentally, as caretaker of the legendary Amazon rain forest, Brazil struggles with the challenge of deforestation. Home to unparalleled biodiversity and thousands of plant and animal species facing the threat of extinction due to habitat loss, the Amazon is under attack from those wanting to clear the forest to make way for cattle ranches and soy plantations. Since the early 1970s, an area the size of France has been deforested, and the rate of destruction increased significantly in the 1990s.

In the last decade the government has taken significant steps to address the problem, aided by a $1 billion grant from Norway to help Brazil make verifiable cuts in its greenhouse gas emissions. Brazil has designated large swaths of the Amazon as protected areas and has beefed up its law-enforcement presence to stop illegal logging and cattle ranching.[20]

However, the government revealed in May that the deforestation rate had risen 27 percent during the nine-month period that ended in April, compared to the same period the previous year. The stunning announcement came as the Brazilian parliament edged toward passing a bill that would relax obligations on farmers to leave a portion of their lands as forest.[21]

Brazil also has begun to break the stranglehold that drug-trafficking gangs have had for decades in the nation's vast urban slums. It has introduced Police Pacification Units — small teams of law enforcement officers embedded in the community to build up the

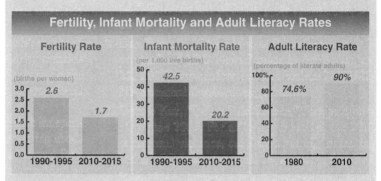

Health, Literacy Rates Improve

Brazil has lowered its average birthrate by about one less child per woman compared to 20 years earlier. The number of infant deaths per 1,000 live births also has decreased by more than 50 percent over the same period. Adults are becoming more educated, with the literacy rate reaching 90 percent in 2010.

Fertility, Infant Mortality and Adult Literacy Rates

Fertility Rate (births per woman): 1990-1995: 2.6; 2010-2015: 1.7

Infant Mortality Rate (per 1,000 live births): 1990-1995: 42.5; 2010-2015: 20.2

Adult Literacy Rate (percentage of literate adults): 1980: 74.6%; 2010: 90%

Sources: U.N. Population Division online database; Human Development Indicators, U.N. Development Programme

residents' trust. In Rio de Janeiro, for instance, the number of murders has declined from 6,323 in 2006 to 4,768 in 2010.[22]

"The locals were afraid of us at first and avoided us. They were worried the program might not be permanent," says Antonio Roberto Cesario de Sa, undersecretary for planning and operational integration. "But as they saw its success, they became more welcoming." Another clear sign of how much progress the city has made came in October 2009, when Rio de Janeiro was selected to host the 2016 Summer Olympic Games, beating out Chicago, Madrid and Tokyo. Not even the presence of ex-Chicago resident President Obama at the final voting in Copenhagen was enough to edge out Rio.[23]

As Brazil continues to make progress on a variety of fronts, here are some of the questions being asked:

Is Brazil's economy a model for developing countries?

Brazil's thriving and highly diversified economy is viewed by many as a role model for developing countries. But others note that Brazil's unique characteristics are not shared by most other under-developed nations.

Brazil built its economic success on three pillars: controlling inflation, having a flexible currency exchange

Illegally harvested logs are confiscated in northern Pará state. Although the government made significant strides against deforestation over the last decade, deforestation unexpectedly jumped 27 percent during the nine-month period ending in April, compared to the same period in 2010.

rate and avoiding excessive public debt, according to Rubens Barbosa, a former Brazilian ambassador to both the United States and United Kingdom who now leads a business development consulting firm in São Paulo. For example, Brazil has transformed itself from a debtor to a net creditor at the International Monetary Fund (IMF).

In addition, Brazil has effectively positioned itself as a world leader in food production, with sugar one of its biggest cash crops. The government relaxed price controls on sugar in 1990, which led to a 250 percent increase in cultivation and helped Brazil become the world's top sugar exporter.[24] And expanding sugarcane production did not contribute to Amazon deforestation, according to Eduardo Leão, executive director of the Brazilian Sugarcane Industry Association, because sugar is grown mostly in the south and center of the country, some 1,550 miles from the Amazon rain forest. Meanwhile, the industry provides about 1 million jobs, he notes, with total revenues about $30 billion a year — $12 billion of that in export revenues.

Given that sugarcane grows well in tropical regions, developing countries in Africa and Asia could follow Brazil's example. Embrapa, the Brazilian government agency for agricultural research, has been sharing some of the country's agricultural technologies with Ghana, Mozambique, Angola and East Timor.[25] According to Fernandes at the World Bank, "we look to Brazil as being a very valuable source of knowledge and experience — in many ways they are ahead of the curve."[26]

For example, he notes that an indigenous crop from the Amazon, cassava, has been successfully introduced in Africa to help boost its food production. Of course, many countries — especially in Africa — face additional challenges, such as civil conflicts, land ownership issues and less fertile soil.

Much of Brazil's sugar is refined to make ethanol. While that has helped to make Brazil more energy independent, some critics worry about diverting such large quantities of food and agricultural tracts into a fuel source instead of using that land to increase food supplies. The use of sugarcane and other biomass to produce ethanol and other biofuels has contributed to a worldwide spike in food prices in recent years, tending to hurt poorer nations the most.[27]

Others say Brazil's trade relationship with China is not a model other countries should emulate. While Brazil exports large quantities of food and raw materials to China, it also imports massive amounts of lower-priced manufactured goods from China. In 2010, 97.5 percent of Chinese exports to Brazil were manufactured products, while 87 percent of Brazil's exports to China were primary products, such as food and raw materials.[28] Brazilian manufacturers find it increasingly hard to compete with the Chinese manufacturers because of China's undervalued currency, coupled with a high tax burden, high cost of borrowing and the poor infrastructure that confront Brazilian businesses.

Last year, for the first time in decades, Brazil exported more commodities than manufactured goods. Manufactured goods' share of Brazil's exports has slipped from 57 percent in 2001 to 39 percent in 2010, while primary commodities' share has increased from 26 percent to 45 percent.[29] Brazil does not rank even in the top 10 among the world's largest exporters of manufactured goods, according to the World Trade Organization (WTO), while China is the second-largest after the EU.[30]

Sotero, at the Brazil Institute, notes that some critics call this a "deindustrialisation model" and are characterizing the China-Brazil relationship as neocolonial.[31]

In other words, there is unease, he says, with a trade relationship in which Brazil exports predominantly raw commodities to China and imports mostly manufactured goods. Moreover, Brazil's economic growth, while impressive, is not nearly as strong as China's — and is much more recent, with China's stretching back to the 1980s. A World Bank report noted that between 1981 and 2005, the percentage of Brazil's population living in poverty declined from 17.1 to 7.8 percent, whereas China's poverty rate plummeted from 84 to 16.3 percent. The report noted, however, that income inequality in China has risen significantly, while it has been reduced in Brazil.[32]

Some see the relationship in a more positive light. According to Mark Langevin, director of BrazilWorks, a Washington-based think tank, "China invests in Brazil — for example in new hydro- and thermo-power plants," and China plans to buy 180 planes from Brazilian aircraft manufacturer Embraer. "The Chinese are not telling Brazilians what to do. There is an interdependency being created," he says. Indeed, overall, Brazil has a trade surplus with China — in contrast to the United States, where Brazil has gone from having a trade surplus to an anticipated $11 billion deficit in 2011.[33]

Brazil's manufacturers, meanwhile, blame their lack of competitiveness on China's undervalued currency, which makes China's products cheaper to buy. Others feel the currency argument is a distraction from Brazil's structural weaknesses that are the true cause of its inability to remain competitive. For example, former Ambassador Barbosa blames Brazil's high overall tax burden, under-investment in infrastructure and high interest rates, which make it hard for businesses to get capital. Moreover, Brazil's strong currency can be an advantage on occasion. For example, when food prices reached an all-time high in 2011 — partly due to growing demand in the emerging BRIC markets of Brazil, Russia, India and China — the strength of Brazil's currency meant there was only a muted impact on domestic prices.[34]

While many developing countries may see Brazil as a role model, Langevin points out that they, for the most part, are not as fortunate as Brazil. "Developing countries do not have as many natural resources so they need to be more careful," he says. For example, the huge, recently discovered oil reserves put Brazil in a special category of countries. And Brazil has so much arable land that even now, as a global leader in exports, it is not producing close to full capacity.

In addition, Langevin notes, many African governments are more corrupt than Brazil, so even if they expand their agro-energy sector, it likely would enrich only an elite group instead of being shared more widely among the population, as has happened in Brazil.

Is Brazil doing enough to stop deforestation?

Brazil's Amazon forestland, which accounts for 30 percent of the Earth's remaining tropical rain forest, continues to disappear at an alarming rate.[35] Between 2000 and 2010, Brazil lost more rain forest than any other country — representing 27 percent of global deforestation. Brazil is now the world's fifth-largest emitter of greenhouse gases, with the removal of forests and their replacement with agricultural lands being the biggest culprit. Over 65 percent of the Atlantic forest around the state of São Paulo has been cleared primarily for agricultural products, especially soybeans, with forests typically slashed and burned, the World Bank noted in a recent report. "Coffee growers, sugarcane farmers and cattle ranchers are some of the major groups responsible for illegal deforestation," it added.[36] On the other hand, Brazil's performance in tackling the deforestation problem steadily improved from 2000-2009, before suddenly regressing in 2010 and 2011.[37]

Despite the ongoing deforestation, former Ambassador Barbosa feels "the government is doing what it can," given the enormous challenges of trying to police a territory "the size of Europe." Nongovernmental organizations should keep up their pressure on Brazil, he says, but "we have to be reasonable in our expectations."

The cattle industry, which clears the forests to make way for large ranches, is a prime culprit. But with worldwide demand for meat at record levels, farmers have a strong economic incentive to get involved in the industry. According to Sarah Shoraka, a deforestation activist at the environmental group Greenpeace, "the cattle industry is the single biggest cause of deforestation in the world and is a disaster for the fight against climate change."[38] Besides eliminating forests, which naturally remove climate-change-inducing "greenhouse gases" — thus helping to counteract global warming — the cattle themselves emit methane, one of the greenhouse gases.

Cultivation of soybeans is also problematic, because forested areas also must be cleared. In an effort to make Brazil more energy independent, the government has been encouraging soy production by subsidizing the refining of soy into biodiesel, a fuel traditionally used by

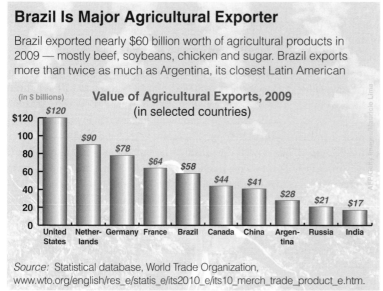

Brazil Is Major Agricultural Exporter

Brazil exported nearly $60 billion worth of agricultural products in 2009 — mostly beef, soybeans, chicken and sugar. Brazil exports more than twice as much as Argentina, its closest Latin American

Value of Agricultural Exports, 2009
(in selected countries)

(in $ billions)

Country	Value
United States	$120
Netherlands	$90
Germany	$78
France	$64
Brazil	$58
Canada	$44
China	$41
Argentina	$28
Russia	$21
India	$17

Source: Statistical database, World Trade Organization, www.wto.org/english/res_e/statis_e/its2010_e/its10_merch_trade_product_e.htm.

trucks in Brazil. Today about 80 percent of the biodiesel produced in Brazil comes from soy. But the subsidization policy indirectly encourages deforestation, environmentalists complain. In contrast, the growth of the ethanol industry, which began in the 1970s in response to the oil crises, does not cause deforestation, farmers and even some environmentalists generally agree, because the sugarcane used for ethanol is not grown in deforested areas.

The government has been doing demonstrably more to prevent deforestation in recent years. According to Steve Schwartzman, director of tropical forest policy at the Environmental Defense Fund (EDF) in Washington, D.C., Brazil's 1988 constitution has helped to preserve the Amazon rain forest because it led to the preservation of large tracts of land for indigenous peoples that cannot be subdivided or sold to loggers and ranchers. Indigenous groups now own about 20 percent of the Amazon — an area twice the size of California, he notes. One indigenous community, the Panara, has managed to preserve a portion of intact forest the size of Delaware, land that cattle ranchers would have liked to exploit, says Schwartzman. The Catholic Church played a helpful role in the process by denouncing ranchers who were intimidating indigenous peoples, and civil society groups that have sprung up since the end of military rule have helped as well, he says.

But Schwartzman gives particular credit to Brazil's former environment minister, Marina Silva, daughter of an Amazonian rubber tapper. Before she took office, the government had focused primarily on building roads in the Amazon, which encouraged deforestation. Silva devised and implemented the first comprehensive program to combat deforestation, creating protected zones covering an area the size of France in the Amazon frontier. She also beefed up law enforcement resources to ensure that ranchers and loggers did not violate the new restrictions. Brazil's deforestation rate plummeted by two-thirds between 2003 and 2010.

Leão, the sugarcane industry official, points out that the government has recently introduced an agricultural zoning system to try to ensure sugarcane cultivation does not cause deforestation. "We support this because we want to send the right signal to the market — that the government is serious about tackling deforestation," he says.

BrazilWorks' Langevin also feels the government "has pretty much done a good job" of slowing deforestation. For example, he says, in Pará and Amapá states the government is encouraging the production of palm oil — a product used in cooking, cosmetics and biodiesel. "They are trying to use already deforested and degraded lands. This approach is more environmentally sustainable than removing forests and replacing them with cattle ranches."

Langevin worries, however, that some Malaysian and Indonesian companies setting up palm oil plantations may not abide by the law requiring 80 percent of the land to be held in reserve.

Asked about Brazil having to rely on $1 billion aid from Norway to deal with the problem of deforestation, Langevin says, "I think at this stage Brazil needs the aid. But once its oil and gas revenues increase, it will have more of its own funds."

From the Inter-American Development Bank, Brazilian natural resources economist Eirivelthon Lima says Brazil "has been very successful, very serious" in measuring and controlling deforestation in the past decade. More than 50 percent of the Amazon rain forest is now protected legally, while the Brazilian government has invested heavily in helicopters, trucks and other equipment needed to enforce the laws.

Lima admits, however, that for a long time prior to that, little effort had been made to enforce a 1965 forestry code that was supposed to prevent deforestation. He adds that while progress has been made in the Amazon, 85 percent of which is still intact, only 8 to 10 percent of Brazil's Atlantic forest is now left. And the government is much less-advanced in devising a system to protect the forests of the *Cerrado*, or savanna, regions, where the forests are less dense than the Amazon, making detecting deforestation more difficult. The IADB is co-funding projects with state governments, including in São Paulo and Acre, aimed at forestry preservation.

However, the announcement in May that satellite images had shown deforestation up 27 percent between August 2010 and April 2011 has stunned environmentalists and politicians alike. The satellite data showed a particularly alarming loss in March and April, when nearly 229 square miles of forest were lost — a 470 percent jump over the same period in 2010. The most dramatic situation was in Mato Grosso, the soy-growing state, where farmers reportedly are using tractors and giant chains to rip up vast tracts of native forest.[39]

According to Andre Muggiat, an Amazon-based campaigner for Greenpeace, "The country is going backwards in terms of forest conservation, definitely." He fears that proposed changes to the country's forestry code set off a "deforestation frenzy." That new law, which would reduce the amount of forest land farmers are required to hold in reserve, could cause "the largest deforestation in the Amazon and in Brazil in general in many years."[40]

But Environment Minister Izabella Teixeira said she is creating a "crisis cabinet" to crack down on illegal logging and that timber and cattle from illegally deforested lands would be seized. "The order is to suffocate environmental crime," she said.[41]

Can Brazil be a superpower?

Brazil is advancing on the global stage militarily, politically and in the trade arena. In foreign policy, for instance, "there is a growing public awareness that Brazil is now a global player," according to Ambassador Shannon.

The Wilson Center's Sotero says he believes Brazil's bid to become a permanent member of the U.N. Security Council will eventually succeed. "I believe the Security Council will be reformed within the next five years, because today it does not reflect global realities," he says.[42]

Sotero argues that this is appropriate, given that "Brazil has always thought and acted globally." Brazil has long provided peacekeeping troops, having taken part in roughly 30 U.N. operations since 1948. Historically, though, Brazil has been more comfortable joining in peacekeeping operations than in peace-enforcing ones, according to *The Economist*.[43]

That seems to be changing, however. Brazil took the lead in a U.N. peace-enforcing mission in Haiti, the U.N.'s third-largest. And since 2005 Brazil has operated a peacekeeping school in Rio de Janeiro, Centro Instrução de Operações de Paz, which has trained 15,000 troops. Brazil's military has much to offer, given its special training in fields such as operating in dense jungles.

Brazil also has beefed up its role in foreign aid. "In search of 'soft power,' Brazil is turning itself into one of the world's biggest aid donors," noted *The Economist*.[44] In Haiti, for instance, Brazil encourages mothers to take their children to school in exchange for free meals. In Angola, it is helping to develop a water supply system, and aid to Mali is targeting improved cotton yields by helping to prevent soil erosion.

Meanwhile, Brazil has developed into a formidable force in international trade. This has been most evident in the ongoing Doha round of trade liberalization talks, launched in 2001 by the World Trade Organization (WTO). At a key ministerial meeting in 2005 in Cancún, Mexico, Brazil blocked a deal being touted by advanced economies and, in doing so, became a champion for developing nations.[45] With the BRIC nations becoming trade superpowers, Brazil has embraced this new order enthusiastically, hosting a BRIC summit in Brasília in April 2010.

At the regional level, Shannon notes, Brazil has taken the lead in promoting integration through the Mercosur trading bloc, the Union of South American Nations summits of South American leaders, and a similar forum that exists at the ministerial level called the South American Defense Council.

Until now, Brazil has focused more on the use of soft power on issues such as foreign aid, climate change and trade than on "hard power" issues like military interventions in foreign countries. It is doubtful whether Brazil has much appetite or aptitude to be a military superpower.

"The Brazilian people have no clue about their government's U.N. Security Council project," according to Luis Bitencourt, a former Brazilian government official and currently a professor of international security at the National Defense University in Washington. "It has not featured on their radar yet. The politicians need to explain to them why we need this and what responsibilities it will bring to Brazil."[46]

Based on current military spending levels — about 1 to 2 percent of annual GDP — military power is not a priority at the moment. In fact, when viewed as a share of the overall economy, Brazil's military spending is lower than that of many of its non-superpower Latin American neighbors, including Chile and Colombia. Brazil may spend more money overall than any other South American country — $26 billion in 2009 — but that is only a fraction of the military budgets of the big global players like the United States ($669 billion), China ($110 billion), France ($67 billion), the United Kingdom ($58 billion) and Russia ($53 billion).[47]

Brazilian social scientist Simon Schwartzman, president of the *Instituto de Estudos do Trabalho e Sociedade* (Institute for Studies on Labor and Society) in Rio de Janeiro believes ordinary Brazilians have little interest in going down the military superpower road.

"Foreign policy is not a big issue for Brazilians. People do not care much about the U.N. Security Council. It's only the intellectuals who are bothered by this," he says.

He does believe the Brazilian public will be comfortable with Brazil participating in more peacekeeping missions. But he doubts Brazil will become more engaged in military conflicts. "We do not have a history of this. The last time we were involved in war was in World War II, when we sent troops to Italy. We do not have problems with our neighbors," he says.

BACKGROUND

Colony to Republic

Modern Brazil traces its origins to a 1494 agreement between Spain and Portugal, the Treaty of Tordesillas, under which the territory that later became Brazil was given to the Portuguese, while Spain was entitled to the rest of the Americas.

On April 22, 1500, Portuguese explorer Pedro Álvares Cabral landed on Brazil's coast, marking the beginning of Portugal's colonization of Brazilian lands.[48] Almost from the beginning, Portuguese colonists imported African slaves into Brazil to tend to sugar plantations.[49]

Beginning in 1580, Spain ruled Portugal — and consequently Brazil — for the next 60 years. When Portugal regained its independence in 1640, Brazil returned to Portuguese rule. But Portugal's grip on its gigantic American colony began to slip during the Napoleonic wars of the early 1800s. In 1807, the Portuguese royal family fled to Rio de Janeiro, accompanied by 15,000 people, including members of the nobility, clergy and military.

During the reign of Dom João of Portugal from 1807-1820, Brazil made progress in commerce, education and finance. In 1821, Dom João returned to Lisbon, leaving his son Dom Pedro in charge in Brazil. In 1822, Brazil became independent from Portugal following a relatively peaceful revolution, and a Brazilian monarchy was established, led by Dom Pedro.[50]

A major milestone in Brazilian history came in 1888, when the country finally abolished slavery — the last Latin American country to do so. But abolition prompted the country's great landowners, who had not been compensated for the loss of their slaves, to withdraw their support from the monarchy. In November 1889, an uprising against the monarchy, spearheaded by the army, forced Pedro II to abdicate, and Brazil became a republic.

Economic Expansion

In the late 1800s, Brazil entered a new phase of economic expansion; huge tracts were cleared, and roads, bridges and railroads were built to accommodate vast grain, sugar and coffee plantations. A resulting economic boom led to a large influx of immigrants in the

CHRONOLOGY

1490s-1880s *Brazil emerges, first as a Portuguese colony, then a monarchy and finally a republic.*

1494 Treaty of Tordesillas divides up the Americas, with Portugal getting Brazil and Spain getting the rest.

1500 Portuguese explorer Pedro Álvares Cabral lands in Brazil, marking the beginning of colonization.

1807 Portuguese royal family flees to Rio de Janeiro during Napoleonic wars.

1822 Brazil gains independence from Portugal after a relatively peaceful revolution and establishes a monarchy under Dom Pedro, son of the King of Portugal.

1888 Brazil is last Latin American country to abolish slavery. Emancipation triggers an army-led uprising, which causes Pedro II to abdicate and Brazil to become a republic.

1930s-1980s *Brazil faces turbulent times as it alternates between democracy and dictatorship while expanding economically.*

1930 Opposition leader Getúlio Vargas seizes power and establishes a dictatorship.

1942 Brazil enters World War II on the side of the allies, deploying 25,000 troops to Italy to help U.S. forces.

1960 Brazil moves its capital from Rio de Janeiro to Brasília, a modernistic, new inland city, in an effort to stimulate inland migration.

1964 Left-leaning Brazilian President João Goulart is ousted in a coup, leading to two decades of semi-authoritarian military rule, during which human-rights abuses and "disappearances" of dissidents become common.

1970 Construction of the 3,300-mile-long Trans-Amazonian Highway begins, opening the region for loggers and farmers and exposing indigenous peoples to outside cultural influences, exploitation and disease.

1979 Military leaders receive amnesty for human-rights violations.

1985 Military rule ends; Brazil begins gradual transition to democracy.

1988 Environmentalist Chico Mendes is assassinated, increasing awareness of Amazon deforestation. . . . New constitution boosts indigenous peoples' rights.

1990s-2000s *Brazil enters era of sustained economic growth and democratic consolidation.*

1991 Brazil, Argentina, Paraguay and Uruguay reduce trade barriers among themselves by creating Mercosur regional trading bloc.

1994 Fernando Henrique Cardoso is elected president; introduces market reforms.

2002 Labor leader Luiz Inácio Lula da Silva is elected president. He continues pro-trade policies but also introduces poverty-reduction programs.

2003 Film exposes severe social problems in Rio de Janeiro's gang-controlled City of God slum.

2009 Brazil's state-owned oil company Petrobras secures $10 billion loan from Chinese Development Bank in return for supplying oil to China.

2010 Earthquake in Haiti leads to strong Brazil-U.S. cooperation in relief effort (January), but U.S. firmly rebuffs Brazil's effort to mediate in Iran nuclear dispute (May). . . . In November, Brazilian authorities wrench control of Rio slum Alemao from drug gangs after new police initiative.

2011 Former guerrilla fighter Dilma Rousseff becomes president (January); limits minimum wages (February). . . . President Barack Obama visits Brazil to help boost trade links (March). . . . Rousseff visits China on trade-oriented trip (April). . . . A 27 percent rise in deforestation is revealed. . . . Government gives next-to-final approval for giant Belo Monte dam, which will flood some indigenous lands (May).

2014 Brazil to host FIFA World Cup in soccer.

2016 Rio de Janeiro to host Summer Olympics.

Hosting World Sporting Events Proves Daunting

Many projects won't be finished in time.

Brazil's performance in hosting two of the world's most prestigious international tournaments — soccer's 2014 FIFA World Cup Finals and the 2016 Summer Olympics — will be judged by many as a measure of how far the country has advanced.

But early reports on Brazil's preparations for the big events are not promising. "Expectations are coming unraveled — fast," wrote Brazil-based Reuters journalist Brian Winter about the country's plans to spend more than $1 trillion "to bring its woeful airports, roads and other infrastructure up to date." The end result, he predicted, is "likely to fall well short" of the government's ambitions. Fewer than half of the planned major projects are expected to be finished on time, he noted.[1]

Brazil's sports minister, Orlando Silva, was similarly pessimistic. "We need to begin to control people's expectations," he said. "The idea that we were going to make up for 30 years without investment in infrastructure in just four years was probably never realistic."[2]

According to Sergio Fausto, executive director of the São Paulo-based Fernando Henrique Cardoso Institute think tank, "the government may need to be more flexible in applying procurement rules [in order] to stay on schedule." Fausto also believes that more public money will need to be spent than originally envisaged, because not as much private investment has materialized as had been anticipated.

Top figures in the football world are getting nervous. "The World Cup is tomorrow, and the Brazilians are thinking it's the day after tomorrow," said Sepp Blatter, president of the Federation International de Football Association (FIFA), the international soccer governing body.[3]

Brazilian soccer legend Pele added that Brazil was "running a huge risk of embarrassing itself" by not being ready for the World Cup.[4]

As for the Olympics, "people do not realize yet what hosting the Games will entail," says Ernesto Araujo, minister counselor at the Brazilian Embassy in Washington. "It is good that the World Cup will come first, because there will be much more to organize with the Olympics."[5]

The Brazilian government expects to spend about $10 billion on World Cup-related improvements.[6] Hosting the event does not require as much construction as the Olympics because Brazil already has enough large soccer stadiums. But they will need to be upgraded. The tournament will be a homecoming, in a way, given that no country is more identified with football than Brazil, having won the cup five times and being the only country to have played in all 19 World Cup tournaments. Brazil hosted the Cup in 1950, when there were 13 participants.

Venues will be dispersed in 12 cities across the country, with the final to be hosted in Maracana Stadium in Rio de Janeiro. However, the project to replace the stadium's roof is already delayed by more than a year.

In choosing recent World Cup hosts, FIFA has favored the major emerging economies: South Africa hosted the 2010 edition and Russia will host the Cup in 2018.

The 2016 Summer Olympics in Rio, will involve at least 100,000 people, including 70,000 volunteers.[7] There will be 10,500 athletes from 205 nations competing in 28 Olympic sports. Rio won the competition to host the Olympics in October 2009, beating out Chicago, Madrid and Tokyo.

Brazil sees hosting the Olympics as a chance to restore Rio to its former glory, before the capital was moved inland to Brasília in 1960. As Carlos Arthur Nuzman, president of the Rio 2016 Organizing Committee, has said, "over these 50 years, too little was done, pretty much nothing. We will have a new Rio, a new Brazil."[8]

The biggest cost facing Brazil's government will be upgrading the nation's transportation infrastructure, which

early 1900s, predominantly from Europe. From 1920-1940, more than 200,000 Japanese immigrated to Brazil, mostly to work on coffee plantations, after the abolition of slavery created a labor shortage. Large urban centers sprang up, such as São Paulo, with a population that rose from 65,000 in 1890 to 350,000 by 1910. In

1932, Brazil and Uruguay became the first Latin American countries to grant women the unrestricted right to vote.[51]

Meanwhile, exploitation of the Amazon rain forest intensified when global demand for rubber surged, fueled by the rise of the automobile industry and the growing

is essential to allow athletes, officials, spectators and tourists to move easily between various venues. As expensive as this will be, Brazil will benefit from the improvements long after the tournaments' closing ceremonies.

As Nuzman has noted, "the state of Rio will improve two subway lines [that will] cross the mountains. The City Council will take care of setting up four bus lines with a high level of service. Finally, we must improve all airports." [9]

Not everyone is as optimistic about the benefits Brazil will derive from hosting the two events. "If Rio follows that pattern of most recent cities that have hosted the games," including Athens and Sydney, they will be "economic losers," said Allen Sanderson, senior economics lecturer at the University of Chicago and an authority on sports economics. The International Olympic Committee often makes cities spend more money than they ordinarily would, he explained, plus special interest groups — developers, contractors and government officials — often try "to get their hands on as much of that money as they can." [10]

And he warned of the danger of "the tail wagging the dog," whereby government decisions on infrastructure investments such as transport or urban development are driven by the games rather than longer-term strategic priorities.

The Brazilian Embassy's Araujo admits there is more at stake than Brazil's reputation as a major events organizer. The comparison on many people's minds will be between Rio in 2016 and the 2008 Summer Olympics in Beijing, hosted by another emerging global giant, China. The Beijing games were generally perceived as having been meticulously planned and executed.

"I think this is Brazil's chance to showcase itself as an open, creative and democratic society," Araujo says. "Our challenge is to show that we can be as well-organized as a more autocratic country like China."

— *Brian Beary*

Brazil plans to spend more than $1 trillion on infrastructure improvements before hosting the 2014 FIFA World Cup and 2016 Summer Olympics. But fewer than half of the proposed major projects are expected to be finished on time. Brasilia's Mane Garrincha stadium, above, is among the facilities under renovation.

[1] Brian Winter, "Brazil's Olympic push isn't winning any medals," Reuters, March 27, 2011, http://graphics.thomsonreuters.com/11/03/Brazil.pdf.

[2] *Ibid.*

[3] Robert Shaw, "Brazil's World Cup 2014 preparations hit by new blow as Maracana project is delayed by at least a year," *The Telegraph*, April 1, 2011, www.telegraph.co.uk/sport/football/teams/brazil/8420222/Brazils-World-Cup-2014-preparations-hit-by-new-blow-as-Maracana-project-is-delayed-by-at-least-a-year.html.

[4] *Ibid.*

[5] Comments made during panel discussion, "Brazil's World Cup and Olympic Hopes," School of Advanced International Studies, The Johns Hopkins University, Washington, D.C., April 25, 2011.

[6] Various news releases, Federation International de Football Association, www.fifa.com/worldcup/index.html.

[7] Organizing Committee for the Rio 2016 Olympic and Paralympic Games, www.rio2016.com.

[8] *Ibid.*

[9] *Ibid.*

[10] "Quarterly Knowledge Report," Vol. 1, Issue 2, Brazil Economic Team, World Bank, December 2009, http://home.uchicago.edu/~arsx/br/Quarterly.pdf.

need for tires. Brazil's rubber boom lasted from about 1890 until 1918. Thousands of poor people were lured into the Amazon to collect rubber, and often were subjected to slave-like conditions.

When other countries, notably British-run Ceylon (today's Sri Lanka) began developing their own rubber

industries, Brazil could not compete, and beginning in 1918 the Brazilian rubber industry collapsed. The former rubber workers who stayed on after the boom became known as *ribeirionhos* (riverside dwellers). They lived near the indigenous Amazonians, but the two communities remained largely distinct. The *ribeirionhos* spoke

AFP/Getty Images/Vanderlei Almeida

Traffic clogs São Paulo's main avenue on May 15, 2006. Brazil's roads, airports, and transportation systems urgently need revamping. The 15-mile road from downtown São Paulo to the airport is so traffic-clogged tourists are advised to leave the city center five hours before their departure in order to reach the airport in time. President Dilma Rousseff's government plans to spend $31 billion on roads, $72 billion on hydropower plants and $19 billion on a bullet train to connect Rio de Janeiro and São Paulo in the coming years as the country prepares to host the 2014 FIFA World Cup and 2016 Summer Olympics.

Portuguese, while the indigenous peoples had their own languages and hunter-gatherer lifestyles. [52]

On Brazil's political scene, opposition leader Getúlio Vargas seized power in 1930 in a bloodless coup. Four years later he pushed through a new constitution that effectively made him a dictator. While Vargas initially sympathized with Adolf Hitler's Nazi Germany, after World War II broke out his allegiances shifted, and on

Aug. 22, 1942, he declared war on Germany and Italy. Brazil sent 25,000 troops to Italy to fight on the side of the Allies; 2,000 of them were killed. [53] In 1945, Vargas was overthrown in a bloodless revolution. He was returned to power following a general election in 1950, but in 1954 he committed suicide while in office.

In the late 1950s, Brazil decided to move its political capital from Rio de Janeiro to Brasília, a modernistic, new city to be built 650 miles northwest of Rio de Janeiro. The move had been approved in the 1891 constitution as part of an effort to draw people from the coast to the interior. Construction of Brasília plunged Brazil into serious debt. On March 31, 1964, Brazil's left-leaning president, João Goulart, was ousted in a coup. Two decades of semi-authoritarian military rule followed.

By the 1960s, Brazil was considered a potentially rich country with untapped, abundant and diverse natural resources. The military government changed that perception by more aggressively developing the economy. For example, it began building roads into the Amazon, starting construction of the Trans-Amazonian Highway in 1970. [54] The road brought people into contact with indigenous Amazon peoples and sparked the widespread deforestation of the rain forest in subsequent decades. The government further contributed to deforestation in the 1970s through various tax incentives and subsidies to cattle ranchers and other businesses. [55]

Government policies aimed at encouraging farmers to move from the south to the *Cerrado* — the tropical savanna region in central Brazil — triggered large-scale migration.

"Environmentalists have accused soy producers and cattle ranchers of degrading the *Cerrado* and encroaching on the Amazon," noted *Christian Science Monitor* reporter Sara Miller Llana. On the other hand, opening the region for agriculture gave farmers new opportunities for economic advancement. For instance, farmer Paulo Roberto Bonato moved to the *Cerrado* in 1977 and eventually came to own a 6,000-hectare (15,000 acres) farm that produces soy, wheat and beans. "My father thought, if we stay in the south, my brothers and I will never have a chance to farm one day," Bonato said. [56]

By the early 1970s, in contrast to the economic stagnation in most of Latin America, Brazil was the fastest-growing economy in the Western Hemisphere, "a booming, headstrong nation that believed its moment in the sun had finally arrived."[57]

However, Brazil's political climate had been repressive since the 1964 coup, with thousands of people being illegally detained and tortured, provoking a surge in anti-government activity. As a guerrilla fighter in the early 1970s, President Rousseff was herself captured, tortured with electric shocks and imprisoned.[58]

But Brazil's government was not alone in perpetrating human-rights abuses against opponents. Many people in Argentina, Chile and Paraguay also were being "disappeared" — or murdered — by military regimes at the time. Indeed, Argentina had some 30,000 victims, compared with "only" about 400 in Brazil.[59]

Democracy and Drugs

Military rule in Brazil continued until 1985, when Brazil began a gradual transition to democracy. By 1995, Brazil's newly elected president, Fernando Henrique Cardoso, had taken office and begun to introduce urgently needed free market-oriented reforms. Excessive government spending had saddled Brazil with crippling inflation and debt. Cardoso's *Plano Real* (Real Plan) stabilized the currency by pegging it to the U.S. dollar. He also restructured banks to make them more stable and privatized many state-owned companies, such as aircraft manufacturer Embraer, to make them more profitable.[60]

In addition, Brazil began integrating with neighboring Argentina, Paraguay and Uruguay, primarily through creation of the Mercosur trading bloc in 1991.

On the environmental front, a watershed moment came in 1988 with the assassination of Chico Mendes, an environmental activist and rubber tapper who had fought to prevent deforestation.

"This became a huge story and changed the way Brazilians viewed deforestation," says the Environmental Defense Fund's Schwartzman. For the first time, they began to see it as "their issue." It would still take several years, however, before the country made concrete progress in reducing deforestation. Between 1970 and 2005, a forested area the size of France was destroyed in the Western Europe-size Amazon.[61]

The 1980s and '90s saw a spike in organized crime, including kidnapping, car theft and burglary, much of it linked to a dramatic increase in the use of cocaine in major urban centers. Drug gangs grew wealthy and powerful — in many cases becoming the de facto local authorities in slum neighborhoods. Turf wars between rival gangs were common. Many young people, lacking job opportunities, joined the gangs. The heavily armed groups turned Brazil into a major drug-trafficking route and caused widespread social problems, as powerfully seen in the 2003 film "City of God."[62]

Police corruption was another major problem, although some progress was made in the 1990s, especially with police reforms in São Paulo.[63] In 1992, Brazilian military police stormed the Carandiru prison to repress a riot, killing 111 inmates. In 1995, a new law made the Brazilian government responsible for crimes committed by its agents, enabling hundreds of families of the "disappeared" to receive financial compensation.[64]

The Lula Years

In October 2002 the election of Lula as president — with 60 percent of the vote — ushered in a new era. Before becoming president, Lula had been a prominent labor leader and an unsuccessful candidate in three previous presidential elections. Although he had leftist origins, Lula ruled more from the center-left and was a strong advocate of free trade.

The Lula years, from 2003-2010, were good for Brazil. The country developed a large trade surplus, enabling it to pay off the $3 billion it owed in foreign debt.[65]

"Lula kept in place the strong macro-economic policy framework he had inherited — the 2000 law on fiscal responsibility — and improved on it," according to de Saraiva of the Inter-American Development Bank. Thus, Lula did not run up government deficits, the state and federal governments cooperated on debt control and privatization of state-level banks led to a better-managed financial sector.

The country continued pursuing greater energy independence. Ethanol output doubled; by 2010 about half of all light vehicles in Brazil — and almost all new cars — had "flex-fuel" engines that enabled them to run on either gasoline or ethanol.[66] And Brazil saw its oil production levels double from roughly a million barrels a day in 1999 to 2 million by 2009.[67]

The 2008 global economic recession had a relatively minor impact on Brazil, despite the reduction in demand for commodities like beef and soybeans. "While Brazil also experienced a contraction in exports, it was accompanied

Poverty Persists

Shortages of affordable housing force millions of Brazilians into slums like Rio de Janeiro's famed City of God (top), featured in a 2003 film. At another Rio slum, Dona Marta, a wall prevents its expansion into a nearby forest (bottom). Some critics say the billions Brazil plans to spend hosting the Olympics and the FIFA World Cup would be better spent improving conditions in Brazil's slums.

by a strong expansion in private consumption and investment above pre-crisis trends," according to the Inter-American Development Bank. While the main drivers of economic growth from 2003-2007 had been exports, they are now consumption, investment and public spending.[68]

To achieve one of his top priorities — reducing poverty — Lula initiated two nationwide programs: *Fome Zero* (Zero Hunger), which gave money to the most needy, and *Bolsa Familia* (Family Fund), which paid low-income families to keep their children in school. The $60 to $70

monthly *Bolsa Familia* subsidy has been an effective income support program, particularly in rural areas, according to social scientist Schwartzman. However, the subsidy has not made much of a difference in urban areas because it is so low, he says, and it has not succeeded in keeping children in school, especially after age 13.

Education was another Lula priority. He tripled government spending on education and doubled the number of students in college. In addition, private universities were obliged to give some scholarships to poor or nonwhite families.[69]

On foreign policy, Lula's leftist origins led him to distance himself from the United States, creating some tensions in the relationship. For example, the United States and Brazil clashed over a constitutional crisis in Honduras in 2009, and again in 2010 when Washington did not appreciate a Turkey-Brazil initiative aimed at resolving the diplomatic standoff with Iran over the latter's nuclear program.[70]

Iran resurfaced in the 2010 presidential campaign when Lula's handpicked successor candidate, Rousseff, had to defend herself against accusations that her mentor Lula had been too close to dictatorships with poor human-rights records, such as Cuba and Iran.[71]

U.S.-Brazil relations were not all bleak, however. Following the 2010 earthquake in Haiti, Brazil cooperated well with the United States in the relief effort.

Lula's administration also made great strides in fighting criminal gangs. In the late 2000s, the Brazilian police implemented a new policy aimed at regaining control of urban areas, notably in Rio de Janeiro.

"We decided not to just arrest the leaders and seize weapons but to actually take back the territory they controlled and reinsert police officers into the community," says de Sa, the security official. "We placed local, young officers there to provide a positive role model for children who until then only had the rich drug traffickers to look up to."

In some areas, military armored cars had to be used to reclaim territory after physical barriers were erected to keep the police out. In November 2010 in Rio's Alemao slum, an operation ended with "euphoric troops waving Brazilian flags from a hilltop they had not controlled in years," according to Reuters. Brazilian newspapers published photos of neighborhood children "doing back-flips into a swimming pool . . . previously owned by a drug lord known as Polegar or 'Thumb,' as smiling troops with assault rifles looked on."[72]

When Lula stepped down due to term limits in December 2010, he had an unparalleled 80 percent approval rating. According to Perry Anderson, a history professor at the University of California, Los Angeles, Lula's success owed much to his exceptional personal gifts: "a mixture of warm social sensibility and cool political calculation."[73]

CURRENT SITUATION

Rousseff Era

Following yet another smooth transition of power, Brazil today is a vibrant and stable country, economically and politically.

Shortly after taking office on Jan. 1, 2011, President Rousseff replaced Lula's foreign Minister Celso Amorim, who had been closely associated with efforts to end Iran's international diplomatic isolation, with Antonio Patriota, a former Brazilian ambassador to the United States.

On domestic issues, Rousseff has sent strong signals that she is interested in investigating human-rights violations committed by the Brazilian military regime from 1964-85. President Lula had originally proposed setting up a truth commission to investigate the abuses, but his plan faltered.[74] Under a 1979 law, the regime's leaders were granted amnesty — justified at the time by the desire to promote reconciliation and a smooth transition to democracy. However, that amnesty is now being called into question, possibly because Rousseff herself was tortured by the regime.[75]

Rousseff also shows signs of being an interventionist on trade and economic issues. For example, she instructed the state-owned oil company Petrobras to increase ethanol production in order to stabilize prices, which had doubled

China Trade Skyrockets

The value of Brazil's imports and exports with China soared during the decade ending in 2010, topping $56 billion, more than 28 times the amount just a decade earlier. Brazil primarily ships commodities to China — notably food and iron ore — while China exports manufactured products to Brazil.

Value of Brazilian Trade With China, 2000 and 2010

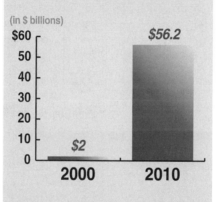

Source: Brazilian Ministry of Development, Industry and Commerce, 2011

in 2010 due in part to increasing domestic demand.

She inherited a strong economy, albeit one with some potential problems. According to the IADB's de Saraiva, public debt is rising, but at 47 percent of gross domestic product the amount is "manageable and relatively stable."

"She has done a good job so far at impressing her own personality on the presidency," says Sergio Fausto, executive director of the Fernando Henrique Cardoso Institute, a São Paulo-based think tank, and an expert on Brazilian politics. "The press is in a honeymoon period with her right now," he adds, in part because the media had grown more negative toward Lula by the end of his term, as accusations mounted that he tolerated corruption and did not support freedom of expression.

Evolving Global Relations

U.S.-Brazil relations, historically quite cordial, have remained generally good, despite some irritants. For example, both sides resent recent protectionist measures taken by one another to promote their domestic biofuels industries. Brazil imposed a tariff on U.S. corn-based ethanol, while the U.S. has imposed a duty — currently 54 cents a gallon — on Brazilian sugar-based ethanol. The EU has imposed a similar tariff of 19 euro-cents per liter on Brazilian ethanol. The United States and Europe are Brazil's No. 1 and 2 markets, respectively, for ethanol exports.

However, sugarcane industry executive Leão notes that the ethanol export market has not expanded much since 2008, partly because domestic demand in Brazil has grown. "We are in a period of consolidation of our industry," he says, with large multinationals like Shell and BP buying up blending facilities to create greater economies of scale.

Indeed, domestic demand has increased so much that Brazil is actually importing corn ethanol from the United States.[76]

In March 2011, Brazil signed "open skies" agreements with both the EU and United States, which aim to open their aviation markets to more cross-border competition.[77] And an upcoming decision by Rousseff could have consequences for Brazil's foreign relations. She is to decide on a lucrative order for fighter planes between the U.S. manufacturer Boeing and France's Rafale.

Although Brazil may be seeking military hardware from U.S. and EU suppliers, its top trading partners today increasingly are the developing and emerging markets in Latin America, Africa and Asia. For example, while Brazil's exports to Russia, India and China accounted for 9 percent of its 2006 exports, that share had nearly doubled by 2009, to 17 percent.[78]

In April 2011, Rousseff visited China on a trade-oriented visit, her first trip outside the Americas as president.[79] China overtook the United States in 2009 as Brazil's largest trade partner and is an increasingly important investment partner. For instance, Petrobras sought a new loan from the Chinese Development Bank, having already borrowed $10 billion from it in 2009. The loan was granted on the condition that Brazil ship oil to China for the next 10 years.[80] Overall, Petrobras needs $224 billion in investments through 2014.

According to the Brazil Institute's Sotero, China is also interested in acquiring Brazilian farmlands to help secure its food supply. "The Brazilian government is looking into the legal rights for foreigners to buy land in Brazil. When U.S. farmers came before, it was not such a big issue, but the debate around China is more sensitive."[81]

Brazil also is investing more overseas, especially in developing countries, where its foreign aid budget continues to rise. "We are encountering Brazil in new places and on new themes — from combating AIDS in Mozambique to promoting democracy in Africa to dealing with Iran's nuclear program," notes U.S. Ambassador Shannon. As a result, advanced economies like the United States are rethinking the kind of relationship they have with Brazil, viewing it more as a development aid partner than a recipient of aid.

Brazil is stepping up its campaign to become a permanent member of the U.N. Security Council. The United States — one of the five existing permanent members — welcomes Brazil's efforts to play a more active role on global security, but it has not yet thrown its support behind this particular campaign.

When President Obama visited Brazil in March 2011, he spoke only in general terms of backing "reforms that make the U.N. Security Council more effective, more efficient, more representative." President Rousseff, standing alongside Obama, stressed how Brazil had "a commitment with peace, democracy and . . . consensus building," and that "tolerance, dialogue [and] flexibility" were key components of the Brazilian mindset.

But former Ambassador Barbosa believes the Brazilian U.N. push is premature. "It is not useful for our government to be campaigning for this right now, because the United States and China are opposed to adding us to the Security Council," he maintains, noting that once the two permanent council members change their minds, "we will be added automatically." If this happens, Barbosa predicts, "Brazil will be a moderator, not a fighter on the Security Council. We will employ soft power, not hard power."

Fighting Crime, Poverty

Brazil's new Police Pacification Units seem to be working well. "Local people are now willing to talk to us," says security official Antonio de Sa. "Women are embracing our cause — we use women to command a lot of our units. When we pacify an area, we hoist the Brazilian flag to show that we have taken the territory back, not for the state, but for the citizens."

So far there are 3,000 units, but the goal is to have 12,500 by 2014, covering 1.2 million people. Some of the units will be assigned to Rio de Janeiro's largest slum, Rocinha, which has 120,000 residents. But while organized crime has been reduced in large cities like Rio and São Paulo, crime is on the upswing in the northern and eastern parts of the country, says social scientist Schwartzman. São Paulo has seen a dramatic improvement in the Paraisopolis (Paradise City) slum. Whereas a famous photograph from 2005 showed corrugated-iron roofs and sewerless streets, today roads are being paved, sewers constructed, drinking water piped in and chic social housing and community parks built. "What is going on in Paraisopolis is emblematic of the changes taking place all over Brazil right now, with an emerging middle class transforming the country's economy — and arguably its

Should Brazil become a permanent Security Council member?

YES
Carlos Eduardo Lins da Silva
Editor, Política Externa São Paulo, Brazil

Written for *CQ Global Researcher,* June 2011

Secretary of State Cordell Hull wrote in his autobiography that President Franklin D. Roosevelt argued in 1944 — during discussions with his World War II allies about the makeup of the future U.N. Security Council — that Brazil should hold one of the permanent seats on the council.

According to Hull, Brazil's size, population, growth potential, involvement in Europe battlefields and the solid help it provided the United Nations in its initial stages fully justified the claim. But opposition by Great Britain and the Soviet Union prevailed, and Brazil was not named a permanent member.

There are more reasons now than there were 67 years ago for Brazil to be among the countries chosen to be included in the Security Council when it is enlarged. Brazil has the world's seventh-largest economy, its GDP per capita is much larger than China's, its position as a regional leader is indisputable and has often been used to avoid conflicts among neighboring South American countries.

For 141 years Brazil has had an outstanding record of peaceful relations with all nine of its border neighbors, has been an important participant in many multilateral forums (such as the World Trade Organization and the G-20), has a constitutional commitment against nuclear arms and is not plagued by religious, ethnic, cultural or political divisions.

Living under a strong democratic regime since 1985, Brazil is confident about its future. It has huge oil reserves, is a leader in biofuels production and in the next 24 years will enjoy the "demographic bonus" — reduced birth rates and expansion of those in the so-called productive bracket (15- to 64-year-olds).

In the last 25 years, Brazil served five times as a rotating member of the Security Council. In the 18 years before Brazil's military dictatorship (1946-1964), it had served on the council three times. Even with its absence from 1964 to 1985, Brazil is among the countries that have been at the council most often — a clear signal of its right to demand a permanent seat there.

In its willingness to further global peace Brazil has sent troops, police forces and civilian personnel to 30 U.N. peacekeeping missions, from the Suez Canal crisis of 1956 until, more recently, the troubles in Haiti and Lebanon.

NO
Ray Walser
Senior Policy Analyst Heritage Foundation

Written for *CQ Global Researcher,* June 2011

Brazil's growing role in international affairs has been impressive, but is she ready yet to play a constructive role if given a permanent seat on the United Nations Security Council? Is Brazil a stable stakeholder in the international system or a builder of coalitions opposed to the United States and the West? And will greater inclusion strengthen the council's ability to preserve international security — or do precisely the opposite?

With one of the world's 10-largest economies and a population of more than 200 million, Brazil carries economic and demographic weight. She has already earned a seat at the international economic table via the G-20. Yet, when it comes to high-stakes international politics, Brazil's progress is less apparent. Brazil's friendship with Castro's Cuba, its abstention in the U.N. on North Korean human rights — and especially its recent enthusiasm for Mahmoud Ahmadinejad's Iran — gives the impression Brazil's democratic convictions do not export well. The joint Brazilian-Turkey nuclear deal of 2010, coupled with Brazil's no vote on U.N. sanctions on Iran, has dampened U.S. enthusiasm for Brazil as a global player. Siding with a terrorist-sponsoring nation does not win real acclaim.

Some assume that expanding the Security Council to include Brazil and others will make the council a more decisive source of authoritative and legitimate responses to threats to international peace. The opposite is likely to occur. Adding additional permanent members will make it harder to achieve swift, effective responses. Friction and gridlock will be more likely. Giving new members the veto power is an even worse idea.

Adding Brazil would dilute U.S. influence on the council and likely foster hostility on many issues the U.S. values. According to the State Department, Brazil voted the same way as the United States last year only a third of the time on key General Assembly votes. This number would not likely improve once Brazil gained permanent admittance to the council.

Yes, expanding the Security Council to include Brazil and others will make the body more representative. But is Brazil inherently more entitled to a seat than Mexico? Will Brazil significantly raise its current 1.6 percent contribution to the U.N. budget?

For now Brazil has ample scope to exercise its influence through regional and global coalitions. A Security Council seat for Brazil now is a bridge too far.

identity," according to Alex Aldridge, a reporter for a British online legal magazine.[82]

Brazil's poverty-reduction policies also have borne fruit. Its extreme poverty rate is at 7 percent, down from 23 percent in 1990 and well below the Latin American average of 13 percent. Neighboring Colombia's rate is 16.5 percent, Mexico's is 11.2 percent and socialist Venezuela has a 9.9 percent rate. Chile's poverty rate of 3.6 percent, however, is half of Brazil's.[83] The minimum wage, which Lula had increased by 60 percent in real terms during his tenure, remains a controversial poverty-reduction policy. In February 2011, President Rousseff limited increases in the minimum wage — currently about $300 month — to about the rate of inflation, scoring a victory against the trade unions and some members of her own coalition. With inflation currently running at 6 percent, Rousseff is worried about overheating the economy.[84]

Schwartzman says regular increases in the minimum wage help to reduce income inequality and shrink the size of the informal (or "black market") economy, which includes street sellers, domestic workers and small shops.

"The informal sector's share of the economy has declined to about 45 percent, so more people are paying taxes," he says. However, he notes, the middle classes are being squeezed, since they tend to pay for private schooling and health care, which is becoming more expensive. The poor, on the other hand, rely more on public education and health care services. A World Bank report concludes that informal-sector wages have risen due to the minimum wage, while staying fairly stable in the formal sector. "The more educated the worker, the less [he] has benefited from the growth in real wages over the last eight years," the report found.[85]

Raising educational expenditures has had mixed results. For example, an Inter-American Development Bank (IADB) study on infant education in six large cities concluded that it was "far from complying with the country's National Parameters for Quality."[86] However, the World Bank report focusing on high-school learning levels found that "few countries have made faster or more sustained progress." It added that "major performance gaps with middle-income countries . . . are closing, such as primary school completion and pre-school coverage."[87]

Despite Brazil's progress on other fronts, its scorecard in one area is distinctly unimpressive: The country's infrastructure urgently needs revamping. The government is rolling out an ambitious infrastructure improvement program, which includes plans to spend $72 billion on hydropower plants, $31 billion on roads and $19 billion on a bullet train to connect Rio de Janeiro and São Paulo.[88] The road from downtown São Paulo to the airport is so traffic-clogged tourists are advised to leave the city center five hours before their departure time for the 15-mile journey. Business travelers rank the terminal as the worst of 26 major airports in Latin America; it is scheduled for replacement in 2014, but that deadline is unlikely to be met.

To implement these ambitious projects, Brazil must attract greater levels of private financing, according to the IADB's de Saraiva. "The tax burden is already high, so it will be harder to raise more public money through increasing taxes," he says. "So far, private capital is not being mobilized enough." The IADB is working with the Brazilian government to address the problem.

After the unexpected spike in deforestation was revealed in May 2011, Brazil's government vowed to clamp down on illegal logging. But if parliament decides to relax the forestry code, President Rousseff must decide whether to allow further agricultural development in rain forest areas or veto a bill that many say would cause even more deforestation.[89]

OUTLOOK

In Lula's Shadow

Observers are debating whether President Rousseff will continue down the path laid out by Lula. Her leadership style is different: She is less charismatic, more low-key and seems more detail-oriented. Whereas Lula looked his most comfortable in factory overalls and mingling with workers, Rousseff looks more at home at global summits.

She outlined her vision at a March 2011 press conference when she said: "My essential commitment is building a middle-class income society, assuring vocational and professional opportunities for the workers and for our immense youth population."[90]

Her immediate challenges include reforming Brazil's over-burdensome tax code and introducing greater budget transparency. On trade, she is expected to try to eliminate trade barriers on commodities and key

Brazilian products such as ethanol, beef, cotton, orange juice and airplanes.

On foreign policy, she is likely to strike a different balance. Lula, while not especially anti-U.S. personally, made a point of being close with leaders who were, such as Venezuela's Hugo Chávez, Cuba's Fidel Castro and Iran's Mahmoud Ahmadinejad. Rousseff appears to be aiming to distance herself from the Iranian regime. She has already said she disagrees with Brazil's previous decision to abstain on U.N. votes about Iran's human-rights record. However, according to social scientist Schwartzman of the Institute for Studies on Labor and Society, "she is very pragmatic so she is not going to become too pro-U.S. either."

Brazil's performance in hosting three huge international events may shape views about how advanced the country is: Aside from the FIFA World Cup and Olympics, Brazil will host the Rio Plus 20 global environmental summit in 2012. The rest of the world will be especially interested in how well Brazil upgrades its infrastructure, which it has pledged to do as part of hosting the three events.

Another question on Brazil's horizon is whether it will revisit a dark chapter in its history: human-rights abuses committed under Brazil's military regime. According to Lula's former human-rights minister, Paulo de Tarso Vannucchi, the debate now revolves around whether to create just a "truth" commission, which would reveal what happened, or a "truth and justice" commission, which would prosecute former officials.[91]

"Personally I favor a truth and justice commission," Vannucchi says. "But that does not mean all people who committed torture will have to be thrown in prison. You could also have some form of restorative justice." So far, Brazil's Supreme Court is upholding the 1979 law granting amnesty for former officials, even though it was enacted under a military dictatorship.

Political analyst Fausto, of the Fernando Henrique Cardoso Institute, predicts Rousseff will be "very committed to upholding freedom of expression and could revise the previous administration's plans to regulate the media." She also will be "less complacent than Lula on corruption in public office," he says. For example, she probably won't continue to give unqualified political backers top jobs in state-owned companies. While the press will welcome this shift, Fausto says, it could weaken her political support and make her more reliant on Brazil performing well economically to stay in power. Meanwhile, Fausto says, Lula will remain an important political actor and could even stand for office again, because the constitution only prohibits a president from serving more than two consecutive terms.

Environmentally, the government will need to develop better economic incentives to discourage people living in the Amazon basin from taking part in activities that lead to deforestation. In addition to Norway, other countries probably will continue to help, and Brazil could become integrated into a global emissions-trading system to cut greenhouse gas emissions such as the one developed by the EU.[92]

Brazil undoubtedly will soon tap into its offshore oil reserves, increasing the risks that the country could become over-reliant on oil revenues or that a catastrophic accident would wreak havoc on the ecosystem. Oil wealth also could cause corruption and bad governance. Shannon K. O'Neill, a fellow at the New York-based Council on Foreign Relations think tank, believes Brazil "has a better chance than most to achieve the vaunted Norwegian model of oil exploitation, and avoid the pitfalls of the Middle East (or closer to home, Venezuela)."[93] In particular, Brazil is lucky to have many other natural resources, reducing the likelihood of oil becoming more of a curse than a blessing.

The big question remains: Can Brazil sustain its economic prosperity and stability in the coming years, or will its growth spurt be temporary?

"There are a lot of reasons to be optimistic about Brazil at the moment," says Charles Johnson, head of the São Paulo office of Chadbourne & Parke, a U.S.-based law firm. "The fundamentals are incredibly strong."

If his prognosis is correct, Brazil will finally render obsolete the old joke: "Brazil is the country of the future — and it always will be."[94]

NOTES

1. Mauro Viero, Brazilian Ambassador to the United States. Comments made at Wilson Center for International Scholars, Washington, D.C., Feb. 28, 2011, during discussion entitled "Prospects for Brazilian-America Relations on the Eve of President Obama's Visit to Brazil."

2. See John Paul Rathbone, "South America's giant comes of age," *Financial Times*, June 28 2010, www.ft.com/cms/s/0/d74d02b6-7d14-11df-8845-00144feabdc0,dwp_uuid=1ab2a3bc-7d38-11df-8845-00144feabdc0.html#axzz1HWckVicv.

3. Brian Winter and Brian Ellsworth, "Brazil and China: A young marriage on the rocks," Reuters, March 1, 2011, http://gulftoday.ae/portal/0f8bce92-92db-4a8a-b4aa-b74c5852eb25.aspx.

4. "Exports of agricultural products of selected economies, 1990-2009," International Trade Statistics 2010, Table II.16, World Trade Organization.

5. *The World Factbook*, CIA.

6. *Ibid.*

7. For background information, see Eliza Barclay, "Crime in Latin America," *CQ Global Researcher*, Sept. 1, 2010, pp. 211-234.

8. Telephone interview, April 11, 2011, with Eduardo Leão, Executive Director of UNICA, Brazilian Sugarcane Industry Association.

9. "Ethanol's Mid-life Crisis," *The Economist*, Sept. 4, 2010, www.economist.com/node/16952914.

10. Comments made at conference "Brazil and Africa: Co-operation for Innovation in Agriculture and What the U.S. Can Do," at U.S. House of Representatives, organized by Woodrow Wilson International Center for Scholars — Brazil Institute, May 16, 2011.

11. Joe Leahy, "Brazil: Platform for growth," *Financial Times*, March 15, 2011, www.ft.com/cms/s/0/fa11320c-4f48-11e0-9038-00144feab49a.html#axzz1HWckVicv.

12. See "Brazil's Foreign Aid Program," *The Economist*, July 15, 2010, www.economist.com/node/16592455/.

13. "Brazil and Africa: Co-operation for Innovation in Agriculture and What the U.S. Can Do," *op. cit.*

14. "Country Profiles & International Human Development Indicators," U.N. Development Programme —The Human Development Indicator ranking combines life expectancy, education and income levels. China is ranked in 89th place, India in 119th.

15. "Social panorama of Latin America, 2010," Table 1, p. 13, Economic Commission for Latin America and the Caribbean, www.eclac.org/publicaciones/xml/1/41801/PSI-socialpanorama2010.pdf.

16. U.N. Population Division online database.

17. Paulo Sotero, "Brazil's Dilma Rousseff faces tough presidential task," BBC News, Jan. 1, 2011, www.bbc.co.uk/news/world-latin-america-11961817.

18. "Corruption Perceptions Index 2010," Transparency International, www.transparency.org/policy_research/surveys_indices/cpi/2010/results.

19. Brian Winter, "Brazil's Olympic push isn't winning any medals," Reuters, March 27, 2011, http://graphics.thomsonreuters.com/11/03/Brazil.pdf.

20. Steve Schwartzman, director of tropical forest policy, Environmental Defense Fund, interview, April 6, 2011.

21. John Lyons, "Brazil Moves to Loosen Amazon-Logging Rules," *The Wall Street Journal*, May 26, 2011, http://online.wsj.com/article/SB10001424052702303654804576345293965158546.html.

22. Roberto Alzir, Brazilian superintendent for operational planning in the State Secretariat of Security. Comments made at seminar entitled "A New Approach to Citizen Security in Brazil — Rio's Pacifying Police Units," Woodrow Wilson International Center for Scholars, Brazil Institute, March 16, 2011. For background, see Barclay, *op. cit.*

23. Juliet Macur, "Rio Wins 2016 Olympics in a First for South America," *The New York Times*, Oct. 9, 2009, www.nytimes.com/2009/10/03/sports/03olympics.html.

24. "Ethanol's Mid-life Crisis," *op. cit.*

25. Sara Miller Llana, "Farming superpower Brazil spreads its know-how," *The Christian Science Monitor*, Nov. 12, 2008, www.csmonitor.com/World/Americas/2008/1112/p01s01-woam.html.

26. "Brazil and Africa: Co-operation for Innovation in Agriculture and What the U.S. Can Do," *op. cit.*

27. Llana, *op. cit.*

28. Paulo Sotero, "Brazil and China: no cause for alarm bells," *FT Brazil Confidential*, April 12, 2011.

29. *Ibid.*

30. "Leading Exporters and Importers of manufactures, 2009," International Trade Statistics 2010, Table II.31, World Trade Organization.

31. Winter and Ellsworth, *op. cit.*

32. Martin Ravallion, "A Comparative Perspective on Poverty Reduction in Brazil, India and China," World Bank, October 2009, Table 1, p. 31. Figures refer to the percentage of the population living on less than $1.25 per day at 2005 Purchasing Power Parity, www-wds.worldbank.org/external/default/WDSContentServer/IW3P/IB/2009/11/30/000158349_20091130085835/Rendered/PDF/WPS5080.pdf.

33. Mauro Viera, Brazilian Ambassador to the United States, comments made at Feb. 28, 2011, discussion at the Woodrow Wilson Center for International Scholars, *op. cit.*

34. Eduardo Lora, Andrew Powell and Pilar Tavella, "How Will the Food Price Shock Affect Inflation in Latin America and the Caribbean," Inter-American Development Bank, April 2011, http://idbdocs.iadb.org/wsdocs/getdocument.aspx?docnum=36144620.

35. "Rain Forest — Incubator of Human Life," National Geographic, http://environment.nationalgeographic.com/environment/habitats/rain-forest-profile.

36. "Brazil — Country Note on Climate Change Aspects in Agriculture," World Bank, December 2009, http://siteresources.worldbank.org/INTLAC/Resources/Climate_BrazilWeb.pdf.

37. See Doug Struck, "Disappearing Forests," *CQ Global Researcher*, Vol. 5. No. 2, Jan. 18, 2011.

38. Fiona Harvey, "The long road to rain forest conservation," *Financial Times*, June 28 2010, www.ft.com/cms/s/0/9195323a-7d13-11df-8845-00144feabdc0,dwp_uuid=1ab2a3bc-7d38-11df-8845-00144feabdc0.html#axzz1HWckVicv.

39. Tom Phillips, "Brazil forms 'crisis cabinet' following unexpected deforestation surge," *The Guardian*, May 20, 2011, www.guardian.co.uk/environment/2011/may/20/brazil-crisis-cabinet-amazon-deforestation.

40. *Ibid.*

41. *Ibid.*

42. Comments made at Feb. 28, 2011 discussion at the Woodrow Wilson Center for International Scholars, *op. cit.*

43. "Policy, not altruism; Brazil and peacekeeping," *The Economist*, Sept. 25, 2010, www.economist.com/node/17095626.

44. "Brazil's Foreign Aid Program," *op. cit.*

45. Perry Anderson, "Lula's Brazil," *London Review of Books*, March 31, 2001, www.lrb.co.uk/v33/n07/perry-anderson/lulas-brazil.

46. Comments from Feb. 28, 2011, discussion "Prospects for Brazilian-America Relations on the Eve of President Obama's Visit to Brazil," *op. cit.*

47. Stockholm International Peace Research Institute, SIPRI Military Expenditure Database, 2009 figures, in constant $US. Database accessed May 27, 2011.

48. For background, see David Masci, "Trouble in South America," *CQ Researcher*, March 14, 2003, pp. 225-248.

49. For background, see "Brazil in Ferment," Richard L. Worsnop, *Editorial Research Reports*, Jan. 15, 1962, available at *CQ Researcher Plus Archive.*

50. For background, see Roland Flamini, "The New Latin America," *CQ Global Researcher*, March 1, 2008, pp. 57-84.

51. "World Chronology of the Recognition of Women's Rights to Vote and to Stand for Election," Inter-Parliamentary Union, www.ipu.org/wmn-e/suffrage.htm.

52. Interview with Steve Schwartzman, Environmental Defense Fund, April 6, 2011.

53. Luis Bitencourt, Dean of Academic Affairs, National Defense University, a former Brazilian government official (1974-99). Comments made at Feb. 28, 2011, discussion at the Wilson Center for International Scholars, *op. cit.*

54. "The World: Transamazonia: The Last Frontier," *Time*, Sept. 13, 1971, www.time.com/time/magazine/article/0,9171,903114-1,00.html.

55. Philip Fearnside, "Deforestation in Brazilian Amazonia: History, Rates, and Consequences,"

Conservation Biology, June, 2005, p. 680, http://philip.inpa.gov.br/publ_livres/Preprints/2005/Cons percent 20Biol-Amazon percent 20deforestation percent 20-percent 20FINAL.pdf.

56. Llana, *op. cit.*

57. For background, see R. C. Schroeder, "Brazil: Awakening Giant," *Editorial Research Reports*, April 12, 1972, available at *CQ Researcher Plus Archive.*

58. Robin Yapp, "Former army captain accused of torturing Brazil's president-elect Dilma Rousseff," *The Telegraph*, Nov. 5, 2010, www.telegraph.co.uk/news/worldnews/southamerica/brazil/8113894/Former-army-captain-accused-of-torturing-Brazils-president-elect-Dilma-Rousseff.html.

59. Remarks made by Sergio Fausto, executive director of the Instituto Fernando Henrique Cardoso, during discussion entitled "Brazil's Truth Commission," Woodrow Wilson International Center for Scholars, March 22, 2011.

60. Alex Aldridge, "Tomorrow's country today," *Legal Week*, Sept. 23, 2010, www.legalweek.com/legal-week/analysis/1734747/latin-america-tomorrows-country.

61. Fearnside, *op. cit.*

62. Antonio Roberto Cesario de Sa, Undersecretary for Planning and Operational Integration, speaking at seminar entitled "A New Approach to Citizen Security in Brazil — Rio's Pacifying Police Units," Woodrow Wilson International Center for Scholars, March 16, 2011.

63. Barclay, *op. cit.*, p. 9.

64. Comments made by Paulo de Tarso Vannucchi, during discussion entitled "Brazil's Truth Commission," Woodrow Wilson International Center for Scholars, March 22, 2011.

65. Flamini, *op. cit.*

66. "Ethanol's Mid-life Crisis," *op. cit.*

67. "BP Statistical Review of World Energy 2010," June 2010, www.bp.com/liveassets/bp_internet/globalbp/globalbp_uk_english/reports_and_publications/statistical_energy_review_2008/STAGING/local_assets/2010_downloads/statistical_review_of_world_energy_full_report_2010.pdf.

68. Alejandro Izquierdo and Ernesto Talvi, "One Region, Two Speeds? Challenges of the New Economic Order for Latin America and the Caribbean," Inter-American Development Bank, March 2011, www.iadb.org/en/research-and-data/publication-details,3169.html?pub_id=IDB-MG-109.

69. Perry Anderson, "Lula's Brazil," *London Review of Books*, March 31, 2001, www.lrb.co.uk/v33/n07/perry-anderson/lulas-brazil.

70. See Fred Kaplan, "Are Brazil and Iran Delusional or Deceptive," *Slate.com*, June 11, 2010, www.slate.com/id/2256762/.

71. Brian Winter, "Brazil's surprise election issue: Iran," Reuters, Aug. 12, 2010, http://af.reuters.com/article/worldNews/idAFTRE67B4IN20100812?pageNumber=1&virtualBrandChannel=0.

72. Brian Winter, "Analysis: Rio raids a critical step for Brazil's economy," Reuters, Nov. 29, 2010, www.reuters.com/article/2010/11/29/us-brazil-violence-idUSTRE6AS3M820101129.

73. Anderson, *op. cit.*

74. For background, see Jina Moore, "Truth Commissions," *CQ Global Researcher*, Jan. 1, 2010, pp. 1-24.

75. Discussion entitled "Brazil's Truth Commission," *op. cit.*

76. Paulo Sotero, comments made at conference "Brazil and Africa: Co-operation for Innovation in Agriculture and What the U.S. Can Do," *op. cit.*

77. Isabelle Smets, "Open Sky-type agreement initialed," *Europolitics*, March 18, 2011; "Strengthening the U.S.-Brazil Economic Relationship," White House, March 19, 2011, www.whitehouse.gov/sites/default/files/uploads/Strengthening_the_US-Brazil_Economic_Relationship.pdf.

78. Izquierdo and Talvi, *op. cit.*

79. Sotero, "Brazil and China: no cause for alarm bells," *op. cit.*

80. Andre Soliani and Michael Forsythe, "Petrobras May Seek China Development Bank Loan After Borrowing $10 Billion" Bloomberg News, April 14, 2011, www.bloomberg.com/news/2011-04-14/

petrobras-in-talks-for-new-loan-from-china-development-bank.html.

81. "Brazil and Africa: Co-operation for Innovation in Agriculture and What the U.S. Can Do," *op. cit.*

82. Aldridge, *op. cit.*

83. "Social panorama of Latin America, 2010," Table 1, Economic Commission for Latin America and the Caribbean, p. 13, www.eclac.org/publicaciones/xml/1/41801/PSI-socialpanorama2010.pdf.

84. "Brazil's fiscal policy: How tough will Dilma be?" *The Economist*, Feb. 17, 2011, www.economist.com/node/18178315.

85. "Brazil Quarterly Knowledge Report," World Bank, April 2011, http://siteresources.worldbank.org/BRAZILEXTN/Resources/322340-1303821749326/Quarterly_Knowledge_Report_1Q_2011.pdf.

86. Aimee Verdisco and Marcelo Perez Alfaro, "Measuring Education Quality in Brazil," Inter-American Development Bank, December 2010, http://idbdocs.iadb.org/wsdocs/getdocument.aspx?docnum=35519645.

87. "Brazil Quarterly Knowledge Report," *op. cit.*

88. Brian Winter, "Brazil's Olympic push isn't winning any medals," *op. cit.*

89. Paulo Adario, "Brazil risks protection record by proposing changes to forest code," *The Guardian*, May 27, 2011, www.guardian.co.uk/environment/2011/may/27/brazil-forest-protection-code.

90. "Remarks by President Obama and President Rousseff of Brazil in Brasília, Brazil," White House Press Office, March 19, 2011, http://m.whitehouse.gov/the-press-office/2011/03/19/remarks-president-obama-and-president-rousseff-brazil-brasilia-brazil.

91. Comments made at discussion entitled "Brazil's Truth Commission," *op. cit.*

92. For background, see Jennifer Weeks, "Carbon Trading," *CQ Global Researcher*, Nov. 1, 2008, pp. 295-320.

93. Shannon K. O'Neill, "Will Brazil Face the Energy Curse," Council on Foreign Relations, March 25, 2011, http://blogs.cfr.org/oneil/2011/03/25/will-brazil-face-the-energy-curse.

94. Aldridge, "Tomorrow's country today," *op. cit.*

BIBLIOGRAPHY

Books

Brainard, Lael, and Leonard Martinez-Diaz, eds., *Brazil as an Economic Superpower? Understanding Brazil's Changing Role in the Global Economy*, Brookings Institution Press, 2009.
Scholars and policymakers from Brazil, Europe and the United States examine the present state and likely future of Brazil's economy, with a focus on agribusiness, energy, trade, social investment and multinational corporations.

Reel, Monte, *The Last of the Tribe: The Epic Quest to Save a Lone Man in the Amazon*, Scribner, 2010.
The South American correspondent for The Washington Post describes the ongoing struggle on the Brazilian frontier between indigenous peoples and land-hungry settlers.

Roett, Riordan, *The New Brazil*, Brookings Institution Press, 2010.
A Johns Hopkins University professor of international relations recounts how Brazil has evolved from a remote Portuguese colony into a regional leader, a respected representative for the developing world and an important partner for the United States and the European Union.

Articles

Anderson, Perry, "Lula's Brazil," *London Review of Books*, Vol. 33, No. 7, March 31, 2011, www.lrb.co.uk/v33/n07/perry-anderson/lulas-brazil.
A profile of the man often described as Brazil's most successful and popular President, Luiz Inácio Lula da Silva, charts his origins as a leftist agitator, his enduring appeal and his policies on issues ranging from trade to poverty reduction to Iran.

Chernela, Janet, "The Politics of Mediation: Local-Global Interactions in the Central Amazon of Brazil," *American Anthropologist*, 2006.
A professor of anthropology at the University of Maryland assesses the international community's success in assisting Amazon peoples, focusing on the effort to preserve an endangered fisheries sector in one particular Amazon community.

Rathbone, John Paul, "South America's giant comes of age," *Financial Times,* **June 28 2010, www.ft.com/ cms/s/0/d74d02b6-7d14-11df-8845-00144feabdc0, dwp_uuid=1ab2a3bc-7d38-11df-8845-00144fe-abdc0.html#axzz1HWckVicv.**
The writer recounts Brazil's remarkable economic and political development since the 1980s and lists the remaining challenges it faces, such as the country's urgent need to improve its transportation infrastructure.

Sotero, Paulo, "Obama's Brazil visit: Fresh start for ties?" *BBC News,* **March 17, 2011, www.bbc.co.uk/ news/world-latin-america-12731912.**
U.S. President Barack Obama's March 2011 visit to Brazil is a sign of how far Brazil has advanced on the global stage.

Winter, Brian, "Brazil's Olympic push isn't winning any medals," *Reuters,* **March 27, 2011, http://graph-ics.thomsonreuters.com/11/03/Brazil.pdf.**
Reuters' São Paulo correspondent explains how Brazil's good intentions to revamp its infrastructure in time for the 2014 FIFA World Cup and 2016 Olympics are running into bureaucratic problems.

Reports and Studies

"Brazil — Country Note on Climate Change Aspects in Agriculture," *World Bank,* **December 2009, http:// siteresources.worldbank.org/INTLAC/Resources/ Climate_BrazilWeb.pdf.**
The report summarizes policy developments that relate to climate change and agriculture in Brazil.

"Brazil Quarterly Knowledge Report," *World Bank,* **April 2011, http://siteresources.worldbank.org/ BRAZILEXTN/Resources/322340-1303821749326/ Quarterly_Knowledge_Report_1Q_2011.pdf.**
A report describes how Brazilians can fix their developmental problems, export and adapt their solutions and upgrade their analytical capacity.

Alston, Lee J., Bernardo Mueller, Marcus Andre Melo and Carlos Pereira, "The Political Economy of Productivity in Brazil," *Inter-American Development Bank,* **March 2010, http://idbdocs.iadb.org/wsdocs/ getdocument.aspx?docnum=35114456.**
A lengthy report explores the link between Brazil's political institutions and its growth and productivity in recent decades.

Ravallion, Martin, "A Comparative Perspective on Poverty Reduction in Brazil, India and China," *World Bank,* **October 2009, www-wds.worldbank. org/external/default/WDSContentServer/IW3P/IB/2 009/11/30/000158349_20091130085835/Rendered/ PDF/WPS5080.pdf.**
The report compares the performances of Brazil, India and China in reducing poverty and income inequality.

Verdisco, Aimee, and Marcelo Pérez Alfaro, "Measuring Education Quality in Brazil," *Inter-American Development Bank,* **December 2010, http://idbdocs. iadb.org/wsdocs/getdocument.aspx?docnum= 35519645.**
Much remains to be done to improve the quality of early childhood education in Brazil.

For More Information

The Brazil Institute, Woodrow Wilson International Center of Scholars, Ronald Reagan Bldg., One Woodrow Wilson Plaza, 1300 Pennsylvania Ave., N.W., Washington, DC 20004-3027; (202) 691-4030; www.wilsoncenter.org. The only country-specific institute in Washington dedicated to Brazil. Hosts the Brazil Portal news aggregator: http://brazilportal.wordpress.com.

BrazilWorks, www.brazilworks.org. A website offering information and analysis about Brazil.

Fernand Braudel School of Economics, Ceará, 2, CEP 01243-010, São Paulo, Brazil; 55 (11) 3824-9633; http://en.braudel.org.br. An educational enterprise that seeks to overcome institutional problems that impede human development in Latin America.

FINEP, The Brazil Innovation Agency, Praia do Flamengo, 200, Rio de Janeiro, RJ CEP 22210-030; www.finep.gov.br/english/folder_ingles.pdf. Branch of the Brazilian Ministry of Science and Technology that promotes innovation.

Fundaçao Getulio Vargas, Praia de Botafogo, 190, Rio de Janeiro, 22250-900; 55 (21) 3799-6000; http://portal.fgv.br/en. Produces diverse publications on Brazil.

Inter-American Development Bank, 1300 New York Ave., N.W., Washington, DC 20577; (202) 623-1000; www.iadb.org. Provides economic studies and statistics on Brazil and Latin America.

UNICA, 1711 N St., N.W., Washington, DC 20036-2801; (202) 506 5299; http://english.unica.com.br. The Brazilian Sugarcane Industry Association.

World Bank, 1818 H St., N.W., Washington, DC 20433; (202) 473-1000; www.worldbank.org. Produces country-specific and country-comparative reports on Brazil's state of development.

Voices From Abroad:

DAVID FLEISCHER

Political Science Professor University of Brasília Brazil

Micromanaging

"I think she is going to be involved a lot more than Lula was involved. Lula had people stand in for him, and Dilma was like [his] prime minister or president adjunct. She is known as a manager."

The Christian Science Monitor November 2010

OSCAR DECOTELLI

Partner, Vision Brazil Investments, Brazil

Not just a commodity

"In the past five years, about 34 million Brazilians entered the middle class. This for a population of 200 million is significant. Brazil is not just a commodity story, but a very strong domestic story."

The New York Times, April 2011

FERNANDO HENRIQUE CARDOSO

Former president, Brazil

Not all credit to Lula

"To be frank, the novelty, the change in terms of the orientation of the Brazilian society and government, was done in my period. Of course, Lula did a series of good things, too. The way he managed the recent international crisis was correct. But I started it. Let's debate, looking eye to eye. I would like to hear from Lula, if he can say to me he created the stabilization in Brazil, or how he created the social programs."

The Washington Post October 2010

El Nuevo Dia/Puerto Rico/Taylor Jones

JOSE ROBERTO BERNASCONI

President National Association of Engineering and Architecture Companies, Brazil

Boosting Brazil's brand

"The government should also focus more on boosting the interest of private business in the World Cup. It is a unique opportunity to boost tourism in the country and to show the 'Brazil brand' abroad."

BBC News, July 2010

FERNANDO HADDAD

Education Minister, Brazil

Education lagging

"I want every child to study much more than I could, much more. And for all of them to get a university diploma, for all of them to have a vocational diploma. . . . Brazil is trying to make up for lost time. While other countries were investing in education we were wasting our time here saying that education was not that important."

The New York Times September 2010

ANDRE MUGGIATI

Amazon Activist Greenpeace, Brazil

Backward looking
"It looked like the country was going one way, a good way for forest conservation — meeting targets, carbon emission reduction. We were really doing fine. But we decided to take a U-turn and go the other way. It is really bad what is happening. The country is going backwards in terms of forest conservation, definitely."

Guardian Unlimited (England) May 2011

WAGNER BELMONTE

Journalism Professor University of Santo Amaro Brazil

Lula forever
"I will vote for him [Lula] forever — for him, Dilma and whoever he supports to continue his work. I hope he comes back to run in 2014, because he will get a standing ovation."

Chicago Tribune, October 2010

FELIPE DE FARIA GÓES

Secretary of Development Rio de Janeiro, Brazil

Sporting events providing resources
"The way we see the World Cup and the Olympic Games is as an opportunity to take these projects off paper and make them reality. We're implementing existing plans that the city has had for many years. Now we have the support and resources for it."

Miami Herald, September 2010

9

India Rising

Ken Moritsugu and Roland Flamini

New residential buildings rise above the slums of Mumbai, formerly known as Bombay. Increasing industrialization and foreign investment have helped create a new middle class in India, but a quarter of the 1.1 billion population still lives on less than $1 a day.

From *CQ Researcher*,
May 2007. (Updated July 21, 2011)

A sea of slums greets passengers landing in teeming Mumbai, where thousands of tiny shacks squeeze right up to the airport fences.

The sprawling metropolis, formerly known as Bombay, is India's business capital. Fortunes are made on the city's soaring stock exchange, so-called Bollywood studios churn out more movies than Hollywood and film stars mingle with the young and wealthy at trendy clubs.

But the flashy goings-on are a world removed from the daily struggle to survive for most of Mumbai's 13 million residents, half of whom live in slums. Indeed, Asia's largest slum, Dharavi, home to 1 million people, sits smack in the middle of the city. Day laborers, who swarm from the impoverished countryside in search of work, sleep on the sidewalks, while others live in makeshift shacks with no electricity, running water or sewer system.

Mumbai epitomizes the two sides of India, one filled with a growing cadre of educated, latte-sipping, cell-phone carrying professionals, the other with often-illiterate workers barely touched by the country's recent economic boom.

"You have 50 percent who are tied into the global economy, and you have 50 percent who don't have hope of owning a house in their lifetime," says Kalpana Sharma, author of the book *Rediscovering Dharavi* and Mumbai bureau chief for *The Hindu*, India's leading liberal newspaper. "The new economy has not touched them."

One of the millions it has touched is Subramanian Pillai. Born and raised in Dharavi, he beckons a visitor up a narrow and steep staircase to a small second-floor room where the two Indias meet.

243

A Crowded Country in a Nuclear Neighborhood

India has 1.1 billion people — nearly four times as many as the United States — squeezed into a country one-third the size. Two of its neighbors — Pakistan on the west and China to the north — are nuclear powers, as is India. While economic growth has pulled many city-dwellers out of poverty, especially in technology centers like Bangalore, much of the rural population is still extremely poor.

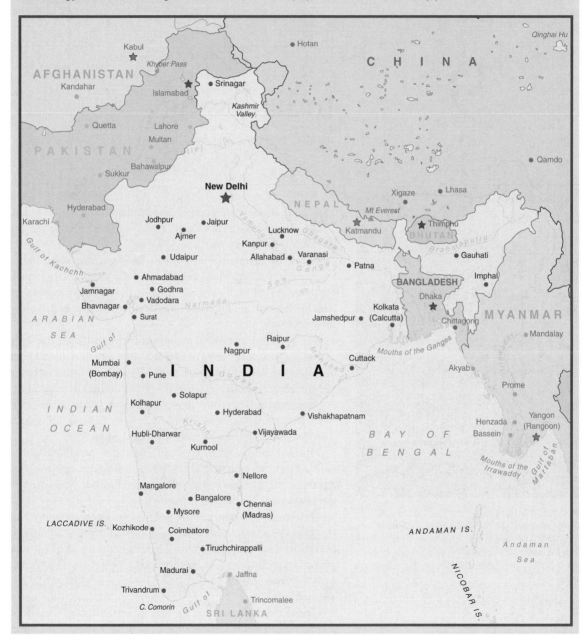

There, in a bare room with concrete walls and floor, Pillai sits doing graphic design on a desktop computer.

A friendly man in his mid-30s, Pillai studied printing technology and learned the trade in a shop. Then he bought a computer, on which he saves his designs — in this case graphics for a pet food box — on a compact disc that he dispatches to a printer. His dream: to be able to buy his own printing machinery and a home for his family outside the slum.

"Ten years back, nobody had a television in their house," he says of his neighborhood. "Now, the economy is growing. Money is coming to people at the bottom. Most people are getting a chance to do something."

Indeed, after two decades of unsteady growth, the economy appears to have shifted into sustained high gear. Gross domestic product (GDP) grew an estimated 9.2 percent for the fiscal year that ended March 31, following a 9 percent rise in the previous year. That puts growth over the last four years at a sizzling 8.6 percent. That's still behind China, which is growing about 10 percent annually.[1]

India has emerged as a global base for outsourcing, carrying out software development and "back office" functions — from call centers to processing health-insurance claims — for American and other overseas companies.

Unlike China, though, where exports power the nation's phenomenal growth, India's expansion has been largely driven by domestic market growth. For several decades, the Indian economy had been hampered by state controls. The loosening of those controls has unleashed an entrepreneurial and consumer boom.

With more than 6 million new connections a month, India surpassed China last year as the fastest-growing market for mobile phones. Auto sales are booming.

India at a Glance

Area: 3.3 million sq. km., slightly more than one-third the size of the United States.

Population: 1.13 billion (July 2007 est.)

Population growth: 1.6 percent per year

Infant mortality: 34.6 deaths per 1,000

Labor force: 509.3 million (2006 est.)

Unemployment rate: 7.8 percent (2006 est.)

Religion: Hindu 80.5 percent; Muslim 13.4 percent; Christian 2.3 percent; Sikh 1.9 percent; the remaining 1.9 percent includes Buddhists and Jains.

Languages: English is used for political and business communication. Hindi is the largest indigenous tongue, spoken by 30 percent of the population. Bengali, Urdu, Telugu and Tamil are among India's 32 other major languages.

Government: The most powerful political leader is the prime minister, who is elected by the lower house (Lok Sabha), which has 543 elected members serving five-year terms. All but 12 of the 250 members of the upper house — the Council of States — are elected by state and territorial legislatures. The remaining 12 are appointed by the president, who is elected by Parliament and state legislatures for a five-year term and has only limited power.

Economy: The economy ranges from subsistence farming and handicraft manufacturing to software and biotechnology industries. The country also has large service and manufacturing sectors, including textiles, chemicals and finance. The gross domestic product was $806 billion in 2005. About 25 percent of the population lived below the poverty line in 2002.

Communications hardware: There are 49.8 million land-line telephones, 69.2 million mobile phones and 1.5 million Internet hosts serving 60 million users.

Source: The World Factbook 2007, Central Intelligence Agency, 2007, and World Development Indicators 2007, World Bank

Indian companies are going global, notably the venerable Tata Group, which gobbled up firms such as Tetley Tea and British steelmaker Corus.[2]

That's a sea change compared to 2002, when growth was "only" 5.4 percent, and the future of India's economic expansion seemed at risk. The government desperately needed to "handle domestic political crises and

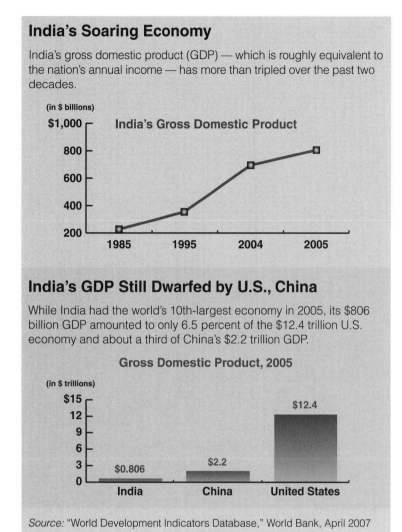

India's Soaring Economy

India's gross domestic product (GDP) — which is roughly equivalent to the nation's annual income — has more than tripled over the past two decades.

(in $ billions)

India's Gross Domestic Product

$1,000
800
600
400
200

1985   1995   2004   2005

India's GDP Still Dwarfed by U.S., China

While India had the world's 10th-largest economy in 2005, its $806 billion GDP amounted to only 6.5 percent of the $12.4 trillion U.S. economy and about a third of China's $2.2 trillion GDP.

Gross Domestic Product, 2005

(in $ trillions)

$15
12
9
6
3
0

$0.806 $2.2 $12.4
India   China   United States

Source: "World Development Indicators Database," World Bank, April 2007

world's 10th-largest economy in 2005, its $806 billion GDP amounted to only 6.5 percent of America's $12.4 trillion economy and about a third of China's $2.2 trillion GDP.[5]

At least for the moment, however, India appears squarely on the right path. Predictions of India emerging as a 21st-century world power — which once seemed fanciful — now appear possible.

In an oft-cited 2003 report, the Wall Street investment firm Goldman Sachs projected that the so-called BRIC nations (Brazil, Russia, India and China) would emerge as major economies over the next half-century, with China as the world's largest by 2050, the United States second and India third.[6]

Earlier this year, however, Goldman revised its findings based on India's improved economic performance. "India's influence on the world economy will be bigger and quicker than implied in our previously published BRICs research," Goldman analysts wrote, adding that India could surpass the U.S. economy by 2050.[7]

As India emerges economically, its foreign relations also are undergoing a transformation.

deadly communal violence, while recharging India's faltering economy," wrote retired ambassador and State Department South Asia specialist Dennis Kux at the time. "Failure to balance these various challenges could . . . slow India's rise to great-power status."[3]

Today, such doubts have faded, both in India and beyond. "There is a new trust, there is a new confidence in India," said Commerce and Industry Minister Kamal Nath, who leads India's international trade negotiations.[4]

Still, the enthusiasm must be tempered by reality. India is growing rapidly, but from a relatively low base. According to the World Bank, while India had the

India came under intense international criticism after conducting successful nuclear tests in 1998 and declaring itself a nuclear weapons state. A United Nations Security Council resolution called on India and Pakistan, which had also conducted tests, to end their nuclear weapons programs. The United States imposed sanctions.

But with the rise of China, India is now being viewed through a different prism. As the United States, Japan and others in the Asia-Pacific region worry that China could become a threat to its neighbors, they increasingly see an economically strong and democratic India as a potential ally should China turn hostile.

That thinking led to a major shift in U.S. policy. The Bush administration, actively wooing India, held out a major carrot in 2005 when President George W. Bush agreed in principle to give India de facto recognition as a nuclear weapons state, something long sought by the Indians. The two countries are trying to hammer out a formal agreement needed under the U.S. Atomic Energy Act to turn that promise into a reality.

"The Bush administration was willing to treat India as a major power and give it a higher billing in the global strategic calculus," wrote C. Raja Mohan, a security analyst in India. "No wonder India found the Bush administration very congenial to its own national interests."[8]

India, which fought a border war with China in 1962, also has concerns about China as a potential threat. So while India continues to resist a formal alliance, it is nonetheless moving closer to the United States, conducting joint military exercises and initially supporting U.S. efforts to prevent Iran from obtaining nuclear weapons.

Even as India moves onto the world stage, however, most Indians remain abysmally poor and far removed from the basic comforts of the new India. "In a country where we talk of 5 million [new] cell phones per month, there are also 300 million people [living] on less than $1 a day," Nath said recently, using the World Bank's measure of extreme poverty.

"Here I [am] speaking to you about WTO," Nath told business leaders in New Delhi, referring to the World Trade Organization. "But when I go back to my own district, which has elected me for 27 years, it's a different world. We may be talking [here] about various formulas in the Doha trade talks, but how does that impact the life of those 300 million or 400 million people who still do not know that there is a thing called the WTO?"

Nevertheless, India has made a dent in its poverty. The percentage of its population living below the government's official poverty line dropped from 36 percent in 1993-94 to 27.5 percent in 2004-05 — or 22 percent according to an alternative survey method.[9] Either way, about 250 million people — a quarter of the population — are extremely poor. Moreover, the government's definition of poverty (anyone earning 43 cents a day or less) is even lower than the World Bank's standard of $1 a day. So many of those living above the official poverty line are still very poor.

IBM Chairman and CEO Samuel J. Palmisano (left) and Indian President A. P. J. Abdul Kalam preside over a company gathering in Bangalore — the center of India's high-tech industry — on June 6, 2006. Low labor costs and the burgeoning technology industry have enticed many U.S. companies to invest in India. With 53,000 employees in 14 cities, India is IBM's second-largest operational base, behind only the United States.

Also troubling has been the slow or even negligible improvement in health, education and other measures of well-being. Malnutrition among young children, for example, remains higher than in sub-Saharan Africa. Forty-six percent of children under age 3 are underweight, according to the Health Ministry, vs. 35 percent in Africa.

A drive to get children to attend school — by such things as offering free lunch — has driven up elementary enrollment, but attendance drops off sharply for junior and senior high. Many poor parents must send older children to work to help feed the family.

And girls suffer disproportionately — even in the new economy — because boys are seen as the ones who will provide for their parents in old age. After girls marry they become beholden to their in-laws, so investing in their education and health is a secondary priority for their parents. Thus, boys get the lion's share of resources in poor families, whether it is receiving a larger portion at mealtime or being sent to school, which usually requires fees, uniforms and books. While 70.2 percent of males were literate in 2001, according to the decennial census, only 48.3 percent of women could read.[10]

Dalits Face Persecution Despite Ban

But some "untouchables" still find success

Fifteen-year-old Mamta Nayak, the first person from her rural Indian village to gain admission to high school, set off every day on her bicycle for the four-mile ride to class.

But there was a problem. She is a dalit, or an "untouchable" in the Hindu caste system. And by tradition, dalits were only allowed to pass on foot through Nanput, a village on her way to school, even though such discrimination has been outlawed for more than 50 years.

Nanput's elders demanded that she stop bicycling through their village, claiming that a dalit riding any vehicle through their village was an insult to them. "They warned me of dire consequences," her father, Ghanashyam Nayak, told an Indian newspaper.[1]

After intense media coverage, the government in the Indian state of Orissa finally intervened and provided police protection — in the form of a female officer on a motor scooter — to ensure that Nayak could bicycle to school. Still, the incident underscores the deep-rooted societal hurdles faced by India's 170 million dalits as they try to join India's economic boom.

India's 3,000-year-old caste system divides Hindus into four groups: priests, warriors, merchants and laborers. Dalits — which means the oppressed — are considered so low they do not even belong to a caste. Traditionally, they were relegated to menial jobs such as sweeping and carting away human excrement, and many still do such work.

After gaining independence in 1947, India outlawed discrimination against dalits and launched programs to improve their lives. But discrimination persists, particularly in rural India. Dalits who try to run for local political office have been threatened and beaten. Mobs have torched and looted entire Dalit villages over a perceived wrong, such as when dalit youths in the town of Gohana were accused of killing a non-dalit in an altercation. "The arson was . . . [their] way of teaching the dalits a lesson," said Vinod Kumar, a dalit whose house was among 54 that were burned.[2]

Just finding a dalit village can be a challenge. One small dalit village, a handful of mud-walled homes with thatched roofs, in the state of Tamil Nadu lies at the end of a sandy path, long after the paved roads have ended. Beyond the enclave lie only fields.

Only 44 percent of dalit households had electricity in 2001, compared to 56 percent in India overall. And while dalit literacy has risen from 37 percent in 1991 to 55 percent in 2001, it still trails the national rate of 65 percent for those age 7 and older. Only 42 percent of dalit females were literate.[3]

The government's biggest program to help dalits is a quota system that reserves 15 percent of government jobs and seats in publicly funded universities for dalits, approximately equal to their proportion of the population. Known as reservations, the quota system has enabled many dalits to move up the economic ladder.

Without adequate education, many migrants from rural areas seem stuck on the first rung of the economic ladder. Their only connection to the new India is that they are building it, brick by brick, often carried on their heads at construction sites in stacks four or five bricks high. "People come to earn money and feed themselves," says Jagjivan Ram, a 28-year-old man who lives alone in the Dharavi slum. "When I can feed myself, I like it here. In my village, there is nothing, so I have no other choice."

Ram cobbled together his windowless, dirt-floor shack with branches, scrap wood and corrugated metal sheets. Without electricity, it is pitch-black inside. He and his neighbors walk on stones or planks to avoid the murky water that flows down narrow gutters in front of their huts.

In the face of these realities, "inclusive growth" has become the mantra of the current government. "Economic growth is not fully reflected in the quality of life of a large number of our people," Indian President A. P. J. Abdul Kalam said in March. "We are looking for inclusive growth for our 1 billion people."[11]

Against that daunting challenge, these are among the key questions being asked about India's economic and social future:

Today, the children of those who entered government service through reservations are reaping the benefits. Dhanai Ram, the son of a farmer, joined the police force in the state of Uttar Pradesh under a quota. He ploughed his earnings into his children's education, not even buying his family a refrigerator. It paid off. Today, his son Yudhishthir Kumar is a computer network specialist in India's burgeoning high-tech industry.

"Reservation helped us a lot," Kumar says. "But we had determination, too, to do something and to prove that if we got an opportunity, we could do better than the upper castes."

But these success stories remain more the exception than the rule. India's economic liberalization has created a new challenge for dalit advancement. When the state dominated the economy, government jobs were regarded by many as the best careers, and the quota system ensured that dalits got a piece of that pie. In today's market economy, however, most new jobs are created in the private sector, prompting the government to propose quotas for private-sector jobs, too.

Fierce resistance from industry put the brakes on that plan. Rather than quotas, industry leaders want the government to improve education for dalits — and the poor generally. But given India's poor education system, that could be a lengthy process.

In the meantime, continuing discrimination against dalits like the bicycle-riding Nayak makes the task that much tougher.

<hr>

[1] Arabinda Mishra, "Dalit Girl Crosses the Hurdle," *The Times of India*, Aug. 20, 2005, and "Girl Rides, With Cops," *The Telegraph*, Sept. 2, 2005.

[2] Basharat Peer, "D for Dalit, D for Defiance," *Tehelka*, Feb. 18, 2006.

[3] "Report of the Task Group on Development of Scheduled Castes and Scheduled Tribes," Government of India, Planning Commission, March 2005, pp. 22-23, 38. Literacy rates are for 2001.

Dalit Christian and Muslim women protest a ruling that reservations — or hiring and education quotas — for the so-called untouchables do not apply to those who converted to Christianity or Islam to avoid discrimination under India's 3,000-year-old Hindu caste system. India's 170 million dalits make up the lowest order in that Hindu system.

Can India match China's economic growth?

India grew in spurts in the 1990s, but never came close to China's torrid growth rates. While many economists believe official Chinese growth statistics were overstated in the early 1990s, they generally agree China expanded rapidly during the decade.[12] India is often described as an elephant, lumbering slowly forward, while China races ahead like a tiger.

Twice during the 1990s, the Indian economy surged, once after a series of economic reforms in the early part of the decade and later during the dot-com boom of the late '90s. Both times, hopes were raised and then dashed, as growth faltered.

Now, after four years of impressive growth, hope is back in fashion. India's four-year average growth rate of 8.6 percent annually represents the best performance since India gained independence from Great Britain in 1947.

Nevertheless, the government has vowed to reach 10 percent growth by the 2011-2012 fiscal year — something economist Surjit Bhalla, who runs the New Delhi asset-management firm Oxus Research and Investments, thinks is possible.[13]

"The likely trend rate of growth is around 9 percent," Bhalla wrote in an in-depth analysis of India's economy. "The inevitability of 10 percent growth is more likely now despite politics and populism."[14]

Such optimism, though, has been tempered by concerns that India's economy could be overheating. "Prices on Fire" screamed the March 5, 2007, cover of the weekly news magazine *India Today* after wholesale prices in early 2007 shot up 6.7 percent over the previous year.[15]

Others wonder whether India's recent growth represents a structural shift or simply the high end of a robust business cycle — bound to return to more earthly levels as the central bank hikes interest rates to tame inflation, which has reached worrisome levels.

Economist Ajay Shah, a former adviser to the Finance Ministry, attributes most of the recent growth to the business cycle. "I don't think that . . . from here on, for the next 20 years, we will get 9.2 percent GDP growth. That's not going to happen."

Economist Arvind Virmani, an adviser to the government's Planning Commission, is not as optimistic as Bhalla either. He puts India's growth in the 7.5 percent range — a rate he is "reasonably confident" can be sustained for the next decade or two "even if everything doesn't go right."

Over the long term, however, Shah sees reasons to hope for truly remarkable growth, but he prefers to use South Korea's impressive rise — rather than China's — as a benchmark for economic ascendancy. India has two advantages over South Korea, he says. As an English-speaking country, it does not face a language barrier when absorbing foreign technology or offering outsourced service jobs to the English-speaking world. Secondly, globalization has accelerated the pace of technological diffusion.

"So when we come out of being a miserable Third World country and are catching up and reaching the frontier, we can do in a generation what took South Korea two generations," says Shah. "India has an opportunity for extremely dramatic rates of growth."

"But that's an opportunity," he warns, "not a reality," and he cautions it's far from guaranteed. Much will depend on whether India can improve its education system and infrastructure. India had only a 61 percent adult literacy rate in 2004, compared to 91 percent in China. Roads and ports are improving but still lag behind China's, creating costly delays in getting goods to market. And perhaps most important, erratic power generation poses a huge hurdle.[16]

Frequent power outages force Indian companies to rely on their own back-up generators, adding to the cost of doing business. Legislation to overhaul the power system passed in 2003, but implementation by the states has been slow. The states own the power companies, and many vested interests benefit from the current system.

Business and political leaders constantly discuss what needs to be done to achieve China's double-digit growth rates. Many hope India can replicate China's success in manufacturing, creating jobs for less-educated workers in industries such as footwear production.

While manufacturing has begun to expand in India, the inadequate road, port and power infrastructure remains a major barrier. Fixing the educational system also is key; even blue-collar workers need a basic education, and manufacturing jobs today increasingly require technical training. Progress is being made in both these areas, but to business leaders, it is often frustratingly slow.

Some Indian commentators say that's the price of democracy. China, with a one-party dictatorship, is able to mandate quick policy shifts. In India, policies can get mired in political debate for years. But some say the democratic process may make India's reforms more durable.

"In 16 years, we had five prime ministers, six governments, but one economic policy," said Nath, the commerce minister. "It is this political consensus which is one of the bedrocks of our reform process. It's not a question of bulldozing reforms. You can bulldoze it through parliament if you have the majority, but how will you bulldoze it through the people?"[17]

Is India doing enough to help its poor?

With economic growth seemingly on autopilot, the government's new "inclusive growth" policy has become a political imperative for the ruling Indian National Congress, or Congress Party, which came to power at the head of a coalition government in 2004. Failure to spread the benefits of growth more widely could spell defeat at the polls in the next national elections, expected by May 2009.

But inclusive growth may be India's greatest social and political challenge. In luxury hotels in New Delhi, leading business groups devote day-long conferences to the subject, with businessmen in expensive suits discussing the future of some of the world's most impoverished people.

With 70 percent of India's population living in the countryside, business leaders realize the country's growth potential will be severely stunted if rural India is left behind. Moreover, an urban-rural divide can spark unrest. Already this year, pockets of farmers have risen up in protest against plans to acquire huge tracts of agricultural land for special economic zones and industrial or commercial development. They fear the developments will benefit corporations, not farmers and their families.

"I am very proud of the fact that we are no longer a sluggish economy," says G. S. Bhalla, an agricultural economist and emeritus professor at Jawaharlal Nehru University in New Delhi. "But growth that ignores a very large section of the people will not do in a democracy."

The growth of agricultural production has, in fact, slowed in the past decade, even as the rest of the economy has gathered steam. While economists have yet to pinpoint the reasons, Bhalla thinks inadequate government spending on agriculture has played a role.

The government has adopted ambitious goals to expand spending on education, health and rural infrastructure, projects applauded by A. K. Shiva Kumar, an economist and member of a council advising the government on development policy. The projects include the National Rural Health Mission, the National Rural Employment Guarantee Scheme and Bharat Nirman (which means "Build India") — a four-year plan to improve roads, telephone service, irrigation, water supply, housing and electricity in rural areas.

So far, though, spending in these areas has fallen short of the goals, Kumar says. India spends about

Poverty Level Drops Dramatically

In a little over a decade, the percentage of Indians living below the poverty line has dropped more than 8 points.

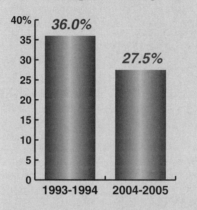

Percentage of Population Living in Poverty

Sources: "National Sample Survey," Government of India Planning Commission; "Poverty declines to 21.8 per cent: NSS," Press Trust of India, March 21, 2007

1 percent of GDP on health, despite a pledge to raise it to 3 percent. By comparison, China spends 2 percent of GDP on health and Brazil, 3.4 percent, while industrialized countries spend 7 to 9 percent. India today spends just over 4 percent of its GDP — about the same as Brazil — on education, even though in the 1960s it vowed to raise that to 6 percent. Industrialized countries, by comparison, spend between 5 and 8 percent of GDP on education.[18]

"India has just not invested adequately in these areas compared to other countries," says Kumar. "You have to increase the amount of spending on these areas. There's no doubt about it."

But, he adds, it's not just a matter of more money. Corruption siphons off significant amounts of government spending into the hands of local politicians and officials. Then-Prime Minister Rajiv Gandhi, whose widow Sonia Gandhi now heads the Congress Party, famously said in the mid-1980s that only 15 percent of government spending for the poor actually reaches the people. Still, India's corruption is not the highest in the world. India ranks 70th in Transparency International's annual index of most corrupt governments, tied with China and Brazil.[19]

Some voices are saying enough is enough. "Throwing money at the problem is not the solution," wrote Aroon Purie, the influential editor-in-chief of *India Today*, in his weekly letter to readers after the fiscal 2007-08 budget proposal was released.[20]

The government needs to monitor social spending to ensure positive results, Purie said. "For all the budgetary allocation on primary education, India still has amongst the lowest literacy rates in this part of the world," he said. "This budget once again caters to the slogan of

CHRONOLOGY

1947–1964 *A newly independent India pursues socialist economic policies and an idealistic, "nonaligned" foreign policy.*

Aug. 15, 1947 India gains independence from Great Britain. Jawaharlal Nehru becomes first prime minister.

1948 Mahatma Gandhi, the non-violent father of Indian independence, is assassinated by a Hindu extremist.

1951 Industries Act requires private companies to obtain permission to expand operations or launch new ones.

1962 China delivers humiliating defeat to India in brief border war along the disputed Tibet and Kashmir frontiers.

1964 Nehru dies in office.

1965–1990 *Indira Gandhi increases state control of the economy and brutally crushes political opponents.*

1966 Nehru's daughter Indira Gandhi becomes prime minister. Aided by the Ford Foundation, the government launches a "Green Revolution," using better seeds and irrigation that eventually enable India to become self-sufficient in grain production.

May 1974 India, which is not a signatory of the Nuclear Non-Proliferation Treaty, conducts its first successful nuclear test.

1975 Gandhi administration declares a "national emergency," leading to a brutal crackdown on political opponents and restrictions on the press.

1977 Voters reject Gandhi and the Congress Party.

1979 India achieves grain self-sufficiency.

1980 Gandhi is returned to office.

1984 Gandhi is assassinated by two of her Sikh bodyguards following her order to storm the Golden Temple, which results in the deaths of hundreds of Sikh pilgrims; her son, Rajiv, becomes prime minister and wins election for a new term.

1991–Present *India begins opening its economy to trade and competition, paving the way for economic growth and a larger international role.*

1991 India launches economic reforms in response to financial crisis.

1992 Hindu mob destroys the Babri Masjid mosque in Ayodhya. Thousands die in sectarian rioting that follows. The incident and ensuing violence are a political turning point, generating a new wave of support for Hindu nationalist parties.

1998 Hindu nationalist Bharatiya Janata Party (BJP) comes to power as head of a coalition government. . . . United States sanctions India and Pakistan after they conduct nuclear tests.

2001–2002 Attack on Indian parliament building leads to heightened India-Pakistan tensions and fears of a nuclear conflict.

May 2004 Indian National Congress party, led by Indira Gandhi's daughter-in-law Sonia Gandhi, unseats the BJP-led coalition in national elections. Former Finance Minister Manmohan Singh becomes prime minister of Congress-led coalition government.

July 2005 President Bush and Prime Minister Singh agree to a nuclear deal at the White House. Details announced during Bush visit to India in March 2006.

February 2006 National Rural Employment Guarantee Act provides 100 days of minimum-wage work each year for any rural household that requests it. Initially launched in 200 of India's 604 districts, it will be expanded nationwide by 2011.

March 2006 Multiple explosions in holy city of Varanasi kill 20; Pakistan-based terror group is primary suspect.

July 2006 Terrorist attacks on Mumbai commuter trains kill more than 200.

December 2006 U.S. Congress approves U.S.-India nuclear deal allowing India to purchase nuclear civilian technology without giving up its nuclear weapons.

March 2007 Economy grows 9.2 percent for the fiscal year ending March 31, the fourth year of high growth. . . . Study finds about one-quarter of Indians live below poverty line, compared to 36 percent in 1994.

2008 U.S. Congress passes, and President George W. Bush signs, agreement to sell peaceful nuclear technology and fuel to India. . . . More than 160 are killed in series of coordinated attacks by militant gunmen in Mumbai tourist and business quarters; India blames Pakistan-based militants.

2009 India Congress Party and allies win large victory in national elections in May, strengthening Prime Minister Manmohan Singh's position. . . . In July, prime ministers of Pakistan and India pledge to cooperate in fight against terrorism, regardless of progress on improving border relations.

2010 Commonwealth Games are held in Delhi, amid criticism of unfinished facilities and poor organization. . . . President Barack Obama visits India, promises to support Indian efforts to gain permanent seat in the U.N. Security Council.

2011 Census puts India's population at 1.2 billion — an increase of 181 million in a decade. . . . Prime ministers of India and Pakistan attend World Cup cricket game between their two countries. . . . In July, three coordinated car bombs explode in Mumbai during rush hour, killing more than 20 and injuring scores of others. . . . Also in July, U.S. Secretary of State Hillary Rodham Clinton travels to Delhi for bilateral talks on terrorism, Afghanistan, China and other regional issues.

inclusive growth but fails to address the core issue of how the inclusion will take place."

A major World Bank review of India's development policies found that while India has set the right priorities and launched appropriate programs, often the programs are not carried out effectively on the ground due to the inefficiency of government agencies. "It is easy to be optimistic about India's economic prospects, but there is growing concern that the basic institutions, organizations, and structures for public sector action are failing — especially for those at the bottom," said the report.[21]

Among the problems, it said, were "corruption, absenteeism, low quality, excessive costs." The bank said "systemic reform," was needed, "not merely expansion of 'business as usual.' "[22]

Even with reform, no one suggests the task would be an easy one. More than 50 percent of Indians are farmers, but they produce only 20 percent of the nation's GDP. And while the rest of the economy races ahead at 9 percent growth rates, agriculture manages to grow at only about 2.5 percent. The only way to keep farmers from falling farther behind is to reduce the number of people in agriculture by shifting them to jobs in faster-growing economic sectors.

But two major obstacles stand in the way. First, with some 300 million workers in farming, creating new jobs for them will take decades. "There is tension between the structural necessity to get a large population out of agriculture and the reality that it's not going to happen for a long time," says Virmani, the government adviser.

Moreover, "a huge number of people have a very high degree of illiteracy" and have inadequate skills to do anything outside of agriculture, says Abhijit Sen, a professor of social sciences at Jawaharlal Nehru University who is on leave to serve on the government's Planning Commission advisory body. "So there is a problem in the short run in even thinking about taking these people into some other activity."

Given those obstacles, the government is following a two-pronged approach: It is trying to increase agriculture productivity to help people in the near future while investing more in educating the next generation of workers. On both fronts, with debt driving some Indian cotton farmers to suicide, progress is limited.

"These turning points in history have not anywhere in the world been easy times to go through," says Sen.

Should India conclude the nuclear deal with the United States?

For the much-trumpeted U.S.-India nuclear deal — announced on March 2, 2006, during a visit by Bush to New Delhi — the devil may be in the details.

New Middle Class Spends Freely

But only 6 percent earn more than $4,500

Kapil Khaneja had a typical middle-class upbringing in New Delhi. A cramped apartment, no family car and 30-hour train rides to vacation at India's tea plantations in Darjeeling.

What a difference a generation makes. Now a manager at an outsourcing firm, Khaneja, 29, bought a used car when he was 21. He upgraded to a new Hyundai a few years later and now is about to move up to a Honda. He sipped wine at Parisian cafes last October on vacation with an American friend. His office colleague, Kamani Sanan, does not think twice about dropping $50 to $100 on a night out. "We work and we spend," she says. "If I like something, I pick it up."

Economic growth is transforming the Indian way of life. Families that always ate at home dine at restaurants and buy Nike sneakers, digital cameras and the latest cellular phones. And as a half-dozen new discount airlines send fares plummeting, they are abandoning India's famously jam-packed trains. Although Khaneja lives with his mother, he inhabits an almost totally different world.

"I don't mind spending the extra buck because I have it," he says, relaxing in one of the Starbucks-like cafes that have sprung up in India's major cities. "Our parents were more driven by necessity than a want for luxuries. It's the difference between needs and desires."

Sanan points out, however, that she and Khaneja are far from average. The new middle class is mostly urban — in a country in which 70 percent of the population is rural — and represents just a sliver of India's total population.

Marketers talk about an Indian middle class of 300 million people, nearly a quarter of the total population of 1.1 billion, but that is widely considered to be inflated. A study by the National Council of Applied Economic Research in New Delhi classified about 6 percent of Indian households as middle class, earning more than $4,500 a year.[1]

Most of the 300 million are what the study called "aspirers." With annual household incomes in the $2,000-to-$4,500 range, they have started the upward climb. Few own a car or an air conditioner; only a third have a refrigerator and 40 percent a color television.

Still, they form part of a new group of consumers, albeit a small one. Companies have responded to their more limited affluence by shrinking product size — little packets of shampoo, for example, are available for the equivalent of a few cents. Cigarette vendors open packs and sell individual cigarettes for three to five rupees (six to 11 cents).

"Companies that have been successful are the ones that have been able to deliver product to homes earning 5,000 to 7,000 rupees ($110 to $150) a month," said Ajit Balakrishnan, the co-founder of Rediff, an Indian Web portal.[2]

Call center employees work the night shift in the small northern city of Mohali. India's emergence as a global base for call centers has helped create a rising middle class, but some researchers say only 6 percent of households have reached the middle class.

Indians' spending power should grow if the country's economy continues to enjoy rapid growth, as expected. Less than 1 percent of households qualify as "rich," with annual incomes above $45,000, but that has not stopped luxury-goods makers from betting on India's future. The first BMW rolled off an assembly line in India this spring. "We see significant sales potential," says Peter Kronschnabl, the executive leading the automaker's entry into India.

Further fueling the spending boom is the spread of consumer credit, a concept that barely existed in India a generation ago. For Khaneja and Sanan's parents, borrowing money is shameful. They look askance as their children pay the bill with a credit card.

"Our parents cannot agree with plastic money," Sanan says. "They still feel like it is borrowing money from someone and that that is not a good thing."

For their parents, buying a house involved borrowing quietly from relatives or private moneylenders who worked on trust, leaving no paper trail. Now, telemarketers besiege Indians on their cellular phones with offers of bank and auto loans.

Khaneja's mother has grown accustomed to her son's credit card. "They've seen it, and they say, 'That's the way they do it,'" he says, "but they still don't approve of the fact that I do it."

---

[1] National Council of Applied Economic Research, *The Great Indian Middle Class* (2004).

[2] Ajit Balakrishnan, interview on "BT Big Thinkers Series," Oct. 3, 2006; www.networked.bt.com/bigthinkers_india.php.

The United States has agreed in principle to provide nuclear power technology and nuclear fuel to India while allowing it to retain its nuclear weapons. In return, India would open its civilian nuclear facilities for the first time to inspections by the International Atomic Energy Agency (IAEA), the international agency entrusted under the 1968 Non-Proliferation Treaty (NPT) with verifying that peaceful nuclear technology is not diverted for weapons use.[23]

Under the treaty, non-nuclear states agreed to refrain from developing nuclear weapons, and in return the five countries that already had tested nuclear weapons when the treaty was signed in 1968 — the United States, the Soviet Union, China, France and Great Britain — promised to share peaceful nuclear technology with nuclear "have-nots." The nuclear "haves" also agreed to reduce and eventually eliminate their own nuclear weapons, a commitment they have largely ignored.

India, which conducted its first nuclear test in 1974 and more advanced tests in 1998, never signed the NPT, which it viewed it as discriminatory since the treaty allowed no new members of the "nuclear club" outside the initial five members.

Critics of the U.S.-India nuclear deal argue that it could undermine the fundamental tenet of the NPT, which induced non-nuclear states to forgo nuclear weapons in return for access to peaceful nuclear technology.

In defending the deal, the Bush administration argued that the benefits of helping to give the South Asian giant energy security while bringing it into the global non-proliferation inspection framework would far outweigh the risks. Moreover, the administration points out, India has been scrupulous about preventing any of its nuclear technology from being transferred to other nations — something its neighbor Pakistan failed to do.[24]

IAEA Director Mohamed ElBaradei called the deal "an important step toward satisfying India's growing need for energy" and said it would "bring India closer as an important partner in the non-proliferation regime."[25]

The deal is also designed to foster closer U.S.-India ties, and is "intended to convey in one fell swoop the abiding American interest in crafting a full and productive partnership with India to advance our common

Rural migrants, many illiterate, come to India's teeming cities seeking work but end up eking out a hardscrabble existence in slums filled with shacks made of scrap wood and corrugated metal, with dirt floors and no electricity or plumbing. The Congress Party has promised to help all Indians benefit from the economic boom, but spending on social programs has fallen short of goals.

goals in this century," said Ashley Tellis, a senior associate at the Carnegie Endowment for International Peace and a former State Department official who helped negotiate the agreement.[26]

But because the deal would set a new precedent within the NPT, some U.S. lawmakers — including leading Republicans — opposed it. Consequently, when Congress approved the deal last December it added conditions that have raised some hackles in India.

"The U.S. Congress, being always overbearing, passed a law called the Hyde Act, which is oppressive and has changed the public mood in India," says Brahma Chellaney, a professor of strategic studies at the Center for Policy Research in New Delhi.

The law exempts India from restrictions in the Atomic Energy Act on the sale of American nuclear materials, equipment and technology to other countries. But the new law allows the United States to nullify the deal if India conducts another nuclear weapons test and to demand return of any nuclear equipment and fuel already delivered to India. Other conditions limit India's ability to stockpile nuclear fuel and reprocess spent fuel. The law also requires the U.S. president to report to Congress on how India is helping to prevent Iran from obtaining nuclear weapons.[27]

Getty Images/Don Emmert

Women spread red chilies to dry in Sertha, a village on the outskirts of Ahmedabad. Despite increasing industrialization, 60 percent of India's 509 million laborers work in agriculture.

"The Indo-U.S. nuclear deal is against India's national interest," former Indian Foreign Minister Yashwant Sinha wrote. "Through this deal, India shall mortgage in perpetuity, for all time to come, its freedom to develop its nuclear technology and the independence of its foreign policy."[28]

Indian proponents of the nuclear deal hope their country's objections will be addressed in ongoing negotiations on an accompanying technical pact. "There are some sticking points," acknowledges Ashok Mehta, a retired Indian Army general, which will "be negotiated and suitably couched in language to assuage each other's security concerns."

The talks, though, appeared to be stuck this spring on some of those very sticking points. If they fail — however unlikely that may seem given the importance both countries place on the deal — it could torpedo the entire agreement.

Opinions vary on how important the U.S. nuclear deal is to meeting India's future energy needs. India already faces power shortages, and the simultaneous rapid growth of the world's two Asian colossi — India and China — portends a squeeze on energy supplies and higher prices.

India must "be able to ensure some degree of energy security over the next two to three decades," says Uday Bhaskar, a retired Indian Navy commodore and an adviser to the government on security issues. "Clearly, you cannot do it without a stable nuclear base."

But others argue that nuclear energy is too expensive for India, which has sizable coal deposits. Even in the most optimistic scenarios, nuclear power would at best meet less than 10 percent of India's energy needs in 2020.

"The Americans are trying to induce India to accept a series of legally binding conditions to obtain this dubious right to import nuclear power reactors for generating electricity, which is a right India can do without," says Chellaney, who was an adviser to the government during the diplomatic brouhaha following India's 1998 nuclear tests.

Most analysts agree, however, that the nuclear deal is significant not only as a means of boosting India's nuclear power sector but also in elevating India's international stature and recognizing India's growing global role.

"[T]his nuclear agreement . . . brings you into the big league," Mehta says. "If this agreement falls through, obviously it dilutes that relationship."

BACKGROUND

Socialist Experiment

If India lives up to its promise and becomes one of the world's major economies, it wouldn't be for the first time.

In 1820, India accounted for 16 percent of global GDP, making it the second largest economy in the world, according to estimates by British-born economic historian Angus Maddison, an emeritus professor at the University of Groningen in the Netherlands. Indian cloth, which made up the vast bulk of the global trade in textiles and apparel, was prized throughout the world.[29]

But even then India was playing second fiddle to China, which accounted for 33 percent of the world economy. The fledgling U.S. economy represented a mere 1.8 percent of the world's GDP.

Then came the Industrial Revolution. While the West roared ahead, today's so-called developing world remained largely stagnant. By 1950, the United States produced 27 percent of global GDP. China's share had plummeted to 4.5 percent; India's, to 4.2 percent.

As Columbia University economist Jeffrey Sachs points out, before the Industrial Revolution "universal poverty" was the norm. [30] But the rise of factories, for all their worker abuses, enabled the Western masses eventually to climb out of poverty.

India, however, was still largely agrarian when it broke free from British colonial rule in 1947, with agriculture accounting for about half of its GDP, says Professor Sen of the Planning Commission. The country's first prime minister, Jawaharlal Nehru, decided the new nation would have to industrialize. Inspired in part by the Soviet model, he envisioned government playing a major role. Power generation was nationalized, and ambitious hydroelectric projects were launched. The government created the now famous Indian Institutes of Technology, inspired by the Massachusetts Institute of Technology.

In 1951 private companies were brought under government control through the Industries Act, which required companies to get official permission to expand production or set up a new business. The law — and subsequent measures — were designed to prevent corporate excesses and keep business working in the nation's interest. [31]

The pervasive regulation, however, had a stultifying effect on private enterprise. Permits and licenses were required at every turn. Critics of Nehru's socialist-leaning polices complained that the British Raj (rule by the British) had been replaced by the "license Raj."

Growth became sluggish, averaging 4.1 percent a year under Nehru, who died in office in 1964. [32] The economy fared even worse after his daughter, Indira Gandhi, became prime minister in 1966. She nationalized banks and further tightened government control

Majority of Indians Are Farmworkers

Despite rising industrialization, India remains largely agricultural: 60 percent of its 509 million labor force — mostly the rural poor — work in agriculture. More than one-quarter are in the service sector, many in call centers or other outsourced employment.

India's Labor Force by Sector, 2003

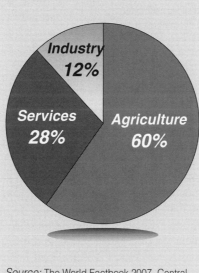

Source: The World Factbook 2007, Central Intelligence Agency

of the economy. The two oil crises of the 1970s added to the economic woes. From 1965 to 1979, growth slumped to 2.9 percent a year.

Economist Shah calls Gandhi's rule "the terrible period of socialism, with all kinds of crazy laws, all kinds of crazy controls." By 1976, says Shah, India had "an incredibly repressive government that was interfering in every part of economic activity."

A bright spot during these tough times was the so-called Green Revolution, the development and introduction of new "high-yield" wheat, rice and other grain varieties, which swept across the developing world in the 1960s, from Mexico to India and eventually Southeast Asia and Africa, with support from the Ford and Rockefeller foundations. After back-to-back droughts led to severe grain shortages in 1965 and 1966, India accelerated efforts to introduce new high-yield grains, train farmers, expand irrigation and increase the use of fertilizers. By significantly improving the harvest per acre, India became self-sufficient in food grains by 1979.

Overall, though, the economy remained in the doldrums. From 1951 to 1980, India eked out only 3.5 percent average annual growth, a record that came to be known derisively as the "Hindu" growth rate.

Reform Era

In 1977, Gandhi and her Congress Party were unceremoniously dumped from office. The immediate reason was the "emergency" her government declared in 1975, during which tens of thousands of political opponents were

AP Photo/Gurinder Osan

Indian Communist Party activists burn an effigy of Wal-Mart Vice Chairmen Mike Duke during an anti-globalization protest in New Delhi on Feb. 22, 2007. Duke was in India to discuss setting up big-box stores across the country. Concerned about the potential loss of cultural identity, many Indians object to the growing presence of foreign retailers.

rounded up and terrorized and the media muzzled — all in the name of law and order.[33]

The crackdown came amid growing labor unrest, coupled with declining popularity for Gandhi, who had brutally broken a nationwide strike by government railway workers the previous year. With an opposition political movement gaining strength, Congress' hold on power appeared vulnerable.

"If Indira Gandhi had thought she could win the 1976 elections, there would not have been an emergency," wrote Tariq Ali, a London-based social commentator. "Its purpose was basically twofold: to safeguard the Congress Party and her own political position while forcibly bringing to an end rural and urban unrest in many parts of the country."[34]

For the first time since independence, Congress was not the ruling party. But the new government quickly unraveled, and Gandhi led Congress back to victory in elections in 1980 and returned as prime minister. This time, she initiated modest economic reforms. After her assassination in 1984, her son, Rajiv Gandhi, succeeded her as prime minister and took India further down the reform path.

If the 1970s were an economic winter, the 1980s were a spring thaw. Growth accelerated to an average of 5.5 percent a year, better than at any time since independence.

Even India's long-struggling farmers were invited to the party, as the Green Revolution came to fruition. Annual growth in agricultural output, which had averaged only 2.3 percent a year from 1951 to 1980, jumped to 4.2 percent in the 1980s.[34]

Farmers traded in their bullock carts for tractors. Agricultural economist Bhalla calls the decade "a golden period" for Indian agriculture. "Farmers benefited immensely," he says. "I belong to a farming community, I was born in a village, I know people who sort of suddenly became rich — you know, tractors and all that. So it's a huge difference in lifestyle."

The 1990s began inauspiciously, however. Mounting government debt under Prime Minister Rajiv Gandhi, who succeeded his mother in 1984, and his successors sparked a financial crisis in 1991.[35] After Iraq invaded Kuwait in 1990, world oil prices soared, and India soon found itself rapidly running short of foreign reserves to buy oil.

Narasimha Rao, who had become prime minister in 1991, turned to respected economist Manmohan Singh, appointing him finance minister. Within a month, Singh had laid out the dire situation: The government had only enough foreign exchange for 13 more days of oil. "He explained the consequences to the Cabinet and he said this is what we have to do," Nath, now the commerce minister, recalled earlier this year.[36]

Rao and Singh took advantage of the crisis to brush aside vested interests and launch a fundamental shift in Indian economic policy. India would abandon Nehru's socialist principles, dismantle the hated license Raj, open the economy to foreign investment and embrace free-market economics.

Although many of the changes have been only partially carried out, they managed to boost India's growth rate in the 1990s to 6.1 percent, according to economist Virmani. "It's very clear now that the shift has happened," he says. "You can show that India is on a higher growth path."

Foreign Policy

As India gained its independence in 1947, the world was fracturing in two. British Prime Minister Winston Churchill had warned of growing Soviet dominance in Eastern Europe during his prescient "Iron Curtain" speech

Has globalization been good for India?

YES Ajay Shah
Economist

Written for *CQ Global Researcher*, April 2007

In my view, globalization has been central to India's growth. In manufacturing, India engaged in substantial unilateral liberalization, removing quantitative restrictions, and brought down customs tariffs from 1991 onwards. Meanwhile, barriers to foreign direct investment (FDI) in almost all manufacturing were removed, and domestic entry barriers were eliminated. These initiatives came together to induce heightened competition in the goods market through new domestic start-ups, competition from foreign firms establishing operations in India and competition from imports.

Thousands of firms died as a consequence of the new levels of competition. From 1996 to 2001, these problems cast a pall over the economy: firms were going bust, profit rates were under attack, investment was sluggish and banks were nervous over non-performing assets. This "trial by fire" seems to have worked wonders for the economy, for the survivors have emerged as more efficient and innovative firms. Many of the winners of this period have gone on to turn themselves into global firms.

Over the last five years, manufacturing exports doubled and gross receipts on the current account tripled. GDP growth rates bounced back from a low of 4.4 percent to more than 8 percent. Globalization was central to these developments.

The next frontier for India lies in opening up the financial sector. Indian finance in 2007 is much like the non-finance sector in the early 1990s. There is a substantial presence of government-owned corporations; there is an elaborate regulatory system where all features of products are prohibited unless explicitly permitted; considerable entry barriers impede domestic start-ups; capital controls greatly impede imports of financial services; and there are barriers to FDI.

The Ministry of Finance recently set up an expert group to explore the possibility of Mumbai becoming an international financial center. This group has argued that India needs to do for finance what was done for the real non-financial economy. By opening up to competition, the Indian financial system will be brought up to world standards of efficiency. This matters disproportionately, because finance is the "brain" of the economy: A better financial sector will give better bang-for-the-buck in converting a 35 percent-of-GDP investment rate to more than 8 percent GDP growth. In addition, there is a significant opportunity for Mumbai to join the ranks of London and New York as one of the world's premiere global financial centers.

NO Vandana Shiva, PhD
Author, Anti-Globalization Activist

Excerpted from "The Suicide Economy of Corporate Globalisation," www.counter-currents.org/glo-shiva050404.htm, February 2004

The Indian peasantry, the largest body of surviving small farmers in the world, today faces a crisis of extinction. . . . Two-thirds of India makes its living from the land. . . . However, as farming is de-linked from the Earth, the soil, the biodiversity and the climate and linked to global corporations and global markets, and the generosity of the Earth is replaced by the greed of corporations, the viability of small farmers and small farms is destroyed. . . .

Two factors have transformed the positive economy of agriculture into a negative economy for peasants — the rising costs of production and the falling prices of farm commodities. Both these factors are rooted in the policies of trade liberalization and corporate globalisation.

In 1998, the World Bank's structural-adjustment policies forced India to open up its seed sector to global corporations like Cargill, Monsanto and Syngenta. The global corporations changed the input economy overnight. Farm-saved seeds were replaced by corporate seeds [that] needed fertilizers and pesticides and could not be saved [from one harvest to the next]. . . . As seed saving is prevented by patents [and] the engineering of seeds with non-renewable traits, seed has to be bought for every planting season. . . . This increases poverty and leads to indebtedness. . . .

The second pressure Indian farmers are facing is the dramatic fall in prices of farm produce as a result of free-trade policies of the World Trade Organization. . . . They have allowed an increase in agribusiness subsidies while preventing countries from protecting their farmers from the dumping of artificially cheap produce. . . . Global prices have dropped . . . due to an increase in subsidies and an increase in market monopolies controlled by a handful of agribusiness corporations. . . . The rigged prices of globally traded agriculture commodities are stealing incomes from poor peasants of the south.

[U]nder globalisation, the farmer is losing her/his social, cultural [and] economic identity as a producer. A farmer is now a "consumer" of costly seeds and costly chemicals sold by powerful global corporations. . . . This combination is leading to corporate feudalism, the most . . . exploitative convergence of global corporate capitalism and local feudalism. . . .

It is necessary to stop this war against small farmers . . . re-write the rules of trade in agriculture [and] change our paradigms of food production. Feeding humanity should not depend on the extinction of farmers and extinction of species.

the previous year in Fulton, Mo. By 1949, Mao Zedong had led the communists to power in China.

Nehru, who was both foreign minister and prime minister, tried to set India on a pacifistic, "nonaligned" course that avoided taking sides in the nascent Cold War. He was a driving force behind a 1955 conference of Asian and African leaders in Bandung, Indonesia, that gave birth to the nonaligned movement.[37]

But Nehru's policy of non-alignment drove the United States to seek out and arm Pakistan, India's arch-rival, as a bulwark against communist expansion in the region. And his idealistic vision came crashing down after China seized disputed Himalayan territory in a brief and humiliating war along the India-China border in 1962.

"The invasion of '62 shattered India's pacifism in one stroke," says Chellaney, of the Center for Policy Research. "India had a military like a police force. It thought that if you seek peace, you will get peace. It did not understand the basic principle of national security: that to have peace, you should be able to defend peace. And therefore '62 was a big revolution in terms of changing Indian military planning and thinking."

Under Indira Gandhi, India moved away from Nehru's idealism toward a more hard-nosed foreign policy.[38] Feeling boxed in by China, Pakistan and the United States, India turned to the Soviet Union for everything from scientific exchanges to fighter aircraft.

Although India remained officially nonaligned, "it is impossible to characterize India's ties with the Soviet Union as anything other than an alliance-like relationship," said security expert Mohan. "India's 1971 peace and friendship treaty with Moscow, which consolidated this relationship, was a structural response to the emergence of what India saw as a U.S.-Pakistan-China axis in its neighborhood."[39]

In 1988 Prime Minister Rajiv Gandhi offered to forgo nuclear weapons if the five original nuclear club members made a long-term commitment to abide by the NPT's Article 6 and begin phasing out their nuclear arsenals. When the United States rejected the offer, the nuclear hawks in New Delhi gained ground.[40]

India upped the ante in May 1998 by conducting advanced nuclear tests and declaring itself a nuclear weapons state. Reaction was largely negative. The United States imposed sanctions, and a unanimous U.N. Security Council called on India and Pakistan — which conducted its own tests two weeks after India — to abandon their

nuclear programs. "We're going to come down on those guys like a ton of bricks," said President Bill Clinton, who later that year called off a planned trip to India.[41]

But by 2000 Clinton's mood had changed; he visited India that March, and many of the sanctions were gradually lifted. Several fundamental changes triggered America's about-face: the end of the Cold War, the Internet-fueled globalization of the economy, India's economic emergence and its fresh approach to foreign policy.

India began to see that building relations with the United States and its economically vibrant neighbors in Southeast Asia would enhance India's future. And its economic emergence suggested to U.S. policymakers that India could play a bigger geopolitical role in Asia.

Although the 60-year-old dispute over Kashmir remains unresolved, the two countries have ratcheted down their warlike rhetoric and taken steps to ease tensions, re-establishing rail and air links, easing travel restrictions and starting a "comprehensive dialogue" on all issues, including Kashmir.

After President Bush took office in 2001, another key element fell into place. U.S. policymakers had long debated whether China was an opportunity or a threat. Clinton leaned toward opportunity; Bush, toward threat. In Bush's worldview, India gained heightened importance as a potential counterweight to Chinese influence in the region.

To entice India into its camp, the Bush administration offered to accept India as a nuclear power. For the Indian foreign-policy establishment, the July 2005 agreement was almost too good to be believed. Mohan called it a "gigantic reversal."[42]

"Within seven years of its nuclear tests, the international community led by the United States was now prepared to accept India's nuclear weapons program," he wrote. "The nuclear non-proliferation wheel had turned full circle."[43]

CURRENT SITUATION
Congress Party Returns

By 2004, the economy appeared to be back on track. "India Shining" was the campaign slogan of the ruling Bharatiya Janata Party (BJP) in parliamentary elections that spring. Re-election for Prime Minister Atal Bihari Vajpayee seemed assured.

In a stunning upset, the Congress Party returned to power under the leadership of Sonia Gandhi, Rajiv

Gandhi's Italian-born widow.* But the party was far short of an outright majority, so it formed a government with the support of the communist and other leftist parties.

Financial markets panicked, fearing the new government would roll back or stall India's pro-market reforms. Calm was restored after Manmohan Singh, the finance minister who had launched India's pro-market reforms in 1991, was named prime minister.

However, while the Congress-led coalition has not gone back on reforms, it has made only slow progress in advancing them. And it has retreated often on planned steps in the face of vocal protests from its leftist allies.

Progress has come in dribs and drabs. After public protests, a proposal to allow foreign companies to own stores in India, which would have opened the doors to the likes of Wal-Mart, was watered down to allow only "single-brand" retailing — a Nike store or Starbucks, for example, but not a department store or supermarket.

India's record on helping the poor remains mixed. More children are attending school, but studies show that educational attainment remains low, says economist Kumar.

Early this year, the government proposed major increases in social spending for the upcoming fiscal year. "Faster economic growth has given us, once again, the opportunity to unfurl the sails and catch the wind," Finance Minister P. Chidambaram said in his annual budget speech to parliament. The government "will deliver on the promise of making growth more inclusive. I believe that, given the right mix of policies, the poor will benefit from growth."[44]

But Kumar says government spending is still far too low. "We have really under-invested, and it [is evident] anywhere you go," he says. A quarter of schools in north India have only one teacher, handling perhaps 80 students in five grades. "It's a joke," he continues. "You have to increase the amount of spending on these areas."

Corruption remains the other over-arching issue. State governments control funding for most social programs, resulting in stark regional differences where officials and politicians siphon off government funds. Northern states such as Uttar Pradesh and Bihar are notably corrupt and lag both in economic growth and various measures of

AFP/Getty Images/Sam Panthaky

Rising beside the Indian Ocean, bustling Mumbai is India's business capital and largest city, with more than 13 million residents. To continue its impressive economic growth, economists say India will have to continue infrastructure improvements, liberalize economic policies and fix its educational system.

poverty, education and health. Much more progress has been made in the south and west where state governments tend to be less corrupt, more efficient and better at attracting private investment.

Neo-Nonalignment

While the nuclear deal with the United States grabbed headlines, India is actively trying to build relations with other powers as well — from China and Japan to Russia and Europe — in a multi-pronged approach that recognizes the U.S. role as the dominant global power.

This spring, for example, the Indian Navy sent five ships to participate in a naval exercise with the United States off Japan. Afterward, three of the Indian vessels made a "friendship" port call in Japan. The two others, described as "less formidable destroyers," headed for a "goodwill" port call in China.

"This aspect of the planning acquires importance as a possible message that India wants to stay engaged with China even while building new bridges with Japan," wrote P. S. Suryanarayana, a Singapore-based correspondent for *The Hindu.*[45]

The relationship with China may be the trickiest. The simultaneous emergence of the two big countries in the same region makes a degree of rivalry all but inevitable. Both need oil and other raw materials to fuel their booming economies, and both may end up competing for the same global resources.

---

*Rajiv had been assassinated in 1991 by a Tamil extremist who opposed his government's support for the Sri Lankan government in its ongoing battle against Tamil separatists.

"The size, the ambitions and the proximity make them natural competitors," says Chellaney at the Center for Policy Research. "These are two large states — huge — and both are coming into their own at the same time in history. It's inevitable that you're going to be competing with each other."

Others concur. "Competition has a certain inevitability," says security adviser Bhaskar. "Whether it's friendly competition or prickly competition, we'll see how the two leaderships address it."

The budding U.S.-India relationship further complicates relations with China. No one is quite sure what China's ambitions are, but the United States sees India as a potential partner to contain China, should its ambitions threaten American interests in Asia. But that thinking apparently does not sit well in Beijing.

"The biggest challenge is going to be China," Bhaskar says. "If India-U.S. moves in a certain direction, it's causing some sort of anxiety in China. India needs to reassure China it's not an alliance or an India-U.S. combine."

Meanwhile, India harbors some of America's wariness toward China, which has concluded a series of agreements with many of India's neighbors that appear aimed at guaranteeing safe passage for energy supplies to China but could have potential military implications. The agreements include helping to finance and build ports in Pakistan, Myanmar, Sri Lanka and Bangladesh as well as a reported agreement to allow Chinese submarines to make port calls in the Maldives. It's a strategy Pentagon analysts call "a string of pearls."

"The Chinese, as part of their strategic and economic interests, are creating corridors on different flanks of India — east, west, north — which, even if they're not designed to contain India, do have strategic implications for India and, willingly or unwillingly, squeeze India strategically," Chellaney says.

"And on top of that, the Chinese are showing increasing interest in the Indian Ocean region," he adds, "where India has been the dominant power. And suddenly, China is appearing from nowhere and actually appearing in a very serious way. So, for Indians, this is a strategic reality that they have to confront."

Fundamentally, Chellaney says, India and China have differing visions of their role in the 21st century. The United States sees itself as the dominant world power,

with power in Asia split between China and India. China wants a multipolar world but seeks to be the dominant power in Asia. India wants multipolarity both globally and in Asia.

In an editorial last year, *The Times of India* termed India's approach "neo-nonalignment." Under the earlier definition, "India ploughed a lonely furrow, as it found itself factored out of everybody's security equation." By taking a neo-nonalignment stance, however, "New Delhi enters into security dialogue with everyone who has interests in South Asia."[46]

OUTLOOK

Full Speed Ahead?

Today it is all but impossible to find a pessimistic voice on India's economic potential. Healthy economic expansion seems assured for the foreseeable future; the only uncertainty is whether the rate of growth will be spectacular or merely steady.

To grow faster, most economists and business leaders say India will have to continue to make infrastructure improvements, liberalize economic policies and fix its education system. Given past experience, that's a tall order. Progress is being made in many areas, but it remains slow.

For example, New Delhi residents and businesses endure frequent power outages, particularly during the peak summer season and increasingly in winter. Even small shops must invest in generators — a costly and inefficient way to keep operations running.

"It's not a threat to basic growth," economist Virmani says. "But beyond a certain point, it's like somebody stepping down on the brakes while you're trying to accelerate."

Business leaders and politicians also engage in much hand-wringing over whether India's continued growth will help the country's poor — a problem for which no easy answer appears on the horizon. Yet signs indicate the notoriously slow Indian elephant may be lumbering toward tackling corruption, which has hindered the delivery of services to all Indians, most notably the poor.

"The nature of public vigilance has dramatically changed," says development adviser Kumar. Citizens have filed a flood of information requests under new right-to-information laws — akin to the U.S. Freedom of Information Act and state sunshine laws — demanding records showing how government money was spent, or misspent. While some requests have been frivolous, others have uncovered malfeasance or forced officials to do their jobs without demanding bribes.

The media, growing exponentially, are shining a new spotlight on official wrongdoing. Some of the new outlets — bordering on the sensational — are aggressive and competitive, often seeking scoops using hidden-camera "sting" operations.

And the Indian public is beginning to exercise a new-found pluck. After the acquittal of a well-connected defendant in a murder trial, protesters took to the streets, forcing authorities to re-open the case. Evidence was found of police complicity in destroying evidence incriminating the defendant. A new trial was held, and the man was convicted.

"That is the strength of our democracy, that these things happen," Virmani says. "They happen slowly, but they will happen because of public pressure."

Still, such instances remain more the exception than the norm. Many Indians continue to pay bribes with hardly a second thought; it's often the only way to get things done.

Virmani echoes other economists and business leaders who say reforming government holds the key to India's future. "The biggest challenge is not these individual things, one particular infrastructure or some other thing, it is governance," he says. "You cannot sustain high growth for several decades without improvements in governance."

UPDATE

Towering over Mumbai is one of the world's largest single-family dwellings: a 400,000-sq. ft., 27-floor high-rise with three helicopter pads, a swimming pool, theater and health club. Built in 2010 by Indian petroleum billionaire Mukesh Ambani, it has spectacular views of the ocean — but also of the sprawling, teeming Dharavi slum featured in the Oscar-winning movie "Slumdog Millionaire."[47]

Shyama Kumar, mother of five, lives in this shanty in a New Delhi slum. The Indian government has made it a priority to reduce by half the number of Indians in extreme poverty by 2015, by spending more on health, education and infrastructure.

More than half the city's 18 million inhabitants eke out a bare and often perilous existence in what is euphemistically called "informal" housing — makeshift slum dwellings often without running water. In Dharavi, with a population of 1 million, up to 18,000 dwellers are crowded into each acre.[48]

Despite years of rapid economic growth, India remains a country of sharp contrasts: While burgeoning millionaire and middle-class sectors enjoy unprecedented prosperity, 30 percent of the nation lives on less than $1 a day.[49]

The poster child for the benefits of globalization, India is expected to overtake China as the world's fastest-growing economy this year, according to the World Bank, while recovering from the 2008 global meltdown faster than the United States or Europe. The bank projects that India's economy will grow this year by 8.2 percent — up from 6.0 percent in 2008 — and could reach 10 percent in the near future.[50]

But built into India's success story is the stark possibility that tens of millions will be left behind, cautioned former Indian Foreign Secretary Shayam Saran. Delhi must seek "the right balance between the demands of a global role and the imperatives of domestic challenges," he wrote. Global ambitions must not undermine India's "ability to deliver the basic development needs of millions of its citizens."[51]

Picking up the challenge, the government has made it a priority to reduce by half the number of Indians in extreme poverty by 2015. Delhi hopes to do this through a program of "increased spending in critical sectors such as health, education, skill development, and infrastructure," according to *The Hindu*, one of the country's leading English-language papers.

But at the same time, says Gareth Price, an India specialist at London's Chatham House think tank, the Indians are under increasing pressure to broaden their country's involvement in world affairs to offset the ascendancy of China and prevent Asia from being dominated by a single power. "Western countries have encouraged India to play a more active global role, as have other emerging powers," Price says.

Washington is applying perhaps the heaviest pressure. Having "clearly overlooked it for a very long time," Price continues, the United States is now making an all-out effort to forge a strategic relationship with India. As the world's largest democracy, "India is easy to like," Price argues. "It has the second-largest caucus in the U.S. Senate, a lot of involvement in U.S. high-tech and a large and influential Indian diaspora, which pushed this trend." The 2.8 million Asian Indians in the United States include more than 200,000 millionaires and the current governor of Louisiana, Bobby Jindal.

Serious U.S.-India rapprochement began in 2005, when Indian Prime Minister Manmohan Singh visited Washington. On that occasion, the Bush administration offered India, already a nuclear power, access to U.S. civilian nuclear technology and fuel, ending a 34-year ban on nuclear trade with India, which has refused to sign the Nuclear Nonproliferation Treaty. The deal involved inspection of Indian civilian, but not military, nuclear facilities.

Six years later, the U.S.-India nuclear accord is still mostly symbolic, due to delays and problems. Most recently, according to a study by the Council on Foreign Relations think tank, U.S. contractors building plants in India have objected to India's stringent new liability laws for nuclear construction, and Delhi had objected to further U.S. restrictions on the transfer of nuclear technology.[52]

But at the same time Washington has stepped up its overtures toward Delhi with a sense of urgency and momentum. In 2009, when Prime Minister Singh paid his second visit to Washington in four years, the Obama White House held its first state dinner in his honor — though the event was overshadowed by a major security breach when an uninvited Washington couple crashed the dinner.

Then, on his Indian visit in 2010, President Barack Obama said the United States supports India's long-standing ambition to achieve permanent member status in the U.N. Security Council and called the bilateral relationship "a defining partnership of the 21st century." India, Obama said, "is not simply emerging. It has emerged."[53]

Meanwhile, the Pentagon — with the tempting prospect that India plans to buy $100 billion worth of new weapons over the next 10 years — has intensified efforts to build a close relationship with the Indian military, similar to what the United States once had with Pakistan. U.S. forces have increased joint military exercises with India, even as Washington announced recently it was suspending aid to Pakistan. U.S.-Pakistan tensions have risen since Islamabad ejected American military aides following the May 2 raid by Navy SEALs on Osama bin Laden's hideout in a military garrison town near Islamabad.

"I believe the U.S.-Indian relationship has the potential to be the cornerstone of Indian and perhaps U.S. engagement in Asia," says Amit Mukherjee, senior fellow at the Institute for Defense Studies and Analyses in Delhi. "We have an amazing convergence of interests."

So why does the relationship continue to be discussed more as a work-in-progress than an established fact? There's a learning curve, says Mukherjee. "Neither country has experience working with the other type of country," he says. "The U.S. doesn't know where to slot India, which is neither NATO, nor major non-NATO. India, in turn, has never allied itself explicitly with any country — for example, sharing military bases."

Chatham House's Price makes the same point. "India is something new for the U.S.," he says. The spirit of nonalignment, once the basis for India's foreign policy, still conditions political thinking. "The Indians don't like patron-client relations, the way the U.S. has been with Pakistan. Most of the political elite don't want an alliance with anyone: They want to be friends with anyone." India, for example, has forged friendships with South Africa, Israel — a regular defense supplier — and

Brazil, its fellow member in the emerging-nation quartet known as BRIC (for Brazil, Russia, India and China).

India's approach leads to the first of several differences with Washington: India's relationship with Iran. Indian Foreign Secretary Nirupama Rao recently called ties with Tehran a "fundamental component" of Indian foreign policy and said U.S. sanctions against Iran adversely affect India's trade and energy security.

The United States also has issues with India's approach to environmental problems. "India's priority remains economic growth," says Price, "and it is likely to do the minimum required in order to avoid international criticism."

Washington got an expensive taste of India's independence recently, when Delhi decided against buying about 160 American F-18 combat planes, opting instead for a European model. The prompt resignation of Washington's ambassador to India was seen as a sign of protest.

"The notion that a major arms purchase should be based on broader strategic considerations — the importance in India's emerging *Weltpolitik* [its role in world politics] — rather than on the merits of the aircraft itself strikes Indian officials as unfair," wrote Shashi Tharoor, a former Indian government minister.[54]

For its part, India has serious reservations about Washington's relationship with Pakistan, its perennial enemy, and with President Obama's exit strategy from Afghanistan. The Indians, for example, want the United States to press Islamabad to crack down on Pakistan-based terrorists who India says killed more than 160 people in attacks in Mumbai's tourist and business areas on Nov. 26, 2008, and then more than 20 in three simultaneous car bombs in the same city this July.[55] While in Mumbai, Obama conceded that Pakistan's progress on countering terrorism was slower than desired.

On July 15, Secretary of State Hillary Rodham Clinton was in Delhi, primarily to brief the Indian government on the planned withdrawal of U.S. and NATO troops from Afghanistan, beginning in 2012. India regards Afghanistan as part of its extended neighborhood and is nervous about what happens there after the pullout. Clinton was also due to report on joint U.S.-Afghan talks with the Taliban — an unwelcome development to which Delhi is resigned.

NOTES

1. "Advance Estimates of National Income, 2006-07," Government of India press release, Feb. 7, 2007, and "Quick Estimates of National Income, Consumption Expenditure, Saving and Capital Formation, 2005-06," Government of India press release, Jan. 31, 2007.

2. Dan Nystedt, "China Mobile Subscribers Top U.S. population," IDG News Service, in *InfoWorld*, Jan. 22, 2007; www.infoworld.com/article/07/01/22/HNchinamobilesubscribers_1.html.

3. Dennis Kux, "India's Fine Balance," *Foreign Affairs*, May/June 2002. For an in-depth look at the 2002 communal violence, see David Masci, "Emerging India," *CQ Researcher*, April 19, 2002, pp. 329-360.

4. Kamal Nath, address to the 79th general meeting of the Federation of Indian Chambers of Commerce and Industry (FICCI), Jan. 9, 2007.

5. "World Development Indicators Database," World Bank, April 23, 2007; http://siteresources.worldbank.org/DATASTATISTICS/Resources/GDP.pdf.

6. Dominic Wilson and Roopa Purushothaman, "Dreaming with Brics: The Path to 2050," Goldman Sachs Global Economics Paper No. 99, Oct. 1, 2003.

7. Tushar Poddar and Eva Yi, "India's Rising Growth Potential," Goldman Sachs Global Economics Paper No. 152, Jan. 22, 2007.

8. C. Raja Mohan, *Impossible Allies: Nuclear India, United States and the Global Order* (2006), pp. 259-260.

9. Government of India press release, "Poverty Estimates for 2004-05," March 21, 2007; www.pib.nic.in/release/release.asp?relid=26316&kwd=poverty.

10. For background, see Masci, "For India's Women, a Hard Life," *op. cit.*, p. 338; and *World Factbook*, Central Intelligence Agency.

11. A. P. J. Abdul Kalam, address at the 81st Annual Day of Shri Ram College of Commerce, March 19, 2007. The office of president is largely ceremonial.

12. While China reported very high growth rates from 1992-1996 — ranging from 10 to 14 percent a year — the statistics were questioned; now some

think China's current official estimates of 9 to 10 percent annual GDP growth may be understated. See Wayne M. Morrison, "China's Economic Conditions," Congressional Research Service, Foreign Affairs, Defense, and Trade Division, Jan. 12, 2006, p. CRS-3. Also see Vaclav Smil, "Podium: It Doesn't Add Up," *AsiaWeek*, Nov. 30, 2001.

13. Government of India Planning Commission, "Towards Faster Growth and More Inclusive Growth: An Approach to the 11th Five Year Plan," 2006. India's fiscal year begins April 1 and ends March 31 of the following year.

14. Surjit S. Bhalla, *Mid-Year Review of the Economy 2006-2007: India at a Structural Break* (2006), p. 84.

15. Shankar Aiyer and Puja Mehra, "Prices Out of Control," *India Today*, March 5, 2007, pp. 34-45.

16. *Human Development Report 2006*, United Nations Development Program (2006), pp. 284-285.

17. Nath, *op. cit.*

18. *Human Development Report 2006*, *op. cit.*, pp. 301-303 and pp. 319-321.

19. "Corruption Perceptions Index 2006," Transparency International (2006); www.transparency.org/policy_ research/surveys_indices/ cpi/2006.

20. Aroon Purie, "From the editor-in-chief," *India Today*, March 12, 2007.

21. *Overview of Indian Development Policy Review: Inclusive Growth and Service Delivery: Building on India's Success*, The World Bank (2006), p. 4.

22. *Ibid.*, pp. 6-7.

23. For background, see Roland Flamini, "Nuclear Proliferation," *CQ Global Researcher*, January 2007, pp. 1-26; also see Rodman D. Griffin, "Nuclear Proliferation," *CQ Researcher*, June 5, 1992, pp. 481-504.

24. With the apparent consent of the government in Islamabad, Pakistani nuclear scientist A. Q. Khan sold black market nuclear plans and materials to Libya, Iran and North Korea. For background, see Flamini, *op. cit.*

25. "IAEA Director Welcomes U.S. and India Nuclear Deal," International Atomic Energy Agency press release, March 2, 2002.

26. Ashley Tellis, "The U.S.-India 'Global Partnership': How Significant for American Interests?" testimony before U.S. House Committee on International Relations, Nov. 16. 2005.

27. For background, see Elaine Monaghan, "2006 Legislative Summary: U.S.-India Nuclear Pact," *CQ Weekly*, Dec. 18, 2006, p. 3350.

28. Yashwant Sinha, "Against National Interest," *India Today*, Dec. 25, 2006.

29. Jeffrey Sachs, *The End of Poverty* (2005), p. 173.

30. *Ibid.*, pp. 26-31.

31. Tariq Ali, *The Nehrus and the Gandhis: An Indian Dynasty* (2004), p. 87.

32. Arvind Virmani, *Propelling India from Socialist Stagnation to Global Power: Volume I* (2006), p. 43. This and subsequent growth figures come from Table 1.1, which breaks down India's growth from 1951 to 2002.

33. Ali, *op. cit.*, pp. 181-187.

34. Virmani, *op. cit.*, p. 56.

35. Gurcharan Das, *India Unbound: The Social and Economic Revolution from Independence to the Global Information Age* (2001), p. 214.

36. Nath, *op. cit.*

37. Ali, *op. cit.*, pp. 93-101.

38. Stephen P. Cohen, *India: Emerging Power* (2001), p. 41.

39. C. Raja Mohan, *Impossible Allies: Nuclear India, United States and the Global Order* (2006), p. 266.

40. See Selig S. Harrison, "How to Regulate Nuclear Weapons; The U.S. Deal with India Could Be a Good Starting Point," *The Washington Post*, April 23, 2006, p. B7.

41. Strobe Talbott, *Engaging India* (2004), p. 52.

42. Mohan, *op. cit.*, p. 15.

43. *Ibid.*, p 7.

44. P. Chidambaram, speech to Parliament, Feb. 28, 2007.

45. P. S. Suryanarayana, "A Wave of Defence Diplomacy," *The Hindu*, March 10, 2007.

46. "Wooing Beijing," *The Times of India*, May 31, 2006.

47. "Most expensive house in the world has 27 floors, ocean and slum views," *Los Angeles Times*, Oct. 25, 2010, http://framework.latimes.com/2010/10/25/ most-expensive-home-in-the-world-has-27-floors-ocean-and-slum-views/.

48. Mark Jacobson, "Mumbai Shadow City," *National Geographic*, May 2007, http://ngm.nationalgeo graphic.com/2007/05/dharavi-mumbai-slum/jacob son-text.

49. Navi Radjou and others, "Indian Tales of Inclusive Business Models," *Harvard Business Review*, Jan. 5, 2011, http://blogs.hbr.org/cs/2011/01/indian_ tales_of_inclusive_busi.html.

50. "Indian economy will grow faster than Chinese in 2012: World Bank," *Times of India*, Jan. 14, 2011, http:// timesofindia.indiatimes.com/business/india-business/ Indian-economy-will-grow-faster-than-Chinese-in-2012-World-Bank/articleshow/7280367.cms.

51. Shayam Saran, "India and China Take Different Roads to World Leadership," *Yale Global*, Nov. 1, 2010, http://yaleglobal.yale.edu/content/india-and-china-different-roads-part-i.

52. Jayshree Bajoria, "The U.S.-India Nuclear Deal," Council on Foreign Relations, Nov. 5, 2010, www .cfr.org/india/us-india-nuclear-deal/p9663.

53. "Obama backs India for permanent UN Security Council seat," BBC News, Nov. 8, 2010, www.bbc .co.uk/news/world-south-asia-11711007.

54. Shashi Tharoor, "Obama dismayed as India rejects arms deal," Al Jazeera, May 12, 2011, www.free republic.com/focus/news/2718878/posts.

55. Amana F. Khan, Rahul Bedi and Rob Crilly, "Co-ordinated bomb attacks bring terror back to streets of Mumbai," *The Daily Telegraph* (London), July 14, 2011, p. 16.

BIBLIOGRAPHY
BOOKS

Ali, Tariq, *The Nehrus and the Gandhis: An Indian Dynasty, Picador*, 2005.
A London-based author and commentator tells the story of one family's dominance of Indian politics.

Bhalla, Surjit S., *Mid-Year Review of the Economy 2006-2007: India at a Structural Break, Shipra Publications*, 2007.
A manager of a New Delhi-based investment fund and former World Bank economist makes the case for India having moved onto a higher growth plane.

Cohen, Stephen P., *India: Emerging Power, Brookings Institution Press*, 2001.
A veteran Indian scholar describes India's emergence as a strategic and military power in Asia and chronicles the course of U.S.-India relations.

Das, Gurcharan, *India Unbound: The Social and Economic Revolution from Independence to the Global Information Age, Alfred A. Knopf*, 2001.
The former CEO of Proctor & Gamble India provides an account laced with personal anecdotes of how India's economic policy and economy have evolved since Independence.

Luce, Edward, *In Spite of the Gods: The Strange Rise of Modern India, Doubleday*, 2007.
A former *Financial Times* South Asia bureau chief examines India's burgeoning growth amid mass poverty and illiteracy, institutional corruption and enduring religious traditions such as the Hindu caste system.

Mohan, C. Raja, *Impossible Allies: Nuclear India, United States and the Global Order, India Research Press*, 2006.
An Indian analyst and columnist for the *Indian Express* newspaper describes how India and the United States came to an agreement on a nuclear deal and his outlook for U.S.-India relations.

Sachs, Jeffrey, *The End of Poverty: How We Can Make it Happen in Our Lifetime, Penguin Books*, 2005.
The famed development economist offers his prescription for eradicating global poverty, based on his experiences in several countries including India.

Talbott, Strobe, *Engaging India: Diplomacy, Democracy and the Bomb, Brookings Institution Press*, 2004.
A former U.S. deputy secretary of State offers a firsthand account of the Clinton administration's negotiations with India after its 1998 nuclear tests.

Virmani, Arvind, *Propelling India from Socialist Stagnation to Global Power, Academic Foundation*, 2006.
An economist and adviser to the Indian government provides a comprehensive look at India's economic performance based heavily on his own pioneering econometric studies.

Articles

Chellaney, Brahma, "Don't Nuke the Facts," *The Times of India*, Jan. 9, 2007.
An Indian analyst says India needs to look closely at the details of the Hyde Act, passed recently by Congress, before agreeing to the U.S.-India nuclear deal.

Mohan, C. Raja, *"India and the Balance of Power," Foreign Affairs*, July/August 2006, p. 17.
A strategic-affairs expert explains India's outlook as it emerges as a more influential player in international affairs.

Reports and Studies

"Economic Survey 2006-2007," *Government of India (Ministry of Finance)*, 2007.
This annual government review gives a detailed overview of the state of India's economy, government spending and receipts, financial and commodity markets and trade.

"Pursuit and Promotion of Science: The Indian Experience," *Indian National Science Academy*, 2001.

The chapter on agriculture describes how the Green Revolution transformed the production of wheat, rice and other agricultural products in India.

"Towards Faster and More Inclusive Growth," *Government of India (Planning Commission)*, December 2006.
A government study describes India's current economic situation and the challenges it faces as it prepares a five-year development plan for 2007-2012.

Shukla, Rajesh K., S. K. Dwivedi and Asha Sharma, "The Great Indian Middle Class," *National Council of Applied Economic Research*, 2004.
A study of 300,000 Indian households finds that 6 percent have reached the middle class.

Tushar, Poddar, and Eva Yi, "India's Rising Growth Potential," *Goldman Sachs Global Economics Paper No. 152*, Jan. 22, 2007.
Financial analysts predict India's influence on the world economy will be bigger and quicker than previously thought.

For More Information

CARE, 27 Hauz Khas Village, New Delhi 110016; (91-11) 2656-6060; www.careindia.org. The Indian affiliate of the aid organization focuses on women and girls.

Carnegie Endowment for International Peace, 1779 Massachusetts Ave., N.W., Washington, DC 20036; (202) 483-7600; www.carnegieendowment.org. Its South Asia project tracks U.S.-India relations and the nuclear deal.

Centre for Policy Research, Dharma Marg, Chanakyapuri, New Delhi 110021; (91-11) 2611-5273; www.cprindia.org. Researches Indian public-policy issues.

Indian Council for Research on International Economic Relations, Core 6A, Fourth Floor, India Habitat Centre, Lodhi Road, New Delhi 110003; (91-11) 2464-5218; www.icrier.org. Conducts research and holds workshops.

The Institute for Defence Studies and Analyses, 1 Development Enclave, Delhi Cantt, New Delhi 110010; (91-11) 2671-7983; www.idsa.in. Conducts research.

Institute of Peace & Conflict Studies, B-7/3 Lower Ground Floor, Safdarjung Enclave, New Delhi 110029; (91-11) 4100-1900; www.ipcs.org. Studies security issues in South Asia.

National Council of Applied Economic Research, Parisila Bhawan, 11 Indraprastha Estate, New Delhi 110002; (91-11) 2337-9861; www.ncaer.org. Leading economic research institution that conducts surveys the Indian economy.

Observer Research Foundation, 20 Rouse Avenue Institutional Area, New Delhi 110002; (91-11) 4352-0020; www.observerindia.com. A public-policy research institute.

Research and Information System for Developing Countries, Zone IV-B, Fourth Floor, Indian Habitat Centre, Lodhi Road, New Delhi 110003; (91-11) 2468-2177; www.ris.org.in. A government-funded research institute.

Voices From Abroad:

RODRIGO DE RATO

Managing Director, International Monetary Fund
March 2005

Needed: 100 million jobs
"India needs to continue to restructure its domestic economy, to allow it to reap the full benefits of globalization. It is sobering to think that India needs to generate in excess of 100 million jobs in the next decade simply to keep the unemployment rate from rising."

BIBEK DEBROY

Secretary General; Progress, Harmony and Development Chamber of Commerce and Industry (India)
January 2006

Government must facilitate growth
"Though the target of single-digit income-poverty ratios in 2012 is a welcome target to have, this will not be possible unless the government creates a facilitating environment for growth and improves delivery of its anti-poverty programmes."

MOHAMED ELBARADEI

Director General, International Atomic Energy Agency
June 2006

No violation of nuclear pact
"The U.S.-India deal . . . does not add to or detract from India's nuclear weapons program, nor does it confer any 'status,' legal or otherwise, on India as a possessor of nuclear weapons. India has never joined the NPT; it has therefore not violated any legal commitment, and it has never encouraged nuclear weapons proliferation."

The International Herald Tribune/Patrick Chappatte

RAHUNATH MASHELKAR

President, Indian National Science Academy
February 2007

The brain drain is over
"During the last three years, more than 30,000 top-class professionals — scientists and engineers — have come back to the country. . . . India is gradually becoming the land of opportunity. . . . The latest Intel chip is not being designed in the U.S. — it's being designed in Bangalore."

KAMAL NATH

Commerce Minister of India
April 2006

Collaboration creates opportunities
"It is only with a conscious multi-pronged, multi-dimensional effort that we can address the massive challenge of finding job opportunities for millions of our unemployed youth, and export-oriented production has a huge potential for generating jobs."

HARUHIKO KURODA

President, Asian Development Bank
November 2006

Inclusion must accompany growth
"Infrastructure development has a crucial role to play if India is to sustain its high growth, which must become more inclusive as the country matures."

ARUNDHATI GHOSE

**Former Indian
Ambassador to the United Nations**
February 2007

Just friends, not allies
"India will never be an ally [of the United States]. . . . But we'll be a friend, which is different. In an alliance there is a leader, and what he says is carried out by the rest of the alliance. . . . [W]here we have common interests, we will work together. Where we disagree, we will continue to disagree."

A.P.J. ABDUL KALAM

President of India
February 2007

Science and technology are top priorities
"The growth of the economy is very important — and if the growth of the economy is important, so is science and technology, because it drives this growth. . . . As science transforms technology, it brings faster development to the nation. That's how, from 1947 onwards, science and technology became the top priority for all the governments."

ARUNDHATI ROY

Author
June 2005

India joining war on terror
"As a spokesperson for the jury of conscience, it would make me uneasy if I did not mention that the government of India is . . . positioning itself as an ally of the United States in its economic policies and the so-called War on Terror."

10

Future of the Euro

Sarah Glazer

An election worker counts ballots after Ireland's general election on Feb. 25, in which the ruling party suffered a crushing defeat amid public anger over the country's economic crisis. Ireland's new prime minister, Enda Kenny, resisted pressure at an EU summit the following month to raise Ireland's low corporate tax rate — which attracts corporations like Google to Dublin — as the price for lowering the interest rate charged by the EU to Ireland for its bailout.

From *CQ Researcher*, May 17, 2011.

W hen two German lawmakers suggested last year that Greece sell off some of its islands and artworks in exchange for a bailout from the European Union, the suggestion caused much hilarity in the European press.

"We give you cash, you give us Corfu . . . and the Acropolis too," cackled a headline in the German newspaper *Bild*. The British *Guardian* couldn't resist calling the proposal "My Big Fat Greek Auction," noting a Greek island could be picked up for as little as $2 million.

Dimitris Droutsas, Greece's deputy foreign minister, was not amused. "Suggestions like this are not appropriate at this time," he told German television.[1]

The dust-up epitomized the conflicts between the weak and the economically strong economies in the eurozone — the 17 European Union (EU) members that have adopted the euro as their currency. The tensions have escalated over the past year as Greece, Ireland and Portugal have received handouts from their EU brethren to help deal with domestic debt and budget crises. Now Greece apparently will need even more money to finance its debt, aggravating tensions and raising questions about whether richer countries will support yet more loans.

"The political understandings that underpin the European Union are beginning to unravel," declared *Financial Times* columnist Gideon Rachman on April 17, the day Finland's nationalist True Finns party — which had campaigned strongly against a bailout for Portugal — made spectacular gains in the general election. The victory intensified doubts at the time over whether Europe could agree on a solution to the debt crisis, since bailouts require

271

Eurozone Power Most of EU Economy

Seventeen of the 27 European Union (EU) members,representing a poulation of about 330 million, have adopted the euro currency.Seven other countries are expected to join the eurozone over the next seven years.Euro countries account for 75 percent of the EU's gross domestic product, making the world's second-most-important currency after the U.S.dollar. Sweden, Denmark and the United Kingdom have declined to join the eurozone. Portugal, ireland and Greece are experiencing debt problem and have asked for bailouts.Some worry Spain could be next

The European Union and the Eurozone

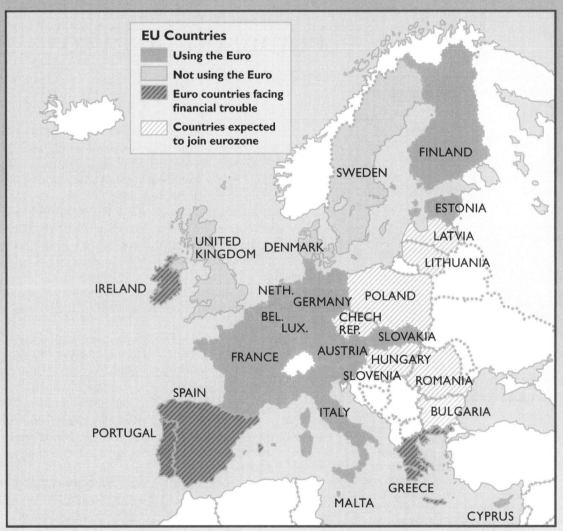

EU Countries

- Using the Euro
- Not using the Euro
- Euro countries facing financial trouble
- Countries expected to join eurozone

ICELAND · FINLAND · SWEDEN · ESTONIA · LATVIA · UNITED KINGDOM · DENMARK · LITHUANIA · IRELAND · NETH. · GERMANY · POLAND · BEL. · LUX. · CHECH REP. · SLOVAKIA · FRANCE · AUSTRIA · HUNGARY · SLOVENIA · ROMANIA · SPAIN · ITALY · BULGARIA · PORTUGAL · MALTA · GREECE · CYPRUS

Source: European Commission

Map by Lewis Agrell

unanimous approval by all 17 members of the eurozone.[2] Those fears were calmed, somewhat, when Finland's Parliament voted May 12 to support the Portugal bailout. But the vote came amid growing opposition in Germany to a possible second bailout for Greece and concerns that all three countries could make return visits to the euro till.

"My fear is the euro could sow seeds of division between members," says Simon Tilford, chief economist at the Centre for European Reform, a London think tank. "My question for the euro is whether it was ever realistic for such a heterogeneous group of nations," he says.

The growing resentments between rich and poor countries feed into a lingering question that has plagued the eurozone experiment since it was created in 1999: Can a common market like the eurozone function without a common government? In the United States, points out Harvard Business School professor of business administration David Moss, "There is a lot of anxiety and anger that Americans feel in bailing out Wall Street banks, but at least they're American banks." In the eurozone, a German voter is just as likely to be asked to bail out the Greek government — or, ultimately, to shore up a Greek bank.

The current crisis grew out of the inability of highly indebted governments like Greece, Ireland and Portugal to raise enough money in the bond markets to pay their debts and government obligations after the global recession sent tax revenues plunging. It began a year ago, when Greece — facing default after revelations that the nation's finances were in much worse shape than the previous administration had claimed — received a €110 billion ($145 billion) bailout loan from the EU and the International Monetary Fund (IMF). Then in November, Ireland — whose hyper-inflated housing bubble burst during the world credit crisis — received a €67.5 billion ($88.42 billion) EU/IMF rescue. Finally, Portugal's Socialist government last month came to the EU hat in

Failing Economies Loaded With Debt

Portugal, Ireland, Greece and Spain failed last year to meet the European Union (EU) goal of limiting countries' public debt to 60 percent of national output, or gross domestic product (GDP). Greece's debt-to-GDP ratio was the EU's highest, at 144 percent of GDP. Nordic countries such as Finland and Sweden had far lower ratios. But Germany, critical of countries with high debts, had a higher ratio than Spain. By comparison, the U.S. debt was 58.9 percent of GDP — just below the EU target.

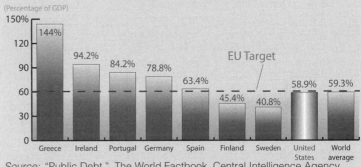

Public Debt for Select Countries
(as a percentage of GDP, 2010 Estimates)

Source: "Public Debt," The World Factbook, Central Intelligence Agency, May 2011

hand, realizing it would not be able to pay its bondholders this June. On May 3, the EU and IMF agreed to loan Portugal €78 billion ($115 billion). The May 14 arrest of IMF Managing Director Dominique Strauss-Kahn on charges of the attempted rape of a New York hotel maid could complicate upcoming EU/IMF talks over revamping Greece's bailout loan, since he was a crucial figure in arranging the bailouts for the three countries.[3]

Despite the bailouts, interest rates for loans to Greece and Portugal have continued to soar, effectively preventing them from resuming normal borrowing. "Apparently bond traders are skeptical of whether those [bailout] guarantees will be sufficient and whether the Germans and other Europeans will stand behind larger and larger guarantees, if they become necessary," says Moss.

In exchange for the bailouts, the EU is demanding painful austerity measures that some economists say could trigger up to 10 more years of recession and huge cuts in treasured pension, unemployment, education and health-care programs. Nevertheless, although EU

'Desperate Generation' Hits the Streets in Portugal

Youths complain of low pay, few jobs.

Twenty-three-year-old João Moreira considered himself lucky to get a job as a school teacher after obtaining his master's degree in education in Porto, Portugal's second-largest city.

But he was appalled when he discovered that he would earn less than the minimum wage. At €330 a month ($440) he is forced to live at home with his mother in his second year of teaching high-school students.

On March 12, Moreira and other recent university graduates used Facebook to organize street demonstrations to protest the dismal economic conditions facing his generation. The protests attracted between 300,000-400,000 demonstrators in Portugal's 10 major cities, surprising even the organizers themselves.

The organizers, all in their 20s, called themselves *geração à rasca* — loosely translated as the "desperate generation" or "generation in a jam." They say they were inspired by the Portuguese band Deolinda's popular song "What a Fool I Am," whose lyrics, "I'm from the unpaid generation," spoke to their precarious work situation.

"There are no jobs for young people in Portugal, and when you have a job, you have a job like mine — a low-paid job," says Moreira. "We can't see a future for ourselves; we have no prospects." Two of his fellow organizers were headed to wealthier countries — Germany and Denmark — to work.

Besides unemployment, demonstrators complained about the lack of job security. The number of so-called "green receipts" jobs — temporary consultant jobs without benefits — has swelled, and the protesters say many are trapped in these jobs for years. Youths also complain of another form of exploitation in their eyes: unpaid or low-paid internships.

"We have 35-year-olds who graduated 10 or 15 years ago who are still in internships because there's no other way of getting into the job market," says Paula Gil, 26, a petite, serious-eyed organizer of the Lisbon protests, who has a master's degree in international relations and is working in a year-long paid internship with a nongovernmental, international development organization.

"It is slavery," when you're working for free, says Gil. In a paid internship like hers, she says, payroll taxes take 50 percent of her pay even though "you don't get access to unemployment insurance or sick leave, you can be fired at any time and you don't get social security benefits."

Such dead-end jobs delay young people's decisions, experts note. "They can't marry because banks won't give them a mortgage," further contributing to Portugal's low fertility rate, observes Ana Catarina Santos, a political journalist for TSF, a radio news station in Lisbon. [1]

But not all university graduates foresee such a grim future. Several graduate students in economics at Nova University School of Business and Economics in Lisbon — Portugal's most selective business school — are optimistic about finding jobs, but expect they probably will have to go abroad to find their "dream job." None had attended the recent demonstrations.

Employers are simply trying to get around Portugal's rigid labor and benefit rules that make it expensive to hire and difficult to fire employees, these students say, echoing the view of the European Union, which is expected to demand that Portugal move towards a more flexible labor

officials in Brussels insist such budget-cutting conditions will prevent defaults, investors recently have come to believe that a Greek default is "inevitable," according to the *Financial Times*.[4]

Indeed, some experts foresee the collapse of banks in wealthier nations like Germany, which loaned billions to the four faltering countries — Portugal, Ireland, Greece and Spain (known by their acronym, the PIGS) — during the credit boom years. Because of those banks' high exposure to troubled governments' bonds, EU leaders want to stave off default at all costs, experts say. The EU's solution is "a Ponzi scheme [that] could in theory go on forever," the former governor of Argentina's central bank, Mario Biejer, recently charged, suggesting that accepting a default might be "preferable to increasing the burden on future taxpayers."[5]

The eurozone was conceived as a way to turn the European Union into a formidable world economic

market. Those labor laws need to change, says Nova student Rafael Barbosa, 21. "When you march against symptoms, nothing will get done," he says.

"It is very difficult for a boss to fire a worker in Portugal because they're protected by law by unions and lawyers," explains Santos, coauthor of the 2010 book, *Dangerous Ideas to Save Portugal*. Under existing law, if an employer fires a worker the boss must pay close to twice the employee's salary for every year worked, Santos notes. If the employer tries to challenge the requirement in court, it could take up to 10 years to get through the appeal process.

Indeed, there's "a cultural expectation" among the Portuguese that they'll have a job for life, especially in the bloated government sector, Santos says. It's partly a legacy of the 1974 revolution against the 42-year dictatorship of António de Oliviera Salazar and of the socialist rhetoric in liberated Portugal's constitution, which strongly guarantees workers' rights. About 13 percent of Portugal's workforce is employed in government jobs, from which it is almost impossible to be fired, according to Santos.

But Portugal's recently requested bailout from the European Union will likely require reform of the country's rigid labor rules — similar to recent labor reforms in Spain — and reductions in worker benefits.

Portugal also has suffered from a decade of poor economic growth, largely the result of its failure to improve the productivity of industries like textiles, which have become increasingly uncompetitive in the face of cheap Chinese exports.

Protest leaders have steered clear of offering political solutions to these economic realities. Their primary purpose, they say, was to start a discussion at the grass roots. They presented parliament with hundreds of survey sheets filled out by protesters, who were asked to suggest solutions. It's unclear what kind of reception their proposals, which Santos expects to be "a bit utopian," will receive from the new government after the June 5 elections. The new

Protesters in downtown Lisbon are just some of the 300,000-400,000 demonstrators who took to the streets of 10 major cities in Portugal on March 12, 2011, to protest the lack of job opportunities for young people. The turnout surprised even the organizers, who used Facebook to advertise the protests.

government will have to devise a strict austerity package to meet EU bailout conditions.

Still, the March demonstrations, notable for their lack of violence, touched a chord among other generations, too. "You could see a 40-year-old mother worried that her sons were unemployed, and you could see pensioners who earn only €300 a month," reports Santos. "It was diverse — each group protesting a different thing, a bit messy but very genuine. It showed Portuguese society has a lot of problems."

— *Sarah Glazer*

[1] The fertility rate refers to the average number of children born per woman in the population during her life. From 2005-2010, Portugal's fertility rate averaged 1.38 children per woman. A fertility rate below 1.8 is considered insufficient to replace the current population. For fertility rates, See "Pensions at a Glance, 2011," Organisation for Economic Co-operation and Development, 2011, p. 163.

power.[6] But the current crisis has highlighted what some economists say is the system's inherent weakness: the failure to form a United States of Europe with overarching power to balance the vast differences in wealth between the poor South and the rich North. The euro imposed a single currency on diverse countries without creating a centralized government with the power to collect taxes and decide how to spend them.

Ardent proponents of the euro knew from the beginning that eventually they would have to create "a federal fiscal system," says British economic historian Niall Ferguson, author of *The Cash Nexus* and a professor of history at Harvard. "But they didn't say it publicly, because no ordinary voter wants to be in the United States of Europe."

"Politicians knew that they risked running afoul of voters if they surrendered too much sovereignty," writes

Mary Elise Sarotte, a professor of International Relations at the University of Southern California.[7] Instead, member countries have continued to guard jealously their power to tax and spend.

The recent deals among EU countries in the wake of the crisis show that member states continue to be reluctant to surrender sovereignty "in key areas such as pensions, labor and wage policy, or taxation," said the European Policy Centre, a Brussels think tank.[8]

EU diplomats say the current crisis presents an opportunity to fix those weaknesses. But some experts say the price demanded by the EU — austerity budgets and repayment of huge loans to the EU — will be so high that debt-laden countries like Portugal, Greece and Ireland will eventually abandon the euro currency.

"It's a question of time before the Irish or the Greeks or the Portuguese say, 'We can't do any more of this [debt- and budget-cutting] adjustment,'" says Desmond Lachman, resident scholar at the American Enterprise Institute (AEI), a conservative think tank in Washington. Or the Germans will simply "get tired of financing this."

The conflict already has had serious political repercussions for leaders in the eurozone. In February, the Irish government fell. A month later Portugal's Socialist Prime Minister José Sócrates was forced to resign. Also in March, German Chancellor Angela Merkel's Christian Democratic Party lost a crucial provincial election in a former party bastion — a loss partly blamed on German voters' resistance to paying higher taxes to rescue crisis-ridden Greece and Ireland.[9]

"The German voter has had enough of writing checks for people in the rest of Europe that he or she regards as lazy," says Ferguson.

Brussels diplomats refer to the tension between what countries must give up to make a common currency work and what is politically feasible as "Juncker's curse," after Luxembourg Prime Minister Jean-Claude Juncker's quip, "We all know what to do, but we don't know how to get re-elected once we have done it."[10]

However, that logjam may have broken, say EU diplomats, citing the recent bailouts and efforts to more closely monitor weaker states' balance sheets to prevent future disasters. "We are strengthening and broadening the surveillance framework of the euro in ways that would not have been thought possible before this crisis,"

maintains Silvia Kofler, minister counselor and head of press and public diplomacy at the EU delegation to the United States.

Yet, those very budget-cutting, debt-reducing measures could force the weaker countries to desert the euro, some fear. At some point, the troubled countries "are going to say, 'We're going through these tremendous recessions in order to pay interest to foreign bankers.' That's a very difficult political sell to maintain," observes Lachman.

And, unlike the U.S. dollar regime, the EU has no common military or coercive power that could be used to force member states to stay in the eurozone, notes Harvard's Moss. "In this country, an attempted secession was put down by force during the Civil War. One has to wonder whether there is a limit to how far integration can go in Europe without a common government and without the threat of coercive power."

"The euro is like a sick patient on the couch, and the doctors don't agree on the diagnosis or prescription," Charles Grant, director of the Centre for European Reform, told a London School of Economics audience on March 15. And the crisis, he noted, comes as Europe's military and diplomatic power are dwindling, along with its economic competitiveness.

The fallout from the crisis has been multifaceted. The seven other EU members expected to adopt the euro sometime in the next seven years may now be less willing to abandon their own currencies.[11] And EU enthusiasm for admitting new, less prosperous countries appears to have cooled somewhat. Meanwhile, right-wing nationalist parties — many of them skeptical of the euro and opposed to helping struggling neighbors — are making big strides across Europe.

Is the eurozone headed for yet more internal conflict or greater unity? Here are some of the questions being posed in governments, academia and the international community:

Will the Eurozone survive in its current form?

Even before Portugal was bracing for a new round of budget cuts in exchange for an EU bailout, some experts were predicting the eurozone's poorest country would defect if the EU's budget discipline became too draconian.

Current EU budget rules require member countries to reduce their public debt to no more than 60 percent of national output — or gross domestic product (GDP)

— and to keep their budget deficits from exceeding 3 percent of GDP.[12]

Portugal, Ireland, Greece and Spain have a long way to go to meet those goals. And reaching them could take up to 10 years of stunted economic growth while they pay back their debts, slash their budgets and raise taxes, some economists say.

Such strict budget and debt ceilings, however, will block the PIGS from using economic tools governments historically have utilized to lift their nations out of recession: deficit spending to stimulate the economy.

"These countries are now forced in a vicious way to use austerity when you shouldn't have it; austerity makes things worse and undermines the political basis of the support you need for the eurozone," says Paul De Grauwe, a professor of economics at the University of Leuven, in Belgium.

Indeed, AEI's Lachman predicts that Greece, Ireland, Portugal and probably Spain will drop out of the eurozone because they won't be able to survive the inevitable years of recession that will follow such austerity programs.

The eurozone "can't survive in its present form," he says. "For me, it's a question of just the timing when that occurs."

Others, such as EU diplomat Kofler, consider the idea of defection "really difficult to take seriously." If a nation left the euro, she says, its "existing debt level would remain in euros, regardless of what new currency it introduced after leaving the euro area." Since the new currency likely would devalue against the euro — by 50 percent according to some estimates — the cost of paying back interest and principal on the existing debt would "skyrocket," she predicts.[13] The result would be steep inflation, collapsed banking sectors and the flight of capital, EU officials warn.[14]

Irish economist David McWilliams, however, advocates that Ireland leave the euro and pay back its debtors in a new devalued Irish currency, essentially forcing debtors to accept a loss. Adopting a new, weaker

currency, McWilliams predicts, would make Ireland "cheaper overnight for people to do business in."[15]

Yet, even an early euroskeptic like economist Ferguson considers exiting too expensive and unlikely, partly because of a widely expressed fear of crisis contagion.

Others cite practical problems like printing new currency and redesigning vending machines. De Grauwe, another early euroskeptic, says these arguments remind him of the stories of Soviet couples who wanted to divorce but couldn't because of the impossibility of finding a second apartment. "You were condemned to stay together, and you hated each other. If that's the future of the eurozone, I'm not optimistic," he says. "In the end, the [weaker countries] will say, 'To hell with it: Even if the practical problems are high, we just don't want it anymore.' "

On the other hand, De Grauwe and other euroskeptics have suggested, stronger economies like Germany are suffering from "integration fatigue" and might leave the eurozone to avoid paying bailout costs. Euro defenders counter that richer countries won't let a collapse happen if only for their own self-interest: Bailouts for

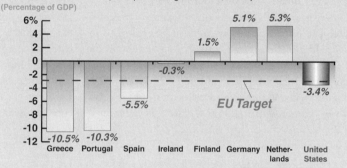

Budget Deficits Hobble Troubled Euro Countries

Portugal, Ireland and Greece are experiencing both debt crises and budget deficits. Greece and Portugal have the biggest deficits — more than 10 percent of their national output, or gross domestic product (GDP). The European Union recommends that member countries' budget shortfalls not exceed 3 percent of GDP. The U.S. budget deficit is 3.4 percent of GDP. Finland, Germany and the Netherlands have budget surpluses.

Budget Deficits (or Surpluses) for Select Countries
(as a percentage of GDP, 2010)

(Percentage of GDP)

Greece -10.5%
Portugal -10.3%
Spain -5.5%
Ireland -0.3%
Finland 1.5%
Germany 5.1%
Netherlands 5.3%
United States -3.4%

EU Target

Source: Organisation for Economic Co-operation and Development

Greece help German banks, which own large amounts of the PIGS' debt in the form of government bonds and loans. If any one of the troubled countries defaults and leaves the euro, German banks would suffer huge losses.[16]

By sharing the euro with poorer economies, Germany also benefits from using a weaker currency, making its exports cheaper than if German exports were priced in a more expensive deutschmark. "It's a great advantage; that's why they'll never leave it," says Carlo Bastasin, an economist and senior fellow at the Brookings Institution, a moderate think tank in Washington.

Observers on both sides say the eurozone is at a critical political juncture. The current crisis is "analogous to the New Deal period in the United States," says Simon Hix, a professor of European and Comparative Politics at the London School of Economics. "There were huge battles over whether the U.S. government would take on . . . fiscal responsibilities [for other states,] because until then the U.S. federal budget was tiny."

And despite the current raging debate, Hix maintains, there's a surprising amount of consensus among political rivals about accepting the EU's new levels of austerity. Even in Portugal, the opposition Social Democratic Party — which is favored to win the June election and which helped sink the government's last austerity package — has accepted the need for bailout austerity.

"If that broad level of consensus carries on in Europe among voters like this, we have a good chance of getting through this," Hix says, "because you have publics that are willing to accept the tough political decisions needed to make these things work."

Skeptics, however, think the strains of trying to yoke such different economies to the euro are fomenting, not calming, new political tensions. "You're getting two Europes: the North that is doing OK and the South that is going down the drain," says Lachman. "That's not the way to have a political union."

Are some countries worse off under the euro?

When it comes to Ireland's current economic crisis, the government's biggest mistake was joining the euro in the first place, according to Sean Barrett, an economist at Trinity College, Dublin.

"Since joining the euro we've conducted an experiment by blowing up the laboratory," he says, pointing out that Ireland went from full employment and a balanced budget before adopting the euro to 14.5 percent unemployment and insolvency today.

As Nobel Prize-winning American economist Milton Friedman warned in 2001, countries need different monetary policies depending on whether their economies are fast-growing and inflationary — which need higher interest rates to cool them down — or slow-growing, needing low rates to help heat up the economy by encouraging borrowing, investment and consumption.[17]

Today Friedman's predictions seem prescient. Known during boom times as the "Celtic Tiger," Ireland was growing exponentially on a virtual tsunami of cheap money during the 1990s-2000s, which triggered a disastrous property bubble. The government should have raised interest rates to slow down the borrowing frenzy, euro critics say, but it no longer had that power since the European Central Bank (ECB) sets interest rates for the euro countries.

"Ireland needed to cool down in the years after it joined the euro, but Germany needed to warm up," notes Barrett. Now the situation is reversed, with the European Central Bank responding more to Germany's fast-growth situation than to Ireland's dismal recession.

ECB President Jean-Claude Trichet encountered a storm of criticism — mainly from Ireland and Spain — when the bank on April 7 raised Europe's interest rates by a quarter of a percentage point to 1.25 percent. The increase was expected to hit the two countries especially hard because of the large number of homeowners with variable-rate mortgages.[18]

"There's a double whammy [in Ireland] for homeowners in that the main banks here can increase their rates but also the European Central Bank can increase its rates," which are reflected in variable-rate mortgages, says Aoife Walsh, spokesperson for Respond! Housing Association, which advises Irish homeowners.

By contrast, Germany welcomed the interest rate hike as a way to cool inflation. Trichet said his action was aimed at the eurozone as a whole, where inflation has exceeded the bank's 2 percent target.

Adopting the euro also meant governments could no longer devalue their own currencies — a primary tool nations use to recover from a recession because it makes their exports cheaper and therefore more competitive. When Ireland devalued its currency, the punt, during its

1990s recession, Barrett notes, it stimulated "pretty strong growth."

In addition, say economists, the EU's Germanic obsession with living within one's budget has shifted attention away from encouraging economic growth, which would require deficit spending.

Portugal, for example, has suffered from a decade of slow growth. After years as Europe's sweatshop, selling cheap shoes and textiles, Portugal recently has found itself underpriced by China. And Portugal's failure to reconfigure its industries as high-end, high-fashion brands, as Italy has done, has forced many small companies to shut down and others to suffer. But that kind of investment seems unlikely when demand is low and the cost of borrowing is high.

During the boom years, with exceptionally low interest rates, those in the weaker eurozone countries were practically "paid to borrow," says Tilford, of London's Centre for European Reform. The resulting borrowing-fueled consumption disguised both the lack of underlying growth and the need for structural reforms, such as making hiring and firing more flexible.

"Spain, Italy and Portugal saw the euro as a way of avoiding reforms and being free of currency crises, but it doesn't shield them from the credit crisis," he says.

By contrast, some non-euro EU economies — notably Sweden, Poland and Britain — grew faster in 2010 than eurozone countries.[19] The U.K. also has embarked on an austerity budget, but it can devalue its currency to make its exports more competitive, which the euro countries aren't free to do.

Other economists say the euro is being blamed unfairly for an economic crash that had more to do with the international credit crisis and the failure of domestic regulators. In the case of Ireland, "joining the euro meant we had greater access" to funding from abroad, acknowledges Philip Lane, a professor of economics at Trinity College, Dublin. German banks lent to Irish banks at low rates, who in turn lent cheaply and recklessly to property developers and homeowners. But, "That doesn't mean we had to take it up. It's the role of the regulator to be the grown-up," he says, by requiring a sensible fit between the income of the borrower and the value of the property, something Ireland's regulators failed to do.

"The world was awash in credit," he says, and borrowing standards were being loosened internationally.

Iceland, for example, experienced a phenomenal credit crash even though it wasn't on the euro, he points out.

Once Ireland got into trouble, he notes, it benefited from eurozone membership by being able to borrow from the European Central Bank when borrowing in the bond markets became too expensive.

John Fitz Gerald, an economist at the Economic and Social Research Institute, a think tank in Dublin, says his group warned as early as 1996 that once on the euro the Irish government would have to take other steps to cool borrowing, like taxing homeowners' mortgage-interest payments.

"It's not rocket science," he says, but the government paid no attention. "Don't blame the euro for bad government. Bad government gives you bad results."

Will the EU approach solve the debt crisis?

"Trouble paying your debt? Here borrow some more: How about €80 billion?" asked the *Financial Times* the day after Portugal asked the EU for a $119 billion loan. The eurozone's policymakers should ask themselves whether overindebted Portugal, Ireland and Greece can really do everything expected of them in drastic austerity plans and still pay back their EU loans on time, the *FT* warned.[20]

Some economists say the EU bailout formula "shows no sign of working," according to *The New York Times*, and some say it's making the problem worse.[21]

Under the weight of steep budget cuts over the past two years, the EU's first bailout recipient, Greece, has suffered a 6-percent contraction in real GDP, while Ireland's economy has shrunk by 11 percent. "This is now seriously undermining those countries' tax bases as well as their political willingness to stay the course of [budget-cutting] adjustment," concluded AEI's Lachman.[22] In fact, he predicts, under the EU's prescription, Greece's economy "will collapse."

Already, "Greece has basically ground to a halt," *FT* writer Vincent Boland said on May 9, after the euro plunged on rumors Greece was in so much trouble it would leave the eurozone.[23]

The EU insistence on governments living within their budgets has deprived these countries of deficit spending, says the University of Leuven's De Grauwe. Deficit spending is used by governments to "make sure those who are unemployed have some purchasing power

New York City detectives hold IMF Managing Director Dominique Strauss-Kahn after he was arrested on May 15 and charged with the attempted rape of a hotel chambermaid. Strauss-Kahn, who is being held without bond, was a crucial figure in advocating the bailouts for Greece as well as Ireland and Portugal, and his arrest could complicate upcoming EU/IMF talks over easing the terms of Greece's bailout loan.

to buy goods and services to permit the economy to start growing again," he says. "You don't do that only out of altruism, but also out of a rational calculus that it stabilizes the economy."

Eurozone ministers acknowledged on May 8 that Greece's bailout was insufficient and that the government would need more EU cash to pay its debts into next year. EU ministers planned to meet in May to find a solution, since it was clear Greece could not borrow in the bond markets at the prohibitively high interest rates it was being charged. Amid heightened speculation that Greece would default, eurozone leaders said they were also considering easing Greece's repayment terms.[24]

That renewed crisis — a year after Greece received its bailout, plus Ireland's recent request for easier payback terms — signal that the bailout approach is failing, critics say. "Greece and Ireland are already bailed out and look like they won't be able to finance themselves next year," because of skyrocketing borrowing costs, says Raoul Ruparel, an analyst at Open Europe, a London think tank focused on the European Union.

Increasingly, some prominent economists are urging that these countries need a restructuring — a polite term for default.

"There needs to be a frank acknowledgement that these debts are unsustainable," says University of California, Berkeley, economist Barry Eichengreen. So far, he says, the EU's emphasis on budget cuts is "reducing the cost of everything but the debt; that's another reason why the current strategy will not work."

With an orderly debt restructuring, much like a personal bankruptcy, the EU could tell the countries' creditors, or bondholders, that if they don't want to suffer a total loss from a likely default, "take 60 cents on the dollar plus a guarantee that this debt is secure" — backed by the full faith and credit of the eurozone member countries.

Once the debt load is reduced in this manner, Eichengreen says, countries like Greece and Ireland can grow again.

A default — or restructuring — would actually be cheaper for Portugal than the current EU-style bailouts, argues a recent paper by Open Europe's Ruparel. The country's overall debt burden would decline, eventually driving down the nation's borrowing costs. It would also shift some of the burden of the loss that default inevitably brings to investors, who would not get back all their money, and away from taxpayers who now are bearing the burden of repaying their government's loans in full.[25]

Ruparel says much of the opposition to restructuring comes from the banking sector, "particularly in Germany, where banks are heavily exposed to these [troubled] countries. The government knows if a restructure were to happen, the banks would suffer serious losses."

In their 2011 book, *This Time Is Different*, American economists Carmen M. Reinhart and Kenneth S. Rogoff find that sovereign defaults have been a common government feature for more than eight centuries. Reinhart says a default could end the market speculation that escalates governments' borrowing costs — and their pain — once and for all. "You may be postponing going to the dentist, and it is not going to be a pretty experience, "says Reinhart, "but once you do, it's over and you move on."

Some economists are horrified by the idea of letting any country default, because they fear failures would spread like a contagious virus. For example, if Portugal defaulted many experts fear Spain, whose banks have high exposure to Portuguese government bonds, would be the next to fall.

Italian economist Bastasin says, "It would be politically disruptive and have terrible consequences on those countries."

EU diplomats have strongly resisted any suggestion of default or restructuring for Greece or Portugal. The EU does not contemplate the possibility of restructuring until 2013, when the EU proposes to establish a permanent bailout fund — the European Stability Mechanism (ESM).

Critics say that's too little too late. And most observers agree the fund wouldn't be big enough to bail out a large economy like Spain. Some experts say they won't worry about the eurozone's future until Spain, a much bigger economy than any of the other PIGS, appears to be in serious trouble. As in Ireland, Spain's housing bubble — concentrated in coastal resort/retirement areas — pulled down home prices. Spanish savings banks are heavily exposed to domestic property losses, so a sharp decline in housing prices could trigger difficulties that could spread to the eurozone. However, Spain has begun to reform its extremely rigid labor market and enacted deficit-controlling cost-cutting measures. So far Spain's borrowing costs have remained below 5 percent, far less than the other PIGS' double digit rates.[26]

Officials in Brussels say the new proposed bailout fund, created from contributions and guarantees from all eurozone countries — represents the kind of "fiscal union" the eurozone has long been criticized for lacking. But De Grauwe, author of the classic textbook *Economics of Monetary Union*, now in its eighth edition, disagrees.

"It's a far cry from the kind of budgetary union the United States would have with automatic transfers" from one state to another, he says. "The ESM is a mechanism to manage crisis not to prevent crisis."

Ironically, when the fund was first proposed last year, it triggered a crisis of its own after investors learned it contemplated restructuring after 2013. Private holders of government bonds feared a default would cost them money. The borrowing costs for struggling eurozone members surged on that news.

As De Grauwe puts it, each time a new country runs into trouble, "we fight, then the markets are uncertain what's going to happen. As a result, they dump bonds of countries in trouble, and we get involved each time in a major financial crisis."

Some economists would favor the introduction of a so-called eurobond, which would be backed by all the countries of the eurozone. That would avoid the kind of market attacks on individual countries' bonds that have occurred in the past year. De Grauwe sees a eurobond as a partial step toward the political union the eurozone has always lacked, yet "more realistic than full budgetary union like in the U.S."

BACKGROUND

Bending Union Rules

History offers few examples of successful efforts among nations to share a single currency on the scale of today's eurozone. It does offer, however, "several examples of monetary unions between sovereign states disintegrating," writes historian Ferguson in his 2001 history of money, *The Cash Nexus.*[27] The unions usually fell apart when one member suffering from deficits bent the rules and began printing its own money, essentially devaluing the currency.

The closest precedent to the eurozone, the so-called Latin Monetary Union (1865-1927), made the coinages of six European governments freely exchangeable within a single area that encompassed France, Belgium, Switzerland, Italy, the Papal States and Greece. Like the eurozone, the Latin Union began with a political motivation — the dream of a "European Union."

Eventually the extravagance of the Italian and Papal governments became too costly for the other member states. The Papal government financed its debts by debasing its coinage, while Italy issued its own paper currency. Under these strains, the union had effectively stopped functioning by World War I and was pronounced dead, belatedly, in the 1920s.[28]

In more recent times, several unions have been short-lived. Around the time of the fall of the Berlin Wall, three separate monetary unions — one among the former members of the Soviet Union, and one each among the countries that make up the former Yugoslavia and Czechoslovakia — broke apart after weaker members raised revenue by printing money. Looking back at that history, Ferguson predicted in 2001 that "the strains caused by unaffordable social security and pension systems," which would grow with Europe's aging population, could similarly break up the eurozone.[29]

Getty Images/Tim Graham

Weeds grow unchecked in the streets and yards of new houses offered at discount prices in Ballindine, County Mayo, Ireland — remnants of the country's hyper-inflated housing bubble that caused average home prices to nearly triple. When the bubble burst, home prices and tax revenues plummeted and Ireland's debt and interest rates skyrocketed, forcing it to seek an EU/IMF rescue.

Governments have long used the tactic of debasing their currencies — which spurred many of the past breakups — to reduce their debts. Ancient Roman emperors had reduced the silver content of the denarius coin by nearly 99 percent between the reign of Marcus Aurelius and the time of Diocletian. Struggling to pay his debts, King Henry VIII in the 1540s reduced the gold and silver content of England's new coins, giving them a face value twice that of the metal they contained.[30]

Today, printing more paper money to devalue one's currency is a technologically advanced way of debasing coinage. But eurozone governments lost the option of devaluing their currency when they adopted the euro — a loss that has exacerbated their current troubles.

Bloodshed Averted

After World War II, European leaders were determined to prevent future bloodshed by creating greater cooperation among their nations. In 1951 six countries — France, Germany, Italy, Netherlands, Belgium and Luxembourg — agreed to run their coal and steel industries under a common plan so no country could create weapons against another. For the first time, the six nations agreed to give up some of their sovereignty in a common effort.

Following the success of the coal and steel treaty, the six nations in 1957 signed the Treaty of Rome, creating the European Economic Community (EEC) or Common Market, pledging cooperation in the free movement of goods, services and people across borders.[31]

Throughout the 1960s and into the '70s, the EEC continued to break down trade barriers and add new members. In 1968 the six Common Market countries removed customs duties on goods imported across their borders. Trade grew rapidly both among the six and with the rest of the world.[32]

By 1988, the Single Market Act contained a commitment to monetary unification but included no deadline for introducing it. The deciding event came in 1989 with the fall of the Berlin Wall and the prospect of a reunified Germany for the first time in 40 years.[33]

Germany's reunification required the consent of the four post-World War II occupying powers: France, Britain, the United States and the Soviet Union. When Germany sought French approval for reunification, the creation of a European monetary union — something long sought by France as a way to increase its own political influence — became France's quid pro quo.

"Now that Germany's land area, population and economic capacity were set to expand at a stroke, it became even more urgent to lock it into Europe" to prevent German imperial ambitions — which had flourished during two world wars — from re-emerging, writes University of California economist Eichengreen.[34]

Why was France so committed to a monetary union? Ferguson notes that one ardent single-currency proponent, French Socialist Jacques Delors, thought the euro would protect Europe's extensive welfare state because all members would be tied to the same highly taxed, "centralized, redistributive and, in some ways, socialist system."[35]

Paradoxically, the eurozone's political leaders have taken more of a free-market approach, judging by recent EU requirements that debt-laden economies slash their social-welfare benefits and reduce expensive payroll taxes paid by businesses for those benefits. "When the countries joined, they effectively signed up to much more liberal [free-market] economic policies — free trade and flexible labor markets — but they don't seem to realize that" or acknowledge it to their voters, says Tilford of London's Centre for European Reform.

Of course, there were also some mutual benefits, even for Germany. "What you got was lower borrowing costs

CHRONOLOGY

1945s-1959s *In aftermath of World War II, European leaders decide to forge greater economic cooperation to prevent more bloodshed.*

1951 Six countries (France, Germany, Italy, the Netherlands, Belgium and Luxembourg) agree to run coal and steel industries under a common pact to prevent one country from forging weapons to use against another.

1957 The six coal and steel compact nations adopt Treaty of Rome, creating the European Economic Community (EEC) — the "Common Market" — to allow free movement of goods and people across borders.

1960-1979 *Economic growth and trade grow rapidly; EEC expands.*

1968 The six EEC members remove customs duties among themselves.

1973 Denmark, Ireland and U.K. join the EEC.

1980s *Berlin Wall falls; Germany agrees to monetary union; EEC membership expands.*

1980 Greece joins EEC, bringing membership to 10.

1986 Portugal and Spain become EEC's 11th and 12th members.

1988 Single Market Act commits to a European monetary union but no deadline for achieving it.

1989 Berlin Wall falls. France approves German reunification in exchange for German agreement to establish a common European currency.

1990s *European Monetary Union and euro established.*

1992 Treaty — signed at Maastricht, Netherlands — re-names EEC the European Community under the newly created European Union (in 2009 the EC is absorbed into the EU), commits it to monetary union by 1999 and sets rules for participating countries.

1997 Stability Pact establishes stricter maximum debt and budget deficit targets for EU members, but they're never enforced.

Jan. 1, 1999 Euro introduced in 11 countries for commercial/financial transactions, but U.K. retains the British pound as its currency.

2000s *World financial crisis dries up credit; housing bubbles burst in Ireland, Spain; EU bails out Greece, Ireland.*

2001 Greece becomes 12th country to join euro but its financial qualifications are later found deceptive.

2002 Euro notes and coins introduced into general circulation.

September 2008 Major financial crisis strikes Europe, as mortgage, credit and housing bubbles burst; Lehman Bros. fails; Irish government guarantees banks' deposits and bonds.

2009 Greece's new government reveals budget deficit is twice what the previous government had reported.

2010 EU and IMF bail out Greece with €110 billion ($160 billion) loan. EU approves new lending to euro countries to prevent the financial crisis from spreading. . . . EU agrees to bail out Ireland (Nov. 28).

2011 José Sócrates' Socialist government in Portugal collapses after his austerity package fails to pass (March 23). . . . EU summit agrees to establish permanent bailout fund to safeguard euro and help struggling countries (March 24-25). . . . Portugal asks EU for bailout (April 6). . . . Greek borrowing costs soar on news it failed to meet its EU deficit-reduction target. Borrowing costs for Portugal and Ireland reach euro-era highs on fears all three countries might default (April 27). . . . EU discusses more aid for Greece (May 7-9). . . . Finnish Parliament supports Portugal bailout, despite opposition from nationalist True Finns party (May 12). . . . IMF head Dominique Strauss-Kahn is arrested for attempted rape in New York, complicating bailout negotiations (May 14). . . . Portugal general election scheduled (June 5). . . . Portugal must redeem €7 billion ($10 billion) in maturing bonds; bailout loan seen as crucial (June 15).

Ireland Struggles With Public and Private Debt

"Reckless lending" and cronyism are blamed.

According to a joke told around Dublin these days, second prize for winning the Irish sweepstakes is five apartments. First prize? Zero apartments.

It's a painful truth that during Ireland's roaring "Celtic Tiger" years, the entire country was caught up in a property-buying frenzy and easy credit — until it all ended in the economic crash of 2008-09.

Since property values plummeted, one of every two homeowners is in "negative equity," with the amount they owe on their mortgage greater than the value of their house. Many families can't pay their debts because they have lost a job, had their salary cut or seen their house value drop by 50 percent from the peak.

"We've seen cases of middle-income families that have their own mortgage to pay plus three more mortgages" on houses they bought to rent out, says Paul Joyce, senior policy researcher at Free Legal Advice Centers (FLAC) in Dublin, a network of volunteer lawyers that advises people on how to get out of debt. During the boom years, investment advisors regularly touted property purchases as a nest egg for retirement, he says. But potential tenants and homebuyers have evaporated, including the immigrant construction workers who returned to Eastern Europe when the housing industry collapsed.

The stories of property magnates and government regulators drinking together at lavish racetrack fundraisers for Fianna Fáil, the previous government's party, are rife — a relationship many blame for a housing bubble the government either didn't see coming or didn't want to burst.[1] "It was cronyism at its worst," says Joan Collins, a member of Parliament who represents Dublin's South Central neighborhood, one of Ireland's poorest. She blames "all this madness" on tax breaks the Fianna Fáil government gave developers to build new housing, hotels and private hospitals.

Less well-known is the extent to which the government turned to private developers to build public housing. The wreckage of that failed effort can be seen at St. Michael's public housing complex in Dublin, where a developer demolished eight of 10 apartment blocks, then walked away bankrupt when the economy crashed, leaving a vast wasteland and former tenants scattered into temporary rentals. "Now a community has been devastated," Collins says.

At one of Dublin's largest public housing complexes, Dolphin House, where residents had long complained of backed-up sewage seeping into their 1940s-era apartments, the City Council also turned to a developer for the solution. The developer planned to replace the existing 436 apartments and build an additional 600 private apartments to be sold to well-heeled professionals, since the location is desirable — just five minutes by light rail from downtown.[2]

The residents were still in the planning stage when the housing bubble burst. The developers vanished. "We missed the boat," admits Veronica Lally, 41, a resident of Dolphin House. "The Dublin City Council is bankrupt. There's no money to maintain these properties," she says, holding little hope for repair of the archaic plumbing system.

Like many Irish taxpayers, Lally, a community employment adviser, expresses rage that she'll be paying thousands of euros in taxes "for a developer that was greedy" and the ensuing bank crisis. She holds government, developers and trade unions equally responsible.[3]

"They got into bed the three of them and ripped the heart out of this country; and young people are shipping off to America and Australia — all our good talent going, because there's nothing here for them," she continues. Now the bankers must be bailed out and the money the government borrowed from the European Union to prop up the banks "paid back to Europe."

Like Dublin's council, the national government made the mistake of failing to build up its budget surpluses during the good times for a rainy day, some economists say.

---

for the indebted nations and a weaker currency for Germany," says Ferguson. That meant German exports were cheaper, making them more competitive.

Until the last 50 years, most Western European countries were not economically viable on their own, and some, like Britain and France, used colonial empires to fuel their domestic economies, points out London School of Economics professor Hix. The Common Market, and later the EU, accomplished the same thing without bloodshed.

Indeed, without the creation of this internal market, the German, French, British and Italian economies "would

"The government should have targeted the housing market by taxing mortgage interest payments. Instead they subsidized mortgage interest payments," says John Fitz Gerald, an economist at the Economic and Social Research Institute, a Dublin think tank. If the government had followed his advice, "they would have given households higher interest rates de facto," he says, which would have made households more cautious about taking on too big a mortgage. Then, "when the economy slowed down, the government would have had a surplus they could have used."

"Reckless lending" by banks is a common phrase heard in Ireland these days. Many blame the failed Anglo-Irish Bank for its maverick lending strategy of dropping traditional credit requirements, such as putting a down payment on a home mortgage — a practice that put pressure on other Irish banks to do the same.

Besides middle-class homeowners, Ireland has a new and growing working class saddled with exorbitant amounts of personal debt, often piled up on multiple credit cards. "A lot of people in working-class areas had access to subprime lenders and to credit they wouldn't have had before," Joyce says. "A lot of individuals won't be able to pay the money back; it was lent quite recklessly with very little regard to lending standards."

Ireland's debt problem is compounded by the fact that the country lacks modern bankruptcy laws that would allow an individual to wipe out his personal debts, Joyce says. And "non-recourse" lending, common in the United States, is totally unknown in Ireland. It allows a homeowner to mail his keys back to the bank and walk away without paying the rest of the mortgage. Even if an Irish bank forecloses on a house and sells it — typically for a fraction of its original value — the homeowner is still responsible for the remainder of the mortgage.

"That's really why people are concerned," says Aoife Walsh, spokesperson for Respond! Housing Association, which advises troubled homeowners. "They know that not only could they lose the roof over their heads, but they'll have this massive debt hanging over them for the rest of their lives."

Although the new Fine Gael/Labour coalition government elected Feb. 25 has pledged to "fast-track" personal bankruptcy reform, no legislation is pending yet. The International

Community organizer Wally Bowden stands in front of an abandoned building at Dolphin House, a public housing complex in Dublin, Ireland. A developer had planned to renovate the complex, add profit-making apartments and turn the building into a private clinic. When the property market crashed, the developer abandoned the project.

Monetary Fund's bailout loan for Ireland, however, called for such legislation to be introduced by March 2012.

— *Sarah Glazer*

[1] Christopher Caldwell, "Not Too Big to Fáil," *The Weekly Standard*, Feb. 21, 2011, www.weeklystandard.com/articles/not-too-big-f-il_547 416.html.

[2] "Dolphin Decides: The Final Report," Dolphin House Community Development Association, 2009, p. 8, www.pcc.ie/dolphindecides/ dolphin.html.

[3] The bill to the government for bailing out Irish banks reached €70 billion in March, equal to €17,000 for each citizen. See Larry Elliott and Jill Treanor, "Ireland forced into new €21 billion bailout by debt crisis," *Guardian*, March 31, 2011, www.guardian.co.uk/world/2011/ mar/31/ireland-new-bailout-euro-crisis?INTCMP=SRCH.

not be large enough to sustain the standards of living which their citizens take for granted," Hix writes.[36]

Birth of the Euro

On Feb. 7, 1992, the Treaty on European Union was signed by the members of the Common Market, under the renamed

European Union, at Maastricht, Netherlands. The treaty established rules for a single currency and set 1999 as the deadline for introducing the euro. Britain was exempted from the currency, while Denmark was to decide by referendum.

Both Britain and Denmark obtained legal exemptions from joining the euro. Denmark, a small but proud

AFP/Getty Images/Louisa GGouliamaki

AFP/Getty Images/Christina Quicler

Strikes and Protests

A man hauls around fake euro notes (top) during a demonstration in Seville called by Spanish unions on June 8, 2010, to protest government austerity cuts. Garbage went uncollected and hospital services were limited throughout the country as thousands of public workers protested the cuts, designed to reduce Spain's deficit. BBVA is Spain's second-largest bank. In Athens, Greece, a cardboard coffin symbolizes the death of the euro during a protest march on March 30, 2010 (bottom). Government austerity measures in Greece have sparked several general strikes and street protests.

country, voted in 2002 not to join the euro.[37] Under Conservative Prime Minister John Major, Britain had participated in an earlier version of monetary union, the European Monetary System. But after a speculators' attack on the pound, Britain took its currency out of the joint system in 1992. "Tony Blair could credit his victory in the 1997 general election to the damage done to the

Conservative government of John Major by the 1992 crisis," Eichengreen writes.

The so-called Maastricht Criteria set conditions for participating in the monetary union, including caps on budget deficits (no more than 3 percent of GDP), public debt (no more than 60 percent of GDP) and limits on inflation and long-term interest rates. But members had trouble following these conditions.

As the University of Southern California's Sarotte has observed, "Policymakers wanted the new currency to succeed and started using the number of members and applicants as an oversimplified metric of success, thereby allowing weaker economies to join without due scrutiny. Such laxness allowed the entry not only of members with debt-to-GDP ratios well in excess of 60 percent (Belgium, Italy) but also of applicants such as Greece, which not only flouted the rules but also falsified its records."[38]

Once accepted into the union, weaker member states could borrow at roughly the same interest rate as Germany, due to the European Central Bank's practice of treating the sovereign debt of all eurozone members equally. This meant that spending increased without regard to what the countries could actually afford.

The budgeting criteria were strengthened, at least in theory, at the request of the Germans in a 1997 Stability Pact, which established fines on those who violated the criteria. But fines have never been imposed, so the Maastricht Criteria have been observed mostly in the breach — even by the Germans.

After German reunification, the high cost of economic reconstruction in East Germany drove up Germany's borrowing costs, forcing Germany to ask, humiliatingly, for lenient implementation of the Stability Pact it had instigated. The EU agreed. Afterward, it was much harder for subsequent German governments to act in a holier-than-thou fashion toward any other member with economic woes. The fact that the French also found themselves in a fiscal hole for much of the 1990s only compounded the problem.

Thus, the Maastricht Criteria were only minimally enforced. But some experts say the caps were unrealistic from the outset. "The aging population of Europe plus the welfare state translated into deficits that were going to be way larger than 3 percent of GDP," says Ferguson, who predicted in 2000 that problems would surface within a decade.

On Jan. 1, 1999, the euro was introduced in 11 countries for commercial and financial transactions. Notes and coins entered general circulation in 2002.

Bubbles and Bailouts

When Greece became the 12th country to adopt the euro in 2001, no one guessed that it held the seeds of a disaster that would severely test the future of the monetary union.

Three years later it was discovered that Greece's financial reports, which had seemed to meet the eurozone's conditions for entry, were inaccurate. And in 2009 Greece's new Socialist government revealed that the national budget deficit would be 12.7 percent of GDP — twice the previous government's estimate, and more than four times larger than the EU's target.

The announcement caused Greece's bond rating to plummet, and the risk of a default surfaced for the first time. This occurred as an international credit and financial crisis was building in 2007 and became official in September 2008, when Lehman Brothers, a big U.S. investment bank, collapsed, and credit dried up around the world.

Starting as early as 2005, imbalances were already building between stolid, economically successful Germany and weaker economies in southern eurozone countries on such crucial measures as competitiveness, trade surpluses and deficits.

With a Greek default looming and fears that such a crisis might prove contagious, European heads of state on April 11, 2010, agreed to establish a crisis mechanism to safeguard the zone's financial stability by lending funds to member states in serious financial distress. On May 2, it was announced that Greece would receive an EU/IMF bailout loan of €110 billion.[39]

On May 9, 2010, officials established the European Financial Stability Facility (EFSF) — a three-year, €440 billion ($592 billion) fund to lend to troubled euro countries (other than Greece). That would be supplemented with a €250 billion ($337 billion) IMF commitment. After recent growing concerns that the fund's lending capacity might be insufficient, EU leaders this March committed themselves to finding a compromise by the summer to boost its lending ability.[40]

Last July 23 the EU announced the results of its "stress tests" on 91 European banks to determine whether the banks were resilient enough to weather future economic shocks. All but seven passed the tests, which the EU represented as a sign of the banks' solidity.[41] But the spectacular crash just a few months later of several Irish banks raised skepticism about the value of future tests.

Between 2003 and 2007 Ireland experienced a property-driven boom. By 2007, average house prices were nearly triple 2000 levels. The Irish economy became increasingly dependent on the construction sector — representing almost a quarter of its economy. By 2007, government revenues were heavily dependent on windfall taxes from the housing market.

When the housing bubble burst, tax revenues plummeted, ending a decade of budget surpluses.[42] But none of this could have happened without German banks lending to Irish banks cheaply and massively.

"People have not commented enough on how unusual it is for banks to get their growth driven by lending from other banks," says William Black, associate professor of economics and law at the University of Missouri, Kansas City, and a former senior financial regulator during the U.S. savings and loan crisis of the 1980s.

As a result, Irish banks grew to be much larger, relative to Ireland's small economy, than U.S. banks.[43]

By the end of September 2008, troubled Irish banks were unable to access financial markets, which were frozen by the international credit crunch. The government agreed to a blanket guarantee on all the banks' deposits as well as to most private bondholders of the six major banks — a move that has been severely criticized for essentially putting the entire burden for bank losses on Irish taxpayers.[44]

Black, an outspoken critic of the move, says bondholders who made risky investments are "supposed to be wiped out. To do anything else is to give people a complete bonanza."

Throughout 2010, the impact of the Greek sovereign debt crisis, coupled with the market's realization that Ireland's generous bank guarantees would severely strain its finances, sent interest rates on Irish government bonds soaring. By autumn it was clear the country was running out of money and was effectively shut out of the financial markets. The government had no choice but to seek help from the new EU bailout fund.

On November 28, the EU and the IMF agreed to bail out Ireland, the second eurozone member to come hat in hand. Under the agreement, it would receive a loan of €67.5 billion ($88.42 billion).[45]

CURRENT SITUATION

Cutting Deals

Eurozone leaders are taking steps to shore up the eurozone's struggling members and will meet in June to put the finishing details on a permanent fund to help future governments that run into difficulty.

But troubles continue to plague countries that have received bailouts and embarked on austerity programs. In April and May, the bond markets were punishing both Ireland and Greece with double-digit interest rates, even as steadfast Germany was paying only around 3.4 percent on its government debt.[46]

Nearly a year after Greece received its bailout deal, its borrowing costs on April 14 had soared to more than 13 percent on 10-year government bonds — the highest since it joined the euro in 2001. The surge followed suggestions by German Finance Minister Wolfgang Schaüble that Greece might have to restructure (default on) its debt. Thus, it appeared increasingly likely that the Greek government would be shut out of the financial markets in 2012, when it needs to raise €25-30 billion ($35 billion-$43 billion).[47]

With a national debt mounting to more than 150 percent of GDP, Greece appeared condemned to years of zero growth and recession, fueled by deep spending cuts and tax increases.[48] Its jobless rate rose to 15.1 percent in January, the highest level since 2004, when the country's national statistics agency began collecting unemployment figures.[49] Given the dismal statistics, European officials admitted on May 7 that Greece probably would need a new cash bailout of tens of billions of euros, possibly with easier repayment terms.[50]

However, EU officials continued to resist any talk of a Greek restructuring plan, even though market speculation that a default was inevitable intensified on May 9, as interest rates on Greek bonds continued to rise.[51]

And in the week following the flurry of EU meetings on the Greek crisis, German leader Merkel, facing opposition to any further bailouts from her junior coalition party, the Free Democrats, denied that Germany was ready to give Greece more aid. She said she was awaiting an EU report on the situation due in June.[52]

EU leaders had already agreed on March 11 to reduce Greece's bailout interest rate by 1 percentage point and extend the payback period to 7.5 years. In exchange, the EU demanded that Greece privatize government assets to yield €50 billion ($69 billion) by 2015 — which led to the German politicians' suggestion, mocked in the press, that Greece sell some of its islands and art treasures.[53]

Some economists said the €50 billion target, amounting to about 20 percent of Greek GDP, would be difficult to reach. As Greece was headed for a revamped bailout in May, European leaders complained that the government's delay in selling off its public holdings was one reason it failed to meet its deficit-reduction target. Intense opposition from public unions over cost-cutting measures also has hampered Greece from meeting EU budget targets.[54]

In March Ireland had refused a similar deal — reducing its bailout loan interest rate — when told it would have to eliminate its corporate tax haven in return. In the wake of the Greek crisis in May, Irish Prime Minister Enda Kenny was intensifying pressure on EU leaders to reduce Ireland's interest bill, saying there was a question as to whether Ireland could repay its bailout loan at the current rate. But in exchange he was once again expected to face pressure from French leaders to "harmonize" Ireland's corporate tax system with the rest of the EU.[55]

France fears that lower-tax regimes like Ireland's could undercut France's own ample social welfare state, says Hix, of the London School of Economics. "In France, a lot of the costs of their generous social welfare state are imposed on business in corporate taxes and in unemployment insurance paid by business," he notes.

Despite the deals cut in early March, EU leaders failed to calm the markets. As the details of the deal trickled out in early March, Moody's downgraded both Greece's and Spain's credit ratings, citing increased risk of default (Greece), and higher estimates of the Spanish banking system's capital needs.

On March 23 Portugal's prime minister resigned after Parliament failed to approve his party's fourth austerity package. The failure was blamed on lack of cooperation from opposition Social Democrats, who are favored to win the June 5th general election.

Then in the run-up to the EU's March 24-25 summit on Portugal's bailout, Portugal's credit rating was downgraded by both the Moody's and Fitch ratings agencies. Standard & Poor's went further, downgrading Portugal's bonds to one notch above junk status on March 29. The actions sent Portugal's borrowing costs soaring, forcing

Would Ireland have been better off without the euro?

YES
Sean Barrett
Senior Lecturer, Economics Department, Trinity College, Dublin, Ireland

Written for *CQ Global Researcher,* May 2011

Ireland joined the euro as a political gesture to a currency that accounted for less than a third of its trade. University of Chicago economist Milton Friedman warned in the *Irish Times* on Sept. 5, 2001, that "the euro was adopted really for political purposes, not economic purposes, as a step towards the myth of the United States of Europe. In fact I believe that its effect will be exactly the opposite. The need for different policies like tightening monetary policy in Ireland or a more flexible monetary policy in Italy will produce political tensions that will make it more difficult to achieve political unity."

Today these tensions have increased German reluctance to fund further rescues after Greece and Ireland. Germany needs higher interest rates in order to curb inflation. Ireland needs lower interest rates to tackle a 14.5 percent unemployment rate. The peripheral countries need a weaker euro to grow, but the euro is strengthening. When Ireland joined as a full-employment, solvent country it did not need either reduced interest rates or the large capital inflow arising from membership.

Friedman was pessimistic about any way out for Ireland. "Ireland is stuck with the euro. How would you break out, and start all over again to establish a new monetary system, the punt?* You are not going to give it up. You have locked yourselves together and thrown away the key."

Having joined the euro without economic analysis, Ireland then celebrated a hard-currency union with soft-currency policies. The Organisation for Economic Co-operation and Development's (OECD) 2008 "Report on Public Management in Ireland" found that between 1995 and 2005 the public-expenditure policies in Ireland and Germany were polar opposites. Real annual public expenditure in Ireland increased by 5 percent a year and contracted by 0.5 percent a year in Germany. Ireland lacked fiscal discipline.

Meanwhile, less than 2 percent of the massive capital inflow resulting from euro membership was invested in industry and agriculture. Ireland had the highest home-price increases in the OECD countries, with Dublin second-hand house prices rising from €104,000 ($121,000) in 1997 to €512,000 ($645,000) in 2006.

Ireland joined the euro without analysis, pursued economic policies the opposite of those of Germany — the bulwark of the euro — and has no exit strategy. It is a lethal policy combination.

* The Irish pound also is known as the punt.

NO
Philip R. Lane
Professor of International Macroeconomics, Trinity College Dublin, Ireland

Written for *CQ Global Researcher,* May 2011

At a superficial level, membership in Europe's Economic and Monetary Union (EMU)* may seem to have directly contributed to the boom-bust cycle in Ireland. However, had Ireland not joined the euro, the current banking crisis could have been amplified by a currency crisis. Moreover, an independent currency would not have offered a guarantee against the onset of the mid-2000s credit boom.

The credit boom affected many non-euro economies in Europe, including Iceland and countries in Central and Eastern Europe. In addition, many nations have experienced twin banking and currency crises, in which collapsing currencies raised the local burden of foreign-currency debts, inducing a more severe crash. Moreover, even under an independent monetary policy, it is not clear that the central bank would have been able to neuter the housing boom solely through its interest rate policy, since a large interest rate hike might have caused a big recession without cooling down the housing market.

Membership in the monetary union also has provided considerable stability during this crisis period. Most directly, the European Central Bank has provided substantial cheap funding to Irish banks during the crisis. In contrast, non-euro countries such as Latvia and Iceland suffered far harsher crises, since these economies had no similar source of external funding. In addition, highly indebted Irish households have benefited from low ECB interest rates during the crisis.

However, it is important to emphasize that Ireland took excessive macroeconomic risks during the first decade of the single currency, particularly by failing to regulate the banking sector to guard against systemic risk factors. This was especially problematic under the EMU, because Irish banks' newly expanded access to area-wide financial markets amplified the scope of their risk-taking. In addition, Ireland's fiscal policy was insufficiently counter-cyclical. These twin policy weaknesses both failed to curb the boom and exacerbated the scale of the crisis. Ireland learned a harsh lesson from the crisis: It should never again tolerate weak banking regulation or imprudent fiscal policies. Indeed, Ireland is now undergoing extensive institutional reforms in order to ensure that such a crisis does not recur in the future.

* The EU-established monetary system that introduced the euro.

the country's caretaker government to seek a bailout loan in April.[56]

In late March eurozone leaders also agreed to create a permanent rescue fund, the European Stability Mechanism (ESM), which in 2013 would replace the temporary fund known as the EFSF. It would have an effective lending capacity of €500 billion ($688 billion). But leaders postponed decisions on the funds' details, saying the effective lending capacity of the temporary fund and of the permanent facility would be finalized by the end of June.[57]

Eurozone leaders also agreed on the so-called Euro Plus Pact — touted earlier in the year by French and German leaders as the Competitiveness Pact — which commits eurozone countries to closer economic cooperation. In provisions that go to the heart of nations' traditional sovereignty, the pact calls on participating states to limit public-sector wage increases, lower taxes on labor, develop a common corporate tax base, revise pension systems with an eye to future costs and establish some form of debt brake in their national fiscal rules.

Both the French and Germans claimed victory, even though the pact did not include any enforcement mechanisms — such as fines or sanctions — included in the original German proposal.

"They've totally watered down the idea that they should all coordinate what they do in their domestic policy," says Hix. "They'll monitor what each other [does] but in a very soft-power way. There's no way they're going to enforce sanctions on what people do with their labor market policies and their tax policy."

By June, new bank stress tests are expected to be carried out by the EU's newly created European Banking Authority, but some observers doubt they will be tough enough to restore confidence in Europe's banking system. The EU's 2010 stress tests were widely criticized when only seven of 91 banks failed the tests. All of Ireland's banks passed the tests, for instance, yet by year's end they required huge bailouts.[58]

Government Killer?

Whether or not the euro is a "government-killing mechanism" as historian Ferguson terms it, several recent government defeats have been attributed to the sovereign debt crises in the euro countries.

In Spain, where unemployment is running at 20 percent, the austerity program arguably made the Socialist Prime Minister José Luis Rodríguez Zapatero so unpopular he has said he won't run for a third term.

Right-wing populist parties — which combine their anti-bailout messages with anti-immigrant sentiments — have made gains, especially in countries with stronger economies. The most recent sign of rising nationalism occurred May 12, when Denmark re-erected border controls with other EU countries, a measure pushed by the right-wing, anti-immigrant Danish People's Party. The action came just as EU interior ministers agreed to reinstate passport controls among 22 EU countries that since 1995 have enjoyed unfettered travel. The measure was designed to restrict the recent flood of North African immigrants fleeing political upheavals and followed an earlier spat between Italy and France over whether the rising tide of Tunisian immigrants arriving on Italy's shores should be able to migrate easily to the other EU countries.[59]

On March 23, the Socialist government of Portuguese Prime Minister Sócrates collapsed after it could not muster support for a fourth austerity package in Parliament. The opposition Social Democrats, now favored to win the June 5 election, particularly opposed cuts that fell hard on pensioners.[60]

Concern about Portugal's ability to pay €7 billion ($10 billion) on bonds maturing on June 15 led to the government's request in April for an EU rescue package, because the newly elected government was not expected to be in place in time for the June deadline.[61] EU officials hoped to approve a final Portuguese rescue package amounting to €78 billion ($115 billion) at a May 16 meeting of eurozone finance ministers.[62] But Finland's finance minister warned that the package must be "harder and more comprehensive than the one the parliament voted against," which included a tax of up to 10 percent on pensions over €1,500 a month and a freeze on smaller pensions.[63]

The latest potential setback for a resolution of the debt crisis came in mid-April, when the True Finns party, which campaigned against a bailout for Portugal, made spectacular gains in the general election. With their jingoistic motto, "The Finnish cow should be milked in Finland," the party rose to a 19 percent share of the vote from only 4 percent in 2007, making it a close third behind the two leading parties. Finland, unlike other countries, requires parliamentary approval to take part in bailouts, which require unanimous support of all 17 eurozone members.[64]

However, on May 12, Finland's Parliament voted to support Portugal's bailout, after the conservative NCP party agreed with the Social Democrats to include conditions requiring Portugal to sell off assets to repay EU countries and to begin talks with private investors.[65] Nevertheless, the True Finns' gains had already triggered a renewed outbreak of the sovereign debt crisis in the eurozone, as the costs of borrowing for debt-laden countries like Greece rose to record levels again.

On May 9, Standard & Poor's downgraded Greece's bond status further into junk status territory — from BB- to B — saying Greece may need to renege on at least half of its €327 billion ($470 billion) debt mountain, implying big losses for investors.[66]

OUTLOOK

Nationalist Obstructionism?

The recent rise of nationalist parties in Europe raises questions about how willing prosperous Europeans will be to bail out their poorer brethren, but also, more broadly, how much unity Europe really wants. Anti-EU rhetoric coupled with anti-immigrant right-wing messages make it appear that this is "Europe's own Tea Party moment."[67]

If nationalism holds sway in any country, a single government could block the rescue packages. Most EU supporters were confident that an effort to put the bailout funds on a firm legal ground, via a pending amendment to remove the EU treaty's prohibition on bailouts, will be approved. But one country could block the change.[68]

In addition, unanimous approval is needed to loan money to any troubled country after 2013, when the permanent bailout fund is set to open. This provision was aimed at reassuring richer eurozone countries like Austria, Finland, Germany and the Netherlands that they can't be forced to provide loans.[69]

Nationalists in debt-laden countries may argue that the bailout austerity measures are too harsh. Will voters stand for such harsh cuts? Ana Caterina Santos, a journalist for the Portuguese radio news station TSF, thinks they will.

"What scares us most is Greece — we don't want to be seen as Greek people," with all the connotations of the profligate southern stereotype, she says. "We have this idea: We Portuguese are more European than the Greeks. [W]e want to prove we can change."

That could be harder than people think. Most Portuguese see free health and education as two sacred untouchables, according to Santos. Unfortunately, that's where the big savings can be found, experts say, along with pensions, which are already very low by European standards.

Europe's lack of unity was further underscored in mid-April when Hungarian Prime Minister Viktor Orbán, whose country currently holds the EU presidency, said the EU's willingness to welcome new members was weaker than at any time in past 15 years.[70]

But the euro's troubles have also given some EU members pause about whether they're ready to adopt the currency, legally a requirement of EU membership (except for Britain and Denmark, which have legal exemptions.)

"The Poles and the Czechs continue to say, 'We'll join.' But they're not going to rush into it," predicts economist Tilford.

"The walking-wounded banks are the second part of the crisis," predicts Ferguson. "Before the end of this year, we'll have to sit down and admit which banks in Europe are bust."

As the continent struggles with the economic crisis, Europe's inferiority complex about its shrinking importance, squeezed between the great economic powers of China and the United States, has intensified. "[W]ill Europe be unable to cope with the dynamism of other regions of the world and be paralyzed at home by national populism and selfishness, leading it to resign itself to being nothing more than a regional power?" Michel Barnier, EU commissioner for the internal market, asked on May 9.

He urged the European Union to move toward greater cooperation, including adopting a common defense policy. "Will Europe be a continent under the influence of the United States, China and even of Russia?" he asked.[71]

To the contrary, according to American economist Eichengreen, the euro — alongside the dollar and the Chinese renminbi — will be one of the three currencies that will dominate world trade in the future. Already, the euro is widely used outside of the eurozone. Some 37 percent of all international bonds are in euros, according to Eichengreen, partly to appeal to European investors.

But what about Europe's failure to come up with an overarching federal government like that in the United States? Won't that hold the eurozone back?

"There are different flavors of capitalism and different flavors of monetary union," says Eichengreen. In his view,

European countries "don't need to turn into a United States of Europe to make a monetary union work."

The eyes of the world are on Europe to see what kind of recipe for unity it will devise and whether it will work.

NOTES

1. Julia Finch, "Greece Told to Sell off Islands and Artwork," *Guardian*, March 4, 2010, www.guardian .co.uk/world/2010/mar/04/greece-greek-islands-auction.

2. Gideon Rachman's Blog, "The European Union in Deep Trouble," *ft.com*, April 17, 2011, http://blogs .ft.com/rachmanblog/2011/04/the-european-union-in-deep-trouble/.

3. "Wires: Portugal Agrees to Bailout Loan," *ft.com*, May 3, 2011, http://ftalphaville.ft.com/blog/2011/05/ 03/558136/wires-portugal-agrees-to-bailout-loan/. Robin Harding, *et al.*, "IMF head's arrest hits debt talks," *Financial Times*, May 15, 2011, www.ft.com/ cms/s/0/415d008c-7e97-11e0-9e98-00144feabdc0 .html#ixzz1MX9YTphe.

4. "Jump in Greek Yields Spurs Restructure Talk," *Financial Times*, May 3, 2011, www.ft.com/cms/ s/0/6cd219e4-75a7-11e0-80d5-00144feabdc0.html# axzz1LUBTvdlc.

5. Mario Biejer, "Europe is running a giant Ponzi scheme," *Financial Times*, May 5, 2011, www.ft.com/ cms/s/0/ee728cb6-773e-11e0-aed6-00144feabdc0 .html#axzz1LUBTvdlc.

6. Estonia became the 17th country to adopt the euro on Jan. 1, 2011. Under EU law, all other members of the 27-nation EU — except for Britain and Denmark — are required to adopt the euro after meeting the budgetary and economic criteria set by the European Union.

7. Mary Elise Sarotte, "Eurozone Crisis as Historical Legacy," *Foreign Affairs*, Sept. 29, 2010, www .foreignaffairs.com/print/66715?page-2.

8. "A Quantum Leap in Economic Governance; But Questions Remain," European Policy Centre, March 28, 2011, pp. 8-9, www.epc.eu/documents/uploads/ pub_1247_post-summit_analysis_-_28_march_2011 .pdf.

9. The state is Baden-Württemberg. A similar defeat occurred in Rhineland-Palatine. See "Germany: The Lights Go Out," *Financial Times*, March 28, 2011, www.ft.com/cms/s/0/828b8746-596b-11e0-bc 39-00144feab49a.html#axzz1JCQeKBqX. Also see, "Angela's Trauma," *The Economist*, March 28, 2010, www.economist.com/blogs/newsbook/2011/03/ germanys_regional_elections?page=1.

10. "The Quest for Prosperity," *The Economist*, March 15, 2007, www.economist.com/node/8808044.

11. For background, see "Europe Will Work," *Nomura Global Economics*, March 2011, p. 19, www.nomura .com/europe/resources/pdf/Europe%20will%20 work%20FINAL_March2011.pdf.

12. GDP is the total value of an economy's output of goods and services. It is considered a key indicator of economic growth.

13. It's estimated that the new currencies of Spain, Portugal and Ireland would fall as much as 50 percent and Greece's as much as 80 percent. See Simon Tilford, "How to Save the Euro," Centre for European Reform, September 2010, p. 14, www.cer.org.uk/ pdf/essay_euro_tilford_14sept10.pdf.

14. *Ibid.*

15. David McWilliams, "Ditching the Euro Could Boost Our Failing Economy," May 6, 2009, www .davidmcwilliams.ie/2009/05/06/ditching-the-euro-could-boost-our-failing-economy.

16. "Europe's Banks: Follow the Money," *The Economist*, April 16, 2011, p. 80, www.economist.com/node/ 18560535?story_id=18560535&CFID=16840511 6&CFTOKEN=43737452.

17. See Conor O'Clery, "U.S. Economist Expounds on Great Euro Mistake," *The Irish Times*, Sept. 5, 2001, p. 17, www.irishtimes.com/newspaper/archive/2001/ 0905/Pg017.html#Ar01700.

18. "Trichet Defends ECB Rate Increase," *Financial Times*, April 7, 2011, www.ft.com/cms/s/0/e4c95f16-6143-11e0-ab25-00144feab49a.html#axzz1Ipf7zFRy.

19. www.economist.com/blog/dailychart/2010/12/ Europes_economies.

20. Lex, "Portugalling: Debts are Not Sustainable," *Financial Times*, April 7, 2011, www.ft.com/cms/

s/3/26efc574-6126-11e0-8899-00144feab49a.html
#axzz1Ipf7zFRy.

21. Steven Erlanger, "In Portugal Crisis, Worries on Europe's 'Debt Trap,'" *The New York Times*, April 8, 2011, www.nytimes.com/2011/04/09/world/europe/09portugal.html?_r=1&scp=1&sq=%22In%20Portugal%20Crisis,%20worries%20on%20europe%27s%20debt%20trap%22&st=cse.

22. Desmond Lachman, "Waiving the Rules for Portugal," *Financial Times*, April 7, 2011, www.ft.com/cms/s/0/e44bab88-6103-11e0-8899-00144feab49a.html#ixzz1JIf33xid.

23. The rumors were denied by both Greek and EU officials. See "Video: Greece Needs Revised Bailout," *ft.com*, May 9, 2011, http://video.ft.com/v/936381701001/Greece-needs-revised-bail-out.

24. Peter Spiegel, *et al.*, "European Officials to Revamp Greek Aid," *Financial Times*, May 8, 2011, www.ft.com/cms/s/0/b445945c-7978-11e0-86bd-00144feabdc0.html#axzz1Lrivh FKc.

25. Raoul Ruparel, "Stopping the Rot? The Cost of a Portuguese Bail-Out and Why it is Better to Move Straight to Restructuring," Open Europe, March 2011, www.openeurope.org.uk/research/portugalrestructure.pdf.

26. FT Alphaville, "A Proclamation from Spain's Ministry of Public Works," *Financial Times*, May 11, 2011, p. 35. Also see Martin Wolf, "The Eurozone's Journey to Defaults," *Financial Times*, May 11, 2011, p. 15.

27. Niall Ferguson, *The Cash Nexus: Money and Power in the Modern World 1700-2000* (2001), p. 340.

28. *Ibid.*, pp. 334-335.

29. *Ibid.*, p. 336. For background, see Alan Greenblatt, "The Graying Planet," *CQ Global Researcher*, March 15, 2011, pp. 133-156; and Sarah Glazer, "Social Welfare in Europe," *CQ Global Researcher*, Aug. 1, 2010, pp. 185-210.

30. Ferguson, *op. cit.*, p. 150.

31. For background, see B. W. Patch, "European Economic Union," *Editorial Research Reports*, March 27, 1957, available at *CQ Researcher Plus Archive.*

32. For background, see I. B. Kobrak, "Common Market: Start of a New Decade," *Editorial Research Reports*, Feb. 8, 1967, available at *CQ Researcher Plus Archive.*

33. For background, see Mary H. Cooper, "A Primer on German Reunification," *Editorial Research Reports*, Dec. 22, 1989, available at *CQ Researcher Plus Archive.*

34. Barry Eichengreen, *Exorbitant Privilege* (2011), pp. 88-89.

35. Delors later became president during the 1980s of the European Commission, a policy-setting branch of the then-Common Market and later the EU, whose membership consists of one commissioner per member state. The presidency of the commission has been compared to the post of prime minister in a parliamentary government.

36. Simon Hix, *What's Wrong with the European Union & How to Fix It* (2010), pp. 10-11, 15.

37. See www.worldpress.org/Europe/232.cfm.

38. Mary Elise Sarotte, "Eurozone Crisis as Historical Legacy," *Foreign Affairs*, Sept. 29, 2010, www.foreignaffairs.com/print/66715?page=2.

39. The €110 billion package, formally agreed to May 10, 2010, consists of €80 billion from euro area countries and €30 billion from the IMF.

40. "A Quantum Leap in Economic Governance, but Questions Remain," European Policy Centre, March 28, 2013, p. 4, www.epc.eu/documents/uploads/pub_1247_post-summit_analysis_-_28_march_2011.pdf.

41. Patrick Jenkins, "Seven Banks Fail EU Stress Tests, *Financial Times*, July 23, 2010, www.ft.com/cms/s/0/c14b9464-9678-11df-9caa-00144feab49a,s01=2.html#axzz1LsWojoIn.

42. Constantin Gurdgiev, *et al.*, "The Irish Economy: Three Strikes and You're Out?" Social Science Research Network, March 6, 2011, http://ssrn.com/abstract=1776190.

43. "How Ireland's Bank Bailout Shook the World," National Public Radio, Nov. 23, 2010, www.npr.org/blogs/money/2010/11/23/131538931/how-the-irish-bank-bailout-shook-the-world.

44. Gurdgiev, *op. cit.*

45. The total rescue package came to €85 billion, including €17.5 billion from the Irish government. Of the €67.5 billion in external assistance: €22.5 billion came from the European Financial Stability Mechanism (EFSM) contributed by EU members; €22.5 billion from the International Monetary Fund (IMF); and €22.5 billion from the European Financial Stability Fund (EFSF) and bilateral loans contributed by eurozone members.

46. See Landon Thomas Jr., "In U.K. Budget Cuts, Test Case for America," *International Herald Tribune*, April 15, 2011, p. 1.

47. Jennifer Hughes, "Greek debt hit by restructuring fears," *Financial Times*, April 14, 2011, www.ft.com/cms/s/0/086d7be6-667b-11e0-ac4d-00144feab49a.html#axzz1JVwZGUMq.

48. "Reuters Breaking Views: Not Yet Time for a Greek Restructuring," *International Herald Tribune*, April 15, 2011, p. 18. See Erlanger, *op. cit.*, for 150 percent figure.

49. "Greece Hit by Fear of Debt Overhaul," *International Herald Tribune*, April 15, 2011, p. 15.

50. Steven Erlanger, "Greek Leader Irked by Speculation on Debt," *The New York Times*, May 7, 2011, www.nytimes.com/2011/05/08/business/global/08greece.html?scp=1&sq=erlanger%20greece&st=cse.

51. *Ibid.* Also See Richard Milne, "S&P Cuts Greece Rating Two Notches," *Financial Times*, May 9, 2011, www.ft.com/cms/s/0/3997499c-7a47-11e0-bc74-00144feabdc0.html#axzz1LrivhFKc.

52. Judy Dempsey, "Germany Rejects Talk of Easing Bailout Terms," *The New York Times*, May 10, 2011, www.nytimes.com/2011/05/11/business/global/11euro.html.

53. Ralph Atkins and Kerin Hope, "Greek Goal of Return to Market in Doubt," *Financial Times*, April 13, 2011, www.ft.com/cms/s/0/c08e2970-65f2-11e0-9d40-00144feab49a.html#axzz1LsWojoIn.

54. Kerin Hope, "Greece in Line of Fire over Inability to Hit Targets," *Financial Times*, May 9, 2011, www.ft.com/cms/s/0/889c47f4-7a60-11e0-af64-00144feabdc0,s01=1.html#axzz1LrivhFKc.

55. Philip Inman, "EU Under pressure to Slash Ruinous Irish and Greek Bailout Bills," *Guardian*, May 9, 2011, www.guardian.co.uk/business/2011/may/09/eu-pressure-slash-irish-greek-bailout-bills?INTCMP=SRCH.

56. European Policy Centre, *op. cit.*, p. 2.

57. *Ibid.*

58. *Ibid.*, pp. 11-12.

59. The May 12 proposal, described as a "last resort" for emergencies, still needs approval from EU prime ministers and the European Parliament. See Ian Traynor, "Europe Moves to End Passport-Free Travel in Migrant Row," *Guardian*, May 12, 2011, www.guardian.co.uk/world/2011/may/12/europe-to-end-passport-free-travel.

60. Raphael Minder, "Austerity Debate Fells Portugal's Premier," *The New York Times*, March 23, 2011, www.nytimes.com/2011/03/24/world/europe/24portugal.html?_r=1&scp=3&sq=Socrates%20resigns&st=cse.

61. Peter Wise, "Portugal's Borrowing Costs Rise," *Financial Times*, April 15, 2011, www.ft.com/cms/s/0/6a38d2a0-675f-11e0-9bb8-00144feab49a.html#axzz1JVwZGUMq.

62. For Portugal's €78 billion package, the EU has pledged a total of €52 billion; the IMF contribution will be €26 billion over three years. See, IMF Survey Magazine, "IMF Outlines Joint Support Plan with EU for Portugal," May 6, 2011, www.imf.org/external/pubs/ft/survey/so/2011/INT050611A.htm.

63. Peter Wise, "Portuguese Prepare for Tighter Belts," *Financial Time*, April 8, 2011, www.ft.com/cms/s/0/4067461c-6211-11e0-8ee4-00144feab49a.html#axzz1JVwZGUMq.

64. See "Frustrated Finland," *Financial Times*, April 18, 2011.

65. "Finnish Parties Agree to Support Bail-out for Portugal," BBC News, May 12, 2011, www.bbc.co.uk/news/world-europe-13372218.

66. Inman, *op. cit.*

67. Peter Spiegel, "Anger Begins to Infect Europe's Prosperous Core," *Financial Times*, April 11, 2011, www.ft.com/cms/s/0/c9ec3d9e-6463-11e0-a69a-00144feab49a.html#axzz1JUlJGMDc.

68. The amendment is needed to counter challenges that have already arisen in German courts. See European Policy Centre, *op. cit.*

69. European Policy Centre, *op. cit.*, p. 5.

70. Stephen Castle, "Hungary Urges Balkan E.U. Entry," *The New York Times*, April 14, 2011, hwww .nytimes.com/2011/04/15/world/europe/15iht-hungary15.html?_r=1&scp=1&sq=Stephen%20 Castle%20Hungary&st=cse.

71. Stephen Castle, "EU Official Urges More Unity," *The New York Times*, May 9, 2011, www.nytimes .com/2011/05/10/world/europe/10iht-union10 .html?_r=1&emc=tnt&tntemail0=y.

BIBLIOGRAPHY

Bibliography

Eichengreen, Barry, *Exorbitant Privilege: The Rise and Fall of the Dollar, Oxford University Press*, 2011.
A professor of economics and political science at the University of California, Berkeley, predicts that the euro will become one of three leading international currencies along with the dollar and the Chinese renminbi.

Ferguson, Niall, *The Cash Nexus: Money and Power in the Modern World, 1700-2000, Penguin*, 2001.
A Harvard professor of international history, who predicted 10 years ago that the eurozone would run into problems, finds that prior attempts to form monetary unions have failed.

McWilliams, David, *Follow the Money: The Tale of the Merchant of Ennis, Gill & Macmillan*, 2010.
In this amusing account of Ireland's economic crash, an Irish columnist says the previous government's finance minister was clueless about how to respond and predicts Ireland will become "a large debt-servicing machine for a generation."

Reinhart, Carmen M., and Kenneth S. Rogoff, *This Time Is Different: Eight Centuries of Financial Folly, Princeton University Press*, 2009.
An economist at the Peterson Institute for International Economics (Reinhart) and a Harvard University professor of economics find that government defaults have been surprisingly frequent over time in their study of 66 countries.

Articles

Erlanger, Steven, "In Portugal's Crisis, Worries on Europe's 'Debt Trap,' " *The New York Times*, April 8, 2011, www.nytimes.com/2011/04/09/world/europe/ 09portugal.html?_r=1&scp=2&sq=steven%20 erlanger%20euro&st=cse.
Economists fear Portugal will follow Greece and Ireland into a "debt trap."

Heise, Michael, "Why the Euro Will Survive," *The Wall Street Journal*, Jan. 6, 2011, http://online.wsj .com/article/SB10001424052748704723104576061 440431381526.html.
The chief economist at Germany's giant Allianz insurance company says breaking up the eurozone would hurt its members, and budget retrenchment for debt-ridden countries will help them in the long run.

Lachman, Desmond, "Waiving the Rules for Portugal," *Financial Times*, April 7, 2011.
A resident fellow at the American Enterprise Institute says austerity budgets imposed on bailout countries like Greece and Ireland are making it harder for those economies to recover.

Lewis, Michael, "When Irish Eyes are Crying," *Vanity Fair*, March 2011, www.vanityfair.com/business/ features/2011/03/michael-lewis-ireland-201103.
In his usual amusing style, journalist Lewis describes how Ireland got into its current economic mess.

McNamara, Kathleen R., "Can the Eurozone be Saved?" *Foreign Affairs*, April 7, 2011, www.foreign affairs.com/articles/67710/kathleen-r-mcnamara/ can-the-eurozone-be-saved.
The director of Georgetown University's Mortara Center for International Studies says the eurozone has failed to create the kind of unified federal government necessary for a monetary union to work, but that a common eurobond will solve the problem.

Münchau, Walter, "The Eurozone's Quack Solutions Will Be No Cure," *Financial Times*, April 24, 2011.
A respected economics columnist says the eurozone's solutions to the debt crisis will not calm the bond market's fears.

Reports and Studies

"Europe Will Work," *Nomura*, March 2011, www
.nomura.com/europe/resources/pdf/Europe%20
will%20work%20FINAL_March2011.pdf.
Asia's largest global investment bank concludes that the
eurozone probably will not break up but needs to
strengthen its governance.

"A Quantum Leap in Economic Governance — But
Questions Remain," *European Policy Centre*, March
28, 2011, www.epc.eu/pub_details.php?cat_id=5&
pub_id=1247.
This summary of the European Union's March summit
agreements on how to tackle the euro debt crisis includes
criticisms of the proposed solutions.

Ruparel, Raoul, "Stopping the Rot? The Cost of a
Portuguese Bail-Out and Why It Is Better to Move
Straight to Restructuring," Open Europe, March
2011, www.openeurope.org.uk.
It would be cheaper for Portugal to default than to accept
a bailout loan from the European Union, concludes an
analyst at the London think tank Open Europe.

Tilford, Simon, "How to Save the Euro," *Centre for
European Reform*, September 2010, www.cer.org
.uk/about_new/about_cerpersonnel_tilford_09
.html.
The gap between the rhetoric of integration and the reality of national interests is proving lethal to the eurozone,
argues the chief economist for a London think tank.

For More Information

Centre for Economic Policy Research, 77 Bastwick St.,
London EC1V 3PZ, United Kingdom; +44 (0)20 7183
8801; www.cepr.org. Network of more than 700 European
researchers who study issues such as the euro. Has set up
VoxEU.org website for commentary by leading economists.

Economics Without Boundaries With David McWilliams;
www.davidmcwilliams.ie/2010/09/08/economics-without-
boundaries-with-david-mcwilliams. Blog of Irish economics
columnist who has been highly critical of the government's
handling of Irish debt and economic crisis.

European Council, Rue de la Loi 175, B-1048 Brussels,
Belgium; (32-2) 281 61 11; www.european-council.europa.
eu/home-page.aspx?lang=en. Composed of the heads of
member states of the European Union; defines the general
political directions and priorities of the EU; posted the March
25 summit agreement on the euro at www.consilium.europa.
eu/uedocs/cms_data/docs/pressdata/en/ec/120296.pdf.

European Union, http://europa.eu/index_en.htm. Web
portal that links to all EU agencies.

**European Union Delegation to the United States of
America**, 2175 K St., N.W., Washington, DC 20037; (202)
862-9500; www.eurunion.org/eu. Provides information about
the EU to Americans.

European Policy Centre, Résidence Palace, 155 rue de la
Loi, B-1040, Brussels, Belgium; +32 (0) 2 231 0340; www
.epc.eu. Independent Brussels think tank devoted to European
integration.

Open Europe, 7 Tufton St., London SW1P 3QN,
U.K.; (44) 207 197 2333; www.openeurope.org.uk.
Independent think tank with offices in London and
Brussels.

Respond! Housing Association, Airmount, Dominick Pl.,
Waterford, Ireland; (353) 0818 357901; www.respond
.ie. Ireland's largest nonprofit public housing association;
has built nearly 5,200 homes nationwide for traditional
families, single-parent families, the elderly, homeless and
disabled.

Voices From Abroad:

DOMINIQUE STRAUSS-KAHN

Managing Director International Monetary Fund

Praise Greece

"The Greek government should be commended for committing to an historic course of action that will give this proud nation a chance of rising above its current troubles and securing a better future for the Greek people."

The Boston Globe, May 2010

ANGELA MERKEL

Chancellor Germany

Germany is ready

"We now have a mechanism of collective solidarity for the euro. And we all are ready, including Germany, to say that we now need a permanent crisis mechanism to protect the euro."

The Washington Post November 2010

SIMON TILFORD

Chief Economist, Centre for European Reform United Kingdom

Euro's Survival

"I don't think it's sustainable in the absence of a much greater degree of political and economic integration. It's very hard for any economy to flourish in the teeth of fiscal austerity of this magnitude — let alone those that can't devalue."

The New York Times November 2010

OLLI REHN

Commissioner for Economic and Monetary Affairs, European Commission

Containing the fire

"The recovery is taking hold, and it is progressing, but at the same time it is essential that we contain the financial

Bulgaria/Christo Komarnitski

bush fires so that they will not turn into a Europe-wide forest fire."

Thai Press Reports December 2010

SIMON WARD

Chief Economist Henderson Global Investors United Kingdom

Weak won't leave

"I don't believe that the weak countries will leave the euro. If it's anyone it'll be Germany, which is worried about financing the bailouts, so it may be attractive for it to return to the deutschemark."

Express on Sunday (U.K.) November 2010

MARKUS KERBER

Professor of Finance Berlin Technical University Germany

Germany is not alone

"German guilt has been turned into too much money over too many years. But this is over. All of a sudden Germans are grasping the figures. The Dutch and the

Austrians are fundamentally in the same situation. They don't want to see the monetary union turn into a transfer union."

The Christian Science Monitor May 2010

COLM MCCARTHY

Lecturer in Economics University College Dublin, Ireland

Blame the real estate bubble
"The credit-fuelled property bubble is the direct and indirect source of Ireland's debt crisis. If the bubble had been prevented by the bankers or their regulators, Ireland would now be suffering a mild recession rather than an existential threat to economic sovereignty."

Sunday Independent (Ireland) November 2010

FRANÇOIS FILLON

Prime Minister, France

Greece is unique
"Portugal's situation is nothing like that of Greece. . . . There is no reason to speculate against Spain and Portugal. . . . These countries' debt is perfectly within the average for the eurozone."

Daily Telegraph (England) May 2010

NICOLAS VERON

Economist Bruegel Belgium

Remaining intact
"The market perception now is the eurozone is not going to break up. We can safely say that if a country left the euro, it would be economically disruptive."

The Associated Press December 2010

11

Evaluating Microfinance

Sarah Glazer

Nolberta Melara of San Marcos, El Salvador, sells her homemade embroidered aprons in shops across the country. She got her start with a $30 loan from a nonprofit microlender. Since the first microfinance bank was established in 1983, thousands of banks and credit cooperatives around the world have been created to help small entrepreneurs. Supporters say microloans lift millions out of poverty, but critics say lenders' exorbitant rates lure many borrowers deeper into debt and may even be creating a microcredit bubble.

From *CQ Researcher*,
April 2010.

Two years ago, Siyawati, a mother of three, lived on a meager income brought in by her husband's work as a construction day laborer in Uttar Pradesh, India's most populous state. Then she got a $212 microfinance loan from SKS India, the country's largest microfinance institution, and invested it in a candle-making machine. That enabled her to increase the number of candles she was making for sale.

Since then, with the help of additional microloans, her small business has become a small factory employing eight people. Her monthly income has risen from $42 to $425, permitting her to send her children to a good school. "She is proud that her expertise could bring her family out of poverty" reports SKS' Web site.[1]

This is the promise of microfinance: helping to end poverty and spur economic development one entrepreneur at a time by offering microloans — typically averaging a few hundred dollars — to help the impoverished, especially women, who lack collateral for a conventional loan. Popular among philanthropists for nearly 30 years, the movement has become increasingly attractive in recent years to equity funds, foreign investors and profit-making banks, drawn by the industry's extraordinary returns on investment, largely due to its high interest and repayment rates of up to 98 percent.[2]

Microlenders' high annual interest rates — averaging around 30 percent but sometimes reaching more than 100 percent — result from the added cost of sending an agent to collect weekly payments on very small loans, often to remote villages. However, microloans

299

Few People in Poor Nations Have Bank Loans

In the world's poorest nations, largely in sub-Saharan Africa, fewer than 5 percent of adults hold bank loans. Credit is more available in China, India and other African countries, where about one in three adults receives a loan. By contrast eight out of 10 adults in the U.S., Japan, Australia and Western Europe have bank loans.

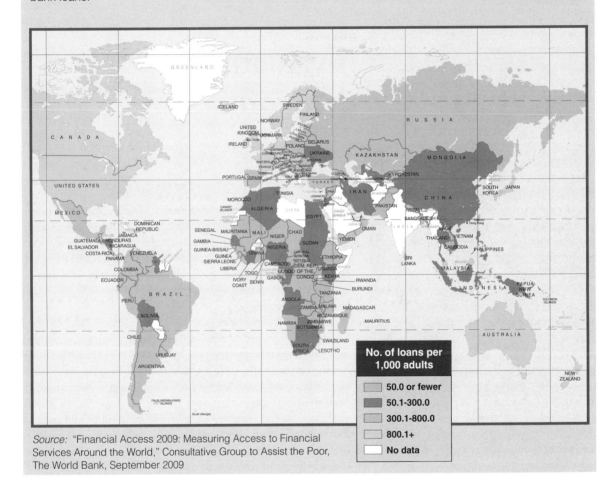

No. of loans per 1,000 adults
- 50.0 or fewer
- 50.1-300.0
- 300.1-800.0
- 800.1+
- No data

Source: "Financial Access 2009: Measuring Access to Financial Services Around the World," Consultative Group to Assist the Poor, The World Bank, September 2009

are generally lower-cost and more reliable than those offered by the moneylenders that many poor villagers and slum-dwellers have depended on for decades.

Countless stories like Siyawati's have attracted billions of dollars in loans — more than $44 billion worldwide in 2008, according to one estimate — creating an average growth rate of 34 percent since 2003.[3]

The idea of microcredit finds its roots in Nobel Prize-winning economist Muhammad Yunus' discovery that even very poor people with no collateral, who would never qualify for a bank loan, could be amazingly diligent in repaying loans. The key, according to Yunus, was for borrowers to band together in small groups of neighbors and guarantee one another's loans. So effective was microcredit as an economic engine in improving the livelihoods of the poor, Yunus famously predicted that it would help create a world where "poverty museums" would be the only place to see poverty.[4]

But increasingly, these cheery anecdotes have been mixed with more disturbing tales of exorbitant interest rates and strong-armed debt recovery practices. Some borrowers who can't make their microloan payments resort to extortionist moneylenders who charge even higher interest rates, sending the borrower ever deeper into debt. Even Yunus' renowned peer-pressure approach has its down side: Members of some neighborhood lending clubs have been known to haul off delinquent debtors' property, attack their houses and ostracize them from their communities.

Malcolm Harper, chairman of M-CRIL, an India-based financial rating company for microfinance lenders, tells of an Indian woman he met in a small village east of Hyderabad. Like many microborrowers, she had taken out a small loan, not for business purposes but to pay for her sister's medical care. Then her husband became ill. When she fell behind on her repayments, the other group members locked her and her young daughters out of their hut. After living on the road for days, she despaired and tried to throw herself and her children into the village well. She was stopped just in time when someone pointed out that she had enough savings with the group to pay off her loan. Her debt was cleared but she was expelled from the group.[5]

The rapid growth of the microfinance sector in recent years and its growing attraction to Western investors have awakened fears that microfinance could create a credit "bubble" akin to the recent U.S. subprime loan craze. Some experts fear that as microfinance institutions seek to reach even more borrowers, especially in areas like southern India where numerous microlenders operate, poor people will be encouraged to take out yet more loans, miring them in a cycle of debt they can never repay.

Microfinance "has put hundreds of millions of people into deeper debt than they were," says Harper. "Now that microfinance is becoming fashionable and

Microlending Totaled at Least $44 Billion

At least $44.2 billion was loaned in 2008 to 86 million impoverished borrowers, mainly in Latin America, Eastern Europe and Central Asia. The loans were made by the 1,400 microfinance institutions (MFIs) — nonprofit organizations, regulated financial institutions and commercial banks — that are tracked by the Microfinance Information Exchange (MIX).

Total MFI Outstanding Loans
(in $ billions)

Sub-Saharan Africa	$3.3
East Asia and Pacific	$8.2
Eastern Europe and Central Asia	$10.0
Latin America	$16.7
Middle East and North Africa	$1.2
South Asia	$4.7
All Regions	$44.2

Source: "Microfinance at a Glance — 2008," Microfinance Information Exchange, Dec. 31, 2009

profitable, a lot more companies are entering the field, and that leads to overborrowing just like it did with house owners in Indianapolis" during the giddy days of subprime mortgages, he maintains. "People are borrowing more than they can afford; it is over-indebting people, and they pay Peter from what they borrow from Paul" — often the high-priced local moneylender.

Because borrowers rarely report their outstanding moneylender debts to microfinance lenders, they may look like better credit risks than they are. Some analysts believe the still-thriving moneylender loans are keeping microcredit loans afloat.[6]

"We fear a bubble," Jacques Grivel of Luxembourg-based Finethic, an investment fund that raises money from institutional investors to channel to microfinance lenders in Latin America, Eastern Europe and Asia, recently told *The Wall Street Journal.* "Too much money is chasing too few good candidates."[7]

But many experts in the field point out that if there really were a credit bubble, it would have had plenty of time over the past 25 years to burst. Instead, microborrowers have consistently maintained high repayment rates. As abusive as it may get, the borrowing group's collective guarantee — known as "solidarity lending" — usually gets people to repay their loans on time.

The borrowers want to maintain access to a highly valued service — reliable loans at lower interest rates than are offered by their local moneylenders.

Yet some fear that for-profit companies will themselves become "microloan sharks," and will charge exorbitant interest, focusing more on profits than on helping the poor, in the words of Jonathan C. Lewis, chair and founder of the nonprofit MicroCredit Enterprises, which makes loans to microlenders.

The commercial industry responds that as more capital and competition enter this market, interest rates will likely come down and more impoverished borrowers can be reached. "There will never be enough donor money to solve the world's ills. We need to find market-driven solutions," says Joan Trant, executive director of the New York-based International Association of Microfinance Investors.

Some question the very premise of microcredit — that it offers an escape from poverty — arguing that China-style economic growth and factory jobs offer the better solution. Defenders respond that while microcredit may not lift everybody completely out of poverty, it has been crucial in tiding families over during economic emergencies like health crises.

For the poorest families, "It's a buffer to prevent them from totally collapsing — going into destitution," says Geeta Rao Gupta, president of the International Center for Research on Women, in Washington, D.C. On that score, critics and supporters alike are starting to emphasize ways to help the poor build savings accounts — which may be more appropriate than expensive loans for tiding families over in emergencies.

In 2005, the international charity Catholic Relief Services announced it would divest its holdings in microcredit and focus on savings. Microcredit was making poor borrowers "poor twice" through high interest rates, in the words of Kim Wilson, former director of the organization's microfinance unit.[8]

Wilson, now a lecturer at Tufts University's Fletcher School, says she was disturbed by the "vigilante" enforcement of loan repayments by fellow borrowers. And she was uncomfortable with microcredit's traditional formula of giving borrowers a new loan as soon as they repaid the old one — leading to a "treadmill" of debt, in her view.

Concerns about extortionist interest rates, deceptive information about the interest charged and abusive collection practices have spurred calls for the kind of consumer protection regulation common in the United States but rare in developing countries. The microfinance industry has taken several steps towards self-regulation — including voluntary codes of conduct and more transparent information about interest rates — in an effort to forestall government regulation.

Most economists believe microloans don't necessarily lift people out of poverty but that the loans help them "manage their poverty better," in the words of David Roodman, a research fellow at the Center for Global Development, in Washington, D.C., who is writing a book on microfinance and maintains a popular blog on the subject (http://blogs.cgdev.org/open_book/).

Microfinance gives the poor "a choice to do something to feed their kids and a chance to have a slightly better life," Lewis says. "We should stop romanticizing it." For the billion people who live on $1 a day, he says, "their economic development question is 'How do I feed my kids today? And do I?' And a lot of days they don't."

Increasingly experts agree that the more than 2 billion people living on less than $2 a day, most without access to banks, deserve access to financial services — not just loans but also savings accounts and insurance, which may help them even more in escaping poverty.[9]

As the industry, academia and the philanthropic world ponder the future of microfinance, here are some of the questions being debated:

Does microcredit help the poor, especially women, out of poverty?

When economist Yunus, the father of microfinance, started giving poor Bangladeshi villagers loans as an experiment in the 1970s, he made some startling discoveries that turned standard economic assumptions on their head. Noticing that even the poorest villages were beehives of small-scale trading, he questioned the conventional wisdom that creating jobs, rather than encouraging entrepreneurial activity, is the best way to help the poor.[10]

"An ever-expanding cycle of economic growth," he predicted, could be created by giving repeat loans to poor borrowers for productive enterprises.[11]

Making loans to women brought more benefits to the family than lending money to men, he discovered.

"When men make money they tend to spend it on themselves" for items like drink and cigarettes, he said, "but when women make money they bring benefits to the whole family" by spending it on their children for schooling and better food.[12]

Yunus, who founded the Grameen Bank in 1983 specifically to make microloans, says "64 percent of our borrowers" who have been with the bank for five years or more have left poverty. By his own simple checklist, a family has risen out of poverty when it has a house with a tin roof, clean drinking water, warm clothes for winter and can afford to send all the children to school.[13]

Yet, according to some researchers, the claim that business microloans lift most families out of poverty is, on average, unfounded.

"Few live up to the mythology that their business grows and they climb out of poverty," says researcher Roodman. "The majority don't climb out of poverty but get some assistance in managing their poverty" by taking out loans that permit them to pay for school fees or medical and other household crises.

Two recent studies of microcredit borrowers, conducted by researchers at the Massachusetts Institute of Technology (MIT) and Yale University, found no improvement in household income or consumption — two standard measures of poverty.[14] Moreover, the researchers found, microcredit often helps men's businesses more than women's and is most helpful to those who already have businesses or are better-off to start with.

Indeed, studies question almost every element of the famous Yunus narrative — from the dominant role of women to the focus on entrepreneurship. One study found that about half of loans made by Grameen Bank are not for business purposes at all, even though they were labeled as such, but go instead to household consumption, such as school fees or medical expenses.[15]

That raises the question: What types of desperate measures will impoverished borrowers take to pay the high interest rates, which can range from 20 percent to over 100 percent, if they're earning no profits? Some go to moneylenders, who charge even higher rates but can quickly produce the cash needed for a loan installment, according to *The Wall Street Journal.* The number of moneylenders in India rose 56 percent from 1995-2006, when microfinance was growing rapidly. "Group pressure makes us go to moneylenders," one woman told *The*

Journal. "If you lag behind, the rest of the group members can't get new loans."[16]

As for empowering women, loans made to the women who show up at the weekly debt collection meetings often get passed on to the male breadwinners in their families, especially in India and Pakistan, according to Sarita Gupta, vice president for global resources and communications at New York-based Women's World Banking, which works with 40 microfinance providers and banks in 28 countries. That's partly because women may perceive their husbands' businesses as the ones most likely to succeed, she suggests, although women may invest in their own enterprises with later loans.

Yet, even if the loans are used for business, most poor women earn too little from their tiny enterprises to make a significant improvement in their lives, argues Aneel Karnani, associate professor of strategy at the University of Michigan's Ross School of Business. In a typical isolated village in India, he points out, "you see a lot of women sitting next to each other selling the same product — bananas" — to equally impoverished villagers.

"They don't earn enough to get lifted out of poverty. [T]he alternative to microfinance is finding jobs for the poor," he asserts. Rather than making tiny loans to five women, it would be more effective to loan one entrepreneur a large enough sum to start a clothing factory that could provide jobs to those five, he argues. Poor entrepreneurs prefer the same thing most people in rich countries want: the security of a salaried job, he says. "They're not entrepreneurs by choice but by necessity," he claims.

Some economists also question whether microfinance can be the engine of economic growth it's touted to be. "We know that broad-based economic growth is the most powerful way to reduce poverty," says Jonathan Morduch, professor of public policy and economics at New York University's (NYU) Wagner School, noting that standard-of-living improvements in China, which has little microfinance, and India, which has a lot, have been driven by growth in gross domestic product. "Frankly, we don't have a sense (even if all the loans went to business) of the degree to which microfinance has contributed to economic growth."

As for Yunus' claim that more than half of Grameen borrowers have left poverty, Morduch says, "The question an economist like myself asks is, 'What would have

Bangladeshi economist Muhammad Yunus was awarded the 2006 Nobel Peace Prize for creating Grameen ("village") Bank, the world's first microcredit bank. The idea grew out of a famine in Bangladesh in the mid-1970s, when Yunus lent $27 of his own money to 42 poor villagers for small enterprises and, to his surprise, all the loans were promptly repaid.

(CGAP), a consortium of government and private development organizations that studies microfinance, concludes the jury is still out as to whether microfinance lifts millions out of poverty. Financial services are, however, "vital tools in helping them to cope with poverty," concluded author Richard Rosenberg, an advisor at CGAP.[17]

Microloans have been used more often to "smooth consumption" over the course of a month of uneven earnings rather than to grow enterprises, studies suggest. But if we find that finding disappointing, it may be because well-to-do Westerners don't have the impoverished person's experience of earning $4 one day and zero the next, Rosenberg suggests.[18]

The microloan can make it possible to eat on that no-earning day. "This is basic survival stuff," says MicroCredit Enterprises founder Lewis.

Will for-profit investors continue to benefit the very poor and women?

Microfinance suddenly became a hot market for Western investors after Banco Compartamos, the largest microfinance lender in Mexico, went public in 2007. Stock in the former nonprofit was soon valued at more than $1.5 billion, offering a mouth-watering rate of return to investors of more than 50 percent a year.[19]

Even more attention-grabbing was the news that Compartamos routinely charged its impoverished borrowers an astoundingly high annual interest rate of more than 100 percent, in sharp contrast to the 31 percent average annual rate charged by microlending institutions worldwide at the time.[20]

Microfinance godfather Yunus, along with others in the industry, was outraged. "Microcredit was created to fight the moneylender, not to become the moneylender," he said.[21]

In an article entitled "Microloan Sharks," MicroCredit Enterprises founder Lewis concurred, "[T]he mission of microfinance is to make a difference in the lives of poor families and to end the scourge of poverty, not build a new asset class based on profiteering."[22]

Yet commercialization boosters say it's just these kinds of highly attractive returns that will draw more capital and more lenders to the sector, permitting it to reach more borrowers. The resulting competition, they say, will ultimately lead to lower interest rates.

happened without Grameen?' This happened at a time when poverty was falling in Bangladesh generally. What's the net impact?"

Microfinance advocates say just because they don't have research evidence that meets the highest standards used by economists doesn't mean microcredit doesn't work. They point to some 25 years of direct experience and growing demand for the loans. "I just think researchers haven't proved it yet," says Alex Counts, president and CEO of the Washington-based Grameen Foundation, which spreads the Grameen philosophy worldwide.

A recent summary of the research from the World Bank-affiliated Consultative Group to Assist the Poor

Does Falling Repayment Rate Signal a Loan Bubble?

Bangladesh-based Grameen Bank, which pioneered providing tiny loans to the poor, is seeing a drop in repayment rates. Founded by Nobel Peace Prize-winner Muhammad Yunus, the bank has nearly doubled its membership rolls since 2004, reaching almost 8 million members in 2009 (bottom). But after the 2008 global recession, the bank reported its collection rate dropped below 97 percent for the first time in recent years, to 96.55 in 2009 (top). Some observers caution this could be a red flag warning that more borrowers will have trouble repaying their loans in the future. But there's been no epidemic of defaults yet in Bangladesh. Even at this new low, repayment rates for microcredit are significantly higher than for American credit card debt, which fell as low as 85.5 percent for Bank of America last year.

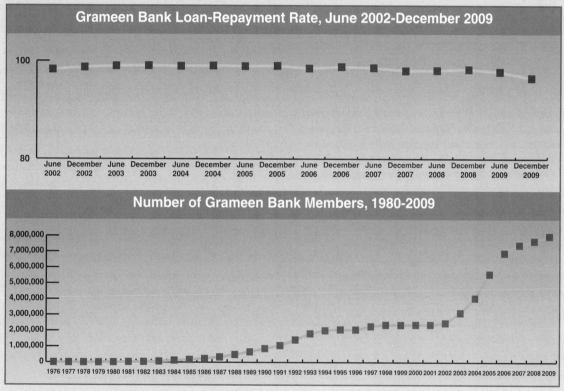

Source: David Roodman, "Grameen Bank, Which Pioneered Loans for the Poor, Has Hit a Repayment Snag," Center for Global Development, February 2010

Even though Compartamos took a lot of heat for its high returns, "you also saw a rush into the Mexican microfinance sector," says Mary Ellen Iskenderian, president and CEO of Women's World Banking, which supports microfinance institutions converting into for-profit banks. "People thought there was money to be made there, and you've seen some real competition," reports Iskenderian, whose organization is starting an equity fund for investors in microfinance institutions.

Bolivia, a microlending market with vigorous competition, has seen some of the world's steepest declines in interest rates, she points out. (Bolivia's rates have dropped from 50 percent in the mid-1990s to just over

The Poor Are Active Money Managers

Financial diaries clarify how the poor manage their money.

People living on $2 a day or less — like Bangladeshi rickshaw driver Hamid and his wife Khadeja — have something in common with the rich: They are also active money managers.

The couple live with their child in one room in the slums of Dhaka, sharing a toilet with seven other families. They survive on an average of 78 cents a day per person. But some days Hamid gets no work and no earnings. To ensure cash flow, they've built up reserves in six different instruments — from money saved at home to a life-insurance policy. [1]

They also have six debts outstanding to lenders ranging from a microlender to the grocer. Between the money they've pushed into savings ($451) and pulled out by taking loans or withdrawing savings ($514), their total turnover ($965) is $125 more than their total income for the year. As a result they have managed to extend each dollar of income earned to $1.15 through a combination of savings, loans and guarding money for others for a fee.

Hamid's story is just one of the 250 portraits gleaned from financial diaries kept by borrowers in Bangladesh, India and South Africa and described by a team of economists in a ground-breaking book last year — changing the way experts think about the "unbanked" poor.

The book, *Portfolios of the Poor*, revealed that while microfinance is often touted as replacing expensive moneylenders for the poor, 88 percent of the loans made actually were taken out through an informal network of friends, relatives and moneylenders — even in Bangladesh where most of the families had access to microfinance banks.

Informal loans, the authors found, sometimes are interest-free, in the cases of relatives, or more flexible, in the case of moneylenders. And loans from microfinance lenders, ostensibly for business enterprises, were frequently used for household needs. Khadeja used part of her microloan to buy gold — a form of secure savings.

Another Bangladeshi rickshaw driver decided that spending his loan to buy his own rickshaw was too risky, because the vehicle could be stolen. Instead, he used the loan to stock up on rice and to buy a cupboard; then he loaned $20 of it to a fellow rickshaw driver for 17.5 percent interest per month, permitting him to make some money.

Moneylenders are often thought to be the main predators on the poor, charging exorbitant interest rates. But the

20 percent as their market grew from about 200,000 borrowers to more than 600,000.)[23]

"You have 1.5 billion potential customers who need access to microfinance," estimates Trant, of the International Association of Microfinance Investors. If you multiply them by a typical microloan size (about $200), you'll need about $300 billion to meet the demand, she says. But with only about $44 billion now in microfinance funding portfolios around the world, that leaves a funding gap of more than $250 billion to reach all the unbanked poor.[24]

"Charity's not going to cover that gap. We have to find business solutions," maintains Trant. "People's enlightened self-interest — if they know they can make a buck while doing some good in the world — that's what's driving investment in microfinance."

Yet scaling up microfinance could just as well create monopolies, warns Lewis, especially in small, impoverished regions that may never support more than one microfinance bank. In those cases, he writes, "A poor woman driven by economic adversity has very little power to negotiate interest rates with a microlender."[25]

Some companies say they plow their increased profits into reducing their interest rates. For example, Compartamos has reduced its interest rates by about 30 percent since 2000, when it was charging 115 percent, according to a spokesman. "As we grow and are more efficient, we move that efficiency to our clients" in the form of lower interest rates, said spokesman Jorge Daniel Manrique Barrigan.[26] Critics point out, however, that the bank's average loan size also has increased over the same time, reducing its servicing cost per loan. Considering the 50 percent return Compartamos has consistently given investors over the years, "they are clearly only passing on a small amount to the poor and keeping much more for themselves," says Chuck

authors were surprised to discover that some of the highest rates in South Africa, for example, were charged by savings clubs. These groups of conservative ladies pool their savings together and then lend a portion of it out at 30 percent per month — over 2,000 percent on an annual basis. That should have yielded hedge-fund sized profits, but because so many loans were not repaid or partly forgiven, the yield came to only about 1 percent a month.

Still, how are poor people able to pay such enormous interest rates? Whether to moneylenders or microfinance banks, interest rates can range from 20 percent to more than 100 percent a year. The authors suggest a 25-cent fee charged for a moneylender loan of $10 for a week may seem reasonable to Hamid, who earns just $2.33 a day as a rickshaw driver, even though on an annual basis, such a loan costs 261 percent per year. That $10 may be the difference between buying new clothes for the Muslim holiday of Eid and going to the mosque in rags.

"It can be a few pennies a week; they're repaying in small bits," explains Jonathan Morduch, a coauthor of *Portfolios* and a professor of public policy and economics at New York University's Wagner School of Business. "Very expensive loans are out for a few weeks, and it's a fee for service — not big." Most microfinance loans made by Bangladesh-based Grameen Bank, a pioneer in microlending, "are 20-40 percent for a year; it's a big chunk of cash you pay back in dribs and drabs."

Many of the diarists also were found to be paying a fee to accumulate their savings in a safe place but earned no interest on their deposits — something a Westerner would find difficult to understand. The fees might be paid to a woman who comes to the village once a week to collect or to a neighbor to act as "money guard," keeping the money out of temptation from a spouse. These savers may not see loans as very different from savings — in each case they are paying a fee each week to procure a large lump sum, the authors note.

But even these nest eggs can disappear. Similarly, informal lenders may not come up with the cash when it's promised. And there can be cheating even among friends.

Having reliable financial tools — whether savings or loans — would make a big difference to those with such low incomes, according to the authors, who find it surprising that cash-flow management has received little attention from the microfinance sector. Although microfinance loans historically have been oriented towards business, the diaries show that households need to borrow for a wide range of needs and "are prepared to find ways of repaying loans from ordinary household cash flow."

— *Sarah Glazer*

[1] Information from this story comes from Daryl Collins, *et al.*, *Portfolios of the Poor: How the World's Poor Live on $2 a Day* (2009).

Waterfield, CEO and founder of MFTransparency, an industry-supported group that reports interest rates.

Lewis says the microfinance sector has split between those who want to commercialize it and his own anti-poverty faction. "We didn't get into this to start banks; we're interested in poverty reduction," he says. "And so we really need to look at the problems the poor have and combine the microfinance services with health, education, financial literacy, malaria bed nets. We need to keep interest rates low; it's not about returns for Western investors."

A recent Women's World Banking study of 25 microfinance institutions seems to confirm his fears. The researchers found that the percentage of women borrowers falls off sharply when nonprofit lenders convert themselves into profit-seeking banks.[27]

That's partly because commercial banks shift to larger loans to improve their profit margins, since they're less costly to administer than very small loans, the report found. And women's loans are typically smaller than men's. Women reinvest less in their businesses than men, because their businesses are smaller, often home-based, with household duties competing for their time. Women also tend to have smaller profit margins than men because they're in highly competitive sectors like food preparation, sewing and beauty salons.[28]

However, the same study also found that more women ended up getting loans from lenders that went commercial, despite being a smaller proportion of the total borrowers — largely because the banks scaled up to serve more people overall, both women and men.

"That's the goal — to reach more people," says Trant. "We want to get economic access to people who haven't had it in the past, whether they're male or female."

The free-enterprise nature of microfinance has attracted millions from investors who see a way to make

Getty Images/Shamik Banerjee

A microcredit borrowers' group in Kolkata, India, meets to make payments on loans. Peer pressure ensures that the poor pay loans promptly. Weekly payments typically are made in public in the village "center," and everyone in the group can be denied subsequent loans if one member defaults.

money while doing good. In 2005, Pierre Omidyar, the billionaire founder of eBay, gave a $100 million donation to Tufts University, specifying it should be invested in microfinance institutions. Omidyar was attracted to microfinance because it demonstrated free-market principles, much like eBay. Omidyar hoped donor funding would become unnecessary once microfinance could raise money in the capital markets, he told *The New Yorker* in 2006.[29]

Yet nonprofits continue to serve poorer borrowers than those sought out by commercial banks, research suggests. Surprisingly, a study of 346 leading microfinance institutions co-authored by NYU economist Morduch found that nonprofit, nongovernmental organizations (NGOs) actually tend to charge higher interest rates — a 25 percent median — compared to banks' 13 percent. That occurs because NGOs' poorer clients take out smaller loans, which are more expensive to administer. "Profit-maximizing investors would have limited interest in most of the institutions that are focusing on the poorest customers and women," the researchers conclude.[30]

"[E]veryone thinks you can do it in a win-win way," helping the poor and maximizing profits at the same time, says Morduch. But in reality, some nonprofits will continue to need donors' help to reach the very poorest.

"There's a lot of stuff going on commercially but it can't reach everybody," he says.

Should microfinance lenders be more tightly regulated?

The astoundingly high interest rates charged by some microlenders have prompted calls for mandated caps on interest rates.

For instance, a populist debtors' rebellion in Nicaragua — the "No Pago" (I Won't Pay) movement — has spurred mass demonstrations protesting high rates and demanding a legal rate ceiling.[31] Part of the outrage stems from the fact that for nearly three decades many microlenders have presented interest rates to illiterate borrowers in a way that makes them look deceptively low.

Until recently, Compartamos charged an annual interest rate of 129 percent, including all up-front fees and taxes, according to a 2008 calculation by MFTransparency's Waterfield.[32] But "Compartamos didn't actually say, 'We charge 129 percent a year.' . . . They said to the borrowers, 'We charge 4 percent a month,' " according to Waterfield.[33]

That 4 percent is deceptively low because it is based on a so-called "flat" rate. Many microfinance lenders charge such flat rates on the entire amount borrowed, but flat fees turn out to be nearly double the annual percentage rate (APR) — the standard used on loans in the United States, which calculates the interest on a declining balance over the life of the loan. For instance, a loan advertised at 36 percent "flat" actually works out to 65.7 percent APR, according to Waterfield.[34] That rate is even higher when up-front fees like security deposits and insurance fees are factored in.[35]

"As soon as some [microlenders] start lying, you've created an environment where everyone else has to lie" within the same regional market, Waterfield says, in order to look as (deceptively) cheap as their competitors. He hopes to break that syndrome by persuading all lenders in a country to submit their interest rates to him in a sealed envelope; then his Web site will disclose all annual rates on the same day.

Compartamos now charges 78.7 percent annually for its core microcredit loan, according to a company spokesman. But Waterfield says even that number is deceptive. Adding taxes and a mandatory 10 percent security deposit brings the rate up to 110 percent annually, he calculates, lower than the 129 percent of two years ago but still breathtakingly high.[36]

"Compartamos has made serious efforts in order to reduce our rates," spokesman Barrigan said in an e-mail. In fact, he notes, the company has lowered its rates "more than 30 percent" since 2000, when it was charging 115 percent annually according to its own calculation, not including tax or up-front fees.

Citing misleading — and sometimes deceptive — practices, Karnani of Michigan's Ross School of Business wants governments to cap the rates microlenders can charge, prohibit abusive debt collection practices and require interest rate disclosure according to a standardized method.[37]

Such legal protections are virtually nonexistent for microborrowers overseas, according to Wilson at Tufts' Fletcher School. By contrast, in the United States, usury laws at the state level limit interest rates, and federal truth-in-lending rules stipulate a consistent method of disclosing rates. The Fair Debt Collection Practices Act attempts to limit harassment of debtors.[38]

But mandated interest rate caps are almost universally opposed by the microfinance industry. If politicians were to set caps too low to cover lenders' costs, microfinance organizations would be forced out of business, Grameen Foundation's Counts contends, and borrowers would be driven into the jaws of unregulated loan sharks.

Nonprofits that offer assistance in health, education and training along with loans would be hit hardest, because those extra program costs would no longer be covered, Counts predicts, "The most vulnerable isolated communities would be driven off the map," he says.

Karnani says these kinds of objections assume that free-market competition is keeping interest rates reasonable. That may be true in a rich country like the United States, where numerous banks compete to drive rates down. But in poor villages "there may be [only] one or two [lenders], so there is no competition," he asserts. "So the tendency is to charge above what would be a competitive rate."

Calls to require transparent disclosure of interest rates find some support among industry practitioners like Waterfield. But he believes his voluntary experiment, launched in 2008, will get the job done faster.

Tattoo artist Filipe Gil started his parlor in Lisbon, Portugal, after receiving a small loan from a private microcredit bank. Unsecured microcredit loans appeal to the poor, who lack the collateral required by commercial banks. High interest rates charged by microlenders are attracting many private investors to the field, and critics say some microcredit lenders use strong-armed collection tactics.

"It will take us a decade to get transparency regulation" in all 100 countries that have microfinance, he says. "But in a couple of weeks I can go to India, we can go to the microfinance institutions and say, 'Why wait for government to tell us to do the right thing? Why don't we ourselves do the right thing?' "

In Cambodia and Bosnia and Herzegovina, the first two countries his organization approached, all lenders agreed to disclose their APR's on his Web site, www.mftransparency.org. However, he concedes, this doesn't necessarily mean their loan officers tell new borrowers the true rate — though he hopes they eventually will.

However, even that information may be insufficient in places like India, where 39 percent of adults are illiterate.[39]

"I want to tell people, 'Here's exactly what you'll pay' in dollars and cents [and] let them figure out that's three meals of food on the table," says Wilson, who points out interest rates may be a hard concept for an illiterate person to grasp.

Media coverage of Indian and Mexican lenders who hired thugs to collect debts has recently drawn attention to abusive debt collection, the other area Karnani wants regulated.[40]

More than 900 microfinance lenders and other organizations have signed an industry code of conduct,
dubbed the Smart Campaign, promising neither to
engage in "abusive or coercive" debt collection, nor to
market loans to people who can't afford them. They also
pledge to present their interest rates in a form under-
standable to clients.[41]

"The main reason for starting the campaign was
watching the U.S. subprime meltdown and recognizing
that it arose from a failure of consumer protection —
and seeing that regulation hadn't stopped it," says
Elisabeth Rhyne, managing director of the Center for
Financial Inclusion, the Washington-based industry
group that initiated the campaign.

Borrowing from the organic and fair trade labeling
movements, Grameen Foundation's Counts has proposed a "certification" for those lenders who agree to
abide by an ethical code — including disclosing their
interest rates and eschewing unethical debt collection.[42]

Karnani is skeptical, especially in the absence of a
government enforcer to assure compliance. "Vague and
platitudinous appeals for self-restraint by companies and
self-regulation by the industry are not effective at protecting microclients," he has charged.[43]

BACKGROUND

Early Beginnings

Efforts to organize financial services for the poor stretch
back to rural credit cooperatives organized in Europe in
the 19th century. By 1910, there were more than 15,000
such institutions operating in small communities in Germany alone.[44]

Members contributed savings to the cooperatives, which
then allocated loans to members who needed money for
investments or living expenses. Participants, whether borrowers or savers, were all shareholders in the cooperative
and made key decisions democratically about interest rates
and loan sizes.

The modern microfinance movement's roots date back
to 1974 when Yunus, then an economics professor in
Bangladesh, became dissatisfied with the free-market theories
he was teaching in the classroom as a solution to ending
poverty. Since the 1950s, foreign aid had been based on
the theory that the route to economic development in poor

countries like Bangladesh was technical assistance in
modernizing their agriculture and industry.

But Yunus noticed that the poorest of the poor in
Jobra, where he was helping farmers improve their crop
yields, received no benefit from his assistance. They owned
no land and eked out a daily living as day laborers, craft
workers or beggars. A village woman, Sufiya Begum, told
Yunus that she relied on a local moneylender for the cash
to make the bamboo stools she sold. But the moneylender
would only give her the cash if she agreed to sell him
what she produced at a price he set. Together with the
high interest on her loan, this left her only two pennies
a day as income.[45]

In an experiment starting in 1976, Yunus decided to
lend $27 of his own money to 42 villagers who were
beholden to moneylenders. When he asked a local bank
to make more such loans, they objected that the borrowers
had no property to offer as collateral and no credit
histories.

Yunus persuaded the bank to make the loans by offering
to act as guarantor. He was "stunned" when the poor paid
back their loans "on time, every time." Unable to persuade
local banks to expand this program further, he created the
now world-renowned Grameen ("village") Bank in 1983,
to lend money to the poor without requiring collateral.[46]

Power of Peer Pressure

The bank grew explosively, largely credited to its innovative group lending, in which poor borrowers acted as
guarantors for one another. Each group consisted of five
friends, all of whom had to approve of a new loan; if a
member defaulted and fellow group members did not pay
off the debt, everyone in the group could be denied
subsequent loans.[47]

This so-called "joint liability" became the most celebrated feature of the Grameen contract, according to
economist Morduch. For many years, microfinance was
linked inextricably to the idea of group lending. It gave
customers incentives to pay promptly, to monitor their
neighbors and to select responsible acquaintances when
forming the groups. The requirement that weekly payments be made in public in the village "center" in the
presence of 10 or 12 such groups, placed even more peer
pressure on timely repayment. To many economists, it
was the linchpin that explained why loans to poor people
without collateral worked.[48]

CHRONOLOGY

1860s-1940s *Credit cooperatives offering savings and low-cost loans to the poor spread from Europe to India, Senegal and the U.S.*

1864 German village mayor Freidrich Raiffeissen pioneers lending to poor farmers through cooperatives.

1904 In British-ruled India, Cooperative Credit Societies Act creates co-ops that lend to poor farmers.

1946 Indian co-ops have 9 million members.

1950s-1970s *Foreign aid focuses on economic development in the Third World.*

1970s Bangladeshi professor Muhammad Yunus begins experimenting with loans to poor villagers.

1974–75 Bangladesh famine leaves many families destitute.

1976 Yunus lends $27 to 42 villagers, launching his lending experiments with the poor; all loans are repaid.

1980s *Bangladeshi banks begin lending to the poor to start tiny businesses; the idea spreads to Latin America, Asia and Africa.*

1983 Yunus creates Grameen Bank in Bangladesh, first bank devoted to making microfinance loans to poor people with no collateral.

1990s *Microfinance lending grows rapidly; Grameen eases lending rules, microfinance becomes more professional.*

1991 Grameen hits millionth member, growing 40 percent per year.

1995 Consultative Group to Assist the Poor, a group of major donors and agencies, created at World Bank.

1997 Microcredit Summit Campaign — a coalition of lenders, donors and advocates — sets goal of reaching 100 million families with microloans.

1998 Worst flood in Bangladesh's history leaves over 30 million homeless, killing over 1,000.

1999 Grameen suffers large-scale defaults.

2000s *Grameen Bank makes microlending more flexible; profit-seeking investors take stakes in microfinance; worldwide credit crisis begins to affect microfinance. Reports of over-indebted microborrowers raise specter of loan "bubble"; microfinance industry initiates consumer-protection efforts to avoid regulation.*

2001 "Grameen II" is introduced, making loan terms more flexible.

2004 Grameen's savings deposits exceed its loans for the first time.

2005 U.N. declares it the Year of Microcredit.

2006 Yunus receives Nobel Peace Prize for bringing microcredit to the poor.

2007 California venture capital firm Sequoia Capital's $11.5 million equity investment in giant microlender SKS India signals attraction to purely profit-seeking investors.

2008 Worldwide credit crisis erupts (March 17). . . . By year-end, growth of new borrowings slows and delinquency rates rise.

2009 First randomized study finds microlending has no impact on poverty (July). . . . *Wall Street Journal* reports poor residents of southern India get "carpet-bombed" with offers of multiple microloans, raising fear of a credit bubble (August). . . . Microlenders criticized for concealing high interest rates with deceptive marketing; industry responds by disclosing true price of microlenders' loans in three countries, at www. mftransparency.org (Oct. 19).

2010 Bill & Melinda Gates Foundation announces $38 million grant to microfinance lenders in 12 countries in Asia, Africa and Latin America to create savings accounts for the very poor — signaling new focus on savings.

Do Microcredit Loans Alleviate Poverty?

New studies question old assumptions.

Many impoverished borrowers rise above the poverty level after receiving a microfinance loan. But was the loan the crucial factor, as advocates have claimed?

Not necessarily, economists have argued. Since people who take small loans tend to be entrepreneurs with drive and ambition, they could have found some other way besides microfinance to better their situation — through social networks, other loans or business aptitude. Dean Karlan, a professor of economics at Yale University, argues that the better question is: "How would their lives have been different had they not received the loan?"[1]

Karlan and economist Jonathan Zinman of Dartmouth College are two of the first researchers to employ the randomized control trial — the gold standard of scientific research — to determine the effectiveness of microfinance. In this approach, one group of people is randomly assigned to receive a loan, and another group gets no loan. Last year, in one of two studies that appear to overturn widely held beliefs about microcredit's power to alleviate poverty, they compared two such groups in the Philippines.[2]

The results were surprising. They found no evidence that household income improved among those who got a loan. Although women are the traditional recipients of microcredit, male borrowers were more likely to increase their small-business profit as a result of their loan. Men also tended to spend their profits on their children's education — in contrast to the conventional wisdom that it's mainly women who can be counted on to do so.

A second study using randomized groups in the slums of urban Hyderabad, India, did see some benefit: Borrowers who already had a business saw some increase in profit. Conducted by economists Abhijat Banerjee and Esther Duflo at the Massachusetts Institute of Technology (MIT),

the study found that overall household spending — a crucial sign of financial health — stayed about the same. The authors found "no impact on health, education or women's decision-making" power in the family — three benefits often claimed for microfinance. For example, households that took a loan were no more likely to have children in school than those that did not.[3]

In at least half the Hyderabad cases, borrowers said they planned to use their loan for a nonbusiness purpose, such as repaying another loan, buying a TV or meeting household expenses. The authors conclude that those borrowers who didn't start a business but increased their consumption when they got a loan "may eventually become poorer" because they are "borrowing against the future."

However, critics said both studies measured a period of time — up to 18 months — that was too short to determine whether poverty would be overcome. "You need about two-and-a-half years worth of loans to see a real impact," says Mary Ellen Iskendarian, CEO of Women's World Banking, which works with 40 microfinance lenders in 28 countries. In Pakistan, she says, that's when "you start to see a substantial improvement in the house: The tin roof goes on or the mud floor becomes wood, or another child is registered for school."

Leading microfinance advocates say the studies can't disprove improvements in people's lives that they've seen with their own eyes. "We don't have the evidence in the sense academics want to have it," partly because randomized trials are expensive, says Susan Davis, president and CEO of BRAC USA, a New York-based nonprofit that supports the leading microlender BRAC. In addition, Bangladesh now has so many microlenders that it's hard to find people who have never received a loan to use as a control group, she points out.

Today Grameen has branches covering virtually all villages in Bangladesh, according to Grameen's Web site. The Grameen bank gives loans to more than 8 million poor people, 97 percent of whom are women. Grameen has long boasted an impressive 98 percent repayment rate, but it recently reported a surprising

drop to just 96.55 percent of loans paid on time at the end of last year.[49]

The 'Debt Treadmill'

Grameen's group lending model has been widely imitated by microfinance institutions around the world. By June

"If I hadn't talked to hundreds and hundreds of microfinance borrowers directly, maybe I wouldn't be such a supporter," says Davis, who lived in Bangladesh for four years. "I'm not worried about what the research says. I could see the difference between a mom who got access to finance in the size of their children," who weren't stunted with malnourishment, she recalls. "We have way too many people who have seen the stories. And the fact that millions want access to the service is an indication of the demand."

Jonathan Morduch, a professor of public policy and economics at New York University's Wagner Graduate School of Public Service, is a longtime skeptic about the traditional claims for microfinance. "The boldest claim for microfinance — that it can single-handedly eliminate a large share of world poverty — outpaces by a long distance the evidence accumulated to date," he said in 2006. [4]

That conclusion is "even more true now," with the release of last year's randomized studies from Yale and MIT, he says. But surprisingly, he also insists that "microfinance could be good in its own right without poverty reduction" by giving poor people the kinds of banking services that permit them to send a child to school or deal with a health problem. Something as simple as having money on hand to go to the hospital for childbirth could have a big impact on infant mortality, he says.

However, the underlying question remains: Would governments and aid agencies make a bigger dent in poverty by spending their money on something else? A year of primary schooling probably helps poor people more than a year of microfinance lending, some experts say. But microfinance costs much less in subsidies. [5]

"What interventions do we have that have even repaid 1 percent of the investment?" asks Jonathan C. Lewis, founder and CEO of the nonprofit MicroCredit Enterprises, which makes loans to microlenders. "Do we have vaccination programs or schools that provide self-financing?"

Carpenter Anil Sutradhr works in the backyard shop he opened in Manikganj, Bangladesh, with a microloan from Grameen Bank. Recent studies have shown that microloans are less effective at decreasing poverty than was widely thought.

As for the recent studies, he concludes, "Every single value that you hold dear you don't measure with a spread sheet. We don't say, 'Before you start school, we need to know what benefit society will get.' We have a general sense this is the way it's going to work."

— *Sarah Glazer*

[1] Dean Karlan, "Measuring Microfinance," *Stanford Social Innovation Review*, Summer 2008, p. 53.

[2] Dean Karlan and Jonathan Zinman, "Expanding Microenterprise Credit Access: Using Randomized Supply Decisions to Estimate the Impacts in Manila," July 2009, http://financialaccess.org/sites/default/files/Expanding%20Credit%20Access%20Manila.pdf.

[3] Abhijit Banerjee, *et al.*, "The Miracle of Microfinance? Evidence from a Randomized Evaluation," October 2009.

[4] Connie Bruck, "A Reporter at Large: Millions for Millions," *The New Yorker*, Oct. 30, 2006.

[5] Richard Rosenberg, "Does Microcredit Really Help Poor People?" January 2010, Focus Note No. 59, Consultative Group to Assist the Poor, www.cgap.org.

2009, microlending had spread to 100 countries, where more than 1,400 microfinance institutions were making loans to more than 86 million borrowers, according to the Microfinance Information Exchange (MIX).

But the model has been criticized in recent years for putting some borrowers into more debt than they could repay and abusively pressuring those who can't repay in time. Loan officers, paid according to how many loans they collect, have sometimes insisted that everyone be held at the village meeting until defaulters paid up. In some cases that meant a rushed visit to an expensive moneylender to come up with the money. In other cases, loan officers

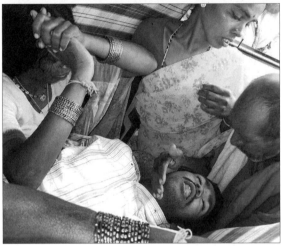

Desperate Microfinance Borrowers

Riot police arrest a farmer in San Benito, Nicaragua, during a January 2009 demonstration in which hundreds of farmers blocked the Pan-American Highway to protest high interest rates charged by microfinance firms (top). Demonstrators associated with Nicaragua's populist "No Pago" (I Won't Pay) rebellion have held mass protests across the country demanding a legal cap on interest rates. In an Indian village in Andhra Pradesh state, family members grieve the suicide death of a 26-year-old farmer, who had been despondent about his debts. In 2006 more than 200 people in the state reportedly committed suicide because of intimidation by microfinance institutions. The government closed down 50 branches of two major microlenders and charged them with extortionate interest rates and intimidating borrowers with strong-armed debt recovery.

harassed borrowers, sometimes refusing to leave someone's house until they came up with the money, according to Anton Simanowitz, a socioeconomist at the University of Sussex Institute of Development Studies in England.

Most microfinance institutions pay cash incentives to loan officers based on how many new clients they bring in and how much money they lend, according to Simanowitz. "It doesn't matter if you're not careful about assessing [the borrower's] ability to repay and their business capacity" when recruiting new clients, he says.

As a result of how they're paid, some loan officers put excessive pressure on borrowers to pay their loans — even in desperate situations. For example, says Simanowitz, a group of women in Kenya had fallen behind in their payments because of a drought. Despite being on the verge of starvation, they sold one of their last chickens to pay their loans.[50]

"That's irresponsible lending . . . accepting money from people selling food when they're starving," says Simanowitz. Theoretically, the business supported by a microloan is expected to generate enough income to repay the loan. But the longer a borrower is with the lender, he says, the more likely are microfinance lenders to "give bigger and bigger loans, so the gap between business and loan size gets bigger until people are extremely vulnerable."

The common practice of pressuring members to take a new loan as soon as they've repaid their last loan also disturbed Wilson, the former director of microfinance for Catholic Relief Services. In 2005, the organization announced that it was withdrawing from the business as a direct investor and lender, citing a fundamental conflict between seeking financial profits and its mission of serving the poor.[51] (The organization still lends technical assistance to microlenders but has shifted emphasis to encouraging savings.) Wilson believes savings, rather than loans, meet the kinds of emergency health and household needs poor families have most often.

"The problem I've seen with most microcredit is they have a formula: once you get a customer hooked, you don't want them to graduate [out of indebtedness] because it's expensive to get that first customer — you've got to do organizing and outreach. Now you've got a live one and don't want to let them go, so you keep selling them more loans. That's a treadmill" of debt, Wilson says.

After the Flood

In 1998 Grameen itself recognized problems with its group lending approach after being hit with large-scale loan defaults following Bangladesh's worst flood in history. When the bank studied which borrowers were defaulting in 1999, it discovered many of them had been struggling to repay for years before the flood.[52]

Recognizing underlying flaws in its approach, Grameen made some radical changes. It began offering more flexible loans — not just for business but also for family needs like student fees — allowing borrowers to change the rigid weekly payment schedule and putting less emphasis on the group to enforce loans.[53]

In 2001 Yunus introduced "Grameen II," which shifted away from the previous inflexible lending system in which every loan term was one year and repayments had to be in weekly installments even if that didn't match the cash flows of many poor households. The new approach removed the requirement that a member borrow continuously. Grameen II also stepped back from the group approach, outlawing an arrangement that makes borrowers responsible for repaying each other's loans.[54]

In addition, the bank intensified its collection of villagers' savings. By the end of 2004, savings deposits amounted to more than its loans for the first time and have continued growing faster than loans.

In 2006, Yunus received the Nobel Peace Prize for his work in microfinance.

CURRENT SITUATION

Rising Delinquencies

Having grown from a small philanthropic movement in the 1970s, microfinance institutions (MFIs) today provide financial services to 86.2 million borrowers and nearly 100 million savers in the developing world.[55] And while dozens of banks in the developed world met their demise during the world financial crisis in mid-2008, the MFIs appeared to be surprisingly nimble.

"No microfinance bank has gone under yet," according to Trant, of the International Association of Microfinance Investors. "We've seen some show stress in repaying loans; but we haven't had a bankruptcy or liquidation."

Iskenderian of Women's World Banking attributes the industry's adaptability to the fact that the microborrowers tend to have small, short-term loans that they can get out of quickly and maintain small inventories so they can shift easily to a new business.

While the industry may have been resilient at first, the most recent reports suggest it is not impervious. By

A Jordanian woman who obtained a microloan from the private Microfund for Women displays her embroidered wares at a microfinance conference in Amman. Studies show that when nonprofit lenders convert themselves into profit-seeking banks, the percentage of female borrowers declines sharply. Commercial banks seek higher profit margins, but women generally operate in highly competitive sectors like food preparation, sewing and beauty salons, which have smaller profit margins.

the end of 2008, the rapid 25 percent annual growth rate in borrowers worldwide had slowed to 15 percent, according to the MIX. A major reason: Rising delinquency rates in some areas forced loan officers to focus on getting current clients to pay their debts rather than attracting new borrowers.[56]

Delinquency rates rose particularly in high-growth markets; Morocco and Bosnia and Herzegovina saw their unpaid loan rate double, though defaults still represented less than 5 percent of their loans.[57]

Contrary to early hopes that they would be insulated from broader economic shocks, microlenders now see themselves as "vulnerable to them through financial markets, credit conditions and the fortunes of their customers," the London-based Centre for the Study of Financial Innovation recently reported. Indeed, a survey of 430 lenders and investors showed that they were most worried about borrowers being unable to repay their loans — a radical change from its last survey in early 2008, when many lenders were growing at double-digit rates.[58]

Fear of growing overindebtedness — borrowers who've taken on more debt than they can repay — dominated the list of concerns. In disturbing echoes of the subprime

Members of the Fikina Kibiashara ("think business") borrowers' group in Nairobi, Kenya, gather to make payments on their microloans. The group's tailors, vegetable and grain vendors and used clothing and wastepaper dealers are just the kind of small entrepreneurs the microfinance movement targets.

mortgage market collapse, many lenders worried that in high-competition regions like Latin America and Asia, where growing numbers of lenders are jockeying for market share, standards for determining the credit-worthiness of borrowers are declining, and more borrowers are defaulting.[59]

In Bosnia and Herzegovina, loan officers are being forced to fill "crazy" monthly quotas of new borrowers, one survey respondent said, based on this come-on: "Just take a loan, you'll pay it back some way."[60]

Looming Crisis?

Even before the international credit crisis hit, there had been growing concern in the industry about regions where borrowers seemed to be over their head in microfinance debt, with rising delinquency rates. A potential repayment crisis is brewing in several "hotspots" — South India, Morocco, Nicaragua and Bosnia and Herzegovina, according to industry experts.[61]

Experts say borrowers owing multiple debts to several microlenders are driving the problem. Typically, microfinance borrowers don't develop individual credit histories. "Group lending . . . the very thing that makes it possible to reach poorer people, means the institution knows less about each individual client," says Rhyne, of the Center for Financial Inclusion.

Could this overlending lead to a bubble like the U.S. subprime crisis? "We should be worried," says the Center

for Global Development's Roodman. Since credit bureaus are rare in these countries, "No one except the borrower has the whole picture," Roodman observes.

In Karnataka, one of the Indian states worst-hit by defaults, the four largest microfinance lenders recently pooled their data to determine how many of their borrowers had multiple loans. They found less of a problem than many imagined. Only 11 percent of borrowers said they were getting loans from two or more institutions, according to the Grameen Foundation's Counts.

Yet, more and more the industry and trade press are asking if a subprime-size bubble could develop. Some argue that a bubble already exists in three states of southern India that account for nearly half of all Indian microclients — Andhra Pradesh, Karnataka and Tamil Nadu — yet are also experiencing some of the fastest growth.[62]

In August *The Wall Street Journal* reported that poor neighborhoods in southern India were being "carpet-bombed" with offers of loans. The reporter found two aspects reminiscent of the subprime bubble: loan officers paid on commission and undocumented loans.[63]

Industry defenders are quick to point out the sector's admirable history of on-time repayment by 98 percent of borrowers. But people living on $2 a day typically have many unreported loans in the informal sector — from moneylenders, storekeepers, friends and family — in addition to one or more microfinance loans.[64]

This is only one of the reasons why Trant, of the International Association of Microfinance Investors, says, "The general consensus is the 98 percent repayment rate is probably not 100 percent realistic." A study by her organization discovered that microfinance organizations often restructured loans — giving borrowers who can't pay extra time — but counted that as part of their renowned 98 percent repayment rate.

Nevertheless, industry experts say, even the highest default rates among microlenders — about 5 to 10 percent of their portfolios — are less than American credit card defaults in the past year, which rose as high as 14.5 percent for Bank of America customers.[65]

Government Crackdowns

As the specter of overindebtedness looms, several governments have introduced consumer protection measures. Some countries in West Africa are encouraging the creation of credit bureaus. Nigeria has imposed interest rate caps

AT ISSUE

Should governments cap microloan interest rates?

YES
Aneel Karnani
Associate Professor of Strategy, Stephen M. Ross School of Business, University of Michigan

Written for *CQ Global Researcher*, April 2010

The microcredit industry resists regulation on the grounds that microcredit is an open and competitive market. I disagree. The industry is characterized by a lack of competition, imperfect information and vulnerable consumers. In an ironic twist on the original microcredit mission, microfinance institutions (MFIs) are making a fortune in microcredit — by exploiting the poor! The government should impose an interest rate ceiling to protect the poor.

Microcredit interest rates are very high. Grameen Bank founder Muhammad Yunus argues that if the interest rate is more than 15 percent above the cost of funds, then it is "too high…. You are moving into the loan shark zone." A study by the Consultative Group to Assist the Poor (CGAP), (a consortium dedicated to promoting microcredit) showed MFIs charge a median interest rate of 28 percent per year, and 5 percent of MFIs charge rates above 50 percent. Generously allowing 10 percent for cost of funds implies that more than half of MFIs charge interest rates that Yunus would consider too high.

High interest rates have made many MFIs very profitable. In the CGAP study, MFIs earned an average 2.1 percent return on assets annually, well above the 1.4 percent earned by banks in the same countries. In 2006 10 percent of MFIs earned a return on equity above 35 percent. These are high profits by any business criteria. Even the CGAP study concludes that MFI profits are high because "the microcredit market is still immature . . . and [has] little competition so far."

The industry responds that the high interest rates are due to high costs. But empirical analysis shows that costs (and prices) vary widely across MFIs in a country. Since this analysis holds the loan size and the environment constant, the cost differential is likely due to some MFIs having unreasonably high controllable costs. In a competitive industry, such wide differentials in costs would not persist, and firms with inefficient operations and high prices would be penalized.

Financial literacy is a major problem for microcredit clients, who are poor, ill-informed and often illiterate and innumerate. The volatile combination of profit-seeking companies, minimal competition and vulnerable borrowers has opened up a dangerous potential for exploiting the poor. MFIs have much market power and can earn monopoly rents. Expecting microcredit organizations to exercise self-restraint and self-regulation is naively optimistic. Regulating interest rates is the only feasible solution. This does not mean that all, or even most, MFIs abuse monopoly power; but enough of them do exploit the poor to warrant regulation.

NO
Alex Counts
President, Grameen Foundation

Written for *CQ Global Researcher*, April 2010

When we hear about poor microfinance clients paying interest rates well above the rates paid by businesses and middle-class consumers, in the same country, it is tempting to argue for government-imposed interest rate caps on microfinance institutions. But I am convinced it would be counterproductive in practice.

Caps might spur some needed innovation and cost-cutting in a few markets if the imposed rate was within striking distance of the rates currently being charged. But in most cases, it would drive microfinance lenders out of business and force their former clients to increase their dependence on moneylenders who can charge rates well above 100 percent annually (as we saw happen in India in 2006).

And the MFIs that survive would likely suspend outreach to the poorest and most isolated clients (where initial transaction costs are highest); cut back on social-empowerment services (mostly related to health and education) that often magnify the poverty-reduction impact of microfinance; and attempt to circumvent the interest rate caps by charging additional fees (effectively negating the cost savings to clients).

Rather than take this crude though possibly popular approach, a more subtle strategy would be preferable. First of all, let competition on a level playing field — rather than government mandates — drive reductions in pricing (as has occurred in Bangladesh and Bolivia, two mature and highly efficient markets where there have been no government-imposed rates). Second, have donors and others invest in industry-wide initiatives that could bring widespread efficiency gains, such as documenting and driving adoption of best practices in (a) low-cost capital mobilization (especially from deposits), (b) optimization of human resources and (c) cutting-edge technology applications.

Grameen Foundation has made significant commitments to all these areas. Governments can play a role by helping to ensure a level playing field by, among other actions, defining price transparency in a way that helps clients find the lowest cost for particular products and requiring microfinance providers to implement consumer protection measures.

Rather than impose interest rates set by bureaucrats and politicians, it would be safer and more in the interests of the poor for governments to work with microfinance stakeholders to accelerate a market-based process that has been under way for years — which is bringing down rates 2-3 percent on an annual basis thanks to competition, media scrutiny, efficiency-enhancing innovation and price transparency.

Women seeking loans in Sauir, Kenya, rest in the shade of an Albizia tree as they wait to speak with a representative from a microcredit lender.

on microlenders. And India has clamped down on what it considers exorbitant rates and abusive debt-collection policies by microlenders.[66]

Such "political interference" worries Latin American microfinance industry leaders, according to a recent survey, some of whom complain that interest rate caps in Colombia and Venezuela are stunting the growth of the market.[67]

In Nicaragua, the "No Pago" movement, supported by thousands of angry borrowers, scored a major victory last October when legislators recommended a bill capping interest rates at 12 percent and giving debtors up to five years to repay loans.[68] The movement in Nicaragua, first sparked by inflammatory remarks against microfinance lenders by President Daniel Ortega, has the industry worried about measures that populist governments might take.

Indeed, according to MFTransparency's Waterfield, fear of government caps is one reason why the industry "lied for three decades" about the interest rates they charge. "If the Ortegas of the world knew what we were really charging, they would freak out and put a limit on interest rates," he says.

India also has cracked down on microfinance organizations over exorbitant rates and abusive debt collection. In Andhra Pradesh more than 200 people committed suicide in 2006 allegedly because of intimidation by microfinance institutions. Government authorities closed down 50 branches of two major microlenders and charged them with extortionist interest rates and intimidating borrowers with strong-armed debt recovery.[69]

Last month, Bangladesh Finance Minister AMA Muhith charged that high interest rates and charges were forcing borrowers to sign up with several microlenders simultaneously to pay back their loans, placing them in a "debt trap." 70 Yunus called on the Bangladesh Microcredit Regulatory Authority to come up with standardized interest rates to establish transparency and remove suspicion among borrowers about interest rates. 71 The authority has announced that it plans to publish microlenders' interest rates regularly and to frame a policy to make rates more transparent. 72

Other than these scattered official efforts, Counts says, no big government backlash has occurred. "There are more threats than outright laws," he says.

Have the recent government actions been effective? "The problem is there's very little ability to enforce regulation in most of the countries in which microfinance operates," says Rhyne. "Most of the time you have a few scattered laws here and there and a very weak regulatory apparatus; it's not clear who is responsible for consumer protection in the financial industry."

OUTLOOK

Soaring Needs

To many in the banking world, microcredit offers enormous opportunity as 2010 marks the beginning of a demographic window in which the developing world's working-age population will surge to its highest point relative to the nonworking old and young. Millions of the "unbanked" will join the formal banking system, and "the need for microfinance will also soar," predicted HSBC Chairman Stephen Green. If all the working-age adults earning $2 a day or less are counted, some estimate the demand for microfinance is already 10 times the current supply.[73]

But many uncertainties hang in the balance, including worries about exploiting the poor to pay Western investors and questions about whether governments will clamp down on the industry.

Revealing microlenders' true interest rates is particularly important now that more profit-oriented investors are getting into the act. "We all agreed to lie [about interest rates] to help the poor, and now we've created the perfect environment for new people to come in and say, 'We can make a lot of money,' " Waterfield, of MFTransparency, says bluntly about his industry. "We're working to rapidly correct that before the damage gets out of control."

Meanwhile, the industry has "a long way to go" before attracting for-profit investors in a big way, according to Tryfan Evans, director of the Omidyar-Tufts Microfinance Fund. Illiterate borrowers placing their thumbprint on a hand-written receipt are a long way from providing Western-style credit ratings. The industry must become far more sophisticated to attract private investors on a large scale.

Despite all the excitement about high profits, average investor returns for microfinance banks overall fall well below the returns for either a commercial bank like Citibank or high-flying Compartamos, according to a recent study. Thus, for the immediate future, the industry probably will continue to depend on "social investors" — those willing to settle for a lower return in exchange for the knowledge they are helping the poor.[74]

And subsidies will continue to be important — perhaps even more so as microlenders struggle with the effects of the worldwide recession. About half of the foreign investment in microfinance in 2008 still came from donors and aid agencies, according to CGAP.[75]

The growing trend of MFIs providing savings accounts to the poor could address concerns that microloans are often used for emergency household needs, rather than entrepreneurial investment. Financial diaries reveal that those living on $2 a day are willing to pay neighbors to guard their savings for emergencies. Citing that finding, the Bill & Melinda Gates Foundation recently provided a $38 million grant to microcredit institutions in 12 countries to encourage them to offer savings accounts for the very poor.[76]

New technology — such as banking via cell phones, which is already widely used in Kenya and the Philippines — could help spread financial services to the poor, potentially offering more flexibility to borrowers than microcredit, with its group attendance requirements and lack of privacy.

Whatever the contributions and faults of the microcredit system, almost everyone agrees that the poor should have access to the same kinds of financial services — whether for credit or savings — that those in the West take for granted.

NOTES

1. See www.sksindia.com.

2. See "Microfinance at a Glance-2008," updated Dec. 31, 2009, Microfinance Information Exchange. www.themix.org/publications/microfinance=glance. The average loan balance per borrower reported by almost 1,400 microlenders is $1,588 — heavily influenced by higher average loans in Eastern Europe and Central Asia. Average loan balances reported by region were Africa: $626; East Asia and Pacific: $684; Eastern Europe and Central Asia: $4,008; Latin America: $1,341; Middle East and North Africa: $746; south Asia: $912.

3. This is the compound average annual growth rate according to "Microfinance at a Glance-2008," Updated Dec. 31, 2009. The $44 billion gross loan portfolio is based on reporting from 1,395 microfinance lenders to the Microfinance Information Exchange, *op. cit.*

4. Muhammad Yunus, "Poverty Is a Threat to Peace," Nobel Peace Prize lecture delivered Oslo, Norway, Dec. 10, 2006, http://nobelprize.org/nobel_prizes/peace/laureates/2006/yunus-lecture-en.html.

5. Malcolm Harper, "Some Final Thoughts," in Thomas Dichter and Malcolm Harper, eds., *What's Wrong with Microfinance?* (2008), p. 257.

6. Ketaki Gokhale, "As Microfinance Grows in India, So do its Rivals," *The Wall Street Journal*, Dec. 15, 2009, http://online.wsj.com/article/SB12605511 7322287513.html.

7. Ketaki Gokhale, "A Global Surge in Tiny Loans Spurs Credit Bubble in a Slum," *The Wall Street Journal*, Aug. 13, 2009, http://online.wsj.com/article/SB125012112518027581.html.

8. Kim Wilson, "The Moneylender's Dilemma," in Dichter and Harper, *op. cit.*, p. 97.

9. The World Bank counted 2.5 billion people living on less than $2 a day in 2005 — two fifths of the world population. See Daryl Collins, *et al.*, *Portfolios of the Poor* (2009), p. 1.

10. Muhammad Yunus, *Creating a World Without Poverty* (2007), p. 54.

11. *Ibid.*, p. 56.

12. *Ibid.*, p. 55.

13. *Ibid.*, pp. 52, 111.

14. For a summary of the studies, See Richard Rosenberg, "Does Microcredit Really Help the Poor?" Focus Note 59, Consultative Group to Assist the Poor, January 2010, www.cgap.org/p/site/c/template.rc/1.9.41443/.

15. Cited in Robert Cull, Asli Demirguc-Kunt and Jonathan Morduch, "Microfinance Meets the Market," *Journal of Economic Perspectives*, January 2009.

16. Gokhale, *op. cit.*, Dec. 15, 2009.

17. Rosenberg, *op. cit.*

18. *Ibid.*

19. Jonathan C. Lewis, "Microloan Sharks," *Stanford Social Innovation Review*, Summer 2008, pp. 55-59, www.mcenterprises.org/userimages/file/microloan_sharks_lewis_stanford_social_innovation_review_2008.pdf.

20. *Ibid.*, p. 56.

21. "Online Extra: Yunus Blasts Compartamos," *Business Week*, Dec. 13, 2007, www.businessweek.com/magazine/content/07_52/b4064045920958.htm.

22. Lewis, *op. cit.*, p. 59.

23. Alex Counts, "Reimagining Microfinance," *Stanford Social Innovation Review*, Summer 2008, pp. 46-53, p. 49, www.ssireview.org/site/printer/reimagining_microfinance/.

24. Similar estimates that worldwide demand for microfinance is about 10 times the current supply are cited in Stephen Green, "People Power," The World in 2010, *The Economist*, p. 142. See "Microfinance at a Glance-2008," *op. cit.*, for estimated loan portfolio of $44 billion worldwide.

25. Lewis, *op. cit.*

26. Email communication, March 16, 2010.

27. Christina Frank, "Stemming the Tide of Mission Drift: Microfinance Transformations and the Double Bottom Line," 2008, Women's World Banking, www.swwb.org/files/pubs/en/stemming_the_tide_of_mission_drift_microfinance_transformations_and_the_Double_Bottom_Line.pdf.

28. *Ibid.*, p. 16.

29. Connie Bruck, "A Reporter at Large: Millions for Millions," *The New Yorker*, Oct. 30, 2006, www.newyorker.com/archive/2006/10/30/061030fa_fact1.

30. Cull, *et al.*, *op. cit.*, abstract.

31. Elyssa Pachico, " 'No Pago' Confronts Microfinance in Nicaragua," Oct. 28, 2009, North American Congress on Latin America, https://nacla.org/node/6180.

32. Chuck Waterfield, "Explanation of Compartamos Interest Rates," May 19, 2008, www.microfin.com/aprcalculations.htm. This rate is the annual percentage rate (APR) — the standard used in the United States.

33. Even that 4 percent — a flat rate — is deceptive, Waterfield explains. If it were calculated on the declining balance, as American banks do, it would be twice as much. See www.mftransparency.org for explanation of the difference between flat and declining balance interest rates.

34. See "Slideshow" at www.mftransparency.org.

35. Aneel Karnani, "Regulate Microcredit to Protect Borrowers," Ross School of Business Working Paper No. 1113, September 2009, http://papers.ssrn.com/sol3/cf_dev/AbsByAuth.cfm?per_id=561150.

36. All interest rates in this paragraph are the annual percentage rate (APR) standard used in the United States.

37. Karnani, *op. cit.*

38. Wilson, *op. cit.*, p. 105.

39. Karnani, *op. cit.*, p. 6.

40. *Ibid.*, pp. 15-16.

41. See Center for Financial Inclusion at www.center forfinancialinclusion.org.

42. Counts, *op. cit.*, p. 48. For background, see Sarah Glazer, "Fair Trade Labeling," *CQ Researcher*, May 18, 2007, pp. 433-456.

43. Karnani, *op. cit*, p. 9.

44. Beatriz Armendáriz and Jonathan Morduch, *The Economics of Microfinance* (2007), pp. 68-69.

45. Yunus, *op. cit.*, pp. 45-47.

46. *Ibid.*, pp. 47-48.

47. Armendáriz and Morduch, *op. cit.*, p. 13. According to Grameen Foundation's Alex Counts, Grameen just barred delinquent borrowers from certain premium loans — not all loans.

48. *Ibid.*, p. 13.

49. Yunus, *op. cit.*, pp. 51, 57. For most recent repayment rate, see www.grameen-info.org.

50. Anton Simanowitz, "What's Behind the Numbers?" *Microfinance Insights*, January 2010. www.microfinance insights.com.

51. Kim Wilson, *op. cit.*

52. Yunus, *op. cit.*, pp. 62-63.

53. *Ibid.*, pp. 62-65.

54. See Collins, *et al.*, *op. cit.*, pp. 154-158, and Yunus, *op. cit*, pp. 63-66.

55. "Fiscal Year 2009 Annual Report," *Microfinance Exchange Inc.*, July 2008-June 2009, p. 10. www.the-mix.org/sites/default/files/Annual%20Report%20 2009_0.pdf. See also, "Fact Sheet," www.themix .org/publications/microfinance-glance.

56. Blaine Stephens "Operating Efficiency: Victim to the Crisis," *The Microbanking Bulletin*, December 2009, Micro Finance Information Exchange, Inc., p. 39, www.themix.org/microbanking-bulletin/ mbb-issue-no-19-december-2009.

57. *Ibid.*

58. "Microfinance Banana Skins 2009," June 2009, Centre for the Study of Financial Innovation, p. 6, www.cgap.org/gm/document-1.9.35203/Micro finance%20Banana%20Skins%202009.pdf.

58. *Ibid.*

59. *Ibid.*, p. 24.

60. *Ibid.*, p. 33.

61. See Simanowitz, *op. cit.*, and Xavier Reille, "The Perils of Uncontrolled Growth," Consultative Group to Assist the Poor, Jan. 11, 2010, http://micro finance.cgap.org/2010/01/11/the-perils-of-uncon trolled-growth/.

62. Daniel Rozas and Sanjay Sinha, "Avoiding a Microfinance Bubble in India: Is Self-Regulation the Answer?" Jan. 10, 2010, Microfinance Focus, www .microfinancefocus.com/news/2010/01/10/avoid ing-a-microfinance-bubble-in-india-is-self-regula tion-the-answer/.

63. Gokhale, *op. cit.*, Aug. 13, 2009.

64. Collins, *et al.*, *op. cit.*

65. See Reuters, "U.S. Credit Card Defaults Up, Signal Consumer Stress," Sept. 15, 2009, www.reuters .com/article/idUSTRE58E6LH20090915.

66. Eric Duflos, "Governments' Responses to the Global Crisis," Nov. 26, 2009, Consultative Group to Assist the Poor, www.cgap.org. See "Governments' role in times of crisis: toward a new paradigm?" http:// microfinance.cgap.org/2009/12/10/governments'- role-in-times-of-crisis-toward-a-new-paradigm/.

67. "Microfinance Banana Skins 2009," *op. cit.*, p. 26.

68. Pachico, *op. cit.* The bill had not been passed at press time.

69. Karnani, *op. cit.*, p. 3.

70. "Strategy of Microcredit Institutions Must be Reviewed: Muhith," *The Daily Star*, March 16, 2010, www.thedailystar.net.

71. "Yunus Calls for Standardised Interest Rate," *The Daily Star*, March 18, 2010, www.thedailystar.net.

72. "Policy on Cards for Microcredit Interest," *The Daily Star*, March 15, 2010, www.thedailystar.net.

73. Green, *op. cit.*, p. 142.

74. Cull, *et al.*, *op. cit.*

75. "Microfinance Funding Continued to Grow in 2008," *op. cit.* The 2008 figures are the most recent available.

76. Bill & Melinda Gates Foundation, "Grant Signals New Movement Towards Savings Accounts for the Poor," Jan. 12, 2010, www.gatesfoundation.org/press-releases/Pages/microfinancing-institutions-helping-poor-save-money-100113.aspx. The foundation cites the financial diaries described in Daryl Collins, *et al.*

BIBLIOGRAPHY

Books

Collins, Daryl, *et al.*, *Portfolios of the Poor: How the World's Poor Live on $2 a Day*, Princeton University Press, 2009.
In this influential study of the poor in Bangladesh, India and South Africa, economists suggest that savings and loans to help the poor survive through a month of uneven earnings may be just as important as the widely heralded microloans for business.

Dichter, Thomas, and Malcolm Harper, eds., *What's Wrong with Microfinance? Practical Action Publishing, Warwickshire England*, 2008.
In this collection of essays, experts discuss problems with microfinance, including abusive behavior toward debtors who can't pay, and Tufts University lecturer Kim Wilson explains why Catholic Relief Services stopped its microcredit program in 2005.

Yunus, Muhammad, *Creating a World Without Poverty*, Public Affairs, 2007.
The Nobel Peace-prize-winning pioneer in modern microfinance describes why he started making loans to the poor and why he sees a future for businesses that care about social benefits, not just profit.

Articles

Bruck, Connie, "A Reporter at Large: Millions for Millions," *The New Yorker*, Oct. 30, 2006.
Bruck describes the debate between free-market entrepreneurs like eBay founder Pierre Omidyar and philanthropic groups over whether microfinance can be a fully commercial profit-making industry.

Harford, Tim, "The Undercover Economist: Perhaps Microfinance isn't Such a Big Deal After All," *Financial Times Weekend Magazine*, Dec. 5/6, 2009.
Pointing to recent studies, Harford writes that the claims that a financial product like microcredit would create millions of entrepreneurs and emancipate women "were always going to be difficult to justify — even if donors tend to lap them up in the search for the next development panacea."

Gokhale, Ketaki, "As Microfinance Grows in India, So Do Its Rivals," *The Wall Street Journal*, Dec. 16, 2009, http://online.wsj.com/article/SB126055117322287513.html.
Moneylenders charging high-interest have multiplied as microfinance has grown, perhaps because the poor use them to pay off their microcredit loans, this article suggests.

Karnani, Aneel, "Regulate Microcredit to Protect Borrowers," Sept 2009, *Ross School of Business Working Paper No. 1133*, http://ssrn.com/abstract=1476957.
An associate professor at the University of Michigan's Ross School of Business argues for government mandates to protect poor borrowers: placing interest rate ceilings on microfinance loans, outlawing abusive debt collection and requiring lenders to disclose annual interest rates to borrowers in a standardized fashion.

Kristof, Nicholas, "The Role of Microfinance," Kristof's *New York Times Blog*, Dec. 28, 2009, http://kristof.blogs.nytime.com/2009/12/29/the-role-of-microfinance.
In a guest piece posted on Kristof's blog, authors of recent MIT and Yale studies say that though they found no impact for microloans on poverty, the borrowers were able to pay for things they previously couldn't afford — like a home TV or a cart for their business.

Reports and Blogs

"Microfinance Banana Skins 2009," *Centre for the Study of Financial Innovation*, 2009, www.csfi.org.uk.
A survey 430 microlenders, investors and experts finds that fear borrowers won't be able to repay their loans tops their list of worries in the wake of the financial crisis.

"Stemming the Tide of Mission Drift: Microfinance Transformations and the Double Bottom Line," *Women's World Banking,* **2008, www.swwb.org/stemming-the-tide-of-mission-drift.**

When nonprofit microfinance groups convert to profit-making banks, the percentage of women borrowers drops, but the total numbers go up as the bank expands its lending.

Karlan, Dean, and Jonathan Zinman, "Expanding Micro-enterprise Credit Access: Using Randomized Supply Decisions to Estimate the Impacts in Manila," July 2009, www.financialaccess.org.

The first research to compare groups randomly to receive microfinance loans — or not — found little effect on poverty among borrowers in the Philippines.

Roodman, David, "David Roodman's Microfinance Open Book Blog," http://blogs.cgdev.org/open_book/.

A research fellow at the Center for Global Development, a think tank in Washington, posts on his blog a critical book he is writing on microfinance, along with reactions. Roodman's blog is one of the best places to follow the microfinance debate.

Rosenberg, Richard, "Does Microcredit Really Help Poor People?" Focus Note No. 59, January 2010, *Consultative Group to Assist the Poor,* **www.cgap.org.**

An adviser to a group of international agencies housed at the World Bank offers a balanced summary of recent research.

For More Information

Center for Financial Inclusion, 1401 New York Ave., N.W., Suite 500, Washington, DC 20005; (202) 393-5113; www.centerforfinancialinclusion.org. An initiative launched by microfinance lender Accion International that has initiated a consumer protection pledge for the industry known as the Smart Campaign.

Consultative Group to Assist the Poor (CGAP), 900 19th St., N.W., Suite 300, Washington, DC 20006; (202) 473-9594; www.cgap.org. A coalition of development agencies and private foundations promoting microfinance, housed at the World Bank.

David Roodman's Microfinance Open Book blog, http://blogs.cgdev.org/open_book/2010. One of the best sources of information about ongoing debates in microfinance, written by a fellow at the Center for Global Development, a Washington think tank, who posts chapters of a book he is writing on microfinance and seeks comments.

Grameen Foundation, 50 F St., N.W., 8th Floor, Washington, DC 20001; (202) 628-3560; www.grameenfoundation.org. Supports microlenders worldwide and promotes the philosophy of the first microfinance bank, Grameen

Bank, founded by economist Muhammad Yunus in Bangladesh.

MFTransparency, 325 N. West End Ave., Lancaster, PA 17603; (717) 475-6733; www.mftransparency.org. A new industry-led effort to disclose the true cost of loans by posting interest rates, country by country.

Microcredit Summit Campaign, Results Educational Fund, 750 First St., N.E., Suite 1040, Washington, DC 20002; (202) 637-9600; www.microcreditsummit.org. A coalition of microfinance practitioners, donors and advocates seeking to provide microcredit to 175 million of the world's poorest families.

Microfinance Information Exchange (MIX), 1901 Pennsylvania Ave., N.W., #307, Washington, DC 20006; (202) 659-9094; www.themix.org. A nonprofit founded by CGAP that receives data from over 1,400 microfinance lenders.

Microfinance Insights, 512, Palm Spring, Link Road, Malad West, Mumbai 400064, India; +91-22-4035 9222; www.microfinanceinsights.com. A widely read trade publication that focuses on the latest trends in microfinance and offers expert opinions and global viewpoints.

Voices From Abroad:

GODWIN EHIGIAMUSOE

Executive Director, Lift Above Poverty, Nigeria

Empowering women and the poor
"Conscious of this reality [that poverty has many root causes], the organisation has over the years evolved into a group of system[s] of robust and viable institutions well-equipped with systems and structures that can effectively deliver sound economic, social and health services for fighting poverty and empowering the poor, especially women, in the society."

Daily Champion (Nigeria) March 2010

Cagle Cartoons/Rainer Hachfeld

VIKRAM AKULA

Founder and Chairman, SKS Microfinance, India

Absolute profitability
"Do we believe that microfinance can be profitable? Absolutely. Do we believe profits have to come at the expense of clients? Absolutely not."

The Times (England) October 2009

DEAN KARLAN

Professor of Economics, Yale University

In reality, microfinance's effect is weak
"Microcredit is not a transformational panacea that is going to lift people out of poverty. There might be little pockets of people who are made better off, but the average effect is weak, if not nonexistent."

The Australian, October 2009

MONIQUE NSANZABAGANWA

Minister of Trade and Commerce, Rwanda

Lenders lack necessary information
"The fact that there are high non-performing loans in the banking and microfinance institutions is proof that

lenders lack credible, comprehensive, easy to obtain and inexpensive credit information."

The New Times (Rwanda) March 2010

XAVIER REILLE

Lead Microfinance Specialist, Consultative Group to Assist the Poor The World Bank

Focus should be on sustainable growth
"Experience shows that microfinance can maintain asset quality, and pay impressive returns, both in terms of profits to investors and as well as improvements in people's lives. Nevertheless, a few countries do show signs of stress and remind us of the need for a much stronger focus on sustainable growth and re-commitment to asset quality."

TechWeb (United States) February 2010

MALACHI KONGUDE

Chief Executive Officer, Tangale Microfinance Nigeria Limited, Nigeria

Microfinance is a path to business and education
"We have been able to disburse loans to farmers to boost their farming business; we give loans to parents to cater for their wards in schools at all levels. . . . Some

parents who cannot afford money to send their wards to school at the beginning of the term/semesters have come to us to get loans, and we are always at their beck and call."

Daily Independent (Nigeria) February 2010

PRASHANT THAKKER

Global Head of Micro-finance, Standard Chartered Bank, England

Microfinance's many benefits

"Asia is the birthplace of microfinance and the largest market for microfinance, whether in terms of potential clients, the number of people near the poverty line or asset size. . . . [Microfinance] offers attractive returns and a reasonable risk, and I'm not even talking about quantifying the social impact of those investments."

The Business Times (Singapore) February 2010

MUHAMMAD YUNUS

Founder, Grameen Bank, Bangladesh

A different kind of bank

"In a traditional bank, the richer you are, the more important you are. With Grameen Bank, the poorer you are, the more important you are. In fact, if you have absolutely nothing — well, you're our best customer! . . . Banks spend a lot of time looking at people's credit history. Our bank is more interested in your future."

Hobart Mercury (Australia) March 2010

12

Religious Fundamentalism

Brian Beary

Burqas enshroud women in Kabul, Afghanistan's capital, reflecting life under strict Islamic regimes like the Taliban. Overthrown in 2001, the radically fundamentalist Taliban has regained control in some parts of the country. In addition to requiring the burqa, it restricts women's movements, prevents men from shaving or girls from being educated and prohibits singing and dancing.

From *CQ Researcher*, February 2009.

Life is far from idyllic in Swat, a lush valley once known as "the Switzerland of Pakistan." Far from Islamabad, the capital, a local leader of the Taliban — the extremist Islamic group that controls parts of the country — uses radio broadcasts to coerce residents into adhering to the Taliban's strict edicts.

"Un-Islamic" activities that are now forbidden — on pain of a lashing or public execution — range from singing and dancing to watching television or sending girls to school. "They control everything through the radio," said one frightened Swat resident who would not give his name. "Everyone waits for the broadcast." And in case any listeners in the once-secular region are considering ignoring Shah Duran's harsh dictates, periodic public assassinations — 70 police officers beheaded in 2008 alone — provide a bone-chilling deterrent.[1]

While the vast majority of the world's religious fundamentalists do not espouse violence as a means of imposing their beliefs, religious fundamentalism — in both its benign and more violent forms — is growing throughout much of the world. Scholars attribute the rise to various factors, including a backlash against perceived Western consumerism and permissiveness. And fundamentalism — the belief in a literal interpretation of holy texts and the rejection of modernism — is rising not only in Muslim societies but also among Christians, Hindus and Jews in certain countries.

Islamic fundamentalism is on the rise in Pakistan, Afghanistan, the Palestinian territories and European nations with large, often discontented Muslim immigrant populations — notably the

Religious Fundamentalism Spans the Globe

Fundamentalists from a variety of world religions are playing an increasingly important role in political and social life in countries on nearly every continent. Generally defined as the belief in a literal interpretation of holy texts and a rejection of modernism, fundamentalism is strongest in the Middle East and in the overwhelmingly Christian United States.

Where Fundamentalism Influences Social and Political Life

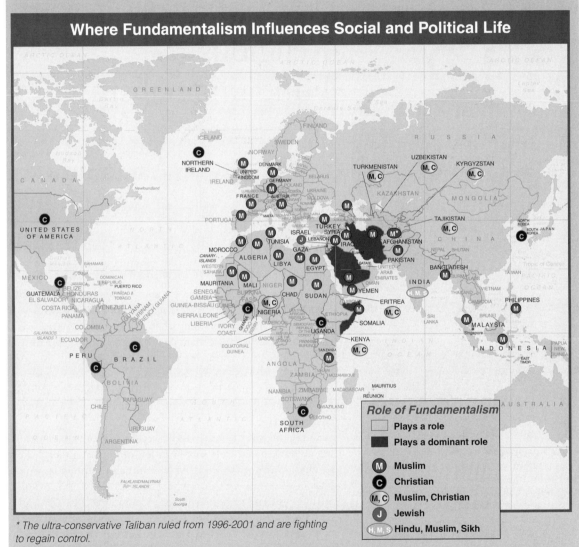

Role of Fundamentalism

- Plays a role
- Plays a dominant role

- **M** Muslim
- **C** Christian
- **M, C** Muslim, Christian
- **J** Jewish
- **H, M, S** Hindu, Muslim, Sikh

* The ultra-conservative Taliban ruled from 1996-2001 and are fighting to regain control.

Sources: U.S. National Counter Terrorism Center, Worldwide Incidents Tracking System, http://wits.nctc.gov; David Cingranelli and David Richards, Cingranelli-Richards (CIRI) Human Rights Dataset, CIRI Human Rights Project, 2007, www.humanrightsdata.org; The Association of Religious Data Archives at Pennsylvania State University, www.thearda.com; Office of the Coordinator for Counterterrorism, Country Reports on Terrorism, United States Department of State, April 2008, www.state.gov/documents/organization/105904.pdf; Peter Katel, "Global Jihad," CQ Researcher, Oct. 14, 2005

United Kingdom, Germany, Denmark, Spain and France, according to Maajid Nawaz, director of the London-based Quilliam Foundation think tank.

In the United States — the birthplace of Christian fundamentalism and the world's most populous predominantly Christian nation — 90 percent of Americans say they believe in God, and a third believe in a literal interpretation of the Bible.[2] Perhaps the most extreme wing of U.S. Christian fundamentalism are the Christian nationalists, who believe the scriptures "must govern every aspect of public and private life," including government, science, history, culture and relationships, according to author Michelle Goldberg, who has studied the splinter group.[3] She says Christian nationalists are "a significant and highly mobilized minority" of U.S. evangelicals that is gaining influence.[4] TV evangelist Pat Robertson is a leading Christian nationalist and "helped put dominionism — the idea that Christians have a God-given right to rule — at the center of the movement to bring evangelicals into politics," she says.[5]

Although the number of the world's Christians who are fundamentalists is not known, about 20 percent of the 2 billion Christians are conservative evangelicals, according to the World Evangelical Alliance (WEA).[6] Evangelicals reject the "fundamentalist" label, and most do not advocate creating a Christian theocracy, but they are the socially conservative wing of the Christian community, championing "family values" and opposing abortion and gay marriage. In recent decades they have exercised considerable political power on social issues in the United States.

Many Religions Have Fundamentalist Groups

Religious fundamentalism comes in many forms around the globe, and many different groups have emerged to push their own type of fundamentalism — a handful through violence. The term "Islamist" is often used to describe fundamentalist Muslims who believe in a literal interpretation of the Koran and want to implement a strict form of Islam in all aspects of life. Some also want to have Islamic law, or sharia, imposed on their societies.

Christian Fundamentalists

- Lord's Resistance Army (LRA), a rebel group in Uganda that wants to establish a Christian nation — **violent**
- Various strands within the evangelical movement worldwide, including the U.S.-based Christian nationalists, who insist the United States was founded as a Christian nation and believe that all aspects of life (including family, religion, education, government, media, entertainment and business) should be taken over by fundamentalist Christians — **rarely violent**
- Society of St. Pius X, followers of Catholic Archbishop Marcel Lefebvre, who reject the Vatican II modernizing reforms — **nonviolent**

Islamic Fundamentalists

- Jihadists, like al Qaeda and its allies across the Muslim world — **violent***
- Locally focused Islamist groups Hezbollah (Lebanon) and Hamas (Gaza) — **violent**
- Revolutionary Islamists, like Hizb-ut-Tahrir (HT), a pan-Islamic Sunni political movement that wants all Muslim countries combined into a unitary Islamic state or caliphate, ruled by Islamic law; has been involved in some coup attempts in Muslim countries and is banned in some states — **sometimes violent**
- Political Islamists, dedicated to the "social and political revivification of Islam" through nonviolent, democratic means. Some factions of the Muslim Brotherhood — the world's largest and oldest international Islamist movement — espouse using peaceful political and educational means to convert Muslim countries into sharia-ruled states, re-establishing the Muslim caliphate. Other factions of the group have endorsed violence from time to time.
- Post-Islamists, such as the AKP, the ruling party in Turkey, which has Islamist roots but has moderated its fundamentalist impulses — **nonviolent**

Judaism

- Haredi, ultra-orthodox Jews — **mostly nonviolent**
- Gush Emunim, aim to reoccupy the biblical Jewish land including Palestinian territories — **sometimes violent**
- Chabad missionaries, who support Jewish communities across the globe — **nonviolent**

Indian subcontinent

- Sikh separatists — **sometimes violent**
- Hindu extremists, anti-Christian/Muslim — **sometimes violent**

For an extensive list of global jihadist groups, see "Inside the Global Jihadist Network," pp. 860-861, in Peter Katel, "Global Jihad," CQ Researcher, Oct. 14, 2005, pp. 857-880.

Sources: Encyclopedia of Fundamentalism; "Foreign Terrorist Organizations," U.S. Department of State

Christians Are a Third of the World's Population

About 20 percent of the world's 2 billion Christians are evangelicals or Pentecostals — many of whom are fundamentalists. But statistics on the number of other fundamentalists are not available. Christians and Muslims together make up more than half the world's population.

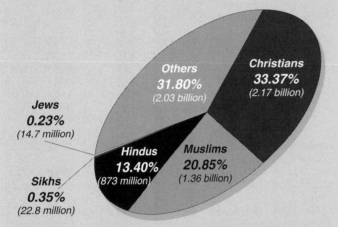

World Population by Religious Affiliation

Christians **33.37%** (2.17 billion)

Others **31.80%** (2.03 billion)

Jews **0.23%** (14.7 million)

Hindus **13.40%** (873 million)

Muslims **20.85%** (1.36 billion)

Sikhs **0.35%** (22.8 million)

Major Concentrations of Religious Denominations
(in millions)

Christians		Hindus		Jews	
United States	247	India	817	United States	5.3
Brazil	170	Nepal	19	Israel/Palestine	5.3
Russia	115	Bangladesh	15	France	0.6
China	101	Indonesia	7	Argentina	0.5
Mexico	100	Sri Lanka	2.5	Canada	0.4
Muslims		**Sikhs**			
Indonesia	178	India	21		
India	155	United Kingdom	0.4		
Pakistan	152	Canada	0.3		
Bangladesh	136	United States	0.3		
Turkey	71	Thailand	0.05		

Sources: World Christian Database, Center for the Study of Global Christianity, Gordon-Conwell Theological Seminary, www.worldchristiandatabase.org/wcd/home.asp; John L. Allen Jr., "McCain's choice a nod not only to women, but post-denominationalists," National Catholic Reporter, Aug. 30, 2008, http://ncrcafe.org/node/2073

— Pentecostals, Anglicans and Baptists — very active in evangelizing," says James Nkansah, a Ghanaian-born Baptist minister who teaches at the Nairobi Evangelical Graduate School of Theology in Kenya. "Even the Catholics are doing it, although they do not call themselves evangelists." A similar trend is occurring in Latin America, especially in Brazil, Guatemala and Peru among the Pentecostals, who stress the importance of the Holy Spirit, faith healing and "speak in tongues" during services.

Both evangelicals and Catholics in Latin America have adopted the basic tenets of U.S.-style evangelicalism, according to Valdir Steuernagel, a Brazilian evangelical Lutheran pastor who is vice president at World Vision International, a Christian humanitarian agency. Like U.S. evangelicals, South American evangelicals passionately oppose gay marriage and abortion, but they do not use the term "fundamentalist," says Steuernagel, because the word "does not help us to reach out to the grassroots."

South Korea also has a thriving evangelical community. A visiting U.S. journalist describes a recent service for about 1,000 people at a popular Korean evangelical church: "It was part rock concert and part revival meeting," with the lead guitarist, "sometimes jumping up and down on the altar platform" like Mick Jagger, recalls Michael Mosettig. [8] Elsewhere in Asia — the world's most religiously diverse continent — Christian missionaries in China have grown their flocks from fewer than 2 million Christians in 1979 to more than 16 million Protestants alone in 2008. [9] It is unknown how many of those are fundamentalists.

Christian evangelicalism is booming in Africa — especially in Anglophone countries like Kenya, Uganda, Nigeria, Ghana and South Africa. [7] "We are all

Among the world's 15 million Jews, about 750,000 are ultra-Orthodox "Haredi" Jews who live in strict accordance with Jewish law. Half of them live in Israel, most of the rest in the United States, while there are small pockets in France, Belgium, the United Kingdom, Canada and Australia. About 80,000 live in the Palestinian territories on Israel's West Bank because they believe it is God's will. [10] The flourishing fundamentalist Chabad movement — whose adherents would prefer to live in a Jewish theocracy governed by religious laws — sends missionaries to support isolated Jewish communities in 80 countries.

"We accept the Israeli state, but we would have liked the Torah to be its constitution," says Belgian-based Rabbi Avi Tawil, an Argentine Chabad missionary. "But we are not Zionists, because we do not encourage every Jew to go to Israel. Our philosophy is, 'Don't run away from your own place — make it better.' "

In India, Hindu fundamentalists insist their vast country should be for Hindus only. In late 2008, a sudden upsurge in fundamentalist Hindu attacks against Christian minorities in the state of Orissa in eastern India ended with 60 Christians killed and 50,000 driven from their homes. [11]

Besides their rejection of Western culture, the faithful embrace fundamentalism out of fear of globalization and consumerism and anger about U.S. action — or inaction — in the Middle East, experts say. Some also believe a strict, religiously oriented government will provide better services than the corrupt, unstable, secular regimes governing their countries. Religious fundamentalism also thrives in societies formerly run by repressive governments. Both Christian and Muslim fundamentalism are spreading in Central Asian republics — particularly Uzbekistan, Kyrgyzstan and Tajikistan — that were once part of the repressive, anti-religious Soviet Union.

Many fundamentalists — such as the Quakers, Amish and Jehovah's Witnesses — oppose violence for any reason. And fundamentalists who call themselves "political Islamists" pursue their goal of the "social and political revivification of Islam" through nonviolent, democratic means, according to Loren Lybarger, an assistant professor of classics and world religions at Ohio University and author of a recent book on Islamism in the Palestinian territories. [12]

In recent years radical Islamic extremists have perpetrated most violence committed by fundamentalists.

From January 2004 to July 2008, for instance, Muslim militants killed 20,182 people, while Christian, Jewish and Hindu extremists together killed only 925, according to a U.S. government database. [13] Most of the Muslim attacks were between Sunni and Shia Muslims fighting for political control of Iraq. [14]

Asmaa Abdol-Hamiz, a Muslim Danish politician and social worker, questions the State Department's statistics. "When Muslims are violent, you always see them identified as Muslims," she points out. "When Christians are violent, you look at the social and psychological reasons."

In addition, according to Radwan Masmoudi, president of the Center for the study of Islam and Democracy, such statistics do not address the "more than one million innocent people" killed in the U.S.-led wars in Iraq and Afghanistan, which, in his view, were instigated due to pressure from Christian fundamentalists in the United States.

Nevertheless, some radical Islamists see violence as the only way to replace secular governments with theocracies. The world's only Muslim theocracy is in Iran. While conservative Shia clerics exert ultimate control, Iranians do have some political voice, electing a parliament and president. In neighboring Saudi Arabia, the ruling royal family is not clerical but supports the ultra-conservative Sunni Wahhabi sect as the state-sponsored religion. Meanwhile, in the Palestinian territories, "there has been a striking migration from more nationalist groups to more self-consciously religious-nationalist groups," wrote Lybarger. [15]

Experts say Muslim militants recently have set their sights on troubled countries like Somalia and nuclear-armed Pakistan as fertile ground for establishing other Islamic states. Some extremist groups, such as Hizb-ut-Tahrir, want to establish a single Islamic theocracy — or caliphate — across the Muslim world, stretching from Indonesia to Morocco.

Still other Muslim fundamentalists living in secular countries such as Britain want their governments to allow Muslims to settle legal disputes in Islamic courts. Islamic law, called sharia, already has been introduced in some areas in Africa, such as northern Nigeria's predominantly Muslim Kano region. [16]

Muslim extremists are not the only fundamentalists wanting to establish theocracies in their countries. The

Jewish Israeli group Kach, for instance, seeks to restore the biblical state of Israel, according to the U.S. State Department's list of foreign terrorist organizations. Hindu fundamentalists want to make India — a secular country with a majority Hindu population that also has many Muslims and Christians — more "Hindu" by promoting traditional Hindu beliefs and customs.

While militant Christian fundamentalist groups are relatively rare, the Lord's Resistance Army (LRA) has led a 20-year campaign to establish a theocracy based on the Ten Commandments in Uganda. The group has abducted hundreds of children and forced them to commit atrocities as soldiers. The group has been blamed for killing hundreds of Ugandans and displacing 2 million people.[17]

In the United States, most Christian fundamentalists are nonviolent, although some have been responsible for sporadic incidents, primarily bombings of abortion clinics. "The irony," says John Green, a senior fellow at the Washington-based Pew Forum on Religion and Public Policy, "is that America is a very violent country where the 'regular' crime rates are actually higher than they are in countries where global jihad is being waged."

Support for violence by Islamic extremists has been declining in the Muslim world in the wake of al Qaeda's bloody anti-Western campaigns, which have killed more Muslims than non-Muslims. U.S. intelligence agencies concluded in November 2008 that al Qaeda "may decay sooner" than previously assumed because of "undeliverable strategic objectives, inability to attract broad-based support and self-destructive actions."[18]

But fundamentalist violence, especially Islamist-inspired, remains a serious threat to world peace. In Iraq, fighting between Sunni and Shia Muslims has killed tens of thousands since 2003 and forced more than 4 million Iraqis to flee their homes. And 20 of the 42 groups on the State Department's list of terrorist organizations are Islamic fundamentalist groups.[19] No Christian or Hindu fundamentalists are included on the terrorist list.

However, Somali-born writer Ayaan Hirsi Ali — herself a target of threats from Islamic fundamentalists — says that while "Christian and Jewish fundamentalists are just as crazy as the Islamists . . . the Islamists are more violent because 99 percent of Muslims think Mohammad is perfect. Christians do not see Jesus in as absolute a way."

As religious fundamentalism continues to thrive around the world, here are some of the key questions experts are grappling with:

Is religious fundamentalism on the rise?

Religious fundamentalism has been on the rise worldwide for 30 years and "remains strong," says Pew's Green.

Fundamentalism is growing throughout the Muslim and Hindu worlds but not in the United States, where its growth has slowed down in recent years, says Martin Marty, a religious history professor at the University of Chicago, who authored a multivolume series on fundamentalism.[20] Christian fundamentalism is strong in Africa and Latin America and is even being exported to industrialized countries. Brazilian Pastor Steuernagel says "evangelical missionaries are going from Brazil, Colombia and Argentina to Northern Hemisphere countries like Spain, Portugal and the United Kingdom. They are going to Asia and Africa too, but there they must combine their missionary activities with aid work."

Islamic fundamentalism, meanwhile, has been growing for decades in the Middle East and Africa. For example, in Egypt the Muslim Brotherhood — which seeks to make all aspects of life in Muslim countries more Islamic, such as by applying sharia law — won 20 percent of the seats in 2005 parliamentary elections — 10 times more than it got in the early 1980s.[21] In Somalia, the Islamist al-Shabaab militia threatens the fragile government.

More moderate Muslims who want to "reform" Islam into a more tolerant, modern religion face an uphill battle, says Iranian-born Shireen Hunter, author of a recent book on reformist voices within Islam. Reformers' Achilles' heel is the fact that "they are often secular and do not understand the Islamic texts as well as the fundamentalists so they cannot compete on the same level," she says.

In Europe, secularism is growing in countries like France and the Netherlands as Christian worship rates plummet, but Turkey has been ruled since 2002 by the Justice and Development Party, which is rooted in political Islam. Though it has vowed to uphold the country's secular constitution, critics say the party harbors a secret fundamentalist agenda, citing as evidence the government's recent relaxation of restrictions on women wearing headscarves at universities.[22]

In Israel, the ultra-Orthodox Jewish population is growing thanks to an extremely high birthrate. Haredi Jews average 7.6 children per woman compared to an average Israeli woman's 2.5 children.[23] And ultra-Orthodox political parties have gained 15 seats in the 120-member Knesset (parliament) since the 1980s, when they had only five.[24] Secularists in the United States saw Christian fundamentalists grow increasingly powerful during the presidency of George W. Bush (2001-2009). Government policies limited access to birth control and abortions, and conservative religious elements in the military began to engage in coercive proselytizing. "From about 2005, I noticed a lot of religious activity: Bible study weeks, a multitude of religious services linked to public holidays that I felt were excessive," says U.S. Army Reserve intelligence officer Laure Williams. In February 2008, she recalls, she was sent by her superiors to a religious conference called "Strong Bonds," where fundamentalist books advocating sexual abstinence, including one called *Thrill of the Chaste*, were distributed. Williams complained to her superiors but did not get a satisfactory response, she says.

In the battle for believers among Christian denominations, "Conservative evangelicals are doing better than denominations like Methodists and Lutherans, whose liberal ideology is poisonous and causing them to implode," says Tennessee-based Southern Baptist preacher Richard Land. "When you make the Ten Commandments the 'Ten Suggestions,' you've got a problem."

However, the tide may be turning, at least in some quarters, in part because the next generation appears to be less religious than its elders. Some see the November 2008 election of President Barack Obama — who got a lot of his support from young voters in states with large evangelical populations where the leaders had endorsed Obama's opponent — as evidence that the reign of the Christian right is over in the United States.

"The sun may be setting on the political influence of fundamentalist churches," wrote *Salon.com* journalist Mike Madden.[25] In fact, the fastest-growing demographic group in the United States is those who claim no religious affiliation; they make up 16 percent of Americans today, compared to 8 percent in the 1980s.[26]

In the Wake of Fundamentalist Violence

Two days of fighting between Christians and fundamentalist Muslims in December destroyed numerous buildings in Jos, Nigeria, (top) and killed more than 300 people. In India's Orissa state, a Christian woman (bottom) searches through the remains of her house, destroyed during attacks by fundamentalist Hindus last October. Sixty Christians were killed and 50,000 driven from their homes.

And in Iran, while the Islamic theocracy is still in charge, "the younger generation is far less religious than the older," says Ahmad Dallal, a professor of Arab and Islamic studies at Georgetown University in Washington, D.C.

Moreover, support for fundamentalist violence — specifically by al Qaeda's global terrorist network — has been declining since 2004.[27] For example, 40 percent of

Radical Muslims Caused Most Terror Attacks

More than 6,000 religiously motivated terrorist attacks in recent years were perpetrated by radical Muslims — far more than any other group. The attacks by Christians were mostly carried out by the Lord's Resistance Army (LRA) in Uganda.

Religious Attacks, Jan. 1, 2004-June 30, 2008

	Killed	Injured	Incidents
Christian	917	371	101
Muslim*	20,182	43,852	6,180
Jewish	5	28	5
Hindu**	3	7	6
Total	**21,107**	**44,258**	**6,292**

* More than 90 percent of the reported attacks on civilians by Sunni and Shia terrorists were by Sunnis. Does not include the Muslim attacks in Mumbai, India, in December 2008, allegedly carried out by Muslim extremists from Pakistan.

** Uncounted are the Hindu extremist attacks on Christian minorities in late 2008 in India, which left more than 60 Christians dead.

Note: Perpetrators do not always claim responsibility, so attributing blame is sometimes impossible. Also, it is often unclear whether the attackers' motivation is purely political or is, in part, the result of criminality.

Sources: National Counter Terrorism Center's Worldwide Incidents Tracking System, http://wits.nctc.gov; Human Security Research Center, School for International Studies, Simon Fraser University, Vancouver, www.hsrgroup.org.

Pakistanis supported suicide bombings in 2004 compared to 5 percent in 2007.[28] Nigeria is an exception: 58 percent of Nigerians in 2007 said they still had confidence in al Qaeda leader Osama bin Laden, who ordered the Sept. 11, 2001, terrorist attacks on the United States. Notably, al Qaeda has not carried out any terrorist attacks in Nigeria. Support for al Qaeda has plummeted in virtually all countries affected by its attacks.[29]

And while the Muslim terrorist group Jemaah Islamiyah remains active in Indonesia — the world's most populous Muslim-majority country — claims of rampant fundamentalism there are overstated, according to a report by the Australian Strategic Policy Institute. The study found that 85 percent of Indonesians oppose the idea of their country becoming an Islamic republic.[30]

Although there has been a "conspicuous cultural flowering of Islam in Indonesia," the report continued, other religions are booming, too. In September 2008, for example, authorities overrode Muslim objections and approved an application for a Christian megachurch that seats more than 4,500 people.[31]

Is religious fundamentalism a reaction to Western permissiveness?

Religious experts disagree about what attracts people to religious fundamentalism, but many say it is a response to rapid modernization and the spread of Western multiculturalism and permissiveness.

"Fundamentalism is a modern reaction against modernity," says Jerusalem-based journalist Gershom Gorenberg. "They react against the idea that the truth is not certain. It's like a new bottle of wine with a label saying 'ancient bottle of wine.'"

Peter Berger, director of the Institute on Culture, Religion and World Affairs at Boston University, says fundamentalism is "an attempt to restore the taken-for-grantedness that has been lost as a result of modernization. We are constantly surrounded by people with other views, other norms, other lifestyles. . . . Some people live with this quite well, but others find it oppressive, and they want to be liberated from the liberation."[32]

Sayyid Qutb, founder of Egypt's Muslim Brotherhood, was repulsed by the sexual permissiveness and consumerism he found in the United States during a visit in 1948.[33] He railed against "this behavior, like animals, which you call 'Free mixing of the sexes'; at this vulgarity which you call 'emancipation of women'; at these unfair and cumbersome laws of marriage and divorce, which are contrary to the demands of practical life. . . . These were the realities of Western life which we encountered."[34]

A similar sentiment was felt by Mujahida, a Palestinian Islamic jihadist who told author Lybarger she worried that her people were losing their soul after the 1993 peace agreement with Israel. "There were bars, nightclubs, loud restaurants serving alcohol, satellite TV beaming American sitcoms, steamy Latin American soap operas [and] casinos in Jericho" to generate tax and employment.[35]

And opposition to abortion and gay rights remain the primary rallying call for U.S. evangelicals. In fact, the late American fundamentalist Baptist preacher Jerry Falwell blamed the 9/11 Islamic terrorist attacks in the United States on pagans, abortionists, feminists and homosexuals who promote an "alternative lifestyle" and want to "secularize America."[36]

In her account of the rise of Christian nationalism, journalist Goldberg said the things Islamic fundamentalists hate most about the West — "its sexual openness, its art, the possibilities for escaping the bonds of family and religion, for inventing one's own life — are what Christian nationalists hate as well."[37]

Pew's Green agrees fundamentalists are irritated by permissive Western culture. "There has always been sin in the world," he says, "but now it seems glorified."

But others say the U.S.-led invasion of Iraq in March 2003 triggered the global surge in violent Islamic militancy. The average annual global death toll between March 2003 to September 2006 from Muslim terrorist attacks jumped 237 percent from the toll between September 2001 to March 2003, according to a study published by Simon Fraser University in Canada.[38]

Moreover, when bin Laden declared war on the United States in a 1998 fatwa, he never mentioned Western culture. Instead, he objected to U.S. military bases in Saudi Arabia, the site of some of Islam's holiest shrines. "The Arabian Peninsula has never — since God made it flat, created its desert and encircled it with seas — been stormed by any forces like the crusader armies now spreading in it like locusts, consuming its riches and destroying its plantations." Bin Laden also railed against Israel — "the Jew's petty state" — and "its occupation of Jerusalem and murder of Muslims there."[39]

Some believe former President George W. Bush's habit of couching the "war on terror" in religious terms helped radical Islamic groups recruit jihadists. *An-Nuur* — a Tanzanian weekly Islamic magazine — noted: "Let us remember President Bush is a saved Christian.

AFP/Getty Images/Simon Maina

Moderate Islamist cleric Sheik Sharif Ahmed became Somalia's new president on Jan. 31, raising hope that the country's long war between religious extremists and moderates would soon end. But the hard-line Islamist al-Shabaab militia later took over the central Somali town of Baidoa and began imposing its harsh brand of Islamic law.

He is one of those who believe Islam should be destroyed."[40]

Nawaz, a former member of the revolutionary Islamist Hizb ut-Tahrir political movement, says fundamentalists' motivation varies depending on where they come from. "Some political Islamists are relatively liberal," says the English-born Nawaz. "It's the Saudis that are religiously conservative. The problem is their vision is being exported elsewhere."

Indeed, since oil prices first skyrocketed in the 1970s, the Saudi regime has used its growing oil wealth to build conservative Islamic schools (madrassas) and mosques around the world. As *New York Times* reporter Barbara Crossette noted, "from the austere Faisal mosque in Islamabad, Pakistan — a gift of the Saudis — to the stark Istiqlal mosque of Jakarta, Indonesia, silhouettes of domes and minarets reminiscent of Arab architecture are replacing Asia's once-eclectic mosques, which came in all shapes and sizes."[41]

What Is a Fundamentalist?

Few claim the tarnished label.

With the word fundamentalism today conjuring up images of cold-blooded suicide bombers as well as anti-abortion zealots, it is hardly surprising that many religious people don't want to be tarred with the fundamentalist brush.

Yet there was a time when traditionalist-minded Christianity wore it as a badge of honor. Baptist clergyman Curtis Lee Laws coined the term in 1910 in his weekly newspaper *Watchman-Examiner*, when he said fundamentalists were those "who still cling to the great fundamentals and who mean to do battle royal for the faith."[1] Several years earlier, Christian theologians had published a series of pamphlets called "The Fundamentals," which defended traditional belief in the Bible's literal truth against modern ideas such as Charles Darwin's theory of evolution.

Essentially a branch within the larger evangelical movement, the fundamentalists felt that the Christian faith would be strengthened if its fundamental tenets were clearly spelled out. Today, while one in three U.S. Christians considers himself an evangelical, "a small and declining percentage would describe themselves as fundamentalist," says Southern Baptist minister Richard Land of Nashville, Tenn. "While most evangelicals support fundamentalist principles, it is unfair to compare them to the Islamists who take up arms and kill people," he says.

Although some may see the label "fundamentalist" as synonymous with radical Islamic extremists, Ahmad Dallal, a professor of Arab and Islamic Studies at Georgetown University in Washington, D.C., notes that the Arabic word for fundamental — *usul* — was never used in this context historically. "There is some logic to applying the word 'fundamental' in an Islamic context, however," he says, because "both the Muslim and Christian fundamentalists emphasize a literal interpretation of the holy texts."

Traditionalist Catholics do not call themselves fundamentalists either. But Professor Martin Marty, a religious history professor at the University of Chicago and author of a multivolume series on fundamentalism, says Catholic followers of French Archbishop Marcel Lefebvre are fundamentalists because they refuse to accept reforms introduced by the Second Vatican Council in 1965. But "theocons" — a group of conservative U.S. Catholic intellectuals — are not fundamentalists, he says, because they accept the so-called Vatican II changes. Theocon George Weigel, a fellow at the Ethics and Public Policy Center in Washington, eschews the word "fundamentalist" because he says it is "a term used by secular people with prejudices, which doesn't illuminate very much."

Al Qaeda leader Osama bin Laden hails the economic losses suffered by the United States after the Sept. 11, 2001, terrorist attacks. "God ordered us to terrorize the infidels, and we terrorized the infidels," bin Laden's spokesman Suleiman Abu Ghaith said in the same video, which was broadcast soon after the attacks that killed nearly 3,000 people.

Neither are religious Jews keen on the term. Rabbi Avi Tawil, director of the Brussels office of the Chabad Jewish missionary movement, says "fundamentalism is about forcing people. We don't do that. We strictly respect Jewish law, which says if someone would like to convert then you have to help them."

Jerusalem-based writer Gershom Gorenberg notes that unlike Christians and Muslims, fundamentalist Jews do not typically advocate reading holy texts literally because their tradition has always been to have multiple interpretations. The term is even harder to apply to Hinduism because — unlike Christianity, Judaism and Islam — whose "fundaments" are their holy texts, Hinduism's origins are shrouded in ancient history, and its core elements are difficult to define.[2]

Yet fundamentalists are united in their aversion to modernism.

As Seyyed Hossein Nasr, an Islamic studies professor at George Washington University, noted: "When I was a young boy in Iran, 50 or 60 years ago . . . the word fundamentalism hadn't been invented. Modernism was just coming into the country."[3]

[1] Brenda E. Brasher, *Encyclopedia of Fundamentalism* (2001), p. 50.

[2] *Ibid.*, p. 222.

[3] His comments were made at a Pew Forum discussion, "Between Relativism and Fundamentalism: Is There a Middle Ground?" March 4, 2008, in Washington, D.C., http://pewforum.org/events/?EventID=172.

Pew Forum surveys have found no single, predominant factor motivating people to turn to Islamic fundamentalism. Thirty five percent of Indonesians blame immorality for the growth in Islamic extremism; 40 percent of Lebanese blame U.S. policies and influence; 39 percent of Moroccans blame poverty and 34 percent of Turks blame a lack of education.[42]

Then there are those who just want to regain their lost power, notes Iranian-born author Hunter. "In Iran, Turkey, Tunisia and Egypt, there was a forced secularization of society," she says. "Religious people lost power — sometimes their jobs, too. They had to develop a new discourse to restore their standing."

Religious fundamentalists in Nigeria are largely motivated by anger at the government for frittering away the country's vast oil supplies through corruption and mismanagement. "When a government fails its people, they turn elsewhere to safeguard themselves and their futures, and in Nigeria . . . they have turned to religion," asserted American religion writer Eliza Griswold.[43]

Many Christian and Muslim leaders preach the "Gospel of prosperity," which encourages Nigerians to better themselves economically. But Kenyan-based Baptist preacher Nkansah says that "while the Gospel brings good health and prosperity," the message can be taken too far. "There are some people in the Christian movement who are too materialistic."

Nkansah argues that evangelism is growing in Africa because "as human beings we all have needs. When people hear Christ came onto this planet to save them, they tend to respond."

But a journalist in Tajikistan says poverty drives Central Asians to radical groups like the Hizb ut-Tahrir (HT). "In the poor regions, especially the Ferghana Valley on the Kyrgyz-Tajik-Uzbek border, HT is very

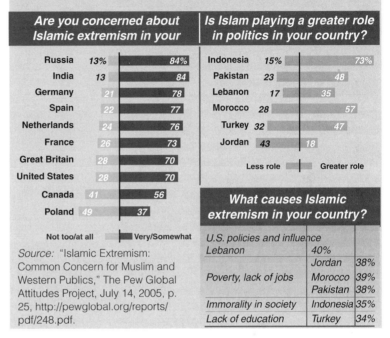

Many Voice Concern About Islamic Extremism

A majority of respondents in nine out of 10 Western countries were "very" or "somewhat" concerned about Islamic extremism in a 2005 poll. Islam was playing a greater role in politics in five out of six Muslim nations, according to the respondents, and most blamed U.S. policies and poverty for the rise in Islamic extremism.

Are you concerned about Islamic extremism in your		
Russia	13%	84%
India	13	84
Germany	21	78
Spain	22	77
Netherlands	24	76
France	26	73
Great Britain	28	70
United States	28	70
Canada	41	56
Poland	49	37

Not too/at all ■ Very/Somewhat

Is Islam playing a greater role in politics in your country?		
Indonesia	15%	73%
Pakistan	23	48
Lebanon	17	35
Morocco	28	57
Turkey	32	47
Jordan	43	18

Less role ■ Greater role

Source: "Islamic Extremism: Common Concern for Muslim and Western Publics," The Pew Global Attitudes Project, July 14, 2005, p. 25, http://pewglobal.org/reports/pdf/248.pdf.

What causes Islamic extremism in your country?		
U.S. policies and influence	Lebanon	40%
Poverty, lack of jobs	Jordan	38%
	Morocco	39%
	Pakistan	38%
Immorality in society	Indonesia	35%
Lack of education	Turkey	34%

active," says the journalist, who asks to remain unnamed for fear of reprisals. "Unemployment pushes people to find consolation in something else, and they find it in religion."

Should religious fundamentalists have a greater voice in government?

Religious fundamentalists who have taken the reins of government — in Iran (since 1979), Afghanistan (1996-2001) and the Gaza Strip (since 2007) — have either supported terrorism or have instituted repressive regimes. Grave human rights abuses have been documented, dissenters tortured, homosexuals hanged, adulterers stoned, music banned and education denied for girls.

Ayaan Hirsi Ali — a Somali-born feminist writer, a former Dutch politician and a fellow at the conservative

AFP/Getty Images/Walter Astrada

Evangelicals from Uganda's Born Again Church are spiritually moved last August while listening to a sermon by Pastor Robert Kayanja, one of Uganda's most prominent evangelical preachers. While Uganda has long been heavily Christian, many churchgoers have switched from mainstream to Pentecostal sects in recent years.

American Enterprise Institute who has denounced her family's Muslim faith — says fundamentalists should be able to compete for the chance to govern. "But we must tell them a system based on Islamic theology is bad," she says. "The problem is that Muslims cannot criticize their moral guide. Mohammad is more than a pope, he is a king. As a classical liberal, I say not even God is beyond criticism."

However, Danish politician Abdol-Hamid, whose parents are Palestinian, argues that because most countries won't talk to Hamas, the ruling party in the Gaza Strip, because of its terrorist activities, "we failed the Palestinians by never giving Hamas a chance." In Denmark, she continues, "We have Christian extremists, and I have to accept them." For instance, she explains, the far-right Danish Peoples Party (DPP) wants to ban the wearing of Muslim headscarves in the Danish parliament, and DPP member of parliament Soren Krarup, a Lutheran priest, says the hijab and the Nazi swastika are both symbols of totalitarianism. Abdol-Hamid hopes to become the first hijab-wearing woman elected to the parliament.

After interviewing Hamas' founding father, Sheikh Ahmed Yassin, Lebanese-born journalist Zaki Chebab wrote that Yassin "was confident that . . . Israel would disappear off the map within three decades," a belief he said came from the Koran.[44]

A Christian fundamentalist came to power in Northern Ireland without dire consequences after the Rev. Ian Paisley — the longtime leader of Ulster's Protestants, who established his own church stressing biblical literalism and once called the pope the "antichrist" — ultimately reconciled his lifelong differences with Northern Irish Catholic leaders and has served amicably with them in government after they offered him political power.[45]

Kenyan-based evangelical Nkansah says "politics is part of life." If a religious person is called into politics in Kenya, he explains, "they should go because that is their vocation." He supports Kenya's model, in which many clergy members, including bishops, enter politics, even though the constitution bans parties based on religion. But evangelical pastor Steuernagel says that in Brazil, religious leaders are increasingly going into politics. "I do not think it is healthy," he says, "but it is happening."

In Central Asia, Islamic parties are only allowed in Tajikistan. But while the Islamic Revival Party has become a significant force there, the party "is neither dangerous nor radical," according to the Tajik journalist, and "does not dream about having a state like Iran."

"It is a delicate game," says fundamentalism expert Marty. "If you have a republican system with a secular constitution, then, yes [fundamentalists must be allowed to have a voice], because they have to respect that constitution. But it's very much a case of 'handle with care.'"

Conservative Catholic theologian George Weigel, a senior fellow at the Ethics and Public Policy Center in Washington, says religious people are entitled to be involved in politics, but "they should translate their religiously informed moral convictions into concepts and words that those who don't share their theological commitments can engage and debate. This is called 'democratic courtesy.' It's also political common sense."

Indeed, religious Muslims not only have the right but also the duty to participate in government, according to Rachid Ghannouchi, a Tunisian-born Islamic thinker. Denouncing countries like Tunisia and Algeria that repress Islamic fundamentalism, Ghannouchi said, "the real problem lies in convincing the ruling regimes . . . of the right of Islamists — just like other political groups — to form political parties, engage in political activities and compete for power or share in power through democratic means."[46]

But ex-Islamist Nawaz warns: "We should not be encouraging Islamists, because every terrorist group has grown out of a nonviolent Islamist group."

Israeli journalist Gorenberg also notes that radical Jewish fundamentalists have repeatedly resorted to violence, citing the case of Baruch Goldstein, a U.S.-born Israeli doctor and supporter of the Kach party who killed 29 Muslims at the tomb of Abraham in Hebron in 1994.

Washington-based Turkish journalist Tulin Daloglu is anxious about her country's future under the ruling Justice and Development Party. "Women are starting to cover their hair in order to get jobs in government," she claims. "The case is not at all proven that Islam and democracy can live in harmony. Turkey is a swing state" in that regard.

Meanwhile, in some Asian and African countries where the rule of law is weak — Pakistan and Somalia for example — many are clamoring for Islamic law. Often the existing government is so dysfunctional that the quick, decisive administration of Islamic law, or sharia, is attractive. In Pakistan, says British journalist Jason Burke, "the choice between slow, corrupt and expensive state legal systems and the religious alternative — rough and ready though it may be — is not hard." Even educated, relatively wealthy women are demanding sharia, he said.[47]

For example, the Taliban has been able to seize control in Pakistan's Swat region because of "an ineffectual and unresponsive civilian government, coupled with military and security forces that, in the view of furious residents, have willingly allowed the militants to spread terror deep into Pakistan."[48]

BACKGROUND

'Great Awakening'

Christian fundamentalist movements trace their origins to the emergence of Protestantism in 16th-century Europe, when the German monk Martin Luther (1483-1546) urged people to return to the basics of studying the Bible.[49] In 1620 a group of fundamentalist Protestants known as the Pilgrims fleeing persecution in England settled in North America and, along with the Puritans who arrived shortly afterwards, greatly influenced the course of Christianity in New England.

In the 1700s, as science began to threaten religion's preeminence, North Americans launched a Protestant revival known as the "Great Awakening," from which the evangelical movement was born. Revivals held throughout the American colonies between 1739 and 1743, offered evangelical, emotionally charged sermons — often in open-air services before large groups — that stressed the need to forge a personal relationship with Jesus Christ. Leaders in the movement included preachers George Whitfield, Gilbert Tennent and Jonathan Edwards.[50]

A similar revival movement — the Sunday school movement — began in the late 18th century, becoming a primary vehicle for evangelism.[51] The term "fundamentalist" originated in the United States when the first of a 12-volume collection of essays called *The Fundamentals* was published in 1910, outlining the core tenets of Christianity.[52] In 1925 fundamentalists were the driving force in the trial of Tennessee schoolteacher John Scopes, who was convicted of breaking a Tennessee law that forbade the teaching of evolution instead of the Bible's version of how the world was created. Even though the fundamentalists won the case, they were lampooned in the popular press, and their credibility and esteem suffered. They withdrew from the limelight and formed their own subculture of churches, Bible colleges, camps and seminaries.

By 1950, the charismatic American Baptist preacher Billy Graham had begun to broaden the fundamentalists' base, and they became masters at harnessing the mass media, especially radio and television. The 1973 U.S. Supreme Court's *Roe v. Wade* ruling legalizing abortion further galvanized evangelicals, leading Baptist preacher Falwell in 1979 to establish the Moral Majority — a conservative political advocacy group.

After his unsuccessful run for president of the United States in 1988, television evangelist and Christian nationalist Robertson formed the Christian Coalition to fight for "family-friendly" policies — specifically policies against homosexuality and abortion. By the mid-1990s the coalition became the most prominent voice in the Christian movement, largely by publishing voter guides on how local politicians voted on specific social issues important to Christian fundamentalists. Many credit the coalition with helping the Republican Party, which had embraced their platform on social issues, to take majority

C H R O N O L O G Y

A.D. 70-1700s *The three great, monotheistic, text-based religions — Christianity, Islam and Judaism — spread worldwide.*

70 Romans destroy the second Jewish temple in Jerusalem, causing Jews to scatter across the globe.

319 Christianity becomes the official religion of the Roman Empire; pagan sacrifices are outlawed.

632 Mohammad dies in Medina, Arabia. . . . Islam begins to spread to the Middle East, Africa, India, Indonesia and Southern Europe.

1730s-40s Evangelical movement is born in the United States in a religious revival known as the "Great Awakening."

1800s-1920s *Fundamentalist impulses are triggered in reaction to scientific developments, modernization and — in the case of Islam — Western colonization.*

1859 British biologist Charles Darwin presents theory of evolution in *On the Origin of Species*, casting doubt on the Bible's account of creation.

1906 African-American evangelist William J. Seymour launches the Azusa Street revival in Los Angeles, sparking the worldwide Pentecostal movement.

1910 American Christian oil magnates Lyman and Milton Stewart commission The Fundamentals, promoting fundamentalist Protestant beliefs that the Bible contains no errors.

1921 Jailed Hindu nationalist Vinayak Damodar Savarkar writes *Hindutva: Who is a Hindu?* — laying the foundation for movements promoting Hindu identity, including the radical Bajrang Dal.

1928 Hasan al-Banna, a schoolteacher in Cairo, Egypt, establishes the Muslim Brotherhood, which calls for all Muslims to make their societies more Islamic.

1940s-1970s *Fundamentalism becomes a significant force in politics and society.*

1948 Israel declares independence, causing millions of Jews — both secular and religious — to return to their spiritual homeland.

1967 Fundamentalist Jews settle in Palestinian territories occupied after the Six-day War, triggering an explosion in Islamic fundamentalism among disgruntled Arabs.

1973 U.S. Supreme Court's *Roe v. Wade* ruling legalizes abortion, galvanizing Christian fundamentalists into political activism.

1979 Islamists overthrow the Shah of Iran and install the world's first Islamic theocracy in modern times.

1980s-2000s *Fundamentalists increasingly endorse violence to further their goals — especially in the Muslim world.*

1984 Indian government storms a Sikh temple, which Sikh militants had occupied, leading two of Prime Minister Indira Gandhi's Sikh bodyguards to murder her.

1994 American Jewish fundamentalist Baruch Goldstein kills 29 Muslims praying at a mosque in the Palestinian city of Hebron.

Sept. 11, 2001 Al Qaeda Islamists kill nearly 3,000 people by flying hijacked planes into the World Trade Center and Pentagon; a third hijacked plane crashes in Pennsylvania.

2002 Sectarian fighting between Hindus and Muslims in Gujarat, India, kills more than 800 people — mostly Muslims.

2006 Palestinians elect Hamas, a radical Islamic party, to lead the government.

2008 Sixty Christians die after outbreak of fundamentalist Hindu violence against Christians in India. . . . Pakistan-based Islamists launch coordinated attacks in Mumbai, India, killing 164 people. . . . Troops from Congo, Uganda and South Sudan launch ongoing joint offensive to crush Uganda's fundamentalist Lord's Resistance Army. . . . Israel launches major attack on Gaza in effort to weaken Hamas, resulting in 1,300 Palestinian deaths.

control of the U.S. Congress in the 1994 midterm elections.[53]

Some U.S. fundamentalists segregated themselves from mainstream society — which they saw as immoral — and educated their children at home.[54] A strand of race-based fundamentalism also emerged, called the Christian Identity movement, which claimed the Bible was the history of the white race and that Jews were the biological descendants of Satan. A Christian Reconstructionist movement, led by preacher Mark Rushdoony, emerged as well, advocating local theocracies that would impose biblical law.[55] The reconstructionists oppose government schools and demand that civil disputes be settled in church courts and that taxes be limited to 10 percent of income (based on the tithe). Through its books, the movement has had a significant influence on other Christian political organizations.[56]

Meanwhile, a fundamentalist Catholic movement emerged in Europe after French Archbishop Marcel Lefebvre refused to accept changes introduced by the Vatican in the 1960s, notably saying Mass in languages other than Latin.[57] Other conservative Catholic movements include Opus Dei, founded by Spanish priest Josemaria Escriva in 1928. Today it is based in Rome, has 75,000 members in 50 countries and appeals to well-educated lay Catholics.[58] In the United States, a group of Catholic intellectuals — including Michael Novak, Weigel and Richard John Neuhaus — became known as the "theocons" and allied themselves with Protestant evangelicals in opposing abortion and gay rights.[59]

Bush's presidency was a high point for U.S. evangelicals. Bush announced during the 2000 campaign that he was a "born again" Christian whose favorite philosopher was Jesus Christ — "because he changed my heart." He also told a Texas evangelist that he felt God had chosen him to run for president, and he was accused of "creeping Christianization" of the federal government by establishing an Office for Faith-Based Initiatives, which critics claimed was just a vehicle for channeling tax dollars to conservative Christian groups.[60]

Bush liberally used religious rhetoric — declaring, for example, after the 9/11 attacks that his mission was "to rid the world of evil."[61] He named Missouri Sen. John Ashcroft, a fellow evangelist, as attorney general and filled his administration with Christian conservatives, such as Monica Goodling, a young Justice Department

official who vetted candidates for executive appointments by checking their views on moral issues like abortion.[62]

Christian missionaries have been evangelizing — spreading their faith — since the 16th century, but fundamentalist strands have grown increasingly prominent in recent decades. Pentecostalism — which began in 1901 when a Kansas Bible studies student, Agnes Ozman, began "speaking in tongues" — is the dominant form of Protestantism in Latin America.[63] In Guatemala, evangelicalism began to overtake the Roman Catholic Church in the 1980s after Catholicism was seen as too European and elitist.[64] Although Pentecostals usually distinguish themselves from run-of-the-mill fundamentalists, both are part of the evangelical family.

In Africa, Christian fundamentalism developed its strongest base in sub-Saharan regions — particularly Nigeria, triggering rising tensions and sporadic violence between the country's Christian and Muslim populations. U.S. Christian fundamentalists have helped to spread an extreme brand of Christianity to Africa, according to Cedric Mayson, director of the African National Congress' Commission for Religious Affairs, in South Africa. "We are extremely concerned about the support given by the U.S. to the proliferation of right-wing Christian fundamentalist groups in Africa," Mayson wrote, as "they are the major threat to peace and stability in Africa."[65]

Uganda became home to the militant Christian fundamentalist Lord's Resistance Army. Its leader Joseph Kony — known as the "altar boy who grew up to be a guerrilla leader" — has transformed an internal Ugandan power struggle into an international conflict by roaming across Sudan and the Democratic Republic of Congo, kidnapping children en route for use as soldiers after slaughtering their parents.[66]

Patrick Makasi, the LRA's former director of operations, called Kony "a religious man" who "all the time . . . is talking about God. Every time he keeps calling many people to teach them about the legends and about God. That is how he leads people."[67]

Islamic Fundamentalism

Originating in the 7th century with the Prophet Mohammad, Islam considers the Koran sacred both in content and form — meaning it should be read in the original

Officials in the 'Stans' Uneasy About Islamization

Education is a key battleground.

"The crowd in the airport parking lot was jubilant despite the cold, with squealing children, busy concession stands and a tangle of idling cars giving the impression of an eager audience before a rock concert," wrote journalist Sabrina Tavernise of a scene in Dushanbe, the capital of Tajikistan.[1]

"But it was religion, not rock 'n roll, that had drawn so many people," she wrote. The families were there to meet relatives returning from the Hajj — the pilgrimage to Mecca that Muslims strive to undertake at least once in their lifetime. Last year, 5,200 Tajiks participated — 10 times more than in 2000.

Since gaining independence from the anti-religious Soviet Union, Tajikistan has been re-embracing its Islamic roots, and a Westerner in the country — who asked to remain unnamed — worries the nation of 7.2 million people may adopt an extreme form of Islam. "Every day you can see on our streets more women wearing the veil and more men with beards," he says.

But while many women in Central Asia today do cover themselves from head to toe, it is "extremely rare" for them to cover their faces as well, which was not unusual in pre-Soviet Tajikistan and Uzbekistan, says Martha Brill Olcott, a senior associate at the Carnegie Endowment for International Peace in Washington, who has traveled there frequently since 1975.

The region is undergoing a wide mix of outside influences, not all of them Islamic, Olcott notes. For example, some women have begun wearing the hijab (a headscarf pinned tightly around the face so as to cover the hair) worn by modern Islamic women in the West, while others, notably in Uzbekistan, imitate secular Western fashions such as short skirts and visible belly piercing.

The Westerner in Tajikistan fears that the government's efforts to block the growing Islamization may be having the opposite effect. Government policies "are too severe," he says. "They give long prison sentences to young men and shut down unregistered mosques. This just strengthens people's resolution to resist an unfair system."

Further, he suggests, "If they developed local economies more, people would not think about radical Islam." Without economic development, "Tajikistan could become another Afghanistan or Iran."

Tajikistan, one of the poorer countries in the region, is in the midst of reverse urbanization due to economic decline, with 77 percent of the population now living in rural areas compared to 63 percent in the mid-1980s.[2] A million Tajiks work in Russia.

In neighboring Uzbekistan, the picture is similar. Olcott likens the California-sized nation of 27 million people to an "ineffective police state. There are restrictions, but people can get around them and — more important — they are not afraid to get around them." She says the government's response is erratic:

The refurbished Juma Mosque in Tashkent, Uzbekistan, reflects Islam's resurgence in Central Asia, where 18 years after the breakup of the former Soviet Union neighboring Iran and Saudi Arabia are exerting their influence on the vast region.

"If you do not draw attention to yourself, you can be an Islamist. But if you preach and open schools or wear very Islamic dress, you can get into trouble."

Christian missionaries are also active in Central Asia. Russian-dubbed broadcasts from U.S. televangelist Pat Robertson are aired throughout the region. According to the Tajikistan-based Westerner, after the 1991 fall of the Soviet Union "Jehovah's Witnesses, Baptists and Adventists came from Russia, Western Europe, South Korea and the United States. The locals were friendly to them because they provided humanitarian aid to poor people." However, authorities in the region have recently clamped down — especially on Jehovah's Witnesses, he says.[3]

In Kazakhstan authorities have cracked down on Protestants and repressed the Hindu-based Hare Krishnas, while in Kyrgyzstan a new law makes it harder to register religious organizations.[4]

In Kyrgyzstan, the authorities are in a quandary about whether to allow a new political movement, the Union of Muslims, to be set up because bringing Islam into politics violates the constitution. Yet union co-founder Tursunbay Bakir Uulu argues that a moderately Islamic party would help stabilize the country. "Currently Hizb-ut-Tahrir is conquering the Issyk-Kul region," he warned. "Religious sects are stepping up their activities. We want moderate Islam, which has nothing to do with anti-religious teaching and which respects values of other world religions, to fill this niche."[5]

The Islamization began in the 1980s, when Soviet President Mikhail Gorbachev eased restrictions on religious worship that had been enforced by the communists for decades. After the Soviet Union's collapse, the relaxation accelerated as the

Central Asian republics became independent nations. Muslim missionaries flocked to the region, and conservative Islamic schools, universities and mosques quickly sprang up, many financed by foundations in oil-rich Arab states like Saudi Arabia, where the ultra-fundamentalist Wahhabi Muslim sect is the state-sponsored religion.[6]

Many Central Asians see embracing conservative Islam as a way to define themselves and reject their Russian-dominated communist past. Curiously, their increasing exposure to secular culture through Russia-based migrant Tajik workers appears to be having a Westernizing influence on the society even as Islam is growing: "Five years ago, I could not wear shorts on the street," said the Westerner in Tajikistan. "Now in summer you can see a lot of Tajik men and even girls wearing shorts in the cities, although not in the villages."

The rise of Islam is strongest in Uzbekistan, Tajikistan and Kyrgyzstan, while Turkmenistan and Kazakhstan have stronger secular traditions. Uzbek authorities initially encouraged Islamization, believing it would help strengthen national identity. But by the late 1990s, they were afraid of losing control to radical elements and began repressing militant groups like the Islamic Movement of Uzbekistan and Hizb-ut-Tahrir.[7] A jailbreak by Islamists in Andijan, the Uzbek capital, in May 2005 triggered violent clashes between government forces and anti-corruption protesters — whom the government claimed were Islamic extremists — resulting in 187 deaths.[8]

Meanwhile, the Saudis are sending Islamic textbooks that promote their own conservative brand of Islam to schools in the region.[9] Saudi-Uzbek ties stretch back to the 1920s, when some Uzbeks fled to Saudi Arabia, according to Olcott.

But Saudi-inspired fundamentalism "is not a major factor" in Turkmenistan yet, says Victoria Clement, an assistant professor of Islamic world history at Western Carolina University, who has lived in Turkmenistan. "There are maybe a few individuals, but the government has not allowed madrasas [Islamic religious schools] since 2003." Even so, she notes, "when I went to the mosques, I saw clerics instructing the kids in the Koran, which technically they should not have been doing [under Turkmen law], but I do not think it was harmful."

Nevertheless, the Turkmen education system is growing more Islamic, Clement says, as new schools follow the model devised by Turkish preacher Fethullah Gulen. "They do not have classes in religion, but they teach a conservative moral code — no drinking, smoking, staying out late at night. I think it is a great alternative to the Islamic madrasas," she says.

Olcott says while the quality of education in the Gulen schools may be good, it is "still very Islamic." Gulen himself now lives in the United States, having left Turkey after being accused of undermining secularism.

The Westerner in Tajikistan notes, however, that in their efforts to stem the growth of radical Islam authorities have a bit of a blind spot when it comes to education. "In most Tajik villages, the children's only teacher is the person who can read the Koran in Arabic, and that is dangerous. The government makes demands about how students look — ties and suits for example — but does not care about what they have in their minds."

Islam Booming in the "Stans"

Several of the nations in Central Asia dubbed "the Stans" are rediscovering their Islamic roots, including Tajikistan and Uzbekistan. The Islamization began in the 1980s, when then Soviet President Mikhail Gorbachev eased restrictions on religious worship.

[1] Sabrina Tavernise, "Independent, Tajiks Revel in Their Faith," *The New York Times*, Jan. 3, 2009, www.nytimes.com/2009/01/04/world/asia/04tajik.html?emc=tnt&tntemail0=y.

[2] *Ibid.*

[3] Felix Corley, "Tajikistan: Jehovah's Witnesses Banned," Forum 18 News Service (Oslo, Norway), Oct. 18, 2007, www.forum18.org/Archive.php?article_id=1036; Felix Corley, "Turkmenistan: Fines, beatings, threats of rape and psychiatric incarceration," Forum 18 News Service (Oslo, Norway), Nov. 25, 2008, www.forum18.org/Archive.php?article_id=1221.

[4] Mushfig Bayram, "Kazakhstan: Police Struggle against Extremism, Separatism and Terrorism — and restaurant meals," Forum 18 News Service, Nov. 21, 2008, www.forum18.org/Archive.php?article_id=1220; and Mushfig Bayram, "Kyrgyzstan: Restrictive Religion Law passes Parliament Unanimously," Forum 18 News Service (Oslo, Norway), Nov. 6, 2008, www.forum18. org/Archive.php?article_id=1215.

[5] "Kyrgyz Experts Say Newly Set Up Union of Muslims Aims for Power," *Delo No* (Kyrgyzstan), BBC Monitoring International Reports, Dec. 9, 2008.

[6] See Martha Brill Olcott and Diora Ziyaeva, "Islam in Uzbekistan: Religious Education and State Ideology," Carnegie Endowment for International Peace, July 2008, www.carnegieendowment.org/publications/index.cfm?fa=view&id=21980&prog=zru.

[7] *Ibid.*, p. 2.

[8] For background, see Kenneth Jost, "Russia and the Former Soviet Republics," *CQ Researcher*, June 17, 2005, pp. 541-564.

[9] *Ibid.*, p. 19.

Getty Images/Chip Somodevilla

Anti-abortion demonstrators carry a statue of the Virgin Mary during the March for Life in Washington, D.C., on Jan. 22, 2009. The rally marked the 35th anniversary of the Supreme Court's landmark Roe v. Wade decision legalizing abortion in the United States. Fundamentalist Christians continue to exert significant influence on U.S. policies governing abortion, birth control and gay rights.

language, Arabic. Muslims also follow the Hadith, Mohammad's more specific instructions on how to live, which were written down after he died. Though Islamic scholars have interpreted both texts for centuries, fundamentalists use the original texts.

The concept of a militant Islamic struggle was developed by scholar Taqi ad-Din Ahmad Ibn Taymiyyah (1263-1328), who called for "holy war" against the conquering, non-Muslim Mongols.[68] The Saudi-born Islamic scholar Muhammed Ibn Abd-al-Wahhab (1703-1792) criticized the Ottoman Empire for corrupting the purity of Islam. The descendants of one of Wahhab's followers, Muhammed Ibn Saud, rule Saudi Arabia today.[69]

Responding to the dominating influence of Western powers that were colonizing the Islamic world at the time, Egyptian schoolteacher Hasan Al-Banna set up the Muslim Brotherhood in 1928 to re-Islamize Egypt. The organization later expanded to other Arab countries and to Sudan.[70] "They copied what the Christian missionaries were doing in Africa by doing social work," notes Islamic studies Professor Dallal. "But they had no vision for 'the state,' and they paid a price for this because the state ultimately suppressed them."

In the 1950s the extremist group Hizb-ut-Tahrir, which advocates a single Islamic state encompassing all predominantly Muslim countries, emerged and spread across the Islamic world. In the mid-1950s, while imprisoned in Egypt by the secular government, the U.S.-educated Egyptian scholar and social reformer Qutb (1906-1966) wrote *Milestones*, his diatribe against the permissiveness of the West, which persuaded many Muslims they needed to get more involved in politics in order to get their governments to make their societies more Islamic. In Pakistan, the politician Sayyid Abul A'la Mawdudi (1903-1979) urged Islamists to restore Islamic law by forming political parties and getting elected to political office, according to Dallal.

The 1973 oil crisis helped to spread conservative Islam by further enriching Saudi Arabia, which set up schools, universities and charities around the world advocating ultraconservative wahhabi Islam. And the 1979 Iranian Revolution — in which the pro-Western Shah Mohammad Reza Pahlavi was deposed in a conservative Shia Muslim revolt led by Ayatollah Ruhollah Khomeini — installed the first Islamic theocracy in the modern era.

In 1991 Islamists were voted into power in Algeria, but the military refused to let them govern, triggering a bloody civil war that the secularists eventually won. In Afghanistan, the ultraconservative Pakistan-sponsored Taliban seized power in 1996 and imposed their strict version of Islamic law — outlawing music, forbidding girls from going to school or leaving their homes without a male relative, forcing women to completely cover their bodies — even their eyes — in public, requiring men to grow beards and destroying all books except the Koran.[71] After the al Qaeda terrorist attacks of 9/11, the United States ousted the Taliban, which had been sheltering bin Laden.

Al Qaeda, a Sunni Muslim group that originated in Saudi Arabia, had been based in Afghanistan since the 1980s, when it helped eject Soviet occupiers, with U.S. aid. But in the 1990s bin Laden redirected his energies against the United State after American troops were stationed in his native Saudi Arabia, home to several sacred Muslim shrines.

After the U.S.-led invasion of Iraq in 2003, al Qaeda urged its followers to switch their attentions to Iraq, which became a magnet for Islamist jihadists. In 2007 al Qaeda attacks in Iraq escalated to such a level of violence — including attacking Shia mosques and repressing local Sunnis — that other Islamic groups like the Muslim Brotherhood repudiated them.[72]

In Europe, meanwhile, beginning in the 1980s the growing Muslim immigrant population began to attach greater importance to its religious identity, and some turned to violence. Algerian extremists set off bombs in Paris subways and trains in 1995-1996; Moroccan-born Islamic terrorists killed 191 people in train bombings in Madrid in 2004; and British-based al Qaeda operatives of mainly Pakistani origin killed 52 people in suicide train and bus bombings in London in 2005.[73] And an al Qaeda cell based in Hamburg, Germany, plotted the 9/11 attacks on the World Trade Center towers and the Pentagon.

The estimated 5 million Muslims in the United States — who are a mix of immigrants and African-Americans — are more moderate than their Western European counterparts.[74] Poverty is likely to have played a role in making European Muslims more radical: Whereas the average income of American Muslims is close to the national average, Muslims' average income lags well behind the national average in Spain, France, Britain and Germany.[75]

Meanwhile, the creation of Israel in 1948 — fiercely opposed by all of its Arab neighbors — and its successive expansions in the Gaza Strip and West Bank have helped to spur Islamic fundamentalism in the region. To Israel's north, the Shia-Muslim Hezbollah group emerged in the 1980s in Lebanon with the goal of destroying Israel and making Lebanon an Islamic state. The Sunni-Muslim group Hamas — an offshoot of the Muslim Brotherhood — won elections in the Palestinian territories in 2006. Hamas, which was launched during the Palestinian uprising against Israel of 1987, has forged strong links with Islamic fundamentalists in Iran and Saudi Arabia.[76]

Fundamentalist Jews

Predating both Islam and Christianity, Judaism takes the Torah and Talmud as its two holy texts and believes that the Prophet Moses received the Ten Commandments — inscribed on stone tablets — from God on Mount Sinai.[77] Fundamentalist Jews believe they are God's chosen people and that God gave them modern-day Israel as their homeland. A defining moment in this narrative is the destruction of the second Jewish Temple in Jerusalem in 70 A.D., which triggered the scattering of Jews throughout the world for nearly 2,000 years.

Jews began returning to their spiritual homeland in significant numbers in the early 1900s with the advent

Members of the ultra-Orthodox Chabad-Lubavitch Jewish fundamentalist movement attend the funeral in Israel of two members of the missionary sect killed last fall during Islamist militant attacks in Mumbai, India.

of Zionism — a predominantly secular political movement to establish a Jewish homeland, founded by the Austro-Hungarian journalist Theodor Herzl in the late 19th century in response to rising anti-Semitism in Europe. The migration was accelerated after Nazi Germany began persecuting the Jewish people in the 1930s in a racially motivated campaign that resulted in the Holocaust and the murder of 6 million Jews and millions of others.[78] Today, a third the world's 15 million Jews live in Israel; most of the rest live in the United States, with substantial Jewish communities in France, Argentina and Canada.

Fundamentalist Jews regret that Israel was established as a secular democracy rather than a theocracy. While most Israelis support the secular model, there is a growing minority of ultra-Orthodox (Haredi) Jews for whom the Torah and Talmud form the core of their identity. They try to observe 613 commandments and wear distinctive garb: long black caftans, side curls and hats for men and long-sleeve dresses, hats, wigs and scarves for women.[79] The Haredim dream of building a new Jewish temple in Jerusalem where the old ones stood, which also happens to be the site of the Dome on the Rock — one of Islam's most revered shrines. The fundamentalist Haredim are represented by several different political parties in Israel — each with a distinct ideology.

A newer strain of Jewish fundamentalism, the Gush Eminum movement, grew out of the 1967 Israeli-Arab War, in which Israel captured large swathes of Syrian,

Islamic Fundamentalism Limits Women's Rights

But Muslim women disagree on the religion's impact.

As a high official in Saudi Arabia, Ahmed Zaki Yamani crafted many of the kingdom's laws, basing them on Wahhabism, the strict form of Islam that is Saudi Arabia's state religion. Under those laws, Muslim judges "have affirmed women's competence in all civil matters," he has written, but "many of them have reservations regarding her political competence." In fact, he added, one of Islam's holiest texts, the Hadith, "considered deficiency a corollary of femaleness."[1]

Since the 1970s, the Saudis have used their vast oil wealth to spread their ultra-conservative form of Islam throughout the Middle East, North Africa and South and Central Asia, including its controversial view of women as unequal to men. Under Saudi Wahhabism, women cannot vote, drive cars or mix freely with men. They also must have a male guardian make many critical decisions on their behalf, which Human Rights Watch called "the most significant impediment to the realization of women's rights in the kingdom."[2]

The advocacy group added that "the religious establishment has consistently paralyzed any efforts to advance women's rights by applying only the most restrictive provisions of Islamic law, while disregarding more progressive interpretations."[3]

In her autobiography, *Infidel*, Somali-born writer and former Dutch politician Ayaan Hirsi Ali writes about how shocked she was as a young girl when her family moved from Somalia's less conservative Islamic society to Saudi Arabia, where females' lives were much more restricted. "Any girl who goes out unaccompanied is up for grabs," she says.

Raised a Muslim but today an outspoken critic of Islam, Hirsi Ali says Saudi Arabia has had a "horrific" influence on the Muslim world — especially on women. In Africa, she says, religious strictures against women going out in public can have dire consequences, because many women must work outside the home for economic reasons.

While Wahhabism is perhaps the most extreme form of Islam, Hirsi Ali doubts any form of Islam is compatible with women's rights. "Islamic feminism is a contradiction in terms," she says. "Islam means 'submission.' This is double for women: She must appeal to God before anyone else. Yet this same God tells your man he can beat you."

In 2004, Dutch filmmaker Theo Van Gogh was murdered by a Muslim man angered by a film he made portraying violence against women in Islamic societies. Hirsi Ali, then a member of the Dutch parliament, had written the script for the movie, and the assassin left a note on Van Gogh's body threatening her.

She believes the entire philosophical underpinnings of Islam are flawed. For example, she says, she had been taught that Muslim women must wear the veil so they will not corrupt men, yet, "when I came to Europe I could not understand how women were not covered, and yet the men were not jumping on them. Then I saw all it took was to educate boys to exercise self-control. They don't do that in Saudi Arabia, Iran and Pakistan."

But forcing women to cover themselves is not the only way conservative Muslim societies infringe on women's rights. Until recently in Pakistan, rape cases could not be prosecuted unless four pious Muslim men were willing to testify that they had witnessed the attack. Without their testimony the victim could be prosecuted for fornication and alleging a false crime, punishable by stoning, lashing or prison.[4]

Ali's views are not shared by Asmaa Abdol-Hamid, a young, Danish Muslim politician of Palestinian parentage who lived in the United Arab Emirates before moving to Denmark at age 6. Covering oneself, she says, "makes women more equal because there is less focus on her body. . . . When you watch an ad on television, it is always women in bikinis selling the car."

A social worker, local council member representing a left-wing party and former television-show host, Abdol-Hamid is a controversial figure in Denmark. She wears a hijab and refuses to shake hands with men. "I prefer to put my hand on my heart," she explains. "That's just my way of greeting them. It's not that shaking hands is un-Islamic."

She has her own view of Islam's emphasis on female submission. "If women want to obey their husbands, it's up to them." However, "I could not live the Arab lifestyle, where the men beat the women. That's not Islam — it's Arab." In a global study of women's rights, Arab states accounted for 10 of the 19 countries with the lowest ranking for women's equality.[5]

Many fundamentalist Muslims say the freedoms advocated by secular women's-rights advocates disrupt the complementary nature of male and female roles that have been the basis of social unity since the rise of Islam. A Palestinian Islamic jihadist, known only as Mujahida, said women should "return to their natural and [Koran-based] functions as child-bearers, home-keepers and educators of the next generation." She rejects women's-rights advocates who urge women to take their abusive husbands to secular courts.

Muslim "family mediators," she said, were best placed to resolve such disputes.[6]

According to the Washington-based Pew Research Center, more than a third of Jordanians and Egyptians oppose allowing women to choose whether or not to veil, although the percentage is falling.[7] Also on the decline: the number of those who support restrictions prohibiting men and women from working in the same workplace.[8] In Saudi Arabia, such restrictions limit womens' employment, because employers must provide separate offices for women.[9]

However, Pew found considerable support in Muslim nations for restricting a woman's right to choose her husband. For example, 55 percent of Pakistanis felt the family, not the woman, should decide.[10]

In Nigeria, Islamic fundamentalism has hurt women's rights, according to Nigerian activist Husseini Abdu. "Although it is difficult separating the Hausa [Nigerian tribe] and Islam patriarchal structure, the reintroduction or politicization of sharia [Islamic law] in northern Nigeria has contributed in reinforcing traditional, religious and cultural prejudices against women," Abdu says.[11] This includes, among other things, the absence of women in the judiciary, discrimination in the standards of evidence in court cases (especially involving adultery) and restrictions in the freedom of association.[12]

Christian countries are not immune from criticism for limiting women's rights. Human Rights Watch found that in Argentina the Catholic Church has had a hand in establishing government policies that restrict women's access to modern contraception, sex education and abortion.[13] And fundamentalist Christian groups have played a significant role in restricting sex education and the availability of birth control and abortion services in the United States.

But while Islamic countries are often criticized for their treatment of women, the world's two most populous Muslim nations, Pakistan and Indonesia, have both elected female leaders in the past — the late Benazir Bhutto in Pakistan and Megawati Sukarnoputri in Indonesia. The world's largest Christian country, the United States, has never had a female president.

In Iran, an Islamic theocracy since 1979, a debate is raging over whether to allow women to inherit real estate, notes Shireen Hunter, an Iranian-born author and visiting scholar at Georgetown University in Washington. "Reformers are also trying to have the age of [marriage] consent raised from 9 to 16 years. This will take time," she says, because "trying to blend Islam and modernity is hard. It is easier to just say, 'Let's go back to fundamentalism.'"

Yet Abdol-Hamid argues that "fundamentalism does not have to be a bad thing. In Islam, going back to the Koran and Hadith would be good."

Ayaan Hirsi Ali (right), a Somali-born former member of the Dutch parliament, has been threatened with death for her outspoken criticism of Islam's treatment of women in Islam. But Danish Muslim politician and social worker Asmaa Abdol-Hamid (left) attributes repressive gender-based policies in Muslim countries to local culture, not the Koran.

Does Hirsi Ali see anything positive about a woman's life in Islamic societies? "I have never seen Muslim women doubt their femininity or sensuality," she says. "Western women question this more. They are less secure. They are always thinking, 'Am I really equal?'"

---

[1] Ahmed Zaki Yamani, "The Political Competence of Women in Islamic Law," pp. 170-177, in John J. Donohue and John L. Esposito, *Islam in Transition: Muslim Perspectives* (2007).

[2] "Perpetual Minors — Human Rights Abuses Stemming from Male Guardianship and Sex Segregation in Saudi Arabia," Human Rights Watch, April 19, 2008, p. 2, www.hrw.org/en/node/62251/section/1.

[3] *Ibid.*

[4] Karen Foerstel, "Women's Rights," *CQ Global Researcher*, May 2008, p. 118.

[5] *Ibid.*

[6] Loren D. Lybarger, *Identity and Religion in Palestine: The Struggle between Islamism and Secularism in the Occupied Territories* (2007), p. 105.

[7] In Jordan, 37 percent of respondents opposed women being allowed to choose whether to veil, compared to 33 percent in Egypt.

[8] The Pew Global Attitudes Project, "World Publics Welcome Global Trade — But Not Immigration," Pew Research Center, Oct. 4, 2007, p. 51, http://pewglobal.org/reports/pdf/258.pdf.

[9] "Perpetual Minors — Human Rights Abuses Stemming from Male Guardianship and Sex Segregation in Saudi Arabia," *op. cit.*, p. 3.

[10] Pew, *op. cit.*, p. 50.

[11] Carina Tertsakian, "Political Shari'a? Human Rights and Islamic Law in Northern Nigeria," Human Rights Watch, Sept. 21, 2004, p. 63, www.hrw.org/en/ reports/2004/09/21/political-shari.

[12] *Ibid.*

[13] See Marianne Mollmann, "Decisions Denied: Women's Access to Contraceptives and Abortion in Argentina," Human Rights Watch, June 14, 2005, www.hrw.org/en/node/11694/section/1.

Egyptian and Jordanian territory. Founded by Rabbi Zvi Yehuda Kook, it believes Israel's victory in that war was a sign that God wanted Jews to settle the captured territories. Israeli authorities initially opposed such actions but did a U-turn in 1977, setting up settlements to create a buffer to protect Israel from hostile Arab neighbors. There now are some 500,000 settlers, and they have become a security headache for the Israeli government, which protects them from attacks from Palestinians who believe they have stolen their land.[80]

Meanwhile the Chabad movement — founded in the 18th century in Lubavitch, Russia, by Rabbi Schoeur Zalman — operates outside of Israel.[81] "They are very religious communities that have become missionaries, even though Jews are not supposed to convert non-Jews, and conversion is very difficult and mostly refused," says Anne Eckstein, a Belgian Jewish journalist. "They are especially active in ex-Soviet countries where the Holocaust and Soviet power wiped out the Jewish community or reduced it to a bare minimum."

Fundamentalism in India

Unlike Christianity, Islam and Judaism, which are monotheistic, Hinduism has thousands of deities representing an absolute power. In addition, it is based not on a single text but the belief that the universe is impersonal and dominated by cosmic energy.[82] Hindu fundamentalism emerged in the early 20th century, partly in reaction to proselytizing by Muslim and Christian missionaries. Some Hindus came to believe that their country needed to be made more Hindu, and that only Hindus could be loyal Indians.

Indian politician Vinayak Damodar Savarkar wrote the book *Hindutva*, the philosophical basis for Hindu fundamentalism.[83] Its cultural pillar is an organization called Vishva Hindu Parishad, founded in 1964, which has had a political wing since the 1980 establishment of the Bharatiya Janata Party, whose leader, Atal Bihari Vajpayee, was prime minister from 1998-2004.

The assertion of Hindu religious identity provoked unease among some of India's 20 million Sikhs, who worship one God and revere the *Adi Granth*, their holy book.[84] Indian Prime Minister Indira Gandhi was murdered in 1984 by two of her Sikh bodyguards in revenge for sending troops to storm the Sikhs' holiest shrine, the Golden Temple, which had been occupied by militant Sikh separatists. Hundreds of people were killed in the botched government operation.[85]

CURRENT SITUATION

Political Battles

Christian conservatives remain a potent force in American political life, even though they appear to have lost some of their political clout with the election of a liberal, pro-choice president and a decidedly more liberal Congress.

In the 2008 U.S. presidential election, evangelicals were briefly buoyed by the nomination of a Christian conservative, Alaska Gov. Sarah Palin, as the Republican vice presidential candidate. But their hopes of having another evangelical in high office were dashed when Palin and her running mate, Sen. John McCain, R-Ariz., were comfortably beaten by their Democratic rivals in November.

Palin was raised as a Pentecostal and regularly attended the Assemblies of God church in Wasilla, Alaska. In a Republican National Convention speech, she stressed the need to govern with a "servant's heart" — which in the evangelical world means Christian humility.[86]

But as details of her religious and political views were revealed, secular Americans began to question her candidacy. Video footage surfaced of her being blessed by a Kenyan pastor in 2005 who prayed for her to be protected from "every form of witchcraft" and for God to "bring finances her way" and to "use her to turn this nation the other way around."[87] Palin was also videotaped speaking at the same church in June 2008, calling a $30 billion gas pipeline project in Alaska "God's will" and the war in Iraq "a task that is from God."[88]

While Palin ultimately may have hurt the Republican ticket more than helping, the passage on Election Day of referenda banning gay marriage in several states — including California — shows that Christian conservatism remains a significant force. And across the American South and heartland, religious conservatives have pressured state and local governments to pass a variety of "family" and faith-based measures, ranging from restrictions on access to birth control and abortion to requirements that "intelligent design" be taught in place of or alongside evolution in schools. The laws have triggered ire — and a slew of lawsuits — on the part of groups intent on retaining the Constitution's separation of church and state.[89]

Is Islamic fundamentalism more dangerous than Christian fundamentalism?

YES
Maajid Nawaz
Director, Quilliam Foundation, London, England

Written for *CQ Global Researcher*, February 2009

While not all Muslim fundamentalists are a threat, certain strands of Muslim fundamentalism are more dangerous than Christian fundamentalism. This is simply a truth we must face up to as Muslims. The first stage of healing is to accept and recognize the sickness within. Until such recognition comes, we are lost.

But if Muslim fundamentalism is only a problem in certain contexts, this is not true of political Islam, or Islamism. Often confused with fundamentalism, political Islamism is a modernist project to politicize religion, rooted in the totalitarian political climate of post-World War I Egypt. But this ideology didn't restrict itself to political goals. Instead, its adherents aspired to create a modern, totalitarian state that was illiberal but not necessarily fundamentalist.

In the 1960s, the Muslim Brotherhood — Egypt's largest Islamist group — failed to impose their non-fundamentalist brand of Islam in Egypt. Instead, they fled to religiously ultra-conservative Saudi Arabia. Here they allied with reactionary fundamentalists. It is from this mix of modernist Islamism and fundamentalism that al Qaeda and jihadist terrorism emerged. It was in Saudi Arabia that Osama bin Laden was taught by Muslim Brotherhood exiles. It was from Saudi Arabia that streams of Muslim fundamentalists traveled to Afghanistan and Pakistan where they fell under the spell of the Egyptian Islamist Abdullah Azzam, another inspiration for bin Laden. The root of the present terrorist danger is the alliance between modernist political Islamists and Muslim fundamentalists.

This global jihadist terrorism — modern in its political ideals and tactics yet medieval in both its religious jurisprudence and justification for violence — is more dangerous than Christian fundamentalism. I believe that such terrorism, far from representing the fundamentals of Islam, is actually un-Islamic. However, a Christian may similarly argue that attacking abortion clinics is un-Christian. We both need to acknowledge the role that religion plays in motivating such individuals.

So, having recognized this problem, how can Muslims tackle it? It is not enough for Muslims to merely take a stand against terrorism and the killing of innocent civilians. This is the very least that should be expected of any decent human being. Muslims must also challenge both conservative fundamentalism and the modern Islamist ideology behind jihadist terrorism. Islamism is to blame, alongside Western support for dictatorships, for the situation we face today.

NO
Radwan Masmoudi
President, Center for the Study of Islam and Democracy, Washington, D.C.

Written for *CQ Global Researcher*, February 2009

The term "fundamentalism" can be misleading, because the overwhelming majority of Muslims believe the Koran is the literal word of God and a guide for the individual, the family and society to follow on everything social, political and economic. In a recent Gallup Poll, more than 75 percent of Muslims — from Morocco to Indonesia — said they believe Islamic laws should be either the only source or one of the main sources of laws in their countries. Under a U.S. definition of "fundamentalism," these people would all be considered "fundamentalists."

However, the overwhelming majority of Muslims are peaceful and reject violence and extremism. In the same poll, more than 85 percent of Muslims surveyed said they believe democracy is the best form of government. Thus, they are not interested in imposing their views on others but wish to live according to the teachings of their religion while respecting people of other religions or opinions. Democracy and respect for human rights — including minority rights and women's rights — are essential in any society that respects and practices Islamic values.

It would be a terrible mistake to consider all fundamentalist Muslims a threat to the United States or to mankind. Radical and violent Muslim extremist groups such as al Qaeda and the Taliban represent a tiny minority of all Muslims and a fringe minority of religious (or fundamentalist) Muslims. These extremist groups are a threat both to their own societies and to the West. But they do not represent the majority opinion among religious-based groups that are struggling to build more Islamic societies through peaceful means.

Many Christian fundamentalist groups have resorted to violence, specifically attacks against abortion clinics in the United States. In addition, prominent Christian fundamentalist leaders, such as John Hagee, Pat Robertson and others say Islam is the enemy and have called for the United States to invade Muslim countries like Iraq, Afghanistan and even Iran. These wars have cost the lives of more than 1 million innocent people in these countries and could still cause further deaths and destruction around the world. The devout of all faiths should condemn the killing of innocents and the self-serving labeling of any religion as the "enemy" against which war should be waged. Surely, one — whether Muslim or Christian — can be extremely devout and religious without calling for violence or hoping for Armageddon.

AFP/Getty Images/Yehuda Raizner

AFP/Getty Images/Gali Tibbon

Jewish Settlements Stir Outrage and Support

Left-wing Israelis criticize Israel last December for allowing fundamentalist Jews to build settlements in the Palestinian territories (top). Evangelicals from the U.S.-based Christians United for Israel movement (bottom) support the settlements during a rally in Jerusalem last April. Many analysts say pressure from American fundamentalist Christians led former President George W. Bush, a born-again Christian, to offer unqualified support for Israel and to invade Iraq — policies that have exacerbated U.S.-Muslim relations

Meanwhile, thousands of conservative Episcopalians in the United States have abandoned their church because of the hierarchy's tolerance of homosexuality and are teaming up with Anglican Protestants in Africa who share their conservative views.[90]

In Latin America, evangelical television preachers are using their fame to launch themselves into politics, notes Dennis Smith, a U.S.-born Presbyterian mission worker who has lived in Guatemala since 1977. He says that in

Brazil, Pentecostal preacher Edir Macedo cut a deal with President Luiz Inacio Lula de Silva in which Macedo got to hand-pick the country's vice president. In Guatemala Harold Caballeros, a Pentecostal who preaches that the Mayan Indians there have made a pact with the devil by clinging to their traditional beliefs, is trying to become president, Smith adds.

In Africa, the Somali parliament on Jan. 31 elected a moderate Islamist cleric, Sheik Sharif Ahmed, as the country's new president. The election occurred just as the hard-line Islamist al-Shabaab militia took control of the central Somali town of Baidoa and began imposing its harsh brand of Islamic law there.[91]

Rising Violence

Attacks on Christian minorities in Iraq and India — and efforts to forcibly convert them — have escalated in recent months.

In November militants said to be from the Pakistan-based Lashkar-e-Taiba carried out a meticulously planned attack in Mumbai, India, killing 164 people in a shooting spree that targeted hotels frequented by Western tourists.[92] Ex-Islamist Nawaz says of the group: "I know them well. They want to reconquer India. They see it as being under Hindu occupation now because it was once ruled by Muslim emperors of Turko-Mongol descent. They use the territorial dispute between India and Pakistan over the sovereignty of Kashmir as a pretext for pursuing their global jihad agenda."

Lisa Curtis, a research fellow for South Asia at the Heritage Foundation in Washington, believes that Pakistan is playing a sinister role here. "The Pakistan military's years of support for jihadist groups fighting in Afghanistan and India," she says, is "intensifying linkages between Pakistani homegrown terrorists and al Qaeda."

India's suspicion that forces within the Pakistani government have given Lashkar-e-Taiba a free rein is further straining an already tense relationship between the two nations.

The Lashkar attackers also killed two young Jewish missionaries, Rabbi Gavriel Holtzberg and his wife Rivkah, in an assault on the Chabad center in Mumbai, where they had been based since 2003. While some accuse the Chabad of proselytizing, Rabbi Avi Tawil, who studied with U.S.-born Gavriel Holtzberg for two years in

Argentina, insists, "He did not force anyone to accept his philosophy. He was doing social work — working with prisoners for example."

But the Mumbai attacks were not the only violence perpetrated by religious extremists in India last year. Between August and December, members of the paramilitary, right-wing Hindu group Bajrang Dal — using the rallying cry "kill Christians and destroy their institutions" — murdered dozens of Christians, including missionaries and priests, burned 3,000 homes and destroyed more than 130 churches in Orissa state.[93] The attackers were angered at proselytizing by Pentecostal missionaries in the region and tried to force Christians to convert back to Hinduism.[94]

Martha Nussbaum, a professor of law and ethics at the University of Chicago and author of the recent book *The Clash Within: Democracy, Religious Violence and India's Future*, writes that no one should be surprised right-wing Hindus "have embraced ethno-religious cleansing." Since the 1930s, "their movement has insisted that India is for Hindus, and that both Muslims and Christians are foreigners who should have second-class status in the nation."[95]

India's bloodiest religiously based violence in recent years was the slaughter of up to 2,000 Muslim civilians by Hindu mobs in Gujarat state in 2002.[96] A Bajrang Dal leader boasted: "There was this pregnant woman, I slit her open. . . . They shouldn't even be allowed to breed. . . . Whoever they are, women, children, whoever . . . thrash them, slash them, burn the bastards. . . . The idea is, don't keep them alive at all; after that, everything is ours."[97]

In Iraq last fall, in the northern city of Mosul, some 400 Christian families were forced to flee their homes after attacks by Sunni Muslim extremists.[98]

In Nigeria, sectarian violence between Christians and Muslims in the city of Jos spiked again in late November, leaving at least 300 dead in the worst clashes since 2004, when 700 people died. Religious violence in Nigeria tends to break out in the "middle belt" between the Muslim north and the predominantly Christian south.[99]

Then in December Israel launched a massive offensive against the Islamist Hamas government in the Gaza Strip, in response to Hamas' continuous rocket attacks into Israel; at least 1,300 Palestinians died during the 22-day assault. An uneasy truce now exists, but Hamas remains defiant,

refusing to accept Israel's right to exist and vowing to fight for the creation of an Islamic Palestinian state in its place.[100]

While most commentators focus on the political dimension of the conflict, Belgian Jewish journalist Anne Eckstein is as concerned about Hamas' religious extremism. "I see nothing in them apart from hatred and death to all who are not Muslims. . . . Jews first but then Christians and everybody else. And those who believe that this is not a war of civilization are very mistaken."

Also in December, troops from, Uganda, southern Sudan and the Democratic Republic of Congo launched a joint offensive to catch Lord's Resistance Army (LRA) leader Kony.[101] The LRA retaliated, massacring hundreds. Kenya-based evangelical Professor Nkansah insists the LRA is "not really religious — no one has ever seen them praying. They are just playing to the Christian communities in Uganda. If they were true Christians, they would not be destroying human life like they are."

Even in areas where religious violence has not broken out, a certain fundamentalist-secular tension exists. In the United Kingdom, for example, a debate has broken out over whether Muslim communities should be allowed to handle family matters — such as divorce and domestic violence cases — in Muslim courts that apply Islamic law. These increasingly common tribunals, despite having no standing under British law, have "become magnets for Muslim women seeking to escape loveless marriages."[102] In Africa, the Tanzanian parliament is having a similar debate, with proponents noting that Kenya, Rwanda and Uganda have had such courts for decades.[103]

In Israel, the majority-secular Jewish population has begun to resent ultra-Orthodox Jewish men who subsist on welfare while immersing themselves in perpetual study of the holy texts. "They claim this is what Jews did in the past, but this is nonsense," says Jerusalem-based journalist Gorenberg, who notes that ultra-Orthodox wives often work outside the home in order to support their very large families. The Haredim are trying to restore ancient Judaism by weaving priestly garments in the traditional way, producing a red heifer using genetic engineering and raising boys in a special compound kept ritually pure for 13 years, says Gorenberg, a fierce critic of fundamentalist Jews.[104]

Many secular Israelis also resent the religious Jews that have settled in the Palestinian territories, arguing they make Muslims hate Israel even more and thus threaten Israel's very security.

OUTLOOK

More of the Same?

Al Qaeda's Egyptian-born chief strategist, Ayman Al-Zawihiri, is very clear about his goal. "The victory of Islam will never take place until a Muslim state is established in the heart of the Islamic world, specifically in the Levant [Eastern Mediterranean], Egypt and the neighboring states of the [Arabian] Peninsula and Iraq."[105]

Former-Islamist Nawaz says such a state would not, as fundamentalists claim, be a return to the past but a modernist creation, having more in common with the totalitarian regimes of 20th-century Europe than with the tolerant Islamic caliphates in the Middle Ages. He thinks Islamists have the greatest chance of seizing power in Egypt and Uzbekistan.

Given the Islamization that she has observed on numerous visits to Uzbekistan, Martha Brill Olcott, a senior associate at the Carnegie Endowment for International Peace in Washington, predicts the country will not remain secular. Because the Muslims there are Sunni, she thinks they will follow an Egyptian or Pakistani model of government.

Georgetown Professor Dallal predicts Iran will remain the world's only theocracy. "I do not think the Iranian model will be replicated," he says. "The religious elite is more institutionalized and entrenched there than elsewhere."

And although young Iranians are more secular than their parents and have been disenchanted with the religious rulers, "We should not assume this is a deep-rooted trend," warns Iranian-born author Hunter. "Look at Arab countries: Forty years ago we thought they were going secular, but not now."

As for Islamist militancy, the signs are mixed. While a Pew survey showed a drop in support for global jihad among Muslims overall, it also found that young Muslims in the United States were more likely to support radical Islam than their parents. Fifteen percent of 18-29-year-olds thought suicide bombing could be justified compared to just 6 percent of those over 30.[106]

And even if, as some analysts suggest, al Qaeda is faltering, other Islamist groups may thrive, such as Hezbollah in Lebanon, Hamas in Gaza and Pakistan's Lashkar-e-Taiba. They attract popular support because they also provide social services, unlike al Qaeda, whose bloody campaigns have alienated most Muslims.[107]

The Israel-Palestine conflict, intractable as ever, will continue to be grist for the Islamist mill. Bin Laden has urged Muslims to "kill the Americans and their allies [and] to liberate the Al-Aqsa Mosque," which is located on the Temple Mount in Jerusalem that Israel has controlled since 1967.[108]

In the Palestinian territories, "Islamist symbols, discourses and practices have become widely disseminated across the factional spectrum," according to Ohio State's Lybarger, but whether it continues depends on the actions of Israel, the United States and other Arab states toward Palestine, he says.[109] Many observers hope President Obama and his newly-appointed Middle East envoy George Mitchell will be able to broker a peace deal, given Obama's aggressive outreach to the Muslim world.

In the United States, the Christian right is likely to remain strong, even as Obama moves to overhaul Bush's faith-based initiatives. Secularists may ask Obama to prohibit groups receiving government funds from discriminating in hiring based on religious beliefs. "Hiring based on religious affiliation is justified," says Stanley Carlson-Thies, director of the Center for Public Justice in Washington, D.C. "Would you ask a senator not to ask about political ideology when selecting staff? A ban would [be] a sweeping change."[110]

Looking farther afield, Baptist minister Land says "by 2025 the majority of Christians . . . will be African, Latin American and Asian. That is where evangelical Christianity is growing fastest." The fastest-growing Christian denominations are in Nigeria, Sudan, Angola, South Africa, India, China and the Philippines, according to the World Christian Database.[111]

But Kenya's Nkansah doubts that Christian-based political parties will emerge in sub-Saharan Africa. "In North Africa almost everyone is Muslim, so it is easier to have Islamic parties. But here, there is more of a mix, and politicians do not want to create unnecessary tensions."

In Guatemala, American Presbyterian missionary Smith says, "Since neither modernity nor democracy has been able to bring security, the rule of law, social tolerance or broad-based economic development" evangelical television preachers will "continue to have great power for the foreseeable future."

Meanwhile, a glimpse of Asia's future might be found in South Korea. "As dusk turns to dark in this capital city," journalist Mosettig wrote, "the skyline glitters with more than the urban lights of office towers and apartment blocks. From the hills that define Seoul's topography and neighborhoods, it is easy to spot lighted electric crosses. They are among the most visible reminders of just how deeply Christianity shapes South Korea."[112]

NOTES

1. Richard A. Oppel Jr. and Pir Zubair Shah, "In Pakistan, Radio Amplifies Terror of Taliban," *The New York Times*, Jan. 24, 2009, www.nytimes .com/2009/01/25/world/asia/25swat.html?_r=1& scp=1&sq=Taliban%20Pakistan &st=cse.

2. "The U.S. Religious Landscape Survey," Pew Forum on Religion and Public Life, Feb. 25, 2008, p. 170, http://religions.pewforum.org.

3. Michelle Goldberg, *Kingdom Coming: The Rise of Christian Nationalism* (2007), p. 7.

4. *Ibid.*, p. 8.

5. Dominionism, Goldberg notes, is derived from a theocratic sect called Christian Reconstructionism, which advocates replacing American civil law with Old Testament biblical law.

6. See World Evangelical Alliance Web site, www .worldevangelicals.org. For background, see David Masci, "Evangelical Christians," *CQ Researcher*, Sept. 14, 2001, pp. 713-736.

7. Quoted in Eliza Griswold, "God's Country," *The Atlantic*, March 2008, www.theatlantic.com/ doc/200803/nigeria.

8. Michael Mossetig, "Among Sea of Glittery Crosses, Christianity Makes Its Mark in South Korea," PBS, Nov. 5, 2007, www.pbs.org/newshour/indepth_ coverage/asia/koreas/2007/report_11-05.html. For background, see Alan Greenblatt and Tracey Powell, "Rise of Megachurches," *CQ Researcher*, Sept. 21, 2007, pp. 769-792.

9. Presentation by Wang Zuoan, China's deputy administrator of religious affairs, Sept. 11, 2008, at the Brookings Institution, Washington, D.C.

10. Estimates provided by Samuel Heilman, Sociology Professor and expert on Jewish fundamentalism at City University of New York.

11. "Christians Attacked in Two States of India" World Evangelical Alliance Web site, Dec. 15, 2008, www .worldevangelicals.org/news/view. htm?id=2277.

12. Loren D. Lybarger, *Identity and Religion in Palestine: The Struggle between Islamism and Secularism in the Occupied Territories* (2007), p. 73.

13. See National Counter Terrorism Center's Worldwide Incidents Tracking System, http://wits.nctc.gov.

14. The Shia, who make up 15 percent of the world's 1.4 billion Muslims, believe only the prophet Mohammad's family and descendants should serve as Muslim leaders (imams). Sunnis — who make up the other 85 percent — believe any Muslim can be an imam. Iran is the world's most Shia-dominated country, while there are also significant Shia communities in Iraq, Turkey, Lebanon, Syria, Kuwait, Bahrain, Saudi Arabia, Yemen, Pakistan and Azerbaijan.

15. Lybarger, *op. cit.*

16. "Sharia stoning for Nigeria man," BBC News, May 17, 2007, http://news.bbc.co.uk/ 2/hi/africa/666 6673.stm.

17. For background, see John Felton, "Child Soldiers," *CQ Global Researcher*, July, 2008.

18. Scott Shane, "Global Forecast by American Intelligence Expects Al Qaeda's Appeal to Falter," *The New York Times*, Nov. 20, 2008, www.nytimes .com/2008/11/21/world/21intel.html?_r=1&emc=tnt &tntemail0=y.

19. "Country Reports on Terrorism," Office of the Coordinator for Counterterrorism, U.S. Department of State, April 2008, www.state.gov/documents/ organization/105904.pdf.

20. Martin Marty and R. Scott Appleby, eds., *Funda-mentalisms Comprehended* (The Fundamentalism Project), 2004, University of Chicago Press.

21. Source: Talk by Egyptian scholar and human rights activist Saad Eddin Ibrahim, at Woodrow Wilson

International Center for Scholars, Washington, D.C., Sept. 8, 2008.

22. For background, see Brian Beary, "Future of Turkey," *CQ Global Researcher*, December 2007.

23. Raja Kamal, "Israel's fundamentalist Jews are multiplying," *The Japan Times*, Aug. 21, 2008, http://search.japantimes.co.jp/cgi-bin/eo 20080821a1.html.

24. *Ibid.*

25. Mike Madden, "Sundown on Colorado fundamentalists," *Salon.com*, Nov. 2, 2008, www.salon.com/news/feature/2008/11/03/newlifechurch/index.html?source=rss&aim=/news/feature.

26. Susan Jacoby, "Religion remains fundamental to US politics," *The Times* (London), Oct. 31, 2008, www.timesonline.co.uk/tol/comment/columnists/guest_contributors/article505 0685.ece.

27. "Human Security Brief 2007," Human Security Report Project, Simon Fraser University, Canada, May 21, 2008, www.humansecuritybrief.info.

28. "Unfavorable views of Jews and Muslims on the Increase in Europe," Pew Research Center, Sept. 17, 2008, p. 4, http://pewglobal. org/reports/pdf/262.pdf.

29. *Ibid.*

30. Andrew MacIntyre and Douglas E. Ramage, "Seeing Indonesia as a normal country: Implications for Australia," Australian Strategic Policy Institute, May 2008, www.aspi.org. au/publications/publication_details.aspx?ContentID=169&pubtype=5.

31. Michael Sullivan, "Megachurch Symbolizes Indonesia's Tolerance," National Public Radio, Oct. 19, 2008, www.npr.org/templates/story/ story.php?storyId=95847081.

32. Comments from Pew Forum on Religion and Public Life discussion, "Between Relativism and Fundamentalism: Is There a Middle Ground?" March 4, 2008, Washington, D.C., http://pewforum.org/events/?EventID=172.

33. Sarah Glazer, "Radical Islam in Europe," *CQ Global Researcher*, November 2007.

34. Sayyid Qutb, *Milestones*, *SIME* (Studies in Islam and the Middle East) *Journal*, 2005, p. 125, http://majalla.org/books/2005/qutb-nilestone.pdf.

35. Lybarger, *op. cit.*

36. See Goldberg, *op. cit.*, p. 8.

37. *Ibid.*, p. 208.

38. "Human Security Brief 2007," *op. cit.*, p. 19.

39. Osama Bin Laden, "Text of Fatwa Urging Jihad Against Americans," Feb. 23, 1998, in John J. Donohue and John L. Esposito, *Islam in Transition: Muslim Perspectives* (2007), pp. 430-432.

40. "Tanzania: Muslim paper says war on terror guise to fight Islam," BBC Worldwide Monitoring, Aug. 24, 2008 (translation from Swahili of article in Tanzanian weekly Islamic newspaper *An-Nuur*, Aug. 15, 2008).

41. Barbara Crossette, "The World: (Mid) East Meets (Far) East; A Challenge to Asia's Own Style of Islam," *The New York Times*, Dec. 30, 2001.

42. Pew Global Attitudes Project, "Islamic Extremism: Common Concern for Muslim and Western Publics," July 14, 2005, p. 25, http:// pewglobal.org/reports/pdf/248.pdf.

43. Griswold, *op. cit.*

44. Zaki Chehab, *Inside Hamas — The Untold Story of the Militant Islamic Movement* (2007), p. 104.

45. Gabriel Almond, Scott Appleby and Emmanuel Sivan, *Strong Religion: The Rise of Fundamentalisms Around the World* (The Fundamentalism Project), The University of Chicago Press, 2003, p. 110.

46. Rachid Ghannouchi, "The Participation of Islamists in a Non-Islamic Government," in Donohue and Esposito, *op. cit.*, pp. 271-278.

47. Jason Burke, "Don't believe myths about sharia law," *The Guardian* (United Kingdom), Feb. 10, 2008, www.guardian.co.uk/ world/2008/feb/10/religion.law1. For background, see Robert Kiener, "Crisis in Pakistan" *CQ Global Researcher*, December 2008, pp. 321-348.

48. Oppel and Shah, *op. cit.*

49. Brenda E. Brasher, *Encyclopedia of Fundamentalism* (2001), p. 397.

50. *Ibid.*, pp. 202-204.

51. *Ibid.*, pp. 465-467.

52. *Ibid.*, p. 186.

53. For background, see the following *CQ Researchers*: Kenneth Jost, "Religion and Politics," Oct. 14, 1994, pp. 889-912; and David Masci, "Religion and Politics," July 30, 2004, pp. 637-660.

54. For background, see Rachel S. Cox, "Home Schooling Debate," *CQ Researcher*, Jan. 17, 2003, pp. 25-48.

55. David Holthouse, "Casting Stones: An Army of radical Christian Reconstructionists is preparing a campaign to convert conservative fundamentalist churches," Southern Law Poverty Center, winter 2005, www.splcenter.org/ intel/intelreport/article .jsp?aid=591.

56. Brasher, *op. cit.*, pp. 407-409.

57. *Ibid.*, p. 86.

58. *Ibid.*

59. Adrian Wooldridge, "The Theocons: Secular America Under Siege," *International Herald Tribune*, Sept. 26, 2006, www.iht.com/articles/2006/09/25/ opinion/booktue.php.

60. See Paul Harris, "Bush says God chose him to lead his nation," *The Guardian*, Nov. 2, 2003, www.guardian .co.uk/world/2003/nov/02/usa.religion; and Melissa Rogers and E. J. Dionne Jr., "Serving People in Need, Safeguarding Religious Freedom: Recommendations for the New Administration on Partnerships with Faith-Based Organizations," The Brookings Institution, December 2008, www.brookings.edu/ papers/2008/12_religion_dionne.aspx. For background, see Sarah Glazer, "Faith-based Initiatives," *CQ Researcher*, May 4, 2001, pp. 377-400.

61. James Carroll, "Religious comfort for bin Laden," *The Boston Globe*, Sept. 15, 2008, www.boston.com/ news/nation/articles/2008/ 09/15/religious_comfort_ for_bin_laden.

62. For background, see Dan Eggen and Paul Kane, "Goodling Says She 'Crossed the Line'; Ex-Justice Aide Criticizes Gonzales While Admitting to Basing Hires on Politics," *The Washington Post*, May 24, 2007, p. A1.

63. Brasher, *op. cit.*, p. 154.

64. Almond, Appleby and Sivan, *op. cit.*, p. 171.

65. Cedric Mayson, "Religious Fundamentalism in South Africa," African National Congress Commission for Religious Affairs, January 2007, http://thebrenthurst- foundation.co.za/Files/terror_talks/Religious%20 Fundamentalism%20in%20SA.pdf.

66. Rob Crilly, "Lord's Resistance Army uses truce to rearm and spread its gospel of fear," *The Times* (London), Dec. 16, 2008, www.timesonline.co.uk/tol/ news/world/africa/article5348890.ece.

67. *Ibid.*

68. Brasher, *op. cit.*, p. 37.

69. For background, see Peter Katel, "Global Jihad," *CQ Researcher*, Oct. 14, 2005, pp. 857-880.

70. Almond, Appleby and Sivan, *op. cit.*, pp. 177-79.

71. Brasher, *op. cit.*, p. 37.

72. "Human Security Brief 2007," *op. cit.*

73. For background, see Glazer, "Radical Islam in Europe," *op. cit.*

74. "World Christian Database," Center for the Study of Global Christianity, Gordon-Conwell Theological Seminary, www.worldchristiandatabase.org/wcd/ home.asp.

75. "Muslim Americans: Middle Class and Mostly Mainstream," Pew Forum on Religion and Public Life, May 22, 2007, p. 4, http://pewforum.org/surveys/ muslim-american.

76. Chehab, *op. cit.*, pp. 134-150.

77. Brasher, *op. cit.*, p. 255.

78. "World Christian Database," *op. cit.*

79. Brasher, *op. cit.*, p. 255.

80. *Ibid.*, p. 204.

81. See American Friends of Lubavitch Washington, D.C., www.afldc.org.

82. Brasher, *op. cit.*, p. 222.

83. Almond, Appleby and Sivan, *op. cit.*, pp. 136-139.

84. *Ibid.*, pp. 157-159.

85. *Ibid.*

86. John L. Allen Jr., "McCain's choice a nod not only to women, but post-denominationalists," *National Catholic Reporter*, Aug. 30, 2008, http://ncrcafe.org/ node/2073.

87. Garance Burke, "Palin once blessed to be free from witchcraft," The Associated Press, Sept. 25, 2008,

http://abcnews.go.com/Politics/wireStory?id=5881256. Video footage at www.youtube.com/watch?v=QIOD5X68lIs.

88. Alexander Schwabe, "Sarah Palin's Religion: God and the Vice-Presidential Candidate," *Spiegel* online, Sept. 10, 2008, www.spiegel.de/international/world/0,1518,577440,00.html. Video footage at www.youtube.com/ watch?v=QG1vPYbRB7k.

89. For background see the following *CQ Researchers*: Marcia Clemmitt, "Intelligent Design," July 29, 2005, pp. 637-660; Kenneth Jost and Kathy Koch, "Abortion Showdowns," Sept. 22, 2006, pp. 769-792; Kenneth Jost, "Abortion Debates," March 21, 2003, pp. 249-272; and Marcia Clemmitt, "Birth-control Debate," June 24, 2005, pp. 565-588.

90. See Karla Adam, "Gay Bishop Dispute Dominates Conference; Anglican Event Ends With Leader's Plea," *The Washington Post*, Aug. 4, 2008, p. A8.

91. Jeffrey Gettleman and Mohammed Ibrahim, "Somalis cheer the selection of a moderate Islamist cleric as President," *The New York Times*, Feb. 1, 2009, www.nytimes.com/2009/02/01/world/africa/01somalia.html.

92. Ramola Talwar Badam, "Official: India received intel on Mumbai attacks," The Associated Press, *Denver Post*, Dec. 1, 2008, www.denverpost.com/business/ci_11111305.

93. Somini Sengupta, "Hindu Threat to Christians: Convert or Flee," *The New York Times*, Oct. 12, 2008, www.nytimes.com/2008/10/13/ world/asia/13india.html?pagewanted=1&_r=1&sq=Christianspercent20India&st=cse&scp=1.

94. "Indian Christians Petition PM for Peace in Orissa at Christmas," World Evangelical Alliance Web site, Dec. 14, 2008, www.worldevangelicals.org/news/view.htm?id=2276.

95. Martha Nussbaum, "Terrorism in India has many faces," *Los Angeles Times*, Nov. 30, 2008, p. A35.

96. For background, see David Masci, "Emerging India," *CQ Researcher*, April 19, 2002, pp. 329-360.

97. Quoted in Nussbaum, *op. cit.*

98. "Iraq: Christians trickling back to their homes in Mosul," IRIN (humanitarian news and analysis service of the U.N. Office for the Coordination of Humanitarian Affairs), Nov. 6, 2008, www.irinnews.org/Report.aspx? ReportId=81317.

99. Ahmed Saka, "Death toll over 300 in Nigerian sectarian violence, The Associated Press, Nov. 29, 2008," www.denverpost.com/breakingnews/ci_11101598.

100. Gilad Shalit, "Hamas rejects Israel's Gaza cease-fire conditions," *Haaretz*, Jan. 28, 2009, www.haaretz.com/hasen/spages/1059593.html.

101. Scott Baldauf, "Africans join forces to fight the LRA," *The Christian Science Monitor*, Dec. 16, 2008, www.csmonitor.com/2008/ 1217/p06s01-woaf.html.

102. Elaine Sciolino, "Britain Grapples With Role for Islamic Justice," *The New York Times*, Nov. 18, 2008, www.nytimes.com/2008/ 11/19/world/europe/19shariah.html?_r=1&emc=tnt&tntemail0=y.

103. "Tanzania: Islamic Courts Debate Splits Legislators," *The Citizen* (newsletter, source: Africa News), Aug. 14, 2008.

104. Gershom Gorenberg, "The Temple Institute of Doom, or Hegel Unzipped," *South Jerusalem* (Blog), July 8, 2008, http://southjerusalem.com/2008/07/the-temple-institute-of-doom-or-hegel-unzipped.

105. See Katel, *op. cit.*, p. 859.

106. "Muslim Americans: Middle Class and Mostly Mainstream," *op. cit.*

107. Scott Shane, "Global Forecast by American Intelligence Expects Al Qaeda's Appeal to Falter," *The New York Times*, Nov. 20, 2008, www.nytimes.com/2008/11/21/world/21intel.html?_r=1&emc=tnt&tntemail0=y.

108. Bin Laden, *op. cit.*

109. Lybarger, *op. cit.*, p. 244.

110. Carlson-Thies was speaking at a discussion on faith-based initiatives organized by the Brookings Institution in Washington, D.C. on Dec. 5, 2008.

111. See 'fastest growing denominations' category in "World Christian Database," *op. cit.*

112. Michael Mosettig, "Among Sea of Glittery Crosses, Christianity Makes its Mark in South Korea," Nov. 5, 2007, Public Broadcasting Service, www.pbs.org/newshour/indepth_coverage/asia/koreas/2007/report_11-05.html.

BIBLIOGRAPHY

Books

Almond, Gabriel A., Scott Appleby and Emmanuel Sivan, *Strong Religion: The Rise of Fundamentalisms Around the World, University of Chicago Press,* **2003.**
Three history professors synthesize the findings of a five-volume project that looks at 75 forms of religious fundamentalism around the world.

Brasher, Brenda E., ed., *Encyclopedia of Fundamentalism, Routledge,* **2001.**
Academics provide an A-Z on Christian fundamentalism — from its origins in the United States to its spread to other countries and religions.

Donohue, John J., and John L. Esposito, *Islam in Transition: Muslim Perspectives, Oxford University Press,* **2007.**
Essays by Muslim thinkers address key questions, such as the role of women in Islam, the relationship between Islam and democracy and the clash between Islam and the West.

Lybarger, Loren D., *Identity and Religion in Palestine: The Struggle between Islamism and Secularism in the Occupied Territories, Princeton University Press,* **2007.**
A U.S. sociologist who spent several years in the Palestinian territories explores how groups promoting fundamentalist Islam have gradually eclipsed secular nationalism as the dominant political force.

Thomas, Pradip Ninan, *Strong Religion, Zealous Media: Christian Fundamentalism and Communication in India, SAGE Publications,* **2008.**
An associate professor of journalism at the University of Queensland, Australia, examines the influence of U.S televangelists in India and the battle for cultural power between Hindu, Muslim and Christian fundamentalists. SAGE is the publisher of *CQ Global Researcher.*

Articles

"The Palestinians: Split by geography and by politics," *The Economist,* **Feb. 23, 2008, www.economist.com/ world/mideast-africa/displaystory.cfm?story_id=10740648.**
The secular organization Fatah controls the West Bank while the Islamist group Hamas is in charge in Gaza.

Crilly, Rob, "Lord's Resistance Army uses truce to rearm and spread its gospel of fear," *The Times* **(London), Dec. 16, 2008, www.timesonline.co.uk/tol/news/world/africa/article5348890.ece.**
A violent military campaign led by Ugandan Christian fundamentalists threatens to destabilize the neighboring region.

Griswold, Eliza, "God's Country," *The Atlantic,* **March 2008, pp. 40-56, www.theatlantic.com/doc/200803/nigeria.**
An author recounts her visit to Nigeria, a deeply religious country where Christian and Muslim clerics compete to grow their flocks, and religious tensions often spill over into violence.

Tavernise, Sabrina, "Independent, Tajiks Revel in Their Faith," *The New York Times,* **Jan. 3, 2009, www.nytimes.com/2009/01/04/world/asia/04tajik.html?emc=tnt&tntemail0=y.**
The Central Asian republic has become increasingly Islamic since its independence from the Soviet Union, with strong influence from Saudi Arabia.

Traynor, Ian, "Denmark's political provocateur: Feminist, socialist, Muslim?" *The Guardian,* **May 16, 2008, www.guardian.co.uk/world/2007/may/16/religion.uk.**
The controversial Danish politician Asmaa Abdol-Hamid, a devout Muslim, hopes to become the first person elected to the Danish parliament to wear the Islamic headscarf.

Reports and Studies

"Islamic Extremism: Common Concern for Muslim and Western Publics," *The Pew Global Attitudes Project,* **July 14, 2005, http://pewglobal.org/reports/pdf/248.pdf.**
A U.S.-based research center surveys public opinion in 17 countries on why Islamic extremism is growing.

MacIntyre, Andrew and Douglas E. Ramage, "Seeing Indonesia as a normal country: Implications for Australia," *Australian Strategic Policy Institute,* **May 2008, www.aspi.org.au/publications/publication_details.aspx?ContentID=169&pubtype=5.**
Two Australian academics argue that claims of rampant Islamic fundamentalism in Indonesia — the world's most populous Muslim country — are exaggerated.

Mayson, Cedric, "Religious Fundamentalism in South Africa," *African National Congress, Commission for Religious Affairs*, January 2007, http://thebren thurstfoundation.co.za/Files/terror_talks/Religious %20Fundamentalism%20in%20SA.pdf.
A South African activist blames growing fundamentalism in South Africa on U.S. Christian fundamentalists.

Olcott, Martha Brill and Diora Ziyaeva, "Islam in Uzbekistan: Religious Education and State Ideology," *Carnegie Endowment for International Peace*, July 2008, www.carnegieendowment.org/publications/ index.cfm?fa=view&id=21980&prog=zru.
Two academics chart the growth of Islam in the Central Asian republic.

For More Information

Association of Evangelicals in Africa, www.aeafrica.org. A continent-wide coalition of 33 national evangelical alliances and 34 mission agencies that aims to "mobilize and unite" evangelicals in Africa for a "total transformation of our communities."

European Jewish Community Centre, 109 Rue Froissart, 1040 Brussels, Belgium; (32) 2-233-1828; www.ejcc.eu. Office of the Chabad Jewish missionary movement's delegation to the European Union.

Evangelical Graduate School of Theology, N.E.G.S.T., P.O. Box 24686, Karen 00502, Nairobi, Kenya; (254) 020-3002415; www.negst.edu. An Evangelical Christian institution devoted to the study of religion in Africa.

Forum 18 News Service, Postboks 6603, Rodeløkka, N-0502 Oslo, Norway; www.forum18.org. News agency reporting on government-sponsored repression of religion in Central Asia.

Organisation of the Islamic Conference, P.O. Box 178, Jeddah 21411, Saudi Arabia; (966) 690-0001; www.oic-oci .org. Intergovernmental organization with 57 member states, which promotes the interests of the Muslim world.

The Oxford Centre for Hindu Studies, 15 Magdalen St., Oxford OX1 3AE, United Kingdom; (44) (0)1865-304-300; www.ochs.org.uk. Experts in Hindu culture, religion, languages, literature, philosophy, history, arts and society.

Pew Forum on Religion and Public Life, 1615 L St., N.W., Suite 700, Washington, DC 20036-5610; (202) 202-419-4550; http://pewforum.org. Publishes surveys on religiosity, including fundamentalist beliefs, conducted around the world.

World Christian Database, BRILL, P.O. Box 9000, 2300 PA Leiden, The Netherlands; (31) (0)71-53-53-566; www.worldchristiandatabase.org. Provides detailed statistical data on numbers of believers, by religious affiliation; linked to U.S.-based Center for the Study of Global Christianity, Gordon-Conwell Theological Seminary.

World Evangelical Alliance, Suite 1153, 13351 Commerce Parkway, Richmond, BC V6V 2X7 Canada; (1) 604-214-8620; www.worldevangelicals.org. Network for evangelical Christian churches around the world.

Worldwide Incidents Tracking System, National Counter Terrorism Center, University of Maryland, College Park, MD 20742; (301) 405-1000; http://wits.nctc.gov. Provides detailed statistics on religiously inspired terrorist attacks across the world from 2004-2008.

Voices From Abroad:

VALERIA MARTANO

Nun, Community of Sant'Egidio, Rome

Putting differences aside

"I want to keep my religion, and you want to keep yours. But instead of emphasizing our differences, which can cause tension, we must start to do something about the real problems faced by humanity."

Jakarta Post (Indonesia),
June 2008

JOHN ALDERDICE

President, Liberal International, London

The prize and price of peace

"Until people in any conflict [have already] begun to turn away from violence as a means of solving their predicament, they are unlikely to be prepared to accept that the prize of peace is worth the price of peace."

Irish Times, August 2008

RUTH KELLY

Communities Secretary, Great Britain

Shutting doors to division

"Success today will hinge on forging a new alliance against violent extremism. We need to reach out and give greater support to the overwhelming majority who are disgusted by terrorist attacks carried out in the name of Islam. The good sense and decency of the vast majority of people in this country has ensured no type of extremism has ever got a mainstream foothold here. But we need to make sure those who stand up don't stand alone. . . . We need to support people in building communities where extremism is resolutely tackled and isolated, and where all doors are shut to those who seek division and violence."

Government News Network (England), April 2007

EMMANUEL UCHECHUKWU IHEAGWAM

Bishop, Anglican Diocese of Egbu, Nigeria

Violence isn't exclusive to any religion

"The Jos saga has clearly demonstrated that violence was not the exclusive preserve of any ethnic or religious group. With what happened in Jos, including the burning of churches and mosques, Nigerians should learn to live in peace, political, ethnic and religious differences notwithstanding."

Vanguard (Nigeria), December 2008

ALEJANDRO SESELOVSKY

Author, Argentina

An appetite for conquest

"The evangelical church has an appetite for conquest, for the social and political conquest that the Catholic Church had 500 years ago."

Turkish Daily News, March 2007

PERVEZ MUSHARRAF

Former President, Pakistan

A possible spread to Europe

"The fight against fundamentalism and terrorism should be continued, because terrorism is a serious threat to the region. There is fear that the wave of this threat will spread to Europe as well."

Tolo TV (Afghanistan), January 2008

STEPHEN SIZER

Pastor, England

Religion must not be used for politics

"So this is really an abuse of religion to further a political agenda. And that's why it's so important for people of faith — Jewish, Muslim and Christian — to work together and focus on what we have in common for the good of humanity and repudiate the use of religion to justify ethnic cleansing or violence, specially against those who are suffering, such as the Palestinians."

Khorasan TV (Iran), November 2007

ABJUL JABBAR

Singer, Bangladesh

Not what we envisaged

"We fought for a country where people from all faiths will be treated equally but here a section of people began shouting that Islam is being ruined for secular ideals. We have failed to protect our achievements. The establishment of democracy, in real sense, not in rhetoric alone, can turn our dreams into reality."

New Age (Bangladesh), March 2008

NECDET

Secularist, Turkey

No such thing as moderate Islam

"There is no such thing as absolute democracy, anywhere. If the AKP takes the presidency, democracy is over here anyway. They haven't changed their stripes. Once an Islamist, always an Islamist. There's no such thing as moderate Islam."

The Nation (Thailand), May 2007

13

Europe's Immigration Turmoil

Sarah Glazer

African migrants at a detention camp in Malta await immigration processing, which can take up to 18 months. Hundreds of African "boat people" arrive each year on the Mediterranean island — the European Union's smallest member state — after risking their lives at sea trying to migrate to the EU, primarily from North Africa.

From *CQ Researcher*, December 2010.

AFP/Getty Images/Robyn Beck

Shooting at mosques and killing *muezzins* aren't usually part of election campaigns in Austria. * But such measures were featured in "Bye Bye Mosque," an online video game launched by the anti-immigrant Freedom Party (FPÖ) during September elections in the industrial state of Styria.

Local party leader Gerhard Kurzmann — who says a multicultural society "can only be a criminal society" — defended the game, which closed with the message "Styria is full of minarets and mosques. So that this doesn't happen (in reality): Vote . . . the FPÖ!"[1]

The game was taken down shortly after protests from the opposing Green Party, which pointed out that there are no minarets in Styria. But Kurzmann's party apparently benefited from the heated debate about the game: For the first time since 2005 the Freedom Party gained a seat in the nine-member provincial government. Even in cosmopolitan Vienna, where the party pushed for referendums banning minarets, it won more than a quarter of the vote in October's provincial elections, spurring speculation the party could dramatically affect national elections in three years.[2]

Fringe factions like the Freedom Party have been gaining support across Western Europe, most surprisingly in two countries traditionally known for their tolerance — Sweden and the Netherlands. And while Swedish and Austrian mainstream parties so far have resisted including such minority parties in their governments, Dutch politician Geert Wilders — charged this year with inciting racial hatred for his rabidly anti-Muslim statements — has become the main power broker in his country's coalition government.[3]

France, Germany and Britain Saw Largest Influx

More than 3.5 million immigrants became permanent citizens of European Union countries between 2004 and 2008, nearly 60 percent of them settling in France, Germany and the United Kingdom. The migrants were from both EU and non-EU countries. Countries with fewer job opportunities, such as Poland and Romania, saw only modest increases.

Number of New Citizens in EU Countries, 2004-2008

Source: Eurostat, August 2010

Rhetoric and anti-immigrant code words once reserved for right-wing, xenophobic parties have seeped into the speeches of mainstream politicians. German Chancellor Angela Merkel's uncharacteristically blunt remark in October that the nation's "multicultural" experiment — to "live happily side-by-side" with foreign workers — has "utterly failed" was widely interpreted as a criticism of the nation's 4 million Muslims, most of Turkish origin. Referring to America's own recent brouhaha over a proposed mosque near Ground Zero, *Boston Globe* religion columnist James Carroll commented, "On both sides of the Atlantic, a rising tide of xenophobic hostility toward immigrants is threatening to swamp the foundation of liberal democracy."[4]

While it's tempting to draw parallels to the recent upsurge in American anti-Muslim hostility, important differences exist between U.S. Muslims — mainly educated and professional — and Europe's Muslims, workers who migrated primarily from rural villages in countries like Turkey, Algeria and Bangladesh. European Muslims are "more like the black communities of the United States — in terms of handicaps and social problems," such as high unemployment, school dropout and welfare dependency rates, notes Shada Islam, senior program executive at the European Policy Centre think tank in Brussels. And Europe's Muslims don't enjoy as much mainstream political support as American Muslims do.

"I haven't heard a single European politician stand up and say what Mayor [Michael] Bloomberg of New York and others say in the United States" in defending Muslims who want to build a mosque near Ground Zero, observes Islam.

European immigration experts are particularly disturbed by the growing power of anti-immigrant parties.

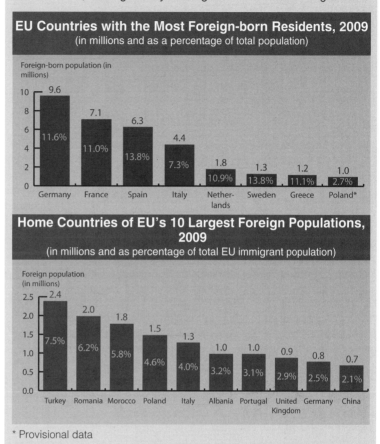

Germany Has the Most Foreign-Born Residents

Nearly 10 million foreign-born residents live in Germany — more than in any other European Union (EU) country. More than 2 million Turks live in the EU, making Turkey the largest source of EU immigrants.

EU Countries with the Most Foreign-born Residents, 2009
(in millions and as a percentage of total population)

Foreign-born population (in millions)

Germany	France	Spain	Italy	Netherlands	Sweden	Greece	Poland*
9.6	7.1	6.3	4.4	1.8	1.3	1.2	1.0
11.6%	11.0%	13.8%	7.3%	10.9%	13.8%	11.1%	2.7%

Home Countries of EU's 10 Largest Foreign Populations, 2009
(in millions and as percentage of total EU immigrant population)

Foreign population (in millions)

Turkey	Romania	Morocco	Poland	Italy	Albania	Portugal	United Kingdom	Germany	China
2.4	2.0	1.8	1.5	1.3	1.0	1.0	0.9	0.8	0.7
7.5%	6.2%	5.8%	4.6%	4.0%	3.2%	3.1%	2.9%	2.5%	2.1%

* Provisional data

Source: Katya Vasileva, "Foreigners Living in the EU Are Diverse and Largely Younger Than the Nationals of the EU Member States," Eurostat, August 2010

For instance, Wilders' party won promises from the new Dutch government to cut immigration from non-Western (presumably Muslim) countries in half and to make it harder for workers from those countries to bring over their spouses. "For the first time we have a government that is singling out a specific group of citizens; . . . it's pure discrimination," says Jan Willem Duyvendak, a sociology professor at the University of Amsterdam.

Even more disturbing, say experts, is the trend of mainstream politicians adopting similar anti-immigrant positions. The National Front, France's most right-wing party,

AFP/Getty Images/Denis Charlet

Afghan migrants receive food handouts from a nongovernmental organization in Calais, France, in November, 2009, after riot police bulldozed a makeshift camp used as a base to sneak across the English Channel into Britain. Resentment toward immigrants has grown in recent years throughout Europe as the weak economy intensifies unemployment.

has declined in popularity since it peaked in 2002, when its leader Jean-Marie Le Pen came in second in presidential elections. But if it no longer garners as much support, that's in part because French President Nicolas Sarkozy "gives people a respectable way" of echoing the party's anti-immigrant sentiments, says Philippe Legrain, the British author of the 2007 book, *Immigrants: Your Country Needs Them.*

"There's a great temptation among mainstream politicians to adopt the rhetoric and the xenophobic diatribes of populist parties," says Islam, who is "very alarmed" by this trend. "People in these uncertain times want to know there is one guilty party," and Muslims have become a convenient scapegoat, she says.

In the past year, anti-immigrant hostility has emerged in various rhetorical and legislative forms in several European countries:

- In the Netherlands, the coalition government that took power in October agreed to Wilders' demands to pursue headscarf bans and measures making it harder for immigrants' spouses to join them. The

agreement followed the strong third-place showing of Wilders' Freedom Party in national elections.[5]

- In France, Sarkozy expelled Romanian and Bulgarian Roma, also known as Gypsies, a move that violated European Union agreements on antidiscrimination and the free movement of EU citizens between countries, according to human rights groups. The parliament banned the public wearing of the Muslim burqa, a full-body covering that exposes only the eyes through a mesh screen.

- In a referendum in Switzerland, nearly 58 percent of voters supported a ban on new minarets on mosques in 2009, and a majority say they want to ban the burqa.[6]

- In Sweden, the anti-immigrant Swedish Democrat Party doubled its support in September from the last election — to nearly 6 percent — allowing members to sit in parliament for the first time. The party's campaign called for banning full-face veils, new mosques and most new immigration from Muslim countries.[7] Also in Sweden, authorities warned in October that in 15 separate shootings this year one or more snipers had targeted "dark-skinned" residents of Malmo, killing one and wounding eight.[8]

- In Britain, Conservative Prime Minister David Cameron was elected after promising to cut immigration from hundreds of thousands to "tens of thousands," and his government temporarily capped non-EU immigration — to become permanent next year.

- In Italy, Roman officials bulldozed 200 Roma squatter camps, which some say was aimed at getting them to leave Italy.[9]

Meanwhile, recent polls show that sizable percentages of Europeans feel immigrants drain welfare benefits, damage the quality of life and make it harder to get jobs. In a *Financial Times* poll in September about 63 percent of Britons thought immigration had harmed the National Health Service and the education system. In Spain, where 20 percent of the workers are jobless, 67 percent of respondents thought immigration made it harder to find a job, and nearly a third said immigration lowers wages.[10]

Paradoxically, Western Europe's anti-immigrant fervor is peaking just as the recession has been slowing immigration and even reversing immigrant flows in some countries. Ireland and Germany, for instance — where booming economies attracted foreign workers for years — are now seeing more out-migration than in-migration, as the economies of those countries slow down or, in the case of Ireland, flounder.[11]

Experts point out that the number of immigrants entering Western Europe from majority Muslim countries is dwarfed by the number coming from non-Muslim countries, especially from the EU. (European Union governments are required by law to accept other EU citizens, as well as all political refugees deemed eligible for political asylum.)[12] For example, Germany now has more people emigrating back to Turkey than Turks entering Germany, and the other countries sending the most migrants to Germany last year — Poland, Romania, Bulgaria and the United States — weren't Muslim at all.[13] Austria, home of the anti-Muslim Freedom Party, has more immigrants arriving from Germany than from Turkey.[14]

Some experts blame growing anti-immigrant hostility on the insecurity voters feel about jobs, pensions and benefits in budget-cutting Europe.[15]

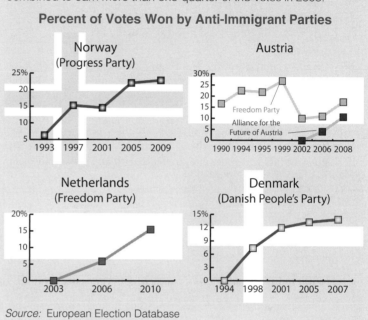

Anti-Immigration Parties Score Election Gains

Right-wing, anti-immigrant political parties have made significant gains in recent parliamentary elections in several traditionally liberal European nations. The Freedom Party in the Netherlands, for example, garnered 16 percent of the vote in the latest election, up from zero percent seven years earlier. Two parties in Austria — the Freedom Party and the Alliance for the Future of Austria — combined to earn more than one-quarter of the votes in 2008.

Percent of Votes Won by Anti-Immigrant Parties

Source: European Election Database

Others say Europeans worry about losing their national identities in increasingly diverse societies that don't subscribe to America's melting-pot cultural heritage.

Sarkozy's mass expulsion of the Roma was widely viewed as a ploy to satisfy right-wing voters, as was his support for banning burqas and stripping French citizenship from naturalized citizens who commit violent crimes. "Sarkozy, with very low approval ratings, is trying to shore up or gain support among the far right and supporters of the National Front," says John R. Bowen, a Washington University, St. Louis, anthropologist and author of the 2007 book *Why the French Don't Like Headscarves.* "The burqa ban looks like it's about Islam, but all of these [initiatives] are really about immigrants and about a deal for the far right."

Still, much of Europe's recent anti-immigrant hostility has focused on Muslims, and that often seems to include Muslims born on the continent or who are citizens. In the Netherlands, Wilders once proposed taxing headscarves for "polluting" the landscape. Similar sentiments in Germany helped to boost former central banker Thilo Sarrazin's new book, *Germany Does Away with Itself,* to the top of bestseller lists. The book claims Muslim immigrants are "dumbing down" society and coming to Germany only for its generous welfare benefits.[16]

"The Turks are taking over Germany . . . with a higher birth rate," Sarrazin has said. "I don't want the country of my grandchildren and great-grandchildren to be largely Muslim, or that Turkish and Arabic will be spoken in large areas, that women will wear headscarves and the daily rhythm is set by the call of the *muezzin.*"[17]

Sarrazin's book dared to break a politically correct silence about Germany's real problems with its Turkish population: high rates of unemployment and welfare dependency combined with low education levels, even among second- and third-generation immigrants.[18] In a survey released in October, 30 percent of respondents believed Germany was "overrun by foreigners" seeking welfare benefits,[19] and 58.4 percent thought German Muslims' religious practices should be "significantly curbed."[20] Newspapers are filled with politicians' statements about Muslim immigrants' inability to integrate — ironically, just when Turkish migration has declined dramatically, and more people are leaving Germany for Turkey than entering.[21]

Some mainstream politicians and economists argue that Western Europe's aging population needs young migrants to expand the work force, pay social security taxes and keep the economy growing, considering Europe's low birth rates and coming retiree bulge. "Europe's feeble demographic outlook" means that continued support of its generous state-funded health and welfare benefits is "incompatible" with the desire to "ring-fence their national cultures with controls on immigration," editorialized Tony Barber, former Brussels bureau chief of the *Financial Times.*[22]

Yet perceptions of immigration are often more about fear and protecting one's culture than about demographics or economics. Statistics "don't address the feeling of unease that voters have [about] 'What kind of society are we developing into? What's happening to our culture?'" says Heather Grabbe, executive director of the Open Society Institute, a think tank in Brussels concerned with immigrants' rights. Much anti-immigrant sentiment perceives Islam as an alien, threatening ideology, even though many Muslims were born in Europe.

"This is not about recent migration," says Grabbe. "This is about several generations of migration and people who are in many cases very well-integrated into communities." And the right's political rhetoric about national identity "hasn't been opposed effectively by any other kind of discussion, particularly on the left."

As Western Europeans struggle with their fears about immigration and its impact on their economies, jobs and culture, here are some of the questions being asked:

Does Europe need its immigrants?

Former central banker Sarrazin's bestseller claiming immigrants "drag down" Germany triggered an eruption in the blogosphere from Germans who say they've had

enough immigration. Yet large swathes of eastern Germany are becoming depopulated due to the country's extremely low birth rate and greater out-migration than in-migration over the last two years.

Demographer Reiner Klingholz, director of the Berlin Institute for Population Development, suggests Germany follow the American example of the Wild West: encourage settlement and "massive" in-migration.[23] Even if Germany could increase its annual net immigration rate back up to the levels of a few years ago (about 100,000-200,000), Klingholz calculates, the population would decline by 12 million by 2050 — a "bloodletting" similar to emptying Germany's 12 largest cities. Young, booming nations like India, China and Brazil will have a clear economic advantage, he says, and when they also begin to age and need to recruit young workers from abroad, there will be no workers left to immigrate into "good old Europe."

The recent fiscal crisis has shined a laser on two trends that will force all European governments deeper into debt: Europe's burgeoning aging population and fertility rates that are too low to replace the current populations.[24] Thus, governments across Europe face the specter of having to support a huge generation of retiring baby boomers with too few young workers to pay the social security taxes needed to support them. Many countries have already turned to immigrants to solve some of their labor shortages, such as Turkish taxi drivers in Berlin and African chambermaids in Italy.

Because immigrants tend to be younger than native-born populations, they can offer an important solution to the looming pension and demographic crises, some experts argue. According to the most recent figures from Eurostat, the EU's statistical office, the median age for foreigners living in the European Union is 34.3, about six years younger than that of the national population.[25] The percentage of older persons in Europe's population is expected to rise even more in nearly all of the EU, primarily because people are living longer and birth rates are declining. But migration will help sustain population growth — where it exists — between now and 2030, according to Eurostat.[26]

In a new report, experts at the Organisation for Economic Co-operation and Development (OECD) in Paris say migration is the key to long-term economic growth. For their own economic self-interest, the report urges, European countries should be opening — not closing — citizenship to foreigners. And, the authors argue, governments should be helping immigrants who have lost jobs by giving them the same unemployment benefits they give to natives — another inflammatory issue among voters this year.[27]

"There is no escaping the fact that more labour migration will be needed in the future in many OECD countries, as the recovery progresses and the current labor market slack is absorbed," said John P. Martin, OECD's director of employment, in an editorial.[28] "In a world where labour is becoming scarcer, immigrants are a valuable resource, and employers need to see this."

Yet skeptics suggest that as more women enter the labor force and as native-born Europeans begin working beyond their traditional retirement age, which is generally in the late 50s, more immigrant workers may not be needed at all. In Austria, life expectancy is now about 20 years past the average retirement age of 58 for women and 59 for men, so many older people probably will remain in the work force years longer than in the past, says Wolfgang Lutz, demographer at the International Institute of Applied Systems Analysis in Laxenburg, Austria, outside Vienna. And as for women entering the work force, countries like Germany and Austria — with their traditions of stay-at-home mothers — have a long way to go to catch up with Scandinavian countries, where women play an equal part with men in the work force, he points out.

"Reforms to labor markets to reduce barriers to working — like childcare policies for women — are going to be more important, quantitatively, than immigration," says Madeleine Sumption, policy analyst at the Migration Policy Institute in Washington, D.C. "If immigration were to solve the problem alone, the scale of numbers you'd have to have coming in would be politically impossible."

It's also possible that technology will improve future productivity, enabling Europe to produce the same amount of goods and services with fewer workers. Under that scenario, says Lutz, "The low birth rate may be the best thing that could happen to Europe. Otherwise there would be lots of unemployment."

Moreover, countries like Germany are getting the wrong kind of migrants — low-skilled, uneducated workers that don't contribute much to the economy or taxes, says Ruud Koopmans, director of migration and integration research at the Social Science Research Center in Berlin. "We need immigrants, it's quite clear; but we do not need the immigrants we are getting so far," he says. "Europe has not succeeded in being attractive

enough for highly skilled immigrants from India or other Asian countries. Usually, we're getting immigrants for whom there are no shortages in the labor market."

Skeptics of the immigration solution also question whether underpaid, low-skilled immigrants can really bail out governments from their pension shortfall, since the taxes they pay will be relatively small due to their low incomes. With immigrants' unemployment rates running at twice those of European natives in the recent crisis, they could eat up more in welfare benefits than they pay in taxes, suggest some experts and anti-immigrant voices in Britain.[29]

A recent British study examined the impact of Eastern European immigration into the U.K., where in 2004 a flood of young Poles and other Eastern Europeans began entering Britain after their countries joined the EU. Although Polish immigrants often generated resentment among working class voters, the study found that immigrants from the new EU countries had actually contributed more in taxes than they consumed in welfare benefits. According to the study, these immigrants were 60 percent less likely than natives to collect state benefits, tax credits or subsidized housing.

"They made a positive contribution to public finance," according to study author Christian Dustmann, professor of economics at University College London. Eastern European immigrants paid 37 percent more in taxes than they received in public goods and services in 2008-2009.[30]

Despite these positive findings, Dustmann doesn't think immigration can solve the problem of aging societies needing younger immigrant labor. "It's only a quick fix," not a long-term solution, he says, because immigrants will eventually age and will also require social security. "I don't think immigrants can solve our demographic problems."

Still, foreign workers could defuse another demographic time bomb, argues author Legrain: the need for workers to care for the elderly. The demand for such workers will skyrocket in the health and elder-care industries, he predicts, as the share of Europe's population over age 80 almost triples by 2050.[31]

"Many of these jobs are low-skilled, low-paid jobs that Europeans don't want to do," he argues. "Who's going to work in the care homes?"

But Sir Andrew Green, chairman of Migration Watch, a British group that wants to cut migration, says access to cheap migrants is precisely why these kinds of jobs are so "appallingly badly paid." He considers it

Homeless Migrants in Britain Feel the Pain

With winter coming, jobless immigrants are sleeping on the street.

When 22-year-old Polish immigrant Michal Aniśko showed up in October at a homeless day shelter in Slough, England, he was a far cry from the stereotypically successful "Polish plumber" often blamed in British tabloids for depriving native workers of jobs.

His weather-beaten face showed the strain of having slept on park benches for four months, ever since returning to this charmless, industrial suburban town outside London — known for its factories, plentiful jobs and big Polish community. After finding only spotty employment in his native Poland for a year, England had drawn him back with memories of an earlier year of steady work in restaurant kitchens, car-washes and construction. But that was before the recession hit Slough; when he returned this summer, the temp agency that had found him those jobs had shut down.

Even the Polish food shop window, which he remembered crammed with help-wanted placards, was comparatively bare. "These days there are only a few jobs posted, and when I ring up, they say someone already took the job," he said through an interpreter. Desperate, Aniśko took an illegal job as a construction day laborer, but when he asked for his pay, his employers beat him up.

Slough is only one barometer of Britain's economic downturn since 2004, when Poland and seven other former Soviet bloc countries joined the European Union and thousands of Poles — just granted the right to work anywhere in the EU — were attracted to England's booming economy. [1] Three or four years ago only one or two Eastern European migrants per day came through the door of Slough's Save Our Homeless shelter seeking a hot meal or a shower.

"We're now looking at 30 or 40 a day using our service, because they're sleeping on the street," Mandy McGuire, who runs the shelter, said in October. Typically, the men, most of them older and more street-hardened than Aniśko, have lived in Slough for four or five years and once earned enough at low-skilled jobs to send money home and rent a room. "But now the work's gone, their accommodations are gone; they're turning to alcohol," McGuire says. "The more they're turning to alcohol, the less employable they're becoming."

London has seen a similar trend. At the latest count, 954 people — about a quarter of those found sleeping on the street — were from Eastern Europe, according to London's Combined Homeless and Information Network. That is more than triple the number counted in 2006-2007. Across the country, 84 percent of homeless day centers have reported an increase in the number of Eastern European migrants using their services, according to Homeless Link, which represents 480 homeless organizations in the U.K. [2]

Because Aniśko's past employers paid in cash, which was off-the-books, he's not eligible for unemployment or housing benefits available to registered immigrants who have worked legally for a year — another contradiction to the widespread British view of immigrants as "welfare scroungers." Aniśko's ineligibility for welfare is typical of homeless migrants from Eastern Europe, either because their jobs are illegal or migrants can't afford the $145 fee to register as a worker, experts say.

The European Commission has said Britain's policy of denying housing, homeless assistance and other social benefits to immigrants from Eastern Europe who have not been registered workers for at least 12 months is discriminatory and violates EU rules on free movement and equal treatment. The United Kingdom has two months to bring its legislation in line with EU law, the commission said on Oct. 28. Otherwise, the commission may decide to refer the U.K. to the EU's Court of Justice. [3]

Also in October, the Polish charity Barka UK offered Aniśko a free plane ticket back to Poland and help finding work there. But he refused, saying it would be even more difficult to find a job back home. Six of his fellow migrants from Slough had accepted Barka's offer and flew home the previous week, according to McGuire.

"immoral" to import what he calls "an underclass" to care for the elderly.

"In the short term it does make elder care affordable," he says, "but in the long term it's a bad policy" that will contribute to Britain's projected population growth and the nation's already crowded highway and mass transit systems. "And we are a small island," he notes, citing statistics showing that Britain is about twice as densely populated as France and about 12 times as crowded as the United States.

While most of Britain's approximately 1 million Polish immigrants have fared well in England, about 20 percent — generally older men who don't speak English — have failed to find a steady source of income, according to Ewa Sadowska, chief executive of Barka UK. [4]

"This is a communist generation that spent most of their lives under a regime where everything was taken care of by the state," she says. Some were lured to London by sham employers who advertised British jobs in Polish newspapers, then took their money and passports when they arrived in England, according to Sadowska.

After the Soviet Union began disintegrating in 1989, Barka UK was founded in Poland by her parents, two psychologists, to help homeless, troubled individuals. Barka was first invited to London in 2007 by one of the local councils in a neighborhood where homeless Polish immigrants were sleeping on the streets. Since then, Barka has been working in a dozen London boroughs and in nearby Slough and Reading at the invitation of local governments, which fund their outreach work.

Besides a free plane ticket, Barka offers help in Poland with alcohol and drug addiction. Unregistered migrants in Britain don't qualify for rehab or detox programs under England's National Health Service. Often, homeless migrants are ashamed to go back home and be seen by their families as economic failures, says Sadowska.

"We help them to understand it's pointless to stay in London and die on the street," says Sadowska. So far, 1,248 mainly Polish migrants have returned to Eastern Europe with Barka's help.

Slough residents have complained of drunken noisemakers and rat infestations at makeshift homeless camps. Slough's local newspaper ran a front-page picture on Sept. 24 of a homeless camp beneath a discarded billboard under the headline "How Can We Be Proud of This?" [5]

Asked if Slough is funding Barka just to export a local nuisance, McGuire said: "We're certainly not saying, 'Go back to Poland and stay there.' We're saying, 'Go back, get yourself sorted out. If you've got an alcohol problem, address that; maybe get trained with a skill that's needed over here so it's comparatively easy to find work.'"

The temperature had just dropped to freezing the previous October night. As winter approaches, McGuire says,

Discouraged by Britain's sagging job market, Polish immigrants in London board a bus to return to Poland on May 20, 2009. Thousands of Polish workers flocked to Britain after Poland's entrance into the European Union in 2004 eliminated barriers to Poles working in other EU countries.

"My personal concern is that those that don't want to go back will be freezing to death out there."

— *Sarah Glazer*

---

[1] The eight Eastern European countries that joined the EU in 2004, thereby granting their citizens working rights in the U.K. are: Czech Republic, Estonia, Hungary, Latvia, Lithuania, Poland, Slovakia and Slovenia. In 2007, Bulgaria and Romania were accepted into the EU, but with only limited working rights in the U.K. The homeless figures in this sidebar include migrants from all new EU countries in Eastern Europe. See www.belfasttelegraph.co.uk/business/help-advice/employment-issues/eu-nationals-and-their-rights-to-work-14314169.html#ixzz13Xz341HR.

[2] "Snap 2010," Homeless Link, www.homeless.org.uk/snap-2010.

[3] "Commission Requests UK to End Discrimination on Other Nationals' Right to Reside as Workers," news release, European Commission, Oct. 28, 2010;

http://ec.europa.eu/social/main.jsp?langId=en&catId=457&newsId=917&furtherNews=yes.

[4] The Civic Institute for Monitoring and Recommendations estimates that about 20 percent of approximately 1 million Polish migrants who live in the U.K. don't speak English, lack a stable income, have health problems (including addictions) and lack access to organized information sources.

[5] "How Can We Be Proud of This?" *Slough Observer*, Sept. 24, 2010, p. 1, www.sloughobserver.co.uk/news/roundup/articles/2010/09/25/48537-how-can-we-be-proud-of-this-/.

Ironically, both sides in the debate admit, when governments try to limit low-skilled immigration, they send culturally hostile signals to the very same high-skilled workers they hope to attract to their country. "If you're an Indian IT specialist, why go to Germany?"

Legrain asks. "Even in a high paid job, you'll be made to feel unwelcome, you'll feel excluded from the rest of society" and will pay higher income tax than in the United States, "where you'll have no problem fitting in."

Germany's Turks Reverse Course

Reflecting Germany's poor job market, 10,000 more people have been emigrating from Germany to Turkey each year since 2008 than have been arriving. German anti-immigrant sentiment is growing, despite the fact that only 30,000 Turks immigrated into Germany last year — about half as many as in 2002.

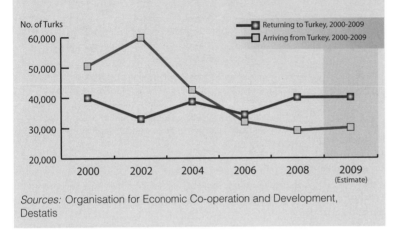

No. of Turks

— ■ — Returning to Turkey, 2000-2009
— □ — Arriving from Turkey, 2000-2009

Sources: Organisation for Economic Co-operation and Development, Destatis

"That's the striking thing: Europe is so terrified of immigrants, and increasingly immigrants don't want to come to Europe," he observes.

Should European governments do more to integrate immigrants?

Chancellor Merkel's remark that multiculturalism has "utterly failed" in Germany reflects a growing sentiment that foreigners and their children should assimilate more into German society. Referring to the nation's majority population as "we," Merkel went on to tell the youth branch of her party, "We feel tied to Christian values. Those who don't accept them don't have a place here." That comment seemed to put the blame squarely on Turks, not Germans, for their failure to assimilate.[32]

Yet, for many years Turkish *Gastarbeiters* (guestworkers) were not even allowed to seek German citizenship, and children born in Germany to Turkish immigrant parents did not automatically become German citizens. A 2000 law that made it easier for Turks to become German citizens spurred an initial surge of applications, but applications have declined steadily in recent years, primarily because Germany does not permit dual citizenship.[33]

Many Turks do not want to give up their Turkish citizenship, even if that means being required to do military service in Turkey.

"We have two nationalisms clashing," says Berlin sociologist Koopmans: "Germans saying, 'You have to make a choice,'" and Turks, who "are also very nationalistic."

Turks without German citizenship cannot vote in Germany or play a part in the political process. "They're still not politically integrated, and that affects the degree of identification of Turks in Germany with their home country," Koopmans acknowledges. First- and second-generation Turkish immigrants share some of the blame for that, he says.

The tendency for Turkish pride to come before German identification was recently illustrated by a widely viewed video clip of young German-speaking Turks booing German-Turkish soccer star Mesut Özil, as he played for the German team in the World Cup.

"Mesut Özil is no Turk!" shouted young Turks decked out in the colors of the Turkish flag, angry at Özil for choosing to play for Germany rather than Turkey. To many Germans, the film clip was yet another sign that Turks don't want to integrate.[34]

But that's not the whole story, says German economist Sabine Beppler-Spahl, an editor at the libertarian German magazine *Novo Argumente*. At her children's predominantly Turkish public school in Berlin, Turkish children arrived waving German flags and rooted for the team during the World Cup, she reports. Germans are just as much to blame for creating two parallel societies, she suggests.

"A lot of middle-class German people moving to the suburbs have virtually no contact with Turks," she says. "Their kids don't go to school with them and don't have Turkish friends in their immediate circle. Middle-class Germans agree with [former German central banker] Sarrazin because they go into the city and see women with headscarves" and are frightened by the sight of young Turks hanging out on the streets, whom they assume are unemployed, on welfare and have criminal tendencies.

In an effort to require greater "integration" of immigrants into their societies, some European governments have begun to require courses on their national culture and language and citizenship tests as a precondition for emigrating to their country. The Netherlands, once known for its tolerance, led the way in this trend in March 2006, requiring applicants for family reunification to take an "integration" test at a Dutch embassy abroad as a precondition for being granted even a temporary residence permit. Since then similar policies have been adopted by Finland, Denmark, Austria, Germany and France.[35]

In the Dutch citizenship tests, would-be immigrants must understand that it is acceptable for unmarried and gay couples to live together, that women enjoy equal rights and that domestic violence (including honor killings and female genital mutilation) will be punished. In the Netherlands, Austria and Germany, religiously conservative Muslims are "a particular target group of these tests," according to a study.[36]

In the Netherlands, "what began as an immigration-integration policy has turned into the opposite: a no-immigration policy," concluded migration expert Christian Joppke, a professor of political science at the American University of Paris. The integration tests and other requirements are aimed at keeping out low-skilled family immigrants, particularly Muslims of Turkish and Moroccan origin, he said.[37]

To Dutch sociologist Duyvendak, such tests are clearly discriminatory. "The wrong answers on these multiple-choice tests . . . have implicit prejudices about Muslims," he says. "People taking the test feel they're depicted as backward and intolerant." Several years ago, the Netherlands garnered international attention for a video it showed would-be immigrants abroad of topless women sunbathing and gay couples kissing. "You can only understand this when you see how monocultural the Dutch are," Duyvendak says, a homogenous culture with clearly progressive values.

But other experts say language requirements and citizenship tests help immigrants achieve economic independence. A recent study by Koopmans found that countries like Germany, Austria and France, which make

AFP/Getty Images/Denis Charlet

A Roma girl plays with her doll on Sept. 8, 2010, in an illegal camp in Lille, France. After France began expelling illegal Roma immigrants in July, the European Parliament on Sept. 9 demanded that France suspend the expulsions. Italian police also recently demolished illegal Roma settlements on the outskirts of Rome in an effort to force the Roma back to Romania and Bulgaria.

welfare benefits or visas dependent on a certain amount of assimilation (such as language tests and obligatory integration courses) tend to produce better results for immigrants than countries like Sweden, with traditionally easy access to citizenship and generous welfare benefits. Countries like Germany, which have stricter immigration prerequisites, have more immigrants who are employed, less crime among immigrants and less residential segregation, Koopmans finds.[38]

While some politicians may see these requirements as a way to keep Muslims out, Koopmans defends them: "It's an attempt by European countries to do something the classical immigration countries like Canada and Australia have done all along, namely selective immigration," or recruiting the highly skilled workers they need, not low-skilled immigrants who will become welfare dependent.

New Integration Policies Seen as Discriminatory

Critics say the tough rules target non-EU immigrants.

British university graduate Emily Churchill began to cry when she heard the announcement that starting this fall, foreign spouses must pass an English test overseas before being allowed to join their British spouses.

Last summer she married an aspiring Palestinian filmmaker named Basel whom she had met while studying abroad in Syria the previous winter and with whom she speaks Arabic. The British government has refused their first two attempts to obtain a visa for him. The English test "epitomized how I felt we'd been treated by the system and the government approach to make spousal immigration as difficult as possible," she says.

In announcing the new requirement, Home Secretary Theresa May said it "will help promote integration, remove cultural barriers and protect public services." [1] But because the rule applies only to non-EU immigrants, Churchill feels it is more about discrimination than integration. "If Basel were British or Italian, we would not be apart," she wrote on a *Guardian* newspaper blog. [2] Under European Union agreements, immigrants from EU member countries are allowed free movement within the EU.

Some experts charge that marriage rules like this — along with strict age limits and required integration courses for would-be immigrant spouses — are discriminatory because they are aimed only at non-EU immigrants. Such restrictions also get vocal support from anti-immigrant politicians with growing electoral power in several European countries. For example, the Netherlands government has agreed in principle to the anti-immigrant Freedom Party's demand to follow Denmark's example by raising the age for immigrant spouses from 21 to 24. The Dutch marriage partner would also have to earn 120 percent of the minimum wage.

"If you're 23 and want to bring your bride from Turkey or Morocco and you don't earn enough, you cannot marry the partner you want," says Jan Willem Duyvendak, a sociology professor at the University of Amsterdam. "Whereas, if you're 24 and want to bring someone from Bulgaria, Rumania or a European country, then it is possible. That shows how discriminatory it is."

But Ruud Koopmans, director of migration research at the Social Science Research Center in Berlin, says the measures are "a good thing because many of these migrants came from rural regions not knowing how to read and write. Almost certainly they will end up dependent on social welfare with integration problems." France, too, has introduced language tests as a prerequisite for entry for prospective marriage migrants. Under pressure from the anti-immigrant Danish People's Party, the Danish government is dropping its age minimum of 24 — but only for those immigrant spouses who speak Danish and have high levels of education and work experience. [3] The policies are aimed at reducing the number of immigrants with low skill levels "for whom there is no demand in the labor market," Koopmans says.

In Germany, newly arrived immigrants from non-EU countries must, at the discretion of immigration authorities, participate in a government-funded integration course that includes 600 hours of German language instruction and a 30-hour orientation on German culture, history and law. Thousands of people are on waiting lists for the courses, but budget cuts suggest the waiting lists will only get longer, according to *Der Spiegel*, Germany's leading news magazine. [4]

Anti-discrimination laws limit the extent to which such restrictions can target only immigrants, Koopmans says, so some countries pass sweeping laws, such as the Dutch decision to abolish welfare benefits for anyone under 27. Though it sounds draconian, the law appears to have improved immigrants' employment rates and reduced dependence on welfare. However, Duyvendak points out, the job market was already booming when the law was passed.

— Sarah Glazer

---

[1] "UK Marriage Visa Applicants will have to pass English tests," June 10, 2010, www.workpermit.com/news/2010-06-10/uk/uk-marriage-visa-applicants-english-language-test.htm.

[2] Emily Churchill, "Being with your spouse is a right, not a privilege," *Guardian*, June 14, 2010, www.guardian.co.uk/commentisfree/2010/jun/14/foreign-spouse-language-tests-immigration-system.

[3] "PM: 24-year-rule expands to points system," *Copenhagen Post Online*, Nov. 8, 2010, www.cphpost.dk/news/politics/90-politics/50410-pm-24-year-rule-expands-to-.

[4] "Migrants on the Waiting List," *Spiegelonline*, Oct. 25, 2010, www.spiegel.de/international/germany/0,1518,725118,00.html and "German Integration Summit Delivers Little," *Spiegelonline*, Nov. 4, 2010, www.spiegel.de/international/germany/0,1518,727238,00.html.

Most of today's European immigration involves relatives of current residents, and governments are trying to make it more difficult for those family members to emigrate. Often the would-be immigrant is a bride-to-be from the home country. Even Muslims born in the Netherlands or Germany tend to import wives from their parents' native land. About 80 percent of second-generation Turks and Moroccans in the Netherlands marry someone from their country of origin, Koopmans notes. Typically, they are highly religious, have low levels of education and can't speak the language of their new country — all factors associated with high welfare dependency and the delay of assimilation for generations.

"The children of these immigrants will be raised in the Berber dialect and start with the same disadvantage as children of the first generation," he says. So language and other assimilation requirements are "good for educational and labor market integration."

Unlike the United States, where the immigrant bears the cost of not learning English — in the form of poorer job prospects — welfare-generous Europe pays the bill, through higher welfare costs if an immigrant doesn't assimilate, Koopmans argues. "That gives receiving societies more of a right to make demands on immigrants than in the United States, where it's your choice," whether to learn English or adjust to American ways, he says.

But Beppler-Spahl says Germany's citizenship tests are a superficial response designed to assuage Germans' fears about immigrants not integrating that doesn't solve the country's real problems. "Our problem is we're not using the potential we have," she says. "If we have young Turkish children, we should ask ourselves, 'Why are they failing in German schools, and what can we do about that?'"

Sarrazin's controversial assertion that Germany is being "dumbed down" by a lower-intelligence population of Turks intensifies the perception that the problem lies with the immigrants rather than with Germany's educational system, she contends. "I don't believe Sarrazin's theory that, 'There's a limited intelligence pool, and we're getting the low end of a nation's limited intelligence pool,'" says Beppler-Spahl. "That's wrong. . . . Why say that people from poor families will stay poor

and will never make it? That's where the racism starts flowing in."

Should immigrants be required to follow local customs?

Liberals, feminists and anti-immigrant conservatives can become strange bedfellows when it comes to one issue in Europe: banning the burqa. Dutch right-wing populist Wilders sounds like some feminists when he argues that the burqa is "a medieval symbol, a symbol against women."[39]

France, which banned headscarves for students attending public schools in 2004, recently banned public wearing of the burqa. Italy, Belgium, the Netherlands, Austria, Denmark and Switzerland have considered similar legislation.

Some see the move as a thinly veiled anti-Muslim policy, others as a strike for women's freedom and integrating Muslims into mainstream society. Washington University anthropologist Bowen described France's national unity around the headscarf ban as stemming from the French philosophy that citizens must all subscribe to the same values. That desire for "shared values" played strongly in the French support of the burqa ban, he says.

"In France everyone is expected to potentially interact with everyone else; wearing a burqa is cutting oneself off from that sort of interaction. That's the justification the justice minister gave when it was being debated," Bowen explains. "All the other arguments — it oppresses women, it's against human dignity — really don't work because no women are complaining. How can you say it harms them if no one's complaining?"

But some Muslim women, like Algerian-American law professor Karima Bennoune, do see the veil as inherently oppressive. She remembers driving into Algiers during the Algerian civil war of the 1990s, when armed fundamentalist groups were killing women who went out unveiled. "I knew that my bare head, like those of the thousands of Algerian women who refused to submit, was marked with a target," she writes.[40]

In a 2007 law review article, Bennoune, who teaches at Rutgers School of Law in Newark, N.J., strongly supported the French headscarf ban. Before the ban, she wrote, gangs of young men in immigrant neighborhoods of Paris had taken to raping young girls who wore

CHRONOLOGY

19th Century *European nations colonize much of the Muslim world, providing source of immigrant labor.*

1830 French control of Algeria, Morocco and Tunisia leads to exodus of Muslim immigrants to France.

1950s-1960s *After deaths of millions of working-age men in World War II, Europe recruits immigrants to rebuild economy. Number of Turkish "guestworkers" in Germany surges. European resentment against immigrants grows.*

1954-55 Germany begins recruiting temporary foreign workers from Italy and Spain, later from Turkey.

1961 Germany signs a recruitment agreement with Turkey to import guest workers for two-year periods.

1970s-1980s *Jobs for immigrants dwindle in recession; Europe limits workers' immigration but lets in families, causing more Muslim immigration. Palestinian intifadas, riots in Britain, Saudi money for fundamentalist Wahhabi teachings stoke religious extremism.*

1974 France, Netherlands institute "immigration stop" policies. Immigration from Muslim countries triples in France, increases tenfold in the Netherlands in next three decades.

1977 France offers to pay immigrants to leave — with little success.

1990s-2000s *Terrorist attacks focus governments to monitor extremism among Muslim residents. Thousands of migrants from Eastern Europe move West; Europe begins requiring immigrants to integrate. Anti-immigrant parties make electoral gains, even as global economic crisis slows immigration to Europe.*

1995-1996 Radical Algerian group seeking Islamist state explodes bombs in Paris subways and trains.

1998 Al Qaeda calls on Muslims to kill Americans and their allies.

2000 Germany makes it easier for Turkish guestworkers and their children to become citizens.

Sep. 11, 2001 Al Qaeda attacks World Trade Center and Pentagon, killing nearly 3,000 people.

2002 Far-right Dutch leader Pim Fortuyn, who criticized Muslims for not assimilating, is murdered.

2004 Thousands of Eastern Europeans move to Western Europe to work. France bans headscarves in schools. . . . Madrid subway bombings kill 191; radical Islamist kills Dutch filmmaker Theo Van Gogh.

2005 London's "7/7" transit bombings kill 52; disaffected African immigrants riot in Paris suburbs.

2006 Netherlands requires applicants for family reunification to pass integration test abroad.

2007 EU admits Bulgaria and Romania but with limited working rights. . . . Radical immigrants try to blow up Glasgow, Scotland, airport. . . . Germany, Denmark foil extremist terrorist plots.

2008 As worldwide recession begins, migration starts to slow.

2009 Swiss ban new minarets on mosques. . . . Immigration to Spain, Ireland falls drastically; unemployment among foreign-born youth exceeds 40 percent in Spain, 37 percent in Sweden.

2010 Anti-immigrant parties make electoral gains in Sweden, Netherlands, Austria. . . . Conservatives take power in Britain with pledge to reduce immigration. . . . French President Sarkozy expels Roma from France. . . . French parliament bans the burqa in public. . . . German bestseller spurs debate on Muslim integration. . . . Migration Policy Institute says European immigration has come to a "virtual halt." . . . British government places temporary ceiling on skilled immigrants from outside EU, prompting industry protests. . . . New Dutch government pledges to halve non-Western immigration. . . . European Commission withdraws threat of legal action against France for expulsion of Roma. . . . France pledges to bring its immigration law in line with EU rules. . . . German Chancellor Merkel says multiculturalism has failed.

miniskirts or went to the movies. Many French Muslim women's groups supported the ban on the grounds that girls were frequently forced by their family or an older brother to wear the headscarf. The French Algerian feminist Fadela Amara called the veil a "visible symbol of subjugation."[41]

More recently, leading German feminists Alice Schwarzer and Necla Kelek came out in support of proposed burqa bans in Germany. Kelek said the garment has nothing to do with religion and comes out of an ideology where "women in public don't have the right to be human."[42]

Human rights groups, however, have generally opposed both headscarf and burqa bans. "Treating pious women like criminals won't help integrate them," said Judith Sunderland, senior researcher with the Europe and Central Asia division of Human Rights Watch in April.[43]

These same human rights groups, Bennoune counters, "would not come out in favor of Christian prayer in American schools . . . or the right to wear a swastika [once a religious symbol, now a political one] in a European classroom, because they understand the potential impact on other students and are able to appreciate the political meaning in context."[44]

Patrick Weil, a University of Paris immigration historian, said the French headscarf ban was largely a reaction to gangs of young Muslim men threatening Muslim girls who did not wear a scarf in school. "The law was endorsed by the majority of Muslims; it preserved the freedom of Muslim girls," maintains Weil, author of the 2008 book *How to Be French, Nationality in the Making Since 1789*, who served on the commission that advised the government to institute the ban. And the law has been enforced over the last six years with very little protest, he has pointed out.[45]

Devout Muslim girls who still want to wear the headscarf can attend the religious schools that operate in France under contract to the government, he points out (though most such schools are Christian): "We have a dual system that works well."

To Weil and other supporters, the headscarf ban was about upholding a basic French principle: separation between government and religion within state schools. But as for adult women walking in the streets, he sees the burqa ban as an assault on women's basic freedom to wear what they want. "I think it's unconstitutional. I don't like the burqa, and very few people in France are in favor of it, but I say these women have the right to go in the street dressed as they wish," he says. "That's a fundamental human right."

Paradoxically, of the fewer than 2,000 women who don burqas in France today, a quarter of them are converts to Islam, and two-thirds have French nationality, according to government estimates.[46]

"These are a small number of young women — several hundred — trying out their relationship to their religion and to the rest of society," Bowen says. "To stigmatize them seems wrong-headed from the point of view of social psychology." Some research indicates that young Muslim women may use headscarves as a way to negotiate with their families for more freedom, to attend university, for example. Banning the veil will, if anything, prompt a more fundamentalist reaction among such women, some critics predict.

After the French Senate passed the burqa ban in September, some Muslim women said they would remain cloistered in their homes rather than go out unveiled, boding badly for increased integration.[47]

In a 2006 court case, *Begum v. Headteacher*, the British House of Lords upheld a British high school's authority to prohibit a young girl from wearing a *jilbab* (a dark cloak) to school and found that the prohibition did not violate human rights.[48] Yet in a country like Britain, with its long tradition of freedom of expression, most people disapprove of the government banning the wearing of burqas in public, judging from polls and recent interviews.[49]

Muslim groups in Britain protested in 2006 when Labour member of Parliament and ex-foreign secretary Jack Straw said he asked Muslim constituents to remove their veils from their faces when they came to his office. Some Muslim community spokesmen claimed Straw was being discriminatory. Straw argued that face-to-face communication was better when you could "see what the other person means, and not just hear what they say."[50]

BACKGROUND

Colonial Roots

Modern Muslim migration in Europe began in the late 19th century as a result of Europe's colonial and trading activities. Those historic patterns largely explain the different ethnic groups that migrated to each country and, to some degree, their acceptance by those societies.

Gypsies Face Poor Education, Discrimination

In traditional clans, girls drop out of school early.

Twenty-four-year-old Sara Kotowicz seems like any other fashionably dressed Londoner finishing her university education. But she is a rare exception in her clan of Polish Roma, or Gypsies. Girls in her large extended family are expected to marry by 15 or 16, have children right away and stop attending school — despite living in 21st-century London.

Kotowicz, whose family migrated to England when she was 11, married at 17, the upper age-limit for acceptable marriage in her family. But her decision to pursue a degree in interior design during her first year of marriage subjected her to severe criticism.

"Within the community you're expected to do the duties of a wife. There's no time for school," says Kotowicz, whose one concession to Gypsy attire is her long black skirt. Each morning as she left for class, she faced a scolding from her mother-in-law — "You should think of washing clothes, looking after your husband" — harassment that drove her and her husband, uncharacteristically, to move out of his family's home.

Throughout Europe, experts say, the lack of education is probably the single greatest impediment to the advancement of the Roma, along with discrimination.[1] British professionals who work with Romanian and Polish Roma immigrants say it's sometimes difficult to convince Roma parents to allow their children to attend school, because in their home countries — Poland, Romania, Hungary and Slovakia — Roma children often were consigned to segregated schools or backwater classes for the mentally handicapped.

For traditional Roma families where girls are commonly expected to marry as early as 14, girls who become mothers enjoy high status, says Michael Stewart, an anthropologist at University College London, who studies the Eastern European Roma. "There's enormous value in traditional Romany communities in becoming mothers — literally reproducing the community" — one that faced extermination under the Nazis and persecution under communist regimes.

"Twenty years ago I never found a 16- or 17-year-old girl who was unmarried," says Heather Ureche, a consultant with the charity Equality, which helps Eastern European Roma migrants in Britain.[2] "Now I do. It's changing slowly, but we still have quite a way to go."

"A lot of people in Eastern Europe say the Roma are not educated, the parents don't want their children in school, don't value education. That's not true — in general," says Stewart. "The problem is they're very badly treated — humiliated and put into separate classes for the hard-to-educate."

In Romania, few Roma children continue school after age 9 or 10, according to Ureche. Moreover, she says, "Roma parents are often worried about sending young girls into coed school settings just after puberty for fear they'll get in trouble with non-Roma boys."

Children in Roma culture generally are given great independence at an early age and are expected to have the maturity needed to be a parent by 14, experts report. "If you're an academically ambitious 13-year-old girl in a traditional Romany family, it is really tough," Stewart observes. "You have a battle on your hands to persuade your parents to let you go on and study." Some younger Roma from traditional families are bucking the trend, such as Viktoria Mohacsi, who represented Hungary as a member of the European Parliament from 2004 to 2009.[3]

Getting a high school education is becoming more acceptable for Roma girls in London, says Kotowicz, who is a youth advocacy worker for the Roma Support Group, a London charity. But she still has trouble persuading teenage girls from her community to continue their education.

By the late 1800s, France, Britain and the Netherlands had gained control over most of the world's Muslims. France conquered Algiers in 1830, eventually leading to French control of Algeria, Morocco and Tunisia. The British colonized India (which included modern-day Pakistan and Bangladesh). The Dutch dominated trade in Southeast Asia, where today's Indonesia — the world's most populous Muslim nation — became a Dutch colony after the Dutch East India Company relinquished control. By the end of the 19th century, France was importing low-paid workers from Algeria and other African territories, while other European countries recruited workers from their colonies and territories.

However, Europe — where residents had long been immigrating to the United States in search of a better life — did not become a major immigrant destination

A recent visit to a house in North London illustrated some of the striking differences in how Romanian Roma families raise their children. As school was letting out, an array of spirited children, ages 4-16, some related to the family and some not, paraded through the tiny kitchen. All seemed perfectly comfortable eating something from the refrigerator, whether they lived there or not.

Unlike British and American culture, where childhood is viewed as a separate phase of life that can last until age 18, for the Roma "young children have enormous autonomy," Stewart explains. "Children are never told off, never told, 'You mustn't do that.' Children learn not to do things through making mistakes rather than through constant correction; the assumption is that by the age of 10 or 13 Romany people are autonomous moral agents — what we would call adults."

These cultural values sometimes create serious problems for Roma families in Britain, says Sywia Ingmire, coordinator of the Roma Support Group. "Children are the responsibility of every adult visiting the home; children are passed from hand to hand," she says. But sometimes "bewildered social workers" think a child is being trafficked. For instance, in 2008 several large extended Roma families were living together in the town of Slough. In a series of dawn raids on 17 houses, 24 Roma adults were arrested, supposedly for taking Roma children from their families and forcing them into a life of crime. But nine days later, none of the 24 adults arrested at the scene had been charged with child trafficking offenses, and all but one child had been returned to the Roma community in Slough.[4]

"These stories about rings of trafficking people are often built more on exaggeration and fantasy than a good empirical basis," says Stewart, who finds that children who beg and steal are a small minority of Europe's Roma population.

Yet the view of Roma children as beggars and thieves is widespread in Europe. In a recent street survey in three cities, more than 60 percent of those questioned associated

School uniforms identify two Roma sisters — Violeta Stelica, 8, (right), and Nicoleta Mihai, 6, (left) — as public school students in North London on Oct. 11, 2010. But in traditional Roma families across Europe, girls often drop out in order to get married, sometimes as early as age 14.

Gypsies with negative activities like thievery. [5]In Europe, Ureche says, prejudice against Gypsies "is the last bastion of racism."

— Sarah Glazer

[1]Angela Doland, "Lack of Schooling Seen as Root of Gypsy Woes," The Associated Press, Oct. 9, 2010, www.google.com/hostednews/ap/article/ALeqM5hA_jAjgctB4r_ZYfw645v7vLBlWAD9IOJLD01?docId=D9IOJLD01.

[2]See Equality's website, at http://equality.uk.com/Welcome.html.

[3]"Interview: Viktoria Mohacsi," *Foreign Policy*, Oct. 20, 2010, www.foreignpolicy.com/articles/2010/10/20/interview_viktoria_mohacsi.

[4]Helen Pidd and Vikram Dodd, "From Brilliant Coup to Cock-up. How the Story of Fagin's Urchins Fell Apart," *Guardian*, Feb. 2, 2008, www.guardian.co.uk/uk/2008/feb/02/immigration.ukcrime.

[5]Heather Ureche, "Racism in a Velvet Glove," *Oxfam Poverty Post*, Sept. 10, 2009, www.oxfamblogs.org/ukpovertypost/2009/09/racism-in-a-velvet-glove%E2%80%A6/.

until the 1950s, when it needed workers to help rebuild cities and economies ravaged by World War II. After the wartime deaths of thousands of working-age men, England sought workers from throughout the British Empire, in part because they would speak English: Indians and Pakistanis came from the 1950s on, Bangladeshis from the 1970s. For much the same reason, in the postwar economic boom, France, Germany and the Netherlands

also recruited immigrants from their former colonies, and in some cases, the mother countries gave preferential treatment to former colonists wanting to enter the country to work.

Some former colonials integrated more quickly into their new home countries than others. Muslims from francophone Africa, for instance, have been more interested in becoming part of France than Turks have been in

For and Against Immigrants

Kurdish immigrants in Rome wave the Kurdistan flag and portraits of their historical leader Abdullah Ocalan during Italy's first nationwide "day without immigrants" strike on March 1, 2010 (top). The rally was one of dozens held around Europe in the last year to protest harsh anti-immigrant measures taken by European governments, which some critics say are particularly targeting Muslim immigrants. Anti-Muslim sentiment was evident in Harrow, North London, on Sept. 11, 2009 (bottom), when riot police quelled clashes between Muslims and anti-Islamic extremists protesting outside a London mosque on the anniversary of the 9/11 attacks in the United States.

Germany, where they have no cultural links, argues Bowen, of Washington University. "The very bitterness of France's colonial history channels Muslims toward demanding inclusion in French society," Bowen wrote. "They, or their parents or grandparents, came from former French territories in North or West Africa, where they learned that they were now part of the grand story of France, albeit in second-class roles."[51]

After World War II, when a devastated Germany needed immigrant labor to help rebuild, Germany's choice of workers would have long-term repercussions. In the mid-1950s, Germany instituted an active immigration policy, first for Italian and Spanish farmworkers.[52] Later, as the economy boomed and industry needed labor, the government turned to North Africa and Turkey for workers, who were expected to stay only two years.

"The German and Austrian governments had recruitment offices in the least-developed rural areas of Anatolia to recruit illiterate Turks because of the false belief that if they can't read, they won't join trade unions and make trouble," explains Viennese demographer Lutz.

But unlike Czech and Ukranian migrants who settled in Austria earlier, Turks did not become absorbed into the society or even learn the language in many cases. "Many Turks didn't think they would stay," Lutz says, "nor did society."

Indeed, most European governments saw the recruitment of immigrant labor as a temporary measure. Temporary "guestworker" programs were initiated in Germany, Belgium and Sweden, recruiting first from Italy and Spain and later from the Mediterranean, North Africa and the Middle East.

Turks made up the largest percentage of German migrants. And the *Gastarbeiter* (guestworker) program was a "hard-currency bonanza" for Turkey, according to author Christopher Caldwell, a columnist for *The Weekly Standard* and *Financial Times* whose book, *Reflections on the Revolution in Europe*, chronicles how Muslims transformed postwar Europe. The Turkish government petitioned hard for inclusion in the program, and the single Turkish men who arrived to work in German mines and steel plants discovered they could make far more money than in Turkey. The number of Turkish guestworkers in Germany burgeoned from 329,000 in 1960 to 2.6 million by 1973, the year the program was discontinued.[53]

But the workers found Germany attractive, and the gap steadily widened between what natives understood the program to mean and what the workers understood. German corporations pressured the government to make the *Gastarbeiter* contracts renewable, to allow workers' families to join them and to permit those that had started families to stay. A "rotation clause" intended to limit a foreign worker's stay in Germany to two years was removed from the German-Turkish guestworker treaty in 1964, partly due to industry pressure.[54]

Europe's acute manpower shortages, however, were not chronic, Caldwell writes. In the 1960s, migrants were manning soon-to-be obsolete linen mills in France and textile mills in England. The jobs would soon be eliminated, creating joblessness among migrants and a growing anti-immigrant reaction.

On April 20, 1968 — two weeks after the assassination of the Rev. Martin Luther King, Jr., triggered riots in Washington, D.C., and other major U.S. cities — Conservative British Parliament member Enoch Powell warned that Britain's growing immigration would lead to similar violent conflicts between immigrants and Britons. Already, he claimed, the native-born English "found themselves made strangers in their own country," and he quoted a constituent's prediction that "in 15 or 20 years' time the black man will have the whip hand over the white man." Citing the poet Virgil, he said, "I seem to see 'the River Tiber foaming with much blood.' "[55]

Powell received enthusiastic letters in response from British natives, and much of the British debate since then has been over whether Powell's "rivers of blood" predictions would prove correct.

'Immigration Stop' Policies

During Germany's 1966-67 recession, many laid-off guestworkers returned home only to find the Turkish economy in crisis. But when the 1973-77 global recession hit, many migrants stayed in their adopted countries, even if they were unemployed — spurring European fears that immigrants would compete for jobs. EU governments between 1973 and 1975 instituted an "immigration stop" policy, aimed at deterring immigration and halting overseas recruitment.[56]

The number of new foreign workers arriving declined, but migration continued — primarily due to extended families joining the original immigrant or new spouses arriving on marriage visas. Today, most immigration into Western Europe involves family migration.

Paradoxically, more immigrants came to Europe during the decades after the "stop" policies were instituted than arrived in the preceding decades, largely because of family immigration. In the Netherlands, the number of first-generation Moroccan and Turkish immigrants increased tenfold in the three decades following the 1974 halt. By 2003, the number of North Africans in France was triple the number from before the government started restricting immigration.[57]

Since then, EU governments have tried repeatedly to discourage immigration. Some, like France, have even offered monetary incentives and continued welfare support to immigrants who return home. Most of the programs ended in failure.[58]

Experts say once an immigration dynamic has been established between countries it is hard to stop. In Belgium, Turkish immigrants from Emirdag settled in Brussels and Ghent, with family and friends living on the same street with their neighbors from back home. Bangladeshis settled in East London, while Pakistanis from Punjab and Kashmir settled in Birmingham and Bradford.[59]

Radical Islam Emerges

During the 1980s some young Muslims, frustrated by job discrimination, turned to their religion as a source of identity. Europe became a target of proselytizing campaigns, helped along by the distribution of Saudi Arabian petrodollars, which financed the construction of new mosques and Islamic schools. Saudi money specifically supported the spread and teaching of the ultra-conservative Wahhabi strand of Islam.[60]

Acts of terrorism in the 1990s and early 2000s fueled fears of radical Islamists. Between 1995 and 1996, radical Algerians exploded bombs on Paris subways and trains, adding to French anti-immigrant sentiment. France and other nations expelled radical Islamists, and members of the French secret services dubbed the British capital "Londonistan" for its role as a refuge for radical Islamist groups.

Then on Feb. 23, 1998, al Qaeda leader Osama bin Laden issued a fatwa stating that all Muslims had a duty to kill Americans and their allies — civilian or military — around the world. Islamic liberation movements worldwide began to shift their emphasis from national revolution to localized, violent terrorism.

The Sept. 11, 2001, attacks on the Pentagon and World Trade Center, in which nearly 3,000 people died, would change forever the way Europeans looked at their Muslim neighbors. Although directed by al Qaeda and carried out by mostly Saudi Arabian jihadists, the attacks had been planned by a group of English-speaking Muslims at a mosque in Hamburg, Germany.

"September 11 turned the spotlight on European Muslims and made people feel insecure; they started looking at Muslims through a security prism," says the European Policy Centre's Shada Islam. Soul-searching about whether Europe was becoming a breeding ground for terrorists intensified after a string of terrorist attacks tied to Muslim extremists: the Madrid subway bombings in 2004; the murder of Dutch filmmaker Theo Van Gogh by a radical Islamist the same year; the "7/7" 2005 London transit bombings that killed 52.

But rather than focus on jobs, education and disaffected youth — the root causes of integration problems — Islam says, the debate about Muslim immigrants was no longer about social disadvantages. Suddenly, "it was as if every Muslim in Europe was a potential terrorist." Islam says the current wave of anti-immigrant, anti-Muslim sentiment would not have "reached this point if September 11 had not happened."

In 2002 far-right Dutch politician Pim Fortuyn (who had criticized Muslims for not assimilating) was murdered by a Dutch man who said he was protecting Muslims. Then in 2004, filmmaker Theo van Gogh, who had made a film critical of the treatment of women by Muslims, was murdered in broad daylight on an Amsterdam street by a Dutch-born son of Moroccan immigrants. As Dutch *Financial Times* columnist Simon Kuper puts it, "violence associated with Muslims suddenly entered the public debate. Nowhere else in Europe has the far right done so well out of 9/11" as in the Netherlands.[61]

In Britain, young Muslims said 9/11 — and the London transit suicide-bomb attacks on July 7, 2005, by radical British Muslims — made them identify as Muslims more than they had before. In 2007, Muslim doctors from India and the Middle East working in Britain tried to blow up the airport in Glasgow, Scotland, and authorities foiled Muslim plots to blow up a U.S. military base in Frankfurt, Germany, and a bomb attack by Muslims in Copenhagen.[62] Polls by the Pew Research Center found that Muslims in France, Spain and Britain were twice as likely as U.S. Muslims to say suicide bombs can be justified.[63]

In 2004, the EU admitted 10 new countries: the Czech Republic, Estonia, Hungary, Latvia, Lithuania, Poland, Slovakia, Slovenia, Cyprus and Malta. Under EU rules, citizens of those countries were free to move to any member country to work, and thousands of Eastern Europeans poured into Western Europe. In 2007, Bulgaria and Romania were admitted, but citizens of those countries do not have full working rights in most EU-15 countries.[64]

While the EU was opening its eastern borders, impoverished West Africans continued to risk their lives to enter Europe from the south. During the early 2000s, scores of Africans drowned when their over-packed small boats capsized en route to Spanish territory. And in 2005, an estimated 11,000 would-be migrants tried to enter Spain by scaling a 10-foot wall surrounding Melilla — a tiny coastal Spanish enclave on Morocco's northern coast. Three immigrants died in the attempts. And in one brazen, pre-dawn incident, about 500 Africans stormed the barrier, using 270 ladders crafted from tree branches. About 100 migrants made it into the Spanish territory before being detained by police.[65]

Examining Multiculturalism

As fear of Muslim extremism and terrorism spread after 9/11, Europeans began to question whether terrorism was caused by a failure to integrate immigrants into society. In their soul-searching, many became increasingly critical of multicultural policies — which sometimes meant government funding of religious and ethnic groups or taking a hands-off attitude toward cultural traditions that may conflict with European laws.

For example, some critics blamed laissez-faire multiculturalism for the failure to prevent up to a dozen suspected "honor killings" every year among Britain's Muslim communities. In these cases, the women were murdered by fathers and brothers, presumably for having "dishonored" the family, such as by dating men outside their ethnic group. One such case particularly spurred outrage: A 20-year-old Kurdish woman, who repeatedly sought help from police, was killed in 2006 by her father and uncle, prompting an investigation into police handling of the case. The Independent Police Complaints Commission found in 2008 that officers had failed to follow up promptly on murder victim Banaz Mahmod's assault allegations, and the Commission recommended "reinforcing" police officers' knowledge about honor-based violence.[66]

Police "may be worried that they will be seen as racist if they interfere in another culture," Diana Sammi, director of the Iranian and Kurdish Women's Rights organization, said at the time.[67]

Globalization Fosters Identity Crisis

"People don't feel at home anymore in their own country."

In the Netherlands, where the same meat-and-potatoes dinner traditionally is eaten night after night, people often "feel threatened" by the mosques and kebab shops proliferating in their neighborhoods, says Floris Vermeulen, who teaches political science at the University of Amsterdam. "Their country is changing, their neighborhoods are changing" and "they don't feel at home anymore in their own country."

Many European countries are experiencing similar national identity crises, as their once monocultural societies — with everyone sharing the same values, ethnicity and food — seem at risk due to the globalization of human migration. That helps explain why Europeans are disturbed at the thought of immigrants living next door who resist interacting with their neighbors. Vermeulen observes wryly, "In many countries this is not considered a problem if they're not killing each other."

But in monocultural societies like Germany or the Netherlands, mainstream politicians want "a new society where everyone has contact and feels the same about all the norms and values." When it comes to a religion like Islam, Vermeulen says, "this is not considered a Dutch, German or northern European value; this is something they have to change. That becomes problematic because how [could] a government . . . change the religious beliefs of a certain people?"

Muslims have been able to resist assimilation with the rest of the society, experts say, partly by importing wives — often illiterate — from their family's village of origin, a custom that has continued into the second and third generation in Germany and the Netherlands. To combat this, European countries have toughened visa requirements for marriage partners. Both the Netherlands and Germany now require spouses to have a basic grasp of the new country's language and pass exams testing their knowledge of the society before they can legally enter. Britain's new

Dominik Wasilewski poses proudly on April 1, 2008, outside the Polish delicatessen where he works in Crewe, England, home to one of Britain's largest Polish communities. Many Europeans feel their once monocultural societies are endangered by the cultural changes caused by increased migration.

Conservative-led government is introducing a pre-entry English test for arriving spouses.

While Ruud Koopmans, director of migration at the Social Science Research Center in Berlin, sees these measures as "very good for integration," economically and socially, others condemn them as discriminatory, aimed mainly at stopping immigrants from Muslim countries. Americans would probably find such pre-entry requirements unduly burdensome, since many of their grandparents entered the country without knowing English.

But Koopmans argues that in Europe's generous welfare societies, where taxpayers bear a heavy burden to support unemployed immigrants, governments have the right to require newcomers to have the necessary tools for employment before entering the country.

— Sarah Glazer

After Sept. 11 and the Fortuyn and Van Gogh murders, even the Netherlands, long considered the leading proponent of multiculturalism, adopted more restrictive immigration policies. Other countries followed suit, including those in Scandinavia, which attempted to limit

arranged marriages from abroad. Since then, women's rights advocates have supported legislation to protect women from forced marriages, which they see as often being linked to honor killings. In Norway, participation in a forced marriage brings up to six years in prison;

German Chancellor Angela Merkel (right) arrives with delegates from immigrant groups for the fourth summit on the integration of foreigners in Germany on Nov. 3, 2010, in Berlin. The summit followed recent heated public debates on immigration policy and the integration of Muslims in Germany, punctuated by Merkel's uncharacteristically blunt October remark that Germany's "multicultural" experiment has "utterly failed" — widely interpreted as a criticism of the nation's 4 million Muslims.

Denmark requires that a spouse brought into the country be at least 24 years old — as must the resident spouse.

Defending these laws, Unni Wikan, a professor of social anthropology at the University of Oslo, said Scandinavian countries felt their values — including the belief in gender equality — were being threatened by Muslim communities that failed to integrate. She said several governments were considering such laws because "we're afraid we're leading toward a society that's breaking up into ethnic tribes."[68]

Islam, of the European Policy Centre, agrees forced marriages and honor killings should be treated as crimes: "Let's not let people off the hook by saying this is tribal tradition." But she adds, "You can do it confrontationally or through a process of consultation; let's not assume every single Muslim believes in these crimes or commits them." For example, grassroots Muslim organizations in Belgium have launched school campaigns to warn young African women returning to their home countries for summer holidays that they could be forced into marriages there.

In the Netherlands, the 90-year-old policy of "pillarization," which permits each faith to set up its own government-funded religious schools and organizations, became increasingly unpopular in the 1990s and 2000s because it was seen as further segregating Muslims from society.

Statistics showed that only one-third of non-EU foreigners in the Netherlands were gainfully employed; the rest were either not in the labor market or depended on social benefits. Welfare-dependency rates among foreigners were 10 times that of the native Dutch, and high-school dropout and residential segregation rates were high as well.[69] In 2004, a Dutch parliamentary inquiry into government policy toward ethnic minorities between 1970 and 2000 came to the damning conclusion that if some migrants succeeded it was "in spite of" government policy.[70]

Because of a long tradition in which the state paid for Catholic and Protestant schools, Dutch sociologist Duyvendak says, "We're struggling: On the one hand, we don't want Muslim schools, but we want to protect our privileges — the state paying for our Catholic and Protestant schools," which are considered academically superior to secular public schools.

In reaction to what it saw as alien Muslim values, the Netherlands demanded that immigrants adopt Dutch progressive values. A new policy of civic integration, starting with its 1998 Newcomer Integration Law, required most non-EU immigrants to participate in a 12-month integration course, including Dutch language and civic education.

The 2002 murder of Fortuyn, who had criticized Muslims for not adopting the country's tolerant attitudes towards homosexuals, helped to turn the Dutch government in an even more draconian direction.[71] After March 2006, applicants for family reunification were required to take an integration test at a Dutch embassy abroad to receive even temporary residence. The policy quickly became a model for the rest of Europe, and variations have been adopted by Finland, Denmark, Austria, Germany, France, Belgium, Portugal and Spain.[72]

The policies generally require newcomers to enroll in civic and language courses, either before or after entering the country. Noncompliance could result in financial penalties or the denial of permanent legal residence. Eventually, the policy morphed into a tool to restrict migration, especially of unskilled migrants or relatives from traditional backgrounds.

For example, in May 2006, after intense debates about honor killings in the Turkish immigrant community and ethnic violence in a Berlin public school, German authorities made attendance at a civic integration course a requirement for naturalization. This reversed a previous trend towards liberalization — most notably, Germany's efforts to make it easier for Turkish guestworkers to become citizens, which began in 2000.[73]

France has been spared a major Muslim terrorist attack since the mid-1990s, leading some French experts to conclude that France does a better job of culturally integrating its Muslim immigrants, who mostly come from francophone Africa. But riots in the poor, largely African suburbs of Paris in 2005 and Grenoble in 2010 — both plagued with high unemployment — presented striking evidence that many of France's Muslims feel economically left behind.

Still, Floris Vermeulen, a Dutch expert on radicalization who teaches political science at the University of Amsterdam, says religious radicalism is much less prevalent in France than elsewhere in Europe. Some immigration experts, including anthropologist Bowen, maintain that the French riots of 2005, spurred by joblessness and discrimination, were driven more by a desire to be part of France, rather than a separatist Muslim movement.

For instance, When French Muslims took to the streets in 2004 to protest the proposed ban on headscarves in French schools, their chant was Francophile: "First, Second, Third-Generation: We don't give a damn: Our home is here!"[74]

CURRENT SITUATION

Rise of Extremists

Anti-immigrant parties are surging in popularity among voters in the Netherlands, Sweden and Austria. Although these remain minority parties, the governing coalitions often need their votes to pass legislation.

"The fall of parliamentary seats into extremist hands represents the biggest shake-up in European politics since the disappearance of communism," Denis MacShane, a Labour member of the British Parliament, recently wrote.[75]

Experts say Europe's progressive social democratic regimes and Britain's liberal Labour government have been defeated because they failed to control immigration.[76]

In the Netherlands, the coalition that emerged from this fall's election joined two center-right parties and did not invite Wilders' anti-immigrant Freedom Party into the coalition. But holding only 52 of the parliament's 150

seats, the coalition needs the support of the Freedom Party's 24 members to pass legislation, making Wilders a kingmaker. In exchange for his party's support, Wilders extracted policy concessions, including consideration of a ban on the Islamic face veil and halving immigration from non-Western (read Muslim) countries. The government also agreed to consider making family reunification and marriage immigration more difficult and to make it harder for people from places like Iraq and Somalia to obtain asylum.

But it's unclear whether international agreements will allow the government to implement all these measures, such as refusing to grant asylum to people from certain countries. "That's problematic for the European Declaration of Human Rights," points out Vermeulen, of the University of Amsterdam. As for cutting immigration, he says, "It's already very difficult to immigrate to the Netherlands. We can't do much more."

In Sweden, the nationalist Swedish Democrats won enough votes in September to gain representation in parliament for the first time. Their campaign had included a controversial TV ad showing an elderly, white Swedish woman in a race for pension/welfare benefits beaten by a stampede of burqa-wearing women pushing strollers. The party's leader, Jimmie Akesson, campaigned for a 90-percent reduction in immigration and described Muslim population growth as the greatest foreign threat to Sweden since World War II. Center-right Prime Minister Fredrik Reinfeldt pledged not to work with the Swedish Democrats even though he failed to achieve a majority.[77]

In Austria, the Freedom Party won enough votes in provincial elections to raise speculation it could have a major impact on Austria's national elections in three years. Formerly led by Nazi-sympathizer Jörg Haider, the party won 17.5 percent of the national vote in 2008.[78]

In Germany, a far-right party has not breached the 5 percent threshold for obtaining representation in the national parliament since World War II, usually attributed to the political elite's fear of a Nazi party re-emerging.[79] But recent surveys suggest up to one-fifth of today's electorate would vote for a party to the right of Merkel's Christian Democrats if it were on the ballot today.[80]

In Britain's May elections, many say the deciding moment came when Labour Prime Minister Gordon Brown was caught on tape privately calling a voter who

Is the French ban on headscarves in schools a good idea?

YES

Rémy Schwartz
Member, French Council of State and Former rapporteur, Stasi Commission on Secularism

From "World on Trial," a series of mock International human rights trials created by Pennsylvania State University's Dickinson School of Law, to be Webcast and broadcast on public television stations worldwide in 2011.

France has always welcomed people from all over the world . . . and everyone can worship as they wish here. We've had many Muslims in our country for a long time; the Mosque of Paris was founded in 1920. Islam is the second religion of France. We have Europe's largest mosque and more mosques than any other European country. . . . We didn't wake up one morning in 2004 and say, "Now we're going to discriminate against Muslims."

It's very rare in France to have unanimous decisions between the Left and the Right . . . but after a 15-year discussion, we said we need to stop what the "older brothers" are doing. Young girls came to us and said, "Protect us, we want to be free — free to wear skirts, free to wear pants and not to be forced to wear headscarves. . . . We want to be able to go to school in tranquility." . . .

It was appropriate to protect young children without forcing them to attend private schools or take correspondence courses. . . . We do not wear religious symbols in schools. We did not set out to discriminate against Muslims. The European Court of Human Rights ruled that we did not discriminate.

And where are the victims? Forty-four students were sent [home] from school out of millions of children, and there hasn't been one single incident for the last couple of years. French laws are always being challenged, and yet this law is one of the few that has unanimous consent throughout the country. Even among the Muslim immigrant population, surveys have shown that 70 percent of French Muslims approve of the law. . . . The French Council of Muslim Faith, which represents 6 million French Muslims, accepted this law.

The law is a victory of democratic French Islam against fundamentalists, who want to impose their vision on others. It's also a victory for these young girls. Go onto the Internet and read what the Stasi Commission did. The hearings were recorded, and young women and girls supported this law, and these immigrant women wanted the protection by the state. The women and girls came to us and said, "Thank you for allowing us to be free."

NO

John R. Bowen
Dunbar-Van Cleve Professor of Arts and Sciences, Washington University, St. Louis; Author of Why the French Don't Like Headscarves (Princeton, 2007) and Can Islam Be French? (Princeton 2009)

Written for *CQ Global Researcher*, December 2010

The headscarf ban is not a good idea. Before the 2004 law, France's highest court had consistently held that Muslim girls or women had a constitutional and a human right to wear headscarves. Since then, France has escaped legal sanctions by saying that the law was enacted to protect Muslim school girls who wanted protection against social pressure to wear a scarf, i.e. that it was not about Islam.

Whatever the merits of this argument, it does not reflect the wide range of claims made by French politicians in favor of the ban. France's leaders on the Right and the Left claimed that headscarves led to the oppression of women, that they favored the entry of political Islam onto French soil and that they were responsible for disorder in the public schools. Quite a lot of trouble to pin on the heads of a few hundred girls seeking to practice their faith! At the same time, sociologists and others who had studied reasons why some Muslim girls wear scarves were ignored.

These wild claims kept politicians from having to tackle real social problems, such as social exclusion, high unemployment and police harassment.

But this easy fix came at a price: It stigmatized Muslims who were exercising their religious freedom. Although many Muslims do not wear headscarves, and many agreed with the law, this is hardly a justification for denying others their religious rights.

It is hard to say to what degree the ban has contributed to a sense among some Muslims that France will never accept their right to be publicly Muslim. The ban started France down a "slippery slope" of attacks on people who may be French but who look or act differently. This past year Parliament enacted a ban on women wearing full face-coverings on the street, a practice that some Muslims consider part of their religion. A minister became so enraged when a woman in face-covering and her husband dared to speak out against a traffic ticket that he tried to deprive the man of his French citizenship.

The president brought down European Union criticism for expelling Roma EU citizens rather than ensure their access to decent housing. Once one denies religious rights, whatever the social justification, it becomes easier to erode them just a bit further the next time.

asked him about Eastern European immigrants "a bigoted woman." Party leaders and critics alike said the comment cost him votes among British workers and helped bring the Conservatives to power.[81]

When it came to confronting immigration, politicians like Brown, who had cut their political teeth on anti-racism and anti-apartheid campaigns in the 1970s and '80s, suffered from a "psychological failure," says Tim Finch, head of migration for the Institute for Public Policy Research, a center-left British think tank. "Labour saw migration and race as two sides of the same coin: Anything about immigration control they found instinctively very difficult," he says. But for Labour's working-class base, "immigration was a proxy for economic insecurity and pressure on public services" like public housing, he says. "Race was not a big element of it."

Britain's two right-wing anti-immigrant parties, the British National Party and the UK Independence Party, captured only 5 percent of the vote, but that was enough to cost the Conservatives a clear majority, according to analyst William Galston at the Brookings Institution in Washington, who attributed their growing percentage to anti-immigration sentiment.[82]

Shortly after the election, Conservative Prime Minister Cameron temporarily reduced non-EU immigration by 5 percent, with a permanent cap to be set next April. But in September the business secretary, Liberal Democrat Vince Cable, complained the cap was "very damaging" to industry and that some companies were relocating abroad.[83] Business leaders said the cap would prevent the hiring of IT specialists from India, investment bankers from the United States and other highly skilled workers from outside Europe.[84]

Because EU agreements require Britain to accept workers from all 27 EU countries, the cap only covers non-EU immigrants, who under Britain's newly restrictive point system are skilled and high-skilled workers. "It's insane economically to chop huge numbers out of that; those are people the economy needs," says Finch.

A parliamentary committee recently reported that — given how few migrants can be capped under international agreements — the proposed cap will cover fewer than 20 percent of long-term migrants. So, while barely affecting Britain's overall migration, the cap could do serious damage to Britain's "knowledge economy," the report said.[85]

Under pressure from business leaders, Prime Minister Cameron was expected to increase the number of non-EU migrants allowed under the cap next year — from about 2,600 a month to 4,000 — the British press reported Nov. 16.[86] The government was expected to shift its attention to limiting the entry of "bogus" students and those getting low-level degrees. After the government effectively barred unskilled workers from outside the EU, "student visas rocketed by 30 per cent to a record 304,000 in just one year, as some applicants used it as an alternative work route," Home Secretary Theresa May said in a speech Nov. 5, adding that students now constitute the majority of non-EU immigrants to the U.K.[87]

In September, the independent Joint Council for the Welfare of Immigrants challenged the cap in court, arguing the government sidestepped parliamentary procedures when it introduced the cap.[88]

Like other European governments, Britain is still struggling to find a magic recipe to promote integration while preventing religious radicalism and, ultimately, terrorism among Muslim youth. In November, May announced that the new government was dismantling the previous Labour government's "Prevent" program, an effort to prevent radicalization of Muslim youth by working in their communities.

"Prevent muddled up work on counterterrorism with the normal work that needs to be done to promote community cohesion and participation," May said on Nov. 3. "Counterterrorism became the dominant way in which government and some communities came to interact. That was wrong; no wonder it alienated so many."[89]

Roma Dispute

In July President Sarkozy sparked an international firestorm when he announced he would dismantle 300 illegal Roma camps in France within three months. Sarkozy's office said the camps were "sources of illegal trafficking, of profoundly shocking living standards, of exploitation of children for begging, prostitution and crime."[90] By October, dozens of camps had been emptied and more than 1,000 inhabitants sent home to Romania and Bulgaria.[91] Last year, 10,000 Roma were returned to the two countries.

EU Justice Commissioner Vivian Reding called the deportations a "disgrace." Citing a leaked memo showing that the French had singled out the Roma for deportation,

Anti-immigrant Sentiment Returns

Politicians blaming immigrants for economic hardship — such as Dutch anti-immigrant leader Geert Wilders (top), whose Freedom Party made surprising gains in June parliamentary elections in the Netherlands — are not new. Conservative British Parliament member Enoch Powell railed against immigrants in the late 1960s and early '70s, triggering demonstrations such as the August 1972 march on the Home Office by meat porters bearing a petition demanding an end to all immigration into Britain (bottom). Between 1973 and 1975, several European governments instituted "immigration stop" policies, aimed at deterring immigration and halting overseas recruitment.

she told the European Parliament: "This is a situation I had thought Europe would not have to witness again after the Second World War."[92]

Initially, the European Commission announced it was investigating France with an eye towards taking it to court for violating EU free movement rules and for discriminating against an ethnic minority in violation of the Charter of Fundamental Rights. But the commission suspended its disciplinary action on Oct. 19, saying the French government had promised to enact legislation by next spring to align French law with EU anti-discrimination principles.[93]

The Open Society Institute's Grabbe called the action "a P.R. disaster, making the commission look weak and France look vindicated."[94]

Rob Kushen, executive director of the European Roma Rights Centre in Budapest, says "France could . . . amend its legislation and still act in a discriminatory way against Roma." The event highlighted the lack of EU enforcement power on immigration issues. "Ultimately, the only serious sanction that carries weight is the threat of expulsion from the EU, and that's such an extraordinary threat that I don't think it's a credible deterrent."

The EU's freedom of movement directive allows member nations to deport immigrants from EU countries after three months if the migrants cannot show they have sufficient employment or resources to support themselves. However, the directive also requires a case-by-case decision before the person can be expelled.

"France in our view is clearly in violation of all those guarantees," says Kushen, because they have been expelling people without individual determinations of immigration status. Even if an immigrant is convicted of a crime, they cannot be deported without an individual investigation, he notes. "The Roma have been accused as an ethnic group of begging, illegally squatting on land," a clear example of ethnic discrimination, says Kushen.

Roma from Bulgaria and Romania are in a catch-22 situation when working abroad, because under a political compromise struck when the two countries were admitted into the EU in 2007, European governments were allowed to limit Bulgarian and Romanian immigrants' rights to work in their countries for up to seven years.[95] Member nations were "horrified at the thought that Bulgaria and Romania would empty out, and every able-bodied citizen would go to Western Europe looking for work," Kushen explains.

Advocates for the Roma agree with France on one thing: Romania and Bulgaria are to blame for discriminating against the Roma in the first place, keeping them impoverished. "As long as unemployment rates are reaching 80 to 90 percent in Roma communities in Romania, people are going to move, try to go somewhere else where life is better," Kushen says.

Migration Slowdown

Ironically, anti-immigrant fervor in Europe is occurring just as the global recession has brought the rapid growth of foreign-born populations in developed countries to "a virtual halt," according to a report released in October by the Migration Policy Institute in Washington, D.C.[96]

Between 2008 and 2009, immigration to Ireland from new EU member states dropped 60 percent while overall EU migration to Spain plummeted by two-thirds. The number of foreign workers caught trying to enter the EU illegally at maritime borders fell by more than 40 percent during the same period and continues to decline.

Skyrocketing unemployment rates mean immigrants no longer see the EU as the land of promise. In 2009, unemployment among foreign-born youth reached 41 percent in Spain and 37 percent in Sweden. And substantial numbers of young, native-born men are leaving countries like Ireland and Greece to look abroad for work.[97]

If immigration is dropping so drastically, why is anti-immigration sentiment running so high in Europe? There's still a sizable immigrant population in Europe, "and the vast majority of those people will not go home as a result of the crisis," says Madeleine Sumption, co-author of the institute's report. "When there are fewer jobs around, it's natural for people to get more anxious about economic security — and immigration is one aspect of that."

OUTLOOK

'Temporary Blip?'

Europe's big unknown is whether the dramatic recent drops in immigration spell the end of an era or are just a temporary blip, according to the Migration Policy Institute report.

"My own view is that immigration levels, at least in the U.K., will not return to the levels of 2005 or 2006 at least for some time," says Sumption, who wrote the chapter on Britain. "In part, this is because the number of workers coming from Eastern Europe was a function of it being a new opportunity for those workers: There was pent up demand combined with a strong economic boom. I don't see those kinds of conditions returning in the next few years."

Increasingly, experts say, fast-growing developing nations like Brazil and China — not the industrialized countries — will drive most of the future worldwide immigration. And traditional immigrant-exporting countries like India and China, with higher projected economic growth than Europe, are expected to attract their highly skilled diaspora back from abroad, according to Sumption.

Press reports have emphasized both the growing anti-immigrant sentiment and government policies pushed by right-wing parties. But some experts, including those at the Migration Policy Institute, expected even harsher restrictions on immigrants in the wake of the global recession.

"Immigrant-receiving countries have not resorted to the protectionism that many initially feared," says the institute's report. For example, while a few governments have offered to pay immigrants to return home, immigrants have been reluctant to accept these offers, so only a few countries adopted such measures.[98]

And legal protections, like the EU's free-movement agreements, will likely hamper efforts to cut the numbers as drastically as right-wing politicians in the Netherlands, Sweden and Britain have pledged to do. At the same time, economic insecurity tends to stir fears about immigrants taking jobs and living off welfare, with much of the resentment aimed at the foreigners already living in their countries.

The European Policy Centre's Islam, a Belgian citizen born in Pakistan, says the biggest problem for Muslims in Europe is, "We're looking at European Muslims not as Europeans but as exotic foreigners who should really not be at home in Europe — which is absolutely the wrong approach to take if you're going to get serious about integration." If Europe's 20 million Muslims are viewed as legal residents who contribute to the mainstream culture, politics and economy, that would change the conversation, she suggests. "Instead, all these diktats are coming up" — about banning burqas and adopting European values —"and Muslims in Europe are feeling very estranged," she says. "It's a suicidal approach."

Meanwhile, as cash-strapped governments prepare to slash welfare benefits — drastically in the case of Britain's new Conservative-led coalition government — some think that Europe's famous social "solidarity" will turn against immigrants, including second- and third-generation populations who may be as European as the natives.

If the immigration debate is truly about what constitutes national identity, Europeans may need to view their countries as places that embrace their Turkish, Polish, Pakistani and African communities in the same way that ethnic street markets, music and restaurants have become part of the accepted fabric and pleasure of European living.

NOTES

1. "FPÖ Behind Muezzin-Shooter Game," *Austrian-Times*, Sept. 1, 2010, www.austriantimes.at/news/General_News/2010-09-01/26447/FP%D6_behind_muezzin-shooter_game. Austria has hundreds of Muslim houses of prayer and community centers but only three mosques with minarets — in Vienna, Bad Voslau and Telfs. The muezzin is the person at a mosque chosen to broadcast the call to prayer from the mosque's minaret for Friday services and five times daily.

2. *Ibid.* The Freedom Party was forced to drop out of the Styrian parliament in 2005 after suffering election losses. See "SPO-FPO Deal Possible," *Austrian Independent*, Sept. 27, 2010, http://austrianindependent.com/news/Politics/2010-09-27/4708/SP%D6-FP%D6_deal_possible_in_Styria. Also see, "Right-wing Triumph in Vienna Shocks Federal Coalition Partners, Oct. 11, 2010, www.austriantimes.at/news/General_News/2010-10-11/27371/Right-wing_triumph_in_Vienna_shocks_federal_coalition_partners.

3. Christopher Bickerton, "Dutch Culture Wars," *The New York Times*, Oct. 22, 2010, www.nytimes.com/2010/10/23/opinion/23iht-edbickerton.html?_r=2&scp=3&sq=Christopher%20Bickerton&st=cse.

4. James Carroll, "The Rising Tides of Xenophobia," *Boston Globe*, Oct. 25, 2010, www.boston.com/bostonglobe/editorial_opinion/oped/articles/2010/10/25/the_rising_tides_of_xenophobia/.

5. "Anti-Establishment Rage is Fueling Populism Everywhere," *Spiegelonline International*, Sept. 29, 2010, www.spiegel.de/international/europe/0,1518,720275,00.html. Also see Ian Traynor, "Dutch Far-Right Party Wins Pledge on Burqa Ban," *The Guardian*, Oct. 1, 2010, www.guardian.co.uk/world/2010/oct/01/dutch-far-right-burqa-ban.

6. "Swiss vote to ban minarets showcases new populism," *The Christian Science Monitor*, Nov. 29, 2009, www.csmonitor.com/World/Europe/2009/1129/p06s05-woeu.html. Also see "Swiss Want to Ban Burka," News24, May 23, 2010, www.news24.com/World/News/Swiss-want-to-ban-burqa-20100523.

7. Anthony Faiola, "Anti-Muslim Feelings Propel Right Wing," *The Washington Post*, Oct. 26, 2010, www.washingtonpost.com/wp-dyn/content/article/2010/10/25/AR2010102505374.html?sid=ST2010102600369.

8. *Ibid.*

9. Stephan Faris, "The Roma's Struggle to Find a Home," *Time*, Sept. 23, 2010, www.time.com/time/world/article/0,8599,2021016,00.html#ixzz13SmqGHDl.

10. James Blitz, "Britons Lead on Hostility to Migrants," *Financial Times*, Sept. 6, 2010, www.ft.com/cms/s/0/231ffb5e-b9fa-11df-8804-00144feabdc0.html#axzz15SUbSd2d.

11. "Migration and Immigrants Two Years after the Financial Collapse," Migration Policy Institute, October 2010, p. 1, www.migrationpolicy.org/news/2010_10_07.php. German migration is negative. "Germany's Population by 2060," Federal Statistical Office, 2009, www.destatis.de/jetspeed/portal/cms/Sites/destatis/Internet/EN/Content/Publikationen/SpecializedPublications/Population/GermanyPopulation2060.psml.

12. About 261,000 people sought asylum in the EU-27 countries in 2009, but only 78,800 were granted legal protection by EU member governments. See "EU Member states granted protection to 78,800 asylum seekers in 2009," Eurostat press release, June 18, 2010, http://epp.eurostat.ec.europa.eu/portal/page/portal/product_results/search_results?mo=containsall&ms=asylum+seekers+&saa=&p_action=SUBMIT&l=us&co=equal&ci=,&po=equal&pi=,.

13. Charles Hawley, "Letter from Berlin: Searching for Facts in Germany's Integration Debate," *Spiegelonline*, Oct. 12, 2010, www.spiegel.de/international/germany/0,1518,722716,00.html.

14. Katya Vasileva, "Foreigners Living in the EU Are Diverse and Largely Younger than the Nationals of the EU Member States," *Eurostat Statistics in Focus*, no.

45, Sept. 7, 2010, p. 5, http://epp.eurostat.ec.europa.eu/cache/ITY_OFFPUB/KS-SF-10-045/EN/KS-SF-10-045-EN.PDF.

15. For background, see Sarah Glazer, "Social Welfare in Europe," *CQ Global Researcher*, Aug. 1, 2010, pp. 185-210.

16. Michael Slackman, "With Film Afghan-German is a Foreigner at Home," *The New York Times*, Oct. 17, 2010, www.nytimes.com/2010/10/18/world/europe/18germany.html.

17. Tony Barber, "European Countries Cannot Have it Both Ways on Immigration," *The Financial Times*, Sept. 3, 2010, www.ft.com/cms/s/0/dab74570-b788-11df-8ef6-00144feabdc0.html.

18. Hawley, *op. cit.*

19. Matthew Clark, "Angela Merkel: Multi-culturalism has 'utterly failed,'" *The Christian Science Monitor*, Oct. 17, 2010, www.csmonitor.com/World/Global-News/2010/1017/Germany-s-Angela-Merkel-Multiculturalism-has-utterly-failed/%28page%29/2.

20. Slackman, *op. cit.*

21. Reiner Klingholz, "Immigration Debate: Germany Needs More Foreigners," *Spiegelonline*, Aug. 30, 2010. See accompanying graphic "A Change of Direction," www.spiegel.de/international/zeitgeist/0,1518,714534,00.html. According to *Der Spiegel*, about 10,000 fewer people emigrated to Germany from Turkey in 2009 than left the country for Turkey.

22. Barber, *op. cit.*

23. Klingholz, *op. cit.*

24. Among Germans the fertility rate has fallen from 2.5 children born to each woman in the 1960s to only 1.4 children — far below the 2.1 rate needed to replace the population.

25. Vasileva, *op. cit.*

26. Migration will compensate for natural population shrinkage in more than half the European regions that are expected to grow, according to Eurostat. See "Regional Population Projections," Eurostat, last modified Oct. 12, 2010, http://epp.eurostat.ec.europa.eu/statistics_explained/index.php/Regional_population_projections.

27. "Economy: Migration Key to Long-Term Economic Growth, Says OECD," Press Release, Organisation for Economic Co-operation and Development, July 12, 2010, www.oecd.org/document/26/0,3343,en_2649_37415_45623194_1_1_1_1,00.html. Also see "International Migration Outlook 2010," OECD, 2010, www.oecd.org/els/migration/imo.

28. John P. Martin, "Editorial: Ensuring that Migrants Are Onboard the Recovery Train," in *ibid.*, pp. 15-17, www.oecd.org/dataoecd/27/0/45593548.pdf.

29. OECD, "International Migration Outlook 2010," *op. cit.* This OECD report finds unemployment for immigrants running about twice the rate for native-born in many countries.

30. Christian Dustmann, *et al.*, "Assessing the Fiscal Costs and Benefits of A8 Migration to the UK," Center for Research and Analysis of Migration, University College London, July 2009, www.econ.ucl.ac.uk/cream/pages/Press_release_A8fiscalimpact.pdf.

31. According to U.N. projections, the share of Europe's population over age 80 will rise from 3.8 percent to 9.5 percent by 2050. Philippe Legrain, "How Immigration Can Help Defuse Europe's Demographic Timebomb," speech delivered in Helsinki, October 2010.

32. Carroll, *op. cit.*

33. "International Migration Outlook 2010," *op. cit.*, p. 206. The new law shortened the time an adult must live legally in Germany before gaining citizenship from 15 years to 8. Under the law, babies born to foreign parents in Germany are considered both German citizens and citizens of their parents' country of origin until age 23. They must reject their parents' citizenship by age 23 or forfeit their German citizenship.

34. "Mesut Özil: Auswärtsspiel in der Heimat," Spiegel TV, Oct. 11, 2010, http://video.spiegel.de/flash/1088559_iphone.mp4. Also see, "Turkish President Criticizes Özil Jeers," *Times Live*, Oct. 16, 2010, www.timeslive.co.za/sport/soccer/article710604.ece/Turkish-president-criticises-Ozil-jeers.

35. Christian Joppke, "Beyond National Models: Civic Integration Policies for Immigrants in Western Europe," *West European Politics*, January 2007,

pp. 1-22, http://dx.doi.org/10.1080/0140238060 1019613.

36. Ines Michalowski, "Citizenship Tests in Five Countries — An Expression of Political Liberalism?" Social Science Research Center Berlin, October 2009, pp. 17, 24, www.wzb.eu/zkd/mit/pdf/dp_sp_iv_ 2009-702.pdfA.

37. Joppke, *op. cit.*, p. 8.

38. Ruud Koopmans, "Trade-Offs between Equality and Difference: Immigrant Integration, Multiculturalism and the Welfare State in Cross-National Perspective," *Journal of Ethnic and Migration Studies*, January 2010, pp. 1-26, http://193.174.6.11/zkd/mit/projects/ projects_Trade_offs.en.htm.

39. "Are Women's Rights Really the Issue?" *Spiegelonline*, June 24, 2010, www.spiegel.de/international/europe/ 0,1518,702668,00.html.

40. Karima Bennoune, "Secularism and Human Rights: A Contextual Analysis of Headscarves, Religious Expression, and Women's Equality under International Law," *Columbia Journal of Transnational Law*, vol. 45, no. 2, April 11, 2007, pp. 367-426.

41. *Ibid.*, p. 415.

42. "Are Women's Rights Really the Issue?" *op. cit.*

43. *Ibid.*

44. Bennoune, *op. cit.*, p. 421.

45. Patrick Weil, "Why the French Laïcité is Liberal," *Cardozo Law Review*, vol. 30:6, pp. 2699-2714, www.cardozolawreview.com/content/30-6/WEIL .30-6.pdf.

46. "French Senate Bans Burka," CBC News, Sept. 14, 2009, www.cbc.ca/world/story/2010/09/14/france- burka-ban.html#ixzz1496l9Pri.

47. *Ibid.*

48. Bennoune, *op. cit.*, p. 371.

49. However, a majority supported banning veils in airport security checks. "Survey Finds Support for Veil Ban," BBC News, Nov. 29, 2006, http://news.bbc .co.uk/1/hi/uk/6194032.stm.

50. "Straw's Veil Comment Sparks Anger," BBC News, Oct. 5, 2006, http://news.bbc.co.uk/1/hi/5410472 .stm.

51. John R. Bowen, "On Building a Multi-Religious Society," *San Francisco Chronicle*, Feb. 5, 2007, http://articles.sfgate.com/2007-02-05/opinion/1723 1341_1_french-muslims-head-scarves-french-people.

52. Leticia Delgado Godoy, "Immigration in Europe: Realities and Policies," Unidad de Politicas Comparadas, Working Paper 02-18. See Christopher Caldwell, *Reflections on the Revolution in Europe: Immigration, Islam, and the West* (2010), p. 25.

53. Caldwell, *op. cit.*, p. 26.

54. Matthew Bartsch, *et al.*, "A Sorry History of Self-Deception and Wasted Opportunities," *Der Spiegel*, Sept. 7, 2010, www.spiegel.de/international/germany/ 0,1518,716067,00.html.

55. Caldwell, *op. cit.*, pp. 4-5.

56. Esther Ben-David, "Europe's Shifting Immigration Dynamic," *Middle East Quarterly*, Spring 2009, pp. 15-24, www.meforum.org/2107/europe-shifting-immigration-dynamic.

57. *Ibid.*

58. *Ibid.*

59. *Ibid.*

60. See Sarah Glazer, "Radical Islam in Europe," *CQ Global Researcher*, Nov. 1, 2007, pp. 265-294.

61. Simon Kuper, "Where is the Netherlands that I Knew?" *Financial Times*, Oct. 16/17, 2010, *Life & Arts*, p. 2, www.ft.com/cms/s/2/badfda56-d672-11df-81f0-00144feabdc0.html#axzz15VNBajlD.

62. Glazer, *op. cit.*, p. 267.

63. Pew Research Center, "Muslim Americans: Middle Class and Mostly Mainstream," 2007, http://pewresearch.org/assets/pdf/muslim-americans.pdf.

64. For background, see Brian Beary, "The New Europe," *CQ Global Researcher*, Aug. 1, 2007, pp. 181-210.

65. Daniel Howden, "Desperate Migrants Lay Siege to Spain's African Border," *The Independent*, Sept. 28, 2005, www.independent.co.uk/news/world/europe/ desperate-migrants-lay-siege-to-spains-african-border-508674.html.

66. "IPCC Concludes Investigation into MPS and West Midlands Police dealings with Banaz Mahmod," Independent Police Complaints Commission, April

2, 2008, www.ipcc.gov.uk/news/pr_020408_banaz_mahmod.htm.

67. Emine Saner, "Dishonorable Acts," *The Guardian*, June 13, 2007, p. 18.

68. Glazer, *op. cit.*, pp. 277-278.

69. Joppke, *op. cit.*, pp. 1, 6.

70. *Ibid.*

71. "Fortuyn Killed to Protect Muslims," *The Telegraph*, March 28, 2003, www.telegraph.co.uk/news/world-news/europe/netherlands/1425944/Fortuyn-killed-to-protect-Muslims.html.

72. Joppke, *op. cit.*, p. 9.

73. *Ibid.*, p. 14.

74. Glazer, *op. cit.*

75. Quoted from Newsweek in James Kirchik, "Europe the Intolerant," *The Wall Street Journal*, Oct. 12, 2010, http://online.wsj.com/article/SB10001424052748704696304575537950006608746.html.

76. Matthew Campbell, "Left's Long Silence on Migration Turns EU to the Right," *The Sunday Times*, Sept. 19, 2010, www.thesundaytimes.co.uk/sto/news/world_news/Europe/article397964.ece.

77. Stephen Castle, "Political Earthquake Shakes Up Sweden," *International Herald Tribune*, Sept. 21, 2010, p. 3.

78. Kirchik, *op. cit.*

79. Michael Slackman, "Germany Hearing Louder Voices from the Far Right," *International Herald Tribune*, Sept. 23, 2010, p. 3.

80. Hawley, *op. cit.*

81. "Gordon Brown 'bigoted woman' comment caught on tape," BBC News, April 28, 2010, http://news.bbc.co.uk/1/hi/8649012.stm.

82. William Galston, "The British Election Was All about Immigration," *The New Republic*, May 11, 2010, www.tnr.com/blog/william-galston/the-british-election-was-all-about-immigration.

83. "Vince Cable: Migrant Cap is Hurting Economy," *The Guardian*, Sept. 17, 2010, www.guardian.co.uk/politics/2010/sep/17/vince-cable-migrant-cap-economy.

84. "Plans to Cap Number of Skilled Workers Under Scrutiny," *Guardian*, Sept. 7, 2010, www.guardian.co.uk/uk/2010/sep/07/plans-cap-migrants-under-scrutiny.

85. Alan Travis, "Immigration Cap Not the Answer to Cutting Net Immigration Figure, Say MPs," *Guardian*, Nov. 3, 2010, www.guardian.co.uk/uk/2010/nov/03/immigration-cap-net-migration-figure.

86. Robert Winnett, *et al.*, "David Cameron Will Bow to Business and Relax Immigration Cap," Nov. 16, 2010, *Daily Telegraph*, 2010, www.telegraph.co.uk/news/newstopics/politics/david-cameron/8132543/David-Cameron-will-bow-to-business-and-relax-immigration-cap.html.

87. "The Home Secretary's Immigration Speech," Office of the Home Secretary, Nov. 5, 2010. www.homeoffice.gov.uk/media-centre/speeches/immigration-speech.

88. Wesley Johnson, "Legal Challenge to Immigration Cap," *The Independent*, Sept. 24, 2010, www.independent.co.uk/news/uk/legal-challenge-to-immigration-cap-2088649.html.

89. Theresa May, "Our Response to the Terrorist Threat," Office of the Home Secretary, Nov. 3, 2010, www.homeoffice.gov.uk/media-centre/speeches/terrorist-response. Also see, Alan Travis, "Theresa May Promises 'Significant' Reform of Counter-Terror Law," *Guardian*, Nov. 4, 2010, p. 20, www.guardian.co.uk/politics/2010/nov/03/theresa-may-counter-terrorism-reform.

90. "Q&A: France Roma Expulsions," BBC News Europe, Sept. 30, 2010, www.bbc.co.uk/news/world-europe-11027288.

91. Matthew Saltmarsh, "EU Panel Suspends Case against France over Roma," *The New York Times*, Oct. 19, 2010, www.nytimes.com/2010/10/20/world/europe/20roma.html?_r=1&scp=2&sq=Matthew%20Saltmarsh&st=cse.

92. "Q&A: France Roma Expulsions," *op. cit.*

93. Saltmarsh, *op. cit.*

94. *Ibid.*

95. For the different rules of EU countries governing Bulgarian and Romanian workers, see European Commission, "Enlargement: Transitional Provisions," http://ec.europa.eu/social/main.jsp?catId=466&langId

=en. For example in the U.K., immigrants generally cannot work unless self-employed, and the restrictions extend to Dec. 31, 2011, but could be extended.

96. "Migration and Immigrants Two Years after the Financial Collapse," *op. cit.*, p. 1.

97. *Ibid.*

98. *Ibid.*, p. 3.

BIBLIOGRAPHY

Books

Bowen, John R., *Why the French Don't Like Headscarves: Islam, the State, and Public Spaces*, **Princeton University Press**, 2007.
In analyzing why the French banned headscarves in schools in 2004, an American anthropologist cites fears — of radical Islam and alien values — and asks how much newcomers must give up to become part of French society.

Caldwell, Christopher, *Reflections on the Revolution in Europe: Immigration, Islam and the West*, **Penguin Books**, 2010.
A columnist for the *Financial Times* and *Weekly Standard* says Muslim immigration is producing "an undesirable cultural alteration" of Europe, which most Europeans don't want and is not economically necessary.

Legrain, Philippe, *Immigrants: Your Country Needs Them*, **Abacus**, 2007.
An economics journalist argues that demand for migrants will rise in aging societies that need a young, cheap work force to do the work that Europeans dislike, such as elder-care, cleaning and child care.

Articles

Barber, Tony, "European Countries cannot have it both ways on immigration," *Financial Times*, Sept. 3, 2010, www.ft.com/cms/s/0/dab74570-b788-11 df-8ef6-00144feabdc0.html#axzz14xtymjdq. (Subscription required)
A former *Financial Times* Brussels bureau chief says aging Europe cannot maintain its expensive social welfare states without immigration.

Batsch, Matthew, "A Sorry History of Self-Deception and Wasted Opportunities," *Spiegelonline*, Sept. 7, 2010, www.spiegel.de/international/germany/0,1518, 716067,00.html.
Germany recruited Turkish workers in the 1960s, tried to send them home in the 1980s and has struggled with what to do with them ever since.

Bennoune, Karima, "Secularism and Human Rights: A Contextual Analysis of Headscarves, Religious Expression, and Women's Equality under International Law," *Columbia Journal of Transnational Law*, Vol. 45. No.2, posted May 2007, http://papers .ssrn.com/sol3/papers.cfm?abstract_id=989066.
A Rutgers University law professor favors the 2004 French ban on headscarves and describes the major legal cases that preceded it.

Klingholz, Reiner, "Germany Needs More Foreigners," *Spiegelonline*, Aug. 30, 2010, www .spiegel.de/international/zeitgeist/0,1518,druck-71.
A German population expert says Germany needs more immigrants, not fewer, if it is to maintain a strong economy, attract skilled workers and populate a country that suffers from a declining birth rate.

Koopmans, Ruud, "Trade-Offs between Equality and Difference: Immigrant Integration, Multiculturalism and the Welfare State in Cross-National Perspective," *Journal of Ethnic and Migration Studies*, January 2010, pp. 1-26, http://dx.doi.org/10.1080/13691830903250881.
A sociologist finds that immigrants in countries that require them to integrate have higher employment rates than those in other countries.

Weil, Patrick, "Why the French Laïcité is Liberal," *Cardozo Law Review*, Vol. 30:6, 2009, pp. 2699-2714, www.cardozolawreview.com/index.php?option=com_ content&view=article&id=116%3Atable-on-contents- 30-6&Itemid=14.
A French immigration historian who advised the French government to institute the headscarf ban says the law is not an attack on liberty.

Reports and Studies

"Foreigners Living in the EU are Diverse and Largely Younger than the Nationals of the EU Member States," *Eurostat*, Sept. 7, 2010, http://epp.eurostat .ec.europa.eu/portal/page/portal/product_details/ publication?p_product_code=KS-SF-10-045.

The statistical arm of the European Commission finds that foreign immigrants are younger than European natives.

"International Migration Outlook 2010," *Organisation for Economic Co-operation and Development*, 2010, www.oecd.org/document/41/0,3343,en_2649_33931_45591593_1_1_1_1,00.html.
The report says migration is the key to long-term economic growth in aging Western countries, and governments should open their citizenship laws and unemployment benefits to migrants to help them weather the recession.

"Migration and Immigrants Two Years after the Financial Collapse: Where Do We Stand?" *Migration Policy Institute*, Oct. 7, 2010, www.migrationpolicy.org/news/2010_10_07.php.
A Washington think tank says migration is slowing to a virtual halt in parts of the European Union, that Ireland has once again become a country of out-migration, and immigrants in Spain and Sweden are suffering high rates of unemployment.

For More Information

European Policy Centre, Résidence Palace, 155 rue de la Loi, B-1040 Brussels, Belgium; (32) (0) 2 231 0340; www.epc.eu. A think tank that focuses on immigration and integration in the European Union.

European Roma Rights Center, Naphegy tér 8, H-1016 Budapest, Hungary; (36) 1 4132200; www.errc.org. Advocates for the legal rights of Roma in Europe.

Eurostat, for English-language inquiries: (44) 20 300 63103; http://epp.eurostat.ec.europa.eu/portal/page/portal/eurostat/home. The statistical office of the European Union; issues migration statistics for the 27 EU countries.

Institute for Public Policy Research, 4th Floor, 13-14 Buckingham St., London WC2N 6DF, United Kingdom; (44) (0) 20 7470 6100; www.ippr.org.uk. A progressive think tank that has a generally positive perspective on immigration to Britain.

Migration Watch, P.O. Box 765, Guildford, GU2 4XN, United Kingdom; (44) (0) 1869 337007; www.migrationwatchuk.com. A think tank that advocates limiting immigration into the U.K.

Open Society Institute-Brussels, Rue d'dalie 9-13, Brussels 1050, Belgium; (32) 2 505.46.46; www.soros.org/initiatives/brussels. In alliance with the Soros Foundation, promotes tolerant democracies and outspokenly supports Roma migrants' rights.

Organisation for Economic Co-operation and Development, 2, rue André Pascal, 75775 Paris, Cedex 16, France; (33) 1 45.24.82.00; www.oecd.org. Represents 33 developed countries; issues frequent reports about migration.

WZB, Social Science Research Center Berlin, Reichpietschufer 50, D-10785 Berlin-Tiergarten, Germany; (49) 30 25491 0; www.wzb.eu/default.en.asp. Conducts research on immigration and integration in Europe.

Voices From Abroad:

PETER TRAPP

Domestic Policy Analyst
Christian Democrats Party, Germany

Give immigrants intelligence tests
"We have to establish criteria for immigration that really benefit our country. In addition to adequate education and job qualifications, one benchmark should be intelligence. I am in favor of intelligence tests for immigrants. We cannot continue to make this issue taboo."

Accra (Ghana) Mail, June 2010

VINCENT GEISSER

Islamic Scholar, French National Center for Scientific Research

Fear of Islam abounds
"Today in Europe the fear of Islam crystallizes all other fears. In Switzerland, it's minarets. In France, it's the veil, the burqa and the beard."

The New York Times December 2009

MARIE BIDET

Former Interior Ministry Officer, France

The new Gypsies
"These Gypsies created an organization with spokesmen. . . . They speak with [the] authorities, something new in France. They are serious, respectable; they vote, they don't want to burn cars, they want everyone living in peace. That's opposite from the traditional image. . . . [I]t can be underlined that they succeed in their approach."

The Christian Science Monitor September 2010

PIERGUIDO VANALLI

Member of Parliament, Italy

Catholic Church has limited vision of immigration
"The Catholic Church does its job. . . . Ours is a different vision. We have to temper the needs of the people

who live in Italy with the problems that excessive immigration brings with it. The church sees only one aspect, whereas we have a broader vision."

Los Angeles Times, July 2010

GUIDO WESTERWELLE

Vice Chancellor, Germany

Also address emigration
"Germany is not a country of immigration but of emigration. The question of what we can do against this emigration is just as important as the question of what immigration policy we want."

Spiegel Online (Germany) October 2010

ROBERTO MALINI

Representative EveryOne NGO, Italy

A cruel strategy on the Roma
"The strategy is clear and simple: Rather than forcing someone on the airplane, authorities keep demolishing Gypsy camps so that eventually Roma people have no place to go and leave the country."

The Christian Science Monitor October 2010

RICCARDO DE CORATO

Vice Mayor, Milan, Italy

The zero solution

"These are dark-skinned people [Roma], not Europeans like you and me. Our final goal is to have zero Gypsy camps in Milan."

The Boston Globe, October 2010

KADRI ECVET TEZCAN

Turkish Ambassador to Austria

Leave the ministry out

"Integration is a cultural and social problem. But in Austria . . . the Ministry for Interior . . . is responsible for integration. That is incredible. The ministry for interior can be in charge of asylum or visas and many security problems. But the minister for interior should stop intervening in the integration process."

Die Presse (Austria) November 2010

THERESA MAY

Home Secretary United Kingdom

No more cheap labor

"We will bring net migration down to the tens of thousands. Our economy will remain open to the best and the brightest in the world, but it's time to stop importing foreign labour on the cheap."

Daily Telegraph (England) October 2010

SILVIO BERLUSCONI

Prime Minister, Italy

A potential new Africa

"Europe runs the risk of turning black from illegal immigration, it could turn into Africa. We need support from the European Union to stop this army trying to get across from Libya, which is their entry point."

The Express (England) September 2010

14

Fourteen-year-old Noor Jehan lies in a Karachi hospital after being shot five times and left in a ditch to die — allegedly by two male cousins. Jehan told reporters that when one of her cousins asked her to marry him and her father refused to consent, the spurned cousin claimed she had had sex with another man and tried to kill her to reclaim his "honor." Jehan died a month later from an abdominal infection, becoming one of the 5,000-20,000 victims murdered each year in so-called honor killings.

From *CQ Researcher*,
April 19, 2011.

Honor Killings

Robert Kiener

In the remote Pakistani province of Baluchistan, three teenage girls — Hameeda, Raheema and Fauzia — fell in love with the wrong people. They apparently wanted to marry husbands of their own choosing rather than the men selected by their local Umrani tribal leaders. Marrying without permission is considered an affront to the honor of the tribe.

Enraged, tribesmen kidnapped the girls, along with two older female relatives of the girls, and drove them all into the desert. The men then dragged the teenagers out of the car, beat them and shot them. But the girls did not die instantly, so their attackers allegedly threw them into a ditch and buried them alive, covering them with sand and rocks. When the older women, aged 45 and 38, objected, they too were shot and buried alive.[1]

Two months later, after a human-rights organization revealed the murders, police opened an investigation. Several men were arrested, including the father, brothers and a cousin of the slain girls. But a local politician defended the murders as "honor killings," justified by tradition — even though such murders have been illegal in Pakistan since 2004. Nevertheless, Israrullah Zehr, a member of parliament from Baluchistan, claimed the killings were part of a "centuries-old tradition" and vowed he would "continue to defend them."[2]

The five victims were just some of the thousands of women and girls around the world who are murdered each year in so-called honor killings: socially sanctioned, premeditated murders — usually by male relatives — due to real or rumored premarital sex or infidelity or for having been raped or sexually abused. Women and girls are also killed for behaving in "immoral" ways — such as talking to

Honor Killings Reported in 26 Countries

Experts say between 5,000 and 20,000 women and girls are killed each year in the name of family honor. Many of the victims are tortured, burned, stoned or strangled. The murders, which often go unpunished, have occurred in at least 26 countries — nine of them Western countries with large immigrant communities, including the United States, Canada, the United Kingdom and Germany.

Countries Where Honor Killings Occur

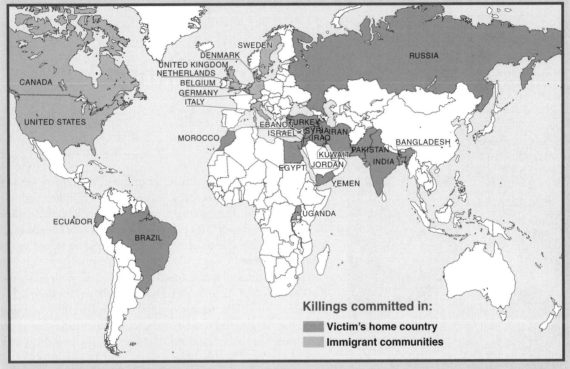

Killings committed in:
- Victim's home country
- Immigrant communities

Sources`: United Nations; news reports

boys, refusing to accept an arranged marriage or marrying outside of their ethnic group. The killer believes that his action cleanses the honor of his family and community.

"Such killings occur when the 'honor' of male members of a household is perceived to have been injured," said I. A. Rehman, secretary general of the Lahore-based Human Rights Commission of Pakistan.[3]

Every week brings new reports of unbelievably cruel honor killings:

- Hena Begum, a 14-year-old Bangladeshi girl, died in February after being publicly flogged. Her crime? She had reportedly been raped by a 40-year-old married cousin.[4] After the rape, family members

reportedly beat her and accused her of having an affair with the cousin. The village council then sentenced her to 100 lashes.[5]

- Karima Metawe, 20, was rumored to have left her home in Alexandria, Egypt, without permission last September. Her two brothers and an uncle strangled her to death in front of her baby "to 'restore' their family's honor."[6]

- As a punishment for "talking to boys," 16-year-old Medine Memi was secretly murdered by her relatives last year in southeastern Turkey. Her body was found in a 6-foot-deep hole under a chicken pen; her hands were tied and her lungs and stomach were filled with soil, indicating she had been buried alive.[7]

Because so many honor killings are never reported — and because international organizations are discouraged from keeping statistics on such politically sensitive practices — no one knows how many honor killings occur each year. The United Nations Population Fund's commonly quoted estimate — up to 5,000 women per year — is thought to be a gross undercount.[8] The figure is closer to 20,000 a year worldwide, according to Diana Nammi, director of the London-based Iranian and Kurdish Women's Rights Organization (IKWRO). Robert Fisk, a Beirut-based journalist, agrees. He wrote a multipart series on honor killings after traveling throughout South Asia and the Middle East studying the practice, which he calls "one of the last great taboos."[9]

During 2010 there were reportedly 960 honor killings in Pakistan alone, according to the U.N. High Commissioner for Refugees.[10] In Syria activists claim up to 200 women die in honor killings annually.[11] In Iraq, more than 12,000 women died in honor killings between 1991 and 2007, according to Aso Kamal, a human-rights activist with the Doaa Network Against Violence.[12]

And honor killings apparently are on the rise, according to many observers. In February Turkey's justice minister shocked the country when he announced that murders of Turkish women had jumped from 66 in 2002 to 953 in just the first seven months of 2009 — a 1,400 percent increase. Some of Turkey's media have labeled the slaughter "Turkey's Shame."[13] Prime Minister Recep Tayipp Erdogan condemned the killings and said there was "no such thing as committing violence in the name of honor." But the killings show no signs of slowing down.[14]

India has also seen a recent resurgence in honor killing, often related to men and women who violate Hindu marriage traditions, such as marrying a partner from a higher or lower caste. As Oxfam International has noted, "every six hours, somewhere in India, a young married woman is burned alive, beaten to death, or driven to commit suicide."[15]

Many experts object to calling the murders "honor" killings. "There is nothing honorable about these killings," says Aisha Gill, a senior lecturer and expert on honor killings at London's Roehampton University. "They are murders, plain and simple. I see the term 'honor killings' as an oxymoron." Some prefer to call the murders "so-called honor killings," "femicide" or "shame killings."

According to Rana Husseini, a Jordanian journalist and author of the riveting 2009 book *Murder in the Name of Honor*, statistics are hard to pin down because "many honor killings are passed off as suicides, accidents and disappearances." For instance, a recent study in Pakistan found that one in five homicides is an honor killing — a total of 1,957 honor killings over four years. But author Muazzani Nasrullah, from Pakistan's highly regarded Aga Khan University in Karachi, noted, "The problem is much more than what is depicted in my paper."[16]

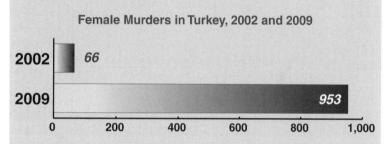

Female Murders Skyrocket in Turkey

Nearly 1,000 women were murdered in Turkey in 2009 — a 1,400 percent increase from 2002, when a religiously conservative Muslim government took power. Most of the murders were stabbings and shootings by family members. No one knows how many of the murders were so-called honor killings, which are illegal in Turkey, but women's-rights advocates say they were probably a large proportion. The government says it has enacted far-reaching gender-equality reforms, but women's groups point out that Turkey, with 74 million people, has only 54 shelters for women escaping violence at home, compared to Germany, which has 800 women's shelters for a population of 82 million.

Female Murders in Turkey, 2002 and 2009

Year	Murders
2002	66
2009	953

Source: Dorian Jones, "Turkey's Murder Rate of Women Skyrockets," Voice of America, February 2011, ww.voanews.com/english/news/europe/Turkeys-Murder-Rate-of-Women-Skyrockets-117093538.html

Loss of Family Honor Can Have Dire Consequences

Intense societal pressure drives many honor killers.

What would lead a father or brother to murder a beloved daughter or sister, in the name of honor? The loss of honor in some traditional societies can have a devastating impact on a family, and perpetrators of honor crimes often say intense community pressure drove them to murder a loved one:

- "I had to protect my children," said an anguished Palestinian mother of nine after putting a plastic bag over her daughter's head and slitting her wrists because the teen had brought shame on the family by being raped and impregnated by a brother. "This is the only way I could protect my family's honor."[1]
- "Honour is the only thing a man has," said a sorrowful Pakistani man, who had strangled his 23-year-old daughter after she ran off with a man from a rival tribe. "I can still hear her screams; she was my favorite daughter. I want to destroy my hands and end my life."[2]
- "I did it to wash with her blood the family honor . . . and in response to the will of society that would not have had any mercy on me if I didn't," said a 25-year-old Palestinian, explaining why he had hanged his sister. "Society taught us from childhood that blood is the only solution to wash the honor."[3]

According to the London-based Centre for Social Cohesion — a nonpartisan organization that studies radicalization and extremism in Britain and studied honor killings in immigrant communities in the U.K. — families with damaged honor can experience a variety of consequences, including:[4]

- **Ostracism** —The family can be ignored or ostracized by the rest of the community. Their children may be rejected at school by fellow members of their cultural, ethnic or religious group.
- **Economic damage** —The family may receive smaller dowries for their children. In some cases, shops and businesses can be boycotted or even physically attacked by community members who believe their collective honor has also been tarnished.
- **Political consequences** — Community leaders and politicians can lose votes, prestige and influence.
- **Loss of self-esteem** — Family members can become depressed or suicidal. Feelings of shame can hamper their interactions with neighbors and friends and negatively affect their work, possibly causing further damage to their social standing.

---

[1] Soraya Sarhaddi Nelson, "Palestinian girl's murder highlights growing number of 'honor killings,'" Knight Ridder, Nov. 16, 2003.

[2] Robert Fisk, "Invisible Massacre: The Crimewave that Shames the World," *The Independent*, Sept. 7, 2010, www.independent.co.uk/opinion/commentators/fisk/invisible-massacre-the-crimewave-that-shames-the-world-2072201.html.

[3] Yotam Feldner, " 'Honor' Murders — Why the Perps Get off Easy," *Middle East Quarterly*, December 2000, pp. 41-50.

[4] "Crimes of the Community: Honour-Based Violence in the UK," Centre for Social Cohesion, 2010, www.socialcohesion.co.uk/files/1229624550_1.pdf.

"Whatever the numbers," says Husseini, "it is clear that honor killings are one of the most serious global problems faced by women today."

Besides murder, other honor-related crimes are committed against women in so-called honor-based traditional societies, including stoning, whipping, acid throwing and forced suicides. According to Navi Pillay, U.N. High Commissioner for Human Rights, "In the name of preserving family 'honor,' women and girls are shot, stoned, burned, buried alive, strangled, smothered and knifed to death with horrifying regularity."[17]

In cultures where honor killings occur, the killings are generally based on the belief that women are objects without rights: Honor may be embodied in the society's women but honor is the property of men, who are responsible for protecting it. As Amnesty International noted, "Women are considered the property of male relatives and seen to embody the honor of the men to whom they 'belong.' Women's bodies are considered the repositories of family honor." A woman suspected of damaging that honor may face punishment or death.

But their murderers often go scot-free. The laws in some countries legitimize the murder of women by their husbands or relatives. In Syria, for example, the penal code grants immunity or a greatly reduced sentence to a man who kills a female relative. Jordan's penal code states, "He who discovers his wife or one of his female relatives committing adultery and kills, wounds or injures one of them, is exempted from any penalty."

Men are sometimes the victim of honor crimes, but such instances are much rarer than honor crimes committed against women. After a Pakistani college student married a woman without the permission of her higher-caste family, the bride's relatives fractured his legs with an ax and slashed his nose and ears. The victim, Mohammed Iqbal, said his attackers screamed, "You have mixed our honor with dirt" as they assaulted him. Last August, the Taliban stoned an Afghan couple to death for committing adultery.[18]

When there is prosecution, the punishments often are lax. A U.N. Commission on Human Rights report noted that the "great majority" of the honor crimes it examined in Pakistan went "unpunished either because no complaint was ever filed by relatives of the victims, or because the police refused to file a complaint." Even in cases where "murderers reportedly surrendered themselves to police with the murder weapon . . . no action was ever taken against them."[19]

Honor killing has been reported in more than a two dozen nations, but primarily occur in South Asia and the Middle East. In recent years honor killings have spread to immigrant communities in Western countries, including France, Germany, Sweden, the United States and the United Kingdom. In the U.K., for example, police investigate up to a dozen honor killings of women each year and estimate that at least 500 cases of other honor crimes, such as beatings or sexual assaults, are committed against women each year in Britain.[20]

Although honor killings are most common in Muslim countries, they also are widespread in non-Muslim cultures. "It is a mistake to see this as a Muslim-only crime," says Husseini. "There are also Christians, Hindus and Sikhs that carry out and condone honor crimes against women." In Turkey's Assyrian Christian community, a newlywed couple was killed by the bride's Christian brother, reportedly "to restore the family honor." The groom was Muslim.[21]

"Violence in the name of honor transcends communities and religions," says Gill.

None of the world's major religions condones honor-related crimes. The practice has traditional and cultural origins, according to experts. Although Muslim scholars say there is no basis in the Quran for honor killing, that doesn't stop some Muslim killers from trying to justify their actions on religious grounds.

"These murders are called 'honor killings' because they are seen by their perpetrators as ways of re-establishing the family's honor, which has been lost by extramarital activity, willing or unwilling, on the part of one of its female members," wrote Kwame Anthony Appiah, a philosophy professor at Princeton University.[22]

In one especially ghastly example, a father in Egypt paraded his daughter's decapitated head through the streets shouting, "I avenged my honor."[23] A Palestinian merchant explained to a reporter, "A woman shamed is like rotting flesh. If it is not cut away, it will consume the body. . . . The whole family will be tainted if she is not killed."[24]

As the numbers of honor killings demonstrate, the pressure on family members to carry out these heinous crimes is immense. "Tradition is a powerful impetus for these perpetrators," explains Husseini. "It supersedes familial love and makes many of these killers feel they have no choice but to attempt to restore their fallen honor."

A few victims are beginning to fight back. Mukhtar Mai, a Pakistani woman, was gang-raped on orders of a village council to restore the honor of a local clan that said Mai's family had violated the clan's honor. But she refused to commit suicide, which was expected of her. Instead, she helped to prosecute her attackers and has become a spokeswoman for the thousands of women who have silently suffered at the hands of so-called honor killers.

"More and more girls and women are being killed every day, and there is so little awareness, punishment or justice," she explains to a visitor in the women's shelter and girls' school she has built in rural Punjab. "The world has to hear their cries. We owe them that much at the very least."

As women around the world continue to suffer at the hands of attackers bent on restoring family "honor," here are some of the questions being asked:

Police present four male relatives of Saima Bibi, 17, who died Jan. 21 in the Punjab city of Bahawalpur, Pakistan. The men are charged with torturing and electrocuting Bibi to death in the name of family honor. She had eloped with a lower-caste neighbor, and a village council ruled that death was the appropriate punishment. Although honor killings are illegal in Pakistan, the U.N. says nearly 1,000 Pakistani women and girls were victims in 2010.

Are honor killings a form of domestic violence?

The chilling murder of 16-year-old Canadian Muslim schoolgirl Aqsa Parvez made headlines around the world in 2007. For many it had all the hallmarks of an honor killing: She allegedly was strangled by her father for refusing to wear a hijab, a traditional Muslim headscarf. Earlier, she had left home and sought refuge in a shelter after telling her friends her father was going to kill her.[25]

Many, however, viewed Aqsa's murder as nothing more than an act of domestic violence. Women are killed in many societies, but the media are too quick to label every Muslim-on-Muslim murder an honor crime, says Mohamed Elmasary, president of the Canadian Islamic Congress. "I don't want the public to think this is really an Islamic issue or an immigrant issue," he said. "It is a teenager issue."[26]

Sheik Alaa El-Sayyed, imam at the Islamic Society of North America in Mississauga, Ontario, agreed. "The bottom line is, it's a domestic violence issue," he said.[27]

Both men claimed that instantly labeling the killing an honor crime unfairly stigmatizes Muslims. "We, as Muslims, are Canadians, and we should be dealt with just like everyone else," El-Sayyed said. "We have rights, duties . . . pros and cons . . . just like all other human beings."[28]

Others disagree. "Like many other Muslims, they are in denial," explains Phyllis Chesler, a professor emerita of psychology and women's studies at the Richmond College of City University of New York who conducted two studies on honor killings for the *Middle East Quarterly.* "Too many Muslims are claiming that honor killings are simply domestic violence. My investigations show that in case after case honor killings are quite distinct from domestic violence."[29]

Chesler insists: "Western domestic violence and honor killings are not the same. An honor killing is a conspiracy planned and carried out by the victim's family of origin who view the killing as heroic. Daughter-stalking, daughter-beating and daughter-killing is not a Western cultural pattern, nor is it valorized. In the West, wife- and daughter-killers are considered criminals, not heroes; wife-killers are not assisted by their parents or in-laws."

She and others list several characteristics of honor killings that distinguish them from domestic abuse:

Planning: Honor killings often follow death threats and may be carefully planned and premeditated. Domestic violence murders usually are spontaneous "crimes of passion."

Reason: The motive given for honor killings is usually that the victim has "dishonored" the spouse or family. Honor is rarely, if ever, a reason given for domestic killings.

Perpetrator: The perpetrator of an honor killing usually does not act alone, as in domestic violence. "There is either an explicit or implicit approval or even encouragement by other members of the family to commit the murder," noted University of California, Berkeley, researcher Rochelle L. Terman. "This is because honor must be restored for the collective, not just the individual."[30]

Perception: While domestic violence is rarely celebrated, many of those who commit or assist in honor killings show little or no remorse. Indeed, a Turkish study of 180 prisoners convicted of honor killings revealed that none regretted their actions. "In some cases, the victim's relatives even praised the perpetrator," said Mazhar Bagli, an associate professor of sociology at Turkey's Dicle University, who supervised the study.[31]

What Does Islam Say About Honor Killings?

Most scholars say Quran does not condone honor crimes.

Because so many honor killings occur in predominantly Muslim countries, many people assume Islam sanctions murders in the name of family or tribal honor. But, according to Islamic experts, the Quran does not support those claims.

"Nothing in the Quran allows honor killings," says Muzammil Siddiqi, chairman of the Islamic Law Council of North America. "They are totally un-Islamic and have nothing to do with the religion."

In fact, he says, the Quran states: "Never should a believer kill a believer. Take not life, which Allah hath made sacred, except by way of justice and law." And while the Quran does teach that a couple who commit adultery should both be flogged "with a hundred stripes," it does not demand death.

Furthermore, says Siddiqi, "Nowhere in the Quran is a family member or anyone but a government authority authorized to carry out any kind of punishment."

Sheikh Muhammad Al-Hanooti — a Muslim scholar and member of the Islamic judicial body, the North American Fiqh Council — explained that in Islam "even in the case of capital punishment, only the government can apply the law through the judicial procedures. No one has the authority to execute the law other than the officers who are in charge."[1]

Such principles contradict what many Muslim honor killers claim: That a man whose family honor has been sullied by a woman must kill her in order to restore honor.

Max Gross, adjunct professor at Georgetown University's Prince Alwaleed bin Talal Center for Muslim-Christian Studies, says, "Many critics of Islam point to the Quran or spurious versions of the *hadith*, the so-called teachings of Muhammad, claiming that Islam justifies honor killings. But scholars agree there is no justification in the Quran for these killings. On the contrary, Muhammad emphasized forgiveness over revenge."

In addition, honor crimes often are carried out based on rumors or suspicions that a female has behaved in an immoral way. However, the Quran forbids anyone from being punished for wrongdoing without conclusive proof: "And those who launch a charge against chaste women, and produce not four witnesses, . . . flog them with eighty stripes and reject their evidence ever after . . . for such men are wicked transgressors."

Nilofar Bakhtiar, a former adviser to Pakistan's prime minister, has said that using Islam to justify honor killings is "rubbish" and blamed such crimes in Pakistan on "the feudal tradition, the culture and the tribal system." She claimed that men "found it very convenient to say that what they don't want to do is 'against Islam' and what they want to do is 'in the name of Islam.'"[2]

Sayyid Syeed, National Director for the Office for Interfaith and Community Alliances for the Islamic Society of North America, says, "Historically, tribal practices such as honor killings were carried out by practitioners who mistakenly believed them to be inspired by Islam."

While the view that women are the property of men, with no rights of their own, does not appear in the Quran, it is deeply rooted in Arab tradition, experts say. Such attitudes facilitate honor crimes, as has Shariah law, which treats women as less than the equals of men.

But as Kwame Anthony Appiah, a Princeton philosophy professor, has noted: "There is almost universal agreement among qualified interpreters of Islam that honor killing is un-Islamic."[3]

Other high-profile Muslims, including Syria's Grand Mufti cleric Ahmad Hassoun, have condemned honor killings.[4] And Lebanon's senior Shiite cleric, the late Grand Ayatollah Mohammed Hussein Fadlallah, last year called the practice of murdering a female relative for alleged sexual misconduct a "vicious phenomenon." He issued a *fatwa*, or a religious ruling, forbidding honor killings. Such crimes, he said, are considered in Islam as "one of the Kabair [severe sins] whose perpetrator deserves to enter Hellfire in the afterlife."[5]

— ***Robert Kiener***

[1] "Honor killing from an Islamic perspective," *OnIslam*, Feb. 22, 2011, www.onislam.net/english/ask-the-scholar/crimes-and-penalties/retaliation-qisas/174426-honor-killing-from-an-islamic-perspective.html.

[2] Jan Strupczewski, "Men distort religion to justify 'honour' killings," Reuters, Dec. 8, 2004, www.ncdsv.org/images/ExpertsMenDistory Religion.pdf.

[3] Kwame Anthony Appiah, *The Honor Code* (2010), p. 153.

[4] Rasha Elass, " 'Honor' killing spurs outcry in Syria," *The Christian Science Monitor*, Feb. 14, 2007, www.csmonitor.com/2007/0214/p07s02-wome.html.

[5] "Fatwa against honor killings," VOA News, Feb. 18, 2010, www.voanews.com/a-41-2007-08-13-voa3-84654512.html.

While some experts, such as Chesler, note that honor killings are "committed mainly by Muslims against Muslims," it is important to note that they can occur across many religions and races. Terman has identified honor killings among Muslims, Christians, Jews, Yazidis, Druze, Sikhs, Hindus and nonbelievers.[32]

"Because so-called honor killings are prevalent among Muslim societies, there is the misconception that they are condoned by Islam," says Husseini, the Jordanian journalist and author of *Murder in the Name of Honor.* Nowhere in the Quran or in any major interpretation of Sharia laws are honor killings prescribed, she says. "Furthermore, many reputable Islamic scholars and clerics have spoken out against the practice of honor killings," noted Terman.[33]

However, some Muslim governments discourage discussion of the topic. The IKWRO's Nammi explains, "Discussions about honor killings in Muslim communities have been taboo for a very long time." Indeed, some activists who are identifying honor killings are accused of stigmatizing Arab communities. They are also accused of perpetuating a Western view of their societies as "primitive" or "backward."

And Islamists who seek "to cover up this sin against Muslim girls and women attack those who would dare expose it as 'Islamophobes,' " says Chesler.

On the other hand, some women's-rights advocates argue that honor killings must be seen in historical perspective. "Until thirty years ago, it was common to hear about honor killings among Italians. But now when a man kills his wife, they call it a crime of passion," said Italian journalist Cinzia Tani. "It's the same concept taking different names: A man kills a woman of his family in order to assert his control over her body. The only difference is that back then the homicide of a woman was 100 percent acceptable."[34]

Canadian journalist Chris Selley said the world should abandon "this ridiculous, self-indulgent debate over the taxonomy of honour killings. Those on the left who abhor the term are right about one thing: A good few of the people who constantly shout it from the rooftops are mostly interested in demonizing Islam. But that doesn't change the fact that honour killings can — over shrieking objections from feminists — rather easily be distinguished from other cases of domestic violence. . . . Ultimately who cares what we call it?"[35]

John Esposito, an authority on Islam at Georgetown University and the author of the 2010 book *The Future of Islam*, and Sheila B. Lalwani, a research fellow at Georgetown University, noted, "Violence against women is a global phenomenon, not a religious one. Nevertheless it deserves the attention of every religious leader and responsible voter; anything less contributes to the denial and complacency that permits it to persist."[36]

Are governments doing enough to deter honor killings?

Many women's advocates say governments are not doing enough to stop the slaughter of between 5,000 and 20,000 women a year in honor killings. "For example," says Nammi, the Iranian and Kurdish women's advocate "many states condone honor killing. It's a disgrace that these laws still exist."

Indeed, many countries have laws legalizing the murder of women by their relatives. For example, Article 220 of the Iranian Criminal Code states: "If a father — or his male ancestors — kill their children, they will not be prosecuted for murder." Last year on International Women's Day, U.N. High Commissioner for Human Rights' Pillay said, "The problem [of honor killings] is exacerbated by the fact that in a number of countries, domestic legal systems . . . still fully or partially exempt individuals guilty of honor killings from punishment.[37]

For example, in Kuwait, "He who surprises his wife in the act of adultery . . . or surprises his daughter, mother or sister in the act of sexual intercourse with a man and immediately kills her . . . shall be punished by prison for a period not more than three years," according to Article 153 of the Penal Code."[38]

The penal code in Jordan says, "[H]e who discovers his wife or one of his female relatives committing adultery and kills, wounds or injures one of them is exempted from any penalty." Article 98 provides for a reduced sentence if the crime was committed in extreme "rage."[39]

In Syria, Article 548, which limited sentences for honor killings to one year, was replaced recently with a law that mandated a minimum sentence of two years.[40]

In Haiti, a husband who immediately murders his wife after discovering her in *flagrante delicto* (committing adultery) in the conjugal abode is to be pardoned. A wife's murder of her husband in similar circumstances is not excused.[41]

Similar laws exist — and have existed — throughout Latin America, Africa and Asia. Until 1980 in Colombia, a husband could legally kill his wife for committing adultery. In Brazil until 1991 wife killings were considered non-criminal "honor killings."[42]

Although there has been pressure to reform such laws, there has been little action. In Jordan activists complained that lax laws encourage honor crimes. "The current law is nothing less than an endorsement for murdering women and girls," said Nadya Khalife, a women's-rights researcher at Human Rights Watch. "The women of Jordan need protection from these vicious acts enshrined in law, not preferential treatment for their killers."[43]

In response, Jordan's Justice Ministry announced it would set up a "special tribunal" to hear these cases. That's not enough, say activists. "Jordan needs to send a strong message to perpetrators that they can no longer get away with murder. It should start by amending the penal code to reflect the seriousness of these crimes and treat them the same as other killings," said Khalife.[44] Efforts to reform Jordan's honor killing laws have repeatedly failed.

Why have these archaic, discriminatory laws been so hard to change? In many cases legislators are reluctant to offend fundamentalist and conservative factions. As the global advocacy movement Violence Is Not Our Culture explains, "As a result of the increased politicization of culture and religion in recent years, governments are increasingly afraid to combat hard-line and conservative elements in their societies."[45]

A Jordanian parliament member who opposed reforming honor crime laws spoke for many when he said, "Women adulterers cause a great threat to our society because they are the main reasons that such acts take place. . . . If men do not find women with whom to commit adultery, then they will become good on their own."[46]

Chechen President Ramzan Kadyrov echoed that view. In 2009 after learning that seven young women had been shot in the head by male relatives and their bodies dumped by the roadside, he said they deserved to die. Claiming the women had "loose morals," Kadyrov said, "If a woman runs around and if a man runs around with her, both of them are killed." He also suggested that a man should be able to murder his daughter if she dishonors the family. "If he doesn't kill her, what kind of man is he? He brings shame on himself!" Kadyrov said, according to Britian's *Independent* newspaper.[47]

Many worry that Kadyrov's approval of honor killings will encourage more murders. "What the president says is law," said Gistam Sakayeva, a Chechen women's-rights activist. "Because the president said this, many will try to gain his favor by killing someone, even if there is no reason."[48]

There have been some small victories, however. In 1993, Tunisia strengthened its laws governing honor crimes. There have been no documented cases of honor crimes in Tunisia for the last 20 years.[49] Turkey has also reformed legislation and is regularly giving life-in-prison sentences to honor killers.

In addition to lax legislation, weak or nonexistent prosecution also permits honor killings to persist. As *The St. Petersburg* [Fla.] *Times* noted, "Police rarely investigate honor crimes, and the handful of perpetrators who are arrested often receive only token punishments. In some settings police may overtly or covertly champion the killers as vindicated men. Elsewhere, police act within a network of conspirators who benefit economically from honor killings."[50]

Says IKWRO's Nammi, "Even if laws are changed, many countries are reluctant to investigate and prosecute honor killers. Time after time these killings are ignored." In Pakistan, for example, honor killings are recognized as a punishable crime, but the laws are only occasionally enforced. According to a recent study, only 10 percent of Pakistan's law enforcement personnel realize that the nation's laws prohibit honor killings.[51]

In fact, one remote rural village court, or *jirga*, in Pakistan, worried that reporting such killings would defame the region, ruled in 2006 that anyone reporting an honor killing to the court or the police should be killed. After ruling that a recent honor killing was "permissible," *jirga* member Malik Faiz Muhammad said, "We stick to our verdict that honour killing is permissible, and those who commit it will not be liable to any punishment. We will also not allow the aggrieved party to report the case to the police or file the case before a court. We will kill those who will violate the *jirga* verdict."[52]

Reuters/Anatolia News Agency/Tevfik Parlak

Sixteen-year-old Medine Memi was buried alive last year in this hole in her backyard in Kahta, a town in the Kurdish region of Turkey. Memi had been missing for 40 days and the hole had been cemented over when police were tipped off that she had been killed by her family. Her father and grandfather were later arrested for the murder. Memi had repeatedly told police that her grandfather was beating her for dishonoring the family by "talking to boys," but each time the police sent her home. Nearly 1,000 women were murdered in Turkey in 2009 — a 1,400 percent jump over 2002. Women's-rights advocates say most of the deaths were probably honor killings.

On the other hand, the United Kingdom, in response to a growing number of honor killings among immigrant communities, created a special unit to investigate closed cases to see if they may have been honor killings.

The U.N.'s Pillay said, "The reality for most victims, including victims of honor killings, is that state institutions fail them and that most perpetrators of domestic violence can rely on a culture of impunity for the acts they commit."[53]

Is the international community doing enough to combat honor killings?

According to a 2000 United Nations Population Fund (UNFPA) report, "perhaps as many as 5,000 women and girls a year are murdered by members of their own families" in honor killings.[54] That is the number most widely used when describing honor killings.

But that estimate hasn't been revised since it was first released in 2000. And it is so low as to be meaningless, according to many women's-rights activists. "It really gets me angry that the United Nations has not seen fit to at least revise that figure," says Nammi. "It is symptomatic of the U.N.'s inaction on honor killings."

"It's very hard to extract the statistic of honor killing from the broader statistic of the murder of women," says Aminata Toure, chief of the UNFPA's Gender, Human Rights and Culture Branch. "Also, states are not very keen on reporting these numbers. However, we are looking at revising our estimate."

Other experts echo Nammi. Says Gill at London's Roehampton University, "The U.N. has been helpful, but not as effective as it should be in terms of ending violence against women. It, and other international organizations, need to go beyond talking the talk and must demonstrate genuine political will to protect vulnerable women. We need to move beyond rhetoric. How many more killings do we need for something to be done?"

Chesler of the City University of New York is blunter: "The United Nations gets nothing done when it comes to honor killings. It hasn't even offered women fleeing honor killers shelter or protection. It is ineffective."

Not so, say U.N. proponents like Jordanian journalist and author Husseini. "The U.N. has been pressing the issue of honor killing," she says, noting that Resolution 57/179, adopted by the General Assembly in 2002, called for nations to "investigate thoroughly, prosecute effectively and document cases of crimes against women committed in the name of honor and punish the perpetrators."[55]

Before that, in 1994, the U.N. Commission on Human Rights appointed a special rapporteur on violence against women, who has gathered testimony on honor killings in several reports since then. Also, both UNICEF and the U.N. Development Fund for Women have programs to address honor killings.

"The United Nations is accomplishing a lot by raising the issue of honor killings [and] helping shed more light on what used to be a taboo subject," says Husseini.

"The United Nations cannot enact a law within a country," points out Toure. "We are doing much to advocate, educate and urge states to have tougher laws regarding honor killings and punish perpetrators. We also support women's organizations to help them speak up."

The United Nations has also made honor crimes a recognized form of violence against women in international-rights law. In 1979 the General Assembly adopted the Convention on the Elimination of all Forms of Discrimination against Women (CEDAW), now commonly viewed as "an international bill of rights for women." (The treaty came into force in 1981, and has been ratified by every developed nation except the United States.)[56]

Honor killings violate rights that CEDAW guarantees to all women, including the right to freely choose a spouse and equality in marriage. Further, the treaty specifically obligates states to defend women from honor crimes and requires states to disqualify "honor" as a legal defense in acts committed against women.[57]

Critics of the convention claim that it is vulnerable to politicization. At a recent U.N. meeting to review Israel's compliance with CEDAW, some Israeli activists attacked Palestinian nongovernmental organizations (NGOs) for failing to raise the issue of honor killings in the Palestinian territories. Paula Kweskin, a legal researcher at the NGO Monitor, a Jerusalem-based research group, claimed that by not reporting on local honor killings, "These groups have abandoned the women they purport to advocate for and, as such, have once again called into question the sincerity of their pursuit of universal human rights."[58]

Nammi, the Iranian and Kurdish women's advocate, said a CEDAW representative had "glossed over" the topic of honor killings in her presentation at a recent international conference on violence against women. When Nammi asked her why, "She told me it was such a sensitive topic that it was better not to talk too much about it. I think it was a case of political correctness gone too far."

Both critics and supporters of the United Nations and other international bodies acknowledge that no international court has sole jurisdiction over honor killings, making it the responsibility of each sovereign state to enforce international human-rights law.

When they have leverage, though, some international bodies do pressure countries to reform their laws on honor killings. For instance, Turkey for years has been seeking membership in the European Union. As one of the prerequisites, the European Council in 2004 pressured Turkey to increase sentences for honor killers.

"Enforcement is the weak link in this issue," says Gill. "We have to put more pressure on the international community to hold states to account in relation to international laws and legal instruments such as CEDAW. Otherwise the laws are meaningless."

BACKGROUND

Early Origins

The tradition that gives rise to honor killing, namely that a woman's chastity is her family's property, can be traced to pre-Christian and pre-Islamic periods. The 3000 B.C. Assyrian legal code in Mesopotamia, for example, held that the father of a defiled virgin could punish her in any way he wished.

The 1752 B.C. Code of Hammurabi, the ancient Babylonian set of laws, justifies honor killing related to sexual crimes. It held that a woman accused of adultery should throw herself into the river, no matter how much, or how little, evidence there was against her. "If the finger is pointed at the wife of a citizen on account of another man, but she has not been caught lying with another man, for her husband's sake — she shall throw herself into the river," the code said. If the woman drowned she was guilty, if she survived she was innocent.

Women had few rights in ancient Rome. According to the Roman law of Paterfamilias, a father had the right to execute his unmarried daughter for any indiscretion — real or perceived. As one writer noted, "A father held the power of life and death over his daughter, and upon marriage that power was transferred to the daughter's husband. Female adultery was a felony under Roman law, and the state actively prosecuted family members and others for not taking action against adulterous female relatives."[59]

Roman law held that married women were the property of their husbands and could be sold into slavery, imprisoned or even killed at their husband's whim. The Roman

AP Photo/Metropolitan Police

Banaz Mahmod, 20, an Iraqi Kurd from south London, was raped, strangled with a boot lace, stuffed into a suitcase and buried in Birmingham, England, in 2006. Her father and uncle later were convicted of ordering Mahmod's murder because they thought she had dishonored the family by leaving an unhappy arranged marriage and falling in love with another man. Two men hired by Mahmod's relatives were later convicted of the murder.

statesman Cato advised a husband who discovered his wife committing adultery to kill her without resorting to the legal system: "If you catch your wife in adultery, you can kill her with impunity; she, however, cannot dare to lay a finger on you if you commit adultery, for it is the law."[60]

Shakespeare's "Titus Andronicus," set in Rome's late empire, portrays the Roman general Titus killing his daughter Lavinia to restore their honor after she was raped and mutilated. As he kills her he cries, "Die, die Lavinia, and thy shame with thee, and with thy shame thy father's sorrow die!"

In India, according to the ancient Laws of Manu, women were considered immoral. Widows were encouraged to throw themselves on the funeral pyre of their husbands (a custom known as *suttee*) to preserve their dead spouse's honor and prevent themselves from living a "life of dishonor." Hindu-Aryan husbands "were entitled to cut off the nose and ears of wives suspected or found

guilty of infidelity — a custom that eerily echoes various cases of 'honor' crimes in the Indian subcontinent across the centuries."[61]

Ancient Aztec laws prescribed a death penalty for women accused of adultery. The sentence was usually carried out by strangulation or stoning. In ancient Peru husbands were pardoned if they killed their wives after finding them committing adultery. Their wives, however, enjoyed no such leniency: They were hung by their feet until dead if they murdered their husbands.[62]

Even children fell victim to what many see as honor killings. In pre-Islamic Arabia fathers sometimes killed their infant daughters to prevent them from possibly bringing dishonor upon the family if they would one day be accused of sexual misconduct outside of marriage. As a proverb said, "The dispatch of daughters is a kindness" and "the burial of daughters is a noble deed."[63] This practice is condemned and explicitly prohibited in the Quran, according to Islamic scholars.

But many experts on honor killing believe the Bible contains clear references to honor killing. For example, Leviticus 21:9 declares, "And the daughter of any priest, if she profane herself by playing the whore, she profaneth her father. She shall be burnt by fire." Others argue that a verse in Exodus (21:17) advocates honor killing: "And he that curseth his father, or his mother, shall surely be put to death."

Medieval Prejudices

Women's status remained low throughout the Middle Ages. In the 13th century the Catholic theologian Thomas Aquinas claimed that women were created only to be "men's helpmate" and promoted the idea that men should use "a necessary object, woman, who is needed to preserve the species and to provide food and drink."[64]

The witchcraft hysteria that spread across Europe between the 14th and 17th centuries exemplifies the extent of women's oppression. As European societies suffered from the Black Plague, the 100 Years War and other troubled times, religious leaders blamed a raft of problems on witches. About 80 percent of the 30,000 to 60,000 people executed for practicing witchcraft were female. As Catholic Inquisitors wrote in the 1480s, "All wickedness

C H R O N O L O G Y

1940s-1980s *Initial efforts are launched to strengthen women's rights.*

1946 United Nations establishes Commission on the Status of Women to promote women's rights around the world.

1979 U.N. General Assembly adopts Convention on the Elimination of all forms of Discrimination Against Women (CEDAW).

1987 India passes Commission of Sati (Prevention) Act, outlawing the once-common Hindu practice of *suttee* — the ritual burning of widows.

1990s *International women's movement focuses on violence against women and girls, including honor killings.*

1990 To gain support from tribal leaders and religious fundamentalists, Iraqi President Saddam Hussein exempts men from punishment for committing honor killings.

1992 CEDAW committee adopts General Recommendation 19, which says governments may be responsible for citizens' "private acts" — such as so-called honor crimes — if the states "fail to act with due diligence to prevent violations of rights, or to investigate and punish acts of violence."

1993 U.N. World Conference on Human Rights adopts the Vienna Convention, which holds that "the human rights of women and the girl-child are an inalienable, integral and indivisible part of human rights."

1995 Fourth World Conference on Women in Beijing calls on states to stop violence against women resulting from "harmful traditional or customary practices, cultural prejudices and extremism."

1998 U.N. Commission on Human Rights condemns honor killing.

1999 Jordan's Queen Noor holds public discussions on honor killings and pronounces them inconsistent with Islam and Jordanian constitutional law, even though parliamentary leaders claim such killings are justifiable.

2000s *Pressure intensifies on governments to outlaw and increase punishment for honor killings.*

2000 U.N. estimates that up to 5,000 women and girls are victims of honor killings each year. . . . Jordanian lawmakers reject proposed law that would impose harsher penalties on honor killers.

2002 U.N. General Assembly Resolution 57/179 calls for "elimination of crimes against women committed in the name of honor." . . . Amnesty International reports that at least three women a day are victims of honor killings in Pakistan, and that the murderers are rarely arrested.

2004 U.K. reopens 117 cases involving Muslim women who may have been victims of honor killings. . . . After pressure from the European Council, Turkey increases punishments for honor killings. . . . U.N. adopts an updated version of Resolution 57/179, acknowledging that girls also can be victims of honor crimes.

2006 Village court in Pakistan rules that reporting an honor killing to the court or the police is punishable by death.

2009 European Parliament describes rise in honor crimes in Europe as an "emergency." . . . Chechen President Ramzan Kadyrov justifies the murders of seven women by claiming they had "loose morals" and are the property of their husbands.

2010 Indian government investigates upsurge in honor killings. . . . Afghan government threatens to close down shelters for women trying to escape honor killings. U.N. High Commissioner for Refugees reports 960 honor killings a year in Pakistan. Other estimates indicate that the number of honor killings worldwide is probably close to 20,000.

2011 Women's-rights advocates in Turkey partly blame honor killings for a 1,400 percent rise in the femicide rate between 2002 and 2009. . . . Phoenix-based Iraqi Muslim is convicted of deliberately running over and killing his daughter with his car after she refused to take part in an arranged marriage.

Honor Crime Survivor Becomes Women's Champion

After gang-rape, she refused to commit suicide.

I t's early morning in the tiny, rural Punjab village of Meerwala, and a handful of women waits patiently outside the Mukhtar Mai Women's Crisis Relief Center. Like thousands of women before them, each of these women has come to this center to seek out the help of an inspiring hero who has become a symbol of strength and resistance to honor crimes.

Women arrive from all over the region with horribly scarred faces, victims of acid attacks by suitors who claim the women have dishonored them by refusing their marriage proposals. Still others have had their ears or noses cut off — a common form of punishment for supposed adulterers. The woman they have come all this way to see is Muhktar Mai, a humble villager who has become famous for courageously standing up for her own rights and now fights for the rights of Pakistani women and women everywhere.

Her story made headlines around the world. In 2002 a village tribe, the Mastois, accused Muhktar's 12-year-old brother of "bringing dishonor" to them by walking unaccompanied with a 30-year old Mastoi woman. The brother later claimed that he had been raped by the Mastois and that they were covering up the rape by falsely claiming he had dishonored them. [1]

The higher-caste tribal elders proclaimed that to restore the Mastois' honor, Mukhtar Mai should be gang-raped.

They told her father Ghulam that if he did not hand over Mukhtar, they would rape all of his daughters.

Accompanied by her father and her brother and clutching her Quran, Mukhtar approached the tribal elders, head bowed, and knelt in front of them. She assumed they would "forgive" her, "because I had done nothing wrong," she remembers.

Instead, four men grabbed her, dragged her into a nearby shed and gang-raped her as others held her father and uncle at gunpoint. When the father protested, the men only laughed. After the attack, the men threw Mukhtar, nearly naked, onto the ground outside. Ghulam wrapped a blanket around his daughter and carried her home.

Defiled and shamed in front of her entire village, Mukhtar felt she had only one option. Reporting the crime to the police would only bring more shame to her family. Honor demanded that she kill herself.

But after lying in bed for three days and contemplating suicide, Mukhtar took courage from her parents and the local mullah — who condemned the rape — and made a startling decision. She decided to live and report the attack to police.

"I will fight them," she bravely told her parents. Her decision was unheard of in rural Punjab, a world where men are rarely punished for such so-called honor crimes against women.

---

is but little to the wickedness of a woman. . . . Women are . . . a structural defect rooted in the original creation." [65]

While women continued to be subjugated elsewhere around the world, their lot began to improve somewhat in the West during the Age of Enlightenment and the Industrial Revolution in the 18th and 19th centuries.

During the 19th century increasing numbers of women began taking jobs outside the home. As a result, governments began to pass laws that both protected

them on the job and granted them more and more legal rights. The British Mines Act of 1842, for example, prohibited women from working underground. John Stuart Mill, a supporter of women's rights and author of the essay "The Subjection of Women," introduced language in the British House of Commons calling for women to be granted the right to vote, but it did not pass.

More governments began giving women long-denied rights. The Married Women's Property Act of 1870

Six of the Mastoi men were found guilty of rape and sentenced to life imprisonment. The case has been appealed several times and is still winding its way through Pakistan's court system, but her attackers remain in jail.

Mukhtar's initial courtroom victory made her an unlikely hero for women's rights in Pakistan. But the meek, low-caste and illiterate woman somehow found the strength and courage to turn her personal tragedy into a triumph for others. She has used her notoriety to build schools, operate a rape-crisis center and bring health care to her destitute part of the country.

In doing so she has struck a chord in the hearts of people around the world. Mukhtar Mai "proves that one woman can change the world," said former American First Lady Laura Bush. Others have compared her to Martin Luther King, Gandhi and Rosa Parks. [2]

Mukhtar has received a slew of international awards, been feted by heads of state and Hollywood superstars and collaborated on a memoir, called *In the Name of Honor: A Memoir.*

More and more women are turning to her for help instead of surrendering themselves to their local *panchayat*, or tribal council. She has almost single-handedly rescued countless Pakistani women from the stranglehold of traditional justice. "Against all odds, this humble peasant woman has led a quiet revolution," says noted Pakistani human-rights activist Aseed Gonur. "She is empowering and emancipating women."

As Mukhtar herself often says, "A mighty river is born from a rainstorm. It just takes someone to be that first drop of rain."

— *Robert Kiener*

AP Photo/Anjum Naveed

Gang-raped on the orders of a Pakistani village council to restore a local clan's honor, Mukhtar Mai refused to commit suicide, as is often expected in such cases, and chose instead to help prosecute her attackers. She has since become a world-renowned opponent of honor killings.

---

[1] Khalid Tanveer, "Thousands of women rally in Pakistan to support rape victim," The Associated Press, March 7, 2005.

[2] Nicholas D. Kristof, "The Rosa Parks for the 21st Century," *The New York Times*, Nov. 8, 2005, p. A27.

and a series of other measures allowed British wives to own property. In 1893, New Zealand became the first nation to grant full suffrage to women, followed over the next two decades by Finland, Norway, Denmark and Iceland. The United States granted women suffrage in 1920. [66]

Honor killings, however, continued. In India, for example, many women were killed during the bloody partition of the country between 1947 and 1950. Indeed, as one writer noted, "The partition years can be seen to

be the beginning of the tradition of honor killing [in India] on a large scale." [67]

Since 1945, when the U.N. was founded, the international human-rights community has alerted the world to the continuing practice of honor-related crimes and begun to encourage interest in change. Honor crimes have been recognized as a form of violence against women in international human-rights law because they violate women's security, right to life and, freedom from torture and cruel, inhuman and degrading treatment.

01/01/2003

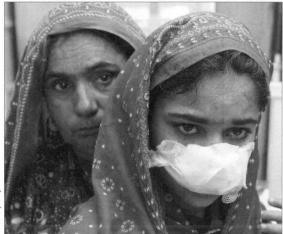

Reuters (both)

Gruesome Aftermath

Honor crimes occur in South Asia's Christian, Hindu, Sikh and Muslim communities. In India, couples involved in socially taboo relationships or marriages outside of their religion or caste are often murdered for sullying the honor of the family or village. That's why villagers in the northern Indian state of Haryana in 2008 allegedly murdered Sunita Devi (top, left), 21, and her partner, Jasbir Singh, 22, who was from another caste. In Pakistan, another type of honor crime involves disfiguring a woman who "shames" a man. Ayesha Baloch, 18, (bottom, right) was dragged to a field in 2006 and held down by her brother-in-law while her husband slit her upper lip and nostril with a knife. The husband claimed she was not a virgin when he married her.

The U.N.'s Convention on the Elimination of all Forms of Discrimination against Women defined discrimination against women as "any distinction, exclusion or restriction made on the basis of sex which has the effect or purpose of impairing or nullifying the recognition, enjoyment or exercise by women, irrespective of their marital status, on a basis of equality of men and women, of human rights and fundamental freedoms in the political, economic, social, cultural, civil or any other field."

Countries that ratified the treaty were legally bound to abolish discriminatory laws against women, take steps to end trafficking of girls and women and ensure women equal access to political and public life.

But CEDAW did not specifically mention violence, so in 1992 General Recommendation 19 defined gender-based violence as a form of discrimination against women and explicitly mentioned "honor crimes."

In 1993 the U.N. Declaration on the Elimination of Violence Against Women strengthened CEDAW by specifically defining "violence against women" as "any act of gender-based violence that results in, or is likely to result in, physical, sexual or psychological harm or suffering to women, including threats of such acts, coercion or arbitrary deprivation of liberty, whether occurring in public or in private life."

The declaration was introduced to pressure states into acknowledging that honor crimes were public, not private, matters. CEDAW also required states to disqualify honor as a legal defense for violence against women. Article Four notes: "States should condemn violence against women and should not invoke any custom, tradition or religious consideration to avoid their obligations with respect to its elimination."

Honor killing also was discussed in 1995 at the U.N.-sponsored Fourth World Conference on Women in Beijing. A resolution called for states to "take urgent action to combat and eliminate violence against women, which is a human-rights violation resulting from harmful traditional or customary practices, cultural prejudices and extremism."

In 2002 the General Assembly adopted Resolution 57/179, which urged states to investigate, document and prosecute honor crimes in order to work "towards the elimination of crimes against women committed in the name of honor." It noted that "states need to intensify efforts to raise awareness of the need to prevent and eliminate crimes against women committed in the name of honor, with the aim of changing the attitudes and behavior that allow such crimes to be committed."[68] An updated version of this resolution adopted in 2004 acknowledged that girls also can be victims of honor crimes.

Killings Spread

Although the United Nations, other international organizations and the media have raised awareness of honor killing, the atrocities continue and are spreading to immigrant communities in Europe and the United States.

In the United Kingdom police estimate that at least 12 women are murdered annually in honor killings. British police are training officers to recognize the tell-tale signs of such crimes. "Honour-based violence is complicated and a sensitive crime to investigate," said Det. Chief Inspector Gerry Campbell of the Metropolitan Police. "It's fathers, brothers, uncles, mums and cousins, and the victim — potential victim — has a fear of criminalising or demonising their family so they can be reluctant to come forward."[69]

With honor killings increasing throughout Europe (mostly within Muslim immigrant communities), the region is only beginning to come to grips with the phenomenon. In 2009 the European Parliamentary Assembly described the outbreak of honor crimes in Europe as an "emergency." Its Resolution 1681 noted, "the problem, far from diminishing, has worsened, including in Europe. It mainly affects women, who are its most frequent victims, both in Europe and the rest of the world, especially in patriarchal and fundamentalist communities and societies." It advised nations to create national action plans to combat violence against women, including violence committed in the name of "honor."[70]

The United States is not immune. Over the last several years at least six men have been accused of committing honor killings in the United States.[71] Faleh Almaleki, an Iranian immigrant, recently was convicted of second-degree murder for running over his 20-year-old daughter, Noor, with his Jeep because she spurned an arranged marriage and insisted on living with her boyfriend.

The late Grand Ayatollah Mohammed Hussein Fadlallah of Lebanon last year called honor killing a "vicious phenomenon" and issued a fatwa, or a religious ruling, forbidding them. He said such crimes are considered in Islam as "one of the Kabair [severe sins] whose perpetrator deserves to enter Hellfire in the afterlife."

AFP/Getty Images/Joseph Barrak

CURRENT SITUATION
Providing Shelter?

"One step forward, two steps back." "Adding insult to injury." "Shameful and dangerous."

That's how women's activists describe the recently proposed law in Afghanistan that would turn the control of women's shelters over to the government. Under the law a woman hoping to enter a shelter would have to obtain the approval of eight different government offices, and the shelters would be run under the Ministry of Women's Affairs.

In a country that already lacks safe and secure facilities to protect women from honor-related crimes or domestic abuse, many see this law as a serious threat to women's lives and freedom. "Shelter administrators say they already get pressure from high-ranking government officials on behalf of families who want the women back in their communities — even when it's likely that the women or girls will be killed when they return," said Quil Lawrence, a reporter for National Public Radio.[72]

Women's-rights activist Saltanat Shalkibayeva holds up a picture of 16-year-old honor-killing victim Morsal Obeidi outside a courthouse in Hamburg, Germany, on Dec. 16, 2008, as the murder trial for Obeidi's brother begins. The Afghan-born Ahmad Obeidi, 23, was accused of stabbing his sister more than 20 times because she didn't live a strict Muslim life. He was sentenced to life in prison. As the verdict was announced, the unrepentant defendant screamed that if the trial had occurred in Afghanistan, he would have been released long ago. The sign behind Shalkibayeva reads, "Say no to power against woman — live free."

The proposed law has reignited the debate about the legality of women's shelters under Muslim law. In October 2010 the Afghan Supreme Court proclaimed that any woman who ran away from home could be charged with adultery or prostitution unless she went to the police or a relative's home. Also, a 2010 television report alleged that women's shelters "are fronts for prostitution."[73]

Age-old prejudices die hard. "You've got a parliament, a cabinet [and] various ministries that are effectively controlled by conservative factions that think very much like the Taliban when it comes to things like women's rights," said Rachel Reid, Afghanistan researcher for Human Rights Watch.[74]

But in other countries, there are some positive developments regarding sheltering women from honor crimes.

In 2010 India's Prime Minister Manmohan Singh ordered a commission to study which penalties for honor killing should be increased, and the nation's Supreme Court asked the national and local governments to report on efforts to stop the crimes. "The Indian government should press ahead to strengthen its laws and make community leaders liable for punishment if their edicts incite so-called honor killings," said Meenakshi Ganguly, South Asia director of Human Rights Watch. "Murder is murder, and customary sentiment should not prevail over basic rights and the laws of the land."[75]

After a surge in the number of honor killings in northern India last year, volunteers banded together to rescue and shelter young men and women threatened with murder for marrying outside of their caste. Named the "Love Commandos," the charity has grown to 2,000 volunteers from all across India.[76]

Marriage-related honor killings occur throughout India. In many cases families would rather kill their children than suffer from the stigma of them marrying a partner considered unsuitable. Often village caste councils sanction the killings.

Nearly every day brings news of caste-related honor killings. For example:

- In Delhi last June a young couple was tied up and tortured to death because the man was from a lower caste than his girlfriend.[77]
- Two months later a newlywed was burned to death in Northern India for marrying against the wishes of his family.[78]
- In January a young couple was slaughtered and left in a field in Tamil Nadu because they were from different castes.[79]

The Love Commandos have rescued hundreds of couples from possible murder and helped them to marry. "In every nook and corner of the country there are couples under threat," said Love Commandos founder Sanjoy Sachdev.[80]

Women's shelters have also sprung up elsewhere, from Asia to Europe to the United Kingdom. But much more needs to be done, according to rights activists. Turkey, for instance, has only 54 shelters for a population of 74 million.[81] "Until we can wipe out this barbaric practice we need to protect and shelter those who are most vulnerable," says Pakistani activist Mai, who runs her own shelter in the rural Punjab and narrowly escaped being a victim of an honor killing.

Legal Efforts

Women's-rights groups say some progress has been made recently in attacking the problem of honor killings. "Both the media and women's-rights activists have helped shine

Are Muslims being unfairly stigmatized in honor crime coverage?

YES
Rana Husseini
Jordanian journalist; Author, Murder in the Name of Honor

Written for *CQ Global Researcher,* April 2011

Ever since the Sept. 11 attacks in the United States, the Western media have become more biased in their coverage of Arabs and Muslims, including in regard to how they report on so-called honor killings.

A so-called honor crime occurs when the family of a woman decides that she has tarnished their reputation and the only way to eliminate this "headache and shame" is to kill her. I have conducted extensive research and readings and concluded that these kinds of murders are not restricted to any country, class or religion. They have been committed recently by members of the Muslim, Christian, Sikh and Yazidi faiths.

Violence against women — including killing for adultery and "illicit" sexual activities — has been the norm since ancient civilizations and later in the world's three main religions: Judaism, Christianity and Islam. All three religions proposed punishments for female [and male] adulterers and "sinners." In the Dark Ages, women were considered witches and were mostly punished or executed for having sex outside the marriage.

The "punishment" of women for "immoral" sexual activities in the West began decreasing after the Industrial Revolution, the creation of the pill, multiple wars and other factors. But Western women still are being killed by their husbands, ex-spouses and boyfriends because of possessiveness, jealousy, suspicion and infidelity — so-called "crimes of passion."

Meanwhile, in the Muslim world, women are murdered for those reasons and for reasons related to family honor. But the crime is motivated by culture and patriarchal beliefs that women are the property of their male guardians. Societies in the Muslim world are still developing and progressing. Women have become more educated and more independent. This has created some clashes with male family members who expect certain roles for females. That was once the case in the West, and it will change eventually in the Muslim world.

Meanwhile, the Western media's coverage of women's issues and domestic violence has been biased toward Muslims. For instance, if the murderer is a Muslim, then he/she is immediately labeled as Muslim. But we are never informed about the religion of a murderer if he/she is Christian, Jewish, atheist, etc.

This labeling will only increase the hatred and fear of Muslims and will further increase intolerance toward religions and traditions between the East and the West. The Western media should take a more objective and responsible approach when covering such issues.

NO
Phyllis Chesler
Emerita Professor of Psychology and Women's Studies, Richmond College, City University of New York

Written for *CQ Global Researcher,* April 2011

Bindu honor killings in India have been covered in the mainstream American media, but Muslim honor killings in the West — such as in Arizona, Georgia, Illinois, Ohio, Missouri, New Jersey, New York, Texas and Virginia — have barely been covered. When they are, experts are quoted insisting that the crime has nothing to do with Islam and that every group does it — even though most honor killings in the West are Muslim-on-Muslim crimes.

Some Muslims say it is unfair for the media to identify a wife- or daughter-murderer as a Muslim because the religion is not listed for all those arrested for domestic femicide. But Western domestic violence and honor killings are not the same. An honor killing is a conspiracy carried out by the victim's family, which views the killing as heroic. Daughter-stalking and daughter-killing are not a Western cultural pattern, nor are they valorized. In the West, wife- and daughter-killers are considered criminals, not heroes; and wife-killers are not assisted by their parents or in-laws.

According to my 2009 and 2010 studies in *Middle East Quarterly,* 58 percent of honor killing victims worldwide were murdered for being "too Western." Thus, an honor killing is part of a war waged by one culture against another. The religious and ideological fanaticism that drove Arab men to fly planes into the World Trade Center is the same fanaticism that drove an Iraqi-American Muslim father to run over his daughter with a two-ton jeep because she refused an arranged marriage and wore makeup and jeans.

True, nothing in "Islam" per se explicitly condones honor killings. However, Muslim leaders have not preached against this crime, and Muslim-majority countries have rarely prosecuted it.

Hindus, not Muslims, are being unfairly stigmatized by media coverage of honor killings. While Hindus, Sikhs and Muslims do perpetrate honor murders in India, Hindu and Sikh immigrants rarely practice the custom in the West. And the Hindu Indian government prosecutes it as a crime. India's Muslim neighbor, Pakistan, resists doing so.

Some fear that singling out only Muslims will stigmatize them. This "politically correct view" is fashionable but also dangerous because if we fail to understand this crime we will never be able to prevent or to prosecute it.

The group Stop Islamization of America uses a photo of slain Texas teenagers Amina and Sarah Said in an anti-honor-killing advertising campaign in Chicago. The Lewisville, Texas, sisters were found shot dead in their father's abandoned cab in a parking lot near Dallas/Fort Worth International Airport on Jan. 1, 2008. Police believe their Egyptian-born father, Yaser Abdel Said — who has been missing since the murder — killed the girls for refusing to accept his culture and religious beliefs. Muslim groups say the murders had nothing to do with Islam.

a light on this problem, which has resulted in some governments being pushed, some shamed, into acting," explains the UNFPA's Toure.

Last November at a conference to celebrate the International Day for the Elimination of Violence against Women, the Kurdish Prime Minister Barham Salih condemned honor killings and promised his government would work to end what he called an "embarrassing" act and the result of "social backwardness and a patriarchal domination."[82] Activists hope he'll keep his word. In 2008 the government amended a law that now regards honor killing as murder. In the past killers had been either let off or given light sentences.

In fact, one of the most high-profile and horrific honor killings occurred in the Kurdish region of Iraq in April 2007, when an angry mob cheered as 17-year-old Duaa Khalil Aswad was stoned to death in the village of Bashiqa, with nearby security personnel watching. Cellphone videos of the murder circulated on the Internet, showing the teenager begging for mercy before a man smashed her skull with a cinder block. Aswad's male

relatives — members of the secretive Yazidi religious sect — are believed to have arranged her death because she had dated a Sunni boy. The Yazidi religion includes elements of Zoroastrianism, Judaism, Christianity and Islam — and forbids interfaith relationships.[83]

Four men (including some of Aswad's relatives) were convicted and sentenced to die for the murder but were released from prison a year later.[84] The case exacerbated sectarian tension, which was rampant at the time in Iraq. Two weeks after the murder, more than 20 Yazidis in nearby Mosul were dragged from a bus and shot to death, allegedly by Sunni gunmen in retribution for Aswad's murder.[85]

Last year a court in the northern India state of Haryana sentenced five men to death and one to life in prison for killing a young couple who married against the wishes of village elders. The capital sentences were the first ever handed down in an honor killing case. Women's-rights activists have hailed the decision, which is a significant break with tradition. "An ugly nexus between politicians, policemen and these self-appointed guardians of tradition — who tend to dominate elected local assemblies as well as unelected caste ones — keeps most honour killings out of court," noted *The Economist*.[86]

Turkey's response to its grim new skyrocketing femicide statistics — admitting the problem and condemning it — is also seen as a step forward. "Too many governments have been reluctant to even speak out about honor killings," says Gill, of London's Roehampton University. "It's a necessary step to stopping this violence."

While Turkey recently strengthened its punishment for honor killings to include life inprisonment, regardless of the age of the murderer, nearby Syria has made what many see as a "token" change in punishing such killers: The two-year sentence was raised to between five and seven years.

Activists have been pressuring the Syrian government to increase the punishment for honor killers, so many saw it as a positive sign when a religious leader publicly condemned such killings and even pushed for longer sentences for those convicted of honor killings.

"He who kills on claims of honour is a killer, and should be punished," said Grand Mufti of Syria Ahmen Badr al-Din Hassoun. "Islamic jurisprudence doesn't allow people to live by their own laws."[87]

OUTLOOK

Needed: Three 'Ps'

Jordanian journalist Husseini began writing about honor killings in 1993. Her investigations, newspaper articles, speeches and book have made her an international expert on the grim subject. She has a perspective on what she insists on calling "so-called honor killings" that few others can rival. Yet, despite all the horrors that she has seen and reported on over the last two decades, she is an optimist.

"I think we are making a lot of progress," she notes. "Twenty years ago no one wanted to talk about this subject. It was denied, hushed up; it was taboo. Today, however, the topic is being debated, and it's featured in the press, on television and even in movies and plays. It's even being talked about on Facebook."

Like other women's-rights proponents, Husseini sees the growing willingness to address the problem of honor killings as the first step in prevention and better prosecution. "These crimes are not going to end overnight; we have to raise awareness, change laws, educate and empower women, convince religious and cultural leaders to condemn the murders, and more. But I see more and more people expressing willingness for better laws and more protection for women. I think there will be less and less of these murders as time goes on."

A recent honor killing prosecution in the United Kingdom supports Husseini's opinion. In December 2009 Mehmet Goren was convicted of murdering his 15-year-old daughter Tulay because he believed she had shamed him.[88] But the conviction only happened after Goren's wife came forward — 10 years after the murder — to testify against her husband.

"She only broke her silence because she was convinced she would be protected," explains London-based women's-rights activist Nammi. "A case like this gives others in the community the courage to come forward and help put an end to these killings. Because of this, and other reasons, I think we will see less honor killings as time goes on."

As Husseini notes, "There is still so much that needs to be done to tackle this crime. These murders are just starting to receive the attention they deserve." Many believe that as more societies modernize, the less prone they will be to accept honor killings. Experts stress the need for "the three P's": prevention, protection and prosecution. On their wish lists are such requirements as:

- Improving the education and emancipation of women,
- Raising legislative, law enforcement and public awareness,
- Researching the causes and consequences of honor killings, and
- Sheltering women threatened with these crimes.

"The more seriously the world takes honor killings, the less they will occur," says Gill, at Roehampton University.

"Violence against women is a pervasive problem across the globe. Honor killing is only one of its many modes, but reforming [the concept of] honor is relevant, I believe, to every form of gendered violence," noted Princeton's Appiah. "Every society needs to sustain codes in which assaulting a woman — assaulting anyone — in your own family is a source of dishonor, a cause of shame."[89]

Pakistan's activist Mai speaks for many women's-rights supporters when she adds, "How important is this? It's a matter of life and death."

NOTES

1. Omar Waraich, "Five women beaten and buried alive in Pakistan 'honour killing,'" Sept. 2, 2008, www.independent.co.uk/news/world/asia/five-women-beaten-and-buried-alive-in-pakistan-honour-killing-915714.html. See also Salman Masood, "Pakistan begins inquiry into deaths of 5 women," *The New York Times*, Sept. 3, 2008; and "Teens buried alive in honor killing," UPI.com, Sept. 5, 2008, www.upi.com/Top_News/2008/09/05/Teens-buried-alive-in-honor-killing/UPI-52141220645085/#ixzz1JKFutCns.

2. *Ibid.*

3. "Pakistan: Hundreds of women die for 'honour' each year," IRIN News, Jan. 27, 2011, www.irin news.org/Report.aspx?ReportID=91753.

4. Michael Winter, "Bangladeshi teen dies from sharia lashing after reportedly being raped," *USA Today*,

Feb. 2, 2011, http://content.usatoday.com/commu nities/ondeadline/post/2011/02/bangladeshi-teen-dies-from-sharia-lashing-after-reportedly-being-raped/1.

5. Anbarasan Ethirajan, "Four arrested after Bangladesh girl 'lashed to death,'" BBC News, Feb. 2, 2011, www.bbc.co.uk/news/world-south-asia-12344959.

6. Manar Ammar, "Egypt: Honor killing hits Alexandria," *Bikyamasr*, Sept. 29, 2010, http://bikya masr.com/wordpress/?p=17594.

7. Robert Tait, "Turkish girl, 16, buried alive 'for talking to boys,'" *Guardian*, Feb. 4, 2010, www.guardian .co.uk/world/2010/feb/04/girl-buried-alive-turkey.

8. "Facts and Figures on Harmful Traditional Practices 2007," UNIFEM, www.unifem.org/gender_issues/ violence_against_women/facts_figures.php?page=4.

9. Robert Fisk, "The crime wave that shames the world," *The Independent*, Sept. 7, 2010, www.independent .co.uk/opinion/commentators/fisk/robert-fisk-the-crimewave-that-shames-the-world-2072201.html.

10. Muhammad Zamir Aassadi, "Violence against women remains high in Pakistan," *The New American*, Feb. 9, 2011, www.thenewamerican.com/ index.php/world-mainmenu-26/asia-mainmenu-33/6246-violence-against-women-remains-high-in-pakistan.

11. "Syria increases punishment for honor killing," *Jerusalem Post*, Jan. 10, 2011, www.jpost.com/ Headlines/Article.aspx?id=203003.

12. "Iraq: Kurdish government promises more action on honour killings," IRIN News, Nov. 27, 2010, www .irinnews.org/report.aspx?ReportId=91216.

13. Dorian Jones, "Turkey's murder rate of women sky-rockets," VOA, Feb. 28, 2011, www.voanews.com/ english/news/europe/Turkeys-Murder-Rate-of-Women-Skyrockets-117093538.html.

14. *Ibid*.

15. "Towards Ending Violence Against Women in South Asia," Oxfam, August 2004, p. 3, www.oxfam.org .uk/resources/issues/gender/downloads/bp66_evaw .pdf.

16. Talea Miller, "Study finds honor killings a major portion of Pakistan's homicides," PBS Newshour,

April PBS 6, 2009, www.pbs.org/newshour/updates/ health/jan-june09/pakistan_0406.html.

17. "Statement by UN High Commissioner for Human Rights, Navi Pillay: Domestic violence and killing in the name of honour," March 8, 2010, www.un.org/ en/events/women/iwd/2010/documents/HCHR_ womenday_2010_statement.pdf.

18. "In-laws incensed by marriage mutilate husband in Pakistan," *Los Angeles Times*, Jan. 4, 2007, http:// articles.latimes.com/2007/jan/04/world/fg-beating4.

19. "Civil and political rights, including the question of disappearances and summary executions," United Nations Commission on Human Rights, Dec. 22, 2003, www2.ohchr.org/english/bodies/chr/ docs/62chr/ecn4-2006-53-Add2.doc.

20. Centre for Social Cohesion, "Crimes of the Community: Honour-based Violence in the UK," Feb. 6, 2008, p. 37, www.socialcohesion.co.uk/ files/1229624550_1.pdf. Also see, "A question of honour: Police say 17,000 women are victims every year," *The Independent*, Feb. 10, 2008, www.inde pendent.co.uk/news/uk/home-news/a-question -of-honour-police-say-17000-women-are-victims-every-year-780522.html.

21. Taner Edis, "Another Honor Killing," *The Secular Outpost*, Dec. 13, 2010, http://secularoutpost .infidels.org/2010/12/another-honor-killing.html.

22. Kwame Anthony Appiah, *The Honor Code* (2010), p. 146.

23. "Honour Killings," "Chapter 3: Ending Violence against Women and Girls," State of the World 2000, U.N. Population Fund, www.unfpa.org/swp/2000/ english/ch03.html.

24. James Emery, "Reputation is everything: Honor Killings Among the Palestinians," *The World & I*, May 2003, www.worldandi.com/newhome/public/ 2003/may/clpub.asp.

25. "Father says killed daughter in Canadian hijab case," Reuters, Dec. 11, 2007, www.reuters.com/article/ 2007/12/11/us-crime-hijab-idUSN11517747 20071211.

26. "Canadian Muslim teen's dad charged in her murder; friends say they clashed over head scarf,"

The Associated Press, Dec. 12, 2007, www.foxnews.com/story/0,2933,316550,00.html.

27. "Muslim leaders say teen's killing was domestic violence," Canadian Press, Dec. 14, 2007, www.cbc.ca/news/canada/toronto/story/2007/12/14/aqsa-parvez.html.

28. *Ibid.*

29. For more information, see Phyllis Chesler, "Are honor killings simply domestic violence," *Middle East Quarterly*, Spring 2009, pp. 61-69, www.meforum.org/2067/are-honor-killings-simply-domestic-violence.

30. Rochelle L. Terman, "To specify or single out: should we use the term 'Honor killing?'" *Muslim World Journal of Human Rights*, Vol. 7, Issue 1, 2010, www.bepress.com/mwjhr/vol7/iss1/art2/.

31. "Honor killing perpetrators welcomed by society, study reveals," *Today's Zaman*, July 12, 2008, www.todayszaman.com/newsDetail_getNewsById.action?load=detay&link=147349&bolum=101www.

32. *Ibid.*

33. *Ibid.*

34. Anna Momigliano, "Honor killing by any other name," *The Nation*, Feb. 2, 2010, www.thenation.com/article/honor-killing-any-other-name.

35. Chris Selley, "Recipe to reduce honor killings," *National Post*, June 18, 2010, www.nationalpost.com/m/blog.html?b=fullcomment.nationalpost.com/2010/06/18/chris-selley-recipe-to-reduce-honour-killings&s=Opinion.

36. John L. Esposito and Sheila B. Lalwani, "Domestic violence: a global problem, not a religious one," *Los Angeles Times*, Oct. 31, 2010, http://articles.latimes.com/2010/oct/31/opinion/la-oew-esposito-lalwani-women-violenc20101031.

37. "Statement by the U.N. High Commissioner for Human Rights, Navi Pillay," *op. cit.*

38. Lynn Welchman, "Extracted provisions from the penal codes of Arab states relevant to 'crimes of honour,'" School of Oriental and African Studies, University of London, www.soas.ac.uk/honour-crimes/resources/file55421.pdf.

39. "Jordan: Tribunals no substitute for reforms on 'honor killings,'" Human Rights Watch, Sept. 3, 2009, www.hrw.org/en/news/2009/09/01/jordan-tribunals-no-substitute-reforms-honor-killings.

40. "Syria amends honour killing law," BBC News, July 2, 2009, http://news.bbc.co.uk/2/hi/middle_east/8130639.stm.

41. Welchman, *op. cit.*

42. "Violence Against Women: Issue of Honor Killing," Legal Service India.com, www.legalserviceindia.com/article/l243-Violence-against-woman--Issue-Of-Honor-killing.html.

43. "Jordan: Tribunals no substitute for reforms on 'honor killings,'" *op. cit.*

44. *Ibid.*

45. "Frequently Asked Questions about honor killing," www.stop-stoning.org/node/12.

46. Quoted in *Broken Bodies, Broken Dreams*, IRIN (2005), p. 140, www.irinnews.org/Report.aspx?ReportId=72831.

47. Lynne Berry, "Chechen president Kadyrov defends honor killings," *St. Petersburg* [Fla.] *Times*, March 3, 2009, www.sptimes.ru/index.php?story_id=28409&action_id=2. See also Fisk, *op. cit.*

48. *Ibid.*

49. *Broken Bodies, Broken Dreams, op. cit.*

50. Berry, *op. cit.*

51. "In the name of honour," *Tribune* [Pakistan], Aug. 12, 2010, http://tribune.com.pk/story/38468/in-the-name-of-honour-2/.

52. Zahid Jan, "Jirga to kill anyone reporting honor killing cases to the police," *Daily Times*, April 29, 2006, www.dailytimes.com.pk/default.asp?page=2006\04\29\story_29-4-2006_pg7_1.

53. "Statement by the U.N. High Commissioner for Human Rights, Navi Pillay," *op. cit.*

54. "State of World Population 2000," *op. cit.*

55. "Honour Related Violence: European Resource Book and good practice," *Kvinnoforum*, 2005, www.endvawnow.org/en/articles/743-roles-and-responsibilities-of-police.html.

56. For background on CEDAW, see Karen Foerstel, "Women's Rights," *CQ Global Researcher*, May 1, 2008, pp. 115-147.

57. "Honor Crimes," MADRE, March 20, 2006, www .madre.org/index/press-room-4/news/honor-crimes-44.html.

58. Paula Kweskin, "NGOs fail Palestinian women at the UN," *In the Moment*, Feb. 24, 2011, www.moment magazine.wordpress.com/2011/02/24.

59. Matthew Goldstein, "The biological roots of heat-of-passion crimes and honor killings," *Politics and the Life Sciences*, September 2002, Vol. 21, No. 2, www.politicsandthelifesciences.org/Contents/ Contents-2002-9/PLS2002-9-3.pdf.

60. Quoted in *ibid.*, p. 29.

61. Umm Rashid, "Honour Crimes and Muslims," *IslamicAwakening.com*, www.islamicawakening.com/ print.php?articleID=1330&.

62. Goldstein, *op. cit.*

63. "Women in pre-Islamic Arabia," Muslim Women's League, September 1995, www.mwlusa.org/topics/ history/herstory.html.

64. For background, see Foerstel, *op. cit.*

65. *Ibid.*

66. *Ibid.*

67. Sango Bidani, "A short note on honour killing in India," *The Himalayan Voice*, Oct. 25, 2020, http:// thehimalayanvoice.blogspot.com/2010/10/honour-killings-on-rise-in-both-nepal.html.

68. "Resolutions adopted by the General Assembly at its 57th Session, United Nations, 2002, www.un.org/ Depts/dhl/resguide/r57.htm.

69. Tracy McVeigh, "Ending the silence on 'honor kill-ing,'" *Observer*, Oct. 25, 2009, www.samoaobserver .ws/index.php?option=com_content&view=article &id=14909:ending-the-silence&catid=64:sunday-reading&Itemid=82.

70. Valentina Colombo, "Honor killings in Europe," Hudson Institute, Feb. 8, 2011, www.hudson-ny.org/ 1849/honor-killings-in-europe.

71 Oren Dorrell, " 'Honor killings' in USA raise con-cerns," *USA Today*, Nov. 30, 2009, www.usatoday .com/news/nation/2009-11-29-honor-killings-in-the-US_N.htm.

72. Quil Lawrence, "Kabul seeks control of women's shelters," National Public Radio, Feb. 21, 2011, www.npr.org/2011/02/21/133865996/kabul-seeks-control-of-womens-shelters.

73. *Ibid.*

74. *Ibid.*

75. "India: prosecute rampant 'honor' killings," Human Rights Watch, July 18, 2010, www.hrw.org/en/ news/2010/07/16/india-prosecute-rampant-honor-killings.

76. Gethin Chamberlain, "Honor killings: saved from India's caste system by Love Commandos," *Observer*, Oct. 10, 2010, www.guardian.co.uk/world/2010/ oct/10/honour-killings-caste-love-commandos.

77. Geerta Pandey, "Indian community torn apart by 'honour killings,' " BBC News, June 16, 2010, www. bbc.co.uk/news/10334529.

78. Chamberlain, *op. cit.*

79. *Ibid.*

80. *Ibid.*

81. Dorian Jones, "Brutal death of 16-year-old reopens debate about honor killings in Turkey," Voice of America, Feb. 15, 2010, www.voanews.com/english/ news/europe/Brutal-Death-of-16-Year-Old-Reopens-Debate-Over-Honor-Killings-in-Turkey-84407947 .html.

82. "Iraq: Kurdish government promises more action on honour killings," IRIN News, Nov. 27, 2010, www .irinnews.org/report.aspx?ReportId=91216.

83. "Iraqi girl's horrific death; Teen's slaying at the hands of a mob highlights religious intolerance that pervades the nation," *Chicago Tribune*, May 22, 2007, p. C1.

84. "Four sentenced to death over Du'a Khalil Aswad honor killing," *Kurdnet.com*, March 30, 2010, www .ekurd.net/mismas/articles/misc2010/3/state3701 .htm.

85. "Iraqi girl's horrific death; Teen's slaying at the hands of a mob highlights religious intolerance that per-vades the nation," *op. cit.*

86. "A disgrace to the village," *The Economist*, April 15, 2010, www.economist.com/realarticleid.cfm?redirect_ id=15912850.

87. "Syria: popular campaign takes aim at 'honour killings,' " IRIN News, Feb. 15, 2011, www.irinnews .org/report.aspx?reportid=25612.

88. "Father convicted of 1999 'honour' killing of his daughter," The Crown Prosecution Service, Dec. 17, 2009, www.cps.gov.uk/news/press_releases/166_09/.

89. Appiah, *op. cit.*, p. 169.

BIBLIOGRAPHY

Books

Appiah, Kwame Anthony, *The Honor Code: How Moral Revolutions Happen*, W. W. Norton & Co., 2010.
A Princeton professor of philosophy offers case studies of "moral revolutions" against four traditional practices: slave trading, dueling, Chinese foot binding and honor killing.

Husseini, Rana, *Murder in the Name of Honor*, Oneworld Publications, 2009.
A Jordanian journalist examines the phenomenon in her own country and around the world.

Mai, Mukhtar, *In the Name of Honor*, Aria Books, 2006.
A rural Pakistani woman describes how she was gang-raped as punishment for her brother's alleged "honor crime." She then successfully prosecuted her attackers.

Articles

Fisk, Robert, "The crime wave that shames the world," *The Independent*, Sept. 7, 2010, www.independent.co.uk/opinion/commentators/fisk/the-crimewave-that-shames-the-world-2072201.html.
A Beirut-based British correspondent examines honor killing in the Middle East and South Asia.

Goldstein, Matthew, "The biological roots of heat-of-passion crimes and honor killings," *Politics and the Life Sciences*, Vol. 21, No. 2, September 2002, pp. 20-37.
The author explores the historical development of honor-based crimes ranging from crimes of passion to honor killings.

Husseini, Rana, "Initiative seeks to change mindset on so-called honour crimes," *The Jordan Times*, Feb. 1, 2011, www.jordantimes.com/?news=34406.
The Jordanian journalist and crusader against honor crimes reports on a recent study of Jordanian attitudes toward such crimes.

Jones, Dorian, "Turkey's murder rate of women skyrockets," *Voice of America*, Feb. 28, 2011, www.voanews.com.
The number of women murdered in Turkey rose 1,400 percent between 2002 and 2009, with many of the crimes attributed to honor killings.

Pandey, Geeta, "Indian community torn apart by 'honour killings,'" *BBC News*, June 16, 2010, www.bbc.co.uk/news/10334529.
An Indian journalist examines the rise of honor killings in New Delhi.

Rose, Jacqueline, "A Piece of White Silk," *London Review of Books*, Nov. 5, 2009, pp. 5-8, www.lrb.co.uk/v31/n21/jacqueline-rose/a-piece-of-white-silk.
In a review of three books on honor killings, Rose explores common misconceptions about the crimes.

Terman, Rochelle L., "To Specify or Single Out: Should We Use the Term 'Honor Killing?'" *Muslim World Journal of Human Rights*, Vol. 7, Issue 1, Article 2, 2010, www.bepress.com/mwjhr/vol7/iss1/art2/.
An academic explores the debate over the use of the term "honor killing."

Reports and Studies

"Crimes of the Community," *Centre for Social Cohesion*, 2010, www.socialcohesion.co.uk/files/1229 624550_1.pdf.
A U.K.-based think tank investigates the characteristics of honor killings that occur in immigrant communities. The report also focuses on forced marriage, domestic violence and female genital mutilation.

"Culture of Discrimination: A Factsheet on Honor Killings," *Amnesty International*, www.amnestyusa.org.
A human-rights organization provides a concise, fact-filled overview of honor killings.

"Harmful Traditional Practices and Implementation of the Law on the Elimination of Violence against Women in Afghanistan," *U.N. Assistance Mission in Afghanistan*, December 2010, http://unama.unmissions.org/Portals/UNAMA/Publication/HTP%20 REPORT_ENG.pdf.
The report documents the prevalence of customary practices that violate women's rights, including honor killings.

"Trapped by Violence," *Amnesty International*, March 2009, www.amnesty.org/en/news-and-updates/feature-stories/trapped-violence-women-iraq-200 90420.

The human-rights organization examines gender-based violence against women in Iraq.

Chesler, Phyllis, "Worldwide Trends in Honor Killings," *Middle East Quarterly*, spring 2010, www.meforum.org/2646/worldwide-trends-in-honor-killings.

A professor emerita of psychology and women's studies at the City University of New York investigates honor killings over a 20-year period.

Patel, Sujan, and Muhammad Gadit, "Kaor-Kari: A Form of Honour Killing in Pakistan," *Transcultural Psychiatry*, 2008, pp. 683-294, http://tps.sagepub.com/content/45/4/683.full.pdf+html.

Pakistan-born academics now in Canada investigate the psychiatric issues associated with honor killings in Pakistan, including its origins, motives and socio-cultural influences.

For More Information

Amnesty International, 1 Easton Street, London, WC1X 0DW, U.K.; +44-20-74135500; www.amnesty.org. International activist movement that campaigns to end human-rights abuses, including honor crimes.

Arab Regional Resource Center on Violence Against Women, P.O. Box 23215, Amman 11115, Jordan; 962 6 5543864; 3www.amanjordan.org. Women's organization that monitors humans-rights abuses in the Middle East.

Center for Social Cohesion, 210 Pentonville Rd., London, N1 9JY, England; (207) 3409641; www.socialcohesion.co.uk. Specializes in studying radicalization and extremism in Britain.

Human Rights Commission of Pakistan, Aiwan-I-Jamjoor, 107-Tipu Block, New Garden Town, Lahore, Pakistan; 92 42 35838341; www.hrcp.cjb.net. Long-established nongovernmental organization that promotes human rights and democratic reforms in Pakistan.

Human Rights Watch, 350 Fifth Ave., New York, N.Y. 10118; (212) 290-4700; www.hrw.org. The largest U.S. human-rights organization; investigates abuses around the world, including honor crimes and honor killings.

Iranian and Kurdish Women's Rights Organization, P.O. Box 65840, London, EC2P 2FS, U.K.; 0207 920 6460; www.ikwro.org.uk. International charity committed to women's equality, human rights and empowerment of women.

United Nations Development Fund for Women, 304 E. 45th St., 15th Floor, New York, NY 10017; (212) 906-6400; www.unifem.org. Promotes women's empowerment and gender equality.

United Nations Office of the High Commissioner for Human Rights, Palais Wilson, 52 rue des Paquis, CH-1201, Geneva, Switzerland; 41 22 917 9220; www.ohchr.org. Supports the work of the U.N. human-rights offices, such as the Human Rights Council.

United Nations Population Fund, 605 Third Ave., New York, NY 10158; (212) 297-5000; www.unfpa.org. International development agency that promotes "the right of every woman, man and child to enjoy a life of health and equal opportunity."

Women for Women International, 4455 Connecticut Ave., N.W., Suite 200, Washington, DC 20008; (202) 737-7705; www.womenforwomen.org. Nonprofit group that helps female victims of violence return to self-sufficiency.

Voices From Abroad:

MARY JOHN

Director, Centre for Women's Development Studies, India

A betrayal of trust

"People pressured into killing believe they otherwise are betraying their community when, in fact, they are betraying their family. They are betraying their authority and the trust of young people in their care. These are guardians killing the young. By calling it 'honour killing,' you rationalise it when, in fact, you are the victim of so-called 'custom.'"

Times of India, June 2010

AHMED NAJDAWI

Attorney, Jordan

Inevitable remorse

"There is remorse, for sure. They commit these crimes, motivated by the cultural aspects. But when time calms them down, they feel regret. Nobody kills a wife or a sister or a daughter without later feeling remorse."

The Independent, September 2010

DHARMENDRA PATHAK

Father of honor killing victim Nirupama Pathak India

Part of our culture

"This is part and parcel of our culture, that you marry into your own caste. Every society has its own culture. Every society has its own traditions."

The New York Times, July 2010

AZZA SULEIMAN

Activist, Center for Egyptian Women's Legal Assistance, Egypt

A lenient law

"In Lebanon and Jordan, they have [laws] that specifically refer to 'honour' killings. But in Egypt, the judge believes he has a special authority, and Article 17 of the law allows judges to use clemency if they wish to reduce sentences — from 25 years, for example, to six months. The religious and traditional background of the judges affects them. . . . This provides leniency for the perpetrators."

The Independent (U.K.) September 2010

SHEIKH HAMZA MANSOUR

Parliamentary Leader, Islamic Action Front, Jordan

Issue is being exaggerated

"This whole issue is being exaggerated, and the reason behind it is not innocent. It's as if the government is giving up our personality to turn us into a Westernised society."

Sunday Independent (Ireland) December 2009

JOHN AUSTIN

Member of Parliament, United Kingdom

Unacceptable

"In Turkey the figures for 2007 show that over 200 women were killed here in the name of family or community honor, and that is frankly unacceptable in a modern Europe."

Thai Press Reports, May 2009

MEWA SINGH MOR

President, Sarv Khap (clan council), India

Destroying social fabric

"It is a shame that so many girls and boys are eloping nowadays, under the influence of TV and movies. Our constitution tells our youth what their rights are but says nothing about their social duties. These couples are like an epidemic. They are destroying our social fabric."

The Washington Post, May 2010

RAVINDER KAUR

Social Science Professor, Indian Institute of Technology, India

The killers are relatives

"What shocks us about such murders is that they are perpetrated by close and trusted relatives, by those who we normally expect to love, nurture and protect us. Family murders strike at our self-image as a society of close-knit, resilient families in a world where we feel the family has largely self-destructed."

Indian Express, July 2010

GUMAN SINGH

Former Judge, Rajasthan High Court, India

A comprehensive law

"The origin of honour killing is not in enmity, rivalry or greed. . . . There is need to cover the entire gamut of this ghastly crime by including all the attendant acts of omission and commission leading to the offence."

The Hindu (India), August 2010

RONA AMBROSE

Minister for Status of Women, Canada

Unacceptable in Canada

"People come to this country to enjoy and embrace the values and opportunities that Canada provides, and as a nation we are proud of the contributions made by our diverse cultural communities. However, killing or mutilating anyone, least of all a family member, is utterly unacceptable under all circumstances and will be prosecuted to the full extent of the law."

Canada Newswire, July 2010

BURAK OZUGERGIN

Spokesman, Ministry of Foreign Affairs, Turkey

Turkey doing its part

"Turkey considered honour killings as a violation of human rights. Together with the United Kingdom, Turkey submitted a draft to the United Nations General Assembly in 2004 to prevent honour killings. Also, the new penal code which was approved by the Turkish parliament in 2004 . . . included many arrangements about gender equality."

Anatolia (news agency) (Turkey), February 2010

15

Social Welfare in Europe

Sarah Glazer

Protesters in London oppose cuts in welfare benefits on April 10, 2010. Generous benefits across Europe are likely to be cut as governments attempt to deal with the economic crisis, which threatens the integrity of the euro. Britain is considering delaying retirement to age 70. The new Conservative-led coalition government has also pointed a finger at the welfare benefits paid for disability, unemployment and housing.

From *CQ Researcher*, August 2010.

G ema Díaz, 34, counted on a range of benefits to supplement her relatively low salary when she took a job as a purchasing agent with the city of Madrid. Now, as Spain initiates a fiscal austerity campaign, she is seeing those benefits eaten away. Her $2,000 a month salary, like those of all public employees, is being cut by 5 percent; her pension is likely to be frozen instead of growing with the cost of living as guaranteed by Spanish law; her subsidized child care will cost more. Even the $3,300 baby bonus she was depending on when her second child is born in August is being eliminated.[1]

Governments across Europe are expected to cut back on their legendarily generous social welfare programs as they attempt to deal with the current economic crisis, most notably mounting deficits that threaten the integrity of the euro. Joining Spain recently in announcing cutbacks and higher taxes are Greece, Italy, Ireland, Portugal, Denmark, France and Great Britain.

Europe's cradle-to-grave welfare provisions — from universal health insurance and subsidized child care to generous unemployment and retirement benefits — have often been proudly touted as "social Europe" — a place where social solidarity and protection from poverty are assured, compared to the more individualistic sink-or-swim philosophy of America.

Conservative economists have long argued that generous welfare states are a drag on European economies, making them less dynamic and less productive than the United States. In exchange for a less secure system for those down on their luck, they argue, the United States provides greater mobility up the income ladder and a more flexible labor market. Historically, people are fired more easily in the

Northern Europe Spends the Most on Public Services

The Scandinavian countries — along with France, Austria, Germany and Belgium — spend more on social services than other European Union (EU) countries. The United States spends 15.9 percent of gross domestic product (GDP) on social services — slightly less than the lowest-spending EU country, the Slovak Republic.

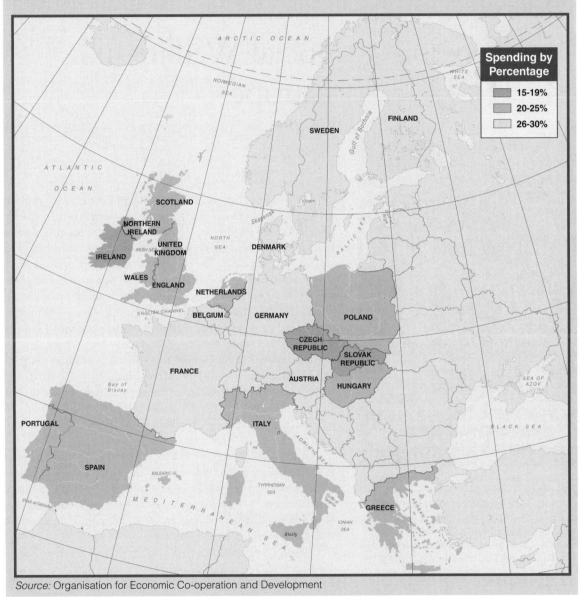

Source: Organisation for Economic Co-operation and Development

United States than in Europe but also hired back more quickly following economic recessions.

Unemployment benefits, which are typically more generous and last longer in Europe, can be followed by welfare payments with no fixed time limit in countries like Britain, Germany and the Netherlands. "The more you spread the safety net, the easier it is to be unemployed and the more people will be unemployed longer," says Vincent R. Reinhart, a resident scholar at the American Enterprise Institute (AEI), a conservative think tank in Washington. "Those economies that have more elaborate safety nets are ones that grow a little slower."

Although the American economy grew faster than Europe's devastated nations in the aftermath of World War II, much of that growth in total national income, or gross domestic product (GDP), was due to America's expanding population and immigration. If measured on a per-person basis, most rich countries actually enjoyed their highest growth rates in the era of the big welfare state, 1975-2006.[2]

Studies of the last 15 years show "European welfare states grew just as fast if not faster than the United States," says Timothy Smeeding, a professor of public affairs and economics at the University of Wisconsin-Madison and coauthor of the new book *Wealth and Welfare States*. Smeeding and his coauthors argue that welfare programs plus capitalism "make nations rich." When public education — not usually considered welfare — is counted along with health care and Social Security, the United States is one of the nations that has benefited from its welfare programs, though tilted heavily toward public education.[3]

And going from rags to riches, long a staple of the American dream, turns out to be easier in welfare-state Europe than the United States, judging from recent international comparisons of men's ability to move out

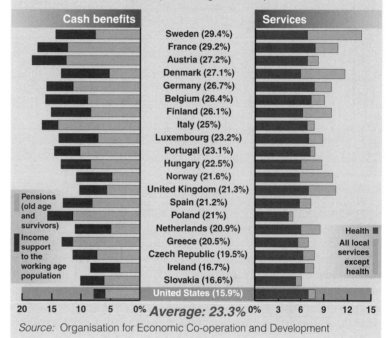

Europe Outspends U.S. on Safety Net

Eighteen selected European Union (EU) countries spend an average of 23 per-cent of their gross domestic product (GDP) on social services, compared with 16 percent spent by the United States. Sweden spends more on its social safety net than any other country in the world.

Public Social Spending by Broad Policy Area, 2005
(as a percentage of GDP)

Source: Organisation for Economic Co-operation and Development

of their father's economic class. Although America boasted greater economic mobility than Europe in the postwar economic boom, since 1975 those at the bottom of the income ladder have had a harder time climbing up as the economy slowed.[4]

One reason may be that the United States has lost its historic lead in education, including the percentage of citizens with college degrees. European countries, many of which offer free preschool education and free university education, have caught up and surpassed the United States, measured by college degrees and test performance.[5]

"The well-to-do in America can afford to do anything they want for their kids (including paying for college). Others can't. We have less mobility in the United States

European Employment Catching Up to U.S.

Employment/population ratios measure the proportion of a country's working-age population that is employed. In European countries with generous welfare programs, such as the United Kingdom and Germany, the employment ratios have caught up over time to the level of the United States. Thirty years earlier, the U.S. ratio was markedly higher than those of Germany and the Netherlands. The trend belies social welfare critics who say welfare programs stifle job growth.

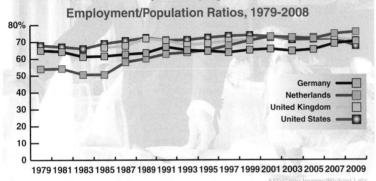

Employment/Population Ratios, 1979-2008

Germany
Netherlands
United Kingdom
United States

AFP/Getty Images/Michael Latz

Source: Organisation for Economic Co-operation and Development

because the main system for mobility — education — doesn't work as well," Smeeding says. And almost all of the growth in income recently has been limited to those Americans with college educations.[6]

Ron Haskins, a conservative champion of American welfare reform at the Brookings Institution think tank, used to believe that Europe was "socialist and soft" on unemployed welfare recipients, he says, but his recent research on work requirements has revealed that Europe "really wants to get people back in the labor force as fast as possible; that's the focus of their policy." Recent trends suggest some European countries are more successful than the United States in getting adults back to work. Since 2002, the United States has dropped from first place in the share of its population that's employed to third behind the Netherlands and Britain, according to Organisation for Economic Co-operation and Development (OECD) data.

In the current economic crisis, to what extent will European governments rethink the generosity of their welfare systems? So far most of the attention has focused on freezing pensions and delaying retirement ages. Europe faces a growing retiree population, but declining fertility rates mean there will be a relatively smaller work force that won't be able to support social security

systems funded by current workers' payroll deductions. Even France, whose government avoids the mention of fiscal austerity, has proposed raising the legal retirement age from 60 to 62.

Despite some proposals to cut other programs, like benefits for children, most experts think it unlikely that European governments will remove the foundations of the welfare state. "So far, I don't think you could find any cutbacks that are in any serious way undermining the cornerstones of the welfare state as such," says Gøsta Esping-Andersen, a prominent welfare expert and sociologist at Pompeu Fabra University in Barcelona. He calls the cutbacks in Spain "desperate measures conceived of as a temporary stopgap" in response to pressure from international markets. "I don't think any of these reforms are aimed at long-term erosion of the welfare state."

But the crisis has revived the long-standing debate over whether welfare states detract from economic growth or contribute to it by providing healthier, better educated, better paid workers. As the recent street protests in Greece, France and Spain indicate, changes to the welfare system could threaten social peace within European countries.

Tougher economic times could lead so-called Eurozone countries to turn against the more marginal members of their society who benefit from the generosity of welfare benefits. Denmark recently capped its monthly per-child cash benefits, a political move aimed at immigrant families with large numbers of children, Danish-born Esping-Andersen says. Denmark's coalition center-right government depends on the anti-immigrant Danish People's Party for support.

"The debate is pretty intense pitching to a rather strong electoral group that thinks we shouldn't coddle immigrants as much as in the past — that they are sucking too much out of the welfare state," he says. The Social Democrats, Denmark's party of the welfare state, "see this as a direct threat to the basic values of solidarity and universalism," he notes.[7]

The European Union's economic interdependence, demonstrated by the current euro crisis, means rich European countries could become more like the United States — less willing to redistribute welfare benefits to poorer, failing countries outside their own homogenous "tribe," Richard Burkhauser, professor of economics at Cornell University, predicts. "My sense is the Swedish tribe thinks they have enough moral cohesion to control all members of their tribe, so they don't have to worry about the behavioral consequences of a guaranteed income in Sweden," he says. Employed Swedes are comfortable paying cash transfers to fellow citizens who don't work, because they attribute it to bad luck, not laziness, most experts agree. But as some countries face mounting debt and unemployment, "even the Swedes won't be willing to do that for the Spanish, let alone the Slovenians," Burkhauser predicts.

Still others say the welfare states are crucial to keeping peace among the bloc's diverse countries. As the recent protests against welfare cuts suggest, if countries like Greece, Spain and Portugal find the violation of their social contract too disruptive, they could defect from the European Union, potentially threatening the euro and the common economic bloc. For some on the Left and much of the French political class, the fear is that "the high-cost social welfare model" can't be maintained by small individual countries in the face of global competition without the combined economic power of the EU, *The Economist* magazine recently noted.[8]

As cuts in social welfare programs are considered across Europe, here are some of the questions being debated:

Do Europe's generous social welfare programs make its economies less productive than the United States?

Economists in the conservative tradition have long argued that Europe's generous welfare lifestyle comes at

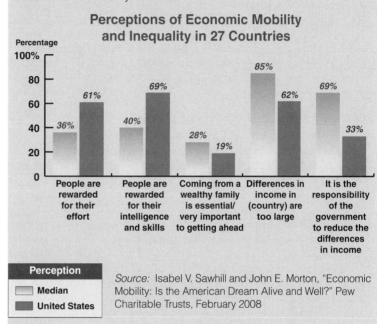

Europeans and Americans See Government's Role Differently

Unlike Americans, most citizens in more than two dozen industrialized countries with generous social programs do not believe hard work gets rewarded. Only 36 percent think hard work is rewarded, compared to 61 percent of Americans. Perhaps not surprisingly, only a third of the Americans surveyed felt the government should address income disparities, versus nearly 70 percent of the respondents in other wealthy countries.

Perceptions of Economic Mobility and Inequality in 27 Countries

Percentage

People are rewarded for their effort: Median 36%, United States 61%
People are rewarded for their intelligence and skills: Median 40%, United States 69%
Coming from a wealthy family is essential/very important to getting ahead: Median 28%, United States 19%
Differences in income in (country) are too large: Median 85%, United States 62%
It is the responsibility of the government to reduce the differences in income: Median 69%, United States 33%

Perception
Median
United States

Source: Isabel V. Sawhill and John E. Morton, "Economic Mobility: Is the American Dream Alive and Well?" Pew Charitable Trusts, February 2008

the cost of economies that don't grow as fast as America's and have higher long-term unemployment. In a series of papers in the 1970s, conservative economist Martin Feldstein, who later served as chief economic adviser to the Reagan administration, argued that unemployment insurance encouraged more people to stay unemployed, that health insurance was inefficient and that Social Security discouraged saving, resulting in a drop in investing and long-term wealth accumulation.[9]

More recently, Swedish economist Assar Lindbeck argued that the Swedish welfare state had become too generous and was responsible for a decline in the Swedish economic growth rate. In theory, there are three main reasons why social insurance programs like unemployment benefits and social security should make capitalist

France's Free Preschools: Do They Guarantee Equality?

The benefits for immigrants appear short-lived.

At the start of the school day, the preschool in Paris' fashionable 5th *arrondissement* feels much like an expensive private school in New York — if a bit more orderly. Well-dressed moms and dads sit with their children at the play-dough table before a whistle signals they should leave. A teacher's aide warmly greets each child, kneeling down to play with the stuffed animals some have brought, which must be put away in a special box until naptime.

Yet, this is a public school, offering a full day of early-childhood education from 8:30 a.m. to 4:30 p.m. for 3-6-year-olds. On a recent Tuesday a three-course hot lunch featured boeuf bourguinon. France's high-quality system of *écoles maternelles* — or preschools — is available free to all income levels, with a nationally standardized curriculum to prepare children for first grade. It is often cited by both the French government and academic researchers as the cornerstone of a system that gives children an equal opportunity in society from the start.

To help working parents, additional wrap-around care is offered after the school day ends until 6:30 p.m. and during school vacations, priced on a sliding income scale. Preschool's standard day is free; extra care is offered at extra charge.

To New Yorker Caroline Gelman, the mother of two boys ages 3 and 6, the contrast to Manhattan — where even well-heeled parents have trouble getting their children into nursery school — is startling. In Manhattan, Gelman had initially wanted to send her older son to the kindergarten at her local public school. Then she paid a visit.

"The school did not seem sufficiently challenging," recalls Gelman, an associate professor of social work at New York's Hunter College, who is living in Paris for a year. "I could not sacrifice my child for my abstract belief in the importance of a public school education. What made me very sad was thinking I had options, and these other kids' families don't. So these [disadvantaged] kids end up there, and you perpetuate this inequality," she notes. "And I think one way that gets addressed here in France is that you have very high-quality child care [for all] very early on."

France's national curriculum requires that children acquire some sophisticated skills before starting primary school at age 6: writing their first name in cursive from memory, copying simple words in cursive and knowing how to sound out consonants and syllables in written words.[1]

The process began gently with this class of 3-year-olds, who learned to recognize their photo next to their name at the beginning of the year. By May most were able to recognize their name label by itself and transfer it to the class attendance list. While children are not expected to read at the *école*, Gelman said her 3-year-old son was given free rein to follow his interest in spelling out classmates' names with plastic letters.

An important hallmark of quality is the education required of teachers: French preschool teachers must have the equivalent of a master's degree in early childhood and

economies less productive: 1) Increasingly burdensome taxation to support welfare programs reduces the incentive to work; 2) Welfare programs distort the true costs of services, by for example, encouraging consumers to use more health care than if they had to pay for it or deciding that working doesn't pay compared to their welfare benefits; 3) The administrative costs of distributing benefits and collecting taxes by government bureaucracies are so inefficient that they add unnecessarily to the overall costs of services.

Just last year, AEI's Reinhart echoed similar concerns: "In Europe there are more protections [for workers], but that makes the economy less flexible. They grow a little slower and have a higher unemployment rate. We've chosen a different point along the trade-off — less safe and faster."

Although it's true that Europe played catch-up with the United States after the devastation of World War II, in recent years the most generous welfare states, especially in Scandinavia, have grown even faster than the U.S. — on

elementary education, which requires a three-year university degree in a subject area followed by at least one year of training at a university-based teacher training institute, where they undergo the same training as prospective elementary school teachers. They also will earn the same salaries, paid vacation and generous health and retirement benefits. As a result of their relatively high pay and greater social status, there is relatively low turnover among French preschool teachers (an important factor in educational quality, according to American research).[2]

About 99 percent of French children attend an *école maternelle* by age 3, although attendance is not obligatory, and a place at one's closest neighborhood school is not guaranteed.

Does the system achieve its mission of giving everyone an equal start, including immigrant children? Having more years of preschool augers greater success for children in their first few years of primary school, but that advantage disappears after about the third or fourth grade for children from poor or immigrant families, according to Gilles Brougère, a professor of education sciences at the University of Paris-North, who is directing the French portion of a five-country study of immigrants in preschool.[3]

"This school culture is a very traditional one," says Brougère. "The teacher is the center of the system; the students have to understand what the teacher asks them and do the activity in the way the teacher wants." As a result, he says, little attention is paid to the individual needs of an immigrant child, who might be having language difficulties, for example. And French teachers often lack warmth, considering hugs the domain of less prestigious child-care workers, his study found.[4]

In addition, French teachers' strong emphasis on following rules may fail to develop the self-motivated pleasure in learning fostered in more child-centered American preschools. "I think we don't care enough about the well-being of the children," Brougère comments. "The child care [aspect] is not considered so important because there is this obsession with learning."

By secondary school, student achievement scores in France are more closely tied to their families' socioeconomic background than in most other wealthy countries.[5] While widely available preschool is an important ingredient of social equality, according to a growing body of research, Brougère says universality is not enough.

"I'm afraid the French system is very oriented towards ranking the children," making distinctions between "good pupils," who follow orders, and "bad pupils" who don't, he observes. The danger, he warns, is that children from immigrant families who may be less at ease with the highly disciplined French school culture will be condemned far too early as "bad pupils."

— *Sarah Glazer*

---

[1] "Votre Enfant à L'Ecole Maternelle," Ministère Education Nationale, 2009-2010, http://media.education.gouv.fr/file/Espace_parent/09/2/guide-parents-maternelle_43092.pdf.

[2] "Focus on Early Learning: Lessons from the French Ecole Maternelles," Economic Opportunity Blueprint, Economic Opportunity Institute, Seattle, Washington, January 2004, eoionline.org. Note: The French government is in the process of changing requirements for preschool teachers to emphasize more time in practical teaching experience in the schools.

[3] The "Children Crossing Borders" study is studying the preschool experience of children of immigrants in five countries, www.childrencrossingborders.org.

[4] Gilles Brougère, *et al.*, "Ecole maternelle (preschool) in France: a cross-cultural perspective," *European Early Childhood Education Research Journal*, September 2008, pp. 371-384.

[5] France is one of six countries, including the United States, where socioeconomic background appears to have the largest influence on students' performance. See "A Family Affair: Intergenerational Social Mobility Across OECD Countries," *Economic Policy Reforms: Going for Growth*, Organisation for Economic Co-operation and Development, 2010, pp. 187-188.

---

a per capita basis. Between 1973 and 2001 the U.S. economy expanded at an average annual rate of 2.9 percent — a higher average rate than Europe's 2.2 percent. (Norway at 3.3 percent was faster than the U.S.) But on a per capita basis, Europe and the United States experienced about the same annual growth — 1.9 percent.[10]

By many measures, Scandinavian countries have had the healthiest economies, including low unemployment, during the latest recession. Sweden, although it had low growth rates in the 1980s and 1990s, had the third-highest growth per capita from 1995 to 2006 (behind Finland and Ireland) among 14 rich nations compared in *Wealth and Welfare States*.[11]

The Nordic welfare states of Denmark, Finland, Norway and Sweden offer generous family-assistance programs, including subsidized child care and a year of paid parental leave. But all four economies have grown faster than the United States over the last 15 years.

"If you compare continental European countries with the U.S. and Britain, you can say that in exchange for more social protection and poverty reduction, they had to pay a price in employment and growth. But once you throw Nordic countries into the mix, you don't see that trade-off at all," says Jonas Pontusson, a professor of politics at Princeton University.

The key difference, he suggests, is that Scandinavian countries don't try to guarantee job security with rigid rules against firing, like the French, but offer serious job retraining along with unemployment insurance to ease the transition to new jobs. "Swedes said the government will not legislate a lot in this area" of employment security, says Pontusson. In France, by contrast, the government requires employers who want to lay off workers to prove the economic case for downsizing or else pay sizable severance packages.

Another difference may be that continental European countries like Germany finance more of their welfare programs through add-ons to paychecks — paid by the employer but deducted from the worker's net pay. "The employer has to pay a huge gross salary — to pay something attractive in net worth," says Jens Alber, a sociologist at the Social Science Research Center in Berlin. "That drives low-wage workers away from work; they're too expensive for employers," he says, and it contributes to high unemployment, especially among the low-skilled.

Sweden remains the most competitive economy in the EU, followed by Finland and Denmark, according to a study released in May by the World Economic Forum, which ranked nations according to indicators like productivity growth and unemployment.[12]

Taking a longer historical view, an even stronger case can be made for the welfare state, advocates argue. Early expansions in welfare states actually increased growth, some studies find. Most of the 14 rich nations studied in *Wealth and Welfare States* had their fastest growth in the era of the welfare state, 1975-2006. Of course, other factors like industrialization played a role in this growth, the authors concede. Still, those who argue that welfare states are strangling growth and productivity "need to explain . . . why growth rates have grown in most rich nations as their welfare states have grown larger," the authors write, throwing down the gauntlet.[13]

Why should welfare programs for the poor, the old and the unemployed encourage productivity? One reason, the authors suggest, is that they provide sufficient economic security that a laid-off worker can afford to remain jobless a little longer and look for a better job that matches his skills, thus improving his productivity. Even public relief programs, by providing a safety net, may "quell discontent," increasing political stability and ultimately productivity.

The authors argue that all rich nations, including the United States, have large welfare states (if you include public education) because they enhance the productivity of capitalism. "Education is so demonstrably productive that including it completely changes the picture" in debates over whether the welfare state reduces productivity, efficiency and growth in economic well-being, they write.

If college education, child care and health insurance are public and free, all income classes have access, not just the rich, welfare state advocates argue. And that has a big effect on upward mobility and productivity.

Economists of all stripes agree that education has great economic benefits in terms of creating more productive workers. But they disagree about whether the best way to do that is through a public education system or a private one — or a quasi-public system using vouchers — which may provide the same services more efficiently for a variety of consumers.

"In many cases, outcomes in the United States and those (welfare state) countries are similar, but Europeans have a greater taste for doing it through the public sector so they have higher taxes," says Burkhauser. For example, his research finds that widows in the United States have about the same income as those in Europe because they supplement public benefits with private pensions and life insurance.

In the trade-off between collective protection and personal liberty (usually in the form of freedom from heavier taxes), Americans have, historically, tended to favor the personal liberty side. "When you mess with people's liberty in the marketplace, it leads to less efficient markets and less growth," Burkhauser asserts, not least because of increased taxation. (In Denmark, historically one of the states with the most lavish spending on welfare, taxes range from 42 to 63 percent of income.)

Model welfare countries like Sweden and Denmark are also smaller and less ethnically diverse than the United States, which makes them more comfortable with social solidarity and supporting those less fortunate, Burkhauser suggests. "It's very hard to make comparisons between [small] countries that are homogeneous in their tastes and preferences to the United States. . . . We're a much less tribal system. They're more tribal there so they're more willing to think in terms of social solidarity than the United States."

Do European welfare states have less social mobility than the United States?

In exchange for a less secure safety net, the United States has historically offered more economic mobility — a better chance of moving from rags to riches — than Europe. And polls show Americans are far more likely to believe that they have more upward mobility than Europeans. About two-thirds of Americans agree that "people are rewarded for intelligence and skill" — the highest percentage across 27 countries. Only about one-fifth of Americans believe that coming from a wealthy family is important to getting ahead — compared to 28 percent among all countries surveyed.[14]

But the historical pattern appears to be changing. Recent studies show that the United States, together with the United Kingdom, has exceptionally low mobility compared to other European countries, if measured by the ability of men to rise above their fathers' economic rank. In the United States and Great Britain about half of parental-earnings advantages are passed on to sons — meaning it would take an average of six generations for family economic advantage to disappear.[15] Fathers' earnings have the least effect on their sons' earnings in Norway, Finland and Denmark, where less than 20 percent of income advantages are passed on to children. One reason may be that in such countries, where incomes are more equal, it's a shorter jump in absolute dollars from the bottom rung to the top.

But if your earnings are higher than your father's — an absolute increase — do you care where you rank on your nation's economic ladder? And if a more vibrant economy is creating an improved standard of living for everyone on the ladder, does your rank really matter that much?

That perspective, often voiced by conservatives, reflects their stronger emphasis on absolute increases in mobility made possible by a growing economy — the belief that "a rising tide lifts all boats." By contrast, "liberals tend to be more focused on relative mobility" — climbing rungs of your society's income ladder — notes John E. Morton, director of the Pew Charitable Trusts' Economic Mobility

Project, which brings together conservatives and liberals to research this issue and discuss policy solutions.

"If we're true to the notion of America as a meritocracy, you want to see some combination of both, because it's not sufficient to have a 'rising tide' if no one is changing places on the ladder," says Morton. "That suggests people are doing better but the meritocracy is broken."

Yet Pew's most recent polls suggest Americans care more about whether they're doing better than their parents in an absolute sense, and they've remained surprisingly optimistic even when polled at a low point in the downturn last year. A 58 percent majority of Americans report having a better standard of living than their parents did at their age, and a majority in most age groups said it will be easier for them to move up the ladder than it had been for their parents.[16]

Julia B. Isaacs, a child and family policies fellow at the Brookings Institution, and author of a recent Pew/Brookings study comparing international economic mobility, says, "I think one reason the American dream — the myth of mobility — has so much power is because it is still experienced by immigrants moving to the country today." And many Americans did experience upward mobility in the boom following World War II.

But since 1970, says Morton, "the rising tide may be slowing." In the post-war period, initiatives like the GI bill, which made college free for returning veterans, also boosted those soldiers' future earnings. "We haven't had that significant a domestic policy initiative around education since then," he observes.

Most experts agree that education — in particular a growing share of the population receiving college education — is the most likely explanation for the superior mobility of Europe today, where college education is often free. In the United States, Pew's study found, a child born to parents on the bottom rung of the income ladder who doesn't get a college degree has only a 5 percent chance of making it to the top fifth of the income ladder. If you get a college degree, the chance of making it to the top almost quadruples (to 19 percent).[17]

"Our education system has really fallen behind compared to European countries. On most comparisons, we're ranked 12th or 14th compared to first — where we used to be," says Haskins, a coauthor of the study. More jobs now require college education, he observes. "The data on the relationship between education and family income is so systematic you could argue that no education group has increased in family income except those with some college and above. High school graduates and high school dropouts have not improved their income on average for 30 to 40 years as a group."

Not everyone is convinced that Europe has raced ahead of the United States on upward mobility. "Just like global warming, the issue is not settled yet," says Burkhauser, who is also an adjunct fellow at the conservative AEI. He cites statistical difficulties in making comparisons between countries, since socialist countries like Sweden tend to track generational income more closely, and studies don't always take into account the years when adults are out of work.

While there have been several international comparisons of relative mobility, there have been fewer of absolute mobility, a question Pew hopes to address with a six-country study coming out later this year.

Finally, there's a question about whether Europe's immigrants — a relatively recent phenomenon for that continent — are sharing in upward mobility. As one sign that they're not, skeptics point to the riots in 2005 and 2007 in Paris' heavily North African suburbs, which are plagued with high unemployment, and riots in July in a similar suburb of Grenoble.

Immigrants' ability to gain economic status remains an open question for some experts since there's a paucity of cross-generational data about recent immigrants. However, Anna D'Addio, an economist at the OECD, says the studies that do exist don't find quite such dazzling results for immigrants — even in the most mobile of countries. "Even in Nordic countries, immigrants don't have the same levels of mobility as the natives. In Sweden, studies show immigrants do not perform as well as natives do," she says.

But neither, she says, do studies support the idea that the United States does much better at assimilating immigrants when it comes to intergenerational mobility. In the United States, immigrants together with blacks have less mobility than white native-born citizens. In general, she finds, "The more unequal a country is [in income] the higher the probability that the mobility across generations is low."

And the United States has long ranked high in income inequality. "Of every dollar of real income growth that was generated between 1976 and 2007, 58 cents went to the top 1 percent of households," according to University of Chicago economist Raghuram Rajan.[18]

Can European welfare states afford their generous benefits?

The rich countries of the European Union have been putting pressure on high-debt countries like Greece, Spain and Portugal to reduce their budget deficits in hopes of reassuring international markets and ensuring the integrity of the euro.

Declining fertility rates and aging populations mean Europe faces a demographic time bomb: It can no longer afford its generous early retirement and pension plans, especially as the baby boom generation moves into retirement, most experts agree. Between 2005 and 2030 the European Union's working-age population, which supports retirees through payroll deductions, will shrink by 20 million, while the number of those over 65 will increase by 40 million.[19]

And many Europeans, especially government employees in France and Spain, retire as early as 50, suggesting governments will be shelling out social security for decades to come.

There's far more consensus about reducing pension liabilities than other cutbacks. Governments in Britain and the Netherlands have proposed delaying retirement — in Britain to the age of 70 for those now 40 — without the kinds of angry street protests seen in France. Still, some object that delayed retirement is more likely to penalize blue-collar workers, who tend to have the worst health. Sixty-five-year-old men living in posh London neighborhoods like Chelsea "can expect to live a further 23 years, while those in [working-class] Glasgow only 14 years," protested British union leader Brendan Barber.[20]

Britain's new Conservative-led coalition government has also pointed a finger at the mounting welfare benefits paid for disability, unemployment and housing. "We as a nation are frankly pretty well bust," Iain Duncan Smith, the Conservative cabinet member in charge of work and pensions, recently told a conference on welfare reform, citing "a looming welfare budget." For the growing number of "workless" households, he said the government has created perverse incentives for welfare beneficiaries not to take a job: For every $10 a recipient earns from a job, the government removes $7-$9 in benefits. "We need to change the culture," Smith asserted.

"A growing number have become dependent on the state and live without work, aspiration and hope."[21]

Although headlines about Britain's welfare "scroungers," or deadbeats, grab headlines, cash benefits to the unemployed barely showed up in the latest government figures estimating Britain's future indebtedness at almost 4 trillion pounds (about $6.1 trillion). The lion's share of the nation's debt is for future state old-age pensions and public-sector pensions for teachers, civil servants and health workers.[22]

"We shouldn't forget that the two really expensive items in the welfare budget are pensions and health care; if you want to go where the money is, that's where you'd go," notes welfare expert Esping-Andersen. "The rest is the peanuts department."

Certain programs like free health coverage in Britain and universal pre-school in France and Scandinavia, are so basic to a society's sense of itself that it seems no political figure, (even a Conservative politician) would suggest cutting them. Britain's new Conservative Prime Minister David Cameron has stuck by his campaign pledge to "ringfence" the National Health Service (NHS) from the 25 percent cuts proposed for most other departments, though Labour's generous annual increases in the NHS budget will come to an end. The decision has come under attack from the British Chamber of Commerce, which charges that "ringfencing health will mean more drastic cuts to important investment elsewhere."[23]

In *Wealth and Welfare States*, the authors argue that welfare programs like health insurance, social security and public education contribute to nations' long-term wealth. "That benefits exceed costs is the primary reason why all rich nations have large welfare states," they conclude.[24] For example, universal child care on the Danish model (all-day and free to low-income parents) boosts maternal employment and "practically pays its own way due to superior female lifetime earnings," according to cost-benefit calculations by Esping-Andersen. When the lifetime benefits of high-quality programs to the children themselves are considered, economists estimate that each $1 spent yields a return of anywhere from $5.60 to $12.[25]

The single most important element in preventing child poverty is mothers working, research by Esping-Andersen finds. The incidence of child poverty falls by a factor of 3 to 4 when mothers work — in particular single mothers. And that becomes far more feasible when, as in Denmark, mothers can count on all-day child care at little or no cost.[26]

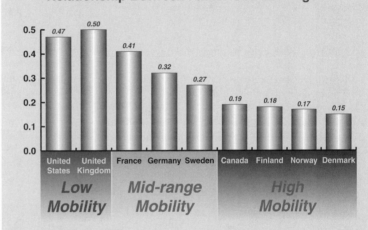

Countries with Higher Social Welfare Spending Have More Upward Mobility

Young people in countries that spend a lot on social programs have higher economic mobility — or a better chance of earning higher wages than their fathers. A young person in the United Kingdom or the United States has a relatively low chance of earning higher wages than his father — a sign of low economic mobility — compared to citizens in countries like Canada, Denmark, Finland and Norway, which spend more on social welfare programs than the UK or the United States. Countries where a son's earnings are similar to his father's are less economically mobile.

Relationship Between Father-Son Earnings *

	United States	United Kingdom	France	Germany	Sweden	Canada	Finland	Norway	Denmark
Score	0.47	0.50	0.41	0.32	0.27	0.19	0.18	0.17	0.15

Low Mobility — Mid-range Mobility — High Mobility

* The higher the score the lower the economic mobility.

Source: Julia B. Isaacs, "International Comparisons of Economic Mobility," Pew Charitable Trusts, February 2008

CHRONOLOGY

19th Century *Conservative German Chancellor Otto von Bismarck, with support of employers, introduces first modern welfare state in late 1880s.*

Early 20th Century *British government introduces unemployment insurance; Denmark leads in old-age insurance, France in unemployment benefits.*

1930s *Great Depression spurs President Franklin D. Roosevelt's New Deal; family-benefits programs spread in Western Europe.*

1931 Sweden introduces paid maternal leave.

1935 United States enacts Social Security, unemployment insurance.

1939 By this year, family allowances have been adopted in Belgium, France, Italy, Spain and the Netherlands.

1940s *World War II ravages economies of Western Europe; welfare state expands with postwar prosperity in Europe.*

1942 Beveridge report to British government recommends health insurance (already in Spain and the Netherlands) and social security.

1948 Britain adopts national system of free medical care for all.

1960s-1970s *Major expansion of welfare programs in Europe; U.S. President Lyndon B. Johnson initiates greatest expansion of welfare state since 1930s; poverty declines in Europe as old-age insurance leaves fewer impoverished.*

1965 Johnson persuades Congress to enact Medicare.

1966 Netherlands adopts paid maternal leave.

1969 Richard M. Nixon becomes president; period of Republican dominance begins, but social insurance and

welfare programs initiated under Johnson continue to swell. . . . U.S. starts to lose world lead in education.

1971 Belgium and Italy adopt paid maternal leave.

1972 Oil embargo by Organization of Petroleum Exporting Countries (OPEC) marks start of stagflation, which conservative economists blame on welfare programs.

1975 Arthur Okun, adviser to President John F. Kennedy, argues in *Equality and Efficiency* that increasing equality results in loss of economic efficiency.

1980s-1990s *Denmark and Sweden achieve universal preschool; U.S. President Ronald Reagan proposes welfare cuts; President Bill Clinton pledges to "end welfare as we know it"; single mothers' employment grows following welfare reform.*

1996 U.S. welfare reforms limit benefits, require work.

1997 Prime Minister Tony Blair and Labour Party take over British government.

1999 Blair announces goal to end child poverty.

2000s *Britain's child-poverty rates fall, but America's stall, then rise; some experts blame welfare work requirements; euro currency crisis focuses on governments' debt.*

2008 Pew report finds less upward mobility in U.S. than Scandinavia, Europe.

2009 Greece reveals serious debt; euro currency threatened. . . . OECD report urges government spending on preschool to improve child well-being.

May 2010 Europe bails out Greece.

June 2010 New British coalition government vows welfare cuts.

July 8, 2010 Greek parliament passes pension cuts.

Recent studies by the OECD have also found a connection between high enrollment in preschool and more mobility, economically and educationally.[27]

But has Europe gone too far in promoting the "social model"? The free-market-oriented *Economist* magazine recently charged that the social model had become "a very expensive" end in itself; it attacked EU leaders who are "calling for Europe to grow purely in order to maintain its social welfare systems. That is a pretty depressing call to arms: become more dynamic so Europe can still afford old-age pensions and unemployment benefits."[28]

Yet, Denmark, which maintains what may be the most generous unemployment scheme in the world, actually creates high employment and better jobs, retorts John Schmitt, senior economist at the Center for Economic and Policy Research, a liberal think tank in Washington. If out of work, a Dane can receive benefits paying up to 90 percent of his former salary for as long as four years, extensive skills retraining, and, if necessary, a subsidized job.[29]

Denmark's famed approach, known as "flexicurity" because it's twinned with flexible hiring and firing rules, comes at a high cost — 5-6 percent of its GDP. But the combination means "unions don't fight tooth and nail on job security issues because they know their members will be looked after" when out of work, Schmitt says. "Denmark has one of the lowest unemployment rates in Europe for the last decade or so."

By contrast in the United States, he says, "If I don't have the resources to wait [for a high-skills job] and I go work at Walmart, I'm not using the skills I have."

"That argument makes sense if you're talking three to six months," concedes Cornell economist Burkhauser, a skeptic of generous benefits, but if it's much longer, skills get rusty and the question becomes "how to wean the unemployed off benefits."

This entire debate is taking place amidst a long-standing disagreement about the best way to get the economy going again — budget cuts, as conservatives advocate, or job stimulation entailing even more government spending, supported by liberal economists. Recent statistics released in Britain showed that without state spending, the nation's economy would have contracted in the first three months of 2010, rather than expanding.[30] "If public spending is behind the recovery, what happens when we cut it?" the liberal *Independent* newspaper asked the day the statistics were released.[31]

BACKGROUND

Rise of Welfare in Britain

Paradoxically, the roots of modern welfare states in both continental Europe and Britain lie in conservative efforts to forestall even more radical visions of a socialist state.[32]

Conservative German Chancellor Otto von Bismarck introduced the first modern welfare state in the 1880s — including sickness insurance and old-age pensions — in an effort to head off calls for more workers' protections from the increasingly popular Socialist Party. Together with German employers, Bismarck introduced the first work-injury insurance program with an eye to reducing class conflict and promoting social stability.[33]

In the Bismarckian model, these benefits are generally financed by deductions from wages. Most of the cash benefits are earnings-related and thus viewed by citizens as an earned right, not a handout.

Social insurance programs to protect against work injury, old age and disability spread through the rest of the wealthy world during the 20th century. This model was adopted by most continental European countries, including France, Austria, Italy, Spain, Belgium and the Netherlands. National health insurance, one of the newest of welfare programs, was adopted mostly after World War II. Paid parental leave, the newest, spread through Europe in the 1960s, '70s and '80s, after originating in Sweden.

In England, the Liberal Party and Winston Churchill, then the Liberals' cabinet member in charge of trade, were responding to fears of an emerging Labour party, as well as the urgings of British socialist thinkers like playwright George Bernard Shaw and Sidney Webb, when they designed the unemployment insurance program, enacted in 1911. "Insurance brought the miracle of averages to the rescue of the masses," Churchill would observe.[34]

The second major introduction of welfare arose when the British government sought advice on rebuilding England after World War II from British economist and government reformer William Beveridge. His 1942 report recommended that the government institute social insurance programs to fight against the five "Giant Evils" of "Want, Disease,

On Welfare Reform, Britain Looks to America

Experts fear progress in reducing child poverty will slow.

"Welfare dependency." "Personal responsibility." "Make work pay." The same rhetoric that accompanied the 1990s welfare reform debate in the United States crops up frequently in the speeches of Britain's new Conservative-led coalition government. Conservative Prime Minister David Cameron campaigned on vows to fix "the Broken Society," pointing to the large number of children growing up in single-parent houses without a history of work.

"We'll demand that job-seekers [on welfare] take responsibility for accepting work when it's offered," Iain Duncan Smith, the former Conservative Party leader who is the new Secretary of State for Work and Pensions, told a conference organized by the free-market think tank Reform on June 30. On the new government's 49th day in office, Smith vowed to enforce financial penalties against welfare recipients who don't take job offers — a sanction he said had "been parked for a while" under the previous Labour government.

But rather than a sudden clampdown on welfare after a soft liberal regime, the new government's recently announced budget represents more continuity than revolution, says Paul Gregg, a professor of economics at the University of Bristol.

"We started moving towards America a few years ago," he says. The Labour government imposed work requirements on single mothers once their youngest child reached 10. The new government has accelerated Labour's plan to reduce the age to 7 by requiring single parents to start working once their youngest child reaches school age of 5, starting this fall. That's still far more generous than the United States, where welfare mothers with infants as young as 6 months old are expected to work, notes Timothy M. Smeeding, a welfare expert at the University of Wisconsin.[1]

In another, even more remarkable sign of continuity in welfare reform policy, the new government is committed to preventing a rise in child poverty, says Jane Waldfogel, a Columbia University professor of social work and public affairs who is a visiting professor at the London School of Economics this summer. To protect the incomes of the poorest families from the tax rises and benefit cuts announced June 22, the government announced it would raise the value of the child tax credit for the poorest and cushion them from middle-class cuts. Cameron has vowed that child poverty would not rise for the next two years, and his government has adopted Labour's goal of eliminating child poverty by 2020, showing "this is now part of the political landscape," says Waldfogel, author of the new book *Britain's War on Poverty*.[2]

Britain succeeded in cutting its child poverty rate in half over the past decade, after the Labour government announced a campaign against child poverty in 1999. It introduced reforms to promote employment and make work pay, such as establishing the nation's first national minimum wage.[3] Welfare mothers were invited to an interview to discuss work (but were not required to take work until recently) and offered much more generous child care than ever before. Employment among single moms jumped by 12 percentage points, about the same rise the United States saw after welfare reform, according to Waldfogel.[4]

However, as both economies became less vigorous in 2000, child poverty in the United States reversed its decline, and began to increase again. But the share of poor children in Britain continued to fall even through last year's recession.

Nevertheless, Britain has the highest share of children living in jobless households in Europe. "We set those children

Ignorance, Squalor and Idleness." He proposed a system of national insurance to cover Britons in cases of ill health, arguing it would improve Britain's competitiveness by moving the costs of health and pensions off corporate ledgers and producing healthier workers.

A national system providing free medical care to all was enacted in 1948 and was closely followed by an expanded social security scheme funded by payroll contributions, based on Beveridge's recommendations.

Welfare Reform

Modern welfare states generally fall into three main categories, according to prominent welfare expert Esping-Andersen. English-speaking countries (including the

on a path of poverty and low achievement at the word Go," Smith said in his June 30 speech.

Yet, the share of children in workless households actually fell significantly as more parents went to work under Labour's reforms, according to Waldfogel. Seeing more mothers working changed traditional British attitudes about a mother's proper role. "This is a country that has a long tradition of mothers staying at home or working part time," she says. "If you listen to Smith it sounds as if that's a legacy of the Labour government; it's actually just the opposite," since Labour introduced a work requirement for mothers for the first time in the history of welfare benefits.

Gregg and Waldfogel predict that the new government's policies will probably mark the end of the successful decade-long decline in child poverty — despite the government's commitment to prevent more children from falling into poverty — in part because the poor are expected to take the biggest hit from projected cuts in public services. Those services, especially free education and child care, are used most heavily by the poor. The projected cuts could result in the poorest 20 percent of families losing the equivalent of nearly 8 percent of their income, compared to less than 3 percent among the wealthiest one-fifth, according to estimates by the *Financial Times* and the Institute for Fiscal Studies, a British think tank.[5] Likewise, an increase in Britain's sales tax, called the Value Added Tax, will hurt the poor the hardest.

British conservatives, borrowing from American conservatives' playbook, have also begun promoting marriage as an antidote to what they see as the grim life chances of children growing up in single-parent families. But most of the research showing children do worse in single-parent families comes from the United States.

"You can't make as strong a case [for that] here in Britain," says Waldfogel, partly because of the UK's strong safety net, which often includes free housing and child care. "So maybe growing up with a single parent actually is not as tough here as in the United States," she speculates. Another factor might be the vast array of free public services in Britain that make life comfortable for even the poorest children — such as local swimming pools with free

Conservative Prime Minister David Cameron has vowed to require more parents on welfare to work but protect children from falling into poverty.

AFP/Getty Images/Raveendran

swimming lessons. But that may come to an end when the government announces additional budget cuts in the fall.

— *Sarah Glazer*

[1]See Rachel Williams, "Budget 2010: Single Parents must work when Child Turns Five," *The Guardian*, June 22, 2010, www.guardian.co.uk/uk/2010/jun/22/budget-single-parents-work-child-five.

[2]See Trevor Mason, "David Cameron not being 'straight' on Budget, says Harriet Harman," *The Independent*, June 23, 2010, www.independent.co.uk/news/uk/politics/david-cameron-not-being-straight-on-budget-says-harriet-harman-2008234.html.

[3]Timothy M. Smeeding and Jane Waldfogel, "Fighting Poverty: Attentive Policy Can Make a Huge Difference," *Journal of Policy Analysis and Management*, January 2010.

[4]Employment among single mothers in the U.S. rose from 62 percent to 73 percent between 1995 and 2000. See Rachel Dunifon, "Welfare Reform and Intergenerational Mobility," 2010. www.economicmobility.org

[5]Chris Giles, "Measures to hit poor the most, think-tank says," *Financial Times*, June 24, 2010, p. 3.

United Kingdom, Ireland, the United States and Canada) generally follow the 19th-century liberal belief in limited government, with heavy reliance on income-based benefits. In the social democratic regimes of the Nordic countries, policy is dominated by the Social Democratic Party's commitment to greater equality, resulting in universal benefits with high floors, regardless of income.

In continental Europe, the conservative belief in preserving both traditional status differences and social peace results in universal benefits closely tied to previous earnings.

Throughout the 20th century, the United States lagged behind other wealthy nations in enacting social insurance programs. The United States did not enact Social Security

AP Photo/Bob Edme

AFP/Getty Images/Marcus Brandt

Street Protests

Hospital workers in Paris protest government plans to raise the retirement age past 60 (top). The May 27, 2010, demonstration was one of many street protests held recently in Europe over changes in the welfare system. In Berlin, demonstrators at the Brandenburg Gate wear "Stop Poverty" signs to protest plans to cut welfare benefits (bottom). Unemployment benefits, which are typically more generous and last longer in Europe, can be followed by welfare payments with no fixed time limit in countries like Britain, Germany and the Netherlands.

and unemployment insurance until 1935, when President Franklin D. Roosevelt introduced the New Deal in response to the Depression. The United States was the last of 14 rich countries to adopt worker's compensation. Unlike most other wealthy countries, it has no universal family allowances, no work-sickness insurance or paid parental leave when children are born. It tends to spend less on cash benefits like unemployment insurance than most other wealthy countries but has until recently been a leader in spending on public education.[35]

In 1997, when the Labour Party took over the British government, there were record-high levels of long-term worklessness and poverty. The party introduced welfare reforms aimed at eradicating child poverty by 2020 and moving single mothers into work, including establishing the first minimum national wage. Under its regime, experts on the left and the right agree, the government succeeded in cutting child poverty in half over the past decade.

"New Labour" politician Prime Minister Tony Blair also adopted the tougher rhetoric of American welfare reform. Influential in this regard was the passage in 1996 of welfare reform legislation in the United States, known as the Personal Responsibility and Work Opportunity Reconciliation Act. Although largely crafted by Republicans, the bill was signed by President Bill Clinton, who had campaigned on the pledge to "End welfare as we know it" and "Make work pay." The new law eliminated the guarantee of receiving welfare, mandated work requirements and imposed strict limits (no more than five years) on the length of time benefits could be received.

By contrast, in Great Britain, single mothers could continue to receive welfare benefits until their youngest child turned 10 without being required to work. Only towards the end of the Labour Party regime was a work requirement introduced for them along with a plan to lower the trigger age for their youngest child to 7.

While welfare reform in the United States led to an increase in the share of single mothers employed (from 62 to 73 percent between 1995 and 2000), its impact on household income is less clear, according to a recent report from the Pew Economic Mobility Project. And although child poverty declined after welfare reform, it has increased since 2000. Most disturbing to experts, the share of single parents with no visible signs of support — neither welfare benefits nor earnings from a job — doubled from 10 percent to 20 percent between 1990 and 2005.[36]

Debating Welfare Success

For decades economists and other experts have been debating whether welfare states are good for the economy, as liberals claim, or a drag on growth, as conservatives contend. In the 1950s many economists were alarmed by the welfare state's rapid expansion, believing it would harm the economy. But their warnings were followed by two decades of unprecedented growth.[37]

Ten years later, many on the Left attacked the welfare state as a failure in eliminating poverty. Postwar prosperity had spurred a major expansion of the welfare state in Europe. Yet in the 1960s and '70s, poverty declined throughout Europe, because pension reforms meant fewer elderly were impoverished.

In the 1970s and '80s, the era of welfare state expansion in Sweden, some pointed to Sweden's success in reducing poverty and inequality while others pointed to the relatively low growth rate that followed that period of expansion.

During the 1970s, American economists weighed in on the negative side. In 1975, in *Equality and Efficiency: The Big Tradeoff*, Arthur Okun, an economic adviser to President John F. Kennedy, argued that trying to increase equality would inevitably lead to a loss in economic efficiency, because transfers from one part of the population to another involved "leaks" like administrative costs and the disincentive effects of taxation.[38]

On the positive side, Nobel Prize-winning economists Kenneth Arrow and Joseph Stiglitz published papers showing why government health insurance produced an increase in economic well-being.

The 1972 OPEC (Organization of Petroleum Exporting Countries) oil crisis marked the start of a new stage of substantial declines in productivity and income growth. By the end of the 1970s, conservative economists like Feldstein, later President Reagan's chief economic officer, were blaming social insurance for the declining economic growth. An OECD conference in the 1980s, "The Welfare State in Crisis," publicized the claims that the welfare state was the cause of inflation and economic stagnation.[39]

Yet the warnings now appear overstated. In the decades since, economies in Europe grew and inflation disappeared, Esping-Andersen has observed.

A long swing right in the United States, starting with Republican Richard M. Nixon's presidential victory in 1968 and peaking with Republican control of the Congress in 2002, "is the key to explaining why at century's end the United States fell further behind in social insurance, lost its lead in education and sank to the bottom in opportunity and equality," the authors of *Wealth and Welfare States* conclude.[40]

Helping Working Mothers

In the postwar era, the early modern welfare state was based on a traditional family model of a male breadwinner and female housewife. Until recently, even Scandinavia's welfare programs were biased toward maintaining the husband's income in bad times. There was little help for the working mother who needed child care or an adult daughter caring for her frail mother.

From the 1970s onward, however, as female employment surged, Scandinavian countries put priority on family services (including subsidized child care and paid parental leave.). In Great Britain and North America, governments instead encouraged tax deductions, a market alternative. The traditional family model was also adopted in the majority of European welfare states.[41]

The female revolution changed all that. Rising educational opportunities for women made them higher earners in the workplace. The birth control revolution, divorce and an overturning of traditional feminine roles all led to female economic independence and increasing numbers of dual-earner households. Europe experienced a huge drop in fertility rates related to the perfect storm for women: working with no prospect of child care.

In the late 1960s, Denmark and Sweden began a massive expansion of subsidized preschool, with universal access achieved by the 1980s. Standards were kept high to cater to the middle class, such as notably low child-teacher ratios in Denmark (10 to 1.)

In the 1990s, "flexicurity" was introduced in Denmark, aimed at reducing long-term unemployment. The approach combined "flexible" labor contracts and relatively little government regulation over hiring and firing with "security" for the unemployed — generous unemployment benefits and retraining programs to get people back to work. The "flexicurity" strategy has been endorsed by the European Union as a common strategy, though more in rhetoric than practice for the continent as a whole.

U.S. vs. EU Spending

Since 1980, EU expenditures on social programs have grown from 16 to 21 percent of GDP, significantly higher than the 15.9 percent in the United States. In France, the figure now is 31 percent, the highest in Europe, with state pensions making up more than 44 percent of the total and health care, 30 percent.[42]

But does the United States really spend less than Europe? "If we include health, education and welfare together we (the United States) spend as much as Europe spends on welfare," says the University of Wisconsin's Smeeding. "We spend less on cash incentives (welfare). We spend more on health than anyone."

More important, he says, Europeans get more for their money when it comes to their standard of living. "If you're European, you never worry about losing health insurance and paying your kids' way through college; every middle-class American family worries about that," Smeeding says. If Americans' private spending from consumers' pockets is counted, the United States actually spends the same proportion of GDP as gold-plated Denmark on social welfare — health, child care and elder care included — Esping-Andersen has calculated.[43]

"The relevant question is not whether we can afford more welfare spending because this will happen anyway. The really relevant question has to do with who are the winners and losers," he has written.[44]

For most of the 19th and 20th centuries, the U.S. was a leader in public education, generally acknowledged as the most productive part of the welfare state. From 1968 to 2006, the United States lost its lead in education, as European nations caught up and even surpassed American college education rates. The result: The United States experienced the most rapid increase in economic inequality among rich nations, according to Smeeding.

"The undereducated work for the educated in America," he says, "delivering food, being a nanny. Many of these jobs don't exist in Europe; the carwash doesn't pay well so they don't have it. A chambermaid in a hotel in Denmark gets four to six weeks' vacation, child care and family leave. A math teacher in Denmark has high respect, high pay and good benefits." The institutions in Scandinavia compress wages and subsidize the unemployed so it's a more equal society, he says, and people on low-wages live better than in the United States.

CURRENT SITUATION

Cuts to Welfare States

The debt crisis currently threatening the euro started last October, when Greece's new government admitted that its predecessor had falsified the national accounts, and the country was racking up an even heavier budget deficit than was feared. It turned out it wasn't the only country in the Eurozone laboring under a heavy debt burden.

Under pressure from the European Union, the governments of Greece, Ireland, Spain, Portugal, Denmark and Italy have all proposed or passed austerity measures to try to reduce their deficits. So far, delaying retirement ages and paring back pensions and public-sector wages are the focus of the largest cuts. Most other core programs, like cash benefits to the unemployed and the sick, subsidized child care and universal preschool, have so far been spared.

For Greece, implementing austerity measures was one of the conditions of receiving 110 billion euros (about $140 billion) in an EU-IMF bailout. In May, the Greek parliament approved legislation that will slash government workers' pay despite violent street protests the previous day leaving three bank workers dead from a gasoline bomb.[45] On July 8, it approved a bill cutting back its generous pension system but with relatively peaceful protests on the streets. The legislation will unify the retirement age at 65 in a country where many now retire before 50 and will calculate pensions on lifetime income, not the highest most recent pay.[46]

Street protests against cuts have also occurred over the past year in France, Spain and Ireland, though with far less violence than in Greece, and were mostly dominated by public-sector workers.[47]

This spring, Spain announced one of the harshest austerity plans in the EU to cut its deficit, partly through a 5 percent cut this year in the salaries of government workers and a near-freeze on hiring. Spain's Socialist President Jose Luis Rodriguez Zapatero was slow to admit the seriousness of the crisis last year, leading to predictions that the country would have to be bailed out like Greece. (In June, Spanish banks were forced to borrow from the European Central Bank at record levels as they faced difficulty raising money in markets worried about their solvency.) But in an about-face, Zapatero this year proposed extending the retirement age by two years to 67.[48]

Although the French government has resisted talk of austerity, President Sarkozy has also proposed delaying the retirement age by two years.

Britain's Reform Moment

In addition to proposing a delay in retirement ages, the new Conservative-led British coalition government is using the debt crisis as an opportunity to impose harsher work

Should the United Kingdom scale back its welfare programs?

YES
Thomas Cawston
Researcher, Reform, a London-based
free-market think tank

Written for *CQ Researcher*, July 2010

The welfare budget must be at the heart of the debate on how to restore the UK's public finances. The government spends more on welfare than anything else. The bill for social protection is now approaching £200 billion, or nearly a third of all governmental expenditure. A large share of this expenditure represents poor value for money and could be reduced without adversely affecting families in need.

Over the past decade the welfare system has lost its way and expanded to attract votes rather than address need. The resulting system of transfers — a money-go-round — does not deliver value for money. Although the UK has one of the most expensive welfare systems in the world, the country is still held back by rising income inequality and low levels of social mobility.

This raises the question of how such an expensive system could lead to such poor policy outcomes. The answer is that poorly made spending, not a lack of spending, is the major social policy problem. Research by Reform has shown that, for example, a large share of welfare spending, conservatively estimated at over £30 billion, goes to wealthier households.

A clear example of poorly made spending is the Winter Fuel Allowance, which is paid to all pensioners irrespective of need and costs £2.7 billion a year. This benefit is even paid to pensioners who avoid British winters and relocate to warmer European Union countries. A Parliamentary review of this spending estimated that close to 90 per cent goes to people who do not need it.

There are many other examples of this poor spending. This includes the £11 billion spent on a universal child benefit although government data show that 97 percent of eligible unemployed families with children already receive a means-tested child tax credit. Another example is the £1 billion spent on free bus passes, which largely benefit wealthier pensioners and pensioners with cars, who can make their own travel arrangements. The list goes on.

In an environment when many private sector workers have lost their jobs, when hundreds of thousands of public sector workers have lost their job security and face pay freezes, when some departmental budgets are facing cuts of up to 40 percent, when housing benefits have been reduced and when more recipients of incapacity benefits will be required to undergo medical tests, asking wealthy families to sacrifice their unnecessary benefits would not only save money but would be the fair thing to do.

NO
Jane Waldfogel
Professor of Social Work and Public Affairs,
Columbia University School of Social Work

Written for *CQ Researcher*, July 2010

Clearly, public spending must be cut. But this does not mean that welfare programs should be scaled back, and in fact, they should not.

Low-income workers are hardest hit by recessions, and tough economic times do not negate government's obligation to protect them, as both Prime Minister David Cameron and Chancellor George Osborne acknowledge. Indeed, while making deep cuts in their June 22 emergency budget, they increased the child tax credit for low income families by £150 per year, to ensure that no children would be made poor by the reforms.

To put this in context, it is helpful to recall that the UK has been aggressively tackling child poverty for the past decade. Between 1999 and 2009, the child poverty rate fell 15 percent in relative terms, and more than 50 percent in absolute terms. Before the Conservatives and Liberal Democrats came into office, they, along with their Labour colleagues, passed a child poverty bill committing future governments to the goal of ending child poverty by 2020. Since coming into office, Cameron has reaffirmed his commitment to this goal, and to advancing social justice.

There are two other compelling reasons to spare welfare programs. The first has to do with the role of public spending as a stimulus. Benefits to low-income families are a win-win — they help buffer families from the worst effects of the recession, and they also help stimulate the economy. Low-income families spend the money they receive, yielding direct benefits to local workers and businesses.

The final reason why welfare benefits should not be scaled back has to do with our collective future. Poverty, particularly if experienced early in childhood and/or for long durations, can scar children for life, sapping aspirations and ambitions, damaging health and development, and curtailing young people's acquisition of needed skills. If we do not invest in children today, we are doomed to have poor children in the future — children who in turn will require more welfare programs and impose other costs on society.

Yes, cutting welfare would save pounds today, but it would cost more in the future, as all of us would pay the price of another generation reared in poverty. Even with the fiscal crisis, a country as rich as the UK can do better than that.

German Family Minister Kristina Schroeder visits a day-care center in Berlin on April 22, 2010. She plans to expand day care to all children under 3 by 2013. The government has rejected politicians' calls to cut day care funding.

requirements on welfare, a change long sought by Conservative Party leaders. The government plans to require a medical test every three years for those on disability benefits, and is suggesting that many recipients who haven't been tested may actually be fit for work. It is also imposing work requirements on single welfare mothers with children age 5 or older. Housing benefits, which were previously based on market rents, will be capped. Finally, the government says it will impose penalties on those welfare and unemployment recipients who don't accept a job offered to them — although welfare experts like British economist Paul Gregg say such refusals are rare.

"We've been using this language 'welfare dependency' and 'making work pay' — quite a lot, but the policy has not reflected it until about two years ago," says Gregg, a professor of economics at the University of Bristol. "The last (Labour) government talked hard but behaved more moderately; the current government is talking hard and acting hard."

As for disability benefits, Gregg says it's true that the number of claims rose from 1975 to 2005 and rose fastest in recessions, which suggests it's at least partly a response to the poor labor market, since incapacity benefits pay more than unemployment benefits and have no work requirement. But the disability community questions how accurate the new medical tests will be. The risk of pushing recipients out is "you're putting some people with health problems out to look for work without the necessary support," Gregg says.

In rhetoric reminiscent of the senior President Bush's "thousand points of light," Prime Minister Cameron has spoken glowingly of a "Big Society" in which voluntary organizations would replace government in providing social services, which he claims they could do more efficiently. On welfare, he's proposed that businesses would be paid on the basis of how many people they get into work. The details of how all these additional services would be funded have remained rather vague, worrying voluntary organizations, which receive about a third of their funding from government. Although Cameron proposed on July 19 to take the money from unclaimed savings accounts in British banks, which could amount to hundreds of millions of dollars, the Association of Chief Executives of Voluntary Organisations, representing over 2,000 nonprofit leaders, warned of "a widening gap between rhetoric and reality as public spending cuts start to bite."[49]

The new wave of austerity cuts comes on the heels of reports from welfare experts all pointing in a similar direction — governments need to spend more on education, opening access for more disadvantaged families to preschool education and college if they want to have an upwardly mobile and economically productive society.

A recent report from the OECD recommends that governments would get far more benefit from investing in the preschool years than the Facebook teen years, when kids' trajectories are already established, but where many governments spend the most. As evidence, it cites the Perry Pre-School experiment — a long-term study of disadvantaged children in the United States. It found an intense program of home visits starting at infancy and quality preschool paid for itself many times over in reduced delinquency and higher educational levels as those children approached adulthood.[50]

"There are few things we can do that are as effective and as cheap," says Simon Chapple, senior economist at OECD and coauthor of the report. But he concedes it's a hard sell when governments are cutting back. "We have aging populations, and children don't vote, to put the bluntest point on it," he says. "It requires political courage to say we'll cover costs now for benefits in 15 to 20 years."

The issue has gotten more traction in connection with the growing concern about the lack of economic mobility in the United States compared to Europe. "When everything is going up, people don't care as much about relative mobility, but when there's less absolute growth these issues become more important," says Isaacs of Brookings.

Under pressure from the European Commission for excessive spending, Denmark's government in May proposed $4 billion worth of austerity measures, including a freeze on pension increases.[51] But its extensive subsidized child-care and preschool program (free to low-income parents) emerged unscathed. "This is very telling that there is absolutely no discussion I can see anywhere in Scandinavia of cutting back on child care. That's untouchable," says welfare expert Esping-Andersen.

The European Model

Ironically, even as Conservative politicians in England are borrowing from America's welfare reform rhetoric, some American experts see Europe as more successful when it comes to reducing poverty and putting people back to work.

The United States leads the wealthy world with high poverty rates, and it has lost its top ranking to the Netherlands as the country with the highest percentage of its population employed.

"How do you have a demanding [welfare] system that doesn't push people at the bottom into destitution? That's something where Europe could be more successful than the United States," says the Brookings Institution's Haskins, who helped write the 1996 American welfare reform bill as staff director of the House Ways and Means subcommittee overseeing welfare, and is studying European work requirements for welfare recipients. He points to the success of "active labor policies" in Germany, the Netherlands and Denmark to put the unemployed back to work with retraining and job help.

Since welfare reform, when the United States enacted tough new work requirements and time limits, the share of single mothers who receive no welfare benefits and no earnings has doubled — a figure Haskins calls "alarming." The easiest way to protect such welfare beneficiaries from destitution, he observes, is "to have a softer system that doesn't push people out the bottom. But then you don't have discipline, and you get all the problems Europe and the United States are trying to solve — dependency on benefits."

Compared to England, where child poverty has declined dramatically in response to Labour government efforts, during America's recession, as jobs got scarcer, "We've seen child poverty go back up again because the safety net is almost completely work-based," says Jane Waldfogel, a professor of social work at Columbia University whio is a visiting professor at the London School of Economics and author of the 2010 book *Britain's War on Poverty.* "That was always the weak spot of welfare reform in the United States: It looked great in a strong economy, but what would it look like when the economy turned down?" she says. "And now we know."

OUTLOOK

'Grand Bargain'

Americans often look with a mixture of envy and amusement at Europe's current turmoil over abandoning its comparatively luxurious welfare benefits. For the French, guaranteeing a comfortable retirement or a 35-hour workweek is akin to banning child labor — "badges of a civilized society" that distinguish it from America, an *Economist* editorial recently opined. Europe may not have the fastest growth, but, "it knows how to look after its sick and elderly, take a long lunch break and abandon the office in August."[52]

Will Europe, like the United States, become less generous in the way it redistributes income? And should it? Some observers, like Cornell economist Burkhauser, think this direction is inevitable as Europe becomes less tribal and less willing to support citizens outside the familiar tribe.

Others, like the market-oriented *Economist*, say Europe has no choice. Europe's free-spending countries have created "an illusion of continual progress by running up hefty debts to finance their welfare state" — with early retirement a particularly "cruel joke" on the next generation. If Germany gets its way, the European Union will start imposing tough penalties on countries seen as fiscally undisciplined, and that could conceivably put even more pressure on Eurozone members to cut budgets.[53]

Yet the lack of welfare state supports like universal child care and quality preschool will perpetuate Europe's baby bust, if nations can't reconcile motherhood and employment. Too few children will result in too few future workers with too little income to pay for retirees, predicts Esping-Andersen, the Danish welfare expert: "Pension reform begins with babies."[54]

David Moss, a professor at Harvard Business School, suggests Europe's policymakers should think not just about economic concerns but also about the social contract their governments have struck. He likens the welfare state to "a grand bargain, where the citizens of European nations agree to open up their economies — and to give up a certain degree of sovereignty — in exchange for social security at home."

Even though cuts will have to be made, particularly in the area of pensions, government officials should be mindful of that "grand bargain," he advises. "If the cuts go too deep, that will end up threatening European integration," he says, and ultimately one of the continent's greatest experiments in peace.

NOTES

1. Suzanne Daley, "Safety Net Frays in Spain, as Elsewhere in Europe," *The New York Times*, June 27, 2010, www.nytimes.com/2010/06/28/world/europe/28spain.html?pagewanted=1.

2. Irwin Garfinkel, Lee Rainwater and Timothy Smeeding, *Wealth and Welfare States: Is America a Laggard or Leader?* (2010), pp. 32-34.

3. *Ibid.*, p. v.

4. Julia B. Isaacs, "International Comparisons of Economic Mobility," Chapter III, p. 1, in Isaacs, *et al.*, "Getting Ahead or Losing Ground: Economic Mobility in America," Brookings and Pew Economic Mobility Project, February 2008, www.economicmobility.org/assets/pdfs/EMP_findings_summary_definitive.pdf.

5. See Garfinkel, *et al.*, *op. cit.*, pp. 80-84 and Organisation for Economic Co-operation and Development.

6. Thirty-eight percent of 55-64-year-olds have an associate degree or higher-a higher percentage than most European countries for that age group. But for 25-34-year-olds, Norway, Ireland, Belgium, Denmark and France have a higher percentage of college graduates, and Spain and the United Kingdom have the same percentage-39.2 percent; "Education at a Glance," Organisation for Economic Co-operation and Development, 2008; "Percentage of Adults with an Associate Degree or Higher by Age Group," data from Timothy Smeeding.

7. Denmark's ruling center-right Liberal Party governs Denmark in a coalition with the Conservative Party and the anti-immigrant Danish People's Party. The Social Democratic Party, Denmark's second largest, has been a strong supporter of redistribution under Denmark's welfare state. See "Denmark Freezes Welfare Payments," *Ice News*, May 30, 2010, www.icenews.is/index.php/2010/05/30/denmark-freezes-welfare-payments/.

8. "Staring into the Abyss," *The Economist*, July 10, 2010, pp. 26-28, www.economist.com/node/16536898.

9. Garfinkel, *et al.*, *op. cit.*, pp. 28-29.

10. Julia B. Isaacs, Pew Economic Mobility Project, Chapter III, citing OECD data.

11. Garfinkel, *et al.*, *op. cit.*, p. 32.

12. "Nordic Nations outshine EU Rivals for Competitiveness, Study Finds," *International Herald Tribune*, May 10, 2010, p. 16.

13. Garfinkel, *et al.*, *op. cit.*, p. 34.

14. Julia B. Isaacs, *op. cit.*, p. 1. The poll results come from the International Social Survey Program, conducted between 1998 and 2001.

15. *Ibid.*, pp. 2-3.

16. "Findings from a National Survey & Focus Groups on Economic Mobility," Economic Mobility Project, Pew Charitable Trusts, March 12, 2009, pp. 9-11, www.economicmobility.org/assets/pdfs/Survey_on_Economic_Mobility_Findings.pdf.

17. "Summary of Findings," Economic Mobility Project," and Fig. 6, "Getting Ahead or Losing Ground: Economic Mobility in America," www.economicmobility.org/assets/pdfs/EMP_findings_summary_definitive.pdf.

18. Quoted from Raghuram Rajan, *Fault Lines* (2010) in Martin Wolf, "Three Years and New Fault Lines Threaten," *Financial Times*, July 13, 2010, www.ft.com/cms/s/0/39c67712-8eb1-11df-8a67-00144feab49a.html.

19. "Staring into the Abyss," *The Economist*, July 10, 2010, p. 27.

20. Jill Sherman and Francis Elliott, "Retirement Age May be Raised Every Five Years," *The Times*, June 25, 2010, p. 1.

21. "Reforming Welfare," Reform conference, London, June 30, 2010, www.reform.co.uk.

22. Sean O'Grady, "Britain's Heavy Burden of Off-Balance-Sheet Liabilities Revealed," *The Independent*, July 14, 2010, p. 4.

23. Katie Allen, "Pledge to Protect NHS Will Hit Recovery, Warns BCC," *The Guardian*, June 14, 2010, p. 27.

24. Garfinkel, *et al.*, *op. cit.*, p. 3.

25. Gosta Esping-Andersen, *The Incomplete Revolution* (2010), p. 139.

26. *Ibid.*, p. 125.

27. Organisation for Economic Co-operation and Development, "A Family Affair: Intergenerational Social Mobility Across OECD Countries," *Economic Policy Reforms, Going for Growth*, 2010.

28. "Staring into the Abyss," *op. cit.*, p. 26.

29. Matt Woolsey, "World's Best Places for Unemployment Pay," *Forbes*, June 27, 2008, www.forbes.com/2008/06/27/unemployment-benefits-world-for-beslife-cx_mw_0627worldunemployment.html.

30. Reuters, "Recession in Britain Bit Harder than Data Showed," *International Herald Tribute*, July 13, 2010, p. 13.

31. David Prosser, "If Public Spending is Behind the Recovery, What Happens When We Cut it?" *The Independent*, July 13, 2010, p. 39.

32. See Garfinkel, *et al.*, *op. cit.*, pp. 30-31, 141.

33. *Ibid.*

34. Garfinkel, *et al.*, *op. cit.*, p. 144. Sidney Webb was a member of the socialist Fabian Society and the civil servant who drafted the unemployment insurance legislation.

35. *Ibid.*, pp. 105-106.

36. Rachel Dunifon, "Welfare Reform and Intergenerational Mobility," Pew Economic Mobility Project, 2010, www.economicmobility.org.

37. Esping-Andersen, *op. cit.*, p. 145.

38. Garfinkel, *et al.*, *op. cit.*, p. 35.

39. Esping-Andersen, *op. cit.*, p. 145.

40. *Ibid.*, pp. 15-16.

41. Esping-Andersen, *op. cit.*, p. 80.

42. Steven Erlanger, "Europeans Fear Crisis Threatens Liberal Benefits," *The New York Times*, May 22, 2010.

43. Esping-Andersen, *op. cit.*, pp. 108-110.

44. *Ibid.*, p. 110.

45. "Greek Parliament Backs Tough Austerity Bill," Reuters, May 10, 2010, http://uk.reuters.com/article/idUKTRE64526A20100506.

46. Landon Thomas Jr., "Greece Approves Pension Overhaul Despite Protests," July 8, 2010, *The New York Times*, www.nytimes.com/2010/07/09/business/global/09drachma.html?_r=2&sq=Greece%20parliament&st=cse&scp=1.

47. "Staring into the Abyss," *op. cit.*, p. 27.

48. See Harold Heckle, "Spain's premier vows to press on with austerity," The Associated Press, July 14, 2010 and Victor Mallet, "Endure Cuts for sake of Spain, urges Zapatero," *Financial Times*, July 15, 2010, p. 8.

49. Brian Brady, "Unclaimed Savings to Fund Tories' Bank Plan," *The Independent*, July 18, 2010, and Association of Chief Executives of Voluntary Organisations ACEVO) press release, "Charity Leaders Welcome Big Society Announcement but Call for Rhetoric/Reality Gap to be Closed," July 20, 2010, www.acevo.org.uk.

50. Organisation for Economic Co-operation and Development, "Doing Better for Children," 2009.

51. Andrew Ward, "Denmark Unveils $4 billion of Budget Cuts," *Financial Times*, May 19, 2010, www.ft.com/cms/s/0/ae65c926-6367-11df-a844-00144feab49a.html.

52. Charlemagne, "Calling Time on Progress," *The Economist*, July 17, 2010, p. 42.

53. Quentin Peel and Ben Hall, "Paris and Berlin Seek to Mend Rift," *Financial Times*, July 15, 2010, p. 8.

54. Esping-Andersen, *op. cit.*, pp. 4, 174.

BIBLIOGRAPHY

Books

Esping-Andersen, Gøsta, *The Incomplete Revolution: Adapting to Women's New Roles*, Polity Press, 2010.
A sociologist at Barcelona's Pompeu Fabra University argues for welfare provisions that make it possible for women both to work and have children as a means to a more productive society.

Garfinkel, Irwin, Lee Rainwater and Timothy Smeeding, *Wealth and Welfare States: Is America a Laggard or Leader?*, Oxford University Press, 2010.
Three leading American welfare experts argue that the socialized programs of welfare states enhance national wealth and that the United States is losing its lead in the most productive aspect of the welfare state — public education.

Haskins, Ron, and Isabel V. Sawhill, *Creating an Opportunity Society*, Brookings Institution Press, 2009.
Children from advanced societies in Europe are less likely to be stuck at the bottom of the income ladder than children in the U.S., according to several experts at the moderate think tank.

Waldfogel, Jane, *Britain's War on Poverty*, Russell Sage Foundation, 2010.
A professor of social work at Columbia University documents the dramatic fall in child poverty in Great Britain following New Labour's welfare reform measures.

Articles

"Staring into the Abyss," *The Economist*, July 10, 2010, p. 26.
The European Union must make structural reforms to its welfare states, including pensions, if it is to survive as an economic entity.

"Too Timid by Half," *The Economist*, May 22, 2010, p. 40.
France's public finances are closer to debt-ridden Greece than Germany.

Atkins, Ralph, "The Gain, Then the Pain, of Life in Euroland," Portugal: Financial Times Special Report, *Financial Times*, July 14, 2010, p. 2.
Once Eurozone membership was about its benefits, but now it's about "tough love" for weaker economies like Greece and Portugal and that could cause national defections.

Erlanger, Steven, "Europeans Fear Crisis Threatens Liberal Benefits," *The New York Times*, May 22, 2010.
The fiscal crisis is forcing EU countries to freeze pensions and cut public sector wages.

Smeeding, Timothy M., and Jane Waldfogel, "Fighting Poverty: Attentive Policy Can Make a Huge Difference," *Journal of Policy Analysis and Management*, January 2010.

Labour government steps — such as longer paid maternity leaves and pre-school — have halved child poverty over a decade even as it rose in the United States.

Thomas Jr., Landon, "Greece Approves Pension Overhaul Despite Protests," July 8, 2010, www.nytimes.com/2010/07/09/business/global/09drachma.html?_r=1&sq=Greece%20parliament&st=cse&scp=1.
The Greek Parliament passed legislation curtailing its generous pension system, but public protests were relatively restrained compared to those in May.

Reports and Studies

"A Family Affair: Intergenerational Social Mobility," Organisation for Economic Co-operation and Development, 2010, www.oecd.org/document/51/0,3343, en_2649_34325_44566259_1_1_1_1,00.html.
It is far easier to climb the ladder and earn more than one's parents in Scandinavia than in the United States or Britain, according to this report, which recommends steps like quality pre-school education to provide more equality and upward mobility.

"Doing Better for Children," Organisation for Economic Co-operation and Development, Sept. 2, 2009, www.oecd.org/document/12/0,3343,en_2649_34819_43545036_1_1_1_1,00.html.
Governments should spend more on children in the first six years of life to ensure equality, says this report, which finds Norway and Finland ranking near the top for child well-being.

"Work-Life in Sweden," Boston College Center for Work and Family, Executive Briefing Series, 2010, www.bc.edu/centers/cwf/research/publications.html#executive brifingseries.
Swedish parents get over a year's paid parental leave and guaranteed public day care, but about one-third say they lack work-life balance, perhaps because gender divisions still exist in workplace attitudes and parenting burdens.

Isaacs, Julia B., *et al.*, "Getting Ahead or Losing Ground: Economic Mobility in America," Brookings Institution, 2008, www.brookings.edu/~/media/Files/rc/reports/2008/02_economic_mobility_sawhill/02_economic_mobility_sawhill.pdf.
The United States is falling behind most European countries when it comes to economic mobility, according to this report, which also questions whether European economies grow more slowly.

For More Information

American Enterprise Institute, 1150 17th St., N.W., Washington, DC 20036; (202) 862-5800; www.aei.org. Washington-based think tank promoting conservative welfare policies.

Brookings Institution, 1775 Massachusetts Ave., N.W., Washington, DC 20036; (202) 797-6000; www.brookings .edu. Washington-based moderate think tank focusing on the well-being of low-income families and children.

Center for Economic and Policy Research, 1611 Connecticut Ave., N.W., Suite 400, Washington, DC 20009; (202) 239-1460; www.cepr.net. Promotes democratic debate on issues of economic and social importance.

Centre for Social Justice, 9 Westminster Palace Gardens, Artillery Row, London SW1P 1RL, England; 020-7340-9650; www.centreforsocialjustice.org.uk. Conservative British think tank seeking effective solutions to poverty in the United Kingdom.

Economic Mobility Project, Pew Charitable Trusts, 901 E St., N.W., 10th Floor, Washington, DC 20004; (202) 540-6390; www.economicmobility.org. Engages both liberal and conservative experts to investigate the status of economic mobility in the United States and other countries.

Economic and Social Research Council, North Star Ave., Swindon, SN2 1UJ, England; 01793-413000; www .esrcsocietytoday.ac.uk. Independent organization funded by the British government researching economic and social issues, including welfare.

Institute for Research on Poverty, University of Wisconsin-Madison, 1180 Observatory Dr., 3412 Social Science Building, Madison, WI 53706; (608) 262-6358; www.irp .wisc.edu. Research center examining poverty and inequality in the United States.

Organisation for Economic Co-operation and Development, 2, Rue André Pascal, 75775 Paris Cedex 16, France; 33-1-45248200; www.oecd.org. Paris-based organization of 31 wealthy nations issuing international comparisons and policy recommendations on economic mobility, income inequality and child well-being.

Reform, 45 Great Peter St., London SW1P 3LT, England; 020-7799-6699; www.reform.co.uk. British free-market think tank sponsoring conferences on welfare reform.

Tobin Project, One Mifflin Place, Suite 240, Cambridge, MA 02138; (617) 547-2600; www.tobinproject.org. Alliance of leading academics seeking to influence policy-makers in areas such as economic regulation and income inequality.

Voices From Abroad:

IAIN BEGG

Professor, European Institute, London School of Economics

An unwillingness to shift

"There has been a lack of willingness to shift away from welfare as social protection towards an approach seen in northern Europe . . . which is welfare as social investment."

Daily Mail (England), May 2010

PAT MCFADDEN

Minister for Business, Innovation and Skills, Great Britain

What is social mobility?

"True class war would be to accept that life chances should be decided because of background or birth. Genuine social mobility is the opposite of class war."

The Observer (England) January 2010

PETER SAUNDERS

Professor Emeritus of Sociology, University of Sussex, England

Today's meritocracy is a myth

"The ideal of promoting social mobility by increasing meritocracy has in the last few years been used to justify some old-style socialist politics which in reality have little or nothing to do with increasing individual opportunities or rewarding effort and ability."

Daily Telegraph (England) June 2010

JAN PIRK

Cardio-surgeon, Czech Republic

Health-care 'rights'

"We have been made [to] believe before the 1989 fall of communism that health care is a free-of-charge service

The Scranton Times-Tribune/John Cole

and the principle 'people have a right to health care' was promoted. However, no one then said that people only had a right to such health care that the state could fund."

Czech News Agency, September 2009

OLIVER ROWLANDS

Head of Retirement for Europe, Middle East and Africa, Aon Consulting

Taking matters into your own hands

"A lot of people will simply be walking blindly into retirement poverty unless they take more of an active interest in their pensions. Governments and some employers are looking at ways to reduce their pensions obligations, so it is imperative that people take more responsibility themselves for their retirement finances."

Daily Telegraph (England), May 2010

ADRIAN FAWCETT

CEO, General Healthcare Group, England

Politicians don't get it

"Health care remains one of the main issues in the minds of voters, but the response so far from politicians is to offer complicated arguments over budgetary funding which completely miss the point. No party has yet set out how it would cope with a rapidly aging population, increasing medical inflation and new and more expensive treatments that will add further pressure over the next few years to what is an already creaking national health-care system."

Daily Telegraph (England), April 2010

HERMAN VAN ROMPUY

President, European Union

New resources required
"The financing of the welfare state, irrespective of the social reform we implement, will require new resources. The possibility of financial levies at European level needs to be seriously reviewed and for the first time ever, the big countries in the Union are open to this."

Daily Mail (England) November 2009

RUTH LISTER

Professor of Social Policy, Loughborough University, England

Inequality leads to more inequality
"Social mobility and meritocracy represent an individualistic, competitive version of social justice, which ignores underlying structures of inequality. Indeed, by legitimating inequality, meritocracy can add to 'the pressures toward increased inequality' to which [Gordon] Brown refers."

The Guardian (England) January 2010

MANTANA LERTCHAITAWEE

Economist, Bank of Thailand

A risky proposition
"The emergence of the sovereign risk crisis in Greece, driven by the unprecedented high level of public debt, is an important warning call for welfare state economies."

Thai Press Reports, June 2010

16

The Graying Planet

Alan Greenblatt

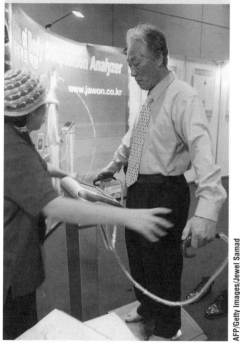

Health check-ups are included at a job fair for senior citizens in Seoul, South Korea. The nation's rapidly aging population threatens economic progress. Experts worldwide say that as workforces shrink and governments raise the retirement age, employers must be more willing to hire and retain older workers.

From *CQ Researcher*, March 15, 2011.

The Fahua Home for the Aged in Shanghai is full to overflowing. Tiny rooms are filled with three to four residents lying in beds crammed so tightly together that they touch. There's hardly room for anyone to walk in.

The tight squeeze is a source of continual surprise to Qing Zhuren, the manager. Traditionally, Chinese elders could depend on their children or grandchildren to take care of them in old age. But decades of strict population controls have brought down China's fertility rate at an unprecedented speed, leaving fewer children to care for their aging parents.[1]

And the size of China's elderly population is set to explode. The number of Chinese over the age of 65 is expected to triple by 2050 — faster than the worldwide aging rate. Over the next 20 years, the number of Chinese 65 and over is projected to reach 167 million — more than half the current U.S. population.

China is experiencing in fast motion what has been happening over decades in Western Europe. Far more people are living longer than ever before, which will eventually turn the traditional familiar population age "pyramid" — with lots of younger people on the bottom helping to support fewer seniors on top — on its head.

The eastern part of Germany, for instance, has seen a precipitous decline in its birth rate, leading to a rapidly aging population. In 1988 — the year before the Berlin Wall fell — 216,000 babies were born in East Germany. In 1994, only 88,000 births were reported.

Populations Worldwide Are Growing Older

European countries and Japan already have older populations than the rest of the world, but developing countries will catch up quickly. By 2050 China and Russia, along with Canada and Europe, will have the highest percentages of elderly populations, followed by India, the Middle East and parts of Africa.

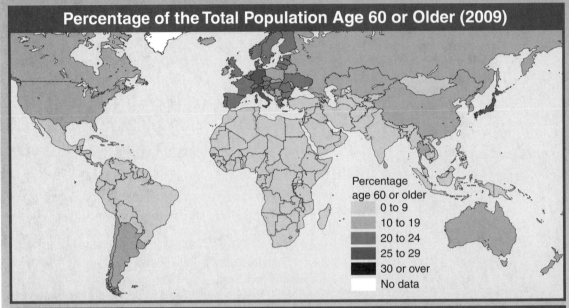

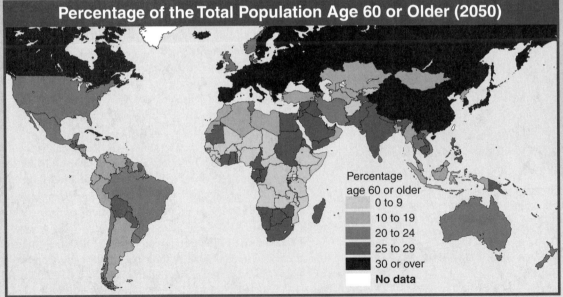

Source: "Population Ageing and Development, 2009," U.N. Department of Economic and Social Affairs, 2009

"There has been nothing comparable in world peacetime history," said Jean-Claude Chesnais, a French demographer.[2]

At one point Eastern Germany's fertility rate — the average number of children born to a given population's women over the course of their lifetimes — plunged below 1. That's well under the "replacement rate" of 2.1, or the average number of births per woman needed to replace the current population. Birthrates have picked up a bit in Eastern Germany, but not by much. In Hoyerswerda, a German city experiencing rapid population decline, schools are closing, and the town's former birth clinic is now a nursing home.

If current demographic trends persist, Germany will lose 83 percent of its native population by 2100. "Germany would have fewer natives than today's Berlin," writes British author and environmental consultant Fred Pearce in his 2010 book *The Coming Population Crash.*[3]

Life Expectancy Rises While Births Decline

Two trends are hastening the "graying" of the world's population: Fewer babies are being born and people are living longer. By 2050, the world's fertility rate (births per woman) is expected to have dropped to about two — less than half the rate in the 1950s. Life expectancy is expected to have increased by 29 years, to an average of 75.5, compared with a century earlier.

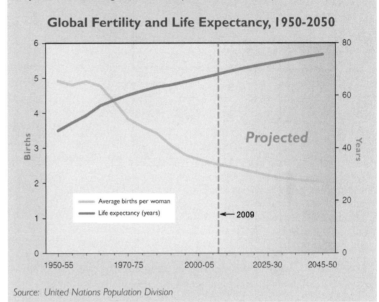

Global Fertility and Life Expectancy, 1950-2050

Source: United Nations Population Division

This year, the oldest members of the post-World War II "baby boom" generation (those born between 1946 and 1964) are turning 65, the vanguard of an aging population that will have immense effects on the workforces and economies in most of today's rich nations.

As people live longer, families are growing smaller. The result is a graying — and eventually shrinking — population. World population is likely to reach 7 billion in the coming months and will continue to grow beyond 8 and perhaps past 9 billion. But by mid-century it's likely to stabilize or start shrinking.

By 2050, the number of children under age 5 is expected to fall by 49 million, while the number of people over 60 will grow by 1.2 billion. In fact, by 2150 the global population could be half what it is now, according to a U.N. projection.[4]

"If you are over 45, you have lived through a period when the world population has doubled," which is both unprecedented and unrepeatable, Pearce argues. If you are under 45, he points out, "you will likely see world population decline for the first time since the plague known as the Black Death, nearly 700 years ago.

"This is the first time in history that we have been able to foresee with some certainty a decline in our numbers," Pearce writes.[5]

Rapid aging is happening first in rich countries. Italy stands to lose even more of its native population than Germany by century's end. Japan was the developed world's youngest nation in 1980 but is now the oldest country on the planet. In fact, Japan's birth rate is so low that its government has forecast that the last Japanese baby will be born in 2959 if existing trends continue.[6]

In Russia, low fertility is combined with a high death rate — caused by various health problems, including HIV/AIDS and alcoholism rates that are among the

A Chinese woman exercises at an outdoor fitness station, one of many in Beijing's residential neighborhoods. Rapidly aging nations like China face enormous challenges, especially as health care costs rise. To keep costs down, officials urge senior citizens to remain fit — both physically and cognitively — for as long as possible.

AFP/Getty Images/Frederic J. Brown

world's highest.[7] Since 1992, Russian deaths have outnumbered births by about 50 percent.[8] As a result, Russia stands to lose about one-third of its population by 2050, "a rate of population decline that has no historical precedent in the absence of pandemic," according to demographers Richard Jackson and Neil Howe of the Global Aging Initiative at the Center for Strategic and International Studies (CSIS).[9]

In most countries, rapidly aging populations are a byproduct of prosperity. Infant mortality rates have been slashed over the past century, while medical advances and improved sanitation and nutrition continue to increase life expectancy.

Throughout most of the 19th century, life expectancy was just 40 years, even in advanced economies. Today, it's 77 in developed countries and 69 worldwide, according to the Population Reference Bureau.[10]

"It's clear that life expectancy is increasing two to three years per decade," says Wolfgang Lutz, director of the Vienna Institute of Demography in Austria. "We're talking about four months per year. People are aging only from January to September."

People are not only living longer but also postponing getting married and having children. "There is a delay in all life-cycle stages: end of education, entry into the labor market, exit from the parental home, entry into union and managing an independent household," said Alessandra De Rose, a demographer at Sapienza University in Rome.[11]

Many women are staying single through their 20s and later. Fewer than 25 percent of American women are now married in their early 20s. Fifty years ago, two-thirds married by then. In Hungary, 30 percent of the women in their 30s are single, compared to 6 percent in their mothers' generation. In Japan, half of all 30-year-old women are unmarried; in South Korea, it's 40 percent.[12]

Women are not only marrying later but having children later — if at all. Over the past century, the average family in developed countries has plunged to half the size of its parents' families, although birthrates are still high in many developing countries.

But while affluent countries are aging faster, developing countries also are starting to age. Half of the world's women are now having two children or fewer — even in some developing countries, such as Iran, Burma, Brazil and Vietnam. "To make people have children they don't want to have, that's beyond the power of any despot," says Phillip Longman, a senior research fellow at the New America Foundation and author of the 2004 book about falling birthrates, *The Empty Cradle*.

Perhaps the most challenging aspect of the aging global population is the fact that longer life expectancies and declining birthrates are shrinking the working-age (15 to 64) population. Some parts of Europe already have fewer than two taxpaying workers per pensioner, making the outlook dismal for the solvency of worker-supported social security systems.

Such a fiscal course is not sustainable, says Jackson, the director of the CSIS Global Aging Initiative. In 1980, there were 62 people between the ages of 50 and 64 for every 100 people between 15 and 29 in developed countries, Jackson says. By 2005, that number had climbed to 94. Over the next 20 years, it will reach 112 and even higher in rapidly aging countries such as Germany and Japan.

And older populations are growing even faster. In developed countries, the 65-79 age group is projected to grow by 57 percent by 2050, while the number of people age 80 and older will rise by 173 percent. The populations of centenarians will rise even faster.[13]

The explosive growth of the oldest population means current expectations about pension levels and access to health care must be painfully adjusted. "The whole premise that has to underlie any social or generational contract is that it be sustainable," Jackson says. "In today's rapidly aging developed countries, the current deal is not sustainable."

As demographers, economists and policymakers prepare for an aging world, here are some of the questions they are debating:

Should official retirement ages be increased?

With the recent near-collapses of the Greek and Irish economies, fiscal policy has become a primary concern across Europe. Faced with rising pension costs and rapidly expanding senior populations, several countries have raised official retirement ages and changed other labor rules affecting older workers.

The list includes not just larger economies such as the United Kingdom, France and Spain but smaller countries such as Bulgaria and Slovenia. "Life expectancy increases by three months every year, and the current pension system does not follow such demographic changes," said Slovenian Labor Minister Ivan Svetlik, who introduced legislation passed late last year to increase the nation's retirement age for all to 65, up from 60 for men and 58 for women.[14]

The idea has been hugely unpopular. A French proposal last fall to increase the age for receiving minimal pension benefits from 60 to 62 (and from 65 to 67 for full benefits) triggered weeks of street protests. On at least two occasions, more than a million people took to the streets, while a blockade of France's main refinery led to fuel shortages at half the nation's gas stations and hundreds of canceled flights.

But the plan, touted by French President Nicolas Sarkozy, prevailed. Now, Sarkozy and German Chancellor Angela Merkel are pushing for a uniform retirement age of 67 across all countries that use the euro.

"As a response to aging populations and sustaining fiscal policies and budgets, raising the retirement age is probably one of the most important policy responses," says Vegard Skirbekk, director of the Age and Cohort

Change Project at the International Institute for Applied Systems Analysis in Laxenburg, Austria.

Nearly all the longevity gains have been added to retirement years, says Lutz, of the Vienna Institute of Demography. "How should those additional years of life be allocated?" he asks. "It seems fair that not all of these years should be allocated to retirement."

But raising the retirement age remains politically unpopular, especially with aging electorates, many of which aren't convinced it's necessary. And even when countries have changed their pension plans, they haven't always stuck. Nearly 30 years ago, the United Kingdom changed its formulas for pension adjustments, pegging them to prices rather than to wages. Over time, the elderly fell behind financially. So in 2007, Britain changed its formula back.

"There's been dramatic progress in Europe and in Japan — unlike the United States — in terms of reducing the long-term burden," says Jackson, at CSIS' Global Aging Initiative. "But it's not clear whether those reforms are politically and socially sustainable."

Even demographers and economists who support later retirement ages say that won't ensure that older people will be able to find continued employment. "You can't have a blank demand that everybody works more," says Ted C. Fishman, author of the 2010 book about global aging, *Shock of Gray*. "But you can have incentives for people who want to work longer."

British author Pearce says seniors must keep their skills up to date and perhaps work in new roles, such as consulting with younger people still working in their field.

Pearce also alludes to a delicate balancing act. If older workers stay in their jobs longer, younger people may feel that they will have less opportunity for advancement. But older workers won't be able to hold onto important positions unless they can maintain their skills.

"Lifelong education can't just be a program that people pay lip service to," says Nicholas Eberstadt, a demographer at the American Enterprise Institute (AEI), a conservative think tank in Washington. "If people want to have a high standard of living, there will have to be some sort of arrangement for continuing learning, because skills that are absorbed in your 20s are out of date by your 40s, let alone your 60s."

Moreover, he says, older people will have to be paid based not on seniority but on their levels of productivity. "If an older person's productivity declines, it will have to be reflected in pay," he says. "The idea of a lifelong [salary] escalator is going to be a nonstarter."

Skirbekk agrees that "in order for individuals to remain competitive" training and education will become increasingly important for aging workers trying to keep up with technological change. And productivity declines will have to be reflected in wage decreases, he says. But employers will have to adjust as well. Companies often are reluctant to hire older workers for fear they will not bring as much energy and stamina to the job and will cost more in health insurance.

Some countries are experimenting with new policies designed to encourage hiring of older workers. As of this April, U.K. employers will no longer be allowed to force qualified workers over age 65 to retire. In January, Singapore passed a law requiring companies to re-hire qualified workers even after they reach the official retirement age of 62, becoming the second country, after Japan, to legislate "re-employment." The following month, the government announced a plan to heavily subsidize the cost of employing lower-wage older workers over the next three years.[15]

"We not only have to change the attitudes of the employees, we might have to change the social benefits they get," says Norbert Walter, former chief economist at Deutsche Bank. "At the same time, we have to educate and help the employers.

"Higher employment of older people will only make good sense if the jobs that the elderly get are appropriate for their age," he says.

China Is Aging Faster Than Rest of World

The proportion of China's population age 65 and older is expected to triple to 24 percent by 2050, while the percentage of the worldwide population age 60 and older is only expected to double during a similar period.

Proportion of Chinese Population age 65 and Older, 2007-2050

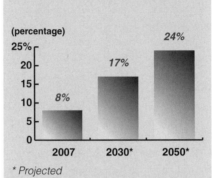

* Projected

Source: "World Population Ageing 2009," U.N. Department of Economic and Social Affairs

Do younger generations bear most of the cost of aging populations?

Christopher Buckley's 2007 novel *Boomsday* opens with a scene in front of a gated retiree community in Florida, where a mob of young people are rioting, angry about having to pay for seniors' Medicare and Social Security benefits. One 29-year-old character suggests a solution to the problem of funding entitlements for older Americans: Pay them to commit suicide.

While the book was darkly satirical, some economists say intergenerational warfare could become a reality. In Germany in 2003, Philipp Mißfelder, the leader of the youth wing of the Christian Democratic Party, sparked a major controversy when he suggested that 85-year-olds should start paying for their own false teeth and hip replacements.

Mißfelder later sought to walk back his remark, saying, "Reform is needed, but there must not be a war between generations."[16] But as societies age, it's difficult to pay for skyrocketing pension and health care costs without putting a growing burden on younger workers.

Such costs will be enormous. Pension costs are likely to double in many developed countries as a share of gross domestic product (GDP), and health care will jump even faster, according to a study, "The Graying of the Great Powers," by CSIS' Jackson and Howe.

If current benefit levels are maintained for the burgeoning number of Japanese seniors, for instance, pension costs in Japan would rise from 8.7 percent of GDP in 2005 to more than 20 percent in 2050. Health care costs would rise even faster — tripling across much of the developed world by 2050.[17]

If wealthy countries weren't already running deficits, they might be able to offer generous solutions that would be less painful for people of all generations, says Walter, the former Deutsche Bank economist.

But that is not the case. "We have not prepared society for the change, and the transition process will be painful and not short," says Walter. "We will have not only younger people protesting but older people as well."

In the United States, cutting popular senior entitlement programs such as Social Security and Medicare remains difficult for politicians to contemplate, so they are proposing serious cuts in programs aimed primarily at younger people, including education and infrastructure. "In a democracy, where every vote counts the same, the elderly have a tendency to vote more frequently than young people," says Lutz, the Austrian demographer.

"It's against their personal interest to reallocate money from pensions to helping the younger people," Lutz says. "The good news is that many surveys show that elderly people who have their own children and grandchildren feel a great intergenerational solidarity and want to help them."

But author Fishman notes that there's a difference between wanting to help the young within one's own family and helping young people in general. "It changes the whole underpinning of projects like public education," Fishman says. "In families, money flows down between generations. In the public realm, money flows up to the older generation."

While the scramble for ever-scarcer resources may have a generational element, it also has a racial and ethnic tinge. In the United States, Hispanics comprise a much larger share of the under-20 population than they do among seniors. The same is true among Muslims in Europe.

Minorities now make up more than two-fifths of all Americans under 18 and will represent a majority of them by 2023, according to William Frey, a demographer at the Brookings Institution, a think tank in

Older Nations Concentrated in Europe

Africa is home to nine of the 10 countries with the largest percentages of young people, while nine of the 10 countries with the oldest populations are in Europe.

Countries With the Youngest and Oldest Populations, 2010

YOUNGEST	% under age 15	OLDEST	% over age 65
Niger	50.1	Japan	22.6
Uganda	48.7	Germany	20.5
Burkina Faso	46.4	Italy	20.4
Congo, Dem. Rep.	46.4	Greece	18.3
Zambia	46.2	Sweden	18.3
Afghanistan	45.9	Portugal	17.9
Malawi	45.9	Austria	17.6
Chad	45.6	Bulgaria	17.6
Somalia	44.9	Belgium	17.4
Tanzania	44.7	Latvia	17.4

Source: "2010 World Population Data Sheet," Population Reference Bureau, 2010

Washington. Non-Hispanic whites, by contrast, make up more than four-fifths of American seniors — a share that will only slip slowly in the future.

"Over time, the major focus in this struggle is likely to be between an aging white population that appears increasingly resistant to taxes and dubious of public spending and a minority population that overwhelmingly views government education, health and social-welfare programs as the best ladder of opportunity for its children," American political reporter Ronald Brownstein wrote in the *National Journal* last year.[18]

And the competition for resources between generations will not always favor the elderly. Younger people may rebel at footing the bill for seniors' entitlements and for the interest on deficits that such programs help cause, CSIS demographer Jackson says.

"Will young, brown people, already sending money home to their country of origin to support their aging parents, cough up an ever-rising share of payrolls to support a population of old Anglos here?" Jackson asks.

'Youth Bulges' Can Spur Violence

"Most of the world's violence and mayhem are committed by young men."

At the same time that European and other developed societies are growing older, "it's the reverse in Arab countries," says Brian Katulis, a senior fellow at the Center for American Progress, a liberal-leaning think tank in Washington.

In fact, the Muslim world has been getting younger in recent years. In Pakistan, Iran and Saudi Arabia — for example — the share of the population made up of young males grew by more than 25 percent since the mid-1990s.[1] That helps to explain, in part, the current political upheaval that has spread from Tunisia and Egypt to Libya, Bahrain and beyond, experts say.

"The problems certainly transcend the 'youth bulge' [a disproportionate share of a nation's population falling between age 15 and 29], but in all these places it starts out with youth discontent," says Ray Takeyh, senior fellow in Middle Eastern studies at the Council on Foreign Relations, a New York-based think tank.

"Well-educated groups of young people who can't find the right jobs and are suppressed by the government . . . are a very strong force for change," says Wolfgang Lutz, an Austrian demographer. Educated youths are also most likely to access social media, the Internet and satellite television, which allows them to see how their countries' economies are faltering compared with the rest of the world.

"The youth component is crucial," says Shadi Hamid, director of research at the Brookings Institution's Doha Center in Qatar. "They're the ones most affected by structural underemployment." And that can lead more readily to discontent than unemployment, he adds, because rising expectations are not being met.

The presence of a large percentage of young people in a country — particularly if they are repressed or economically frustrated — has played out in a variety of eras and locales, from the French Revolution to the Parisian *banlieues* — the suburbs where riots among youths have broken out in recent years. "Certainly the presence of a large youth bulge can be destabilizing," says Richard Jackson, a senior fellow at the Center for Strategic and International Studies.

In addition, demographic studies statistically establish "what we've intuitively known all along," he says, "which is that most of the world's violence and mayhem are committed by young men."

Countries where people 15 to 29 made up more than 40 percent of the adult population were more than twice as likely to see civil conflict during the 1990s, according to a study by Population Action International, a Washington-based organization that advocates family planning.[2]

Young people are more prone to engage in civil disobedience for several reasons. For one thing, their risks are

Many observers are growing concerned that programs benefiting the elderly are coming under attack. Most attempts at changing pension rules target current workers to avoid hurting those who are already retired and wouldn't have time to adjust to the new rules. But policymakers increasingly are contemplating changes that would affect current retirees, since they are the source of existing deficit pressures.

Longman, at the New America Foundation, warns that poverty rates among the elderly may soon rise rapidly due to cuts in government programs, reversing trends dating back to the 1960s. And, he points out, in countries where pension and health costs have driven taxes to exorbitant levels, more and more economic activity takes place off the books.

"That's a large part of what's happening in Greece and Italy," he says. "Pension costs are too high, and younger people trade with younger people in an underground [tax-free] economy. In that sense, the young win, or hurt less than the elderly."

Can aging nations increase their birthrates?

Some nations are aging so rapidly — with birthrates too low to replace the current child-bearing generation — that they fall into what Austrian demographer Lutz calls "the fertility trap."

After fertility rates are low for a generation or so, small families become the norm, and it's difficult to raise them back up. More and more women choose to have fewer children — or none at all. In countries such as

often smaller. Many don't yet have families they would have to worry about supporting from a jail cell. They also suffer more in an economic downturn. During the recent recession, youth unemployment has spiked much higher than the workforce as a whole — a particularly acute problem in Arab countries, where jobless rates are among the world's highest.

In Saudi Arabia, unemployment among men is 10 percent, but among college-educated men the number leaps to 44 percent.[3] "If you're a young person coming of age in a country with a large youthful population, your prospects often are not very good," says Elizabeth Leahy Madsen, a senior research associate with Population Action International.

Some countries have enjoyed a "youth advantage," Madsen says, by investing in education and putting their young people to work. In the 1980s and '90s, for instance, the East Asian "tiger" economies — such as Thailand, Indonesia and South Korea — were able to shift from agriculture to more knowledge-based economies by investing in their suddenly abundant youthful human capital.

But the job market must keep up with the rise in educated youth. Most countries now experiencing a youth bulge — such as sub-Saharan Africa, Pakistan and Afghanistan — are not creating jobs fast enough to keep up with population growth, leading to mass frustration. Many societies now under siege have invested heavily in educating their young people but have not provided them with enough to do after graduation.

"We're talking about people who are college-educated and ambitious and want to accomplish something with

Young Egyptians participate in an anti-government rally in Cairo on Feb. 25, part of the revolution that ousted President Hosni Mubarak. Egypt's "youth bulge" has been instrumental in organizing the recent protests. With young people making up 29 percent of the country's population, many young Egyptians can't find jobs.

their lives," says Hamid. "But the jobs aren't out there, so they have to be taxi drivers."

— *Alan Greenblatt*

[1] Fred Pearce, *The Coming Population Crash* (2010), p. 198.

[2] Richard P. Cincotta, Robert Engelman and Daniele Anastasion, "The Security Demographic: Population and Civil Conflict After the Cold War," Population Action International, 2003, p. 13, www.populationaction .org/Publications/Reports/The_Security_Demographic/The_Security_ Demographic_Population_and_Civil_Conflict_After_the_Cold_War.pdf.

[3] Deborah Amos, "Rise of Education Lifts Arab Youths' Expectations," National Public Radio, Feb. 18, 2011; www.npr.org/2011/02/18/133 779699/rise-of-education-lifts-arab-youths-expectations.

Germany and Japan, according to AEI's Eberstadt, the number of women who end up having no children at all is approaching 30 percent.[19]

In response, numerous countries — including Australia, Poland, South Korea and Spain — have introduced programs recently to raise the birth rate by encouraging women to have more children.

Germany has built more state-financed day care centers and created a parental leave policy in 2007. Spain offers parents "baby bonuses," while Japan has allowed shorter work days for women with children. In Singapore, the official family-planning slogan has shifted from "Stop at Two" to "Three Children or More If You Can Afford It."[20]

But while programs to discourage child-bearing have worked in some countries, such as China's "one child"

policy, it's been harder to encourage women to have more children. "You can keep people from having babies through coercive state measures," says AEI's Eberstadt. "It's harder to make them have babies."

And heavy-handed government efforts to control child-bearing can have horrific, unintended consequences. China's one-child policy, for instance, has been blamed for a rise in female infanticide because of a cultural preference for boys. And in the 1960s, Romanian President Nicolae Ceausescu banned contraception and abortion in an effort to boost population growth. Thousands of women who had more babies than they could support abandoned them in Romania's 600 state orphanages. The notoriously overcrowded institutions housed an estimated 100,000 children — often

AFP/Getty Images/Remy Gabalda

Crowds march in Toulouse, France, during nationwide strikes on June 24, 2010, to protest President Nicolas Sarkozy's plan to raise the retirement age from 60 to 62. France's state-run pension system has been under increasing pressure because people are living longer, according to Sarkozy. The plan was approved in October.

malnourished, neglected and physically or sexually abused.[21]

Still, offering incentives to boost birthrates is not a new idea. The ancient Romans offered money to families with many children, penalized bachelors and encouraged immigration by offering citizenship to immigrants. Fifteen centuries later, Jean-Baptiste Colbert, Louis XIV's finance minister, offered up the same basic menu. "Leaders have been perpetually disappointed by their population policies," CSIS analysts Jackson and Howe conclude.[22]

Falling birthrates are driven by deeply rooted social and economic developments, so a few financial incentives — what Eberstadt calls "baby bribes" — aren't going to convince people to have multiple children. At most, policies such as tax incentives merely change people's timing, economists say.

Jackson says pro-natal policies can be effective, but they must be permanent. And they can be expensive. Countries such as France and Sweden that offer extensive government support to families with children spend 3 to 4 percent of GDP on such programs — double the rate of less-generous countries such as Germany and Japan.

Immigration also can help counter population aging. If not for its immigrant population, Canada's demographic profile would look like Germany's. Instead, it looks more like the United States, an immigration magnet

with a relatively high fertility rate by today's rich-nation standards.

But immigrants also grow old. Typically, within a generation or two their fertility rates come to mirror those of their new nation's population. "Foreign-born women have a higher fertility rate than Spanish women," says Margarita Delgado, a sociologist at the Spanish National Research Council. "However, it doesn't take long for this to decrease and get closer to Spanish women's behavior."[23]

Also, there aren't that many young immigrants to go around. With few exceptions, most of the world's populations are aging, even relatively young countries, such as those in Africa, the Muslim world and Latin America. So, while immigrants can help lower the median age of a tiny country like Singapore, there aren't enough available to curb aging in, say, China.

Some scholars suggest that policies making it easier for women to balance work with child-rearing are the most helpful.

Traditionally, women were more concerned with child-bearing and other family concerns than working outside the home. Now that they have opportunities for jobs and careers, Jackson says, it's important that governments and employers make it easier for workers to balance their family and working lives. "You would assume that having a female workforce . . . means fewer babies, but the opposite is actually true," Jackson says. When it's easier for women to balance work and family — and get some help at home from their spouses — women are more likely to have a second or third child. But, if women are forced to choose between family and work, many today choose to work — or to delay procreation long enough to make having multiple children unlikely.

"It's important that employers understand that the employee is a human being integrated into a family, with prior family obligations," says former Deutsche Bank chief economist Walter.

According to Eberstadt, "the best single predictor of fertility in different societies" is not external factors — such as availability of contraceptives or women's workforce participation — but cultural preferences. "It's desired family size as reported by women of childbearing age."

Perhaps that's why high fertility rates are more commonly found in religious communities. Religious fundamentalists tend to produce more babies. Heavily Mormon

Utah has a birth rate 50 percent larger than more secular-minded Vermont. "In Israel, in 1948, 4 percent of the population was ultra-Orthodox," Longman says. "Now, they're already up to 16 percent of the children of Israel."

Most monotheistic religions promote or even mandate large families. Many were founded at a time when nations or tribes were often surrounded by hostile neighbors, so large populations were viewed as defense against attack.

"Injunctions similar to Jehovah's command, 'Increase and multiply,' are found in the religions of practically every nation," Charles E. Strangeland wrote in his history of population doctrines more than a century ago.[24]

Experts predict heightened competition for resources among groups with widely differing fertility rates within the same country. Alexandra Parrs, a French scholar of the Middle East who lectures at The Johns Hopkins School of Advanced International Studies in Washington, D.C., notes that in Bahrain the Shiites have roughly double the fertility rate of Sunnis. The split between the ruling Sunni and the majority — and faster-growing — Shiite population is a major factor underlying the recent unrest in Bahrain.

"The Shia don't have power, and they outnumber the people who are trying to rule over them," Parrs says. "Hence, their anger."

Even religious orthodoxy, however, may not be enough to slow the trend toward smaller families. "Iran is usually not seen as a poster child for secularization, but its birth rate is way below replacement levels," Eberstadt says. "Tehran's birth rate is lower than New York's."

Summing up, Jackson says, "Nobody thinks you can dramatically raise the fertility rate through government policies. If children are not part of your life plan, you're not going to do anything with incentives to change that."

But, he warns, "If you don't raise birth-rates, there's no long-term solution."

BACKGROUND

Demographic Transitions

For most of human history, Fishman points out in *Shock of Gray*, people who lived past 45 had beaten the odds. Life expectancy barely budged from 25 years in Roman times to 30 years at the dawn of the 20th century.[25]

Up until the Industrial Revolution, people who were 65 or older never comprised more than 3 or 4 percent of the population. Today, they average 16 percent in the developed world — and their share is expected to rise to nearly 25 percent by 2030.[26] Demographers call such shifts from historic norms "demographic transitions."

A confluence of factors has led to the current transition. Aging was once largely synonymous with death. Older people were both rarer and more vulnerable to sudden death due to such things as infectious diseases and poor sanitation. But even as modern medicine has conquered diseases that afflict the old, it has done even more to address infant mortality. Pearce points out in *The Coming Population Crash* that when he was born, 150 out of every 1,000 babies worldwide died before celebrating their first birthdays. That number today is down to 50.[27]

With fewer people dying young, life expectancy has increased. And healthier babies have coincided with other societal and economic factors to bring birthrates down. As prosperity grows, death rates fall and people feel less pressure to have large numbers of children to help support them in their old age.

Meanwhile, women's roles have changed in most countries. Many now balance reproduction with concerns and responsibilities outside the home. Contraceptives are more widely available, while abortion has become legal and available in many countries.

Finally, as societies urbanize, fewer families need to have multiple children to help work in the fields. And the advent of pensions and other social-insurance programs means parents no longer need large families to support them as they age.

Population Boosterism

Concern that women aren't having enough children is not new. From around 1450 to 1750, write Jackson and Howe in "The Graying of the Great Powers," monarchs "showcased an unparalleled obsession" with the connection between demographics and geopolitics. Population growth was seen as a predominant source of strength, both for nations and for leaders. Kings Henry IV of France and Frederick the Great of Prussia, for instance, believed that crowded nurseries translated into large armies and navies.[28]

By the late 18th century, however, opinion among the intelligentsia began to shift away from population boosterism. By then, much of Europe had begun its demographic transition, with mortality rates dropping as living standards improved.

In England, the population doubled between 1750 and 1800 and then again between 1800 and 1830, reaching 24 million.[29] Population growth emerged as a pressing concern, particularly after the 1798 publication of British economist Thomas Malthus' hugely influential *An Essay on the Principle of Population*. Malthus argued that growing populations drain resources and ultimately impoverish societies. Among other things, Malthusian theory led to fear that social-welfare policies would encourage the poor to have more children.

"Dependent poverty ought to be held disgraceful," Malthus wrote. "A man who is born into a world already possessed, if he cannot get subsistence from his parents, or if the society do [sic] not want his labor, has no claim of right to the smallest portion of food and, in fact, has no business to be where he is. At nature's mighty feast there is no cover for him. She tells him to be gone."[30]

Malthus turned out to be wrong. Resources were no more finite than population levels. The Industrial Revolution helped increase the world's "carrying capacity" for feeding growing numbers of people — and increased demand for labor.

Still, concerns about population growth outstripping the supply of food and other essentials persisted well into the 20th century. Eugenics, or the attempt to control the qualities of the population by discouraging reproduction among those with so-called undesirable traits, became official policy in many countries early in the century. Japan, for instance, forcibly sterilized tens of thousands of criminals, lepers and those with mental illness. Sweden also sterilized the mentally ill. Between World War I and World War II, 60,000 "feebleminded" people were sterilized in the United States, and some laws prevented the mentally ill from marrying.[31]

After the defeat of Nazi Germany in World War II revealed the horrific extent of the regime's eugenics experimentation — designed to create an Aryan master race partly through genocide against "undesirable" populations — eugenics became a disgraced notion. In its 1948 Universal Declaration of Human Rights, the United Nations banned forced sterilization, among other practices.

Population Control

After World War II, fast-rising populations led to renewed concerns that the planet was filling up too fast. Countries such as Indonesia, El Salvador, Nigeria, Brazil, Turkey and Kenya were on course to double their populations within a generation.

From the 1940s to the '60s, both the U.S. government and private groups such as the Rockefeller Foundation sponsored family-planning efforts around the world. Mortality rates came down quickly in India after World War II and independence from the U.K., thanks largely to an effort to eradicate malaria. Fertility rates, meanwhile, were climbing fast. With births outnumbering deaths by a 2-to-1 ratio, government officials worried that population growth would prove economically devastating.

"We produce more and more food, but also more and more children," complained Jawaharlal Nehru, India's first prime minister. "I wish we produced fewer children."[32]

In 1952, Nehru released a population-control plan that encouraged vasectomies. In the coming decades, states such as Kerala and Gujarat organized mass vasectomy camps, carrying out tens of thousands of vasectomies. Some states sought to impose sterilization, requiring, for instance, that couples show proof of sterilization when seeking new housing.

Neighboring China also grew concerned about population growth. The postwar communist regime of Mao Zedong had had enormous success with health initiatives, including mass distribution of vaccines and antibodies and improved sewers. China immunized almost a half-billion people against smallpox and trained 750,000 midwives in sterile techniques.

"The results were dramatic," Pearce writes. "In Mao's first eight years in charge, Chinese life expectancy rose from 35 to 50 years."[33]

With deaths down and births up, China had a growth spurt, its population spiking from 583 million in 1953 to 700 million a decade later. In 1979, Mao's successor Deng Xiaoping introduced the "one-child policy," which limited families to one child each.

Every unit of population — every farm, workplace and street — faced limits on the number of babies they

C H R O N O L O G Y

1940s-1970s *Fast-growing populations lead to worries about overcrowding and government programs to limit fertility.*

1946 First of the 78 million American baby boomers are born; other English-speaking countries also see higher fertility rates after World War II.

1952 Indian Prime Minister Jawaharlal Nehru creates the world's first comprehensive population-control plan, promoting vasectomies.

1970 Developing countries' average fertility rate reaches 5.1 percent; it will drop to 2.9 percent by 2005.

1979 China launches its one-child policy. . . . After Iran's Islamic Revolution, government initiates programs to encourage high fertility and rapid population growth.

1980s-1990s *As the baby boom winds down, birth-rates slow. . . . The specter of aging populations emerges as a growing concern.*

1980 With only 9 percent of its population over 65, Japan is the youngest among developed countries; within 25 years it will become the world's oldest country.

1992 Abortions in Russia outnumber live births by more than 2-to-1; total births will decline by 40 percent over the next 15 years.

1994 World Bank publishes *Averting the Old Age Crisis*, promoting pension privatization in more than 30 countries.

2000s *The effects of aging are beginning to be felt as growth declines among working-age populations.*

2004 The percentage of women with no children rises from 10 percent to 16 percent in the United States, and to 18 percent among Germans.

2005 In developed countries, the share of the working-age population peaks at 61 percent. . . . Life expectancy reaches 77 in the United States and 82 in Japan.

2006 Russian government says it will raise fertility rates and reduce mortality by 2025.

2007 To encourage more women to have babies, Germany introduces a new parental-leave benefit. . . . United Kingdom reverses course on a program to index pension benefits to prices rather than wages.

2009 Japan's fertility rate drops to 1.21, among the world's lowest.

2010s *Governments begin to formulate policies to deal with their aging societies.*

2010 France raises the retirement age from 60 to 62. . . . Average life expectancy in developing regions reaches 67 except in sub-Saharan Africa, where it has tumbled due to AIDS. . . . Russia's population, expected to decline rapidly due to low birthrates and high mortality, is already 7 million below 1991 levels. . . . A study finds that 40 percent of Americans age 50 to 64 have difficulty performing basic physical tasks.

2011 United Kingdom changes compulsory retirement rules so that employers will no longer be able to force qualified workers to retire at 65. . . . In January, Spain strikes a deal with the country's two largest unions to raise the retirement age to 67. . . . Singapore announces subsidies for employers who hire low-wage older workers. . . . China is considering allowing elderly parents to demand that courts order their children to visit and look after them. . . . "Youth bulge" in Arab world contributes to unrest throughout the Middle East and North Africa.

2015 Working-age populations are projected to begin declining in the developed world, with the United States the sole major exception.

2025 Population growth will stall or decline in every major developed country except the United States, which will also be the only developed country with more children under 20 than elderly over 65.

2030 Developed countries will have 42 seniors for every 100 working-age adults.

2050 The median age is expected to reach 56 in Japan, 49 in Western Europe and 40 in the United States.

Aging Trends Affect Economic Migration

Laborers seek work in countries with older populations.

It's a bit like the weather. Just as high- and low-pressure zones move air around, differences in aging rates among countries also affect the rate of human migration.

"Instead of air pressure, you can talk about median age," says Richard Jackson, director of the Global Aging Initiative at the Center for Strategic and International Studies in Washington, D.C. "You'll tend to see population flow from countries with lower median ages to countries with higher median ages."

That's especially true in today's world, where some countries are aging rapidly and the economies in countries with higher shares of young people — such as Uganda and Afghanistan — cannot employ them all. Most immigrants leave their countries for economic reasons, although a small percentage leaves to escape political persecution.

Prior to 1990, most migrants were in developing countries, but that is no longer the case. In the past 20 years, the number of immigrants entering developed countries has more than doubled — from 48 million to 100 million — while immigrants in developing countries only rose from 52 million to 65 million, according to Stefano Zamagni, an economist at the University of Bologna, Italy.[1]

The list of countries with mismatches between labor and jobs changes over time. Fifty years ago, Spain saw a large share of its population leaving in search of work abroad. In those days, foreign-born residents were rarities in Spain — just one out of every 500 persons in 1953. Today, 12 percent of Spain's population — nearly one in eight — is foreign born.

With its elderly population on the rise, Spain now needs to import workers. A dozen years ago, Ecuadorians were scarce in Spain. Today, some 700,000 Ecuadorians live there — a major chunk of Ecuador's expatriate population.[2]

For aging countries, attracting and keeping foreign workers at the height of their earning powers is hugely attractive economically, says Ted C. Fishman, author of the 2010 book *Shock of Gray*. The workers' home countries also benefit: Remittances — money sent home by so-called guest workers abroad — make up an important or even leading share of GDP in countries that export labor.

But countries don't like to see huge percentages of their populations go abroad — particularly the working-age cohort that is both the most productive and the most likely to leave. But incentive programs — instituted in countries ranging from the Czech Republic to the Philippines — have failed to keep workers at home.

In the receiving countries, meanwhile, there is always the risk of a backlash developing against immigrants, who often are seen as a threat to native workers' jobs or a country's values. Several European countries have been experiencing such a backlash since the economic recession began in 2008.[3]

Echoing remarks made by his French and German counterparts, British Prime Minister David Cameron complained in February that "multiculturalism" had led to segregation and encouraged radicalization of Muslim youths. "We have failed to provide a vision of society to which they feel they want to belong," Cameron said. "We have even tolerated these segregated communities behaving in ways that run counter to our values."[4]

"The prime minister was speaking to the pressure to limit the number of migrants coming in," says Fred Pearce, an author and consultant in Great Britain. That sentiment runs

were allowed. Women who were illegally pregnant were often forced to have abortions, sometimes after being abducted and taken to clinics in the dead of night.[34]

Falling Fertility

China's crackdown caused a dramatic decline in birthrates. In 1963, 43 children were born per 1,000 people. By 2003, it had dropped to just 12. Over that same 40-year period, China's fertility rate has dropped from about 6 to below 2. The government estimates that during the first 30 years of the one-child policy, China added 400 million fewer people to its population than it otherwise would have.[35] Partly as a result, China's population today is aging faster than the rest of the globe. Worldwide, the percentage of the over-60 population will double — from 11 percent in 2009 to 22 percent in 2050. But in China the percentage of the over-65 population will triple between 2007 and 2050 — to 24 percent.[36]

Meanwhile, fertility rates have been dropping in many countries for decades, interrupted only by a postwar baby

counter to the coming economic reality of aging populations. "Others, including the mayor of London, are saying that we need more migrants, they're needed in the economy."

Aside from the political push-pull regarding immigration, there also are large economic forces at play. Partly due to the high pension and health care costs associated with supporting older populations, multinational corporations may prefer to move more of their operations to countries with young workers, rather than have workers migrate in search of jobs.

"It's true that people move around in an aging world," Fishman says. "But capital also moves in an aging world, seeking young people unencumbered by age-related expenses."

And developing countries whose young people have long gone abroad for work are starting to catch up with the developed world — both in terms of aging and, to some extent, in terms of standards of living. People don't like to emigrate, so the differences in standards of living must be great enough to convince them it's worth it to pack up and move.

In Mexico, the number of children under 4 has been falling rapidly for 15 years. As the country starts to age, it won't be subject to the same level of population pressures that have contributed greatly to mass emigration over the past half-century.

"Unidirectional migration [within] Europe has stopped," says Wolfgang Lutz, leader of the World Population Program at the International Institute for Applied Systems Analysis in Austria. "In the 1970s, thousands moved from Italy to Germany and from Portugal to France or Luxembourg.

"Today, movement between those countries is free, and people in Portugal are still earning a quarter less than in Germany, but hardly anyone is coming for a higher wage."

Still, given the prospect of labor shortages in the aging rich world and continuing poverty in most of the countries

AFP/Getty Images/Roberto Salomone

Would-be immigrants — probably from North Africa — approach the Italian island of Lampedusa on March 7, 2011. In the past 20 years, the number of job-seeking immigrants entering developed countries like Italy has more than doubled, from 48 million to 100 million. Job prospects are better in nations with aging workforces.

with the lion's share of births, economic migration appears bound to continue and even accelerate in coming years.

"As long as there are big economic differences between countries, there's going to be an incentive for migration," says Nicholas Eberstadt, a demographer at the conservative American Enterprise Institute think tank in Washington.

— Alan Greenblatt

---

[1] Stefano Zamagni, "On the Move," *SAISPHERE*, 2010-2011, School for Advanced International Studies, The Johns Hopkins University, p. 66.

[2] Ted C. Fishman, *Shock of Gray* (2010), p. 95.

[3] For background, see Sarah Glazer, "Europe's Immigration Turmoil," *CQ Global Researcher*, Dec. 1, 2010, pp. 289-320.

[4] John F. Burns, "Prime Minister Criticizes British 'Multiculturalism' as Allowing Extremism," *The New York Times*, Feb. 6, 2011, p. A6; www.nytimes.com/2011/02/06/world/europe/06britain.html.

boom that was especially pronounced in the United States and other English-speaking countries.

From 1950 to 1973, the world's population grew by an unprecedented average of 2 percent a year.[37] But demographers increasingly believe the subsequent "baby bust" will prove more the norm than the preceding boom. Fertility rates, in fact, have fallen almost continuously since the 19th century. Where it was once common to find fertility rates of 4 to 6 or even 7 in the United States and Western Europe, by the 1930s most had dropped

closer to 2. And since 1930, the average number of children born to each succeeding cohort of women ending their child-bearing years declined in nearly every developed country.[38]

Today, much of the world is not just getting old, but dramatically older. The United Nation projects that by 2025 life expectancy will rise to 84 in the developed world — up from today's 79.

Some demographers believe that the U.N. estimate is too low, because it assumes life expectancy will increase by only 1.2 years per decade, or about half the rate over the past 50 years.

CURRENT SITUATION

Aging States

Although every developed country is aging — along with most less-developed countries — they are not all aging at the same rate or in the same way. The United States is aging more slowly than Western Europe, for instance. The U.S. birth rate is the highest in the developed world, remaining close to replacement levels, and the country remains a powerful draw for immigrants, who tend to be younger than the native-born population.

While the rest of the developed world is set to lose 18 million people by midcentury, the United States is on course to gain 119 million. By 2025, it will be the only major developed country with more people under 20 than over 65 — and, thus, the only one with a working-age population that will continue to grow.[39]

By some measurements, the United States is in comparatively good shape on pensions. Social Security eats up only about half as much of GDP as more generous pension programs in France, Germany and Italy. And American men over 65 are at least three times as likely to continue working as older men in those countries.

The bad news, however, is that U.S. pension funds — both public and private — are underfunded by trillions of dollars.

Older Population to Double by 2050

The proportion of the world population age 60 and older is expected to double to 22 percent by 2050. The number of individuals age 80 and older is expected to nearly quadruple to almost 400 million during the same period.

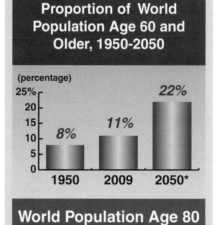

Proportion of World Population Age 60 and Older, 1950-2050

(percentage)

- 1950: 8%
- 2009: 11%
- 2050*: 22%

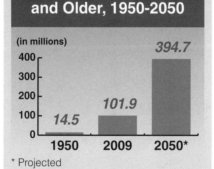

World Population Age 80 and Older, 1950-2050

(in millions)

- 1950: 14.5
- 2009: 101.9
- 2050*: 394.7

* Projected

Source: "World Population Ageing 2009," U.N. Department of Economic and Social Affairs

"This has made American companies relatively uncompetitive when compared to their international counterparts, which have much more flexibility in the labor space and have not had the burden of pension costs anywhere to the degree that Western industrial companies have," said Dambisa Moyo, a Zambian international economist who has worked for Goldman Sachs and the World Bank.[40]

And the United States faces other looming age-related fiscal challenges, because health costs through Medicare and other programs far outweigh those in other countries. "The U.S., demographically, looks pretty good on paper compared to anyone else," says Longman, of the New America Foundation, "until you remember our health care encumbrance. We can't afford to get old, even a little."

Exporting Jobs

Japan, by contrast, is aging at warp speed. In 1980, Japan was the youngest of the developed countries. Now, it is the oldest country on Earth. Japan has the world's highest life expectancy — 83 — with birthrates below any other developed nation except Italy and Spain.

In 1963, there were 100 centenarians in all of Japan. By 2050, their ranks are projected to reach 1 million. Already, more than a fifth of Japan's population is over 65 — a percentage that will double by midcentury.[41] Meanwhile, Japan recorded only about 40 percent as many births in 2008 as it did 60 years earlier.[42]

Should official retirement ages be raised?

YES
Ursula von der Leyen
Minister, Labor and Social Affairs Germany

Written for *CQ Global Researcher*, March 2011

Tomorrow's working world will be different from the one we know today. The German population is getting smaller and older. By 2030, the number of 20- to-64-year-olds will have declined by more than 6 million, while the number of those 65 and older will have risen by over 5 million.

Persistent low birthrates and longer life expectancy are to blame. By 2030, men age 65 can expect to live 19 additional years on average and women almost another 23 years — up more than two years from present rates.

Raising the standard retirement age is not just a pension-policy measure. It is also intended to convey a clear message to society and business and industry: Change your attitudes toward the potential of older employees and take appropriate action.

Demographic change will cause a substantial contraction of the labor pool, which will also be considerably older. The future task for businesses, social partners and policymakers will be to create suitable conditions for an aging labor force to maximize productivity and innovation. This can be done if company labor organization and workplace design are tailored to the specific abilities and competencies of older employees.

Longer life expectancy also means more years in good health. The aim must be to share the burden resulting from demographic change equitably among all generations. Strengthening the generational contract will avoid distribution conflicts between young and old, provided the necessary change of course is made early on. If this is not done in good time, larger adjustments will be needed later.

To safeguard social welfare and international competitiveness, we must harness more future labor potential through greater labor-force participation by older people. Switzerland and the Scandinavian countries have proven that it is not only necessary but also feasible to adjust the supply of and demand for jobs to the abilities and needs of different age groups.

Longer lifetimes also mean an increase in the time people remain healthy and capable in older age. Developments on the labor market in recent years confirm the federal government's view that labor-force participation and labor-market opportunities have much improved for the older generation. With their adherence to the new standard retirement age, policymakers have laid a firm foundation for the realignment now under way.

NO
Florian Blank, PhD
Senior Researcher, Institute of Economic and Social Research Hans-Böckler-Foundation Düsseldorf, Germany

Written for *CQ Global Researcher*, March 2011

In 2007, the German government decided to raise the standard retirement age in the public pension insurance system from 65 to 67 by 2029. The main reason — as stated by the government — is that demographic change threatens the pension insurance fund's finances. The decision provoked fierce criticism, especially from trade unions, and probably contributed to the electoral loss of the Social Democrats in 2009.

German society, like others, is aging, and it seems to be widely accepted that this process will affect the social security system, too. However, raising the retirement age does not seem to be an adequate reaction. Not only is it seen as an affront by many future retirees, but it obscures other possible responses.

Demographic change and pension finances are not directly linked. In a contribution-based system, pension finances are heavily influenced by employment and wages. Enabling more people to keep a well-paying job until reaching the retirement age of 65 would directly affect pension finances. But today, only 38.4 percent of those between the ages of 60 and 65 are employed, and only 23.4 percent have a job subject to social insurance.

Raising the retirement age before substantially increasing labor market participation of elderly workers is putting the cart before the horse — and certain groups of employees will still need public support and ways to leave the labor market before age 65, even if employment rates of older workers rise.

Furthermore, according to government's calculations, raising the retirement age will lower future contribution rates by 0.5 percentage points while increasing future pension benefits by 0.6 percentage points.

These seem to be pretty small advantages, compared with the anxiety associated with worrying about potentially being forced to leave the workforce early due to illness, and thus receive smaller benefits.

So raising the retirement age does not tackle the real problem of how to keep people on the job and stabilize contributions through good jobs and decent wages. And since the impact on retirement incomes of raising the retirement age is ambiguous, it does not answer the question of how to guarantee retirement without financial worries.

The number of Chinese senior citizens is projected to triple by 2050 — faster than the worldwide aging rate. Within 20 years, the number of Chinese over age 65 is expected to reach 167 million — more than half the current population of the United States.

Traditionally, Japanese sons take in their aging parents, but this has created a vicious circle when it comes to the nation's aging population. Women put off getting married longer because they fear getting sandwiched between the responsibilities of caring for aging in-laws and their own children, which has translated into more women having fewer children.

Indeed, some Japanese demographers say nearly a third of the current generation of young women will have no children at all. "Some people believe the Japanese economy's lack of growth in the last couple of decades may be traceable to its aging population," says Pearce, the British author.

Japan has sought to attract some immigrants, particularly descendants of Japanese who emigrated to Latin America 100 years ago when Japan had a surplus working-age population. But the country's xenophobic immigration policies and cultural mores remain highly restrictive toward foreigners.

Instead, Japanese companies are exporting manufacturing jobs to countries with younger workers. Already, 20,000 Japanese companies have operations in China, employing 1 million people. "The model for Japan in the future is to make money from Japanese factories in foreign places where other people will do the work," said Masanao Takahashi, whose company, Taisei Industries, supplies steel parts.[43]

'Six Elders Per Child'

But China will not be able to indefinitely take up the slack left by other countries' aging workforces. China is aging so fast that some observers wonder whether it will grow old before it can grow rich enough to support an older population.

"Each country, as it develops, seems to age faster than its neighbors," *Shock of Gray* author Fishman says. "China is aging faster than South Korea, which aged faster than Japan."

China has what some demographers call a 4-2-1 problem. That is, each young adult today may be responsible for supporting not just two parents, but four grandparents, as well. "The one-child policy could just as accurately be called the 'Six Elders Per Child' policy," Fishman writes.[44]

From 1980 to 2010 — when China was growing incredibly fast — the country's working-age population grew by about 1.8 percent per year, until it reached 72 percent of the overall population. But that percentage will peak in 2016, and by 2030 it will be shrinking by nearly 1 percent a year.[45]

Already, Beijing's 60,000 nursing home beds are filled, unable to meet the needs of 2.3 million senior citizens. Nationwide, China has fewer than half as many elder-care beds per 1,000 people over 65 than is the average in developed countries.[46]

The suicide rate among Chinese elderly has been growing rapidly, and the government is considering allowing elderly parents to sue their children if they don't visit regularly.[47] "Their old-age poverty will be a big issue in the '20s and '30s of this century," predicts Walter, the former chief economist at Deutsche Bank.

Other economists note that China's aging is happening much more rapidly than occurred in the West. "China will be growing old before it becomes affluent and before it's had time to put in place the protections of a modern welfare state," the CSIS' Jackson says.

Aging Workforces

China now has three young workers — age 20 to 29 — for every two older workers age 55 to 64. Twenty years from now, that ratio will be reversed.[48]

By that time, China will be facing some of the same issues already bedeviling older societies. Economic growth has been tied strongly to employment growth — something few countries can count on in the coming decades.

CSIS analysts Jackson and Howe estimate that the lack of growth in working-age populations will markedly slow economic growth. While the U.S. GDP doubled during the 22 years leading up to the 2008 worldwide recession, experts say it will take 33 years for that to happen again, due, in part, to the aging workforce. Western Europe's economy will be hit even harder, taking an estimated 64 years to double, while Japan's will take "an incredible 168 years," according to Jackson and Howe.[49]

Severe economic consequences will become evident as the age pyramid continues to invert, with those ages 50-to-80-plus making up an increasingly large share of populations. Not only will pension and health care costs continue to escalate, but there will be less innovation and entrepreneurship, since younger workers are disproportionately responsible for such activities.

And many of today's comparatively young countries, such as Egypt and China, are facing "marriage squeezes" in coming years, with the share of men who will remain single rising rapidly to well above 20 percent. In China, this may be in part because of the gender selection that favored boy babies during the one-child policy period.[50] Worldwide, say researchers, as many as 100 million females are "missing" in cultures that traditionally prefer boy babies, due to selective abortions and female infanticide — usually by poisoning or starvation.[51]

Global aging also affects international and internal migration. "Virtually all the additional population, as we go from 7 to 9 billion people, will be urban," says author Fishman, "and urban families rarely have more than two children."

And while Western countries such as the U.K. and Germany had a century-and-a-half to adjust to their demographic transitions, newly emerging countries will see that sort of change telescoped into one or, at most, two generations, says Jackson, potentially triggering social upheaval. "These are societies experiencing a kind of future shock," he says.

Societies are just beginning to grapple with the effects of an aging world — and doing what they can to prevent it. "Have babies — Allah wants it," Turkey's prime minister, Recep Tayyip Erdogan, told a 2002 gathering in Istanbul, reacting to proposals to expand the use of contraception. "To recommend to people to not procreate is straight-out treason to the state."[52]

OUTLOOK
Age Adjustment

Aging populations — barely on the radar screens of most policymakers a decade ago — will become central to

> "We have not prepared society for the change, and the transition process will be painful and not short. We will have not only younger people protesting but older people as well."
>
> — *Norbert Walter, former chief economist, Deutsche Bank*

fiscal, economic and security discussions over the next decade, especially in the developed world. "It will be a decade of economic crisis and economic stagnation in most of the developed world," says Jackson, director of the CSIS Global Aging Initiative. "We will be coming to terms in a real way with the diminished economic and geopolitical stature of current [rich] countries."

Jackson believes aging societies will have to renegotiate social contracts that are no longer sustainable, triggering epochal arguments about who will bear the burden of paying for pensions and health care. Many observers worry that most societies may have already waited too long to start such debates.

"This issue is no longer neglected, but we have not yet reached a comprehensive willingness to respond in a profound way," says Walter, the former Deutsche Bank chief economist. "I'm 66, and when I say that we, the older, have to work longer hours, I get very nasty e-mails from my age cohort, even sometimes from organized groups. If I were a politician, they would be nastier."

Adjusting to aging populations won't be easy, but neither will it necessarily be all bad, suggests Pearce, the British author. It will be a problem "if we just blunder into an aging population without changing our attitudes toward the old," he says. "But if societies help . . . make it easier for older people to keep working — whether full time or in second careers as consultants — they will benefit. We will want to use the skills of old people more wisely. It may happen almost without us noticing, in the way the dominance of the youth culture crept up on us."

The elderly must stay fit longer, both physically and cognitively, says Lutz, the Austrian demographer. That presents some challenges. According to the U.S. Centers for Disease Control and Prevention, even in the United States — where older people are more inclined to keep working after age 60 than in most Western European countries — only one American in five stays physically active on a regular basis.[53] According to a recent study by the RAND Corporation think tank and the University of Michigan, more than 40 percent of Americans aged 50 to 64 have difficulty performing simple physical tasks such as walking a quarter-mile or climbing 10 steps — a big increase from a decade ago.[54]

But, Lutz says, older societies could end up being more peaceful, since seniors suffer fewer problems such as crime and drug abuse. And having fewer children may actually be a good thing, because more per capita can be spent on their education. "This can even overcompensate for their smaller numbers," Lutz says.

"Aging is part of the prosperity equation," notes *Shock of Gray* author Fishman. "I'm not sure we want to reverse this entirely."

Rapidly aging populations will present especially enormous challenges as the cost of their health care goes up. A recent Johns Hopkins University study, for instance, projected that the number of cases of Alzheimer's Disease — the debilitating form of dementia among the elderly that eventually requires the equivalent of full-time nursing home care for the patient — will quadruple by 2050, with one in 85 persons worldwide suffering from the disease.[55]

It will also require some attitude adjustment as societies learn to take full advantage of older workers' knowledge, rather than putting them out to pasture. According to a recent Wellesley College study, more over-55 workers who need to work longer than expected due to losses in their retirement savings accounts may be forced to retire than will be able to hang onto their jobs.[56]

For aging societies to prosper, many habits — including ageism and the desire of the old to seek retirement and leisure — must change. "The big thing is how to get through these first times when we're older," Fishman says, "and figure out how to reap the benefits of being older."

NOTES

1. Phenola Lawrence, "Double-Whammy: Aging China Has Fewer Children to Care for It," *Chicago Tribune*, June 30, 2010, p. 30; www.mcclatchydc .com/2010/06/24/96489/double-whammy-aging-china-has.html.

2. Quoted in Fred Pearce, *The Coming Population Crash* (2010), p. 89.

3. *Ibid.*, p. 247.

4. Phillip Longman, "Think Again: Global Aging," *Foreign Policy*, November 2010, www.foreignpolicy .com/articles/2010/10/11/think_again_global_aging.

5. Pearce, *op. cit.*, p. xviii.

6. Longman, *op. cit.*

7. Bulat Akhmetkarimov, "In Russia, Ambitions vs. Demography," *SAISPHERE*, 2010-2011, p. 14.

8. Nicholas Eberstadt, "The Demographic Future," *Foreign Affairs*, November-December 2010, p. 54.

9. Richard Jackson and Neil Howe, "The Graying of the Great Powers," 2008, p. 3.

10. "2010 World Population Data Sheet," Population Reference Bureau, 2010, www.prb.org/Publications/ Datasheets/2010/2010wpds.aspx.

11. Pearce, *op. cit.*, p. 98.

12. *Ibid.*, p. 122.

13. Fishman, *op. cit.*, p. 69.

14. "Slovenia Adopts Pension System Reform, Raises Retirement Age," Agence France-Presse, Dec. 14, 2010.

15. Jeremy Au Yong, "One-off Subsidy for Hiring Low-Wage Older Workers," *The Straits Times*, Feb. 19, 2011, http://justice4workerssingapore.blogspot.com/ 2011/02/budget-2011-cpf-contributionswage.html.

16. Jack Ewing, "Germany: Revolt of the Young," *Business Week*, Sept. 22, 2003, www.businessweek.com/ magazine/content/03_38/b3850051_mz014.htm.

17. Jackson and Howe, *op. cit.*, p. 64.

18. Ronald Brownstein, "The Gray and the Brown: The Generational Mismatch," *National Journal*, July 24, 2010; www.nationaljournal.com/magazine/the-gray -and-the-brown-the-generational-mismatch-2010 0724.

19. Stefan Theil, "Beyond Babies," *Newsweek International*, Sept. 4, 2006, www.newsweek.com/2006/09/03/ beyond-babies.html.

20. Michael Cardiosk, "Singapore's Aging Population," Yahoo.com, April 19, 2009, www.associatedcontent .com/article/1621347/singapores_aging_population_ the_stop.html?cat=9.

21. Kate McGeown, "What happened to Romania's orphans?" BBC News, http://news.bbc.co.uk/2/hi/europe/4629589.stm.

22. Jackson and Howe, *op. cit.*, p. 26.

23. Delgado was interviewed via email with translation assistance by Cecilia Cortes-Earle.

24. Charles E. Strangeland, *Pre-Malthusian Doctrines of Population* (1904), p. 40.

25. Fishman, *op. cit.*, p. 13.

26. Jackson and Howe, *op. cit.*, p. 7.

27. Pearce, *op. cit.*, p. xvi.

28. Jackson and Howe, *op. cit.*, p. 22.

29. Pearce, *op. cit.*, p. 6.

30. *Ibid.*, p. 5.

31. *Ibid.*, p. 24.

32. *Ibid.*, p. 59.

33. *Ibid.*, p. 77.

34. Louisa Lim, "Cases of Forced Abortions Surface in China," National Public Radio, April 23, 2007, www.npr.org/templates/story/story.php?storyId=9766870.

35. Fishman, *op. cit.*, p. 306.

36. "World Population Ageing, 2009" Population Division, United Nations Department of Economic and Social Affairs, 2010, www.un.org/esa/population/publications/WPA2009/WPA2009-report.pdf; "Asian Demographic and Human Capital Data Sheet, 2008," Asian MetaCentre, www.populationasia.org.

37. Jackson and Howe, *op. cit.*, p. 25.

38. *Ibid.*, p. 46.

39. *Ibid.*, p. 40

40. "Pensions Dull America's Global Edge, Economist Says," National Public Radio, Feb. 18, 2011, www.npr.org/2011/02/18/133860435/Pensions-May-No-Longer-Be-Sustainable.

41. Fishman, *op. cit.*, p. 144.

42. Eberstadt, *op. cit.*

43. Fishman, *op. cit.*, p. 185.

44. *Ibid.*, p. 308.

45. Nicholas Eberstadt, "The Demographic Risks to China's Long-Term Economic Outlook," Swiss Re: Centre for Global Dialogue, Jan. 24, 2011, http://cgd.swissre.com/global_dialogue/topics/ageing_longevity/Demographic_risks_to_China.html.

46. Lan Fang, "Future Starts to Age: China's Elderly," *Caixin Online*, Sept. 6, 2010, www.marketwatch.com/story/china-begins-to-suffer-aging-population-pressures-2010-09-06.

47. Sharon LaFraniere, "China Might Force Visits to Mom and Dad," *The New York Times*, Jan. 29, 2011, www.nytimes.com/2011/01/30/world/asia/30beijing.html?_r=1&ref=asia.

48. Eberstadt, "The Demographic Risks to China's Long-Term Economic Outlook," *op. cit.*

49. Jackson and Howe, *op. cit.*, p. 75.

50. Ching-Ching Ni, "The World; China Confronts Its Daunting Gender Gap; Officials seek corrective measures as a one-child policy and a preference for male offspring mean men now significantly out-number women," *Los Angeles Times*, Jan. 21, 2005, p. A6.

51. Nicolas Kristoff, "Stark Data On Women: 100 Million Are Missing," *The New York Times*, Nov. 5, 1991, www.nytimes.com/1991/11/05/science/stark-data-on-women-100-million-are-missing.html.

52. "Contraception Is Treason, Turkish Islamist Leader Says," Agence France-Presse, Feb. 16, 2002.

53. Fishman, *op. cit.*, p. 29.

54. Linda G. Martin, Robert F. Schoeni and Patricia M. Andreski, "Trends in Disability and Related Chronic Conditions Among People Ages Fifty to Sixty-Four," *Health Affairs*, April 2010, p. 725. For background, see Beth Baker, "Treating Alzheimer's," *CQ Researcher*, March 4, 2011, pp. 193-216.

55. Ron Brookmeyer, *et al.*, "Forecasting the Global Burden of Alzheimer's Disease," Johns Hopkins University Department of Biostatistics, 2007, http://works.bepress.com/cgi/viewcontent.cgi?article=1022&context=rbrookmeyer.

56. Kelly Evans and Sarah Needleman, "For Older Workers, a Reluctant Retirement," *The Wall Street Journal*, Dec. 8, 2009, http://online.wsj.com/article/SB126022997361080981.html.

BIBLIOGRAPHY

Books

Fishman, Ted C., *Shock of Gray*, Scribner, 2010.
A former financial trader describes how aging is presenting fiscal, health and economic challenges to countries like Japan, China and the United States.

Longman, Phillip, *The Empty Cradle: How Falling Birthrates Threaten World Prosperity (and What to Do About It)*, Basic Books, 2004.
A senior fellow at the New America Foundation examines why birthrates are falling and suggests that societies find economical ways to reward child-bearing to bring rates back up.

Pearce, Fred, *The Coming Population Crash and Our Planet's Surprising Future*, Beacon Press, 2010.
A development and environmental consultant for *New Scientist* magazine traces the history of population shifts and examines past state-sponsored efforts at population control.

Willetts, David, *The Pinch*, Atlantic Books, 2010.
A member of the British parliament examines the implications of the fact that the postwar baby boomers are running up retirement bills that younger generations will have to pay.

Articles

Anderson, Gerald F., and Peter Sotir Hussey, "Population Aging: A Comparison Among Industrialized Countries," *Health Affairs*, May/June 2000, p. 191, http://content.healthaffairs.org/content/19/3/191.
Johns Hopkins University researchers compare countries' health spending, long-term care and retirement policies.

Brownstein, Ronald, "The Gray and the Brown: The Generational Mismatch," *National Journal*, July 24, 2010, www.nationaljournal.com/magazine/the-gray-and-the-brown-the-generational-mismatch-20100724.
The United States is seeing a divergence in attitudes and priorities between a heavily nonwhite population of younger people and an overwhelmingly white cohort of older people.

Eberstadt, Nicholas, "The Demographic Future: What Population Growth — and Decline — Means for the Global Economy," *Foreign Affairs*, November-December 2010, p. 54.
A demographer at the American Enterprise Institute says the "coming demographic challenge of stagnant and aging populations" threatens to put constraints on economies worldwide.

Longman, Phillip, "Think Again: Global Aging," *Foreign Policy*, November 2010, www.foreignpolicy.com/articles/2010/10/11/think_again_global_aging.
A senior fellow at the New America Foundation tries to sort out facts and myths about aging populations, pointing out that aging is not just a rich-world phenomenon. Moreover, he says, seniors can work longer only if their health improves.

Studies and Reports

"Foreshadowing the Future? The Impact of Demography," *SAISPHERE*, The Johns Hopkins University School of Advanced International Studies, 2010-2011.
SAIS scholars focus on demographic topics, many related to aging and showing its effects on health, migration and military strategy (both in general and in individual countries and regions such as Russia, Japan and Latin America).

"World Population Aging 2009," United Nations Population Division, 2010, www.un.org/esa/population/publications/WPA2009/WPA2009-report.pdf.
The latest in a series of U.N. studies finds that aging of societies is pervasive, profound and irreversible because fertility rates will not return to higher past levels.

Cincotta, Richard P., Robert Engelman and Daniele Anastasion, "The Security Demographic: Population and Civil Conflict After the Cold War," Population Action International, 2003, www.populationaction.org/Publications/Reports/The_Security_Demographic/The_Security_Demographic_Population_and_Civil_Conflict_After_the_Cold_War.pdf.
Civil conflicts between 1970 and 2000 were often sparked by demographic factors, such as youth bulges.

Haub, Carl, "2010 World Population Data Sheet," Population Reference Bureau, July 2010, www.prb.org/pdf10/10wpds_eng.pdf.
The cost of entitlements and other supports for aging populations will burden working-age people in the coming decades.

Jackson, Richard, *et al.*, "The Graying of the Great Powers: Demography and Geopolitics in the 21st Century," Center for Strategic and International Studies, 2008.
This comprehensive survey of aging trends in the developed and developing world projects how global aging will affect economic growth, national security and "social mood."

Lutz, Wolfgang, Vegard Skirbekk and Maria Rita Testa, "Forces that May Lead to Further Postponement and Fewer Births in Europe," International Institute for Applied Systems Analysis, March 2007, www.iiasa.ac.at/Admin/PUB/Documents/RP-07-001.pdf.
Three Austrian demographers say governments must revise assumptions about ideal family size and income expectations in order to avoid the "trap" of low fertility rates.

For More Information

Berlin Institute for Population and Development, Schillerstrasse 59, 10627 Berlin, Germany; 49 302 232 4645; www.berlin-institut.org. An independent institute that researches and publishes studies examining the impact of international demographic changes, including aging, on sustainable development.

Center for Strategic and International Studies, Global Aging Initiative, 1800 K St., N.W., Washington, DC 20006; (202) 887-0200; www.csis.org/gai. Explores the fiscal, economic, social and geopolitical implications of population aging.

China Ageing International Development Foundation, Room 1907, Tower B, Winterlesscenter, No.1 West Dawang Rd., Chaoyang District, 100026 Beijing, China; 10 65388759; www.caidf.org.cn. Manages several funds that aimed at serving aging populations in areas such as health.

International Longevity Center, 60 E. 86th St., New York, NY 10028; (212) 288-1468; www.ilcusa.org/. Conducts research and advocates for maximizing the benefits of the current age boom.

The Johns Hopkins University, School of Advanced International Studies, 1740 Massachusetts Ave., N.W., Washington, DC 20036; (202) 663-5600; www.sais-jhu.edu. Is sponsoring a "year of demography," holding lectures and conferences devoted to global aging and other demographic issues. Devoted entire 2010 issue of SAISPHERE magazine to "the impact of demography."

Oxford Institute of Aging, 66 Banbury Rd., Oxford OX26PR, United Kingdom; 44 (0) 1865 612800; www.ageing.ox.ac.uk. Institution that studies the effects of demographic change on income, health and other issues in the U.K. and in the less-developed world.

Population Action International, 1300 19th St., N.W., Suite 200, Washington, DC 20036; (202) 557-3400; www.populationaction.org. A research and advocacy group that aims to improve access to family planning and reproductive health care around the world.

Stanford University Center on Longevity, Landau Building, 579 Serra Mall, Stanford, CA 94305; (650) 736-8643; http://longevity.stanford.edu/. Focuses on improving quality of life, from early childhood to old age. Its Global Aging Program conducts research on the geopolitical impacts of different aging trends in developed and less-developed regions.

United Nations Population Division, 2 United Nations Plaza, Rm. DC2-1950, New York, NY 10017; (212) 963-3179; www.un.org/esa/population/. Monitors a broad range of areas within the field of population; has produced a series of conferences and publications related to aging.

U.S. Census Bureau, 4600 Silver Hill Rd., Washington, DC 20233; 1 (301) 763-4636; www.census.gov/ipc/www/idb/. Population Division's International Data Base publishes various demographic indicators for countries and areas of the world with populations above 5,000.

World Population Program, International Institute for Applied Systems Analysis, Schlossplatz 1, A-2361 Laxenburg, Austria; 43 2236 807 0; www.iiasa.ac.at. Studies how population trends influence society, the economy and the natural environment.

Voices From Abroad:

YUAN XIN

Professor of Population Studies, Nankai University China

Sacrificing for country

"China implemented its family planning policy and achieved its objective within three decades, which will, in turn, intensify some side effects. In China, the family planning policy rapidly sped up the process, with many having made or having been forced to make, a personal sacrifice to help achieve the national goal."

The Statesman (India) September 2010

HENRY KAJURA

Public Service Minister Uganda

Youth must be guided

"I agree with the members [of parliament], we cannot run a country by the youth, the youth have to be guided by older people. This is the reason why we want to establish a Civil Service College to help the youth get competence before they get jobs."

The Monitor (Uganda), July 2010

ANNE O'REILLY

Chief Executive, Age NI* Northern Ireland

Raise the retirement age

"Ageing is a global phenomenon. We believe it to be a demographic bounty that offers exciting opportunities. Policies like the default retirement age must be scrapped to ensure that there are no barriers to the full and equal participation of older people in Northern Ireland. The default retirement age is acutely ageist,

---

* A nonprofit that deals with problems affecting the elderly.

counter-intuitive and stamps an expiry date on thousands of older workers."

Belfast (Northern Ireland) Telegraph, April 2010

XIE LINGLI

Director, Shanghai Population and Family Planning Commission China

Elder care a serious issue

"Compared to families with multiple children, the offspring in single child [Chinese] families have to bear the burden of elderly parents on their own. The problem of how to provide for the aged is a serious issue."

Chinadaily.com.cn, June 2010

ANATOLIY KINAKH

Director, Ukrainian League of Industrialists and Entrepreneurs

The meaning of pension reform

"The retirement age is a part of the problem, and the government, unfortunately, is going about it the wrong way.

Ask anyone on the street what pension reform in Ukraine is all about, and, unfortunately, the answer will be this: An increase in the retirement age for women. But that's wrong."

Interfax news agency (Russia) December 2010

GIYAS GOKKENT

Chief Economist, National Bank of Abu Dhabi United Arab Emirates

Older population = slower growth
"Conceptually, growth is a function of a growth in inputs such as labour and productivity. An older population profile suggests slower growth and, therefore, slower economic growth."

Gulf News (United Arab Emirates), January 2011

BARRY DESKER, DEAN

S. Rajaratnam School of International Studies, Nanyang Technological University, Singapore

Sources of rebellion
  "The youth uprising in Egypt draws attention to the impact of similar youth bulges as a result of rapid population increases over the past 20 years. . . . The authoritarian policies and lack of employment opportunities in many of these states will fuel youth rebellion. . . . The volatile mix in the greater Middle East makes this the region with the highest potential for political violence and conflict."

Straits Times (Singapore) February 2011

KIM ENG TAN

Credit Analyst, Standard & Poor's, South Korea

Pension reforms needed
"The proportion of China's population contributing to the government's revenue is likely to begin to fall soon. Unless China is able to carry through reforms in its health-care and pension financing systems, it may have to increase government funding in these areas."

Yonhap (news agency) (South Korea), October 2010